Santa Anna of Mexico

Santa Anna
of Mexico

WILL FOWLER

UNIVERSITY OF NEBRASKA PRESS | LINCOLN AND LONDON

Library of Congress
Cataloging-in-Publication
Data

Fowler, Will.
Santa Anna of Mexico /
Will Fowler.
p. cm.
Includes bibliographical
references and index.
ISBN-13: 978-0-8032-1120-9
(hardcover: alk. paper)
1. Santa Anna, Antonio López de, 1794–1876.
2. Mexico—History—1821–1861.
3. Presidents—Mexico—Biography.
4. Generals—Mexico—Biography. I. Title.
F1232.S232F69   2007
972'.04092—dc22
[B]
2007016104

Set in Quadraat by Bob Reitz.
Designed by R. W. Boeche.

for Tom, Ed, and Flo

Contents

Illustrations

Preface

Santa Anna remains to this day the leader all Mexicans (and Texans) love to hate. The view that he "was the exclusive cause of all of Mexico's misfortunes" following the country's independence from Spain still goes unquestioned by many. Misleadingly described as "eleven times" president of Mexico, he is consistently depicted as a traitor, a turncoat, and a tyrant. He was the traitor who allegedly recognized the independence of Texas in captivity (1836), who lost the Mexican-American War (1846–48) for a fistful of dollars, and who shamelessly sold parts of Mexico to the United States in the Treaty of La Mesilla (1853). He was the bloodthirsty general who ordered the sanguinary assault on the Alamo and who ordered the execution of all the Texans taken prisoner at Goliad in 1836. He was the opportunistic turncoat who changed sides whenever it suited him, depending on which faction was most likely to rise to power, without upholding any consistent political ideals. He was also a despotic tyrant, the "Attila of Mexican civilization," the "Napoleon of the West." So goes the black legend that has come to dominate much of historiography's portrayal of Santa Anna's military and political career. He was demonized by Mexicans who wanted a scapegoat for losing the Mexican-American War and by Americans who needed a hate figure to justify their military involvement in Mexico. The time has come to deconstruct these myths. Otherwise it is impossible to understand Mexican history during the early national period. If Santa Anna was such a monster, how can we explain his repeated comebacks or that so many different factions invited him at one stage or another to come to the country's rescue? This new biography aims to set the record straight.

Santa Anna's life was both long and eventful. He was involved in most of the major events that unfolded between the final years of colonial rule and the consolidation of the modern nation-state that Mexico went on to become in the latter half of the nineteenth century. At a time of great uncertainty and instability, when issues of authority and legitimacy remained unresolved and divisive, Santa Anna emerged, as did so many other strongmen in Spanish America at large, as the much sought after arbitrator and necessary gendarme of his nascent country. Born in Xalapa (21 February 1794), in the province of Veracruz, Santa Anna joined the royalist army as a cadet in 1810. Like so many creole officers he embraced the cause of independence following the proclamation of the 1821 Plan of Iguala and was mainly responsible for liberating his home province. Once independence was achieved he initiated four revolts (1822, 1823, 1828 and 1832) before being elected president of the republic. Thereafter he was president on six different occasions (1833–35, 1839, 1841–43, 1843–44, 1846–47, and 1853–55), although he always preferred to retire to his haciendas in Veracruz whenever he had the chance. His military victories included repulsing a Spanish and a French invasion (1829 and 1838, respectively) and slaughtering the Texan rebels at the Alamo (1836). His defeats included the battle of San Jacinto (1836), which led to the independence of Texas, and the Mexican-American War (1846–48), whereby Mexico lost half of its national territory. His political views evolved from upholding a liberal agenda to supporting a conservative one as the different constitutions failed to give Mexico a stable political system. Exiled following his 1853–55 dictatorship, he tried unsuccessfully to return to Mexico on two occasions before he was allowed back in 1874. Having been one of the most influential *caudillos* in Mexico at the height of his career, he died impoverished and forgotten in Mexico City on 21 June 1876.

To revise the way in which this historical character has been portrayed is no easy task. His vilification has been so thorough and effective that the process of deconstructing the numerous lies that have been told and retold about him takes time. Only by going back to the primary sources does one begin to appreciate the extent to which Santa Anna's life has been misrepresented. To note just two examples: he did not recognize the independence of Texas in the Treaty of

Velasco, and he did not fight the Mexican-American War with an aim to lose.

My main purpose is to understand Santa Anna in as sober, detached, and balanced a way possible, building on my seventeen-year-long research into the politics of independent Mexico and, in particular, into the ideas and actions of the *santanistas*. Over the last thirty years what were once described as the "forgotten years" have received at last the attention they deserved. By incorporating into this revisionist biography the many recent findings made in the historiography it is possible to understand Santa Anna's actions better. With the knowledge we have acquired about regional politics in Mexico, political ideas and behavior, actions that were once deemed contradictory or enigmatic, have come to make sense. For instance, his transformations are interpreted paying close attention to the chronology. Responding to what I once defined as the stages of Hope (1821–28), Disenchantment (1828–35), Profound Disillusion (1835–47), and Despair (1847–53), Santa Anna's political evolution is congruent when we understand how he was influenced by the traumatic experience of the first national decades.

In a similar revisionist vein I also give significant attention to his activities in his home province. If Santa Anna became the leading caudillo of his day, this was in great measure due to the power he acquired in his home province as its leading military chieftain, landowner, and political leader. Because of the discoveries I made in the regional archives of Veracruz, his relationship with the region is given great importance. His life in the army is also given prominence. His rise to power was consistently backed by the *veracruzanos*, but it was also promoted by a number of high-ranking officers. His symbiotic relationship with the regular army, which mirrored his relationship with the elite and people of Veracruz, is a recurrent theme in this biography. I propose that his involvement in politics was always as a member of the military. He was a landowner and an army man. To see him as a politician is a mistake. He spent more time on his hacienda and in the barracks than he did in the National Palace. We need to appreciate that while the political class converged in the national and state legislatures to discuss the future of Mexico, Santa Anna was more often than not looking after his land, initiating or quelling revolts, or preparing to fight foreign armies. We will not understand his antipolitics, his view of himself as an arbitrator, his reluctance to govern the country, if we do not accept that his lands and the army were his main concerns.

The Santa Anna who emerges in this book is neither a diabolical dictator nor a benign, selfless, patriotic patriarch. He was courageous and he risked his life for his country. He even lost a leg fighting for Mexico. He was also notoriously corrupt and amassed a formidable fortune at the height of his career by lining his pockets with government funds. He was charismatic and charming. He was also forceful and ruthless. He was ingeniously deceptive and yet stubbornly reckless. He features here as the intelligent and contradictory leader that he was; a middle-class provincial *criollo* who became a high-ranking officer, a large landowner (*hacendado*), and a president. Not a traitor, nor a turncoat, and not always a tyrant; this is the story of a general, a landowner, and a leader who tried to prosper personally *and* help his country develop at a time of severe and repeated crises, as the colony that was New Spain gave way to a young, troubled, besieged, and beleaguered Mexican nation.

Acknowledgments

I could not have written this book without the help of a number of individuals and institutions. I am extremely grateful to my editor Heather Lundine. I thank her for having faith in this book and for her first-class editorial work. At the University of Nebraska Press I would also like to thank Bridget Barry, Joeth Zucco, and Sally E. Antrobus. My colleagues in the Spanish Department at St. Andrews, as ever, deserve a mention for their unwavering support and for their collegiality. The same goes to my students, who over the years have not minded becoming santanistas for a semester. I must also thank the many historians who very generously shared their thoughts and notes with me during the period in which I wrote this book. I am immensely grateful to the following: Cath Andrews, Tim Anna, Christon Archer, Linda Arnold, Carmen Blázquez Domínguez, Jesús Hernández Jaimes, Timothy Johnson, Marco Antonio Landavazo, Juan Ortiz Escamilla, Gabriel Torres, Eric Van Young, Josefina Zoraida Vázquez, and Verónica Zárate Toscano. I should also like to thank Alfredo Ávila, who spoke to Santa Anna's descendant Margarita O'Reilly Pavón on my behalf, took the time to photograph the documents held in her private collection and forward them to me as e-mail attachments, and who eventually introduced us in January 2005. I am grateful to Doña Margarita for having allowed us access to her collection in the first place. Likewise I am indebted to another of Santa Anna's descendants, Hugo Villalobos Velasco, with whom I came in contact following an extraordinary series of coincidences. The portrait of Santa Anna that figures on the cover of this book belongs to his private collection. I thank him for bringing it to my attention and for allowing me to reproduce it here.

I am also deeply indebted to Anne Staples, Michael Costeloe, and the two anonymous reviewers Heather Lundine approached in the fall of 2005. Professor Staples generously allowed me to stay at her place in Mexico City and dedicated countless hours to challenging my views during the months I spent there. Her ideas and insights were extremely helpful in allowing me to clarify my own interpretation of Santa Anna's life. Professor Costeloe kindly and patiently read through the entire first draft of this biography (which was 320,000 words long). His comments and suggestions proved extremely helpful when it came to editing the original text. I hasten to add that the book's faults remain my own. That they are not even greater is due to his help and to the extremely thorough comments I received from the two anonymous reviewers who read the third draft.

I would also like to thank Anne Staples's husband, Renán Pérez, for his hospitality. In a similar vein, I thank Diana Pérez, Rubén Tenorio's family, Juan Arturo Rivera, Esther Mandujano, Juanito Rivera Mandujano, Jorge Sánchez Mejorada, and Pedro and Alma Jiménez for having made my field work in Mexico such a pleasurable experience.

I must note my gratitude to all those librarians and archivists who, over the years, have made my research possible. I am immensely grateful to the following: Margaret Grundy at the Main Library, University of St. Andrews; Alison Hill at the British Library; the six Archivo Histórico de la Secretaría de la Defensa Nacional officers General de Brigada DEM Salvador Cienfuegos Zepeda, Sargento 1 Auxiliar Historiador María Luisa Alavés Cataño, Sargento 1 Auxiliar Escribiente Ernesto Carvajal, Sargento 1 Auxiliar Historiador Rafael Flores Álvarez, Sargento 2 Archivista José Antonio González Garduño, and Subteniente Historiador Sergio Martínez Torres; Lic. Roberto Beristain at the Archivo General de la Nación; Dr. Manuel Ramos Medina at the Centro de Estudios de Historia de México CONDUMEX; Lic. Alejandro M. Riquelme Zamorano and Eloísa Olivo at Archivo Histórico Municipal del Ayuntamiento de Xalapa; Lic. Griselda Avendaño at the Archivo de Notarías de la Biblioteca Central de la Universidad Veracruzana; Jane Garner, Santiago Hernández de León, Michael Hironymous, Ann Lozano, and Carmen Sacomani at the Nettie Lee Benson Latin American Collection, University of Texas at Austin; and Daniel Z. Kreisman at the Kreisman Gallery, Woodstock, Illinois. I would like to thank Simon Milner at the British Council in Mexico City for writing me the letter of recommendation I needed to gain access to some of the more guarded archives in Mexico.

The research that made this biography possible could not have been carried out without the financial backing of a number of institutions. Thanks to a British Academy Larger Research Grant I was able to spend six months working in the regional archives of Veracruz. Three research awards from the Carnegie Trust for the Universities of Scotland allowed me to return to Mexico at critical junctures. My own university's School of Modern Languages Research and Travel Fund proved important in covering my frequent travel to Santa Anna's homeland and my accommodation expenses. Finally, the Arts and Humanities Research Board Research Leave Award I was given in 2004 freed me from all teaching and administrative duties, enabling me to extend my sabbatical over a period of two whole semesters. The privilege of being able to dedicate myself exclusively to writing this book was one for which I remain profoundly grateful.

I would also like to thank my family. My father, who died in 2002, would no doubt have found a number of Shakespearean qualities in Santa Anna, as the archetypal flawed hero of tragedies. I thank him and my mother, Rosa María Laffitte, for their support. I thank my parents-in-law, Susan and Peter Wilkes, who have backed me in equal measure over the last seventeen years. Last but not least, I thank Caroline and our children. They made all of this worthwhile. It is to Tom, Ed, and Flo that I dedicate this book. The childhood of all three was marked in one way or another by Santa Anna. Six months in Xalapa, years of coming and going, long e-mails, repeated trips to the airport . . . I hope they were all worth it.

Introduction

Traitor, Turncoat, and Tyrant

The Gulf of Mexico port of Veracruz, with its notoriously insalubrious climate, was awash with light the morning of 7 October 1867. The sky was an impossible blue. Like pterodactyls from a previous era, pelicans could be seen gliding over the fortified island of San Juan de Ulúa, occasionally plunging into the shark-infested sea. Palm trees lining the waterfront in tropical splendor stood perfectly still in the morning sun. The fierce and feared *norte*, the strong wind that often prevented ships from docking, was not blowing that day. Instead the still air was humid and stifling. Smoke from gentlemen's cigars lingered around them, hanging oppressively over their troubled minds.

In the main theater of Veracruz, seventy-three-year-old General Antonio López de Santa Anna stood accused of high treason. It was the first day of the court-martial. He had been captured by the Mexican liberal forces in Yucatán in mid-July after attempting yet another remarkable political comeback. This time it was not to be. The hero of independence, six times president of the republic, who over the previous four decades had repeatedly and in the most extraordinary of circumstances succeeded in returning to power, was this time unable to pull off another miraculous recovery.

Colonel José Guadalupe Alba, the chief prosecutor, called for Santa Anna to be sentenced to death. He accused the septuagenarian and one-legged warrior of inciting the French intervention (1862–67) that had led to the imposition of a Habsburg prince, Archduke Ferdinand Maximilian, on the Mexican throne. He accused Santa Anna of recognizing the illegal empire that was forged and of then changing sides and fighting for the Republicans who had forbidden his joining their struggle. He was a traitor, a turncoat, and a tyrant. If he was found guilty and the draconian law of 25 January 1862 was applied, Santa Anna's days were numbered. The aging liberator of Veracruz, "founder of the Republic," who had been forced to have his left leg amputated after he was badly wounded repulsing a French incursion into the port in December 1838, could not believe there were Mexicans who dared accuse him of treason. He was one of the strongmen, one of the chieftains, one of the *caudillos* of the War of Independence (1810–21). He had "spilt his blood in [Mexico's] defense."[1] Here was a man who believed he should be celebrated as one of Mexico's greatest men. At the height of his career he had been paraded around the streets of Veracruz on people's shoulders. And yet, that October morning, it looked very much as though he was to be condemned as a despicable criminal. Although Santa Anna would miraculously succeed in escaping the death sentence in the fall of 1867, his reputation as a traitor would accompany him for the rest of his life. To this day, more than 130 years since he died an impoverished and ostracized man in Mexico City, in the early hours of 21 June 1876, Santa Anna's name continues to be associated with treachery, tyranny, and deceit.

In Mexico this has to do with the way history is taught in schools, portrayed in the media, and commemorated on certain chosen dates. There are heroes and there are villains. History is like a Diego Rivera mural in which some people and events have been dramatically idealized, while others have been deliberately satanized. What is lacking is an overriding detached view whereby people can contemplate their history without a need to pass sentence, as a landscape in which there were not always obvious rights and wrongs, good and bad choices, saintly and demonic characters. What continues to elude the Mexican educational system is a predisposition to accept that reality is often murky, that not all heroes are virtuous, and that some villains are probably misguided (or unlucky) rather than evil.

The annual liturgy of fiestas ritualistically reinforces this view of the past: 5 May, 16 September, and 20 November. Street names repeated in every Mexican town further confirm this official version. Those who are honored during the fiesta *del grito* on the evening of 15 September, who have deserved a statue, whose faces have figured on peso coins, who have had a plaza named after them, become almost sacrosanct in the way that they are venerated. In contrast, those who do not figure on street maps, whose names appear in the school history textbooks only as villains, are irredeemable.

Antonio López de Santa Anna remains one of the most controversial and vilified figures of Mexican history. His career has not yet been granted a balanced evaluation. There are no monuments, statues, or streets that carry his name in the entire republic. Even the museum on the former grounds of his *hacienda* El Encero, outside the town of Xalapa in the state of Veracruz, does not have a plaque to indicate that Santa Anna lived in the area for several years. Although children across the republic sing the national anthem at school every Monday morning, few are told that it was commissioned by Santa Anna. It goes without saying that the stanzas contained in the original celebrating the virtues of Santa Anna are no longer sung. Purposefully forgotten by the authorities, he continues to appear, in school textbooks and in most historical accounts, as the leader all Mexicans (and Texans) love to hate. Any legend surrounding him can only be described as a black one. The view that he "was the exclusive cause of all of Mexico's misfortunes" still goes unquestioned by many.[2]

Santa Anna is ever represented as the unpatriotic traitor who deliberately lost the Mexican-American War in exchange for a fistful of dollars and who sold parts of Mexico to its northern neighbor in the Treaty of La Mesilla or Gadsden Purchase (1853), shamelessly pocketing the profits, his signature becoming associated with corrupt and damaging transactions.[3] Representative of this view is the conclusion of Enrique Serna's best-selling novel about Santa Anna, *El seductor de la patria* (The mother country's seducer, 1999). The character of Santa Anna predictably confesses at the end to having treated the country as if "she" were a whore: "I stole her bread and sustenance. I became rich on her poverty and her pain. . . . I have never given a damn about Mexico and her people."[4] He is the sanguinary general (as depicted in John Wayne's 1960 and John Lee Hancock's 2004 films about the battle at the Alamo) who led the bloody assault on the fortified mission and subsequently ordered the execution of Texans captured at Goliad. He appears, moreover, as the incompetent general who allowed the Texans to defeat the Mexican Army in 1836 while having a siesta at San Jacinto when Samuel Houston's troops were only a mile away.

Furthermore, Santa Anna is invariably presented as an opportunistic turncoat who changed sides according to necessity. He is presented as having been a royalist, an insurgent, a monarchist, a republican, a federalist, a centralist, a liberal, and a conservative, depending upon which faction was most likely to rise to power, without upholding any consistent political ideals. Proponents of such a view tend to ignore the fact that most of Santa Anna's contemporaries also changed sides as the hopes of the 1820s degenerated into the despair of the 1840s. It was a period of change, uncertainty, and experimentation, which of necessity meant that no faction remained static in its demands, and everybody's political stance evolved in response to the different stages of hope, disenchantment, profound disillusion, and despair.[5]

Santa Anna is also remembered for the 1853–55 repressive dictatorship in which he became His Serene Highness (*Su Alteza Serenísima*) and was particularly brutal in his attempts to crush the Revolution of Ayutla (1854–55). As exemplified in the title Felipe Cazals gave his 2000 film about the last days of Santa Anna's life, *Su Alteza Serenísima*, Mexicans have come to associate the caudillo with this pseudomonarchic personal appellation. Conveniently they overlook the fact that it was first donned by the idolized "father of Independence," Miguel Hidalgo y Costilla. To a great extent we owe Santa Anna's depiction as a despotic tyrant to one of his enemies, liberal ideologue José María Luis Mora, who developed the highly influential view that Santa Anna "certainly desired *absolute* power" from as early as 1833. Mora called him the "Attila of Mexican civilization" and argued that he championed the cause of the privileged classes, that of the "military and clerical oligarchy." His party, in Mora's words, was made up of selfish and self-promoting high-ranking officers who had no other aim but to ensure that Santa Anna was granted absolute power. Regardless of self-contradiction, Mora also criticized Santa Anna for retiring to his hacienda instead of exercising the power he had been awarded.[6]

However, it is both misleading and inaccurate to state that dictatorships were characteristic of nineteenth-century Mexico. With reference to Santa Anna, historian Michael Costeloe reminds us that "despite the opportunities in 1834, 1841 and again in December 1842, he made no obvious or known attempt to establish a permanent military dictatorship."[7] Although Santa Anna is often referred to as a dictator, he acted as a dictator on only three occasions. In 1834, following the Plan of Cuernavaca (25 May), Santa Anna assumed dictatorial powers in order to reverse most of the reforms that had been passed under Vice President Valentín Gómez Farías. In 1841, following the overthrow of General Anastasio Bustamante's government (1837–41), and as was stipulated in the Bases de Tacubaya (6 October), he served as dictator until the 1843 Constitution was approved and put in place (8 June 1843). Neither in 1834 nor in 1841 was it his intention to impose a perpetual dictatorship. On both occasions a constituent congress was formed in order to draft a new constitution. It was only in 1853 that he actually attempted to forge a long-lasting dictatorship. It is this last dictatorship, characterized by its extravagance and brutal repression, that most people remember.

Moreover, his recurrent depiction as a womanizer, a gambler, and an irresponsible regional chieftain who appropriated the national treasury on the six different occasions he served as president (or eleven, according to the traditional historiography), means there is little that would appear redeemable in his career.[8] His faults are portrayed as having been so great, and his role in national politics so influential (the 1821–55 period in question continues to be called the "Age of Santa Anna"), that he has served the official Mexican version of events to account painlessly for the loss of half of its national territory in 1848. Santa Anna has become the ideal scapegoat, to be held responsible for all that went wrong after Mexico became independent from Spain. He has been so useful to this end, serving as everybody's trump card that, as noted by historian Josefina Zoraida Vázquez, if he had not existed, they would have had to invent him.[9]

Having said this, back in the nineteenth century and until the definitive triumph of Benito Juárez's faction in 1867, the view of Santa Anna was more varied. Although he was indeed vilified by a considerable number of his contemporaries, the majority admired him at one stage or another. Santa Anna was known as the liberator of Veracruz. Having defected to the insurgent cause, following the proclamation of the Plan of Iguala (24 February 1821), he played a major role in liberating his home province from royalist control. He also acquired fame, albeit not entirely justified, as the author of Agustín I's downfall and the founder of the Republic of Mexico. Santa Anna's role in the Republican revolt of 2 December 1822 allowed him to state on numerous occasions that he was "the first caudillo to proclaim the Republic."[10]

Moreover, on 11 September 1829 Santa Anna, together with General Manuel Mier y Terán, succeeded in defeating a Spanish expedition that had landed in Tampico in July with the intention of reconquering Mexico for Ferdinand VII. Santa Anna's victory became one of the most insistently celebrated military exploits of the early national period, and thanks to his ideologue, propagandist, and informant José María Tornel, he subsequently became known as "el héroe de Tampico." He also led the Mexican victory of 5 December 1838, on this occasion against French troops who had occupied the port of Veracruz, during the so-called French Pastry War (March 1838–April 1839). At the time, Santa Anna's role in the battle and the loss of his leg allowed him to regain his previous heroic reputation.[11]

He was celebrated with more fiestas than any other Mexican hero, living or dead, between 1821 and 1855. His popularity with the masses was indeed great, particularly in the state of Veracruz. As was noted by one British traveler, Santa Anna was "a great territorial lord, a *nong-tong-paw* of the state of Veracruz. Wherever you go, you hear of his name, and are made acquainted with his possessions of every kind."[12] Santa Anna's populism certainly served the all-important purpose of making him figure as "a man of the people." The pilgrimages that were organized to venerate the remains of his amputated leg, buried in the cemetery of Santa Paula on 27 September 1842 with all the pomp and circumstance such an occasion merited, offer a striking sense of the extent to which Santa Anna acquired a Messianic status at the height of his popularity. Although some may deem it controversial to say so, it remains the case that almost anybody who was somebody in independent Mexico was a *santanista* at one point or another. He was actively sought and invited to assume the presidency by a wide range of factions at different junctures, including by radical liberals such as Valentín Gómez Farías (1833 and 1846), moderates such as Ignacio Comonfort,

Mariano Otero, and José Joaquín de Herrera (1847), and conservatives such as Lucas Alamán (1853). There were even British diplomats, such as Percy Doyle, who could not wait for Santa Anna to return to power. As he wrote in a letter to Lord John Russell in 1853: "It is to be hoped that General Santa Anna will come shortly, and that he will be able to restore order in this country, for, should such not be the case, I know of no men of sufficient weight capable of doing so."[13]

What becomes apparent is that there was obviously more to the Santa Anna phenomenon than has been generally acknowledged. A more sober look at his life shows that most of the noted accusations are inaccurate and misleading. They also make it extremely difficult for us to understand this period. If Santa Anna was nothing other than a despicable traitor, turncoat, and tyrant, how can we understand his repeated rise to power, the popularity and influence he enjoyed? Historian Christon I. Archer poignantly asks: "How could a leader survive despite overwhelming defeats as military commander and apparently inexplicable personal political shifts from liberal to reactionary conservative . . . ? If he was an incompetent fool, how could he endure crisis after crisis to regain power? If he was a traitor, how did he avoid the firing squads that terminated the lives of others?"[14] It is worth remembering how he impressed the observant Spanish minister plenipotentiary's Scottish wife, Fanny Calderón de la Barca, who after meeting Santa Anna in December 1839 described him as

> a gentlemanly, good-looking, quietly-dressed, rather melancholy-looking person, with one leg, apparently somewhat of an invalid, and to us the most interesting person in the group. He has a sallow complexion, fine dark eyes, soft and penetrating, and an interesting expression of face. Knowing nothing of his past history, one would have said a philosopher, living in dignified retirement—one who had tried the world, and found that all was vanity—one who had suffered ingratitude, and who, if he were persuaded to emerge from his retreat, would only do so, Cincinnatus-like, to benefit his country.[15]

On meeting him again two years later, in 1841, Madame Calderón de la Barca did not find that she had misjudged him following their first encounter: "He retains the same interesting, resigned, and rather melancholy expression; the same quiet voice and grave but agreeable manner; and surrounded by pompous officers, he alone looked quiet, gentlemanly and high bred." It was clear to her that Santa Anna was in a league of his own; she noted that his "name has a prestige, whether for good or for evil, that no other possesses."[16] Privately she admitted that he was an "energetic robber," but this did not prevent him from being a cut above the rest of his contemporaries.[17] What becomes obvious is that it is important that we rethink the role Santa Anna played in Mexican politics following independence.

Although numerous biographies of Santa Anna exist, it is clear that there is a need for a new study to take on board the findings made in the relevant historiography over the last thirty years; to go beyond the myths that continue to cloud our understanding of the period; to interpret Santa Anna's transformations, paying close attention to the chronology; to focus on his activities in his home province of Veracruz; and to understand his role from the perspective of the period in which he moved.[18]

Santa Anna's long and meaningful relationship with Veracruz deserves to be looked at more closely. Most biographies focus on his activities either in the capital or on the battlefield and eschew the many years he remained out of public scrutiny at his haciendas in Veracruz (Manga de Clavo and El Encero). He spent far more time in Veracruz than he did in Mexico City. Why was he so reluctant to leave Veracruz? Why did he abandon the presidency, time and again, instead of consolidating his rise to power from the capital? If he was truly interested in power itself, would it not have made more sense for him to take hold of the executive with an iron grip? As Conservative ideologue Lucas Alamán stressed to him in March 1853, the Conservative party definitely wanted him to stay in the capital, for they feared that if he retired to Manga de Clavo, as was customary, the government would be left "in hands that may well make a mockery of authority."[19] And what did he do in Veracruz as hacendado, military commander-general, state governor, and vice-governor? What policies did he implement in the region? Who were his allies? Which factions did he favor? And how did his political behavior in his bailiwick in Veracruz tally with his actions at a national level?

An aspect of his career that is emphasized in this biography is precisely Santa Anna's success as an important rancher and landowner in Veracruz. This was a key region in the Mexican political economy of the early nineteenth century. His success as a rancher and the critical geopolitical position of his estates were vital in enabling him to become such a major political actor in early republican Mexico. They allowed him to figure as a potentially valuable political ally or as a dangerous political foe by those of his contemporaries who took to the boards of the Mexican political stage following independence.

This is also a biography that builds on my own seventeen-year-long research into the politics of independent Mexico and into the ideas and actions of the santanistas. Concentrating on his most consistent followers and in particular on the political career of Santa Anna's intellectual informer, propagandist, ideologue, and master conspirator, six times Minister of War José María Tornel, I developed an interpretation of the evolving antiparties, antipolitics, and nationalist, populist ideology that the caudillo's movement came to endorse. I have argued that the santanistas did have a political agenda, inferring therefore that Santa Anna did also, even if he was "a man of action, not a political thinker."[20] I have also stressed the importance of chronology in a number of studies, reiterating the point that people change in response to events, experiences, triumphs, and failures. This logic was applied not only to the santanistas but also to a wide range of politicians and factions. Responding to what I have defined as the stages of hope (1821–28), disenchantment (1828–35), profound disillusion (1835–47), and despair (1847–53), santanistas like Tornel went from advocating a radical liberal agenda in the 1820s to defending a diametrically opposed reactionary one in the 1850s. Experience took its toll on the generosity of early beliefs. The time has now come to apply these findings to Santa Anna himself, recognizing that he did uphold a political ideology. Inevitably, Santa Anna's political outlook changed as the experience of the first national decades scarred him, both figuratively and literally.[21]

To a great extent this biography is a reworking of documents that have been studied before in the numerous studies that exist on Santa Anna. It therefore constitutes a fresh look at well-used sources, challenging the hegemonic myths that surround his career and attempting to provide a balanced account of Santa Anna's contribution to nineteenth-century Mexican politics. Nevertheless, this study does benefit from discoveries made in the "untapped" regional archives of Veracruz, bringing to light new information about Santa Anna's career. It also benefits from the time and opportunity I was awarded to work in the Archivo Histórico of the Mexican Ministry of Defense. Consequently, although this is first and foremost a revisionist biography of Santa Anna, it does offer new insights into the caudillo's life, in particular with regard to his activities in his bailiwick of Veracruz and the numerous military engagements in which he was involved.

This is definitely not a hagiography of Santa Anna. There is no intention here of inspiring the Mexican government to erect a statue in Santa Anna's honor or to persuade local authorities to rename an avenue after him. My main purpose is to understand Santa Anna in a sober, detached, and balanced way. The following pages are thus aimed at doing away with all the clichés and politically motivated myths that obscure our understanding of his actions and decisions. I seek to embrace the latest trends in the historiography and in so doing to provide a revised account of his life, including new insights into his activities in Veracruz. And I aim to bear in mind that he was neither alone nor unique as a Spanish American caudillo and that his political behavior was paralleled by that of other strong leaders of his time.

In brief, the Santa Anna who emerges in this book is neither a diabolical dictator nor a benign selfless patriotic patriarch. He features as the intelligent and contradictory leader that he was; a middle-class criollo, high-ranking officer, politician, and hacendado. The stress, if any, is on seeing him as a landowner and as someone who changed, not necessarily for devious aspirational reasons but because his context was one of constant motion, where the solutions that were thought up one day were abandoned the next, in the face of their failure. Santa Anna was not a traitor, nor a turncoat, and not always a tyrant; this is the story of a landowner, general, and political leader who tried to prosper personally and help his country develop at a time of severe and repeated crises, as the colony that was New Spain gave way to a young, troubled, besieged, and beleaguered Mexican nation.

Part 1
Santa Anna's Early Life, 1794–1823

You, standing, Cruz, thirteen years old, on the edge of life. You, green eyes, thin arms, hair coppered by the sun. You, friend of a forgotten mulatto.

You will be the world's name. You will hear Lunero's call. You engage the infinite depthless freshness of the universe. You will hear the clang of mule-shoes. In you the earth and the stars touch.

Carlos Fuentes, *The Death of Artemio Cruz*

1. Between the Volcano and the Sea, 1794–1810

Santa Anna must have known he stood a good chance of facing a firing squad later that month, as the chief prosecutor's words reverberated around the packed theater of Veracruz. The Zapotec constitutional president and iron-willed leader of the Liberals, lawyer Benito Juárez, was determined to exterminate anyone who stood in the way of his reformist project. He had shown no mercy toward the three iconic Conservatives who were executed outside Querétaro, on the Cerro de las Campanas, at dawn on 19 June. Letters had flooded in from Europe begging him to spare Maximilian's life. Juárez would have none of it. It did not matter that Maximilian was an Austrian prince or that the 1857 Constitution banned the death penalty for political offenses. Maximilian was tried by court-martial under the harsh law of 25 January 1862, found guilty of attacking the nation, and shot dead.

Juárez wanted the world to know that this was the fate that awaited those European imperialist adventurers who dared intervene in Mexico. He also wanted Mexicans to know that he was not prepared to spare the lives of those nationals who dared take up arms against his Liberal republic. Miguel Miramón, the dashing Conservative general who returned to Mexico to assist Maximilian in his hour of reckoning, knowing that his was a lost cause, and Juárez's Indian nemesis, the ultra-Catholic nationalist Otomí general Tomás Mejía, both faced the firing squad alongside the ill-starred Habsburg archduke-cum-emperor of Mexico. What chance did Santa Anna have of escaping the death penalty when such eminent men had all been tried and killed?

On 8 October 1867, it was the turn of the accused to make his case. A distinguished lawyer from Santa Anna's hometown of Xalapa, Joaquín M. Alcalde, represented him.[1] Alcalde was a gifted speaker and he knew Santa Anna well, even though he was only thirty-four years old. We can only speculate about what Santa Anna made of the fact that most of the men present at his court-martial had not even been born when he took on the task of liberating his home province during the War of Independence forty-six years earlier. Judging by his comments on Juárez, who was born in 1806, Santa Anna could not have been amused: "Where was he? Where could that scoundrel be found when I was conquering Mexico's independence, founding the Republic on the burning beaches of Veracruz with my own sword?"[2] How could these young men judge him? What did they know of his past? What did they know of Mexico's recent history? Some of them were only toddlers when he was leading his troops into the fray.

Alcalde was born in 1833, the same year Santa Anna was elected president of the republic for the first time. Even in his case, dedicated as he was to defending the seventy-three-year-old general, there were bound to be gaps in his understanding of events. Could he do justice to Santa Anna's defense when he had no empirical memory of some of the caudillo's greatest exploits? How could he appreciate what it had meant for Santa Anna to repulse Barradas's Spanish expedition of 1829? Graduating in law in Mexico City, Alcalde had served as an auditor for the Ministry of War in the northern province of Sinaloa in 1854 under Santa Anna's last government. He had later become a member of the Liberal party, serving as deputy in Congress under Juárez's government. He could talk confidently about Santa Anna's dictatorship. But as for the general's early sacrifices and services—Alcalde had been only five years old when Santa Anna lost his leg defending Veracruz from the French.

Wide gaps notwithstanding, Alcalde was a *xalapeño* and a *veracruzano*, and as such he must have been brought up to know that Santa Anna was his region's favorite son and most important landowner. By the time Alcalde was ten, Santa Anna owned most of the land that spread from the port of Veracruz up the mountain to the beautiful highland town of Xalapa. It was no doubt as a veracruzano that Alcalde pitched his defense of the old man, and he did so with great passion and conviction. According to one source he spoke without interruption "from eleven in the morning until seven in the evening."[3] As Alcalde's oratorical skills were put to the test in a lengthy panegyric account of Santa Anna's glorious past, the caudillo's mind must have flooded with memories. His lawyer's main argument was that they were placing on trial one of the republic's greatest warriors and leaders of all time. To accuse him of treason was incongruous. In tandem with Alcalde's words, the caudillo's thoughts must have drifted back to his youth, to the origins of his career in the army, to the beginning of his intense love affair with his home province of Veracruz . . .

Antonio de Padua María Severino López Santa Anna was born on 21 February 1794 in Xalapa.[4] The town was and continues to be the administrative and political center of the state (formerly intendancy and province) of Veracruz. Xalapa is 105 kilometers from the port of Veracruz, following what was at the time a particularly bumpy road that rapidly climbed to over 1,300 meters above sea level, past sand dunes, swamps, and a series of ravines and steep hills covered with low and largely spiny forest characterized by tangled vegetation. As one English traveler noted in his journal in 1823, "It took four days to travel a distance an English stagecoach on English roads would have covered comfortably in twenty-eight hours, carrying double the weight."[5]

According to the intrepid Prussian scientist and explorer Alexander von Humboldt, Xalapa's population in 1803 was thirteen thousand inhabitants, and like Orizaba, also high up on the *cordillera*, it benefited from being in the temperate region. The "beau climat de Xalapa" was in fact noteworthy, because of the striking abundance of fruit trees that resulted.[6] As the U.S. minister plenipotentiary, Waddy Thompson, observed in the 1840s: "All the tropical fruits grow there, and are cultivated with great care and taste. It is not exaggeration to say that it is impossible . . . to conceive of climate so elysian."[7] Because of its altitude, although nobody could explain why at the time, Xalapa was beyond the reach of yellow fever. Humboldt reckoned that the area affected by this dreaded tropical disease ended at the hacienda of El Encero (which Santa Anna would eventually acquire in 1842), at 928 meters above sea level. Therefore, Xalapa was praised not only for its wealth of tropical fruit (bananas, mangos, avocados, limes, chiles) but for its "healthy airs." It is not surprising that toward the end of the colonial period, because of fear of the "*vómito negro*," most Spanish and Veracruzan merchants settled in Xalapa even when their businesses operated from the port. If there were a complaint, and Humboldt was but one of the travelers to make it, this invariably concerned the thick fog in which Xalapa was and is so often immersed.[8]

Situated in the middle of a highland tropical forest, described by local biologists as a *bosque de niebla* (cloud forest), Xalapa's microclimate is characterized by its constant drizzle and its famous all-encompassing humidity. As a result it is justifiably known as the "City of Flowers." When the sun comes out, views are spectacular. To the east one can just see Veracruz and the blue of the Gulf of Mexico on a clear day. Towering high above Xalapa to the west are the Cofre de Perote at 4,250 meters and the volcano Citlaltépetl, better known as the Peak of Orizaba, which at 5,747 meters is the highest mountain in Mexico.[9]

Madame Calderón de la Barca's description of Xalapa, written in 1839, is worth quoting in full, since it offers an eloquent portrait of what Santa Anna's birthplace was like:

> [It] consists of little more than a few steep streets, very old, with some large and excellent houses, the best as usual belonging to English merchants, and many to those of Veracruz, who come to live in or near Jalapa, during the reign of the "vómito." There are some old churches, a very old convent of Franciscan monks, and a well-supplied marketplace. Everywhere there are flowers—roses creeping over the old walls, Indian girls making green garlands for the virgin and saints, flowers in the shops, flowers at the windows, but, above all, everywhere one of the most splendid mountain views in the world.[10]

By the time of Santa Anna's birth in 1794, most accounts appear to concur that the city was beginning to show signs of having seen better days. The fair for which it was famous during most of the eighteenth century had ceased to take place in 1778. Xalapa was in the middle of a recession when Santa Anna was born. The town nevertheless benefited from the open support of Viceroy José de Iturrigaray (1803–1808), who in 1804 ensured that his Real Tribunal del Consulado backed the interests of the Xalapa-based business class of Veracruz. The centuries-long dispute between the two mountain towns of the province, Xalapa and Orizaba, over which route the main Veracruz–Mexico City road should take, was thus settled for the first half of the nineteenth century. Until the railway diverted traffic away from Xalapa and along the Orizaba route in the 1860s, Xalapa remained, alongside the port, the main financial center of Veracruz, with a particularly vibrant market.[11]

Local lore has it that Santa Anna was born in the spacious house that is now a branch of Banco Banamex in Xalapa's *centrô histórico*, overlooking the intersection where the streets called Xalapeños Ilustres and Zamora join together to become Calle Enríquez. Although Santa Anna was to spend the greater part of his childhood and youth in Veracruz, the bonds that were to tie him to Xalapa would be long-lasting. Most of his siblings settled in Xalapa once they came of age. His sister Francisca López de Santa Anna lived on the Calle del Ganado and owned another good-sized house, which she had to vacate during Emperor Agustín I's visit to Xalapa in November 1822. His sister Merced also had a property in Xalapa, which she used as her permanent base, and to which she retired toward the end of her life, having acquired two other houses in Campeche and Yucatán. His brother Manuel lived in Xalapa until his premature death, in 1828, on the ship that was taking him into exile in Peru following his involvement in the Plan of Montaño.[12]

Santa Anna ensured that he had his own base in Xalapa for much of his life, despite the fact that he lived mainly on his haciendas Manga de Clavo (1825–42) and El Encero (1842–47) or in Mexico City. By 1824 he occupied the largest house in Xalapa, and whenever he stopped there in later years on his way to or from the capital, his stay would be celebrated with fiestas, and a military band would play music for him outside his windows. Xalapa was also to acquire great financial importance for Santa Anna, since he would trust members of the town's elite with his life's savings. Dionisio J. de Velasco, Ramón Muñoz, and Manuel de Viya y Cosío were three xalapeño financiers who looked after his assets. Another key entrepreneur to whom he entrusted his money was the xalapeño José Julián Gutiérrez. His economic and political relationship with Xalapa would be all-important. Revolts such as Santa Anna's uprisings of 12 September 1828 or 9 September 1841 would enjoy the crucial financial backing of some of Xalapa's better-off merchants: individuals such as Bernabé Elías and Bernardo Sayago. Certain business activities, such as the development of a textile industry in Xalapa in the 1830s–40s, were made possible as a result of his patronage and protection when in power. On those occasions when he served as vice-governor, governor, and/or military commander of the province, he made a point of establishing himself in Xalapa.[13]

However, Santa Anna was only three years old when his family left Xalapa to go to Teziutlán (on the border between the present-day states of Veracruz and Puebla, to the northwest of Xalapa) in 1797. Although the family returned to Xalapa in 1799, they did not stay there long, moving to Santa Anna's parents' hometown of Veracruz in 1800. His mother Doña Manuela did take him and his siblings back to Xalapa when he was thirteen (1807–1809), but by 1810 he was back in the port. Therefore, although he was a *xalapeño de origen* and would certainly endeavor in subsequent years to support the local community of his birthplace, when the key years he spent in the port are considered, Santa Anna became, with time, more of a *porteño* and a veracruzano than a xalapeño. His affinity with the port would be such that on several occasions he stated that he had had "the good fortune of seeing the first light in that city," leading more than one historian to say he was born in Veracruz.[14]

Veracruz was entirely different from the City of Flowers. Beautiful to some, morbidly fascinating to others, but above all feared by most foreign travelers, Veracruz remained for much of the nineteenth century a disturbingly threatening city. Until yellow fever was contained and eradicated at the beginning of the twentieth century, Veracruz was not a place visitors thought it wise to stop for long. Anybody who had not been born and bred in the region was at risk of catching the disease, and it was both nasty and deadly. From a military perspective, yellow fever was Mexico's best defense against foreign aggression. There was the fortress-prison of San Juan de Ulúa, lying "low on the water, in the midst of the harbourage, having for its base nothing more elevated than a mere sandbank," fortified in the 1770s and 1780s to repulse a much-feared British attack.[15] The violent *nortes* protected the port as well. These were northerly gale force winds that made coming ashore impossible at regular intervals during the dry season. However, there was nothing like yellow fever to act as a deterrent for any planned invasion, as the Spaniards would discover to their cost when between 1811 and 1818, of the forty thousand troops dispatched to Spain's American colonies to quell the revolutions of independence, most died of disease. While locals were mysteriously immune to the *vómito*, outsiders, whether foreign or from the Altiplano, were not.[16]

Having spent part of his childhood in Veracruz, Santa Anna had developed an immunity to yellow fever. This ostensibly minor detail would prove extremely important in later years. It gave him a significant advantage over any nonlocal adversaries who engaged him in battle in the disease-infested areas of Veracruz and Tampico. While for his enemies it was of paramount importance to obtain a quick victory in order to leave the region as soon as possible, Santa Anna could afford to make a siege last indefinitely, knowing he and his *jarocho* troops would not be wiped out by the disease. His immunity to yellow fever would play a major part in his military successes against sieges of the port by Colonel José de Echávarri and General José María Calderón in 1822–23 and 1832, respectively, and in his victory over the Spanish expedition of Brigadier Isidro Barradas in Tampico in 1829.

Veracruz was bigger than Xalapa. Its population was sixteen thousand when Humboldt visited the port in 1803, although it would fall dramatically once the War of Independence began, reaching a low of 6,828 souls by 1831. It was also noisier, dirtier, and when the merchant fleets arrived, incredibly busy. For a couple of months the port would fill with people; Indians and *mestizos* (racially mixed Spanish Americans of Spanish-Indian descent) would flock to Veracruz looking for work, to sell their merchandise, to observe the strange foreigners disembark, "crowding, jostling, and nearly throwing each other into the water, . . . gazing with faces of intense curiosity."[17] Then when the fleet left, Veracruz would go strangely quiet, and unemployment would bring with it all those vices so often equated with porteño life: slovenliness, drunkenness, petty crime, antisocial behavior, and a marked addiction to gambling, dancing fandangos, brawling, and fornication.[18]

The racial composition of the population was far more varied in the port than in the mountain town of Xalapa. Given that most whites (*crio-*

llos and Europeans) did not settle at the coast because of their fear of yellow fever, their presence was not as noticeable. In contrast, the streets of Veracruz were full of mestizos and had a significant Afro-Mexican-Caribbean population deriving from people originally brought as slaves to work in the sugar cane and cotton plantations of the lowlands.[19]

Despite the fact that Veracruz was one of the greatest Spanish American ports of its time, accommodating almost all the commerce between Spain and New Spain, it was a surprisingly "melancholy, délabré and forlorn, . . . miserable, black-looking city, with hordes of large black birds, called *sopilotes* . . . flying heavily along in search of carrion."[20] The city of Veracruz simply did not prosper apace with the commercial and maritime traffic of its port. Little time or thought was given to the city's architectural potential. It was a walled cluster of wooden huts, storehouses, and coarse barracks. The unhealthy climate had clearly impeded its urban development, with the propertied classes establishing themselves and spending their pesos up in the highlands, out of reach of the *vómito*. The port was thus reduced to being a quay and a wharf for the loading and unloading of merchandise. In a sense, the real port was in Xalapa or in Mexico City. All of New Spain's imports (wine, oil, mercury, iron, clothes, fine cloths, paper, books), and its exports (silver, cochineal, leather, indigo, wool, wood, sugar, tobacco, vanilla, coffee) merely passed through, almost always in transit, seldom unloaded for the consumption of the locals.[21]

Veracruz did not impress Fanny Calderón de la Barca. Without having gone ashore, she was struck by "all its ugliness" as her boat neared the port. Once in Veracruz she found the mosquitoes and the heat prevented her from sleeping at night. During the day, she said, "nothing can exceed the sadness of the aspect of this city and of its environs." She could not believe "those who speak of Vera Cruz as having been a gay and delightful residence in former days," and was perplexed by the people she met (including foreigners) who, having resided there for a while, "almost invariably become attached to it." She was also taken by the pride veracruzanos displayed for their hometown (and Santa Anna would be no different): "as for those born here, they are the truest of patriots, holding up Vera Cruz as superior to all other parts of the world."[22]

Santa Anna's affective, military, and political relationship with Veracruz is one of the recurrent themes of this biography. Unlike Doña Fanny and the many foreigners who speedily passed through the port, terrified of catching yellow fever and unimpressed by the city's rudimentary architecture, Santa Anna evidently grew to love Veracruz and thrive there. As he stressed in a letter to his mentor and Spanish commander, José García Dávila, when he was forced to besiege the port at the head of his liberating army after having joined the insurgency in 1821, tears filled his eyes at the thought of having to spill Veracruzan blood. Veracruz was the home of his "siblings, comrades in arms, friends."[23]

The value of the produce and goods that made their way through Veracruz would provide Santa Anna, in years to come, with one of his most significant advantages. When he revolted against the order of the day, his base in Veracruz enabled him to seize the customs houses of the port and, in so doing, fund his uprisings as well as deprive the national government of much needed resources with which to defend itself. *Pronunciamientos* that were resourced with funds expropriated from the customs houses of the port seldom failed. Those uprisings that started elsewhere in the republic, without control of the key customs posts of Veracruz, San Luis Potosí, or Guadalajara only exceptionally succeeded in achieving their aims.[24]

It is impossible to understand the port of Veracruz without considering its two roads to Mexico City. Take away the roads to the capital of New Spain, and Veracruz would have been like Campeche or Tampico. The roads gave Veracruz its strategic importance as well as its particular character. After 1804, and for the greater part of the early national period, to think of Veracruz was to think of the Veracruz-Xalapa road to Mexico City. The port existed as it did because of that road, and it gave meaning to the road and Xalapa, because of its predominant role as the portal of New Spain's and subsequently Mexico's trade with Spain and the world. Focusing on this conceptualization of Veracruz and Xalapa, and their intrinsic closely-knit relationship and interdependence, means that Santa Anna emerges as their natural leader, and by default the obvious caudillo of central Veracruz. His family, both on his father's side, the López Santa Annas, and on his mother's side, the Pérez Lebrones, originated from the port but worked and lived in Xalapa at different junctures. Santa Anna's own early life stretched to include both towns, leading him to develop a critical sense of allegiance that spread from the City of Flowers down to the sea and back up again. By 1844 Santa Anna owned most of the land between Xalapa and Veracruz. He developed a highly symbiotic relationship with its inhabitants as the hands-on grand hacendado of the region. In the same way that to think of Veracruz was to think of the road to Xalapa and vice versa, by the early 1840s it could be said that to think of Veracruz-Xalapa was to think of Santa Anna and vice versa.

His childhood and adolescence in Xalapa, Teziutlán, and Veracruz gave him certain advantages over a number of his contemporaries, when it came to the power struggles in which he was to star following independence. Being a veracruzano in the early national period worked in his favor. His strategically important links with the economic elite, the merchant class, and the proto-industrialists of Xalapa, originating from his family's networks and the acquaintances he made as a young man, would prove invaluable. His immunity to yellow fever and the understanding he acquired of the resources that could be used (and abused) in the customs houses of the port would also be key factors in assisting him in his repeated rise to power. His social background would help him even though he did not originate from an affluent household.

Santa Anna was born into a middle-class creole family. Although his baptism certificate did not include the noble "de" that he would add later on, members of the family such as his uncle Ángel López de Santa Anna, used the "de" from as early as 1789. His father, the Licenciado Antonio López Santa Anna, was a porteño, born in Veracruz in 1761, son of another Antonio López Santa Anna and Rosa Pérez de Acal. His mother, Manuela Pérez Lebrón, was the daughter of Antonio Pérez Lebrón and Isabel Cortés, and she was also a veracruzana. The origins of the family remain unknown. Proof of this is that the speculative interpretations of several of Santa Anna's biographers lead to such different conclusions, with the family's origins being traced back to Florida, the Basque country, Galicia, Portugal, France, and even a Gypsy household.[25]

What is known for certain is that Santa Anna's family had resided in the region for at least two generations by the time he was born. There is evidence of the López de Santa Annas' presence in Veracruz from as early as 1744.[26] Also clear is that the family was by all appearances and in all social senses "white" and consequently belonged to the *criollo* class of Veracruz. Worth noting, albeit impossible to prove, is the suggestion hinted at by biographer Wilfrid Callcott that Santa Anna may have had a shade of mestizo in him. In describing Santa Anna's mother, Callcott noted that she "is reported to have been an excellent woman, but with no especial social standing. Most claim that she was of pure creole stock, though others assert that there was some Indian blood in her veins."[27] On the father's side of the family, the grandmother's surname Acal makes one wonder as well.[28] If Santa Anna was a mestizo, or was even perceived as having been one by the *jarochos*, regardless of his own views on his individual ethnicity, his popular appeal could be easily explained. Other nineteenth-century Spanish American caudillos (e.g., Rafael Carrera in Guatemala, 1814–65; José Antonio Páez in Venezuela, 1790–1873; and Andrés de Santa Cruz in Peru and Bolivia, 1792–1865) acquired a large following among the popular classes precisely because, in being mestizos, they were perceived as the natural representatives of the "people." Since this cannot be demonstrated, we cannot use this assumption when accounting for Santa Anna's popularity.

Lic. Antonio López Santa Anna (i.e., Santa Anna *père*), born in Veracruz in 1761, was a university graduate, registered as a lawyer before the Real Audiencia, who worked mainly as a mortgage broker in Veracruz but who was involved in other commercial activities. He also held several minor bureaucratic posts, at intervals. He was a public clerk and served as a subdelegate in the intendancy for the viceregal authorities. As a young man he was the government's subdelegate in La Antigua (Veracruz). It was as interim subdelegate that he was posted to Teziutlán in 1797, which was a relatively undistinguished post. In many senses, Santa Anna *père* was a typical Veracruzan middle-class criollo, who served the Spanish merchant elite dominating the port and whose interests were closely linked to theirs. By all accounts he prospered at the service of the viceregal authorities and consequently belonged to that particular *costeño* Caribbean creole class who felt they had more to lose than to gain by turning against their Spanish patrons and commercial partners. It may also be presumed that he was a fairly healthy man, since at the age of fifty-seven, on 3 June 1818, he married the twenty-three-year-old Dolores Zanso y Pintado, four years after the death of his first wife, Doña Manuela (29 October 1814).[29]

Santa Anna *père's* two brothers, Ángel and José, were similarly profoundly associated with the Spanish political, religious, and commercial class of the region. Ángel López de Santa Anna was a public clerk (*escribano*) in the town hall of the port from as early as 1789. He also served the army in the area as a minor bureaucrat. Don Antonio did not bear any grudges against the viceregal authorities as far as we know, but some documents have been found suggesting that Don Ángel's loyalty was put to the test in 1807. There is evidence that he became highly aggrieved by the way the town council of Veracruz prevented him from moving to Mexico City, where it was his intention to join the viceregal bureaucracy in the capital. He wrote a vigorous protest to the governor of the intendancy of Veracruz, Pedro Telmo Landero, on 14 January 1807, accusing the town council of deliberately and maliciously placing obstacles in the way of his career. It is clear from this that the Santa Annas, or at least some of the members of the family, like so many other creoles at the time, were directly affected by the discriminatory practices that were introduced with the Bourbon reforms of the latter half of the eighteenth century.[30]

Uncle José, an ordained priest who looked after several parishes during his life, in both Veracruz and Puebla, was the black sheep of the family. Having succeeded in acquiring a respectable position in the community as a parish priest, he went on to spend most of his time in the tribunals of the Inquisition, defending himself from a whole range of accusations. In the suggestive words of one biographer, Father José, otherwise known as the "bullfighter priest" (*Padre torero*), "did not respect either virgins, married women, or widows."[31] Unlike Don Ángel, whose problems with the authorities in 1807 stemmed in all likelihood from the peninsular-creole divide prevalent at the time, Father José's sexual appetite and corrupt practices were almost solely to blame for his dealings with the Inquisition.[32]

In Enrique Serna's novelization of Santa Anna's life, he features Santa

Anna's mother's mortification over the way people knew and talked about Uncle José's scandalous depravity, and yet he overlooks the fact that Doña Manuela was herself involved in an investigation by the Inquisition. From what can be gathered, Santa Anna's mother was one to stand up for her friends, even when this entailed defending them from the Santo Oficio. Although she was described as a lady, known both in Xalapa and Veracruz for her "good, and religious customs," she was not prepared to let the Inquisition punish her neighbors Benito Díaz and Josefa Ximénez for having enjoyed a good party. As may be gathered from the accusation and her own interrogation, one night in 1809, in Xalapa, Doña Manuela's neighbors and some rowdy friends ended an evening of merrymaking by singing the "Napoleon March." According to the accusation, people heard the partying crowd profane "in a song, the holy name of God." Doña Manuela did not deny that there had been singing, but she persuaded the Inquisition that the profanity had come from some passers-by in the street, and not her neighbors. Although little else is known about her, several of Santa Anna's biographers appear to concur on the fact that Doña Manuela sided with Antonio *fils*, rather than Antonio *père*, when the young Antonio rebelled against his father's decision to make him into a respectable shopkeeper, and the young man asked to be enrolled in the army. Likewise, it is generally accepted that it was Doña Manuela's long-term acquaintance with Governor José García Dávila that led to the authorities overlooking his age, so that he could become a cadet in 1810, a year earlier than was permissible by law.[33]

Santa Anna was one of seven children. He had four sisters, Francisca, Merced, Guadalupe, and Mariana, and two brothers, Joaquín and Manuel. Little is known about Guadalupe, Mariana, or Joaquín López de Santa Anna. There is every indication that Santa Anna's siblings (with the exception of Joaquín) were born in Veracruz before or after the family's residence in Xalapa (1794–97, 1799). Merced married into the army, becoming the wife of General Francisco de Paula Toro.

We know that Francisca was born in the port in October 1791 and that she married three times. Francisca's first husband was a high-ranking officer, Lieutenant Colonel José Ventura García Figueroa, of the Provincial Infantry Regiment of Toluca. After he died, she married a lawyer, the Licenciado José Agustín de Castro. Her early experience of married life was traumatic. Her first son, José Ventura Figueroa, died a premature death. Her first two husbands died young, moreover, in a matter of six years, between 1810 and 1816, resulting in her struggling to keep herself and her surviving children afloat. She made as much clear in 1820, in her attempts to ensure that the town council of Xalapa repaid her the 350 pesos real that her second husband had lent the corporation in 1813 to build the fountain in the main square. Subsequently she married Colonel Ricardo Dromundo, who in turn left her, resulting in her spending several years struggling to ensure that he paid her upkeep.

Francisca was undoubtedly the sister to whom Santa Anna was closest. Evidence of this is that on 15 September 1820, she granted her brother Antonio full powers of attorney to represent and defend her in her bid to recoup all the money she was entitled to inherit from her deceased son's estate. And it was Francisca who, on her brother's account and because she was suspected of actively plotting to bring him back to power, was imprisoned in Mexico City in the summer of 1832. Also close was his brother Manuel, who joined the army two years after Santa Anna and became deeply involved in the political scene of Xalapa, in tandem with his brother, in the aftermath of independence.[34]

In brief, Santa Anna belonged to a traditional and relatively typical provincial middle-class creole family of the time. They had little property, except for an *escribanía* in Veracruz owned by Uncle Ángel. Both Santa Anna *père* and Uncle Ángel held public appointments but not of the first rank. Likewise they had the means to have access to education, and moved within traditional middle-class areas of economic participation, gaining employment at the lower end of the legal profession, in the regional bureaucracy, and in the clergy. While viceregal clerks and bureaucrats enjoyed the benefit of being among the few economic groups in colonial society to have stable and safe employment, their means were modest, albeit comfortable. They were in no sense rich, earning between five hundred and eight hundred pesos per annum.[35]

From the perspective of the revolutionary years that lay ahead, it was precisely the middle class of New Spain that would become the driving intellectual force behind the anticolonial movement. As second-class creole lawyers and priests (*de segundo orden*), they were enlightened and had high aspirations, and yet they were not wealthy. Colonial legislation prevented them from pursuing a "lucrative and honorable career." They were, in macro terms, the social class most acutely aware of the fact that as long as the rules governing colonial society did not change, they would be unable to fulfill their dreams and vocation.[36] Nevertheless, although Santa Anna's family was economically middle class, it was, to quote one historian, "linked by real or pretended bonds of service, friendship, and race to the Spanish merchant class of the port." Unlike the disgruntled middle-class creoles who joined the insurgency from the start, "the López de Santa Annas accepted the colonial class structure with every hope of succeeding within it." This view may be confirmed by Santa Anna *père*'s friendly relationship with the prominent Cos family of Veracruz, and Doña Manuela's acquaintance with Intendant José García Dávila, together with the Santa Annas' links to other politically and commercially influential Spanish merchant families of the region. The "family saw themselves as aligned to the peninsular elite, whom they served, and were in turn recognized as belonging."[37]

Considering the ambivalent position in which Santa Anna's family found itself once the war broke out, it may be possible to appreciate why Santa Anna was initially a tireless counterinsurgent, and yet nonetheless capable, with time, of turning against the colonial order. Uncle Ángel's frustrated attempt to rise in the colonial bureaucracy by moving to Mexico City, and even Doña Manuela's refusal to aid the Inquisition, may provide indications that Santa Anna's family, for all its Spanish affinities, did harbor some of those middle-class creole resentments that found expression in the violence of the 1810–21 civil war.

Looking beyond the War of Independence, Santa Anna's provincial middle-class origins would prove important in accounting for the caudillo's popular appeal and for the difficult relationship he developed with the long-established elite of the capital. His popularity was initially based on heroic status acquired on the battlefield. A career in the military was fundamental in allowing someone from a middle-class background to leap up the social hierarchy in a way that no other profession made possible. His popularity was cultivated by his own populist conduct— frequenting cockfights and often being seen mingling with the masses. However, also important in giving him a certain aura of "democratic" legitimacy was the fact that his career in itself demonstrated that with independence you no longer had to be a member of the white capital-based aristocracy to aspire to occupy the National Palace.[38]

However, as a middle-class soldier from Veracruz, Santa Anna would also find Mexico City with its "pretentious" and arrogant political class both daunting and hostile. In a society where social and racial distinctions were so prominent, it is impossible to overlook the tensions that must have been more than apparent between Santa Anna, the provincial son of a second-class bureaucrat, and the Mexico City—based "pseudo-aristocrats" who inhabited the corridors of the National Palace. José María Tornel (also of middle-class origins, being the son of a shopkeeper), was perfectly aware of the divide that existed between Santa Anna and himself and the Mexico City elite:

> In this capital of the republic there remains an old political class that learned its science of government in the school of the viceroys . . . , that practices its art and plays with us, the men of the revolution, helping us to rise only to overthrow us, depending on its selfish interests. This brotherhood, as invisible as it is successful in its calculations, is the same one that for different reasons, and depending on the circumstances, has maintained a constant and decisive influence in the affairs of state. Does it please this class, for instance, to praise and hail General Santa Anna? We then have him turned into a Cirus, the glorious restorer of the temple; another Constantine, founder of the cult; a great and noble hero capable of personifying all alone the glory of the nation. Is it in their interest to destroy him and insult him? Then we are told he is a traitor, the one who lost Texas, one of those tiring tyrants who exhaust human patience.[39]

A significant proportion of politicians born and bred in the provinces found, during the early national period, that besides being a tight and impenetrable set, the elite of the capital could be a particularly influential force in national politics.[40] Santa Anna's middle-class provincial background accounted, in part, for his dislike of the capital and for his propensity to leave Mexico City whenever he had the chance.

It was very much a middle-class decision to turn the teenage Santa Anna into a shopkeeper. Santa Anna *père* was not impressed with his son's progress at school and asked the influential port merchant José Cos to do him the favor of giving his restless son a useful and respectable job in one of Cos's shops. According to one of his contemporaries, fellow student Francisco Lerdo de Tejada, Santa Anna and his brother Manuel were "quarrelsome" children who enjoyed bullying their peers.[41] However, if his school years were short, his stint at working behind a counter was shorter. Santa Anna turned against his father and categorically stated that he had not been born to be a "ragman (*trapero*)."[42] As he would put it sixty-four years later when recalling his childhood, "From my first years, I was inclined toward the glorious career at arms and felt a true vocation for army life. I gained my parents' consent and became a gentleman [*caballero*] cadet in the Fixed Infantry Regiment of Veracruz."[43] On 6 July 1810, a sixteen-year-old Santa Anna joined the army. What could have been a quiet and anonymous life of nurturing and serving his own shop's clientele in Veracruz was irretrievably lost the moment the young Antonio López de Santa Anna walked into the barracks of the port and fastened the buttons of his uniform.

2. An Officer and a Gentleman, 1810–1821

In the early hours of 16 September 1810, the bells of the parish church of Dolores began to chime and went on chiming until everybody in the village was awake and aware that something unusual was afoot. In the dark of night, with the bells ringing and the dogs barking, the villagers made their way to church, confused, holding up burning torches and lanterns to find out what was happening, the cold mountain air thick with fear and speculation. Waiting for them at the pulpit was their fiery priest, Father Miguel Hidalgo y Costilla. Here was a creole cleric, born in the mid-eighteenth century and brought up on a hacienda in what is now the state of Guanajuato, who had developed strong affinities with the land and its laborers. He had studied theology in Valladolid (present-day Morelia) and had become a priest renowned for his radical tendencies. He deliberately gave up a successful academic career in the prestigious Diocesan College of Valladolid to pursue his vocation as a rural priest. He cared about social injustice, agrarian discontent, and the welfare of Indians and other marginal sectors of society. He was also opposed to the manner in which the enlightened Spanish monarchy had assaulted the Church over the last fifty years.

Like those of many of his Spanish American contemporaries, Hidalgo's revolutionary impulses were a reaction to over half a century of Bourbon reforms. By the time Napoleon Bonaparte ordered the occupation of the Iberian Peninsula and took King Ferdinand VII prisoner in Bayonne, in 1808, unleashing the constitutional crisis that inspired the Spanish American revolutions of independence, parts of Mexico were ready for a revolution. The Bourbon reforms, initiated under the rule of Charles III (1759–88), had resulted in the existence of acute creole, mestizo, Indian, and slave discontent. Bourbon political, economic, military, and religious policies had succeeded in alienating the majority of the colonial population. The American War of Independence (1775–83) had become a source of inspiration for many creoles. The French Revolution (1789) had been equally influential in spreading beliefs that promoted the need for equality, liberty, and fraternity. From as early as 1808, Hidalgo had actively conspired to give a new lease of life to Viceroy José de Iturrigaray's failed attempt to create a creole-led junta that could govern the colony in the king's absence.

In the middle of the night of 15 September, Hidalgo heard that the Querétaro conspiracy had been discovered and that the viceregal authorities had sent orders to arrest all those involved. That included him. At dawn, before his sleepy-eyed congregation, Hidalgo launched his Cry (grito) of Dolores, initiating the Mexican Revolution of Independence. Entrusting his cause to the Virgin of Guadalupe, he called for an end to bad government and death to all Spaniards, claiming he was being loyal to the captive monarch by taking such drastic action. The revolutionary whirlwind and bloodbath he unleashed in what are now the states of Guanajuato, Jalisco, Querétaro, Michoacán, and Hidalgo were to be characterized by appalling violence. Although initially supported by creoles, he soon lost their support once news spread of how Hidalgo's spontaneous army of fifty thousand assaulted properties large and small, regardless of whether they belonged to creoles or Europeans, killing anybody who stood in their way.

Santa Anna had joined the army as a cadet on 6 July 1810, at the age of sixteen, two months and ten days before the Mexican War of Independence erupted.[1] His youth and early manhood, his critical formative years, would unfold during one of the most violent periods of Mexican history. By the time independence was proclaimed, with Agustín de Iturbide's march into Mexico City at the head of the Army of the Three Guarantees on 27 September 1821, Santa Anna was a hardened twenty-seven-year-old colonel. The years that privileged individuals spend, in times of peace, developing a sense of identity and purpose in senior school, university, and later in their chosen profession, Santa Anna spent fighting Indians, insurgents, and eventually royalists. It is hardly surprising that he developed such a strong attachment to the army.

Although Veracruz historian Carmen Blázquez Domínguez may be exaggerating, her statement that news of Miguel Hidalgo's revolt was received "with indifference" in the province of Veracruz appears to be accurate.[2] On hearing of the uprising on 5 October 1810, the town councils (*ayuntamientos*) of Veracruz and Xalapa manifested their loyalty to the viceroyalty. The few attempts by a handful of veracruzanos to emulate the insurgents in the Bajío (Guanajuato and Michoacán) came to nothing. There was no revolutionary activity in the province until May 1811. In September that year some rebels entered into action near Perote, and by October other revolutionary-led violent clashes were recorded in Mutuapa, Teocelo, Xico, and Ixhuacán. However, the revolution did not make itself felt in Santa Anna's home province until mid-1812, when several guerrilla forces started to operate on the Perote-Xalapa-Veracruz road.

Apart from the insurgent attack on Orizaba, led by Hidalgo's successor, Father José María Morelos, the insurgency in Veracruz was characterized by hit-and-run operations. Two military conspiracies being plotted in the garrisons of Veracruz (13 March 1812) and Perote (8 June 1812) were discovered, and their instigators executed. The War of Independence in Veracruz was a very different affair to the War of Independence in the Bajío or the southern regions now the states of Morelos, Guerrero, and Oaxaca. The extreme violence of the assaults on main urban centers was felt only in Orizaba (29 October 1812). Santa Anna's hometowns of Xalapa and Veracruz were spared the horrors of revolutionary violence. Similarly, the province of Veracruz did not witness any major clash of arms. Full-scale pitched battles with their corresponding high death tolls were avoided.

For Santa Anna and his family, therefore, the experience of the war was far removed from that of the haunted generation that suffered its traumatic events in the Bajío. Evidently, the Santa Annas' commercial interests were deeply affected. However, they did not see, as Lucas Alamán did in Guanajuato (28 September 1810), Hidalgo's revolutionary hordes rampage into the city center, killing over three hundred people, yelling "a cry of death and desolation . . . having heard it over a thousand times during the first days of my youth, after all this time, it still reverberates in my ears with its terrifying echo."[3] Santa Anna was not in Veracruz between March 1811 and November 1815 and was not involved in the few significant skirmishes that took place there. He was not involved in any of the key campaigns of the War of Independence either, given that he was posted in the remote provinces of Nuevo Santander (Tamaulipas) and Texas. This alone would mean that it would not be as difficult for him as it was for others to change sides in 1821. He had not actually fought against "old" insurgents such as José María Tornel, Vicente Guerrero, or Nicolás Bravo.

Santa Anna's peripheral participation in the War of Independence may also account for the ease with which he was able to gain the support of both former insurgents and royalists in later years. Following independence, he had no surviving enemies bearing personal grudges outside Texas, unlike Generals Anastasio Bustamante and Vicente Guerrero, for instance, whose actions during the war were both remembered and resented by their insurgent and royalist adversaries, respectively.

Nicolás Bravo's campaigns in Veracruz at the head of three thousand insurgents from August 1812 to October 1813, during Santa Anna's absence, were successful in disrupting the flow of trade between the port and the Altiplano, but they failed to capture either Xalapa or Alvarado. The same may be said of Guadalupe Victoria's actions as leader of the Veracruzan insurgency (1814–18). The government's convoys were regularly attacked near Puente del Rey, and there were minor yet constant raids in and about central Veracruz. Since Veracruz lay outside the main theater of events, it is not surprising that revolutionary activity faltered there following the capture and execution of the key insurgent leaders. By 1818, moreover, the amnesty that Viceroy Juan Ruiz de Apodaca (1817–21) offered to every insurgent who gave up his arms and swore allegiance to the Crown proved effective in reducing further the dwindling numbers of insurgents in the field. From a peak of eighty thousand insurgents during the most dynamic period of the revolution (1810–15), by 1816 there were no more than eight thousand poorly armed insurgents left.[4] The main urban centers of Veracruz—Veracruz, Xalapa, Orizaba, Córdoba, Alvarado, and Tlacotalpan—remained firmly in royalist hands.

Notwithstanding the comparatively small scale of the insurgent activity in the region, the effectiveness of the small bands of guerrillas that operated between 1816 and 1821 must not be underestimated. Constant rebel interruption of the communications system seriously undermined the main source of wealth of the social groups who controlled the regional politics and economy of Veracruz. This stalemate eventually made the creole merchant class of Veracruz permeable to the ideas of the insurgents. Santa Anna's experience of the War of Independence in Veracruz (1816–21) would be characterized by attrition, confronting an enemy that often avoided direct confrontation and succeeded in disappearing into the tangled vegetation of the province. His eventual conversion to the cause of independence was influenced, no doubt, by four to five years of failing to eradicate the insurgency in the area. Equally important must have been the fact that his family's commercial interests had suffered significantly. For a creole, after nine long years of insurgency during which trade had been badly affected, and with no end in sight, changing sides would not have been an outrageous option.[5]

Developments in Spain further complicated matters, creating divisions within both the royalist and the patriot forces. In 1812 the rebel junta in Cádiz, Spain, drafted what could easily be defined as one of the most progressive constitutions of the period. With liberals in power in Cádiz and representing the legitimate government of Spain, responses in the colonies to the 1812 Constitution were fraught with contradictions. When the Constitution was first implemented in Spanish America in 1813, many liberal creoles preferred to remain attached to this new progressive Spain, rather than support independence movements that, in some cases, appeared to be led by reactionary clerical traditionalists. For many Spanish administrators, in contrast, the implementation of the Constitution was a blow to their attempts to crush the revolts, since it enabled the population at large, *castas* (racially mixed people) and creoles alike, to elect their subversive representatives in the Cortes (Spanish parliament). Once Ferdinand VII returned to power and revoked the Constitution in 1814, imposing a return to despotism, the Spanish forces in the colonies became divided between those who were liberals and those who were absolutists. Their divisions became further exacerbated in 1820, when a liberal revolt in Spain succeeded in forcing the monarch to impose the 1812 charter all over again, only to overthrow it once more in 1823.[6]

It is difficult to know what the sixteen-year-old Santa Anna made of the news of Hidalgo's revolt, when it reached Veracruz in October 1810. Judging from the relish with which he abandoned the good life of his hacienda or the National Palace in later years to be close to the roar of the cannons, he was probably excited about the prospect of getting away from his father and of seeing some action. The Fixed Infantry Regiment of Veracruz in which he served until 7 April 1821 was different from other Mexican infantry regiments since it was conceived of as a stationary unit, permanently based at the port. Its troops consisted mainly of locals immune to the tropical diseases that affected the coastal area. There was a certain Veracruzan esprit de corps about the regiment, predominantly made up as it was of *jarochos*. Santa Anna's comrades in arms, many of whom would subsequently become loyal santanistas, included veracruzanos such as Sergeant Major José de Cos (of the great merchant family), Pedro Landero, Pedro Lemus, and Ciriaco Vázquez. During the following eleven years, Santa Anna proved himself a courageous soldier and rose fast in rank, becoming a lieutenant colonel (*teniente coronel*) in the royalist army by the time he opted to join the insurgency.[7]

His first slice of the action came only eight months after he enrolled and not quite three weeks after his seventeenth birthday. Under the orders of Colonel Joaquín de Arredondo y Mioño, Santa Anna set sail on 13 March 1811 on one of the three schooners that mobilized the five hundred troops chosen to pacify Nuevo Santander and the Provincias Internas de Oriente (the present-day states of Tamaulipas, Nuevo León, and San Luis Potosí). Arredondo's mission was initially to prevent Father Hidalgo, who was making his way north following his defeat at the battle of Puente Calderón (17 January 1811), from reaching the United States. He also had orders to put an end to several Indian-led rebellions in the region. Following news of the Gutiérrez-Magee Expedition (November 1812–August 1813), Arredondo became responsible for leading the forces that crushed this early bid for Texan independence.[8]

At the time, Joaquín de Arredondo had a reputation for being effective, sanguinary, and difficult to control. Santa Anna would have plenty of opportunity to see this reputation confirmed. Arredondo's effectiveness was proven by the success of his campaign. Between 1811 and 1817 Arredondo destroyed the main pockets of Indian-insurgent resistance in the northern provinces that were under his control, he crushed the Gutiérrez-Magee Texan rebellion, and he defeated Francisco Javier Mina's ill-fated 1817 revolutionary expedition in Soto la Marina. His ruthlessness and taste for blood found expression in the way that he repeatedly had all prisoners executed, regardless of their numbers or whether he had promised to spare their lives. Like other high-ranking officers at the time, Arredondo used the context of the war as a pretext to ignore the local authorities (town councils, provincial deputations, etc.) and impose his will, and he came close to turning the region into his personal fiefdom after he established his headquarters in Monterrey (1814). He did as he pleased and displayed complete disregard for the local governments. Viceroy Félix María Calleja, pleased with his success, approved his methods, and Calleja's successor, Juan Ruíz de Apodaca, found he could do little to curb Arredondo's autonomy.[9]

Arredondo was also a compulsive womanizer and prankster. According to one telling anecdote, he enjoyed amusing his female companions by ordering his bugler to sound the reveille, waking his troops with a fright in the middle of the night. It is evident from Santa Anna's subsequent behavior that Arredondo became a role model for him. Santa Anna would, with time, acquire a similar reputation for being effective, sanguinary, and difficult to control.[10]

A storm at sea forced Arredondo's 1811 expedition to disembark in Tampico. His men were forced to make their way to Aguayo (present-day Ciudad Victoria) on foot. They reached the rebel-held town in early April 1811, and Santa Anna experienced the adrenaline rush of combat for the first time. Judging from the readiness with which he repeatedly entered the fray thereafter, he must have been hooked on the raw, violent excitement of the battlefield from the start. Establishing what would become common practice for the rest of the campaign, the royalist forces summarily executed rebel leaders captured. From Aguayo, Santa Anna's battalion went on to Jaumabe and Palmillas, where they defeated the guerrilla force of one Villerías at Estanque de Colorado (9

May 1811) and the band of one Iturbe the following day. Notwithstanding the fact that he had been present at only three skirmishes, Santa Anna's zest for fighting did not go unnoticed. He was mentioned for the first time, together with two other cadets, for distinguishing himself on the battlefield.[11]

Given little time to rest, and urged to pursue Villerías, who had managed to escape despite his defeat at Estanque de Colorado, Arredondo led his men to Mateguala, where the insurgent and his surviving followers were killed in action (13 May 1811). Displaying the kind of inexhaustible energy, obsessive determination, and downright stubbornness that would come to be associated with Santa Anna, Arredondo did not waste any time. Without allowing his men to recover from the marches of Aguayo, Jaumabe, Palmillas, Estanque de Colorado, and Mateguala, he proceeded to attack and seize the village of Tula (21–22 May), where an insurgent band was camped. Arredondo noted in a letter to Viceroy Francisco Javier de Venegas that his force had just completed a march of seventy leagues (about 280 kilometers) in eleven days, with little water and over particularly bad roads. Santa Anna was singled out again, together with three other junior officers. The young officer had "had enough constancy to suffer the inconveniences of continuous marches, giving an example in this way to the troops, and demonstrating the most vivid desires to give credit to their valor."[12]

In July of the same year Arredondo's army headed toward San Luis Potosí to pacify the Sierra Gorda. Santa Anna was placed in a platoon under the orders of Colonel Cayetano Quintero and Captain José Daicemberger. Forming part of Daicemberger's detachment of twenty-four men, he was involved in a number of skirmishes with the Indian tribes of the area. It was with Daicemberger, and side by side with his comrade in arms Pedro Lemus, that he fought against the Indian rebel leaders Desiderio Zárate and el indio Rafael in the battle of Amoladeras (29 August 1811). This was the first major confrontation in which he participated, and he showed great "spirit . . . under fire."[13] It was in the action of Amoladeras that he received his first wound: an arrow injured his left hand.[14]

For the next eighteen months Santa Anna continued to serve under Colonel Quintero, waging war on the Indian communities of the Sierra

Gorda. He was recommended for promotion on 5 January 1812, and this was approved on 6 February. By the time of his eighteenth birthday (21 February 1812), Santa Anna was a lieutenant, had been involved in eight clashes of arms, and had received a wound, and Quintero was beginning to entrust him with minor commands.[15]

In the spring of 1813 news reached Arredondo that a revolt had erupted in the faraway province of Texas, led by Augustus Magee and Bernardo Gutiérrez de Lara. Gutiérrez de Lara took San Antonio de Béxar and defied the viceregal authorities by demanding the independence of Texas. Arredondo set out for Laredo in early June. The long march to Texas, which Santa Anna would notoriously undertake on another occasion at a later stage in his life, lasted almost two months. His first Texan campaign, under the orders of Arredondo, began on 26 July 1813.[16]

Santa Anna distinguished himself in the battle of Medina (18 August 1813), earning himself the distinction of being awarded a "shield by his Commander General, and approved by His Excellency the Viceroy."[17] It was a particularly bloody affair, and it was decisive in crushing the Texan rebellion. Arredondo's troops numbered 1,830 (635 infantry, 1,195 cavalry). Led by Cuban rebel José Álvarez de Toledo, the Texan army did not amount to more than 1,400 rebels, although some accounts claim they outnumbered the royalist forces. The fighting lasted four hours. Most of Álvarez de Toledo's militias were wiped out. Those taken prisoner were shot that day and the next, until none of them were left alive. Arredondo's troops then moved into San Antonio de Béxar, where anybody suspected of subversive activities was also executed.[18]

Santa Anna's participation in Arredondo's Texan campaign was to have a long-lasting effect on him. Apart from learning from Arredondo what appeared to be the most effective way of destroying a Texan revolt, his involvement in the conflict resulted in his developing a personal attachment to the region. The politicians who favored the option of recognizing the independence of Texas in the mid-1840s had never been there. The remote province of Texas was an abstract consideration. They did not have a mental picture of the vast territory they were prepared to negotiate away. For Santa Anna, Texas was not a concept; it was a reality. He had seen with his own eyes "the beauty of this country," one which "surpasses all description"; with its "hills covered in grass," "oak forests," and "in the early evening . . . one of the loveliest arrays that can be observed in the heavens."[19] Moreover, Texas became associated in his mind with one of his early triumphs, the victory of Medina. Texas meant something to him, with his memories of the landscape and the associations it bore with his early exploits in the army, at the age of nineteen. When the Texans revolted again, in 1835, he would personally take it upon himself to crush them.

During Arredondo's stay in San Antonio de Béxar, during the lazy days that followed the victory of Medina, Santa Anna found himself passing the time playing cards and gambling. During one game he lost heavily. He resorted to forging the signatures of Colonel Quintero and General Arredondo to withdraw the necessary pesos from the company's funds to cover his losses—and was found out. In his defense he stressed that he was helping out a brother officer in distress and, in so doing, was maintaining the honor of his regiment. His offense was not punished, and he was able to pay part of his debts thanks to Jaime Garza, the surgeon of his regiment, who lent him the sum of three hundred pesos. This was still not enough, and he was forced to sell everything he had with him, said to have been worth a thousand pesos, "including his sabre," being left with only two old suits of clothes. The scandal of the forgery came out into the open in 1820, when the surgeon petitioned the viceroy to force Santa Anna to repay him the long overdue loan of three hundred pesos. Garza's protest was also forwarded to Governor José García Dávila. By then, however, Santa Anna was Dávila's protégé, and he had already gained Apodaca's favor. Santa Anna replied to the accusation on 8 June 1820, claiming that more than the sum due had been taken in the form of property and that Garza was lying. His version of the events was accepted, and nothing came of the affair.[20]

In the spring of 1814 Arredondo established his headquarters in Monterrey, and Santa Anna followed him there, together with the main bulk of his forces. For the next year and a half his service entailed chasing rebels, roaming Indian bands, and bandits. It became clear that having succeeded in pacifying the Provincias Internas de Oriente, those men who belonged to the Fixed Infantry Regiment of Veracruz were no longer needed in Monterrey. Veracruz, in contrast, was under strain.

The population in the port was declining fast. By 1818, there were 8,934 inhabitants in a port that had boasted 15,000 eight years earlier. Frightened members of the Spanish population were leaving in droves, taking with them their capital and commercial networks. The disruption caused by the insurgent guerrilla bands operating along the Veracruz-Xalapa-Perote road was undermining the economic infrastructure of the province. The royalist forces were hard-pressed to recruit men.[21]

Following four years spent in Tamaulipas, the Sierra Gorda, Texas, and Nuevo León (1811–15), Santa Anna returned to Veracruz on 20 November 1815, a year after his mother died. Knowing how difficult it is for war veterans to adapt to life away from the theater of war, one can only imagine what this homecoming of sorts must have been like for the twenty-one-year-old Santa Anna. On 1 March 1816, José García Dávila left Mexico City to assume the governorship of Veracruz for a second stint. By all accounts Santa Anna soon became the "closest aide-de-camp of the new governor, Don José García Dávila."[22] It had been Dávila who had overlooked Santa Anna's age in 1810 as a favor to Doña Manuela; the governor was already acquainted with Santa Anna and now took the young officer under his wing. They developed a close working relationship. On two occasions, separated by more than fifty years, Santa Anna went as far as stating that José García Dávila had been like a father to him.[23] Dávila, like Arredondo, was impressed by Santa Anna and praised him regularly in the dispatches he sent to the viceroy.

Little is known about Santa Anna's activities in the port from when he arrived in November 1815 until he was involved in a clash of arms in September 1816. One biographer speculates that he spent these months womanizing and reading Julius Caesar's account of the Gallic Wars as well as other classic texts held in Dávila's library. While one can believe the first part of the statement, given the promiscuity of his later years, it is highly unlikely that Santa Anna, man of action, settled down to read the works of Plutarch, Cicero, or Virgil. According to the brilliant and sardonic mid-nineteenth-century journalist Guillermo Prieto, Santa Anna had read only one book in his entire life.[24]

In 1816, after the Spanish expeditionary Infantry Regiment of Barcelona had failed to make any progress in its war against the guerrillas of

Veracruz, Brigadier Fernando Mijares y Mancebo decided to change his strategy. The Barcelona infantry, decimated by disease, was replaced in Veracruz by a militia force of locals, led by officers of the permanent army, called the Realistas del Camino Real (Royalists of the Royal Highway). Their duties included protecting the Veracruz-Xalapa stretch of the Veracruz–Mexico City road and pursuing guerrilla bands. Santa Anna, an obvious candidate for leading a battalion of this description, grasped the opportunity to become one of the more effective counterinsurgents in the region. In September 1816 he obtained his first results. At the head of thirty lancers he captured the sanguinary rebel chieftain José Parada. On September 8 he defeated another band of rebels near Boca del Río, and José García Dávila commended to Viceroy Apodaca the courage, dedication, and effectiveness of this young and intrepid officer. By the end of the month Dávila established a permanent detachment of royalists in Boca del Río, and Santa Anna was given its command because of his "proven fidelity and patriotism."[25]

In October 1816 Santa Anna left Veracruz on a search-and-destroy mission at the head of 192 men. He fought the insurgents based in the Pueblo de Cotaxtla and San Campus, in a three-day campaign (20–22 October 1816) that led to the vital capture of rebel chieftain Francisco de Paula, the death of several insurgents, and the seizure of a large cache of arms. He was promoted to captain, and his brother Manuel, who also participated in the expedition, was promoted to first lieutenant. A month later, showing no signs of tiring, he led the assault on and capture of Boquilla de Piedras (24 November 1816). He commanded this royalist squadron until he joined the Army of the Three Guarantees in 1821.[26]

Although a number of biographies claim that Santa Anna returned to Tamaulipas to fight under Arredondo against Francisco Javier Mina's expedition in April 1817, and that he became Viceroy Juan Ruíz de Apodaca's personal aide-de-camp in Mexico City, no evidence has been found to substantiate these claims. He remained in Veracruz during these years and had his first run-in with his lifelong foe José Antonio Rincón. When Dávila was temporarily replaced as governor by Ignacio Cincúnegui, Santa Anna fell out of favor with the local bigwigs. Cincúnegui placed Colonel José Antonio Rincón at the head of the port garrison from January to June 1818, and together they ostracized Santa Anna. They prevented him from being given any responsibility in the defense of Veracruz. It is certainly possible that Rincón and Cincúnegui, among other veracruzanos, had started to feel that Santa Anna was beginning to acquire too prominent a role in the region. Jealousy could equally have accounted for Rincón and Cincúnegui's aversion.[27] There might have also been a family feud between the Rincones and the Santa Annas that dated back to the time of Antonio's childhood in Xalapa.

In January 1818 Santa Anna started to correspond with Viceroy Apodaca. Unable to pursue his plans while Cincúnegui was interim governor, he decided to bypass his immediate superior by writing directly to Apodaca. The ambitious young officer was full of ideas, desperate to implement them, frustrated by the obstacles Cincúnegui was placing in his way, and hopeful that Apodaca might listen to him and overrule the interim governor's orders. As well as writing to the viceroy he returned to Xalapa, where he met with the captain general of the province, Ciriaco de Llano, to press his case. De Llano, obeying orders from Apodaca, intervened on Santa Anna's behalf, giving him written instructions to take to Cincúnegui, confirming that he was to be placed in charge of a militia unit. The militia unit he was to command thereafter with considerable success, formed of amnestied insurgents and the inhabitants of villages located just outside the port city, was to be the Realistas de Extramuros de Veracruz y Pueblo de la Boca del Río.[28]

Cincúnegui was not amused by Santa Anna's successful bypassing of his authority, and he dragged his feet over giving the young officer the command of the agreed militia unit. Santa Anna wasted no time in complaining to both De Llano and the viceroy about Cincúnegui's disobedience, and this time Apodaca replied in person. Santa Anna's delight at receiving Apodaca's support found ample expression in the letters he wrote both to the viceroy and De Llano, warmly thanking them for having intervened on his behalf. Apodaca acknowledged Santa Anna's gratitude as well as his stubborn determination to serve the army and the *good cause*. This acquaintanceship was to serve Santa Anna well when, in the fall of 1818, he was formally accused of insubordination and was in a position to go to the capital to seek the viceroy's personal pardon.[29]

Before Santa Anna's misdemeanor took place in November that year, he enjoyed a couple of resounding successes and had one humiliating defeat. In June 1818, in command of the flying militia unit of Extramuros, he defeated a gang of rebels entrenched in Boca del Río. On 22 August 1818, riding with a force of fifty men, he routed another band of insurgents in the proximity of the haciendas del Jato and Joluca. On 11 September 1818, however, more than two hundred mounted insurgents, led by Valentino Guzmán and Marcos Benavides, launched an attack within sight of the walls of Veracruz. They burned two houses, stole cattle, and left several inflammatory proclamations behind, one of which directly threatened Santa Anna. Santa Anna's Realistas de Extramuros, together with pickets from the Fixed Infantry of Veracruz, raced out to engage in combat with the rebels. The support he was expecting from the Infantry Battalion of Asturias, however, was not forthcoming. Dangerously exposed and outnumbered, he had no choice but to beat a hasty retreat. Prolific journalist, diarist, and idiosyncratic republican politician Carlos María de Bustamante, in prison in San Juan de Ulúa at the time, described Santa Anna's undignified escape "thanks to his horse's speed, losing his hat [as he fled]."

Santa Anna was furious with the governor of Veracruz at his failure to send out the main force of the Asturias infantry. Against a backdrop of infighting between Santa Anna and Cincúnegui, one wonders whether Cincúnegui deliberately hesitated in sending out the Infantry Battalion of Asturias, in the hope that Santa Anna would get killed. In a strongly worded letter to Apodaca, Santa Anna condemned the governor for his apathy and for displaying a marked absence of resolve. He also demanded that he be given fifty regular soldiers from the Fixed Regiment of Veracruz, who would form a rapid response unit, ready at any time to back his one hundred militia troops. He defended his request by adding that he was convinced the regulars would serve to train the militia and to give them greater fighting confidence. Although this request was rejected, it is evident that thanks to all these letters, he had become a familiar name in Apodaca's quarters by the time he most needed the viceroy's personal intervention.[30]

In November 1818 Santa Anna raided Venta de Arriba, in the proximity of the port, and captured a particularly sanguinary guerrilla chieftain, Francisco de Asís. Applying Arredondo's methods, he personally escorted Asís to a point outside the city walls and had him executed by firing squad before the local inhabitants. Asís should have been offered the opportunity to repent and take the amnesty. Cincúnegui seized this opportunity, claiming that Santa Anna's execution of Asís was an unforgivable breach of discipline, and reported him to the commander general of Puebla and Veracruz, Brigadier Ciriaco de Llano. De Llano had no choice but to suspend Santa Anna. Showing no lack of initiative, Santa Anna set off to Mexico City, "without a licence, to represent before Your Excellency the grievances herewith referred to." He argued that Asís was a "pernicious and sanguinary chief" who deserved to be executed. He also claimed he was close to capturing the much-sought-after insurgent leader Guadalupe Victoria. He could not pursue these activities if he was suspended. The priests and communities from outside the walls of Veracruz and Boca del Río certified that he fulfilled his duties with "efficiency and exactitude." Surely he deserved praise for his labors, not punishment. He was the victim of a conspiracy. Governor Cincúnegui and Lieutenant Colonel José Rincón were doing everything they could to malign him. The fact that he had gone to Mexico City without permission was also being seized upon to pervert the course of justice.[31] General Pascual Liñán intervened on Santa Anna's behalf. He described Santa Anna as being "active, zealous, indefatigable in his service, and of very good military knowledge." Liñán also stressed that he was young: "it is not strange that on some occasions he may have exceeded his powers."[32] Although the exact date of Santa Anna's rendezvous with Apodaca is unknown, it worked. Following this visit to the capital and Liñán's timely intervention, the viceroy granted Santa Anna permission to return to his command and ensured that there would be no further legal action.

Reinstated at the head of his flying squadron, Santa Anna returned to his line of duty with his customary zest and enthusiasm. In the first weeks of 1819 he set out at the head of seventy horsemen to raid a large insurgent stronghold. During five hectic days of marches and countermarches, they searched the districts of Rajabandera, Campos de Baja, Banderas, Tamarindo, Paso de Fierro, Soyolapa, and Paso de Naranjo, seeking out guerrilla leaders Manuel Salvador, Félix González, and

Mariano Cenobio. The operation resulted in a major victory, demonstrating that Apodaca had made the right decision. All three insurgent chieftains, together with a priest and 230 armed men, surrendered and begged for amnesty.[33]

Less than a month later, in early February, Santa Anna set out to find and capture the elusive and highly prized insurgent leader Guadalupe Victoria. With seventy newly amnestied cavalry forced to dismount and use machetes to open a trail through the thick vegetation, Santa Anna made his way into the Sierra de Masatiopa, through Soyolapa, Río Blanco, and Rincón Papaya. As they made their way toward Masatiopa and La Laguna, penetrating the region surrounding Aguas de Azufre, more insurgents handed themselves in, seeking amnesty. Even the Indians of Masatiopa surrendered to Santa Anna. He stopped in Córdoba to rest and gather information. Here he was told that Victoria was almost alone by now, crippled by poor health, reduced to eating roasted papayas and little else. Santa Anna was not feeling well himself, yet he persevered in his search of the area. Victoria, ill or not, managed to avoid capture. Other insurgents on the run, however, such as Cleto, Casas, and Bonilla, handed themselves in.[34]

Santa Anna's successes coincided with the appointment of Pascual de Liñán as interim governor of the Intendancy of Veracruz in 1819. Under Liñán, Dávila also returned to assume control of the port. In contrast to the state of play of the previous two years, it was now Santa Anna's turn to enjoy the benefits of being favored by those in power in Veracruz, while Rincón and Cincúnegui were demoted to a secondary role. One of the interesting ways in which Liñán advanced Santa Anna's career was by assigning him the responsibility of organizing the reestablishment of the abandoned towns of Medellín and Xamapa, as well as founding a new one at Loma de Santa María, with over three hundred amnestied insurgents. Santa Anna's ability to govern the newly formed settlements—the villages of Medellín, Xamapa, San Diego, and Tamarindo, and the 593 families that came to inhabit them—showed that there was much more to him than just courage, boundless energy, and raw ambition.

Pascual de Liñán was a perceptive man. Having arrived in New Spain in 1817, he had not taken long to appreciate "that land was the key element in pacifying the province and in achieving the resettlement of the insurgents. Without agrarian reform to distribute agricultural land to the uprooted population, the cycle of insurgency would continue without end."[35] Santa Anna, with plots of land to distribute among the amnestied insurgents, became the most popular and sought after royalist officer of the region. Rebels now started to surrender to him en masse. Transformed into a royalist land reform administrator, he chose the sites of settlements, planned the organization of communities, assigned plots, helped with construction of churches at Xamapa, San Diego, and Tamarindo (Medellín's original church was still standing), and imposed his own idiosyncratic system of governance, forging, for want of a better term, a mini-military autocracy in all four communities.

His responsibilities were far-reaching, ranging from architectural design to pastoral care. He was in all but name the ruler of the settlements. He was a hands-on, interventionist ruler. He told the settlers what to grow (beans, bananas, maize, rice) and where. He went into Veracruz to recruit teachers for the communities' schools. He budgeted for the construction of churches (1,000 pesos each) and houses erected in 1819 (51 in Medellín, 47 in Xamapa, 113 in San Diego, and 23 in Tamarindo). He ensured that the three bigger communities also had shops (four in Medellín and two each in Xamapa and San Diego). As Santa Anna informed his superiors with unquestionable pride: "I forced and compelled the inhabitants [of these communities] to build each his own house, with a kitchen and a yard, giving each family the necessary land in relation to their circumstances." He also convinced them to plant their vegetable fields around the villages. After a year and seven months, "of working with these indomitable people, enemies of all subjugation," he liked to think that he had personally been responsible for "reducing them to live together in villages and subject entirely to the norms of the most civilized society."[36]

Liñán gave him extensive powers to run the four agricultural communities of Medellín, Xamapa, San Diego, and Tamarindo, and Santa Anna did not shy from using them. He placed his brother Manuel and three other cronies at the head of the newly formed communities.[37] He set about imposing a tightly controlled administrative system with a strong militaristic slant. All men in the settlements between the ages of sixteen and fifty were obliged to serve in a royalist militia. They were given the responsibility of patrolling their communities regularly. One of the explanations he gave for not allowing the fields surrounding each village to spread too far was that nobody would ever be too far away to return and protect the community from an unforeseen attack. Families were also encouraged to produce extra food to feed the militias. In San Diego he supervised the construction of an octagonal fort that could hold fifty soldiers. In all four villages he also made sure that a large shed was constructed where one hundred men could take refuge under siege. He gave his designated subordinates the authority to monitor the movements of all community residents. Nobody could leave or enter without the written authorization of their military commander. All weapons were stored in the village barracks. The villagers could use them as long as they had been issued a license and were obliged to return them every day after use. He also decreed that within Medellín, Xamapa, San Diego, and Tamarindo, all legal authority relating to military matters lay with him and his subordinates. They could override any decisions made by the local magistrates. His obsession with maintaining rigid controls and sustaining militias that were ready for action at all times may have been indicative of his pronounced militarism but probably had more to do with wartime conditions.

Within a few months the four agricultural communities Santa Anna had established were thriving. By June 1819 Medellín had a population of 63 families (245 persons), Xamapa 83 (297 persons), San Diego 200 (250 persons), and Tamarindo 50 (175 persons). A year later, in July 1820, Santa Anna recorded that Medellín had a population of 112 families, Xamapa 140, San Diego 287, and Tamarindo 54. For two years, until the end of 1820, there were no instances of residents returning to the insurgency, and life in the communities was not touched by conflict. By 1820 these villages were sending cartloads of vegetables to Veracruz. San Diego, the largest of the four, benefiting from its proximity to the *camino real* (highway), enjoyed heightened prosperity. To quote historian Christon I. Archer, "They became models of constructive counterinsurgency planning and established Santa Anna as a regional leader with a significant following outside the port city."[38]

There is certainly enough evidence to suggest that Santa Anna succeeded in acquiring and developing strong leadership skills during his time as royalist land reform administrator. José García Dávila was persuaded that Santa Anna deserved to be promoted for his efforts.[39] For some, however, it was as the commander of these villages that he first crossed the thin line separating the strongman from the despot. On 5 January 1820, Marcos Benavides (the very same Benavides who had humiliated Santa Anna on the plains of Veracruz in September 1818) and four others complained to García Dávila. They accused Santa Anna of being a "despot." He was forcing fourteen civilians, on a weekly basis and without pay, to work on the construction of the officers' houses. To add insult to injury he was making them build a large yard where he intended to keep cattle. And to make matters worse he was selling them hay at ridiculously expensive prices. For Benavides, Santa Anna's tyranny was perfectly captured by the way he turned round on hearing that some people were suffering hunger because of his punishments, and retorted: "Let them die. They might learn then that my orders are sacred."[40] Had it not been for the fact that the town council of Veracruz, as a corporation, started to whinge about Santa Anna's antics in the summer of 1820, Benavides's accusations could have been attributed to his personal dislike of the incipient caudillo.

In August and September 1820, however, the town council joined Benavides's men in asking the governor for help and protection from Santa Anna. Its members discussed the complaints made about his cruel treatment of one Casimiro de Arenaza. He had "violently ridden roughshod" over Arenaza as well as other people from San Diego. He had imprisoned a number of them, on 14 August 1819, for not having their passports with them. The people of San Diego were said to live in fear of him and his cattle-rustling bandit friends Crisanto de Castro and Rafael Villa. Equally sinister was that Arenaza's witnesses were being persecuted, since Santa Anna and his men knew they were intending to make a formal complaint. Arenaza was so scared that he was staying in Veracruz, to the detriment of his commercial interests. During his absence his shop had been broken into and 220 pesos' worth of goods had been stolen. As was forcefully expressed by Councilor Manuel de Viya y Cosío, they needed to replace Santa Anna with "a trustworthy leader, capable of repressing these excesses." In a letter to Dávila, Viya y Cosío added that not only was it imperative for Santa Anna to be removed from office; it was essential that he was not given a similar post in any other part of the province. The minutes of the town council of Veracruz and the correspondence they generated show that even before Santa Anna acquired a prominent role in politics, there were people who considered him to have despotic tendencies. Dávila appeased the town council by replacing Santa Anna as head of San Diego, but no legal action was taken against him. To Dávila, who defended his protégé and paid little attention to the town council's tongue-wagging, Santa Anna was not a tyrant, just a strong and effective leader—the view of all those who would follow him in years to come. It is interesting to note that by the 1840s, even the angry Manuel de Viya y Cosío had changed his tune and had become one of Santa Anna's most trusted bankers.[41]

By the time of his twenty-seventh birthday, Santa Anna was a promising lieutenant of grenadiers in the royalist army. The son of a provincial middle-class creole family had grown into a man who already inspired strong emotions in the people who met him. He was described as being impulsive, quarrelsome, courageous, disobedient, energetic, despotic, talented, impetuous, arrogant, and good-looking. His character, as might have been expected, was multifaceted and complex. He was a dedicated and tireless royalist counterinsurgent, prepared to endure all kinds of hardships to capture the insurgents who hid in the thick insect-ridden chaparral of Veracruz. He was also a keen village administrator, who dedicated day and night to ensuring that the communities for which he was responsible had fresh water, adequate kitchens, an enclosure for their chickens, and a novel system of governance. And yet at the same time he was also a troublemaker with despotic tendencies; a wild kid who gambled away a fortune in San Antonio de Béxar and forged his commanders' signatures to cover his losses. He was manipulative, wily, and extremely good at extricating himself from tight corners. For biographer Rafael F. Muñoz he was a "sensual player," whose "tropical temperament" enabled him to be capable of both "the most intense activity" and "the most complete indolence," without there being a contradiction.[42] He was also a man of actions, not words. This side of his character would become a hallmark of his idiosyncratic presidential style once he rose to power in the 1830s. He was certainly brave: a dedicated and energetic officer. There is little doubt that he enjoyed that excitement to which certain soldiers become addicted and which can be found only in the thick of the battlefield. As he reiterated in his memoirs, it was always an "honor to lead the vanguard" forces. He definitely "preferred the dangers of war to the seducing and desirable palace life."[43]

He had boundless stamina as well. Santa Anna was one to enjoy a challenge. He must have responded well to being described by his superiors as "indefatigable." According to Liñán, it was Santa Anna's "energy, hard work and vigilance" that made him outstanding.[44] He was also evidently stubborn. His perseverance as a counterinsurgent exemplified this. The fact that he would not give up easily, even if this entailed breaking rules or bypassing one's immediate superiors, is apparent. Worthy of mention was his predisposition to write to the highest authorities (i.e., the viceroy) if he considered this necessary. Santa Anna was ambitious, and like most young officers, impatient to gain praise and, through heroic feats, join the "swift road to promotion and advancement in every arm."[45] As he recalled, to gain such a promotion was the "golden dream of his ardent youth."[46] He was confident of his own abilities and thought highly of himself. It is significant that his respect of authority did not amount to subservience. Even as a young man, he showed signs that he believed in authority so long as this authority recognized his merits and backed his actions. Otherwise he was ready to seek ways around it; and he was not shy about knocking on the viceroy's door if help was required. It is possible that this was a lesson he learned from Arredondo: in this new and exciting revolutionary age, high-ranking officers could be choosers. Authority was now in the eye of the beholder. It could be questioned, challenged, overcome, and ultimately appropriated. For Santa Anna and his generation, the mystique of authority lay no longer in the genealogy of kings or the prestige of hierarchy. Authority was there for the taking, and the strongest bidder could take all if he played his cards right in what had become a dog-eat-dog world by the teens of the century. He could be ruthless, as the execution of Asís exemplified. This sanguinary streak in his character clearly struck a chord of fear in the population.

However, he was also effective without resorting to violence in persuading insurgents to hand themselves in and actually join his militia unit. He himself claimed that this was his "natural inclination," to use "persuasion rather than a show of arms."[47] Prieto, despite being a consistent critic of the caudillo, could not help noting Santa Anna's hypnotic charisma: "When he was in high spirits his words acquired a charm of their own as he caressed them with his *jarocho* accent; his large and penetrating dark eyes were the ones to do the persuading rather than his words, and his easy and swift gestures transformed him into an irresistible seducer."[48] The respect his men accorded him must have arisen from Santa Anna's zeal. He led from the front and by example. If his men suffered, so did he. He was not one to give orders from a comfortable and ventilated room, protected and well attended, behind the thick walls of a guarded garrison. He gained his men's loyalty and obedience by being prepared to endure the same hardships as they did, pursuing insurgents into the dense insect-ridden tropical forest of central Veracruz. The lancers of the Extramuros–Boca del Río unit could not complain about their commander's laziness, cowardice, or unwillingness to fight. If anything, they must have moaned about their leader's high expectations, his tirelessness, the way he pushed himself and them, and his resolve to keep going when all the rest were desperate to catch their breath.

He now also had more than ten years' experience in the armed forces. His formative years had gone by in marches, battles, and sentry duty. He had seen action in Tamaulipas, the Sierra Gorda, and even in the remote northern province of Texas. He had acquired a taste for violence and had no doubt learned a thing or two from his superiors, especially from Arredondo. He had spent over five years pacifying central Veracruz. He had become familiar with the terrain, the dense bush, the swampy coastline, the thorny vegetation. He had learned to live with the biting insects and the torrid temperatures. He had come to know the people of the region well. Through his two years of work at the head of the settlements of Medellín, Xamapa, San Diego, and Tamarindo, he had gained valuable experience as a leader. On paper, everything seemed to indicate that he was one of Spain's most dedicated defenders in the region. Governor Dávila treated him as if Santa Anna were his own son. He had even been awarded the Shield of Honor and Certificate of the Royal and Distinguished Order of Isabella the Catholic for his services.[49] As Santa Anna himself recognized, he was "pampered by the viceregal government," and his "gratitude knew no limits."[50] Then, three days after his twenty-seventh birthday, on 24 February 1821, Agustín de Iturbide and Vicente Guerrero launched the Plan of Iguala. And everything changed.

3. Liberator of Veracruz, Founder of the Republic, 1821–1823

By the end of 1820 the War of Independence had reached a stalemate. The insurgents, though few and dispersed, remained unbeaten. To many high-ranking creole royalist officers it was obvious that peace would not be restored until Mexico became independent. It was in this context of exhaustion and uncertainty that negotiations began between the handsome and astute creole royalist commander Agustín de Iturbide and the defiant Afro-Mexican insurgent leader Vicente Guerrero in December. The negotiations focused initially on the restoration of the 1812 Constitution. Guerrero was not prepared to surrender, and he was not confident about events in Spain. He feared that the liberals who had forced Ferdinand VII to restore the 1812 charter in the wake of Rafael Riego's 1820 revolt would be overthrown before they could accomplish their aims. Nor did the 1812 Constitution offer citizenship rights to mulattos like himself. Iturbide offered to propose to the Cortes that mulattos be given such rights, in exchange for Guerrero putting down his arms. Guerrero did not believe the Cortes would listen. He was prepared to place himself under Iturbide's command if he endorsed the cause of independence. On 24 February 1821, Iturbide opted to run with Guerrero's proposal and proclaimed the Plan of Iguala.[1]

The Plan of Iguala was an incredibly seductive proposal. With the vague promise of Three Guarantees of religion, independence, and union—(i.e., that Roman Catholicism would be the official religion; that Mexico would be independent; and that all Spaniards could continue to live unharmed in Mexico, enjoying equality before the law)—Iturbide brought old insurgents and old royalists together, even though they opted to join forces for very different reasons. According to some accounts, Santa Anna was acquainted with Iturbide and was already conspiring to bring about independence by the time news of the Plan of Iguala reached Veracruz. No evidence, however, has been found to support such a claim. News of the 24 February 1821 Plan of Iguala reached Veracruz on 5 March, and Santa Anna did not immediately embrace it. Instead he led his regiment to Orizaba following orders to replace Colonel Francisco Hevia.[2]

As he made his way there, on 21 March 1821 under the towering presence of the volcano Citlaltépetl, he became acquainted with José María Tornel y Mendívil. It was the beginning of a long and extremely productive friendship between two men whose careers would become profoundly intertwined over the next thirty years. They had a great deal in common. They were both in their twenties, Tornel being one year younger. Like Santa Anna, Tornel was a creole veracruzano (born in the rival mountain town of Orizaba) from a middle-class family with links to commercial sectors of the province. They were both ambitious military men and compulsive schemers, who also enjoyed the company of women (in years to come, the two of them would have notorious extramarital relationships) and a good night out, although Tornel preferred the theater to Santa Anna's favored cockfights. Santa Anna was renowned for his charm, Tornel for his eloquent, impassioned writing. Their friendship was to last until Tornel's death. The only significant difference between them at the time, and it was not a minor one, was that Tornel had fought for the insurgents (1813–14). However, he had accepted the amnesty in 1815, following his imprisonment in 1814, and had kept a low profile until he offered himself to Santa Anna's regiment in 1821. Santa Anna would go on to name Tornel his personal secretary, making him treasurer as well as chief postmaster of the province. The fact that they immediately became close friends is evidenced in Santa Anna's willingness to give Tornel full powers of attorney to represent him in 1822.[3]

On reaching the highland town of Orizaba, Santa Anna confronted Francisco Miranda and José Joaquín de Herrera's reinforcements, from 23 to 29 March. On the 29th, having held out for six days and fortified his forces in the Carmen convent, he notoriously changed sides and joined Herrera. In his own rather vague words, "the Plan of Iguala appeared, proclaimed by Colonel Agustín de Iturbide on 24 February 1821, and I hastened to support it, because I wanted to contribute my grain of sand to the great work of our political regeneration."[4]

Tornel's acceptance of the Plan of Iguala was understandable since he had been an insurgent initially. Santa Anna's conversion from royalist to insurgent, however, was not such an obvious step, even considering that it was under Iturbide's Army of the Three Guarantees. Santa Anna had been a dedicated defender of the colony and had also developed a close relationship with General García Dávila. To change sides represented a major betrayal, and a personal one at that.

Santa Anna's conversion to the cause of independence was preceded and followed by that of almost all the creoles in the royalist army, after the Plan of Iguala was proclaimed. He was one of eighty-five thousand men at arms who changed sides. After eleven years of war, his family's commercial interests had undoubtedly suffered. With no end to the disruptive effects of war in sight, unless independence was endorsed, it is not difficult to appreciate the logic of Santa Anna's conversion, under the broad and consensual terms of Iguala. Against the backdrop of frustration created by the unsatisfactory restoration of the 1812 charter, and with the viceregal authorities dragging their feet over its implementation, Santa Anna came to the conclusion—probably persuaded in part by his friend Tornel—that independence was a viable and desirable option. One source suggests that Tornel was already writing speeches in support of the Plan of Iguala by 18 March, several days before he and Santa Anna openly defected to the rebel cause. Santa Anna would admit years later that "when Sr. Herrera presented himself at Orizaba, I had already for many months been discussing independence with army officers and pardoned insurgents."[5]

Three factors must have influenced him. The first was Tornel. Orizaba was Tornel's hometown, and he probably tried to talk Santa Anna out of attacking a community that was supporting independence and from where Tornel had secretly supported the guerrilla bands after he had been amnestied (1815–17). The second was José Joaquín de Herrera's influence. On 26 March Herrera met with Santa Anna to persuade him to change sides. Herrera explained to him in exhaustive detail exactly what the Plan of Iguala entailed. The third was that his defection would be rewarded with a further promotion, this time to the rank of colonel. Once Santa Anna accepted Herrera's offer, he set about fighting for his new cause with characteristic zeal.[6]

He helped Herrera liberate Córdoba a couple of days later, then headed down toward the coast, where Santa Anna already counted a strong number of supporters. At the head of six hundred troops he liberated Alvarado on 25 April. The people there welcomed him "with an inexplicable joy: they all cried at the same time long live independence and the troops who defend it." He set in motion the preparations to send an emissary to the United States giving himself political attributes with which nobody had invested him. His army doubled to twelve hundred men. His ability to mobilize the *jarochos* and the so-called dangerous classes was becoming apparent.[7]

At the end of the month Santa Anna moved north toward Veracruz. On his way there he met Guadalupe Victoria in La Soledad (now Soledad de Doblado). The great insurgent leader, who had been living in hiding for thirty months, "naked like Adam; alone, ill, . . . with little else to eat except grass and tree-roots," was found by some Indians, who persuaded him to abandon his secret retreat, given that the political context had changed so dramatically.[8] He presented himself before Santa Anna to offer his services. Displaying remarkable shrewdness, the incipient caudillo, rather than accept Victoria's offer, immediately gave the command of the province to Victoria and placed himself under the famous revolutionary's orders. Victoria, after all, had been the original leader of the insurgency in Veracruz. In so doing, Santa Anna succeeded in associating himself in the eyes of the mestizo and Indian popular classes of central Veracruz with this hero of independence, making his conversion to the cause of independence ring true. Had naked ambition been the motivation behind his betrayal of the royalist cause, he would not have offered his commanding position to Victoria. It would not be long before he made some significant political gains out of this gesture.[9]

News that a royalist division was besieging Herrera in Córdoba prevented him from assaulting the port in early May. He made his way back up the mountains to Córdoba to assist Herrera in the action of 19–20 May and forced the royalists to lift their siege and flee inland. Iturbide awarded Santa Anna the *Córdoba cross*, and shortly after, despite his original act of deference toward Victoria, he became the self-appointed commander general of the Province of Veracruz. For this appointment to be recognized, two things needed to happen. The first was for Victoria to leave Veracruz, which he did by going to meet with Iturbide in San Juan del Río. The second was that Santa Anna had to overcome Herrera's objections. Herrera accused him of calling himself commander general of Veracruz without Iturbide's approval. Santa Anna replied that since the end of April, Guadalupe Victoria had granted him the command of the army in absentia. If the province was under his orders this was because of his "influence, sleepless nights, and money." He told Herrera to be satisfied as the commander general of Puebla and asked Herrera to leave him alone in Veracruz. Herrera reluctantly returned to Puebla, and Santa Anna set about liberating Xalapa.[10]

Following news of the Plan of Iguala, the people of Xalapa were ready for independence, as evidenced by the reports that the royalist parapets and defenses erected by day were regularly sabotaged at night. Nevertheless, Commander Juan de Orbegoso's royalist garrison was not ready to surrender. Santa Anna arrived on the outskirts of his birthplace on 27 May and launched his attack at dawn two days later. After three hours of combat, Orbegoso surrendered. This being Santa Anna's hometown, his liberating army was particularly well behaved. On the 30th he went to meet the town council and concurred with its members that every effort would be dedicated to preserving the "tranquility, well-being, and comfort of the people of this town." A thanksgiving mass and a *Te Deum* were held and sung in the principal church of Xalapa.[11]

As new commander general of Xalapa, Santa Anna asked the Xalapa elite for a 12,000-peso loan to sustain his army. He recognized that it was a high figure but justified it by arguing that he did not expect to ask for another loan thereafter. The town council replied that with difficulty they might manage to raise 6,000 pesos. They were to learn very fast that Santa Anna was not one to accept "no" for an answer. If his deference toward Victoria shows that he was already becoming a cunning politician, the manner in which he obtained the 12,000 pesos shows that by 1821 he had also become a particularly forceful character. By 24 June, after a number of tense meetings with an intransigent and menacing Santa Anna, the town council had coughed up the full sum of 12,000 pesos despite several attempts to avoid payment.[12]

He obtained the grudging support of the elite by ensuring that their commercial interests were not harmed by his troops, while he became the hero of the popular classes by abolishing the taxes that most affected them. Being the protagonist of numerous celebrations also gave him an aura of authority that no other local chieftain acquired. He decreed exemption of maize, beans, smoked chiles, barley, and straw from all taxation. Although a number of taxes were maintained and some were even introduced to pay for the costs of his troops, these were targeted at the wealthier members of Xalapan society. He was also quick to give his followers positions of responsibility in key areas. Without yet having received confirmation from Iturbide that he was the commander general of the province, he took it upon himself to behave as such. Representative of his growing popular appeal in the region, most of his men were mestizo and mulatto peasants from the coast who grew "the bare basics" to survive. The fact that they did not own land meant they were free and ready to follow him in his military adventures.[13]

On 24 June, Santa Anna informed the town council that he was leaving Xalapa to liberate Veracruz and that he was leaving Diego Leño in charge of the town garrison. The decision to assault the port was his, and he proceeded with his planned attack before Iturbide could reply to him. As he stated to the Liberator, it was essential to liberate the port before reinforcements were sent from Havana. On the fields of El Encero he harangued his troops with a speech that was probably written by Carlos María de Bustamante, who joined him temporarily as his ghostwriter in Xalapa. He addressed the troops as his comrades and soldiers. Through Bustamante's pre-Hispanic motifs, they were called upon to bring to a happy end the reconquest of their freedom and independence, avenging the suffering the conquistadors had inflicted upon their ancestors. Taking Veracruz became a truly momentous feat that would "change the face of two worlds, recovering the glorious prestige of which we were dispossessed for three hundred years." They were to fight "with the fury of a climate that devours men." He also stressed that in order to attain a glorious victory that would make the triumphs of Cortés and Alvarado pale into insignificance, they needed to be disciplined. On 25 June, his army made its way down the mountain toward the coast.[14]

On the 27th Santa Anna reached the outskirts of the port. He issued letters to the "European inhabitants of Veracruz" and to the soldiers who guarded its walls. He stressed that he did not want to be responsible for a massacre. He did not want to hurt Veracruz, since he was himself a veracruzano. Proof that no harm would come to Veracruz lay in the example of Xalapa, where commercial activities were thriving following the town's liberation. He reminded the *porteños* of his generosity in not imposing a siege on Veracruz. He expressed his sadness that they appeared reluctant to listen to him, and his anger that they had mistreated those among them who favored independence, and those who supported the 1812 Constitution. He offered them one last chance to surrender. If they rejected his generous offer they would inevitably "suffer the horrors of war, and [would] not be able to blame [him] for them." He urged the recently arrived reinforcements from Cuba to desert, reminding them that the longer they stayed, the longer they were exposing themselves to the dangerous "heat, mosquitoes and death" of Veracruz.[15]

He also addressed a letter to José García Dávila, who according to Tornel was "his friend and benefactor" and to whom he awarded the respect due to a father. However callous he may have been, it could not have been easy for Santa Anna to take on the man who, as a favor to his mother, had allowed him to join the army as a cadet in the first place. He offered Dávila his respect and affection: "I have always thought of myself as your son." Under Dávila he had prospered in the army. Thanks to Dávila, his enemies [i.e., the Rincones] had been unable to disarm him. He admitted it was difficult finding himself outside Veracruz, preparing to launch an attack on a leader it had been his honor to serve. He was pained at the thought of fighting his own people: "Such are the horrendous consequences of a civil revolution." He knew Dávila understood deep down that despite the debt he owed the Spaniard, it was Santa Anna's duty to stand by his nation as her son and citizen. His only hope was that Dávila might surrender. They would then be able to embrace each other. He would be able to kiss the hand that had done so much for his family and the people of Veracruz.[16]

Dávila was not amused. He placed, of all people, Lieutenant Colonel José Rincón at the head of the garrison's troops to repulse Santa Anna. He also said of his former protégé, in a proclamation, that he was a perfidious, treacherous, and scheming inexperienced youth who, blinded by ambition, was prepared to sacrifice the precious lives of over three hundred Americans (Mexicans).[17] We do not know how Santa Anna felt when he read Dávila's vitriolic description of him, or what he made of Dávila's decision to place José Rincón up against him. What is evident is that Santa Anna was now even more committed to liberating Veracruz, whatever the cost. The impetuousness with which he led the major assault of 7 July 1821 may substantiate the view that he was fighting with his heart, not his head.

Santa Anna displayed the kind of courage, tenacity, and bloody-mindedness that had characterized his reckless actions under Arredondo. According to one account, he was the first in and the last out. His bravery was recognized by Iturbide, who awarded him the Cross of the First Epoch. According to Dávila's dispatch, while Santa Anna's valor was not disputed, the strategy he employed was. It seemed as if he did not care about exposing his men's lives. He entered Veracruz at the head of his men at 2:00 in the morning, under the torrential rain. He succeeded in advancing as far as the market square, with his men firing their guns, playing martial songs as they went. They placed a cannon in the middle of the street and blasted part of the city center away as they opened fire on Dávila's house. The royalists fought back, and the streets of the town center became littered with debris and corpses. The combat lasted three hours. Santa Anna's cavalry detachment, led by his brother Manuel, then lost their nerve, panicked, and retreated in disorder, ignoring their commander's shouts. The fleeing cavalry scared the rest of Santa Anna's men, who also beat a hasty retreat. According to Dávila, over one hundred of Santa Anna's men died in the assault, while only four royalists were killed. No mention was made of the civilians who died caught in the line of fire.[18]

Frustrated, Santa Anna retreated to Córdoba. From here he followed the course of the war in Tabasco and kept Iturbide abreast of developments in Villahermosa as well as of his army's victories in Corral Nuevo, Acayucan, and Coatzacualcos. While he was in Córdoba news reached him that the newly appointed political head of New Spain, Juan O'Donojú, had arrived in Veracruz on 30 July and was willing to meet with Iturbide. A truce was called, and Santa Anna was able to enter Veracruz on 5 August to see O'Donojú and organize a meeting between the Spaniard and Iturbide. Arrangements for such an encounter were set in motion.[19]

Santa Anna personally escorted O'Donojú to Córdoba. If one is to believe his own account of the negotiations that preceded the encounter between O'Donojú and Iturbide, and the signing of the Treaties of Córdoba (24 August), his role was all-important. He inculcated in O'Donojú the need to see Iturbide. He wrote extensive letters to Iturbide to obtain a groundbreaking peaceful result. He was responsible for O'Donojú's safety. Both Iturbide and O'Donojú insisted he was present at their negotiations. With the Treaties of Córdoba, in which O'Donojú recognized the independence of Mexico in return for Iturbide's assurance that the Mexican throne would be offered to a member of the Bourbon dynasty, to quote Santa Anna, "the war came to an end." He returned to Xalapa, where on the 31st he presided over the fiesta that celebrated the signing of the treaties.[20]

Following the Treaties of Córdoba, only four garrisons remained in Spanish control: Mexico City, Perote, Veracruz, and San Juan de Ulúa. Iturbide, O'Donojú, Guerrero, and the main bulk of the Army of the Three Guarantees made their way toward the capital. Santa Anna took it upon himself to liberate Perote, Veracruz, and San Juan de Ulúa. He carried out a reconnaissance expedition to and around the large fortress of San Carlos (Perote), between 9 and 15 September, and then returned to Xalapa to organize his troops before launching the assault of 7 October. It was during late September, while Mexico City was being liberated and before Santa Anna attacked Perote and Veracruz, that he became embroiled in a confrontation with the town council of Xalapa.[21]

On 28 September, Councilor José Antonio Agrazar called an extraordinary town council meeting at 8:00 in the evening. Santa Anna had insulted him. On the 10th the town council had decreed that one Domingo de la Rocha pay a 100-peso fine. As he could not, it had been agreed that Rocha's goods would be confiscated to the value of 100 pesos. Rocha's wife went to see Santa Anna to plead for help. Santa Anna, busy making his preparations for the attack on Perote, determined that Rocha's property should not be confiscated before the accused could make his appeal. Agrazar took no notice, since Santa Anna did not have the power to overrule the town council, and proceeded with the confiscation. At this point Santa Anna intervened. On hearing that Agrazar had ignored his recommendation, he summoned the councilor. He insulted Agrazar and said that had he known at the time that the councilor had dared to ignore his orders, he would have had a patrol bring him to Santa Anna tied to their horses' tails. He demanded that Rocha's property was returned. Having endured Santa Anna's forceful demands since the end of May, the town council found this the final straw. The council decided not to deal with Santa Anna unless he could provide written evidence that he was the political chief of the province: "the argument that he is the *jefe político* because he is a military commander is not valid."[22]

The following day Santa Anna, who must have found this kind of distraction particularly irritating as he planned the attacks on Perote and Veracruz, called a meeting at 6:00 in the evening to talk things over. The town council refused to meet him on the grounds that he had not yet provided written evidence that he was in a position to give them orders. Santa Anna was not one to put up with earnest and self-important civilians. He forced them to hear him out at eight o'clock that night, trying to smooth things over by turning on his tropical charm. He said it had never been his intention to ride roughshod over the corporation, and that he believed the law must be respected and upheld, but Sr. Agrazar should not have ignored his plea. The law did allow for appeals to be made. As for raising his voice, he admitted that Sr. Agrazar may well have thought Santa Anna had shouted, but he spoke in a loud voice by nature. He then reminded them that he had consistently protected Xalapa and that it should have been obvious to them that he acted with their best interests at heart. As for the suggestion that his political power could be questioned, Santa Anna displayed a certain degree of incredulity. Were they serious about expecting to see a written order? Did Iturbide have them himself? He was the *jefe* because Iturbide liaised with him. It was as simple as that. If they were not going to recognize him as the *jefe*, who were they going to report to? To Dávila? The war had not finished. Written confirmation of his position was bound to come, but time was needed for the new order to settle.[23]

On 1 October, as if the matter had been amicably settled and forgotten, Santa Anna demanded to be provided with 20,000 rations of biscuits, beans, rice, and other foodstuffs for his troops on the eve of the liberation of Perote. The town council refused to cooperate. They reminded him that it was originally agreed that the 12,000 pesos they had paid him was a one-off loan. No others would follow. They recommended he look for his rations in Perote. In the meantime the town council wrote a letter to Iturbide, begging him to replace Santa Anna with someone else. This letter was to be followed by others in which the councilors reiterated that it was imperative he be ousted as commander general of the province.[24]

On the 2nd, news reached Xalapa of Iturbide's liberation of Mexico City (27 September 1821). It was agreed that this major event would be celebrated on the 5th, with a solemn ceremony in the church, and that the townspeople of Xalapa would light up their houses for three consecutive nights. One can only imagine the tensions that must have intruded upon the joy of the occasion as Santa Anna made his way to the church, side by side with the members of the town council. Indicative perhaps that his control of Xalapa was slipping was that on that very same day, the royalist Colonel Manuel de la Concha was murdered just outside the city walls. De la Concha had surrendered and had been issued a passport by Santa Anna, together with assurances that he would be protected. His murder caused enough of a shock for Santa Anna to feel impelled to publish a manifesto that condemned the crime and exonerated himself from any blame in the matter. Concha had ignored his orders and exposed himself to danger by leaving Xalapa at dawn that day, on his own.[25]

On 6 October, Antonio López de Santa Anna Pérez de Lebrón, "Lieutenant Colonel of the Imperial Army of the Three Guarantees, Commander General of the Province of Veracruz, Sub-Inspector of its troops, and Political Chief of the same," led his army up the mountains to the desolate, foggy, and cold plain of Perote.[26] Despite his soldiers' suffering from hunger and the bitter cold of the mountains, he claimed they were ready to suffer anything "except subservience or slavery."[27]

On the 7th, without much of a struggle, they liberated Perote. From Perote Santa Anna wrote to the town council of Veracruz to inform them that he was going to bring his army down to the port. He stressed that it was not his intention to hurt the people of Veracruz or their property, but they were warned that they had little choice but to surrender.[28] On the 20th he was outside the port's walls.

Much to his disappointment, the meeting he held with Dávila was not successful. Dávila was determined to deny Santa Anna the satisfaction of being the one to liberate the port. Santa Anna was clearly prepared to lay waste the port if that was what it would take to crush Dávila's stubborn resistance. He claimed he had done everything in his power to prevent a bloodbath. Although José Rincón was inside the city walls, placed at the head of the royalist forces by Dávila to irritate Santa Anna, his brother Manuel Rincón was outside, having joined the Army of the Three Guarantees. Dávila, in another move to spite Santa Anna, wrote to inform Iturbide that he would surrender the port only if Manuel Rincón were placed at the head of the liberating forces. Iturbide acquiesced to bring about a speedy capitulation, and Manuel Rincón replaced Santa Anna as commander in chief of the liberating forces outside Veracruz. A few days later, Iturbide replaced Santa Anna as commander general of the province with the very same Rincón.[29]

Dávila left the port on 26 October and retreated to San Juan de Ulúa. The town council of Veracruz then agreed to negotiate the terms of their capitulation with Manuel Rincón, who was to be given the political command of the city, and who would no doubt negotiate with Santa Anna over the timing of the entrance of the troops. Santa Anna took these maneuvers by Dávila, Rincón, and Iturbide in his stride and did not challenge Rincón's ascendancy. He did, however, ensure that regardless of what was written on paper, it was he whom the porteños saw liberating the port. He also ensured that this was made known throughout Mexico. He wrote a proclamation that Tornel published in Mexico City in November, in which he celebrated the glorious liberation of "his birthplace" and prided himself on having liberated the province with so little bloodshed.[30]

On 28 October, despite the fact that Manuel Rincón was the appointed commander of the liberating army of Veracruz, Santa Anna was recognized as the chief destined to take possession of the port, which he did at 9:00 in the morning, leading the liberating army into the main square of Veracruz. He must have enjoyed leading the festivities, presiding at the mass and Te Deum held in the cathedral, with his troops firing three volleys of artillery, bearing in mind all of Dávila's exertions to spoil this day for him. He may not have been the liberator of Veracruz on paper, but he certainly came across as such for those who saw him ride in on the 28th. From the perspective of the rest of the country, and thanks to Tornel, he was recognized as the Liberator of Veracruz.[31]

Unlike Rincón, Santa Anna benefited from having a brilliant writer at his service. As far as publicity went, his achievements once he joined the Army of the Three Guarantees were heralded and publicized like those of no other veracruzano. Tornel compared Santa Anna to Julius Caesar. He was the "hero of the province of Veracruz." He was the "young immortal who . . . has lavished Veracruz with the benefits of the independent system." The country was indebted to him, and he was barely twenty-six years old (not true). He was "brave and moderate." He did not fear death, just despotism. Santa Anna was one of the "military caudillos" whose interests were "identified with those of the people [he] had saved," who "belonged to the people," and whose "supreme law was the good health and redemption of the mother country." He was one of "those liberal and virtuous men" who would attack despotism even in its last entrenchments."[32]

The Spaniards were to hang onto the island fortress of San Juan de Ulúa until 1825. Santa Anna's bid for power in his home province would suffer several setbacks. From his perspective, at the end of October 1821, this was unimportant. Mexico was independent. Veracruz was free. Regardless of what Dávila, Rincón, and Iturbide said or did, Santa Anna was the popular hero of the province, the Liberator of Veracruz. He must also have been aware by then that with independence, the traditional rules governing political authority, legitimacy, and hierarchy were dead. Under the colony it would have been impossible for him to become viceroy or supreme magistrate of the region. With independence, anything was possible. One cannot help wondering at what point this thought struck the young Santa Anna, with all its extraordinary implications. If a high-ranking creole officer like Iturbide could go from being a royalist colonel to Emperor Agustín I, what was there to stop him from doing the same? In a telling letter dated 14 November 1821, Manuel Rincón told Iturbide that Santa Anna was "drunk without doubt of ambition" and that he was promoting seditious sentiments among the *jarochos*. The most popular cry in Veracruz had become "Long live Santa Anna and death to the rest."[33]

With Manuel Rincón serving as *jefe militar y político* of the province, Santa Anna decided to visit Mexico City. His trip to the capital was brief and uneventful. It was rumored that he attempted to seduce Iturbide's sister, the sexagenarian Doña Nicolasa, but no evidence has been found to substantiate this. In all probability this piece of gossip was invented by his enemies to convey the idea that he was so ambitious as to be prepared to marry a woman more than twice his age, just to become a member of the future emperor's family. He returned to Xalapa in early 1823, where he was given the command of the town garrison.[34]

Having reveled in the exalted title of Liberator of Veracruz, Santa Anna now found himself reduced to the humble position of commander of Xalapa. Much to the dismay of the town council, they were once more forced to deal with him on a daily basis. They begged the captain general of Puebla and Veracruz, Domingo Luaces, to adopt "the most opportune remedies so that this town may be free of the evil doings . . . to which Antonio López de Santa Anna has exposed it." He was no longer described as the prudent man of the spring of 1821. Instead he was characterized by his "vindictive spirit," and actions that were "despotic and rash." They went as far as stating that it was impossible to describe his personality in any detail for "such a portrait would be so black" that no one would believe it. The town council's delight when he was finally replaced by brigadier José María Lobato, on 10 May 1822, was effusively expressed.[35]

However, by the end of the summer of 1822, they were forced to endure him as their *jefe político* again. In the hope of starting a new relationship with Santa Anna, the town council actually congratulated him on his appointment. The town council of Veracruz, in contrast, decided to be as awkward as possible toward him when he arrived in the port on 29 September and informed them he was replacing Brigadier Manuel Rincón. When he told the town council he expected the investiture cer-

emony to take place on the morning of the 30th, the town council replied they could do no such thing without seeing his credentials. Santa
Anna duly presented these, but the corporation said they were not acceptable. They wrote to the minister of interior, José Manuel de Herrera, expressing the constitutional reasons why Santa Anna could not
replace Rincón. To their chagrin, Herrera replied confirming that Santa
Anna was in charge, and the town council invested him on 10 October.
It goes without saying that they had not endeared themselves to him.[36]

Santa Anna's fraught relationship with the *iturbidista* town councils
of Xalapa and Veracruz no doubt contributed to his increasing irritation with the emperor's supporters and, by default, with the emperor
himself. It was a relationship that is not always easy to understand with
its multiple layers of complex regional allegiances and Santa Anna's
taste for bluffing and double-bluffing his adversaries. An example of
this may be found in the way Santa Anna insisted, in a letter he addressed to Iturbide in February 1822, that the town council of Xalapa
was a den of anti-iturbidistas, entirely opposed to independence, and
which praised the republican Victoria. The contradictions involved in
this statement illustrate how difficult it is to decipher what was actually going through Santa Anna's mind. The councilors could be anti-
iturbidistas *and* supporters of Victoria, who had gone back into hiding
after escaping from prison, where he had been incarcerated for his involvement in a republican conspiracy toward the end of 1821. However
they could not be supporters of Victoria *and* opposed to independence.
Given that the town council was iturbidista and Santa Anna's loyalty to
the emperor was somewhat strained after the appointment of Manuel
Rincón as liberator of the port and commander general of the province,
the whole accusation becomes even more absurd. Santa Anna was evidently trying to create distrust between Iturbide and his supporters in
Xalapa.[37]

His aversion to the town councils may have been partially personal,
but it also originated from a conflict of interests that mirrored the tensions between the town councils and the Provincial Deputation.[38] The
bottom line, in ideological terms, was that Santa Anna and the Provincial Deputation believed it was up to them to determine the future of Veracruz, and not to someone in a remote city on the Altiplano. The town

councils, afraid of submitting to a context where caudillos like Santa Anna could become profoundly influential at a regional level, preferred to defend a strong national leader. The paradox of their choice lay in the fact that a strong centralized government could remove officers like Santa Anna and yet, because of their distance, could not control the town councils' own everyday running of their community, as a local strongman might. Supporting Iturbide ideally entailed disempowering local caudillos and giving the town councils greater freedom to govern as they pleased. In brief, while Iturbide was struggling to forge a new monarchy in the capital, the town councils of the empire were struggling to dominate the political scene in Veracruz. It should not come as a surprise that between January and April 1823, during and briefly after Santa Anna's revolt of 2 December 1822, Santa Anna opted to head and empower the Provincial Deputation of Veracruz.[39]

Equally important in inspiring Santa Anna eventually to turn against Iturbide was the personal animosity that developed between the two men. It is not difficult to understand Santa Anna's disappointment with Iturbide, considering that after all his efforts to emancipate the region, he had been abruptly replaced by Rincón. He wanted his hard work, self-sacrifice, and merits to be duly recognized. His dissatisfaction must have been exacerbated by Iturbide's failure to promote him, despite showering multiple promotions upon just about everyone else when he came to power. By the time Santa Anna was promoted to general, the damage was done. It was a case of too little, too late. The letters that came and went between Iturbide and Santa Anna from January to May 1822 demonstrate that while Santa Anna was obsessed with promotion, Iturbide was obsessed with seeing Victoria captured and San Juan de Ulúa taken. Each was prepared to comply with the other's request, providing his own request was granted first. Iturbide's approach could be reduced to "catch me Victoria and I'll make you brigadier"; Santa Anna's was "make me brigadier and I'll catch you Victoria."[40]

In May 1822, coinciding with Iturbide's move to become emperor, Santa Anna was promoted to brigadier general.[41] However, Santa Anna was not grateful and compliant. He was still unsatisfied. He wanted to be commander general of the province again. As noted, Iturbide gave him his job back in October 1822. Iturbide was mistaken, however, if he thought this would finally win over Santa Anna's loyalty. By then Santa Anna no longer respected him. One wonders whether he ceased to respect him the day Iturbide listened to Dávila, Rincón, and the town council of Xalapa and had Santa Anna replaced as commander general of Veracruz back in October 1821.

Santa Anna did not deliver Victoria, and probably had no intention of doing so. He did, however, try to take San Juan de Ulúa, following his appointment as military commander general of Veracruz on 25 September 1822. His strategy of 27 October 1822 displayed a new side to his character. Not only was he cunning; he had a vivid imagination. His brilliant yet unsuccessful stratagem consisted of persuading Francisco Lemaur, the new Spanish commander posted at the head of San Juan de Ulúa, that he was prepared to surrender the port. For him to do so, the Spanish troops in San Juan de Ulúa had to enter Veracruz at night, through the bastions of Concepción and Santiago. Once Lemaur went ahead with his part of the agreement, Santa Anna's planned ambush would be set in motion. The Spaniards were to be taken prisoner the moment they disembarked. Santa Anna's troops, wearing the Spaniards' uniforms, were then to head across the harbor to San Juan de Ulúa and take the island garrison by surprise. Lemaur, who did not know at the time that Santa Anna had been trying to bribe the troops in San Juan de Ulúa into defecting, fell for the trap.[42]

The plan, however, did not work. What was more, the newly appointed captain general of Puebla, Oaxaca, and Veracruz, José Antonio de Echávarri, came to the conclusion that Santa Anna deliberately botched the plan so as to get him killed. While Lemaur sent a large contingent of troops to the bastions of Concepción and Santiago, Santa Anna and Echávarri's men failed to implement their part of the plan effectively. The Spanish troops, on realizing that an ambush was awaiting them, opened fire on the port, and two hours of combat ensued. Although the intended capture of San Juan de Ulúa did not take place, Santa Anna was able to claim that his forces had successfully repulsed the Spaniards' attempt to take Veracruz. Both the port and Xalapa, following his instructions, celebrated "a Te Deum Laudamus for the brilliant action" of 27 October, whereby Santa Anna's men had repulsed more than four hundred Spanish troops. Both Santa Anna and Echávarri were awarded special medals for their triumph. Echávarri was even promoted to field marshal, and Santa Anna was made general *con letras* (with letters).[43]

Santa Anna's October "victory" notwithstanding, the regional power struggle involving him, Rincón, and Echávarri became so acerbic that Iturbide found it necessary to see Santa Anna in person. Iturbide believed Echávarri's account of events and felt compelled to remove Santa Anna.[44] Rumor also had it that by October 1822, "most of the officers in [Santa Anna's] regiment were republicans, and were restrained from declaring themselves against the emperor, only by their colonel, Santa Ana [sic], who possesses great influence over the troops."[45] Hoping to avoid provoking him into rebellion, Iturbide chose to meet him in Xalapa and "reward" him with a post in Mexico City, rather than demote him in writing.

On seeing Santa Anna's reception—arriving in Xalapa on a white horse, at the head of his officers, under a shower of flowers and celebrated by the masses—Iturbide became aware of the extraordinary power Santa Anna wielded in his home province. Iturbide is alleged to have commented: "This scoundrel is the true emperor here."[46] Iturbide was put out by this, and according to Santa Anna, one of the imperial officers tried to put him in his place by reprimanding him for sitting in the presence of Agustín I, the emperor. Iturbide informed Santa Anna that he was to be replaced as commander general and that he was to accompany the emperor's party to Mexico City. When Santa Anna replied that he lacked the necessary money to go there and then, Iturbide went as far as offering him five hundred pesos in cash. Santa Anna insisted that he needed to attend to some personal affairs first; he promised to go to the capital as soon as these were settled. When Iturbide left Xalapa on 1 December, Santa Anna raced to the port of Veracruz and launched his republican revolt the following day.[47]

In Santa Anna's words, Iturbide offended his military honor and forced him to see with his own eyes "absolutism with all its ferocity." It was then that he decided "to reinstate seriously the nation's sacred rights."[48] On hearing of Santa Anna's rebellion, the imperial authorities were quick to state that he gave the insurrectionary call to arms for reasons they were unable to discern, since, not having any fixed ideas, he could proclaim a republic as well as call for a European prince and the need to revert to Spanish rule.[49]

The reasons Santa Anna gave for rebelling against Iturbide would not be characterized by any expressions of personal ambition or resentment. In his defense, he admitted that at the beginning of 1822, "educated under the monarchy, [we] were not ready for the change" entailed in endorsing a republican system. However, by the end of the year he, like so many others, had realized that if they proclaimed the republic, the nation would be the "arbiter of its own destiny." He made use of the outspoken republican former Colombian ambassador, Miguel Santa María, to write the Plan of Veracruz of 6 December and placed himself at the forefront of the republican movement. Although there is little doubt that he was avenging Iturbide's mistreatment of him, as well as the town councils' repeated attempts to jeopardize his rise to power in the province, there was more to his revolt than a strictly personal agenda.[50]

In the letter he addressed to Iturbide on 6 December 1822, he explained that he was rebelling because he was opposed to absolutism. He had not fought so hard for this. Iturbide's dissolution of Congress (31 October 1822) was an infringement of the constitutional rights of the nation. He accused the emperor of preventing commerce from prospering and of failing to regenerate the nation's mines and economy and condemned him for the vile and despotic manner in which he had treated the deputies he had imprisoned and exiled. He attacked Iturbide for the way he had behaved in Xalapa. He denounced Iturbide's ostentation. It was an insult to the nation, at a time of need, to see the emperor throwing money away on his lavish court.[51]

On 2 December 1822, at the head of Infantry Regiment Number 8, Santa Anna launched the revolt from the port of Veracruz. The revolt did not receive the immediate support he expected. He turned to San Juan de Ulúa for help. As he told the town council of Veracruz, Lemaur "was about to enter into harmonious relations with this port, signing a treaty that may guarantee reciprocal interests." In an act of good faith, he freed the wounded Spanish prisoners held in the hospital, allowed the exchange of capital and goods between the island garrison and the port, and promised treaties of reciprocity. However, Lemaur refused to enter into any formal negotiations with the republicans.[52]

Tornel, based in Mexico City since September 1821 and fearing that the Spaniards would use the instability caused by the revolt to attempt the reconquest of New Spain, wrote publicly to Santa Anna to ask him to put down his arms. Although Alvarado and La Antigua seconded the revolt at the coast, nobody else followed their example. Santa Anna's attempt to give the revolution some momentum by taking Orizaba at the head of eight hundred men did not go according to plan. The town council and its inhabitants refused to back him. Only "the down and out" *jarochos* conscripted in Orizaba joined his republican army. He attempted to liberate Xalapa on 21 December, having routed an imperial force at Plan del Río on the 19th. However, the Xalapan incursion turned out to be a costly defeat. General José María Calderón, with whom Santa Anna would have several other violent encounters in 1828 and 1832, refused to join the republican plan. Many of the men who had joined him after surrendering to his forces in Plan del Río deserted him. Santa Anna and his loyal troops found themselves surrounded in the Church of San José on the town's outskirts. They fought bravely from five to eleven in the morning. When they ran out of ammunition they were forced to escape by mounting a frantic cavalry charge out of Xalapa. Having failed to spread the revolution inland, Santa Anna retreated back to Veracruz where, at the head of six hundred men, he opted to sit out the siege to which three thousand imperial troops subjected the port to for a month and ten days. In a bid to garner the support of the mestizos and Indians of central Veracruz, he recognized Victoria as the leader of the rebellion.[53]

In the port, the revolt took the inhabitants by surprise. The town council and the Provincial Deputation supported the plan initially, since Santa Anna convinced them that the uprising had the backing of a number of influential military leaders. He also reassured them by showing them a letter from Lemaur, in which he promised not to attack Veracruz while the revolt lasted. Typically, he made a point of stating that he would personally guarantee the welfare of the people and that commerce would be protected. When it became apparent that most of his reassurances were meaningless, the corporation of the port found itself in the awkward position of not knowing how to distance itself from the rebellion. In one of the public meetings held, several veracruzanos challenged Santa Anna and manifested their opposition to the revolt. He had them arrested. The town council sought an alternative way out by asking Guadalupe Victoria, as leader of the revolt, to take over the port and replace him. This was not possible since Victoria was supporting the revolt by holding the post at Puente Nacional and was not prepared to undermine his ally's authority. There was also an attempt on the part of some of the port's officers to bring about a counterrevolution within the city walls, but this came to nothing.[54]

News of the problems facing Santa Anna reached the imperial troops who arrived outside the port at the end of December. Luis Cortázar, one of the commanders of the besieging army, was confident the port would fall in a matter of days. The scouts he sent out on the 28th to reconnoiter Santa Anna's defenses returned amazed at having seen the sea for the first time, and amused by the way Santa Anna had his troops in a constant state of alarm. Cortázar thought it funny that the rebel leader had taunted him with a letter warning that Santa Anna would yet surprise him.[55]

Despite the complaints of the imperial soldiers—who described Xalapa as the "urinal of the world" and who made it known that they wanted to attack the port immediately so that they could return to the Altiplano as soon as possible, and get away from the "cursed *vómito*"— Cortázar decided to wait for Colonel Echávarri to organize his troops. On 27 December Echávarri took possession of Casa Mata. Echávarri also thought the rebels would succumb easily. He wrote to the town council of Veracruz to demand that they surrender and rebel against "the sinister ideas . . . Santa Anna" professed and did not understand. Echávarri wrote to them again on the 29th, lamenting that "Santa Anna by ignoring the calls of the people and consulting his capriciousness alone will inflict [upon Veracruz] all the disasters consequent upon a siege." It was only after Echávarri wrote a third and furious letter, later the same day, demanding to know why the town council was refusing to reply to him, that the corporation sent him a laconic missive asking him not to be cruel to Veracruz. They pointed out that the siege could not harm the port since Santa Anna had made sure they were well provided for, for at least two months.[56]

Santa Anna decided to use a devious strategy similar to the one he had employed unsuccessfully the previous October. On this occasion it worked to a certain degree. He made Echávarri think some of his troops were about to betray him. The "traitors" (Santa Anna's close friends Crisanto de Castro and Bernardino del Junco) wrote to Echávarri to tell him they were prepared to let his men "enter the port at night without causing a stir." Castro, in charge of the bastion of Santiago, and Junco in San José, were ready to hand these positions over to Echávarri as long as he committed four to five hundred men to entering Veracruz by the Escuela Práctica and the bastions mentioned. Although they warned Echávarri that Santa Anna's brother Manuel (who married in Veracruz during the siege!) was also based in Santiago, they promised to immobilize him. The plan was to ambush Echávarri's men once they had committed themselves.

Echávarri, who had almost lost his life in the October farce, did not entirely trust Castro and Junco since, as he noted, "I am not entirely oblivious to the favorite intrigues of the Proclaimer of the Republic." However, it was too good an opportunity to miss, if what they said was true. News of the problems Santa Anna had faced during December must have niggled at the back of Echávarri's mind. He opted for a compromise. He did not commit all his troops, and he avoided the bastions of Santiago and San José. But he did send a company on 2 January 1823 in through the gates by the Escuela Práctica, and, as he feared, these men were mowed down by Santa Anna's gunfire. In his frustration, Echávarri wrote to the town council to tell them this treacherous scheme proved in itself that it pleased Santa Anna to see the blood of his countrymen spilled.[57]

The action of the 2nd worked in Santa Anna's favor. It gave Veracruz a much needed confidence boost. He won over the support of those who doubted him. His troops were to prove stubbornly loyal. Echávarri tried to explain their reluctance to betray Santa Anna by saying he had "bought" them with "booze and flattery." Echávarri excused his failure to assault the port on humanitarian grounds, claiming he did not want to be responsible for bloodshed. He was also beginning to find the hardship of the campaign difficult to bear. In a letter dated 11 January, he complained that he had not had the chance to undress for fifteen days and that his skin was covered in insect bites. He was also evidently terrified of catching the deadly *vómito*.[58]

From Casa Mata Echávarri persevered in his attempts to forge a plan with those dissident porteños who appeared to be willing to hand over the city behind Santa Anna's back, but there were not enough of them. The majority was prepared to stick it out with Santa Anna, convinced that Echávarri's troops would pillage the city if they were allowed in. Santa Anna appears to have persuaded them that he represented the "American" cause of liberty. Echávarri was a "*gachupín*" (a derogatory term for Spaniard), who "upholds in his poisoned heart the darkest ideas, and who will never offer the Americans a favorable action since he only joined the Plan of Iguala to further his career and because he thought the Bourbons would come to govern us."[59]

The reasons why Echávarri then decided to lift the siege and issue his own anti-Iturbide revolt remain uncertain. It is possible that he realized he could not take the port. There is also evidence that he had recently joined the Scottish Masons, and given that their lodges opted to use Santa Anna's revolt to further their own political project, Echávarri had little choice but to turn against Iturbide. Much to Santa Anna's delight, on 1 February 1823, Echávarri called a truce and issued his own Plan of Casa Mata. The Plan of Casa Mata dropped the republican standard proposed in the Plan of Veracruz but demanded the restoration of the Congress. Critical to the success of the Plan of Casa Mata was its tenth article, which stated that the Provincial Deputation of Veracruz was to have full control over all administrative issues in the region. Its defense of the powers of the Veracruz Provincial Deputation inspired all the other provincial deputations in Mexico, resentful of the manner in which Iturbide had curtailed their sphere of influence, to come out with proclamations of allegiance.[60]

On 2 February Santa Anna and Victoria joined the Plan of Casa Mata, even though it did not mention the need to impose a republic. Santa Anna could claim to have survived the siege. Iturbide's imperial army had failed to bring him to his knees. The Provincial Deputation of Veracruz was also quick to come out in support of the Plan of Casa Mata. It was not long before all the main garrisons in the country did the same, and Iturbide was left with little choice but to restore the Congress, abdicate, and go into exile in Europe. On 24 February Santa Anna took five hundred men with him to Tampico to propagate the revolution against

Iturbide and take control of the customs house there. As Iturbide set sail to Italy, a resilient, resourceful, and increasingly confident Santa Anna made his way to San Luis Potosí.[61]

Once Congress met after Iturbide's departure, Santa Anna's original republican proposal, much to the surprise of the Bourbonists who backed the Plan of Casa Mata, started to gain acceptance among the members of the Mexican political class. As noted by the santanista lawyer, politician, and writer José María Bocanegra, while in 1822 republicanism was supported by a rather hesitant minority, by April 1823 the newly convened Congress "openly manifested from the beginning a particularly pronounced republican spirit."[62] Carlos María de Bustamante noted in his diary that Providence had given them Iturbide so that they learned to detest all the monarchs in the world.[63] Santa Anna's revolt gave the political class the confidence they had been missing in 1821 and 1822 to defend the creation of a republic. It is true that the Plan of Casa Mata, with its less radical demands, and its federalist undertones, proved all-important in uniting the opposition against Iturbide. Without the Plan of Casa Mata, it is not certain that the emperor would have fallen. However, by the same token, the importance of Santa Anna's republican revolt should not be underestimated. It was the first open and aggressive defense of a republican system in Mexico. Having given a loud and clear voice to the republican cause, Santa Anna's proposal was ultimately the most influential once Iturbide was out of the way.

The success of the revolt enabled Santa Anna to say on numerous occasions that he was "in our history . . . the first to proclaim the Republic."[64] For many of his contemporaries he became known as the Founder of the Republic. At the age of twenty-nine, he could well boast about his life and achievements. Whatever hopes his father may have had in store for him, he had more than surpassed them. The places he had seen and the events in which he had participated were already rich and varied. They made the thought of the mortgage broker's son living a quiet life as a shopkeeper in Veracruz somewhat difficult to imagine. He was the Liberator of Veracruz and Founder of the Republic. More than twelve years of service in Tamaulipas, Texas, and Veracruz had transformed him into a hardened soldier. His devotion to army life, his sense of belonging to and respect for the army as an institution, together with his love of combat all stemmed from the experience of these critical years. Likewise, as a counterinsurgent, land administrator, liberator, commander general, and triumphant republican rebel, he had developed an intense and complex relationship with the people of his home province. Although there were still influential veracruzanos who did not trust him, and his father's perspective is unknown, he had acquired an all-important understanding of the region's terrain and needs, the grudging support of the elite, and a large following among the popular classes. He was also very much in his prime. The U.S. envoy, Joel Roberts Poinsett, who met him briefly in October 1822, described him as "a man of about thirty years of age, of middle stature, slightly yet well made, and possessing a very intelligent and expressive countenance."[65]

The irony was that despite his extraordinary successes, he was still little more than just another ambitious high-ranking officer at the time. Although in the spring of 1823 he was on his way to being known to many as the Liberator of Veracruz and the Founder of the Republic, he did not obtain any tangible political gains. Thanks to his exertions, and in the wake of the Plan of Casa Mata, the Provincial Deputation went on to tame the town councils of Veracruz and Xalapa, and Mexico became a republic. But power eluded him both at a regional and at a national level. Guadalupe Victoria and Miguel Barragán were to be the regional chieftains of Veracruz before him. Victoria would also make it to the presidency first. Six years later, however, Santa Anna was not only the indisputable strongman of Veracruz; he was also the most celebrated living hero in Mexico. The next decade was to prove vital in transforming him into a caudillo.

Part 2
The Making of a *Caudillo*, 1823–1832

As to the town leperos, sir, the sight of his black whiskers and white teeth was enough for them. They quailed before him, sir. That's what the force of character will do for you.

That man seems to have a particular talent for being on the spot whenever there is something picturesque to be done.

And it is curious to have met a man for whom the value of life seems to consist in personal prestige.

Joseph Conrad, Nostromo

4. A Federalist on the Periphery, 1823–1825

The ten years that unfolded between Santa Anna's departure to Tampico on 19 March 1823 and his election to the presidency of the Mexican Federal Republic in 1833 were to prove decisive. They were critical in establishing him as a caudillo at a national as well as at a regional level. They gave him the kind of fame that would allow him to overcome a series of notorious setbacks. The prestige he acquired in the 1820s would make a strong mark on the psyche of his contemporaries.[1]

It was during these years that he became the true caudillo of Veracruz. Guadalupe Victoria went to the capital to become president (1824–29) and did not pursue a political role in the province. Miguel Barragán was discredited for his involvement in the failed revolt of Montaño (1827–28). José Joaquín de Herrera moved away from Veracruz, holding a variety of military and political posts in other regions of the republic, ceasing to pose a challenge to Santa Anna's emergent authority in the province.[2] Santa Anna overcame the power and influence the Rincón brothers had in the port and Xalapa in the bitter dispute that was played out in the summer of 1827. His grip over the region became all the stronger after he bought the hacienda of Manga de Clavo and was appointed acting governor (1827–29).

Following Iturbide's abdication and departure into exile, a temporary triumvirate was formed by Generals Nicolás Bravo, Guadalupe Victoria, and Pedro Celestino Negrete (1823–24). The restored Congress (closed down by Iturbide) was asked to arrange for the election of a Constituent Congress. It was as this new order came into place that Santa Anna made his way to the northern city of San Luis Potosí, in the spring of

1823. Tornel claimed it was the provisional government, established following Iturbide's abdication on 19 March 1823, that sent him to San Luis Potosí so that he could not use his "brilliant 8th regiment" against it. However, the evidence suggests that he went, following Victoria's instructions, to promote the Plan of Casa Mata and to cut off the escape route north, were Iturbide to attempt to flee to the United States.[3]

Santa Anna's expedition landed in Tampico on 1 April 1823 and set out the next day to San Luis Potosí. While he had come to be treated as "the emperor" of Veracruz in his hometown, in San Luis Potosí his arrival at the head of 1,541 men was not welcome. The local troops were hostile toward his army, and the next few weeks were to prove difficult. Men from his cavalry became involved in a violent quarrel with members of his infantry, and to make matters worse the local garrison joined the fray in support of the cavalry unit. Following one street skirmish between the troops of San Luis Potosí and Santa Anna's men, on the night of 12 May, the commander general of the city, the Marquis of Jaral de Berrio, went into hiding, leaving his position vacant. Santa Anna asked the town council to elect a substitute, and the corporation, probably fearful of the veracruzano general, chose to appoint him commander general, "being the highest ranking officer in the town."

It was a decision they would soon regret. There was the perennial problem of maintaining and feeding Santa Anna's troops. He became embroiled in a dispute with the local political head, José Díaz de León, over his request for eighty-five horses, five hundred pack animals, and a hundred wagons. On hearing that his request would not be granted, he confiscated two hundred animals from the ranchos outside San Luis Potosí. He also lost any support he might have had among the members of the local elite by appropriating the bar silver in the local treasury, confiscating up to thirty thousand pesos. One letter of protest that reached the minister of war in the summer of 1823 complained that Santa Anna had stolen twenty-seven bars of silver that one Francisco Oyarzín was transporting from Durango to the capital. Santa Anna's pastimes did not endear him to the local community either. If one source is to be believed, he spent most nights gambling with former insurgent leader Ignacio López Rayón and José María Bárcena, and "indiscreetly" making love to the women of upright and prudish San Luis Potosí.[4]

In an attempt to introduce some harmony into a fraught San Luis Potosí and among his feuding troops, he ordered that a major banquet be held in the Alameda de Bracamonte, in the city center. Unfortunately, a drunken brawl broke out between his men, leading to six deaths. By the time Santa Anna launched his Plan of San Luis Potosí on 5 June 1823, the local Twelfth Regiment not only refused to back him; it took over the church towers and other vantage points and openly defied him, to the cry of "Death to Santa Anna! Death to the Veracruz Jews! Long live the Twelfth."[5]

His decision to start another *pronunciamiento*, only six months after he had revolted against Iturbide, deserves some consideration. Why did he rise up in arms to demand that the Constituent Congress forge a *federal* republic? Why did he choose to do so then? Why did he choose to stage the uprising in San Luis Potosí, of all places? In ideological terms there was certainly consistency in his demands. The republican 1822 Plan of Veracruz and the 1823 Plan of Casa Mata with its defense of Congress and the federalist provincial deputations, were all in tune with the demands he made in the Plan of San Luis Potosí. In repudiating Iturbide's empire he had become a republican (the Founder of the Republic, in fact!), and he was intent on promoting the federalist agenda he had defended by siding with, and even leading, the Provincial Deputation of Veracruz against the centralist-*iturbidista* town councils of Xalapa and Veracruz. The centralist politician Carlos María de Bustamante, forgetting how he had praised Santa Anna's republican virtues in the days following his revolt of 2 December 1822, claimed that "it may be assured, [Santa Anna] ignored the meaning of the word [federalism]."[6] All the evidence points, nevertheless, to the fact that Santa Anna, as a strongman from the provinces, knew only too well what a federalist system could do for Veracruz and himself. He was to remain a federalist, at heart, throughout his life. The occasions when he defended a centralist agenda were for pragmatic reasons but also coincided with contexts in which he was in a position to fill his cabinet in Mexico City with veracruzanos.

The timing of the revolt and the choice of location are less easy to explain. Unlike Veracruz, which he knew well, San Luis Potosí did not present him with any of the advantages of starting a revolt from a city in his home province. The evidence suggests that Santa Anna's plan had been agreed upon beforehand between Guadalupe Victoria, Vicente Guerrero, and himself. In other words, obeying Victoria, Santa Anna went to San Luis Potosí to cut off Iturbide's foreseen escape north and to follow up the Plan of Casa Mata with a federalist revolt.[7]

As early as April 1823 there were those who feared that Santa Anna was planning on being proclaimed absolute ruler of Mexico and that he wanted to be crowned Antonio the First. No proof has been found to substantiate this piece of hearsay. The view that he opted to rebel with the purpose of making himself noticed, on the other hand, is persuasive. Following the Plan of Casa Mata, Nicolás Bravo, Guadalupe Victoria, and Pedro Celestino Negrete, among others, had gained greater prominence in terms of national politics. Santa Anna wanted to remind the political class in the capital that he also had a stake in the new country's politics. He believed in the virtues of a federalist republican system, he had agreed with Victoria to promote this system with a *pronunciamiento*, and he was in San Luis Potosí because there had been the fear that Iturbide would try to escape to the United States. Congress was in the process of determining what system to follow, and Santa Anna could not allow the centralists to control the proceedings. He was far removed from the corridors of power, and it was a way of reminding the emergent Mexican political class that he was a prominent figure who deserved to be taken into consideration.[8]

In the Plan of San Luis Potosí, the ideological link between this uprising and Santa Anna's 1822 revolt was established from the beginning. His men had been with him on the previous occasion. He stressed that they were anxious to be given laws. He celebrated the fact that Congress had listened to the provinces and had moved ahead with the plan to form a Constituent Congress. However, he was nervous about the prospect of an impasse. If the creation of the Constituent Congress took too long and there was a morass between the closure of the current Congress and the beginning of the new one, there could be trouble. He feared that prospective tyrants in the mold of Iturbide could turn this political vacuum to their advantage and attempt to impose "antiliberal" measures. He noted that he was not prepared to expose the country again to such a threat and that he could not be indifferent to the country's needs.

He admitted that he could not possibly aspire to become a legislator. For such an ominous task he claimed to lack the "necessary talents." He was just a soldier, and his sole intention, through the proclamation of the Plan of San Luis Potosí, was to ensure that Congress gave Mexico the Constitution it deserved. Although this is the kind of statement that has often been disregarded as insincere, it is important not to lose sight of the fact that there was coherence in his words. The Plan of San Luis Potosí was not about bringing him to power or making him emperor. It limited itself to coercing Congress into creating a federal republic. There is absolutely no evidence that he attempted to take over the nascent country's presidency in the 1820s.

In the plan's first article he gave his army the title of "Protector of Mexican Liberty." In the second he stated that it was this army's aim to protect religion as well as the other two guarantees of the Plan of Iguala, respecting property, security, and equality, sustaining order and peace. In article 3 he demanded that the election of members of the Constituent Congress be carried out freely, without restrictions, enabling the provinces to grant their respective representatives full powers and detailed instructions to forge the nation's Constitution. In the fourth article he stressed that his army's obligation was to defend the provinces' will to forge a federal republic. And in the fifth article he requested that while the new Congress was being formed, power should reside in the provincial deputations. As noted in article 11, in proclaiming this plan, the army was bearing witness to its liberal ideas. The plan concluded with him expressing his desire to free the country of new disasters, and to prevent monarchists and centralists from gaining power, ignoring the clamor of the provinces that desired to be constituted under a federal system. He would not surrender until Mexico was constituted freely, and as long as the imminent danger that threatened it at the time was not repudiated.[9]

As a result of his failure to establish a good relationship with the local authorities and garrison, the immediate response to his revolt was not what he had hoped for. The San Luis Potosí–based Twelfth Regiment defied him, leading to a day of street fighting before he was able to consolidate his control of the town. He succeeded in gaining the upper hand only after the Twelfth Regiment abandoned San Luis Potosí, preferring to leave than to obey his orders. His men were attacked, as well, in the villages of Santiago and Tlaxcala, during a foray in search of men and provisions. Santa Anna had these villages punished and destroyed in true Arredondo fashion, drafting all the Indians who survived the massacre and did not manage to escape into the mountains.[10]

In the meantime, Generals Pedro Celestino Negrete and Nicolás Bravo started their march north to suppress Santa Anna's revolt, and Congress, on 12 June, determined to give Mexico a federal constitution. The decision of the Congress did not result from the revolt, although the Plan of San Luis Potosí must have been on the deputies' minds. Lucas Alamán, as minister of relations, wrote to Santa Anna condemning his actions, and General Gabriel Armijo moved his troops to San Luis Potosí to besiege the town. Armijo's siege of San Luis Potosí started on 12 June and lasted until Santa Anna agreed to submit to the government on 23 June. News of Congress's move to forge a federal republic meant that he could call an end to his revolt. This he did on 6 July 1823, publishing several pamphlets to justify his actions. As he stressed in one leaflet, he was bringing the uprising to an end since "it was well-known that the election [of members of the Constituent Congress] demanded unanimously by the Provinces, is now being carried out . . ., and the Sovereign Congress is working in conformity with the general will."[11]

Santa Anna left San Luis Potosí on 10 July and was replaced by General Gabriel Armijo as commander general. He was escorted to Mexico City, where he was put under house arrest for just over a month (the area of restriction was then extended to the boundaries of Mexico City) and placed on trial on 18 August. The case dragged on for most of the fall. He wrote a lengthy *Manifesto* in his own defense and stood up for those men who had backed him during the rebellion. He also fell ill during this period, claiming that Mexico City affected his health. He asked for permission to leave the capital briefly in December, to recuperate in the spa of Atotonilco. This license was granted, but he was forced to return to the capital soon after.[12]

A certain sense of the absurd pervaded the proceedings, given that Santa Anna was being tried for demanding the creation of a federal republic, which was indeed being established by the government at the time. This was ultimately acknowledged in Judge Ignacio Alvarado's summing up comments, when he exonerated Santa Anna, almost seven months later, on 22 March 1824: "No charge could or may stand against Sr. Santa Anna, . . . instead he deserves for his *pronunciamiento* of San Luis the same considerations he was awarded for his *grito* of Veracruz [2 December 1822]."[13]

On 23 January 1824 General José María Lobato, another xalapeño, started a revolt in Mexico City, demanding the dismissal from public office of all Spaniards. Lobato's plan was an early expression of a grievance shared by many *criollos* that the Plan of Iguala allowed the Spaniards to retain too powerful a presence in the government bureaucracy. It also aimed to force the removal of two alleged Hispanophiles, Miguel Domínguez and José Mariano Michelena, from the Triumvirate (supreme executive power) they had become part of standing in for Bravo and Victoria. With Lobato in control of the capital's garrison, and having taken over the convent of the Belemitas, his coup represented an immediate threat to the national government. Lobato listed all the high-ranking officers who backed him and made the mistake of including Santa Anna. Santa Anna, still on trial and residing in Mexico City, was livid. Tornel, who had defended Santa Anna during the trial, displayed his commitment to ensuring that the caudillo's reputation was not tainted by going to the convent of the Belemitas in person, where he struck Santa Anna's name off Lobato's plan. According to Tornel, Lobato lied about Santa Anna's intentions to give his *pronunciamiento* more prestige.[14]

Santa Anna did not remain silent either. The day after Lobato issued his *pronunciamiento*, Santa Anna marched into Congress and, displaying his taste for the theatrical, offered his life and his sword to the government to crush the uprising. Keen to quell the revolt, Congress agreed to allow him to join Vicente Guerrero, the tough mulatto warrior from the south, thus showing that his loyalty was not doubted. Santa Anna and Guerrero suppressed the revolt in three days, reinstating the general in the confidence of Congress. Although Lobato surrendered before Santa Anna went into action, the impact of his intervention should not be underestimated. In the words of historian Timothy Anna, "The mutiny almost immediately began to buckle when . . . Santa Anna issued a flurry of statements insisting that, although he had been listed as one of the mutineers, he was loyal to the Congress."[15]

In the light of Santa Anna's subsequent stance over the laws that were approved by Congress in 1827 to expel most Spaniards from Mexico, and which he implemented in Veracruz (1828–29), it is worth pausing to consider the reasons why Santa Anna was not ready to support Lobato's anti-Spanish revolt in 1824. Santa Anna's standpoint on this issue was particularly ambivalent. In 1828 he ensured that his Spanish relatives and associates in Veracuz were exempted, and yet he was particularly zealous in expelling those Spaniards he did not like. In essence, his view on the expulsion question evolved in tandem with that of most of his contemporaries. By 1827, in the wake of the discovery of a Spanish plot to reconquer Mexico, many politicians who had previously endorsed the Plan of Iguala's fundamental defense of "Union" came around to believing that the *gachupines* had abused the Mexicans' goodwill. However, Lobato's revolt was premature. The demands may have been the same, but the context was different. Santa Anna, like Tornel, Guerrero, and Victoria, came to see the need for such drastic measures in the late 1820s, but like them, he was not yet ready to support this course of action. In a letter he addressed to Lobato at the time, he admitted to sympathizing with the cause but stressed that an armed petition could only harm the country at this juncture. Mirroring the joint effort by Santa Anna and Guerrero to quell Lobato's revolt, in August 1824 Tornel and (then presidential candidate) Victoria led the forces that peacefully put an end to Colonels Antonio and Manuel León's revolt in Oaxaca demanding the expulsion of Spaniards. Santa Anna's stance on the expulsion question, in 1824, was in line with that of Victoria, Guerrero and Tornel, among others.[16]

As the Constituent Congress worked toward the drafting of what was to become the 1824 Constitution, it is evident that the political class in the capital thought it wise to remove Santa Anna to somewhere where it would prove difficult for him to interfere with the discussions and outcome. It was agreed that he should be made commander general of the faraway province of Yucatán, which at the time included the present-day states of Campeche and Quintana Roo. The authorities felt they could not punish him for his federalist revolt of 5 June 1823 and considered him to be loyal to the government. However, there was unease about his propensity to use force to make his views heard. Two revolts in a matter of six months were not something that could be easily overlooked. The commission that appointed him military commander of Yucatán stated in their orders that he could not leave the state without their written permission.[17]

Santa Anna went back to Xalapa to arrange his affairs before setting off to remote Yucatán. He left Xalapa on 29 April and embarked on the sloop *Iguala*, in the port of Veracruz, on 17 May 1824. He must have known that he was heading for a troubled region. On 15 February the rivalry between the two main cities and garrisons of Campeche and Mérida had degenerated into violence. The political class in Campeche was determined to force the state legislature, based in Mérida, to comply with the federal government's directive to sever all commercial relations between Yucatán and Havana. In tandem, the political and commercial class in Mérida, dependent on trade with Spanish-dominated Cuba, was not prepared to allow the national government or the *campechanos* to cut their main source of trade. Two thousand men under the orders of José Segundo Carvajal made their way to Campeche from Mérida to place the city's town council and garrison under siege. Although news of Santa Anna's appointment led to a standoff between the warring factions, Yucatán was on the verge of civil war when he reached its humid tropical coast.[18]

While Santa Anna was in distant Yucatán, the 1824 Federal Constitution was completed and approved. General Guadalupe Victoria was elected first president of the republic, and what I have described as the "stage of hope" (1821–28) got well under way.[19] The presidential elections that were organized in the summer of 1824 were carried out with a generalized sense of goodwill, hope, and optimism. The progressive nature of the constitution needs to be highlighted. Not even in the United States was there universal male suffrage. The electoral victory of Victoria was celebrated by radicals and traditionalists alike. To quote Lucas Alamán: "President Victoria found himself . . . in the most prosperous of circumstances: the Republic was enjoying a period of peace, the factions had been repressed, and the hope of a happy future burned in everybody's hearts."[20] The first two years of Victoria's presidency were particularly promising ones. The Mexican government received large loans from several British investors in 1825 and 1826. Although

Mexico defaulted on the dividend payments as early as October 1827—
with the corresponding debt becoming a major problem both for the
country's subsequent governments and for the British investors (until
it was liquidated in 1888!)—at the time, the loans gave Victoria's government an auspicious beginning. The reforms and policies that were
debated in the Chamber of Deputies and the Senate were proposed and
discussed with a strong commitment to representative and enlightened
values. Philanthropic enterprises such as the Compañía Lancasteriana
started to offer free primary education to the children of the less privileged sectors of society with the full support of most, if not all, of the
politicians of the period. The disillusion that was to characterize the
writings of so many Mexican intellectuals in the 1840s provides a star-
tling contrast with the high hopes and enlightened expectations that
featured with so much passion in the pamphlets they published in the
mid-1820s. The freedom of the press that was guaranteed in the 1824
Constitution further allowed for the development of a highly exciting
and combative press.[21]

While José María Tornel became fully immersed in the vibrant political life of the capital, serving as President Victoria's personal secretary
and subsequently as a deputy in Congress, Santa Anna remained on the
periphery. His experience of the early years of the federal republic was
significantly different from that of the political class established in Mexico City. He arrived in Campeche on 18 May 1824 and was pleased that
on hearing of his imminent arrival, the besieging troops from Mérida
had withdrawn. In the speech he addressed the people of Yucatán, he
stressed that it was his mission to bring peace. Although he lamented
the rivalry that existed between Mérida and Campeche, he celebrated
Mérida's willingness to hold their fire and listen to the voice of reason. Santa Anna waxed lyrical about independence and the virtues of a
political system that was federal, republican, and liberal. However, he
warned the *yucatecos* that should they continue to fight each other, their
ills would only get worse. He celebrated the importance of the army because it was the only institution that could guarantee peace. He begged
of the people of Yucatán a predisposition to seek "reconciliation."[22]

It is interesting to see how Santa Anna liked to project himself at
the time. In another speech to the troops in Campeche, he reminded

them that he was "the first to swear on the sandy beaches of Veracruz to ruin the tyrants" who oppressed Mexico. It was he who after "many sacrifices and dangers contemplated the fierce enemy of the mother country defeated and humiliated." It was he who, determined to forge a federal republic, initiated the "revolutionary movement that bore such prosperous results." He was "the friend of Liberty" and was welcomed as such by the people of Campeche, who saw themselves as the "lovers of American liberty."[23] It may be tempting to give little or no credence to his words. Nevertheless, Santa Anna was not being entirely dishonest. He may have been simplifying the causes and effects of the recent events and exaggerating his own importance. He may even have been deceiving himself into believing that he was exclusively responsible for liberating Veracruz, bringing down Iturbide, founding a republic, and giving its political class the confidence it needed to forge a federal and liberal constitution. Nonetheless, it remains true that he had risked his life fighting to liberate Veracruz, found a republic, and give its political charter a federalist slant.

It did not take long for Santa Anna to realize that he might have been a little hasty in his initial optimistic assessment of the situation in Yucatán. Dependent as it was on its commercial relations with Cuba, the region was left in a financial quandary by the rupture with Spain. Santa Anna was shocked by the poverty of the area. In a letter he wrote only ten days after arriving in Campeche, he made it clear that if the national government wanted Campeche to remain loyal to the federal government, financial aid was urgently required. He hoped a thousand pesos would serve, to begin with, to show that the Mexican nation cared about the garrison there. However, there was little that could resolve the profound hatred that divided Campeche from Mérida. Campeche, he thought, was republican, federalist, and a devout defender of independence. Mérida, on the other hand, sympathized with Spain. While Campeche traded with Veracruz and New Orleans and was commercially dependent on Mexico, Mérida's market was almost entirely dependent on Cuba. The only way forward that he could think of was for him to visit Mérida personally.[24]

In Mérida Santa Anna was shocked to find poverty even worse than in Campeche. Although he liked to flatter himself by believing that he was personally responsible for peace in Yucatán, the dire straits of the peninsula haunted him. The only effective solution Santa Anna could think of was that the government relieve Mérida's poverty with a subsidy of 100,000 pesos. In a particularly thorough report he wrote in Calkiní on 9 July 1824, he reiterated this concern: "Its poverty is general, which is why it deserves . . . the most serious attention from the federal government." Given that Yucatán was the poorest state of the republic, it was important that it was treated with care, even if this entailed awarding it particular "exemptions and privileges." If the national government did not find a way of aiding the province (and he insisted that 100,000 pesos were necessary to begin with), he feared that Yucatán would seek its own independence from Mexico. This was not idle talk. Until 1 July 1823, when present-day Guatemala, El Salvador, Honduras, Nicaragua, and Costa Rica came together as the United Provinces of Central America, these countries had been part of Iturbide's Mexican Empire. Santa Anna admitted to finding it extremely difficult to solve the many problems that afflicted the region. He described himself as continuously walking on quicksand. Yucatán presented itself before his imagination like a "mortar bomb" that would explode if he did not find a way of defusing it. The declaration of war on Spain and the belief that all trade with Cuba should be brought to an end was, in his words, "the [main] problem or the Pandora's box" of Yucatán.[25]

He saw the logic in postponing the national government's decree to suspend all trade with Spain, even if it meant he could be accused of undermining his country's rejection of Spanish imperialism. This was no doubt the kind of "exemption" and "privilege" he was thinking of when he drafted his report of 9 July. Such a view was consistent with Santa Anna's federalism. The whole point of a federalist system was that local circumstances and problems differed from region to region and required different solutions. What worked in Mexico City or even in Veracruz did not necessarily work in Yucatán.[26] In the distant capital, Carlos María de Bustamante argued in Congress that it was highly detrimental to the country's national sovereignty that Yucatán was not complying with the decree of 8 October 1823, whereby war had been declared on Spain following Lemaur's bombardment of Veracruz from the island garrison of San Juan de Ulúa. In Yucatán Santa Anna wrote to the state legislature from Calkiní, on 30 June 1824, that he had been persuaded by its deputies to suspend temporarily the execution of the federal decree. The political elite in Campeche was not impressed with Santa Anna's decision to back Mérida's demand to postpone the implementation of the ban on Spanish trade. However, it served to gain him the support of the yucateco congress. Following Francisco Antonio Tarrazo's resignation in the first week of July, the Congress of Yucatán, based in Mérida, elected Santa Anna their second constitutional governor.[27]

Santa Anna was sworn in as governor of Yucatán on 20 July 1824. He gave the expected promise to do everything within his means for the well-being of Yucatán. Worthy of note is that he also stressed that he intended to rely on the state legislature for advice and direction. He even went as far as confessing what was not entirely untrue, given the experience of the previous ten years: that he was "only accustomed to leading masses of soldiers." He "ignore[d] the science of politicians and statesmen."[28] He was certainly consistent in depicting himself as an army man, a liberator, an arbitrator, even a pacifier—but not a politician.

He was nevertheless uneasy about having to postpone a decree in which he ultimately believed. It was for this reason that he came up with a solution that could please both the federal government and those people of Yucatán who depended on trade with Cuba. Displaying yet again a formidable imagination and a tendency to think, where possible, in big, ambitious terms, Santa Anna offered to retain the region's commerce with Cuba by liberating the island from Spanish domination. There was the added bonus that in freeing Cuba, the garrison of San Juan de Ulúa—which was to remain under Spanish control until 17 November 1825 and which continued to cause serious problems to trade, exacting a duty of 8 percent on the invoice prices of all merchant ships' cargoes that entered the harbor—would cease to receive food and reinforcements from Havana.[29]

Santa Anna's fantastic plan to send an expedition from Yucatán to liberate Cuba was undoubtedly cunning and not necessarily unfeasible. José de San Martín's plan to liberate Peru, after first freeing Chile by crossing the towering Andes at the passes of Los Patos and Uspallata, and Simón Bolívar's plan to liberate Venezuela after first freeing Colombia, by crossing the mighty cordillera over the Páramo de Pisba, had been even more far-fetched and yet had been successful. Santa Anna went as far as preparing five hundred men for the planned expedition. In a report he wrote on 18 August 1824, he stressed that now was the ideal time to launch an invasion, given that news had reached him of major discontent on the island. He dispatched his friend from his days in the Fixed Infantry Regiment of Veracruz, Pedro Lemus, to Mexico City to form a Junta Promotora de la Libertad Cubana (Junta to promote Cuban liberty) and to present before Congress, on 8 October, a proposal to form an Ejército Protector de la Libertad Cubana (Protecting army of Cuban liberty). Former royalist officer and moderate federalist liberal politician General Manuel Gómez Pedraza, then minister of war, notoriously said at the time that the government should back Santa Anna's wild plan, for it would be beneficial whatever the outcome. If Santa Anna liberated Cuba, it would be a great gain for Mexico. If Santa Anna died in this patriotic ordeal, everybody would gain.[30]

The Mérida elite, whose commercial ties to Cuba were essentially Spanish ties, seriously opposed Santa Anna's plan and condemned him in secret session in the Yucatán legislature on 30 September, accusing him of abusing the Declaration of War on Spain, of misusing funds sent for his troops, and of sustaining an army that was too large for the region's needs. In the end, despite the fact that the Colombian government was disposed to support Santa Anna's Cuban adventure by sending a parallel expedition to liberate Puerto Rico, the national government decided not to support the scheme.

It is worth noting that Guadalupe Victoria did back Santa Anna's proposal. Providing another example of the affinities Victoria and Santa Anna shared, the president had himself belonged to a secret society whose sole purpose was to free Cuba. Before moving to Mexico City, Victoria had been the "strong male" (*varón fuerte*) of the Xalapa-based Masonic society known as the Black Eagle (Gran Legión del Águila Negra), set up to bring about Cuban independence. Given that Victoria defended Santa Anna's proposal, in spite of the fact that the entire political class in the capital (with the notable exception of Tornel) thought it was a preposterous idea, suggests that he was probably in on the scheme. A pattern may certainly be seen to be emerging as regards Santa Anna and Victoria's relationship at the time. Santa Anna could have been following Victoria's lead when he pronounced himself in favor of the republic on 2 December 1822, and again in favor of a federalist system on 5 June 1823. It is equally possible that his Cuban dream had originally been conceived in Victoria's mind. Santa Anna did not give up the idea, despite the government's opposition, and in January 1825 he was still writing to Victoria about the benefits of sending a liberating expedition.[31]

With the Cuban project stalled, Santa Anna was no longer able to postpone indefinitely the implementation of the trade ban on Spain, and by default on Cuba. On 9 October the supreme government's order telling him to stop stalling in the implementation of the relevant decree reached him. Santa Anna, therefore, as governor and commander general of Yucatán, was finally responsible for bringing all commercial transactions between Mérida and Havana to an end. Surprisingly, for the following four months, the much feared impact such a piece of legislation was expected to have on the region did not make itself felt. The swearing in of the 1824 Constitution found Santa Anna in Yucatán, and he led the major ceremony held in the state congress on 21 November.

In the speeches during the occasion it is interesting to see how Santa Anna's career and exploits were already beginning to be introduced into the fabric of the national narrative and, by default, into the collective psyche of his contemporaries. In terms of its importance, 21 November 1824 was equated with 2 December 1822. Implicit throughout the speech Santa Anna addressed to the Congress of Yucatán was the fact that without his 1822 revolt of Veracruz, Mexico would not be a republic. Those present in the legislative chambers of Yucatán that day would not be in the enviable position of swearing their allegiance to their immortal Magna Carta. At least Santa Anna, if not the rest of the yucateco political class, had come to view his contribution to the formation of a constitutionally governed, liberal, federal, and republican Mexico as both pivotal and heroic.[32]

As can be seen from the letters Santa Anna wrote from Yucatán, he succeeded in reestablishing "unity, peace, and rest" in the region. However, he was frustrated at the lack of support he received from the national government and grew increasingly obsessed with the idea of returning to Veracruz. Between July 1824 and February 1825 Santa Anna wrote four lengthy letters requesting permission to leave. In the last letter, and no doubt in response to all his previous letters having been ignored, Santa Anna claimed his health was broken. Despite not having received a single reply for the last four months, he had no choice but to demand to be relieved from his post in Yucatán. He was finally recalled in April 1825. According to a confidential letter Lucas Alamán wrote to Pablo Obregón, it was the manner in which Santa Anna had governed Yucatán, ignoring the national government's orders and instructions, that finally persuaded Victoria's cabinet to order his return. According to several other sources, however, the government's real fear was that as long as Santa Anna was based in Yucatán, there was the real concern that he would attempt to liberate Cuba regardless of what orders he was given. He was thus appointed director of engineers in the capital. Consequently, Santa Anna resigned as civil and military commander of Yucatán on 25 April 1825, two days after the liberal constitution of the State of Yucatán was approved (23 April 1825) with his blessing. He declined the post of director of engineers soon after he reached the capital, in June 1825, claiming that he lacked the education and qualifications for such a job, and returned to his home province of Veracruz. The true solution to the Mérida-Campeche divide, proposed by three deputies led by Joaquín Cásares y Armas on 2 September 1824—that Yucatán should be divided into two different states—would not be fulfilled until 1862.[33]

Back in Veracruz, Santa Anna chose to give politics a rest. From the summer of 1825 to the summer of 1827 he channeled his energy into running his hacienda and looking after his young wife. However, although he stayed away from the political theater of events, he found other ways of increasing his influence in his home province. Marrying into an important Spanish merchant family was one way in which he furthered his career, both financially and through the patron-clientele networks he established as a result. Buying a large hacienda was another. With time, as he came to own most of the land between Xalapa and Veracruz, Santa Anna became the main provider of employment, produce, and patronage in the region. He had gained the admiration of the *jarochos* for the way he had pacified the province in 1819–20. He was already recognized as the Liberator of Veracruz. During the next two years his relationship with the region, with its different levels of dependency, was to become even more significant through his emergence as one of the province's main *hacendados*, or landowners. This prominent role would be further highlighted by the manner in which he used the political impasse of 1827 to his advantage. Building on his heroic past and making the most of the political experience he had acquired in Yucatán, Santa Anna was to become the indisputable caudillo of Veracruz, using his stake in the local economy and his eventual involvement in local politics to consolidate his hold on regional power.

5. Among the Jarochos, 1825–1828

Most of the caudillos who came to dominate politics in Spanish America following the achievement of independence used the power they acquired in their regions to take on the national government. Juan Manuel de Rosas was the leader of the *gauchos* of the province of Buenos Aires before launching his bid for power. José Antonio Páez was the undisputed strongman of the Apure plains in Venezuela. They dominated their home provinces because of the prominence they achieved there during the wars of independence or because they belonged to families who owned the largest haciendas in the area. They established resilient networks of patronage that transformed them into the "natural" leaders of their province. Invariably, they obtained the undying support of their fellow *jarochos/llaneros/gauchos* by ensuring that this support was rewarded. At a regional level this meant employment, land concessions, and the benefits of having a landowner who would not let the national government's decrees harm local interests. For the aspiring caudillo the nurturing of a reliable regional bastion of support was essential. Without the aid of local finance and troops, it would be impossible to overthrow a national government.

Santa Anna's very particular *jarocho* affinities, paired with the notoriety he had acquired in the region as its tireless land administrator and intrepid liberator, placed him in good stead to become the province's favorite strongman. However, for him to become the undisputed chieftain of Veracruz he needed to strengthen his financial links with the region so that the welfare of the majority of *jarochos* depended on that of their caudillo. It was also important that he defeat his political rivals.

Given the strategic commercial importance of Veracruz as Mexico's key portal to the outside world, it followed that whoever controlled the region would be in a strong position to influence national politics. Most politicians must have realized this, and during a significant part of the early national period, the relationship of the political class with Santa Anna would reflect as much. Once he became the strongman of Veracruz, those who aspired to reside in the National Palace found that they had to come up with ways of controlling him and, by default, Veracruz. This could entail alliances even if they did not share his political beliefs. It would also explain the fear and respect the political class felt toward him. Santa Anna became the caudillo of Veracruz by becoming a *hacendado*, by marrying into a strategically well placed family, and by winning the regional power struggle that was played out in the summer of 1827. He consolidated his hold on Veracruz, becoming the state's acting governor.

He acquired the hacienda Manga de Clavo, outside Veracruz on the road to Xalapa, in August 1825, for 10,000 pesos; it would be worth 25,000 pesos twenty years later. Unfortunately, the deeds for the purchase of the hacienda have not been found. The absence of documentary evidence and the fact that the hacienda was partly burned down during the U.S.-Mexican War and subsequently broken up in the 1860s make it difficult to determine where it stood. According to Fanny Calderón de la Barca, the hacienda was "twelve leagues square," or approximately 73.6 square kilometers (46 square miles), and the main house was only three hours away from the port by stagecoach. Waddy Thompson claimed that Santa Anna's hacienda spread over 112 square kilometers (70 square miles) by 1842. In Doña Fanny's words, "The house [was] pretty, slight-looking, and kept in nice order." According to Thompson the land around the house was "of good quality, and would produce cotton and sugar most profitably." He noted that little of it was in cultivation, however, since "Santa Anna owns immense herds of cattle, some forty or fifty thousand head, which graze upon it."[1]

Manga de Clavo became Santa Anna's main home and haven between 1825 and 1842. Although far from the capital, it was on the route between Veracruz and Mexico City, enabling him to meet all the important personages who made their way up to and down from the Altiplano. It was here, according to the Spanish spy and adventurer Eugenio de Aviraneta, that Santa Anna held court, with Manga de Clavo becoming "the center of all meetings." Here he spent most of his time between the date of its purchase and his 1841–43 presidency, when he was not rebelling, quelling revolts, or fighting foreign aggressors. As time went by he channeled his wealth and energy into purchasing all the ranches and haciendas that spread around Manga de Clavo, so that by 1839, he was the largest landowner of Veracruz.[2]

Between 1825 and 1827 Santa Anna kept out of sight.[3] It certainly must have been a liberating experience for him not to have to endure the hardships of barracks life anymore. No longer was he required to endure the stress of leading a revolt, or the challenge of reconciling the warring factions of remote Yucatán. His time was his own. However, it would be wrong to believe that he spent these two years idly lazing about on one of his hammocks, gently swinging time away in the shade on his hacienda veranda, listening to his canaries sing from the cages that covered the walls. Instead he looked after his hacienda, attended to the needs of his young wife, and dedicated some energy to his very favorite pastime: cockfighting.

Doña Fanny was one of several foreigners to be struck by Santa Anna's "game-cocks" and how they were "kept with especial care, cock-fighting being the favourite recreation of Santa Anna's." Waddy Thompson's impressions on seeing Santa Anna's cockerels are worth quoting in full, for they provide a picturesque insight into the caudillo's preferred pastime (as well as an example of his characteristic charismatic attentiveness):

> When I first visited him at Encerro [sic], he was examining his chicken cocks, having a large main then depending—he went round the coops and examined every fowl, and gave directions as to his feed; some to have a little more, others to be stinted. There was one of very great beauty, of the color of the partridge, only with the feathers tipped with black, instead of yellow or white; and the male in all respects like the female, except in size. He asked me if we had any such in this country, and when I told him that we had not, he said

that if that one gained his fight he would send him to me,—
he was the only one of fifteen which did not lose his fight;
and shortly after my return, when I visited New York, I found
the foul there.

Guillermo Prieto provides one of the most vivid and enduring portraits of Santa Anna's love of cockfights and gambling, only on this
occasion far from his Veracruzan retreat, and in the midst of the hurly-
burly of the then famous fiesta of San Agustín de las Cuevas, south of
Mexico City (Tlalpan):

> Santa Anna was the soul of this emporium of chaos and li-
> centiousness. You just had to see him during the cockfight,
> surrounded by the tycoons of speculation and usury, call-
> ing the bets, taking other people's money, mingling with
> third-rank employees and low-rank officers; he asked for
> money, did not pay, his undignified tricks and cheats were
> celebrated, and when the heat of the game languished, the
> fair sex granted its smiles and accompanied our "hero" in
> his pranks.

It is more than probable that Santa Anna spent many a day between
1825 and 1827 looking after his cockerels and enjoying the excitement
of cockfights in the company of his *jarocho* friends.[4]

However, judging from the detailed instructions he gave his tenants,
it is evident that he spent most of his time looking after his properties.
Santa Anna was not an absentee hacendado. He was not one of those
rich Mexico City tycoons who bought a hacienda as an investment, as a
status symbol, or because it was fashionable. The man who had proven
himself such a dedicated and hardworking land administrator in Medellín, Xamapa, San Diego, and Tamarindo was very much a hands-on
landowner. He rode up and down his lands, checking that the cattle,
horses, mules, sheep, and chickens were all fed and well looked after.
He gave strict orders as to where and when sugar cane could be grown,
cattle butchered, and wood felled. If his supervision of his hacienda
resulted in the night finding him too far from the main house to return before dark, his tenants knew that he expected them to let him stay

over. On these occasions one suspects he entertained his tenants with stories of his adventures, enjoying himself with his peons' dances and songs, the harps, guitars and *zapateado* (stamping) of Veracruz filling the night with lively *sones jarochos*. The fact that he went on to father several illegitimate children in the region suggests that he also entertained himself on the nights he spent away from home in the company of the *veracruzanas* living on his estate.[5]

In 1825 Santa Anna married his first wife, the fourteen-year-old María Inés de la Paz García (1811–44).[6] She came from an affluent Spanish family. Santa Anna did not attend the wedding ceremony. He legally empowered his future father-in-law, Juan Manuel García, to take his place at his wedding in Alvarado in September 1825. This was a marriage of convenience. Santa Anna's reluctance to attend his own wedding certainly displays an acute absence of enthusiasm for the romantic and religious pomp and ceremony of the occasion. He was interested in the financial benefits of the alliance. Inés García's dowry allowed him to underwrite the purchase of Manga de Clavo in 1825 and included one hundred head of cattle. According to his second will (1867), Doña Inés's dowry amounted to six thousand pesos in country property. Given that less than a month after Doña Inés's death he proposed to Dolores Tosta, the view that he was not emotionally attached to his first wife would strike us as having some credence. As one scholar reminds us, after independence: "family alliances . . . emerged as particularly appealing and powerful means of ordering one's social and, more to the point, political worlds."[7]

Santa Anna was also notoriously unfaithful. Apart from the four legitimate children to whom Inés García gave birth (Guadalupe, María del Carmen, Manuel, and Antonio), the following women claimed to have had children of his: Nazaria Santos, Rafaela Morenza, María Cesárea, and Amanda Sandoval. In Santa Anna's last will (29 October 1874) he admitted to having fathered four illegitimate children (Paula, Merced, Petra, and José). One of his biographers found another: Pedro López de Santa Anna, and my own research in the regional archives of Veracruz led to the discovery of two more: Ángel and Agustina Rosa López de Santa Anna. Santa Anna's sexual appetite was well known at the time, as were some of the ploys he used to seduce unsuspecting women. According to one account, the only time he actually went through with the motions of a wedding was during his 1836 Texan campaign, when he paid a soldier to dress up as a priest and pretend to marry him to a woman from San Antonio who had promised to let the *señor presidente* sleep with her only if he joined hands with her in matrimony.[8]

It is difficult to venture an interpretation of Santa Anna's marriage to Doña Inés. Some glimpses of their private life have survived the passing of time. For instance, she was actively involved in administrating the hacienda during Santa Anna's absences. When in October 1828 General José Antonio Rincón, acting as commander general of Veracruz, expropriated Manga de Clavo during Santa Anna's absence, allegedly as a punishment for his 12 September revolt of Perote, he very deliberately prevented Doña Inés from managing the hacienda, and the consequences were dire. Santa Anna also stated in his 1867 will that Doña Inés "was almost always on our country properties advancing their interests, preferring this work to being in Mexico City, where she could have taken advantage of all the pleasures and delight which that beautiful capital offers."[9]

Perhaps the clearest indication that she did administer Manga de Clavo can be found in the fact that the hacienda, like the other properties that Santa Anna bought subsequently, fell into disrepair and abandonment following Doña Inés's death in 1844. Santa Anna's second wife was a refined Mexico City lady who preferred to live in the capital than on the family haciendas. Had Manga de Clavo, together with his other properties, been managed by his sons-in-law, José de Arrillaga and Francisco de Paula Castro, before Doña Inés's death, as they were following his first exile in 1845, there is no explanation as to their subsequent deterioration. In all likelihood, Doña Inés managed the hacienda on the occasions her husband was not around and actually enjoyed the life of the *hacendada*.[10]

The portrait Fanny Calderón de la Barca provides of her is one of a happy and relaxed lady. She describes Doña Inés as "tall, thin, and, at that early hour of the morning, dressed to receive us in clear white muslin, with white satin shoes, and with very splendid diamond earrings, brooch and rings. She was very polite, and introduced her daughter Guadalupe, a miniature of her mamma, in features and costume." Being Santa Anna's wife did, of course, mean that as well as enjoying the freedom of having a largely absentee husband, she could enjoy certain luxuries. The house may have been "large, cool, agreeable . . . with little furniture," but she could afford to wear the latest fashions and provide a splendid banquet. The breakfast she offered the Calderón de la Barcas that morning was "very handsome, consisting of innumerable Spanish dishes, meat and vegetables, fish and fowl, fruits and sweetmeats, all served in white and gold French porcelain, with coffee, wines, etc." She had officers she could boss around and was emancipated enough to enjoy smoking with the men: "After breakfast, the Señora having dispatched an officer for her cigar-case, which was gold, with a diamond latch, offered me a cigar, which I having declined, she lighted her own, a little paper 'cigarito,' and the gentlemen followed her good example." The image Doña Fanny leaves is certainly not that of an oppressed, neglected, and ill-treated woman. Several weeks after the encounter, Doña Inés followed up the acquaintance by writing Doña Fanny "a very polite letter." She was more than happy to look after her husband's public relations.[11]

We do not know whether she loved her husband or the extent to which she was distressed by his notorious infidelity. Having established from his behavior (his absence during the wedding, his promiscuity, and the speed with which he remarried) that his emotional attachment to her does not appear to have been significant, it is striking to find in the one letter that survives from their correspondence a marked warmth in the language he used when addressing her. As a prisoner in Orazimba, Texas, in the fall of 1836, he repeatedly calls her "my darling wife," warns her that his former secretary Ramón Martínez Caro can falsify his signature, and that he is adopting an entirely new one, and asks her to take good care of the children. Although this is not enough to support any judgment on Santa Anna's feelings towards her, it may serve to remind us that life is far more complex than may be hinted at in a biography like this one. It is highly possible that despite having grown to love his wife and cherish his family, he still continued to enjoy his brief affairs with other women. There is certainly ample evidence that he adored his children and that they reciprocated his love. It would be difficult to believe that he felt no affection toward the mother of his beloved children.[12]

Moreover, male fidelity was highly uncommon. According to one German traveler, "fidelity on the part of the husbands must be 'among the scarcest virtues to be found in Mexico,'"; that observer blamed the hot climate for this! As another European noted, although "between married couples one may observe a reciprocal attention, . . . fidelity, especially on the part of the husband, does not merit any consideration." Proof of the degree to which male adultery was almost accepted as inevitable in all marriages is that it was seldom used as a justification for divorce. Given that adultery was in a sense the norm, Santa Anna's antics may not have been as mortifying for Doña Inés as we might be inclined to think, especially if the marriage was one of convenience to begin with.[13]

Probably the most striking aspect of Doña Inés's life was the extent to which she came to be adored by the Mexican people. It is difficult to fathom how she became such a public figure given that she spent most of her life with her children at Manga de Clavo. Nevertheless, in 1842, when news spread that she was "dangerously ill," a procession of over twenty thousand people was held for her in Mexico City. Waddy Thompson was himself an admirer of this "lady of rare virtue," and attributed to her influence the fact that a number of Texan prisoners were eventually released from Perote earlier that year. When she died of pneumonia two years later at the age of thirty-three, while staying in Puebla, the public outpouring of grief was phenomenal. A huge funeral procession was held in Puebla, where she was buried. Parallel processions and masses took place for her throughout the country. In Xalapa the town council spared no expense in the events organized to mourn her death. Inscriptions, sonnets, and octaves circulated, praising her for having been "a model of maternal love, virtue and faithfulness," "a noble soul." One pamphlet, hinting at the possibility that people may have thought she regularly advised her husband when she was alive, prayed that she would "from heaven [continue to] guide the steps of her husband."[14]

It was during Santa Anna's temporary retirement at Manga de Clavo (1825–27) that the republic started to face its first significant problems. Following the 1824 elections two factions developed, which became bitterly opposed in the summer of 1826: the *yorkinos* and the *escoceses*. The *escoceses* belonged to a Masonic Rite that was first established in Mexico in 1813 by defenders of the 1812 Constitution. They were enlightened liberals whose main concern was to reconcile tradition with modernity while securing the major jobs that emerged with independence for the members of their lodges. Although initially perceived as a kind of loosely defined liberal political organization, which had played a significant role in bringing down Iturbide's empire, advocating an anti-absolutist agenda, they came to represent the forum where the more traditionalist (and affluent) members of the creole elite discussed politics. The Masonic Rite of York, formally consolidated in Mexico in 1825 through the exertions of U.S. Minister Plenipotentiary Joel Poinsett, was far more populist, with the stress on promoting U.S., as opposed to European, political values. They were also concerned with securing government posts for their members. Given that the Plan of Iguala had guaranteed the permanence of Spaniards in many bureaucratic positions, the *yorkinos* became characterized by their aversion to the Spanish and their demand for expulsion laws that would allow the members of their lodges to take over those posts vacated by the expelled Spaniards.[15]

It would be wrong to assume that the yorkinos represented a liberal agenda and that the escoceses did not. Entire lodges belonging to the Scottish Rite of Masons joined the newly formed Rite of York. The membership of the Rite of York was politically heterogeneous—old royalists such as General Manuel Gómez Pedraza together with old insurgents such as Tornel became yorkinos. In broad terms, and it must be stressed that exceptions abounded, the yorkinos favored a federalist system, and the escoceses did not. If anything they were divided by the pace of reform. The yorkinos appeared more willing to seize the day and attempt to reform Mexico overnight, whereas the escoceses preferred a more gradualist approach.[16]

By 1826 the congressional elections were fought out between these two factions, and the politics of the subsequent two years (1826–28) witnessed an accentuated power struggle between members of these two parties in the buildup to the 1828 presidential elections. The 1826 elections witnessed high levels of popular participation, and a dramatic increase of seats in the Chamber of Deputies went to the yorkinos. Their increasing power had several effects. It unnerved escoceses such as the vice president, former insurgent leader General Nicolás Bravo, who started to plot a revolt that might bring an end to the influence of the yorkinos. It gave the yorkinos a boost of confidence that incited them to radicalize their demands.[17]

On 19 January 1827 a Spanish conspiracy to return Mexico to its previous status as a Spanish colony was discovered. News of the Father Arenas conspiracy, as it became known, gave the more radical yorkinos the ammunition they needed to press forward with the expulsion laws. On 10 May Congress approved the first of these, and the feuding between the factions grew increasingly acerbic, as witnessed in the press. By the time the second and more radical set of expulsion laws was passed, on 20 December 1827, the rivalry between the two parties had reached breaking point. The increasingly acrimonious nature of the political divide in Mexico City found its own expression in the provinces. The major difference between Veracruz and the rest of the republic was that while the yorkinos had come to dominate the national government, the regional government of Veracruz was controlled by escoceses. Miguel Barragán, a leading *escocés* and subsequently *novenario* (representing yet another Masonic entity), had become governor of Veracruz on 20 May 1824. To make matters all the more tense, the leader of the Veracruzan yorkinos (and Santa Anna's personal enemy), Manuel Rincón, was the vice-governor.[18]

Santa Anna's political friends in Mexico City had all become yorkinos. Tornel was the master of one of the lodges in Mexico City. Together with José María Bocanegra he became the editor of the radical anti-Spanish newspaper El *Amigo del Pueblo*. In the context of Mexico City it made sense for Tornel, as a liberal republican federalist, to join the increasingly dominant Rite of York. Guadalupe Victoria, without wanting to join any of the factions in his bid to lead the country impartially, decided nonetheless to fill their lodges with his friends so that he could influence them. These included allies such as Tornel (Victoria's personal secretary, a deputy in Congress from 1826 to 1828, and Santa Anna's legal representative in the capital), José Ignacio Esteva (another veracruzano, the minister of finance, and the grand master of the Rite of York), and independence warrior General Vicente Guerrero. In Veracruz, however, Santa Anna's political allies and relatives were all escoceses.[19]

Manuel López de Santa Anna was one of the editors of escocés newspaper *El Veracruzano Libre*. Its regular writers included Pedro Landero, José María de la Portilla, Ciriaco Vázquez, and Tomás Pastoriza, all of whom would become regular santanistas. We know that Santa Anna became a yorkino in 1825, having been an escocés beforehand, and actually bought the Veracruzan yorkino newspaper *El Mercurio*, even though there is no evidence that he contributed to it. This was consistent with the actions and ideas of his allies in the capital (Tornel and Guerrero). His newspaper, paralleling Tornel's writings in the capital, provoked significant resentment among the Spanish and escocés population of Veracruz. And yet the local yorkinos accused him of conspiring with the escoceses and the Spanish merchants to bring down Victoria. Representative of the ambivalent stand he adopted in Veracruz is that he was elected vice-governor of Veracruz, on 6 September 1827, by a Scottish Rite–dominated legislature under the interim governorship of radical yorkino general Vicente Guerrero (August–October 1827).[20]

If we are to accept the view that the Veracruzan escoceses were united by their defense of a centralist agenda, it is difficult to accept that Santa Anna was an escocés at the time. He owned the main yorkino newspaper. Unlike for his brother, no evidence was found to link him to the 1827–28 escocés conspiracy to bring down Victoria and bring Bravo to power. Santa Anna was a die-hard federalist. One of the reasons he turned on Iturbide was his commitment to forging a federalist political system. He had led the 1823 federalist revolt of San Luis Potosí and had shown in Yucatán a disposition to accept that local circumstances did not always make the implementation of decrees issued in a capital thousands of kilometers away a straightforward affair; he was prepared to postpone them. He was an admirer and friend of Victoria, as evidenced by the way he offered Victoria the leadership of his troops in 1821 and 1822, and Santa Anna went to San Luis Potosí on Victoria's orders. His friend and informer Tornel was Victoria's personal secretary, a leading yorkino. The unsubstantiated accusation that Santa Anna was an escocés in 1827 is consequently difficult to believe. At a national level, he was a yorkino both in ideological terms and in terms of his personal allegiances. It was at a regional level that the profession of his political faith became difficult to express.[21]

Personal issues prevented him from supporting Rincón's party. His brother was an escocés. His father-in-law's friends and commercial partners were either Spaniards or escoceses (or both). Aviraneta, for once, appears to have been telling the truth when he stated that in the midst of the feuding that encompassed the region between the local factions of escoceses and yorkinos, "Santa Anna, secluded in his hacienda Manga de Clavo, remained aloof, without manifesting himself in favor of either of the two parties." Tornel concurs with Aviraneta on this point, stating that Santa Anna, disdainful of all Masonic lodges, was neither a yorkino nor an escocés by then. He hated all the divisive factions and sects. His political loyalty was to Guadalupe Victoria's national government and the figure of Vicente Guerrero. His only links to the Veracruzan escoceses were those of friendship and kinship. Tornel was adamant, bearing in mind Santa Anna's subsequent support of Guerrero at the battle of Tulancingo (7 January 1828), that had Santa Anna been an escocés in 1827, Barragán, his brother Manuel, and others would have accused him of betraying them, something they never did. He sympathized with the government and the yorkinos but did everything possible within the context of Veracruz to protect the lives and interests of his friends and relatives, without ever committing himself to supporting their political cause.[22]

There was a certain parallel between Victoria's so-called amalgamationist stance at a national level, whereby he refused to join either of the Masonic factions and worked toward including representatives from both sides in his cabinet, and Santa Anna's own balancing act in Veracruz. In the same way that Victoria belonged to neither faction and attempted to lead the country in an impartial manner, Santa Anna tried to steer Veracruz away from the dangerous divisions generated by Masonic-inspired party politics. That his brother was an escocés, that the dominant faction in Veracruz was the escocés one, and that the Rincones controlled the local yorkino lodges all just made Santa Anna's position difficult.

It was as the opposition between the factions started to reach breaking point that Victoria decided to transfer the Veracruzan minister of finance and grand master of the Rite of York, José Ignacio Esteva, to his home province, making him treasurer general of the port. Santa

Anna's newspaper El Mercurio claimed that Esteva's appointment followed the repeated requests of the (escocés-dominated) state legislature for the minister to be given this post. This was not true. Barragán, at the head of the escoceses of Veracruz and making the most of his post as governor, led the state legislature to decree on 29 May, only four days after Esteva's arrival, that he was *persona non grata* and that for fear of his presence inspiring a breakdown of peace and order in the province, he was under orders to depart the state immediately. There was also the contested issue that in a federal system like theirs, the national government could not make any such appointments in the states. That privilege belonged to the state legislatures. This was the angle Santa Anna adopted when he came out of his retirement to support the state legislature's decision publicly. He also decided to close down his own newspaper, El Mercurio, on 1 June.[23]

Esteva left Veracruz, denying that his departure was a result of his expulsion by the state legislature. The yorkinos in Veracruz soon launched their counterattack, furious that the escoceses had succeeded in expelling their grand master from the province and angry that Santa Anna had allowed the escoceses to silence their main newspaper. Their offensive centered on accusing a number of prominent politicians, including Barragán and Santa Anna, of being involved in a conspiracy to bring down the government. Using this as a pretext, Colonel José Antonio Rincón, military commander of Veracruz, dispatched his troops around the port on 25 June 1827 to ensure that order was not disturbed (and to intimidate the increasingly vociferous escoceses). A mob sacked Manuel López de Santa Anna's El Veracruzano Libre with the apparent support of Colonel Rincón on the night of 25 July 1827, following the publication of several articles that criticized him. Manuel López de Santa Anna protested this scandalous infringement of freedom of the press, both to his brother and to Governor Miguel Barragán. Santa Anna did not hesitate to come out of retirement to offer his services to the state legislature.[24]

Two days after the incident he was prepared to replace José Antonio Rincón as commander general of the port while the events of 25 July were investigated. This move was proposed and approved by Governor Barragán, much to Rincón's indignation. Barragán claimed in his letter to the minister of war that he was not at all surprised, since José Antonio Rincón's "violent character" was well known in the region. Rincón protested that the whole affair was a premeditated conspiracy. He denied sending in his officers to wreck the newspaper's printing house. He claimed that Manuel López de Santa Anna, Pedro Landero, José María de la Portilla, and Ciriaco Vázquez, together with Barragán, were involved in a conspiracy to overthrow Guadalupe Victoria's government and make Nicolás Bravo president. He stated that it had been his men's interception of some compromising letters that had led Manuel López de Santa Anna to wreck his own business and maliciously accuse Rincón of doing so. Defiant, Rincón escaped prison and took refuge in the barracks of the Ninth Battalion outside the port, on the 31st. From there he issued a *pronunciamiento* in which he demanded justice and officially withdrew his recognition of the state authorities, noting that he would obey only the federal government.[25]

Barragán, in a bid to show that Rincón's allegations were false, and frustrated with the federal government's ambivalence, resigned as governor on 4 August and was replaced temporarily on the 7th by Vicente Guerrero. While Santa Anna, as commander general, arrived in Veracruz on 2 August and ensured that Rincón could not leave his barracks in Boca del Río, Guerrero opted to investigate the accusations that had seriously marred the political fabric of the province. The fact that Guadalupe Victoria allowed Santa Anna to assume responsibility for restoring order in the port demonstrates that, at least in Victoria's mind, the accusation that he was involved in an escocés conspiracy was not true. Guerrero resolved to dispatch José Antonio Rincón and his crony Captain Juan Soto to Mexico City to be interrogated. He also resolved to place colonels Landero, Portilla, Vázquez, and Manuel López de Santa Anna on trial for conspiring to bring down the federal government.[26]

Santa Anna was furious about accusations that were made against him in a pamphlet entitled *Prisión de los Generales Santa Anna y Barragán en la plaza de Veracruz*, concerned with the events of 25 July, and demanded the libelous authors be punished. On 29 August 1827 he wrote the first of two long letters of protest. In the first he depicted himself as a true patriot who did not shy away from serving his country when he was needed. Having seen Mexico achieve its independence and forge a political system with "liberal institutions," he had considered his work done. He had resigned from his posts as commander general of Yucatán and director general of engineers. He was not ambitious for power, as his critics made him out to be. All he wanted was to retire to his hacienda, as he had done for the previous two years.

He had reemerged from his voluntary retirement only because he felt his services were required. In the same way that he had offered to help when news reached him of a filibuster expedition in Texas earlier that year, he had been ready to go into action the moment he heard of Rincón's abuses of 25 July. Called to bring peace and order to Veracruz, he had responded immediately. If all Mexicans did the same and were not blinded by "the party spirit, personal resentments and spitefulness, the lowest and filthiest of passions, vile and shameful adulation," the republic would be able to enjoy the "happy system that governs it." His sole concerns were "the true interests of the mother country and not those of the parties." To prove that all of this was true, now that peace had been restored in Veracruz, he wanted to be relieved as commander general of the port. He was to retire to his hacienda, where "from my domestic retirement I will remain true to my principles, abandoning it only when independence, liberty or the happy federal system is endangered."[27]

His anger, the following day, on hearing that his brother Manuel had been arrested was also expressed in forceful terms. Manuel was arrested on the night of 28 August. Santa Anna felt it right that his brother's conduct should be investigated. The sooner his innocence was proven the better. What was unacceptable was that he had been forcefully arrested and treated like a bandit. Equally upsetting was that he had then been locked up in a garrison held by the insubordinate Ninth Battalion. The chief prosecutor, Pablo Unda, moreover, was a renowned supporter of Rincón's faction. This was the trouble with party politics: "the parties . . . unfortunately agitate the mother country." He wanted his brother to be punished if he was found guilty, but he wanted the trial to be impartial. How could justice be accorded in this context? The strong words he used actually led Guerrero to reprimand him for employing a tone that could be almost described as insubordination.[28]

Nevertheless, it was while Guerrero was acting governor of Veracruz that Santa Anna was elected vice-governor, on 6 September 1827. Two days after this appointment he stood down as commander general of the port, claiming that his health needed a change of airs. This did not prevent him from serving as acting governor following Guerrero's return to Mexico City, even though he did request permission to retire to Manga de Clavo for a brief spell in mid-October 1827. Santa Anna's reputation came out intact, if not augmented, following the 1827 Rincón affair. In contrast, Colonel José Antonio Rincón had to face a court-martial that lasted until April 1828, by which time, although exonerated, he had lost his influence over the port.[29]

Before Congress approved the expulsion laws of December 1827, Santa Anna apparently promised his Spanish relations and friends in Veracruz that he would do everything possible to spare them from the effects of any adverse legislation. Apparently he even encouraged Spanish merchants such as Francisco Rivas to pay him to "sort everything out." Through his marriage to Inés, it is evident that he had strong financial (as well as emotional) ties to certain members of the Spanish community in the province. It was through Don Juan Manuel, his "uncouth Galician" father-in-law, that Santa Anna became in the eyes of "the rich merchants of Veracruz" their leading defender. When it became his duty as governor of Veracruz in 1828 to implement the expulsion laws, he dragged his feet over expelling his Spanish friends and those Spaniards who enjoyed the military *fuero* (privilege or immunity).[30]

His federalism, expressed in Yucatán through his attempts to delay the federal decree to end all commercial ties with Cuba, found expression in Veracruz in his parallel efforts to interpret the expulsion laws from a regional perspective. As he made clear in his first decree as vice-governor, on 15 December 1827, the time accorded to the Spaniards in the state of Veracruz to arrange their affairs before being expelled was to be determined by the state legislature and not the national Congress. A tendency to use the laws to his advantage may be seen in the way that, paradoxically, he was particularly effective in implementing the laws when dealing with specific Spaniards. In those cases where he hastily expelled Spaniards, such as 205 *gachupines* who had been exempted, there was the suspicion that he was targeting individuals he did not like, arbitrarily describing them as "dangerous" without providing any evidence to substantiate the claim. Tornel, as governor of the Federal

District (Mexico City) in 1828, was similarly active, expelling and exempting high numbers of Spaniards. In Tornel's case there is every indication that he accepted bribes to exempt those Spaniards who were willing to pay to stay.[31]

The Plan of Montaño (23 December 1827) was a clear expression of the extent to which the political atmosphere of the republic was becoming profoundly violent and unstable by the end of 1827. Instigated by the escoceses and the *novenarios*, the Plan of Montaño proposed to abolish all Masonic organizations, especially the Rite of York; to change the members of the cabinet, so that it was less radical; to expel Poinsett from Mexico; and to ensure that the federal constitution was abided by in full, stressing that this was not a centralist revolt and that it was not the intention of the rebels to overthrow the existing political system. The timing of the revolt, three days after the expulsion laws of 20 December had come into force, worked against the rebels. Tornel, acting as president of the Chamber of Deputies, deliberately used the sequence of events in his speech of 1 January 1828 to draw the inevitable yet erroneous conclusion that the revolt was a pro-Spanish reaction to Congress's deliberations. Vice President General Nicolás Bravo, a former insurgent Tornel knew full well was not a pro-Spanish reactionary, assumed the leadership of Manuel Montaño's revolt and took the town of Tulancingo, to the northeast of Mexico City.[32]

Santa Anna's links to the Spanish community in Veracruz, and his brother's affiliation to the local Scottish Rite Masons, have led a number of historians to state that he initially supported the Plan of Montaño. Several of his contemporaries were convinced that when he set out to meet the rebels of Montaño, his intention was to join the uprising. Montaño himself claimed later that Bravo had assured him Santa Anna had pledged to support the revolt. However, Montaño also said the same of Vicente Guerrero, José María Calderón, and Manuel de Mier y Terán. Santa Anna did not support the revolt, leading the same historians to claim this was an example of his characteristic opportunism.[33]

Considering Santa Anna's support of the national government and his yorkino affinities, this commonly held interpretation would appear to be inaccurate. His personal affinities with the escoceses of Veracruz did not amount to his being an active supporter of their revolutionary plans. The close ties that linked him to Guadalupe Victoria, Vicente Guerrero, and José María Tornel make the suggestion that he was prepared to support Bravo highly dubious. Judging from his actions alone, if there was a cause for which he was prepared to fight, it was that of Guadalupe Victoria's yorkino-dominated government. On 2 January 1828 he wrote to the government from Huamantla condemning the movement, offering his services to the government. He also wrote to tell Vicente Guerrero that Guerrero had his full support. He joined Guerrero in the assault on Tulancingo of 7 January 1828, which led to Bravo's surrender and capture, and for this act of loyalty Santa Anna was appointed acting governor of Veracruz.[34]

Unaware of the outcome of the battle of Tulancingo, on 8 January 1828 Barragán, Santa Anna's brother Manuel, and a faction of Veracruzan escoceses, in tandem with the state legislature, pronounced themselves in favor of the Plan of Montaño. When news reached Xalapa of Bravo's defeat, Barragán and Manuel López de Santa Anna opted to flee and hid briefly at Manga de Clavo before they were found and arrested on 2 February by Colonel Crisanto Castro. The fact that they hid at Manga de Clavo confirms the expressed view that Santa Anna had throughout the troubles done everything possible to help his escocés friends and relatives without committing himself to supporting their cause. If they had felt in any way betrayed by Santa Anna's involvement in the action of Tulancingo, it would make their choice of a hiding place difficult to understand. It is evident that Santa Anna, his brother, and Miguel Barragán were capable of making a distinction between friendship and politics.[35]

One of the results of Tulancingo was that Nicolás Bravo and sixteen others were sentenced to exile in Guayaquil and Perú. The hardships of the journey were such that Santa Anna's brother Manuel died during the journey, as did Bravo's only son. We do not know how Santa Anna reacted to news of his brother's death. However much he may have grieved for Manuel, it did not lead him to switch allegiances and oppose the faction that had condemned his brother to exile.[36]

Santa Anna returned from Tulancingo in late January 1828 and became the acting governor (vice-governor) of Veracruz. Despite the fact that his archenemy General Manuel Rincón was named governor, in lieu of Barragán, on 23 January 1828, it was Santa Anna who actively governed Veracruz from 28 January until 5 September 1828. His election by the state congress proves that he was seen as a leader whose ambivalent past allowed him to create bridges between the divided factions. He was perceived as being able to ensure that the federal government in Mexico City was obeyed *and* that local escocés interests were protected *at the same time*. In the same way that Santa Anna was able to bring together Victoria's insurgents and his royalist division in 1821, or conciliate between the divided factions of Yucatán in 1824, he was now capable of inspiring a realignment of allegiances between the defeated escoceses and the triumphant yet minority faction of yorkinos.[37]

Santa Anna was a very energetic governor. Evidently most of the reforms and decrees that were passed at the time may be attributed to the Xalapa-based Congress of Veracruz, rather than to him personally. Nevertheless, given that he was not known for letting civilians dictate his actions, it must be assumed that he believed in their decrees. Had he not agreed with the measures proposed, there is little doubt that he would have made his opposition to them known. As acting governor he took great interest in promoting trade in the region and ordered the celebration of trade fairs throughout the province. He also made a point of coming across as a strong leader, a champion of order. Among the first dispositions he made was one that required all town councils in Veracruz to take the necessary measures to strengthen their police forces and bring an end to banditry. He demanded that efforts be made to improve and mend the cities' streets and sidewalks. He supported the state congress's attempts to construct and reconstruct a number of roads affecting the routes to Coatepec, Papantla, Jalacingo, Tlapacoyan, Xalapa, Orizaba, Córdoba, and Huatusco. He also backed the irrigation project to channel water from the River Metlac into Córdoba. And he ordered the port authorities to clean up filthy and unhealthy streets.[38]

He asked for the town councils to raise funds to mend the brig *Guerrero* and strengthen the province's armed forces. In a similar vein he pressed the town councils to waste no time in forming their own corresponding local militias, reinstating the procedures established on 8 April 1823. He attempted to tighten his control of the region by ordering that for any civil servant to leave a department, it was necessary to request written permission from the governor. He was particular about ensuring that all financial matters were scrutinized with care and pushed through decrees such as that of 8 February, which created a number of bureaucratic posts in the customs houses of Veracruz, Alvarado, Pueblo Viejo de Tampico, and Coatzacoalcos. As stipulated in a subsequent law, the administrator general and his accountant were accountable to the state government and were obliged to inform the authorities of all of their transactions. He also kept an eagle eye on the corporations' finances. As an example he personally chased up any outstanding debts, such as the town council of Xalapa's overdue payment of 682 pesos and 4 reales to the town's judge and judiciary. By the same token, he encouraged the town councils of the state to raise their own taxes. A case in point was the decree of 18 March 1828, whereby the town corporations became entitled to tax all rum-producing factories under their jurisdiction.[39]

He showed concern for education as well. He was a patron of the philanthropic educational Compañía Lancasteriana in 1823. In line with his lifelong commitment to improving the new country's educational system, he gave his full backing to a series of decrees aimed at improving education in the province. A general education plan for Veracruz was approved under him, and the state congress committed itself to injecting the necessary funds to kick-start a number of so-called national schools throughout Veracruz (three primary schools in each of the twelve districts [cantones] that made up the state). Furthermore, 30,000 pesos per annum were allocated for the maintenance of the Lancasterian schools in the region. Santa Anna also stressed that a Drawing Academy should be established. Likewise, he backed one Claudio Francisco Goján's claim, as one of the teachers of the local Escuela Pía in Xalapa, for 25 pesos and 5 reales to be paid to cover the cost of the school's utensils. During the period in which Santa Anna was most active as governor, the president of the Veracruzan Chamber of Deputies was Tornel's brother, José Julián. Tornel himself was vice president of the Compañía Lancasteriana at the time.[40]

Santa Anna demanded that a cemetery be erected behind the San José barracks in Xalapa and went on to play an active role in raising funds for it as well as in the planning and building stages. One wonders whether Santa Anna's son's poor health had anything to do with his obsession about completing the cemetery. He certainly maintained good relations with the town council, lavishing its members with his praise whenever possible.[41]

The town council of Xalapa in 1828 was dominated by yorkino supporters of presidential candidate Vicente Guerrero and their vice-governor Santa Anna. In a speech Santa Anna made at the time, it is possible to discern the anti-party standpoint that would become a constant in his political manifestations: "Let us banish party and personal hatreds; let us be generous; the Mexican is an idolater of liberty, he may err, but he is not disloyal; . . . let us not give the enemies of the Republic days of glory; we are persuaded that in order to progress, we need tranquility, obedience, and union."[42] His factional ambivalence, which may be equated with Victoria's own amalgamationist stance, found expression in his reiterated view of himself as an impartial mediator. Stemming from his military career, far removed from the daily diatribes of city party politics, he already projected a belief in himself and the armed forces as representing a standpoint that was *above* factional interests. He was also in a position now to make his presence felt in the wider context of national politics. He was a feted hero of the War of Independence, a hacendado, and a successful arbitrator. His success was confirmed by his position as a much-respected governor of Veracruz. The highly controversial presidential elections of 1828 and the Spanish armed intervention of 1829 would provide him with the opportunity to consolidate his position as regional strongman and place him in good stead to become a national caudillo in the 1830s.

6. General of Tricks, 1828–1832

The battle of Tulancingo represented the end of the *escoceses* as a credible option and led to a realignment of political allegiances. The yorkinos, having based their entire propaganda between 1825 and 1827 on an anti-escocés/anti-Spanish platform, now found themselves without their old enemy and in need of replacing their offensive politics with beliefs that consolidated their hegemony. This need to define the politics of *yorkismo* brought to light the divisions that existed within what had been a loosely defined liberal Masonic faction with radical/populist tendencies. By April these divisions became apparent. In the buildup to the presidential elections the radical *yorkinos* started to campaign in favor of former insurgent, mulatto general Vicente Guerrero. The more moderate yorkinos turned against their own lodges and joined the ex-escoceses in supporting former royalist, Caucasian, and well-to-do liberal general Manuel Gómez Pedraza.

By mid-September, after six months of vitriolic campaigning, it became clear that Gómez Pedraza was going to win. This realization must be qualified. Gómez Pedraza was going to win only because the outcome of the elections was based on an indirect system that left it up to the creole representatives of each state legislature to determine the winner. Each of the nineteen state legislatures (except Durango) cast two votes, one for president, one for vice president. Manuel Gómez Pedraza, with eleven, beat Guerrero by three votes. As was noted by radical politician Lorenzo de Zavala, "had the elections [been based] on individual suffrage, [Guerrero] would have received an immense majority of votes in his favor." This was a view shared by many, including Santa Anna.[1]

According to one piece of gossip, Santa Anna strongly resented the manner in which Guerrero favored José Antonio Rincón during the three months Guerrero resided in Xalapa (August to October 1827), visiting his rival regularly at Rincón's house on the Calle del Toronjo. Even if this were true, his allegiance to Guerrero ran deeper than this. Their politics had followed similar paths following the proclamation of the Plan of Iguala. Guerrero had been one of the few high-ranking officers to support Santa Anna's revolt of 2 December 1822 prior to the Plan of Casa Mata. Together with Victoria, Guerrero had also sympathized with Santa Anna's 1823 federalist *pronunciamiento*. They had already joined forces twice, in Mexico City in 1824 against Lobato, and in Tulancingo in 1828 against Bravo. When Guerrero was elected governor by the state congress of Veracruz on 9 May 1828, replacing an absent Manuel Rincón, he let Santa Anna take care of the day-to-day running of the state government.

Like Victoria, as one of the insurgent leaders whose support for independence had not wavered, Guerrero had an aura about him that impressed Santa Anna. In April 1828 Santa Anna persuaded the state legislature to donate Guerrero a valuable hacienda in recognition of his services to the nation. If we are to believe Aviraneta, Santa Anna and Guerrero made a secret pact on the eve of the presidential elections of 1828 that if Guerrero did not win, Santa Anna would revolt against Gómez Pedraza's faction. In return Guerrero was to make Santa Anna minister of war. Santa Anna's yorkino sympathies, downplayed in the regional context of Veracruz, were to find forceful expression that September.[2]

As acting governor he attempted to ensure that the local legislature cast its vote in favor of Guerrero. Throughout the summer of 1828, he wrote a number of secret letters to the town councils of the region urging them to vote for the insurgent hero. He gained the support of Veracruz, Xalapa, and Orizaba. He also attempted to bribe and threaten a number of deputies in the state congress. When this failed, the town council of Xalapa, now fully behind Santa Anna, stated that they no longer recognized the state congress. The state congressmen in turn replied by deposing Santa Anna on 5 September 1828. Therefore on 11 September Santa Anna left Xalapa at the head of eight hundred men and arrived in Perote on the 12th, where he was welcomed with forty-two cannon volleys. It was from here that he launched what was to be his third *pronunciamiento*. On this occasion he demanded that Guerrero be made president, since "the people everywhere have made their intentions sufficiently clear." Given that the voice of the majority was not being respected, the people had little choice but to join the army in this cry for justice. He blamed the defeated Spanish faction for conspiring to bring down the constitutional government. He criticized Victoria for doing little to prevent the ascendancy of this "anti-national party." He accused Gómez Pedraza of being a hypocrite, "always inclined to [defend] an aristocratic system," bribed by the gold of the Spaniards. He called for the election of Gómez Pedraza to be annulled, as he was "the declared enemy of our federal institutions"; for all Spaniards to be expelled from Mexico since they were "the origin of all our problems"; and for Guerrero to be elected president.[3]

Santa Anna had under his command the Second Squadron and the Fifth Battalion. He also had with him two pieces of artillery. On the dawn of the 14th, following a foray into the Hacienda of San Marco, near Nopaluca, three hundred of his cavalry captured a government convoy carrying fifteen thousand pesos to Xalapa. Toward the end of the month, he crushed the government troops posted in the Hacienda del Molino. According to one witness, Santa Anna used a filthy trick to defeat Colonel Pablo Unda (the *rinconista* high-ranking officer who had prosecuted Santa Anna's brother Manuel in 1827). He entered the hacienda saying he wanted to talk and then placed his sword on Colonel Unda's chest and arrested him, forcing his troops to join the rebels. Santa Anna characteristically made a point of speaking to each and every one of Unda's troops to rally them to his cause.[4]

Guadalupe Victoria publicly condemned the revolt and demanded that the Mexican people stand by the Constitution. He did not condemn Santa Anna personally. Despite his restraint, stemming from his friendship toward Santa Anna, the government decreed that the caudillo of Veracruz was an outlaw and that he faced the death penalty unless he surrendered. According to Carlos María de Bustamante, General Manuel Rincón received orders from Victoria not to defeat Santa Anna. He claimed that this was the reason why Rincón did not rout Santa Anna when he had the chance. Although this is difficult to believe, the suggestion highlights how people saw between Victoria and Santa Anna a definite and special bond.[5]

Once more, the support Santa Anna was expecting was not forthcoming. Minister of War and triumphant presidential candidate Gómez Pedraza dispatched Santa Anna's personal enemy, General Manuel Rincón, at the head of two thousand men to besiege the garrison in Perote. Rincón camped at the Hacienda del Molino outside the Fortress of San Carlos (Perote). From there, Rincón wrote to inform Santa Anna that he was an outlaw and had little choice but to surrender. Santa Anna's reply of 30 September 1828 denoted both his heart-felt commitment to supporting Guerrero and the personal animosity he felt toward Rincón: "It has always been your part to oppose true public opinion, because your personal resentments declared you long ago my personal enemy. The well-deserving Guerrero is not only in the hearts of the veracruzanos; he is the idol of all those who repudiate aristocratic privileges, and who without doubt include more than six million in the Republic."[6]

Rincón did not attack. In contrast, Santa Anna made daring excursions outside the walls of the fortress to obtain supplies. Impatient, Gómez Pedraza sent General José María Calderón to the area of conflict. Informed of Calderón's arrival on the outskirts of Perote, Santa Anna realized that if he did not break the siege, he would be defeated. Lieutenant Colonel José Antonio Mejía proposed that they flee to Oaxaca, convinced that their revolt would be seconded there. As a result, on the night of 19 October, three days after a full moon dissuaded him from putting his escape plan into practice, Santa Anna led his army out of the fortress and past the besieging troops without their noticing. While Rincón scratched his head in disbelief on the morning of the 20th, Santa Anna arrived in San Andrés Chalchicomula to the sound of church bells, fireworks, and military music, having escaped from the thirty-seven-day siege of Perote. He sent Lieutenant Colonels Mariano Arista and José Antonio Mejía to Orizaba to force a 10,000-peso loan on the vicinity (they succeeded in obtaining 1,300 pesos), and from there moved on to Tehuacán (raising 8,000 pesos), and thereafter to the beautiful colonial city of Oaxaca, which he entered on 6 November 1828.[7]

General Manuel Rincón, who took an "inexplicable" amount of time to muster his troops and pursue Santa Anna, finally reached Oaxaca in mid-November. The battle for Oaxaca began on the hills of Montoya but soon reached the city itself. The streets became littered with corpses, and Rincón took the corn exchange, the convent of San Juan de Dios, the hospital, and San Felipe church as well as a significant part of the city. Despite the triumphalism of Rincón's dispatch, Santa Anna's forces remained in control of the garrison of la Soledad and the convents of Santo Domingo and del Carmen. Faced with a stalemate, Santa Anna wrote to Rincón on 20 November to suggest that they join forces. He feared a Spanish invasion was imminent, and the longer they fought each other, the greater the Spaniards' chances of succeeding would be. Rincón, after a good ten years of personal rivalry, was not prepared to enter into negotiations with Santa Anna and allowed Calderón to take over as leader of the government forces in the field.[8]

Two examples of Santa Anna's cunning antics date from the showdown in Oaxaca, though both may be apocryphal. The first is that he dressed as a woman to enter Rincón and Calderón's side of the city and get a close view of the enemy positions. The second is that one night, he and his men succeeded in climbing into the convent of San Francisco, where Calderón attended mass during the siege. On 29 November, disguised as monks and within the convent walls, his troops ambushed the congregation. But Calderón was not there that day. They settled for a large "voluntary" contribution instead.[9]

Negotiations began again on 2 December 1828. Santa Anna was prepared to submit to the government if the rebels were amnestied. Calderón was prepared to intercede for them before Congress if they put down their arms first. This was not good enough. Both parties eventually agreed upon an armistice on 11 December. Three days later news reached Oaxaca of the revolt of La Acordada barracks (30 November) and the Parián Riot (4 December), which submerged the capital in a state of anarchy. Calderón and Santa Anna decided to put aside their differences and head together to Mexico City to do everything possible to restore peace in the capital. This gallant resolution was short-lived, for the next day the news of the riot was superseded with details of Manuel Gómez Pedraza's resignation and escape and the triumph of Guerrero's faction.[10]

Santa Anna was still prepared to return to Mexico City, but Calderón was not. In fact, Calderón did not know what to do. He adamantly refused to join sides with the "outlaw" he had been fighting for the better part of two months. With a beautiful sense of irony, Santa Anna turned the tables and demanded, on behalf of the national government he represented, that Calderón put down his arms and obey the legally constituted authorities of the republic. If Calderón did not do so, Santa Anna would have no choice but to treat him as a criminal. It goes without saying that by the morning of the 16th, the armistice was broken.[11]

Calderón voiced his despair in a heartfelt letter to Guadalupe Victoria on the 19th. How could he now find himself at the front of the defeated faction? How could he, of all people, have gone from being the champion of the constitutional government to being a common outlaw? He grudgingly insinuated that he would subject himself to Victoria's orders, even though he was still determined to put up a fight against his nemesis. Santa Anna was in high spirits. In a wonderfully confident letter he addressed to Guerrero on the 20th, he stated that his positions were impregnable and he had eight hundred brave men and more than enough armament and munitions. On the following day he went on to write, with a palpable sense of glee, a stream of letters to Calderón as well as to the various leading authorities in Oaxaca to remind them that it was now he who represented the legitimate government. Calderón was nothing but an outlaw. As he wrote to the minister of war, his troops were the ones defending the national government, unlike Calderón's rebel troops, and should receive their pay.[12]

On Christmas day 1828, Calderón's frustration found expression in a major attack on Santa Anna's part of the city. Santa Anna's troops fought back in what became a long and bloody affair. The fighting went on into the night and the following day. The people of Oaxaca suffered greatly, trapped in between Santa Anna's and Calderón's forces. Even Santa Anna was not oblivious to the massacre of innocent *oaxaqueños*. With contempt he noted that it was ironic that Calderón could have claimed his men were the "jealous defenders of law and order." He requested the immediate dispatch of around five hundred reinforcements in order to obliterate Calderón's forces. Two days later, after both armies had inflicted significant pain and losses upon Oaxaca and each other, it became apparent that they could not go on like this. The two generals finally came face to face at 4:00 in the afternoon and signed a peace treaty. Calderón was allowed to go to Puebla to see for himself whether "the Supreme Government was [acting] freely."[13]

On 3 January 1829, Santa Anna informed the government that he intended to leave Oaxaca. He was pleased that Calderón had left, and that the government was to send him 700 new uniforms (500 for his infantry, 200 for his cavalry). He did not leave until the 9th, as he felt his presence was necessary to ensure that peace truly had been restored to the city. He went to Mexico City, where he attended a banquet with Guerrero on the 23rd. According to one source it was during the meal that Guerrero told Santa Anna he intended to appoint him minister of war when Guerrero took over the presidency in April (a promise that according to Aviraneta had been made back in 1828, prior to the elections). The fact that he appointed General Francisco Moctezuma instead was to irritate Santa Anna considerably, according to one biographer.

Nevertheless, Santa Anna's support of Guerrero was rewarded once the mulatto hero of independence became president. Guerrero restored him to the post of governor and commander general of Veracruz, two positions that, in a sense, meant much more to him than a role in the cabinet in Mexico City. On 29 August 1829, as Santa Anna confronted Isidro Barradas's invading expeditionary army, he was promoted to general of division for his "extraordinary ability." In March Congress formally canceled the decree that had made him an outlaw. Santa Anna returned to Veracruz, where he assumed the post of governor once more on 23 March 1829. Evidence of the fact that he continued to hold Guerrero in high esteem is that he asked the president to become his daughter Guadalupe's godfather, following her birth on 13 March.[14]

Although it was not Santa Anna's revolt of Perote that brought Guerrero to the presidency but the revolt of La Acordada, in the capital, the former soon assumed greater significance in the minds of his contemporaries. Replicating the manner in which the revolt of Veracruz (2 December 1822) became associated with the fall of Iturbide—overshadowing the determining impact of the Plan of Casa Mata (1 February 1823)—it was the Plan of Perote (12 September 1828), rather than the Revolt of La Acordada (30 November 1828), that became popularly known as the one that prevented the "unjust" election of Gómez Pedraza. To quote El *Fénix de la Libertad*: "The campaign in Oaxaca in 1828 . . . will forever honor [Santa Anna] as the captain of such a small division. With it he made the large army that pursued him respect and fear him; he escaped from Perote taking heavy artillery with him without being heard by the besiegers; he went from there to Santo Domingo de Oaxaca . . . [where] with a handful of men he carried out all kinds of opportune and astute sorties." The newspaper compared Santa Anna to Hannibal and called him "the General of Tricks [*ardides*]."[15]

Back in his bailiwick, serving as governor, Santa Anna was once more characteristically energetic and masterful in his leadership of the State of Veracruz. The triumph of the *guerrerista* faction worked in his favor. The Congress of Veracruz was now fully behind him, decreeing that he be considered "a hero of the State [*benemérito del estado*]," and that all the men who accompanied him in his "heroic *pronunciamiento*" were awarded a blue sash inscribed with the words: "The State of Veracruz for proven patriotism."[16]

Santa Anna was beginning to sense his growing importance both in Veracruz and the republic at large. In a speech he addressed to the veracruzanos on 10 February 1829, it is possible to discern a new maturity in his voice. The outcome of the revolt of Perote had given him new confidence as he reassumed his post of governor. Santa Anna's 1829 oration contained four themes that would become recurrent in subsequent santanista political writings. It was an openly populist manifestation, a passionately veracruzano piece of oratory. It was rabidly anti-parties and anti-politics. He presented himself as a national (super)hero and endeared himself to his audience by presenting himself as one of them. He referred to the people of Veracruz as his "friends" and "compatriots" who had taught him "to be a man." Together, he said, they had crushed Spanish despotism in 1821 and brought an end to Iturbide's homegrown tyranny. Emphasizing his undying love of Veracruz, he explained that he had risen against the arrogant aristocratic and tyrannical ambitions of Gómez Pedraza *because he was a true veracruzano*, and true veracruzanos did not sit back and watch the suffering of the mother country with indifference. He made a point of noting that the country's recent troubles could not be blamed on one man alone. Mexico's problems stemmed from the divisive behavior of its political parties. Unlike himself, who was interested in the good of the country, Mexico's parties were interested only in themselves:

> [My] heart only seeks peace and unity, it joyfully gives in to the redeeming idea of a general and fraternal reconciliation; that the kiss of true peace among Mexicans of all parties, serves as the medicine which may cure all of our ills before they infect us. . . . The ridiculous names which have so far been given to the parties tear the nation apart; let there be only one . . . the party of the true Mexican patriots. Let us prepare for a great national reconciliation, because only this will serve as the anchor of our hopes.

Probably with the assistance of speechwriter Tornel, Santa Anna figured in his own narrative of the recent events as the selfless patriot who had defeated foreign and domestic tyrants alike. Although he stressed that they owed their allegiance to Guerrero, "called to occupy the [presidential seat] . . . out of justice," he himself was the real protagonist of his speech.[17]

An insight into his views on the political role of the Church emerges in one of the first public statements he circulated as governor, on 11 April 1829. His private thoughts on the importance of the Roman Catholic faith did not prevent him, as a politician, from supporting anticlerical measures. In the *Circular* of 11 April, he expressed in forceful terms a belief in curtailing the political influence of the Church. He was in line ideologically with the president's faction. He did not share the proclerical views of the ex-escoceses, novenarios, moderate yorkinos, and traditionalists who were beginning to rally around the figure of General Anastasio Bustamante, under the guidance of the brilliant conservative ideologue Lucas Alamán.

It had been brought to his attention that a number of priests were discussing political issues in their sermons. He felt it was objectionable that they were attacking the current government from the pulpit. He made it clear that at a time when the nation's wounds needed to be healed, and the Church should be encouraging its flock to cooperate, he would not turn a blind eye to the priests' misconduct. He brought to the veracruzanos' attention the law of 20 March 1801, which punished priests who promoted dangerous beliefs. He would apply it to any priest found guilty of altering the peace of the province. He asked the virtuous and peace-loving people of Veracruz to denounce any priests who attempted to break "the perfect union, sighed for by the lovers of national prosperity."[18]

Once more, Santa Anna dedicated his energies to promoting trade, reinforcing the part-time civilian provincial militias, in consonance with radical liberal belief, and building a cemetery (on this occasion in Cosamaloapan). A certain amount of time was accorded to redefining the privileges and responsibilities of the state judiciary and amending the political makeup of some of Veracruz's districts (e.g., Santiago Tuxtla became a *cantón* of Acayucan). As was highlighted in the agenda for the "extraordinary" state congressional session of 1 July (before news of the arrival of a Spanish military expedition diverted Santa Anna's and the legislature's attention from their projected reforms), their main concerns revolved around preserving peace and order; organizing the state's finances, judicial system, and local militias; dividing the state's territory; reforming the federal and state constitutions; and addressing the economic needs of the congress.[19]

Much of Santa Anna's time as governor was dedicated to implementing the 1828 expulsion laws. As we have seen, his stance toward these had initially been ambivalent. In many instances he hesitated in applying the laws, lending a hand to members of the Spanish community of Veracruz with whom he had ties. In other cases he abused the laws to expel Spaniards he did not like. In 1829 he became particularly active both in applying the laws and in explaining the rights and obligations of those affected. Despite his previous hesitation, Santa Anna expelled more Spaniards than any other governor at the time, issuing nearly half the passports in Mexico for the period. He issued two circulars in 1829 that sought to give greater efficiency to the expulsion. Santa Anna was no longer playing the part of the lenient caudillo. He had exonerated those Spaniards who were close to him and could now pursue this reinvigorated hard-line stance. With the *guerrerista* faction in power, both at a national and at a regional level, Santa Anna's anti-Spanish stance coincided with that of the authorities.[20]

Even so, there were rumors of tensions. In a fascinating although unreliable report dispatched to the *Times* of London from Veracruz, a striking account of the uneasy relationship that existed between Santa Anna and Guerrero's government emerges:

> The Government of Mexico is distrustful of Santa Anna and Santa Anna is distrustful of the government since the appointment of Guerrero to the presidency. Santa Anna has been appointed Minister of War, but is not gone, and will not go to Mexico to take possession of this portfolio. It is thought that he intends making the state of Vera-Cruz an independent sovereignty. This plan is not badly conceived: he would have thus the key and the treasury of the country, as Vera-Cruz is the only part to which strangers come. Santa Anna is a young man, about 30 years of age, enterprising, ambitious, and despotic, under the appearance of affability; it is thought here that he thinks of making himself dictator, and that he is the only man able to hold with a firm hand the reins of government in a country where there exists such a struggle of opinions. . . . He has about 4,000 men under his command. He is called here, and he likes to hear himself styled, the Mexican Napoleon.[21]

Santa Anna did not take any action to promote the independence of Veracruz or to overthrow Guerrero. However, like Tornel and Bocanegra, who also served Guerrero's government in different capacities, he started to feel unease toward the middle of 1829 when a number of radical proposals met with the approval of both Congress and the president. Tornel felt that Guerrero, by being too "tolerant and fair," allowed certain radical yorkinos to take advantage. Santa Anna was committed to seeing Minister of Finance Zavala removed from the cabinet. Zavala's radical reforms taxed the large landowners, reduced the salaries of both governors and high-ranking officers, abolished the tobacco monopoly, and expropriated the property of the Jesuits and the Inquisition. Tornel and the santanistas saw him as too radical, although this did not prevent them, as Tornel put it, from identifying themselves with "the men of 1829." Santa Anna's political concerns, however, were put on hold, as his main concern that summer was to repulse an attempt on the part of Ferdinand VII's government to reconquer Mexico.[22]

As early as June Santa Anna knew that the Spaniards were planning an invasion of Mexico. At the time everything seemed to suggest that the landing would take place in Yucatán. Rumors of the projected invasion reached the capital, and while Tornel, as governor of the Federal District, called for the capital's militias to be armed and drilled, Carlos María de Bustamante claimed Santa Anna had invented the whole story as an excuse to raise funds to take on the government. On this occasion, however, the rumors were well-founded.[23]

Santa Anna went into action the moment news reached him, on 1 August, that Barradas had disembarked at Cabo Rojo, close to Tampico, on 28 July at the head of 3,500 men. In three days he raised a forced loan of 20,000 pesos from the business class of Veracruz and took possession of all the boats that could be mobilized, regardless of whether they belonged to merchant or fishing fleets. The names of some of the ships he appropriated show that he did not care whether they were foreign: *Louisiana, Trinidad, William,* and *Splendid* were four transports he "borrowed" that were of British or U.S. origin.[24]

He set sail for Tampico on 9 August, a week before Congress actually authorized the mobilization of Veracruzan troops to the state of Tampico. His cavalry, about six hundred strong, was ordered to head north overland to the Pánuco River, where they were to meet up with the seaborne infantry. His improvised flotilla got as far as Tuxpan on the 19th, and from there proceeded along the lagoon of Tamiahua until it reached Pueblo Viejo, two kilometers from Tampico. He was itching to engage in battle the moment they arrived. In the early hours of the 20th Santa Anna and Colonel Pedro Landero contemplated the enemy's positions. They resisted the temptation of attacking as dawn was breaking, and a gunshot gave away their position. This did not deter Santa Anna from leading fifteen hundred men across the river the following night, conducting his first attack on Tampico, with street fighting taking place well into the next day (21 August 1829).[25]

The battle of the 21st was bloody. What Santa Anna did not know was that General Isidro Barradas and the main bulk of his forces had vacated Tampico to explore the route to Altamira, several kilometers to the north. When the Spanish forces under siege asked for an interview, Santa Anna called a truce under the assumption that Barradas was about to surrender. He met with Spanish Colonel José Miguel Salomón in downtown Tampico. According to Aviraneta, who was present at the meeting, Santa Anna did not drink much alcohol, only a glass of wine, ate little, and after two hours made it clear that he would not accept anything except the Spaniards' unconditional surrender. At this point, the roar of Barradas's cannons was heard, and news reached him that the brigadier's forces had returned to Tampico and cut off his escape route. He was quick to realize that he had been lured into Tampico under false pretenses and that he could be made prisoner.

Displaying his usual talent for improvisation and deception, Santa Anna took two quick decisions. He dispatched Colonel José Antonio Mejía back to his headquarters with orders that he should return with a forged letter stating that reinforcements from Mexico City had just arrived. He made his way to the French consul's house, where he was protected by the flag of truce. Barradas was in no position to crush Santa Anna's trapped forces. A month in the region had decimated his army with disease. The reinforcements he was expecting had not arrived. The local population had deserted the towns, leaving the expedition without provisions. Barradas's hopes that the Mexicans would celebrate his arrival, despairing of the horrors of independent life, had proven unfounded. Barradas pinned his hopes on persuading Santa Anna to change sides.[26]

Santa Anna entered into another round of negotiations that day. Barradas offered him the title of duke of Tampico. Aware of his own precarious situation, he asked for some time to consider the offer. According to eyewitness Aviraneta, Santa Anna "tricked the brigadier [Barradas] with his customary astuteness." Toward the end of the talks, Mejía returned with the forged letter. On seeing the document, and fearing an attack, Barradas insisted that Santa Anna return to his camp in Pueblo Viejo to think things over. This he did, escaping from what could have amounted to a particularly embarrassing episode.[27]

Once back in safety, he wrote to inform Barradas that he could not accept anything other than the Spaniards' unconditional surrender. The clash of arms of 20–21 August and the subsequent meetings proved to be of great importance. Any hopes the Spaniards may have held that their invasion would be welcomed by the local population were now dead. They were up against a defiant and reckless adversary. Santa Anna was able to see the Spaniards' weaknesses with his own eyes— their lack of food and the effect the tropical diseases of the region were having upon them.[28]

Following the clash of arms of 20–21 August General Manuel de Mier y Terán arrived with six hundred reinforcements from Altamira and placed his troops on the *rancho* Doña Cecilia, between Tampico and the fortress of La Barra, preventing Barradas from making an escape back out to sea. As a result, by 8 September, Santa Anna was ready to present Barradas and his men with an ultimatum: either they surrendered or they would face an assault. The deadline was one o'clock on 10 September.

On the 9th a hurricane hit the coast of Tamaulipas and submerged the siege in a whirlwind of rain and gales. In Mier y Terán's report, he described how his troops' tents were blown away, how their fortifications were destroyed, and how half of their ammunition was spoiled by the torrential rain: "The whole land, up to the horizon, is a sea." Mier y Terán thought the best course of action was to wait, regardless of the ultimatum. Disease, the climate, and isolation were all powerful weapons at their disposition. Santa Anna did not listen, and on 10 September, under heavy rain, he ordered the bloody assault that led to Barradas's surrender. "Drenched from head to toe and having eaten nothing since the previous day," Santa Anna ordered the assault to the cry of "To the Fortress or to hell!"[29]

The battle raged on through the night and the next day until, on the 11th, Barradas surrendered at 3:00 P.M. Despite his previous misgivings, Mier y Terán recognized that Santa Anna's assault was a "masterful coup of audacity." Santa Anna attributed the victory to his men. In the treaty that was signed on 11 September 1829, Barradas surrendered his forces' weapons and flag and agreed to return to Cuba, while the Mexican government consented to safeguarding the Spaniards' lives and properties. Santa Anna could have let the siege go on and succeeded in obtaining Barradas's surrender without inflicting the carnage of 10–11 September. However, in political terms, news of a resounding

Lithograph of Santa Anna in 1829, the Hero of Tampico. Includes his autograph. Courtesy of Nettie Lee Benson Latin American Collection, University of Texas at Austin.

victory attained in a heroic assault proved to be far more effective. Santa Anna's victory over the Spanish expedition shook Mexico to the core and transformed him into a living legend.[30] One of Guillermo Prieto's earliest memories would be precisely the commotion that shook the capital the night the news of Santa Anna's victory at Tampico reached Mexico City:

> The city awoke at an unearthly hour in the middle of the night to the roar of the cannons, the pealing of bells in all of the churches, the splendid lights that lit up the most far-away cabins and the highest of palaces, the cheers, the immense rejoicing of all the classes of society. "Barradas has surrendered," shouted the newspaper boys as they ran in all directions; people who did not know each other embraced;

> the shopkeepers, in their doorways, uncorked bottles and
> toasted with whoever passed by; the reveilles sounded; the
> fireworks lit up the sky and there were times that the [ex-
> pression of] pleasure sounded just like a storm.[31]

The celebration of Santa Anna's victory acquired dimensions that
far surpassed anything that had preceded it. He arrived in Veracruz
on the 24th, where he was given a wildly enthusiastic reception. According to the *Times*, he was "met with the reception of a god."[32] There
were repeated celebrations in Xalapa throughout September, October,
and November. The state congresses of Veracruz and Puebla, as well as
the national government, conferred upon him the prestigious title of
Benemérito de la patria (Hero of the mother country). He was called the
Victor of Tampico. The States of Jalisco and Zacatecas made him their
"favorite citizen," Guanajuato gave him a sword with a golden hilt, and
a small pyramid was erected in Tampico, on the spot where Barradas
surrendered, with an inscription that stated: "On the shores of the Pánuco national independence was guaranteed on 11 September 1829."
Congress awarded him a cross, inscribed with the words "He who defeated Spanish pride in Tampico," and Tampico was renamed Santa
Anna de Tamaulipas. As noted in an 1842 edict outlining the order of
ceremonies for the festivities of 16 and 11 September in Xalapa: on the
16th, in Dolores, the "terrible cry for freedom was heard," on the 11th,
freedom "was guaranteed forever in the brilliant action of Tampico." A
year after the event itself, notwithstanding the fact that General Anastasio Bustamante was in power, the Congress of Veracruz decreed that 11
September would be an annual holiday. In national terms 11 September
became a yearly fiesta whenever the santanistas were in power. He had
become "immortal," the "Champion of Zempoala," the "mainstay of
the people," "the illustrious victor."[33]

The cult of Santa Anna got under way in the aftermath of Tampico.
Through the use of fiestas, paintings, monuments, speeches, and pamphlets, his followers transformed him into a national hero. It is evident
that defeating the Spanish invasion was an important feat, worthy of
the celebrations it inspired. However, Santa Anna benefited from having a number of gifted writers determined to provide a narrative of his

heroic actions. With Tornel in command of the capital, Santa Anna's victory became a legendary event. He ordered marches, *Te Deums*, and fiestas, and decreed that 25, 26, and 27 September were to be dedicated to celebrating Santa Anna's victory. With a propagandist like Tornel at his disposal, Santa Anna began to acquire a mythical status that no other general enjoyed. Mier y Terán, who played an equally important role in defeating Barradas, did not feature as prominently in the celebrations. He did not have someone like Tornel to wax lyrical about his virtues. Representative of this is Carlos Paris's famous 1835 oil painting of the battle. Santa Anna appears in the center of the scene, holding the baton of power, giving orders to a mounted soldier, with Mier y Terán, significantly, standing behind him.[34]

Following the victory of Tampico, rumors started to abound that a plot to overthrow Guerrero's government was under way. Despite the temporary explosion of national unity brought about by the conflict, Guerrero's presidency was being undermined by the divisions that emerged among the yorkinos who had propelled him to power. The radicalism of Zavala, as minister of finance, and the influence that his contemporaries came to believe he had, were certainly a cause for discontent. Guerrero's own political agenda, paired with his racial and social background, lay at the heart of a growing concern among the criollo political class that his government represented the "dangerous classes." The majority of the *hombres de bien*, including many moderate yorkinos, were disenchanted with, if not afraid of, the threat posed by Guerrero's cabinet's more radical proposals. Their unease became all the more acute after Guerrero was awarded emergency powers during the Barradas invasion. Since Guerrero refused to renounce these powers after the Spaniards surrendered, and used them to pass a range of reforms without consulting Congress (including the abolition of slavery on 16 September 1829), the hostility toward his government became all the more virulent. He was perceived as a radical and as a dictator. The traditionalist factions, including ex-escoceses and those yorkinos who had supported Gómez Pedraza's candidacy, found themselves conspiring in the fall of 1829 to overthrow Guerrero's unconstitutional government.[35]

Some historians, believing that Santa Anna coveted the post of min-

ister of war, have suggested that following the campaign of Tampico he
retreated to Veracruz harboring a grudge against Guerrero. Considering the affinities between Santa Anna and his *compadre* Guerrero, it is
difficult to believe that he was instrumental in the plot to overthrow
a president he had played such a key part in bringing to power. Nevertheless, the gossip of the time hinted at this being the case, and on
29 October 1829 Santa Anna and Vice President Anastasio Bustamante
issued a joint statement denying that they had any revolutionary plans
or were planning to overturn the Guerrero administration. It is true
that Santa Anna disapproved of certain members of Guerrero's cabinet (namely, Zavala) and had told him as much. It is also clear that he
was aware of the preparations for the forthcoming revolution. The key
instigators of the impending rebellion were in his hometown, at the
head of a Reserve Army that had been positioned there following news
of Barradas's landing. However, as would become clear once the revolt erupted with the proclamation of the Plan of Xalapa (4 December
1829), his concerns about Guerrero's ministers did not amount to his
believing in overthrowing the government.[36]

Indicative of how popular Santa Anna was by the end of 1829 is that
the revolutionary Plan of Xalapa invited him, in its seventh article, to
head the rebel army with General Anastasio Bustamante. Equally significant, in the light of the repeated allegation that he was an unprinci-
pled ambitious general who coveted absolute power, is that he declined
the offer. In the wake of the triumph of Tampico, had Santa Anna been
intent on becoming president, now would have been the time to take
on the national government. Instead, although he stated that he sympathized with the demands in the Plan of Xalapa, he opted to rally his
troops to the defense of Guerrero.[37]

The Plan of Xalapa was a traditionalist reaction to Guerrero's presidency and the radical proposals that were made in the fall of 1829.
However, there was nothing in it that could be defined as characteristic
of a reactionary political standpoint. Article 1 professed that it was the
duty of the army to defend the federal pact. Article 2 asserted that all
laws should be strictly abided by. Article 3 demanded that the president
renounce his use of emergency powers and that Congress was reinstated. Article 4 claimed that all those government officials whom pub-

lic opinion rejected should be removed from office. For Santa Anna to state that he sympathized with the plan's demands was not particularly reactionary. It is probable that he did believe in what the Plan of Xalapa was intended to achieve.

What Santa Anna was opposed to was the faction behind the Plan of Xalapa, although initially he did not state this openly. He stressed that he was opposed to the means by which the rebels were hoping to bring the plan's aspirations to fruition. Unaware of the irony of his words, he publicly condemned all revolutions as the true cause of the country's troubled state and stressed the suffering caused to the nation by so many *pronunciamientos*. Santa Anna actually made a vow never again to place himself at the head of a revolution. In practice, he set about preparing his defense of the government. The state congress, in support of his planned measures, made him civil *and* military governor of Veracruz, and as such, on 15 December, he declared that he would allow the overthrow of Guerrero only over his dead body.[38]

Faithful to their liberal principles and their allegiance to Guerrero's presidency, José María Bocanegra and Tornel stood by Guerrero's government. Bocanegra served as acting president (17–23 December 1829) while Guerrero left the capital to fight the rebels. Tornel, on his way to the United States to serve as Mexican minister plenipotentiary, met with Bustamante at the hacienda of La Joya and tried to persuade him to abandon the revolt but failed. Santa Anna set off with his troops toward Mexico City to aid the president. However, many of his soldiers must have suspected that he was not backing the winning horse, since most of his troops uncharacteristically deserted him. News reached him of Guerrero's retreat to the south, and on 3 January 1830 he resigned from all his political and military positions.[39]

With Bustamante's military victory confirmed (30 December 1829), Santa Anna retired to Manga de Clavo. Tornel, who saw him before departing for the United States, stated that the caudillo was "working on ways in which he could bring about a counterrevolution with uncertain . . . and scarce resources."[40] Two years were to pass before he did so. The time was not right, and Santa Anna sensed this. With Guerrero's side having lost this power struggle, and Santa Anna unwilling to be part of General Bustamante's traditionalist government, it made sense to retreat to his hacienda. His adored daughter Guadalupe, who had been born in 1829, was also just a baby, and if we are to believe him, there was nothing he liked more than looking after his land surrounded by the warmth of his family.[41]

He did make sure that he received his full pay as general of division and brigadier during his retirement, despite having ceased to be in service on 17 January 1830.[42] In a letter to a friend of his, dating from this time (9 April 1831), he stated that:

> In regard to my country, I cannot tell you anything, because it is now sixteen months since I have abandoned public affairs and retired to this farm, which is my own property, where I desire nothing but the peace and welfare of the country, and my own tranquility. I never enjoyed more satisfaction than during the time of my retirement, in the bosom of my adored family. I enjoy the necessary comforts of life, and look with horror upon high stations; so it is that in this corner I am nothing else than a spectator of what is passing in the world.[43]

Tending to his cockerels, riding the length and breadth of his estate, checking on his cattle, delighting in the view of the Pico de Orizaba on the horizon on a clear day, resting in a hammock under the palm trees, seeing little Guadalupe learn to walk, speak her first words—little would appear to have changed since he had last retired from public life in 1825. And yet, so much had indeed changed.

Santa Anna was now a fully-fledged caudillo. He was a military hero, at a regional and at a national level. He was now not only the Liberator of Veracruz and the Founder of the Republic but also the Hero of Tampico. Thanks to him, so the story went, Mexican independence had finally been guaranteed. He was adored by the *jarochos* and had also gained the respect of the political class in Yucatán and Veracruz, for being a resourceful arbitrator, an impartial leader who could find points of consensus between the warring factions. He had avoided party politics wherever possible. He saw himself as a soldier, not a legislator. He was there to remind the political class of its duty to respect the so-called general will, whether this constituted forging a federal constitution or ensuring that the truly popular candidate was given the presidency. Unlike so many politicians of the period, he had not spent more than a few months in Mexico City. For many army officers, this alone made him a true patriot leader and arbitrator. From their perspective, while the political class destroyed the achievements of independence, moaning and whinging in Congress, dividing the people with factional disputes, Santa Anna was risking his life for the mother country.

His attention had been centered on looking after his hacienda, leading his troops into the fray—in San Luis Potosí in 1823, Mexico City (1824), Tulancingo, Perote, and Oaxaca (1828), and Tampico (1829)—and gaining valuable political experience in the complex regional governments of Yucatán and Veracruz. Although the view that he was interested in acquiring absolute power was voiced from as early as 1823, the evidence does not confirm this. Had he been as desperate to become the country's first magistrate as his critics made him out to be, he would not have retired from public life on returning from Yucatán in 1825. He would have used the Plan of Xalapa to take the presidency.

Santa Anna was a federalist and a republican. His federalism had found ample expression in the way that he had listened to the concerns of the *yucatecos* and the *jarochos* and postponed the implementation of federal laws that harmed local interests. His ambivalence over ending Mérida's trade with Cuba and in implementing the 1827 expulsion laws in Veracruz stemmed from his tendency to pay attention to the regional context in which he moved. At a national level his loyalty had been saved for Victoria and Guerrero. The conflict of interests that had surfaced as a result of the Veracruzan escocés-yorkino configuration may have given rise to some confusion about his true political allegiances, but he had overcome the problems this had created. Within the context of Veracruz, he had outwitted the other regional caudillos (namely Miguel Barragán and the Rincón brothers), in part through their own mistakes, in part through his own anti-political/anti-parties stance. In becoming a hacendado, Santa Anna had also strengthened his ties with the *jarochos*.

From the perspective of the capital, there is no doubt that by 1830 Santa Anna was perceived by many as the providential man who had sparked off the most significant transformations in Mexico's political system. It did not matter whether this perception was inaccurate. The fall of Iturbide was seen as a consequence of Santa Anna's Plan of Veracruz (2 December 1822). The adoption of a federal constitution was likewise seen to stem from his Plan of San Luis Potosí (5 June 1823). Santa Anna had been the first to rebel in Perote (12 September 1828) against the electoral results that the majority deemed to be an inaccurate interpretation of the will of the people. After the glorious victory of Tampico (11 September 1829), he had become the most praised general of the period. Recognition of all of this had come in the invitation in the Plan of Xalapa for him to lead the revolt. Santa Anna, displaying more integrity than is often attributed to him, declined. His repeated withdrawal to the provinces after intervening in the country's politics with his *pronunciamientos* of 1822, 1823, and 1828, also gave credence to his claim that he did not aspire to power. He was an impartial arbitrator who intervened when his help was needed. Evidently, it was only a matter of time before such a hero was called upon to become president. By 1833 Santa Anna would acquiesce. Before that, however, he would lead yet another revolt; one that would unleash upon the republic its worst civil conflict since the War of Independence: the *impulso de Veracruz* of 2 January 1832.

Part 3
The Returns of the Phoenix, 1832–1841

He survived fourteen attempts on his life, seventy-three
ambushes, and a firing squad. He lived through a dose of
strychnine in his coffee that was enough to kill a horse.

Gabriel García Márquez, *One Hundred Years of Solitude*

Well, that is the Media Luna from one end to the other.
All the land you can see, as you might say. And all of that
expanse belongs to him.

Juan Rulfo, *Pedro Páramo*

7. The Absentee President, 1832–1835

From 1830 to 1832 the party of order, as it became known, took over the government. Under the guidance of Lucas Alamán, General Anastasio Bustamante's government curtailed the power of the federal states and limited the universality of male suffrage to more clearly defined property-owning citizens. The traditionalist politicians who had been ostracized since the 1826 congressional elections, former royalists, escoceses, and centralists made an important comeback. It was an administration determined to protect Church and army, empower the national government, and put the radical liberals who had dominated politics under the Victoria and Guerrero presidencies in their place. Several attempts were made to inject new life into the Mexican economy through the creation of a bank, the Banco de Avío (16 October 1830), assisting Mexico's dormant industry with protectionist policies. The initial economic success of the administration's policies was fairly impressive.[1]

However, Bustamante's government soon became characterized by its repression. The tide of opinion turned against the government when it authorized the execution of Guerrero (14 February 1831). The execution of a high-ranking officer who was also an ex-president of the republic, an action with no parallel since Emperor Agustín I's execution in Padilla (19 July 1824), turned the majority of those moderates who had initially supported the party of order against Bustamante's government. As Santa Anna would put it, Bustamante's government was characterized by "thirty months of arbitrariness and despotism." Not yet aware that his comrade in arms was dead, Santa Anna wrote to Busta-

mante the day after Guerrero's execution, reminding Bustamante that
Guerrero was his daughter's godfather, that their families were united
by ties of kinship, and urging the vice president to spare Guerrero's
life. The death of the great insurgent leader of the south must have been
a bitter blow.[2]

From as early as 1829 it was clear that Santa Anna did not sympathize
with the party of order. When the Plan of Xalapa (4 December 1829)
was launched, he stood by Guerrero. Although he was approached on
several occasions by Bustamante's administration, he maintained a
significant distance from the government. It was only after Tornel returned from the United States in late 1831, where he had served as Mexican minister plenipotentiary for over a year, that Santa Anna, making
the most of the government's increasing unpopularity, left Manga de
Clavo and accepted the invitation to lead the 2 January *pronunciamiento*
of Veracruz.[3]

The plan, drafted and written by Ciriaco Vázquez, among others,
stated that the rebels supported the federal constitution; that Bustamante should renew his cabinet, since it was dominated by centralists
responsible for tolerating unforgivable crimes against the country's
civil rights; that Santa Anna would be offered the leadership of the revolt; and that they awaited his orders once he took over the *pronunciamiento*. This he did the following day. On 3 January Santa Anna entered
Veracruz "amid the universal acclamations of the People" and placed
himself at the head of the uprising.[4]

Despite the fact that he had been away from the political scene for
two years, his popularity in Veracruz remained extraordinary: "so great
was the enthusiasm manifested in favour of the cause which he has
been called to espouse that it was late before he could attend his official
duties." According to one eyewitness account of the revolt, he took care
to ensure that his troops were well-behaved and that no harm came to
the commercial establishments in the port. He also made a point of
keeping key players in the business community informed of his movements. Importantly, he ensured his troops' loyalty through the regular
payment of their salaries.[5]

He also made it known that he feared Bustamante's administration
was attempting to overthrow the federal Constitution. This was to prove

an effective way of mustering support against the government, even if it was not an entirely truthful allegation. The alarm felt had become acute in the more openly federalist states of the republic, namely Veracruz, Tamaulipas, Jalisco, and Zacatecas, that the Bustamante regime was intent on wresting power away from their respective legislatures. Santa Anna was to make the most of their resolve to prevent this from taking place, along with the indignation caused by Guerrero's execution, to rally a rebel army strong enough to bring down the government.[6]

Nevertheless, to begin with, in the letters he sent Bustamante he depicted himself as a mediator. He claimed he did not want this protest to escalate into violence and that all he requested was that Bustamante renew his cabinet with men "whose national prestige is commendable." He also wrote to all the key military commanders of the republic. If Sebastián Camacho (Relations), Melchor Múzquiz (War), Francisco García (Finance), and Dr. Valentín Gómez Farías (Justice and Ecclesiastical Affairs) were to replace the current ministers, public opinion would be satisfied and the revolt could be brought to an end. He even wrote to some of the ministers under the ostensible belief that they would see the logic of resigning. In one such letter he addressed to Lucas Alamán, he urged Alamán to stand down in what amounted to "a light sacrifice given the great benefits that will be obtained from such an action." He also published a pamphlet on 7 January outlining these points for the attention of the general public: "All you ask for is a change of ministers. I could not do less than . . . support your petition."[7]

His choice of ministers deserves comment. With the exception of Camacho, he had not had the chance to become acquainted with any of these politicians. He had spent most of the 1820s far removed from Mexico City. How could he have known that these were commendable individuals? Why did he believe that they deserved to be backed by a military uprising? This was one of several instances in which Tornel, in great measure, influenced his politics. The choice of ministers is proof that he was following advice from Tornel and Bocanegra. Tornel was a close friend of Camacho. He was also close to Melchor Múzquiz, who like him had studied in the Colegio de San Ildefonso. Bocanegra, Tornel's best friend in Mexico City—a minister under Guerrero, a moderate, a federalist, and a consistent santanista, who had returned to Zacatecas following the 1829 revolt—was a close friend of Gómez Farías and Governor Francisco García. Santa Anna was obviously opposed to the Bustamante administration. However, he relied on the advice of Tornel and Bocanegra when presenting a list of desirable ministers. All four politicians were federalists and moderates, either yorkinos who had become unsettled by their faction's radicalization in the wake of the battle of Tulancingo or members of the independent faction, the *imparciales*, formed in 1828 to counter the increasing influence of the more extreme branch within the dominant Rite of York. Gómez Farías was not yet the radical liberal he was to become in the mid-1840s.[8]

By March Santa Anna's revolt was to receive the support of the militias in Zacatecas, led by Gómez Farías and García. It is true that the alliance that was forged between the Zacatecan federalists and the santanistas in 1832 was to a certain extent a "marriage of convenience," but they nevertheless shared more ideological aims than has generally been acknowledged. Bocanegra and Gómez Farías had been close friends since their years as deputies for Zacatecas in Iturbide's Congress. Given that Santa Anna and the santanistas had been federalists since 1823, supported the 1824 Constitution, and had advocated a moderate agenda within the more radical movement that came to power after the La Acordada revolt, it is not surprising that they had common reasons for opposing Bustamante's government and joining forces with Gómez Farías. Regardless of Bustamante's own moderate agenda, his government was made up of former escoceses, reactionary priests, and centralists who were threatening to reform the Constitution and empower the national government in Mexico City. In contrast, Gómez Farías was an ex-*iturbidista*, a federalist, a supporter of the 1824 charter, and a reformist who had opposed the radical yorkinos by forming with Francisco García the faction of the *imparciales* in 1828, and who still did not want to be associated with the radicals in 1832. Santa Anna thus led the campaign in the east of the country, Bocanegra assisted García and Gómez Farías with the revolt in the north, and Tornel served as a point of contact between the two rebel armies in Mexico City.[9]

By launching the revolt in Veracruz, Santa Anna was able to hold the government to ransom. He appropriated 279,000 pesos, took charge of the port's customs receipts, and fortified his position in the port. Most veracruzanos were confident that he would win. As was noted by Joseph Welsh, the British vice-consul in Veracruz, "General Santa Anna's troops are in high spirits, and little doubt can, I believe, be entertained of the result being favourable to them."[10] On 21 February the government troops dispatched to quell the uprising arrived outside the port's city walls. None other than General José María Calderón led them. Santa Anna was his usual hyperactive self. On the night of the 24th he was able to fall upon a government convoy outside the port, making away with 20,000 pesos, sixty-mules'-worth of provisions, and according to one pamphlet, around three hundred prisoners who asked to join Santa Anna's cause.[11]

However, on 3 March, he suffered his first major defeat. The battle of Tolome was the first of the four major pitched battles that took place during the 1832 Civil War. Fought between General José María Calderón's government regular troops and Santa Anna's federalist civic militias, the battle lasted seven hours and the death toll was high. On the 1st, Santa Anna had heard that the government troops had raised their camp and were retiring toward Puente, to escape yellow fever. He marched out with around fourteen hundred men and by the afternoon of the 2nd caught up with them in Manantial. That night he "passed them, cutting off their supplies, water and retreat to Puente," and called on them to surrender. On the 3rd Calderón, having "taken up a strong position at Loma Alta near Tolome, where he has raised parapets and placed his artillery," repulsed Santa Anna's attack.[12]

The fighting was fierce, with bayonet charges, and the battlefield was strewn with bodies. Only hours after the clash, Calderón counted up to 462 dead santanista soldiers. Colonels Pedro Landero and Juan Andonegui were among them. Santanista Colonel Manuel Fernández Castrillón had been captured. The damage inflicted upon Santa Anna's forces was significant. Calderón's troops had come out of the battle in relatively better shape, although seventy-five men had died, and a further 166 lay badly wounded, including Colonel Antonio Gaona. The heightened violence that characterized the 1832 Civil War is captured in one of Calderón's dispatches in which he noted that despite his men's efforts, there were too many corpses for them to bury and burn. The terrain was difficult, with steep ravines and thick forest. There were corpses that were impossible to reach, and the stench had become unbearable. He resolved to move on to Paso de Ovejas, leaving those corpses they had been unable to bury to decay in the tropical heat of March.[13]

Surprisingly, the high spirits of Santa Anna's followers were not dented by news of the defeat. One Domingo Ramela taunted Calderón with a letter in which he stated: "Your Division's momentary triumph in Tolome has had no influence [upon us]; instead it has given our soldiers greater devotion [to our cause], as well as inspiring the common people to take up arms. If you dare come to this city as you threaten you will, you will encounter the most obstinate resistance."[14] Only weeks after the defeat, "the government troops have already commenced deserting again," while in contrast "the enthusiasm of the troops and inhabitants in general [in Veracruz] is very great."[15] Santa Anna, too, was defiant. In an address to his troops that he circulated the day after the battle, he blamed Calderón's temporary victory on lady luck. He noted the sadness he felt for their brothers whose blood had been spilled but affirmed that definitive victory would still be theirs.[16]

Calderón's army was still a strong force to contend with. However, he did not consolidate his victory with an assault on the port because of the issue of the insalubrious climate. Santa Anna's *jarochos* were immune to yellow fever, but Calderón's troops were not. After attempting to lay siege to Veracruz again, Calderón ordered his division's retreat to Xalapa on 13 May. Yellow fever alone had decimated his army. According to one source Calderón lost up to a thousand men to the dreaded disease. Faced with the news of Calderón's mixed fortunes in Veracruz and his decision to retreat, the denounced cabinet ministers resigned on 17 May. Their decision to stand down came too late. By then Santa Anna's revolt had acquired the support of garrisons in other states, namely Tamaulipas, Zacatecas, Durango, and Coahuila-Texas. Moreover, Santa Anna had increased his demands, in part to accommodate those made by the rebels in Zacatecas and Jalisco, who were asking for General Manuel Gómez Pedraza to resume his place as constitutionally elected president. Santa Anna was now asking Bustamante to resign and for Gómez Pedraza to return to Mexico from exile to complete the term in office that had been aborted as a result of the 1828 revolt.[17]

He stated publicly that he had offered to mediate between the rebels and the government and that Bustamante had responded by sending his personal enemy General Calderón against him. The sanguinary 1828 clash of Oaxaca was not forgotten. Consequently, the only way forward was to bring back the legitimate president, even if it was for just one day. He informed Sebastián Camacho that he had sent Joaquín Castillo y Lanzas, with six thousand pesos, to the United States to find Gómez Pedraza and offer him the presidency once the revolt was over. Camacho could not help noting that this could not have been Santa Anna's original idea, for the two men hated each other.[18]

Santa Anna's decision to back Gómez Pedraza's return to power was pragmatic. He was aware of the irony of the situation—that he, of all people, was now demanding that the constitutionally elected president against whom he had revolted in 1828 be allowed to complete his term in office (which technically ended in April 1833). As he wrote to reassure his supporters in the capital: "with regard Pedraza's return . . . there is nothing to fear, since if there is anyone who should fear his return, it is me . . . and I am certain that he will not attack the individual tranquility of our citizens. . . . Tell those upset [supporters of ours] to make the same sacrifice as me, and to wait for a happy outcome once power is enshrined in legality."[19] In adding this constitutionalist twist to his revolt, he was able to garner far more support throughout the republic, and he also gave the rebellion a legitimacy it had originally lacked. By restoring the deposed president, he could claim he was returning Mexico to its former constitutional path (conveniently ignoring the fact that he had contributed to the country losing its way in the first place). Knowing that the president could not be reelected and that Gómez Pedraza's spell in the National Palace would be short, it was also a way of setting up the possibility of rising to the presidency by electoral means, after Bustamante had been overthrown.[20]

On 11 June Santa Anna initiated a new incursion past the enemy lines, succeeding in advancing as far as the hacienda he would eventually acquire: El Encero on the outskirts of Xalapa. Calderón was quick to march his army to his enemy's location. An armistice was signed between them to allow Guadalupe Victoria and Sebastián Camacho to act as intermediaries and hold a meeting with Santa Anna on the night of 13 June, at Puente Nacional. The encounter came to nothing. Santa Anna was not prepared to moderate his demands. General José Antonio Facio replaced General Calderón at the head of the government forces and, warned of Santa Anna's intention to proceed toward the capital, mobilized his troops to higher ground. He set up his camp on the slopes of the Maltrata mountain and established his headquarters at San Andrés Chalchicomula.[21]

By the beginning of August Santa Anna was in Orizaba at the head of three thousand men. Despite the fact that Gómez Pedraza's initial reply to his invitation had not been favorable, the caudillo refused to give up. He sent another letter on 9 August to the exiled president in Bedford Springs, Pennsylvania, stressing that the garrisons of Zacatecas, Jalisco, Durango, Sonora, Sinaloa, Tabasco, and many others in the states of San Luis Potosí, Querétaro, and Mexico, were openly supporting the *pronunciamiento* of 5 July, whereby Veracruz and San Juan de Ulúa had called for the return of Gómez Pedraza.[22]

General José Antonio Facio was twenty kilometers away, hoping to prevent Santa Anna from proceeding with his climb up onto the Altiplano. Santa Anna was confident that his force would crush any resistance that stood in their way. He had more men than Facio, and their enthusiasm knew no bounds. As well as having his own troops and the recruits he was able to muster from Córdoba and Orizaba, his old comrade in arms José Antonio Mejía had sent him reinforcements from Tampico, where the garrison had been up in arms since March. Santa Anna's confidence was well founded. When the two armies finally did confront each other at San Agustín del Palmar, on 29 September 1832, he routed Facio's forces. Of the eight hundred men sent against Santa Anna, few survived. Those who did were taken prisoner. Santa Anna took some pleasure in having "completely ridiculed that idiot and no less arrogant Facio."[23]

It was as he made his way to Mexico City that his sister Francisca was arrested and imprisoned in the capital, accused of conspiring to bring down the government. A significant number of individuals were planning to bribe the troops in the Mexico City garrison of La Ciudadela and launch a santanista coup on 22 July. Francisca aided them by serving as the go-between for her brother and the rebels. The interception of a let-

ter compromised Doña Francisca, resulting in her being one of the few
women to be locked up in prison for political reasons in nineteenth-
century Mexico.[24]

By October Santa Anna had taken Amozoc and was in a position to
occupy Puebla on the 4th, which he did after opening fire on the City of
Angels. Here he reorganized his troops and proceeded to obtain the surrender of the government soldiers at Atlixco, before starting the climb
to the Valley of Mexico. He was pleased to see his army reinforced by the
arrival of General Gabriel Valencia, who at the head of six hundred men
decided to join the caudillo's march to the capital. With a four-thousand-
strong army, he made his way into the south of the Valley and between 20
and 22 October occupied Tlalpan, Coyoacán, San Ángel, and Tacubaya
(all present-day districts of Mexico City). Before his advance into the city
center, news reached him that General Bustamante, returning from his
victory in the north at the battle of El Gallinero (18 September 1832), was
in the proximity of San Juan del Río, in the state of Querétaro. Santa Anna
decided to go and meet him rather than occupy the capital. It was around
this time that the letter he had long been awaiting reached him. Gómez
Pedraza was on his way back to Mexico.[25]

Santa Anna and Bustamante's armies confronted each other on 6
November at the battle of the Rancho de Posadas in the state of Puebla.
This was another gruesome clash. The result, however, was inconclusive.
Bustamante followed this engagement by attacking Santa Anna's headquarters at Casa Blanca. After five hours of intense fighting, Santa Anna's
men repulsed the offensive and the vice president retreated to Tequis-
quiac. Santa Anna gave chase to Bustamante's forces, and both armies
found themselves zigzagging their way in between the states of Puebla
and Mexico until, on 23 December 1832 after a further indecisive skirmish, General Luis Cortázar persuaded Santa Anna and Bustamante to
sit down together and enter into talks at the hacienda of Zavaleta.[26]

The terms of the Treaty of Zavaleta that brought the 1832 Civil War to
an end were, to quote historian Catherine Andrews, "more conciliatory
than Santa Anna had originally intended."[27] Nevertheless, although he
did not emerge as the victor in the document that was signed on 23 December, the ultimate result of the end of the war was his election to the
presidency in 1833. The peace treaty stressed that the army's aim was to

sustain the existing federal system, to ensure that elections were called following on from those held in 1828, to recognize Gómez Pedraza as the legitimate president of the republic until 1 April 1833, and to offer a general amnesty to all parties involved.[28]

Santa Anna and Gómez Pedraza entered Mexico City triumphantly on 3 January 1833. Anastasio Bustamante was also part of the charade. The constitutional order Santa Anna had interrupted in September 1828 was now restored. The caudillo, donning the title of Liberator, stressed that his mission was accomplished, and he retired to Manga de Clavo claiming that all he aspired to was to give up his sword for the plow. Removed from the political machinations of the capital, he witnessed Gómez Pedraza's brief spell in power and the congressional and presidential elections of 1833. By making Gómez Pedraza president, Santa Anna and the Zacatecan federalists succeeded in giving constitutional legitimacy to their revolt and created the right circumstances for a new round of elections. Not surprisingly, the two favored candidates were Santa Anna and Dr. Gómez Farías, both of whom had played a major part in leading the revolution.[29]

Indicative of Santa Anna's popularity at the time is that sixteen of the eighteen state legislatures voted for him. Only Chihuahua and Guanajuato did not. Suggestive of his absence of ambition is that he claimed he was unwell and was unable to be in Mexico City for the start of his term in office on 1 April 1833. Some contemporary observers suspected he already knew that he was going to have a hard time presiding over a radical Congress with which he did not entirely sympathize. Carlos María de Bustamante believed his reluctance to return to the capital was "deliberate, mysterious, and perverse" and that he was plotting to overthrow the government by force after it had caused enough of a stir during his absence.[30] Although this latter claim was premature, it reflected a perceived ambiguity in Santa Anna's relationship with the triumphant radical federalists he had brought to power.[31]

In a letter Santa Anna wrote to Gómez Farías in March 1833, it would appear that he was not waiting impatiently to become president, even if he appeared to have revolted and orchestrated Gómez Pedraza's return precisely so that he could become the First Magistrate of the Republic. For a man so often described as desperate to acquire absolute power, his behavior was rather that of a coy mistress. He was not intending on taking the reins of government should he win the elections. Instead he was hoping Gómez Farías would: "You, my good friend, can take charge, supposing you are elected Vice President, and the election [of president] falls upon me. Then the Mexican people will have nothing more they could wish for, or anything to fear with regards their liberties."[32]

He was not present at his investiture for his first term in office as president of the republic. It was the newly elected vice president, Gómez Farías, who stepped in as acting head of state on 1 April 1833. When Santa Anna did finally arrive in Mexico City ready to assume the presidency, on 15 May 1833, he did not remain in the capital for long either. Considering the little time he actually spent at the head of the nation between 1833 and 1835, it is surprising that he has been blamed for so many of the problems that surfaced at the time. He was not in Mexico City long enough to give the country a direction that could be described as his own. The 1833–34 government was more Gómez Farías's project. In fact, the 1833–34 government was the construct of its radical Congress. As I have argued elsewhere, Gómez Farías was a moderate vice president at the head of a radical administration. Thereafter, although Santa Anna used the 1834 Plan of Cuernavaca to take on emergency powers and put a forceful end to Congress's rampant reformism, he continued to leave the executive in the hands of others. Even the measures that were put in place between April 1834 and October 1835 cannot rightly be attributed to him but derive from the centralist Congress that replaced the radical one and from the acting president, General Miguel Barragán. Although Santa Anna was the elected president (1833–36), he did not actually serve as president for more than a few months, making a mockery of the accusations that he was a tyrant or that he was personally responsible for the eventual change to centralism. As is demonstrated by the ensuing narrative of Santa Anna's activities during this period, his time was spent either quelling revolts or taking care of his hacienda.[33]

His absence notwithstanding, there are some indications of what he thought the country needed and how he hoped this could be achieved. His characteristic populism found early expression in his gift of two thousand pesos per year to the public education fund that was created

in April 1833. Likewise an early indication of his belief in forging national political traditions with cults to particular patriotic heroes may
be found in his decision to have Agustín de Iturbide's remains disinterred and transferred to Mexico City. In a series of letters he addressed
to Gómez Farías between February and November 1833, he made a
number of his views known. He did not see himself as being capable
of taking care of the day-to-day running of the country. Such a claim
may be doubted, of course, but it did echo previous statements of this
ilk. He repeatedly told Gómez Farías that he trusted the physician's
knowledge of political and financial matters, and that it was preferable
for the "reins of government not to be in the hands of a poor soldier
like me, but in those of a citizen like you, known for his virtues and
enlightenment." He did let Gómez Farías preside over the country until
Congress's radical proposals attacked the army. The British minister
plenipotentiary was of the mind that Santa Anna was easily "fatigued
with the cares of office, to which he has never been accustomed."[34]

He was consistent in stressing his "hatred of tyranny" and "inclination toward the popular form [of government]." He was particularly
concerned about the dreadful state of the treasury and insisted that
the crisis needed "a radical solution." He was to return to this point
throughout Gómez Farías's term in office as acting president, for there
was "nothing worse than to be at the head of a government lacking in
resources." The government's financial system needed "to be radically
reformed." The taxes that would come to characterize his later presidencies, namely his 1841–43 and 1853–55 administrations, were being
hinted at as early as April 1833.[35]

As regards the reforms Congress proposed concerning the Church,
he was not opposed to them. As long as the reforms were adopted slowly,
ensuring that all violent disorders were avoided, he sympathized with
the need to tax church wealth in order to cover the treasury's expenses.
Already in 1829 he had shown no qualms in telling the members of
the Church to keep out of politics. The santanistas shared, to a certain
extent, the anticlericalism of the 1833–34 Congress. They believed in
secularizing education and, like the radicals, were of the opinion that
it was the Church's obligation to finance the state and the army. This
disposition on his part to allow the radical Congress of 1833 to carry

on with its anticlerical reforms led one observer to believe that "Santa Anna is not a free agent, but rather . . . he is now completely a tool in the hands of the violent party." It was only when Congress directed its attention to the army that he intervened.[36]

In regard to the army, he did nevertheless try to reform it as well, in accordance with Gómez Farías's views. Coinciding with his return to the presidency on 27 October 1833, he made Tornel minister of war (6– 19 November 1833) and put forward the reform of 16 November. Adopting extraordinary powers, he decreed that the regular army was to be reduced from twelve to ten battalions, and from twelve to six regiments, and that the mounted artillery brigade was to be abolished. From then on, there could be only eight generals and twelve brigadiers in the entire regular army. There is no doubt that Tornel and Santa Anna were hoping to anticipate Congress's own proposal and appease the radicals' demands. Congress accepted the reform but went on to propose its own more draconian rationalization in the spring of 1834, bringing matters to a head. Nevertheless, his predisposition to enter into the spirit of the times and propose a reform of the army of his own accord is worthy of mention.[37]

Concerning Texas, Santa Anna received *empresario* Stephen Austin in Mexico City on 5 November. His government did not grant Austin's request for Texas to be awarded independent statehood, separating the province from Coahuila. However, it authorized him to permit the entry of more U.S. immigrants, supported his colonization companies, and encouraged him to press ahead with his intended reforms of the state legal system. In the case of the highly controversial Ley del Caso (23 June 1833), whereby fifty-one politicians, including Anastasio Bustamante, were accused of upholding unpatriotic beliefs and expelled from the republic, Gómez Farías claimed that Santa Anna was the law's true author and that he played a major part in choosing who was exiled. Gómez Farías also claimed that it was Santa Anna, and not he, who first sanctioned Congress's ecclesiastical reforms.[38]

Despite the liberal affinities Santa Anna shared with Gómez Farías, the santanista-federalist alliance was soon to be placed under strain. The main bone of contention lay in Congress's behavior. According to liberal José María Luis Mora, the majority of deputies were "angry and

violent men who lacked any sense of propriety."[39] They wanted to reform the nation too fast, by the santanistas' standards. In Bocanegra's
words: "There are those who say let's finish with what is old and start
everything anew; but these with poor intelligence, or better said, in bad
faith, do nothing other than destroy, reaching extremes in which neither man nor God is respected." Bocanegra, who joined the government as minister of finance (16 May–12 December 1833), supported
Gómez Farías's intentions of "verifying a change in the republic, which
varying its political nature, prepared the ground so that in the long run
the establishment of true democratic principles would be possible."
He believed that the council formed around Gómez Farías consisted
of individuals whose "respectability and reputation" were well known.
However, what was required was that regardless of "which policy was
pursued its implementation was slow."[40]

With Santa Anna allegedly convalescing in Manga de Clavo and Bocanegra at the head of the ministry of finance, it took only one month
for Congress to provoke a major political crisis. In a chaotic series of
proposals, Congress put Bustamante's cabinet on trial for the execution of Guerrero (contravening the agreements made in the Treaty of
Zavaleta), nationalized the duke of Monteleone's properties, and decreed that the Mexican government could appoint all ecclesiastical
posts (thus exercising the patronato; that is, the right to appoint ecclesiastical posts, which had previously been the king's prerogative). The
press exacerbated the increasing tension by either advocating truly radical measures, such as the abolition of military and church privileges
(proposing an end to the fueros), or embracing an aggressive reactionary agenda, inviting the regular army to close down Congress in the
name of their sacred religion.[41]

Less than two months after the new government had been formed,
on 26 May 1833, Ignacio Escalada, at the head of the garrison in Morelia, issued the plan that carried his name demanding that the Church
and army fueros were protected, and that Santa Anna act as the protector of his cause. Santa Anna published a Manifestación two days later
in which he made it clear that he did not endorse Escalada's plan and
that he considered the rebels' fears unreasonable. He stressed that neither the Church nor the army would be attacked. His would be a gov-

ernment characterized by its "conciliatory system." Notwithstanding these assurances, Escalada's revolt was followed on 1 June by another similar plan. General Gabriel Durán launched a *pronunciamiento* in Tlalpan demanding that Santa Anna be made Supreme Dictator of Mexico. Santa Anna's reaction to Durán's revolt was also prompt and unambiguous. He issued a statement in which he stressed that despite the rebels' invoking of his name in their cause, he was against any attempt to undermine the Constitution. He wrote a personal letter to Durán demanding that he put down his arms immediately. He then set off to the south of Mexico City at the head of fifty chosen dragoons on 2 June. Durán retreated to Tenango and displayed no intention of abandoning his revolt, even if several of his men deserted him after hearing of Santa Anna's condemnation of the plan. It was after Santa Anna's division was reinforced by men from General Mariano Arista's column that events took a particularly disconcerting course.[42]

On 8 June 1833, in the town of Huejotzingo, Arista espoused Durán's cause and issued his own plan, promising to defend the privileges of both army and Church and to make Santa Anna "Supreme Dictator . . . to cure all the ills that the nation suffers today." He sent Colonel Tomás Moreno to see Santa Anna as he approached Yautepec and offer him the plan. Despite Santa Anna's protests, Arista's men and his fifty dragoons celebrated the plan and forced their hero to accompany them to meet up with General Durán, cheering and proclaiming him Supreme Dictator along the way.[43]

According to Santa Anna, Durán made him a prisoner on the outskirts of Cuautla when he went to meet Durán to ask for an end to the revolt. Durán assured Santa Anna that he would obey only if Santa Anna agreed to become dictator. Santa Anna would have us believe that he was appalled by such an offer. He claims he was unable to hide his displeasure and was consequently locked up and placed under guard. If we are to believe him, he was able to escape from the hacienda de Buenavista on the night of 11 June. Somewhere around 9:00 P.M. Lieutenant Gerónimo Cardona, together with one Manuel Rojano, helped him flee in disguise. Riding throughout the night in the direction of Puebla, he reached the City of the Angels at one o'clock on the morning of the 13th.[44]

The moment news reached Gómez Farías of Santa Anna's apparent abduction, he issued a statement, on 7 June, to inform the country of this and to confirm his belief that while it was not known whether Santa Anna had authorized such an uprising, he would surely offer Mexico and the world resounding proof of his commitment to upholding his duties in the most honorable of ways. The fact that Gómez Farías said "surely" suggests that he did not know himself whether the president was privy to the rebels' plans. In all likelihood, he was making his own doubts known so as to provoke Santa Anna into declaring his allegiance to the government as forcefully as possible.[45]

Arista denied that Santa Anna was held prisoner. Had he or anyone under his command as much as put a hand on Santa Anna, they would have incurred the wrath of the entire division. This he stated in a letter dated the 12th, the morning after Santa Anna had escaped. Not knowing where Santa Anna was, and still hoping his hero would be present at the planned reunion of rebel troops the following day, Arista wrote to Manuel Gómez Pedraza to inform him that he was prepared to hand himself in if Santa Anna was not willing to join the plan.[46]

It is tempting not to believe Santa Anna when he claimed he was opposed to the plans of Durán and Arista. Would these men have risked so much without believing that he backed them? Could they have plotted to make him dictator without asking him whether he wanted to be given such powers? The generally accepted view is that he was in on the plan, and that only when it became apparent that it had not garnered enough support did he rally to the defense of the constitutional government. In all likelihood he was aware of Arista and Durán's plans, and it is equally probable that he was flattered and tempted by them. Perhaps he did egg them on, curious to see what might happen. According to British Minister Plenipotentiary Richard Pakenham: "Perhaps the truth may turn out to be that General Santa Anna, unwilling to take an active and open part in a question in which his own personal aggrandizement is concerned, has consented to remain neutral, at least at the outset, with the intention of ultimately adhering to that side which may appear to obtain most favour in public opinion, and thus close the contest without the effusion of blood."[47]

However, if we are to judge Santa Anna by his actions rather than speculate on what he may or may not have hinted to the rebels, then there is only one clear interpretation of the events: he was opposed to the revolutionaries' movement and did not aspire to be made absolute ruler of the republic. The violent manner in which he pursued the rebels to Guanajuato and took the city by assault, after he managed to escape captivity on 11 June 1833, would appear to prove that he believed in defending the constitutional government at the time.[48]

In the *Manifiesto* Santa Anna published at the end of June he certainly made it clear that he was opposed to the revolutionary plans of Morelia, Tlalpan, and Chalco. He stated that he despised all dictatorships. Had the rebels forgotten who he was? He reminded them that it was he, "the friend of liberty," who had called for an end to Iturbide's abuses in December 1822; it was he who had been among the first to demand the proclamation of a liberal political system. To say that the Mexican people could only be governed by a tyrant, he claimed, amounted to saying that they were not civilized, that they were unable to be governed according to laws and principles. He pledged never to be the oppressor of the Mexican people. He professed a belief in being consistent in the application of the law and, above all, moderate in the field of government actions.

The fact that these words were accompanied by the warning that religious wars were the worst of all was a double-edged warning: aimed as much at the radical anticlerical Congress of 1833 as it was at Durán and Arista. In a pious nation like Mexico, he stressed, religion was its dearest concern. He did not support the revolutionary demands to have him proclaimed dictator and remained the federalist liberal republican he had been in all of his actions since 1822. He was displeased with Dublán and Arista for unleashing this particular demon. The people could easily be manipulated when it came to matters of the faith. However, he was uncomfortable with the proposals that were being discussed in Congress. Between the lines it is possible to discern Santa Anna's dislike of the radicals who had taken over Congress. He was prepared to leave his retirement and accept his political responsibilities as an arbitrator, rather than as the leader of a particular party. He had accepted his election as president because he was resolved to mediate between the belligerent factions, establishing himself as a peaceful arbiter. It was his intention to act with impartiality, and to ensure that justice prevailed, as enshrined in the laws and principles of their society. His view of himself as a high-ranking officer who was above party politics was not new, but the fact that he was applying this principle to his function as president was. Given the political climate in which these views were voiced, he was distancing himself not only from the rebels who wanted to protect the *fueros* and make him dictator but also from the radicals in Congress. Already in 1833, only months after having been elected president for the first time, Santa Anna was very much his own man.[49]

After a brief spell in the capital he left Mexico City on 10 July, at the head of twenty-four hundred men, to crush Durán and Arista's revolt, since they had not handed themselves in. As his army headed toward the northwest in the summer of 1833, a cholera epidemic hit Mexico City. In a speech he addressed to his troops in Querétaro on 10 August 1833, he noted the extent to which the deaths caused by the dreaded illness had seriously affected him. He used the mention of the epidemic to give his words of encouragement to his men greater resonance. Their heroism in pursuing the "enemies of our laws and institutions" became all the more pronounced during the time of cholera.[50]

The fourth anniversary of Santa Anna's "glorious action of Tampico" found him in Ciudad Allende (San Miguel de Allende) as his army proceeded north into the state of Guanajuato. He had his troops line up for inspection and harangued them from his horse, succeeding in generating the kind of enthusiasm he was hoping for as his forces drew closer to Durán and Arista's hounded divisions. His words were welcomed with a roar of cheers from his soldiers, with gunshots, and with repeated salutes to independence, the federation, liberty, and the supreme powers of the union. In the dawn of 2 October 1833 he left Silao and made his way to the hacienda de Cuevas, where he knew Durán was hiding. Durán escaped to the gully known as the Cañada del Marfil. Santa Anna, on the 4th, found a way of climbing up to a position above Durán's men without being seen. From there his troops opened fire on the rebels, taking both the hill of Los Tumultos and all of the rebel positions in the gully by nightfall. Durán fled in time, taking refuge with his men in Guanajuato. At five o'clock the following day (5 October), Santa Anna proceeded toward Guanajuato and routed the men

Durán left behind holding the fort of Gerona on the city's outskirts. While Arista opted to wait for Santa Anna in Guanajuato at the head of a thousand men, Durán fled south with five hundred horsemen. Santa Anna informed the government of Durán's movements, urging it to take action to intercept him before he reached Oaxaca, and decided to stay and take on Arista.[51]

His presence outside Guanajuato unnerved the town council's president, Fernando Chico, who wrote to beg him not to take the city by assault. Santa Anna replied with a particularly cryptic letter that leads me to believe he was offering Chico a bribe: "I could provide you the goods you so clearly deserve," as long as he let Santa Anna in. Chico did not have the nerve or was not in a position to acquiesce to Santa Anna's offer. As a result, the people of Guanajuato and Arista's rebel army looked on throughout the 6th as Santa Anna mobilized his army around the city. Arista's resolve wavered, and he asked to speak to Santa Anna. Santa Anna sent General José Antonio Mejía and Juan Arago to parlay. Arista was prepared to surrender as long as he and his men were offered an amnesty. Santa Anna rejected the request, stating that either they surrender or face a major assault the next day. Arista opted to fight, and on the following night (7 October), the full horror of war was unleashed upon the streets of Guanajuato.[52]

Santa Anna and Generals José Antonio Mejía and Martín Perfecto de Cos led the three-pronged attack on the city.[53] The action lasted an hour and a half, at the end of which Arista and his remaining four hundred men surrendered. According to Santa Anna's dispatch, only nine of his men died in the assault. His army went on to celebrate the victory with a parade that took place in the center of Guanajuato while Generals Esteban Moctezuma and José de la Cuesta were sent, at the head of a thousand men, to capture Durán. In Santa Anna's address to the people of Guanajuato he encouraged them to rejoice and celebrate the renewal of their freedom. He made a point of thanking them for having supported and aided his campaign to "reconquer [their] liberty."[54]

On 21 October 1833 he made his way into Querétaro and at four in the afternoon was given a rapturous welcome. The church bells peeled, and the crowds gathered to see and cheer him and to "demonstrate their gratitude." By the 27th he was back in Mexico City and ready to assume the baton of power, at least until 15 December, when he returned to Veracruz. Santa Anna recalled returning to Mexico City following his victory in Guanajuato with a sense of foreboding. He was uneasy about the increasing radicalism of Congress. He was also aware that society in general was becoming anxious about their proposals and noticeably obstinate in its growing opposition. Congress had certainly been busy between 12 June and 6 November, proposing and passing a wide range of highly controversial anticlerical laws.[55]

Santa Anna did not challenge Congress, however, or reprimand Gómez Farías for allowing the legislature to push forward such a range of radical measures. Although he was uneasy about the government's extremist agenda, he was not in principle opposed to his government's determination to finance its project with Church funds. Nevertheless, unless Congress moderated its reformist drive, sooner or later he would be driven to take action, especially since the discontent caused by the legislation was mounting, both among the traditionalist elite and among the church-going popular classes. On 2 December 1833, in Chichihualco, General Nicolás Bravo launched his own *pronunciamiento* against the government, calling for the defense of ecclesiastical and military *fueros* and for the creation of a new constituent congress. The stakes were rising. Santa Anna wrote to Bravo to ask him to put down his arms and to avoid being used as the instrument of ill-advised rebels. However, for the time being, he opted to delay any drastic decisions. He did not head for Chichihualco to crush the revolt, nor did he take on his radical Congress. He conveniently claimed his health was frail and was given permission to retire to Manga de Clavo, which he did on 16 December 1833.[56]

Not long after he left, Tornel started to plot the downfall of the Gómez Farías administration. Gómez Farías was aware that Tornel was writing letters to Santa Anna, keeping him informed of events, involved in a conspiracy to close down Congress. A critical bone of contention was Congress's move in January and February 1834 to reduce the national regular army and increase the state civic militias. By March 1834, almost a year since the 1833 government had been formed, the divergence in the political standpoints of Santa Anna and Gómez Farías finally made itself felt. On 12 March 1834 Santa Anna wrote Gómez

Farías an openly critical letter, calling for restraint. He accused the vice president of having ignored him. Why should anybody respect authority if no attention was paid to the Executive? He stressed that he was opposed to all forms of tyranny. He also underlined the fact that he had been irritated by the disdain he had been shown, and that public opinion was being seriously divided. If the mounting discord between the president and the vice president became public knowledge, he dreaded the consequences. He feared the enemies of progress would seize the day. Gómez Farías ignored Santa Anna's warnings. Moreover, on 16 April the president and acting president's vitriolic letters were read out in Congress, and it suddenly became apparent that the country's supreme magistrates could no longer see eye to eye.[57]

There was a certain inevitability about what happened next, even when one suspects that Santa Anna did not want to bring his enemies of 1828, '29, and '32 back to power. If only Gómez Farías's cabinet had managed to restrain Congress's demands, if only the reformist agenda of '33 had been pursued in a less confrontational manner, one wonders whether Santa Anna would have been willing to close down Congress and banish his vice president into exile. His quandary was that of attempting to pursue Victoria's moderate liberal course at a time of extremes. The violence of the 1832 Civil War showed how polarized society had become. Old grudges dating from the War of Independence remained unresolved. Former patriots had executed Iturbide in 1824. Former royalists had avenged Iturbide's death, executing the co-signatory of Iguala, Guerrero, in 1831. Santa Anna, whose experience of the War of Independence had taken place in the peripheral provinces of Veracruz, Tamaulipas, Nuevo León, and Texas, was not part of this ongoing cycle of vendettas. His sympathies lay with Victoria and Guerrero's factions. He was a federalist, a republican, and, ultimately, a moderate liberal. He had spent almost the whole of 1832 fighting Bustamante's government precisely because he was opposed to the party of order. And yet, the Congress that had been formed in 1833 was not the one he had hoped for. It did not matter that the cabinet included men whose reformist ideas he shared; individuals such as Bocanegra and even Gómez Farías. The moderates in charge of the cabinet, and I include Gómez Farías among them, were unable to control Congress. It became imperative for Santa Anna to intervene before someone else did, someone like General Bravo, whom he had fought against in Tulancingo six years before. In this sense, it would be preferable for him to close down Congress rather than leave the job to one of the more reactionary generals associated with Bustamante's faction. As long as he was president, he hoped he could ensure that the government did not swing entirely back into the hands of what Mora defined as the "party of reaction [*retroceso*]."[58]

Santa Anna returned to Mexico City on 24 April 1834. He challenged some of the measures being discussed by Congress but did not resort to force immediately. It was clear, however, that he was going to take action. As he stated in a *Manifesto* he issued on 29 April, he was not the servile supporter of the disorganizing plans of the demagogues. The nation had elected him president to "contain or moderate precipitated decisions or excessive passion." He promised to defend religion, liberty, security, and all the rights guaranteed by the Constitution. He was against the "rigors of tyranny in the same way that [he was] opposed to the exterminating excesses of an ill-understood liberty." His main concern lay in the impact "the immature introduction of [certain] reforms" was having on the country. Congress's response was to ignore Santa Anna's summons to meet on 21 May. The time for action had come.[59]

Tornel went to Cuernavaca with his brother-in-law, Miguel Diez Bonilla, and drafted the plan that was proclaimed on 25 May 1834, calling for "Religion, the *fueros*, and Santa Anna" and demanding a reversal of Congress's policies. According to the plan's five articles, in response to the "atrocious chaos, confusion and disorder" the country was in as a direct result of the legislature's behavior, its advocates (Tornel and colleagues) wanted to ensure that (1) all decrees issued against individuals (the Ley del Caso) and the Church, and in favor of Masonic sects were abolished; (2) all laws violating the Constitution and the general will were reversed; (3) Santa Anna be given the authority to execute these demands; (4) all deputies who favored these deeply unpopular reforms were removed from office and replaced by others following the corresponding procedures specified in the 1824 Constitution; and that (5) Santa Anna would have those forces who defended the plan at his service to ensure that it was executed accordingly. Tornel played a major role in coordinating the outpouring of support for the Plan of Cuernavaca that followed its proclamation, from a wide range of garrisons. According to an embittered Mora, Tornel pulled this off by promising "mountains of gold to those who proclaimed, protected or even just accepted" the Plan of Cuernavaca.[60]

Even without this careful orchestration, the Plan of Cuernavaca was popular. The mobilization that took place was such that it would be hard to believe that the fall of the radical 1833–34 administration was entirely Tornel and Santa Anna's doing. Evidently there were those who believed this shift in the country's politics was entirely Santa Anna's fault. Nevertheless, the evidence does point toward a broader consensus of rejection. Large sections of the population as well as the army were not yet ready to embrace Congress's radical attack on Church and army. There was no instance of a garrison opposing the plan, and the 316 plans of allegiance it received between May and August 1834 included a high proportion of civilian-led groupings (such as town councils, municipalities, and regional councils).[61]

Following the Plan of Cuernavaca, Santa Anna gave himself extraordinary powers, closed down Congress, dismissed Gómez Farías and his advisors, and set about reversing most of the laws passed by the radical Congress. For a second time, and on this occasion with even greater support, Santa Anna had the opportunity of becoming dictator and of taking draconian measures to consolidate his hold on power in the capital. Many high-ranking officers like Durán and Arista were ready to make him Absolute Ruler. He had the backing of the Church and the more powerful sectors of society. Santa Anna, however, did not seize this opportunity, demonstrating yet again that he was not actually interested in being the new country's director. As he recalled: "The President was invested with emergency powers while a new Congress was formed."[62]

In a letter he addressed José Fernando Ramírez, in reply to his correspondent's concern that he had betrayed his liberal ideals and was on the verge of becoming a tyrant, the caudillo replied:

> I have not joined any party that may have as its main aim to destroy the mother country, nor will I ever cooperate [with one] as a blind instrument; without abandoning that in-

> dependence that characterizes me, and consulting the true
> interests of the mother country, I have always acted in accor-
> dance with the inspirations of my heart, which is inclined
> toward doing good; and it is this conviction that gives me
> strength not to succumb in the middle of all those lies my
> personal enemies throw in my direction . . . striving hard to
> attribute sinister motives to my actions. . . . [They claim] I
> am opposed to the reforms; this is not true: I am opposed to
> the speed with which those laws are dictated . . . serving as a
> pretext to alter a [peace and] order it is my duty to preserve.

He argued that he was temporarily putting a stop to Congress's legislation because "it is my obligation to prevent a destructive religious
war from erupting." Again, Santa Anna was consistent. The barely disguised warning to Congress that he had issued a year earlier when addressing the rebels who were intent on declaring him Supreme Dictator
had not been heeded. He did not oppose the reforms in themselves, at
least those that did not harm the army. He had made his own reformist
proposals known to Gómez Farías, backing the government's drive to
raise revenue by enforcing contributions from the Church. However,
he was opposed to the pace of the reforms and, seeing himself as the
nation's pacifier, arbiter, and guarantor of order, felt impelled to intervene.[63]

Notwithstanding his assurances, the way in which the army and the
political class in the capital celebrated his saint's day that year is indicative of the extent to which people believed or wanted to believe that
he was the country's savior. On 13 June 1834, the streets of the capital
became crowded with a cheering multitude wearing blue and white rib-
bons that read: "Long live Religion and the Illustrious Santa Anna."
They converged in the main square of Mexico City, before the National
Palace, and spent most of the morning cheering their hero. That evening Santa Anna went to see the Mexican premiere of the opera *Zelmira*
and was honored in a hymn the santanista poet Ignacio Sierra y Rosso
composed as a tribute to him.[64]

Santa Anna brought about a reshuffle in the cabinet and set in motion
the procedures for a new Congress to be formed. Although the Church

and the army's *fueros* were preserved, the Church was made to pay for the support the santanistas guaranteed them in imposing the Plan of Cuernavaca. As historian Barbara Tenenbaum reminds us, "Nine days after the proclamation of the Plan of Cuernavaca, the Church agreed to provide Santa Anna between 30,000 and 40,000 pesos, on a monthly basis, over a period of six months."[65] The santanistas succeeded in achieving what the radicals had failed to do: forcing the Church to assist the republic's daily fiscal needs with its funds and properties. The difference was that they did this by making Church loans a prerequisite for their guaranteed defense of Church privileges. They did not openly attack the Church, as the radicals had done.

For the remainder of the year Santa Anna oversaw the implementation of the Plan of Cuernavaca, seeing to it that all the pockets of resistance in the republic were dealt with, that the controversial laws of 1833–34 were overturned, and that elections for a new Congress were duly arranged. Once Santa Anna felt that peace and order had truly been reestablished and that the newly elected members of the government could be left to their own devices, true to form, he opted to return to his hacienda. On 4 January 1835, the new Congress met, and on the 28th Santa Anna left the presidency in the hands of his old friend Miguel Barragán and retired to Manga de Clavo once more.[66]

8. The Warrior President, 1835–1837

Santa Anna remained an absentee president following the demise of the 1833–34 radical administration. The return of the men of 1830–32 to the corridors of power did not inspire him to stay in Mexico City. At the end of January 1835 he turned his back on politics to tend to his hacienda. He was as uncomfortable with the centralists' antics as he had been with those of the radicals. For the next two years (1835–37), he spent hardly any time in the capital and was in fact absent when the 6th Constitutional Congress brought an end to the 1824 Constitution. Although he has been blamed for the change to centralism, he was not actually present during any of the deliberations that led to the abolition of the federalist charter or the elaboration of the 1836 Constitution.[1]

In accordance with its deputies' traditionalist agenda, the 1835 Congress was determined to strengthen the regular army. On 31 March 1835 Congress passed a bill ordering the discharge of local militias in the country. The government in Zacatecas interpreted the law as confirmation that the centralists in Congress were on their way to overturning the 1824 Constitution. On 30 March, preempting the government's resolution, Francisco García, governor of Zacatecas, raised the standard of revolt by decreeing that "the [state] government is awarded the faculty to make use of its civic militia to repulse any aggression that may be attempted against it." Having returned to Manga de Clavo only three months earlier, Santa Anna nonetheless made his way back to the capital on 9 April on hearing the news of this *pronunciamiento*. He did not, however, return to Mexico City in order to preside over the republic but to acquire permission to quell the rebellion in person.[2]

His resolution to crush the Zacatecan uprising is striking when one remembers how Francisco García and his state militias had supported Santa Anna's 1832 revolt. García together with Gómez Farías and Bocanegra had launched their own anti-*bustamantista pronunciamiento* when he most needed their help: in the wake of the battle of Tolome. Two men who had been with García at the time, Manuel González Cosío and Marcos Esparza, could not help expressing their astonishment when they saw the energy he invested in bringing the 1835 *pronunciamiento* of Zacatecas to an end: "it is even more surprising, nay, even inconceivable, that Your Excellency, of all people, who has received such testimonies of benevolence, support, and love from the Zacatecans, has become, almost by magic, their cruellest enemy, the instrument of their degradation and ruin."[3]

Apart from his public statements about the need to preserve law and order, there is little that may help us understand his motivation. As a professional soldier he did not want the regular army weakened. Now that he was president (albeit an absentee one) he did not want his government's authority threatened by subversive state militias. However, there appears to have been more to his resolve than this. Santa Anna did not forgive disloyalty. He expected his allies to be faithful even if he changed sides. He punished Arista for breaking rank in 1833. He would punish Mejía in 1839 for betraying him in 1835. He was punishing Zacatecas for not accepting the new order he had contributed to creating following the Plan of Cuernavaca.

On 18 April 1835 Santa Anna left Mexico City to force Zacatecas into submission. He entered León on the 24th, moved on to Aguascalientes thereafter, and by 7 May 1835, his army was ready for action. Formed into three infantry divisions and one of cavalry, it consisted of 172 sappers, 2,000 infantrymen, 1,000 cavalrymen, and 18 pieces of artillery mustered by 140 gunmen. He led his men to the plain of Guadalupe, outside Zacatecas, where, on 10 May, at nine o'clock in the morning, the enemy lines were first seen. On observing García's forces, he was not impressed. However, he did not rush into an attack and, in fact, altered his original plan after he had reconnoitered the rebels' positions more carefully.

Using the cover of night to launch his assault on Guadalupe, he commenced the attack at 2:00 A.M. Ten pieces of artillery opened fire on the left flank, preventing García's forces from retreating into Zacatecas. Having opened a breach in the rebels' fortifications, two infantry divisions moved in. At the same time a cavalry charge took care of the right enemy flank and cut off their rearguard positions. A center infantry division presented García with "a wall of fire and steel." Santa Anna led a portion of troops into Zacatecas to take hold of its military garrisons. After two hours of combat, Guadalupe and Zacatecas were taken. The government forces had suffered a death toll of around one hundred men. The rebels had been routed. Figures for their casualties were not provided, although Santa Anna noted that 150 officers had been taken prisoner. The 2,443 *zacatecanos* who surrendered were allowed to go free. Santa Anna did not mention the pillage to which Zacatecas was subjected that day. The troops' plunder of Zacatecas was brutal, leaving in the region a deep-seated hatred of Santa Anna that would last for the rest of his lifetime. According to one source the caudillo expropriated the silver mine of Fresnillo in all but name, and had cartloads of silver bars dispatched from there to Manga de Clavo. He made a killing selling the expropriated silver to his protégés. The government lost out to the tune of 180,000 pesos, while some of his friends, like Tornel, came out rather well with earnings rising to 90,000 pesos.[4]

Following Santa Anna's victory in Zacatecas, he went on a tour of celebration and was hailed as a hero in Aguascalientes, Guadalajara, and Morelia. The government named him *Benemérito de la patria*. He returned to Mexico City on 21 June but again did not stay long. After celebrating his victory and meeting up with Barragán, Tornel, and his friends, he returned to Manga de Clavo on the 30th. He did not mind leaving his retreat to quell a revolt, but when forced to choose between presiding over the country and looking after his hacienda in the glorious sunshine of Veracruz, Santa Anna favored the latter. He clearly enjoyed the adrenaline rush of the battlefield and the life of the hacendado in his idyllic haven of Veracruz. Chasing up cabinet meeting minutes and haggling with congressmen in the dark corridors of the National Palace, on the other hand, bored him to distraction.[5]

For many it had become obvious that the experience of the First Federal Republic had been a failure. Since 1828 revolution had followed revolution, and it had become clear that the 1824 Constitution had failed to establish a stable, long-lasting political system suited to the needs and customs of the Mexican people. Santanistas like Tornel and Bocanegra arrived at the conclusion that the reality of their country demanded that they change its political system. Mexico needed a new constitution that did not go against the general will, did not create a context in which political upheavals were commonplace, and took into account "the habits, customs, and even preoccupations of the people." As was professed in the *pronunciamiento* of Orizaba (19 May 1835), it was essential that they terminate the federal system, "adopting [instead] another form of government more in tune with the people's needs, demands, and customs, and which can better guarantee our independence, internal peace and the Catholic religion we believe in."[6]

Tornel, the minister of war (1835–37), became a committed centralist. For him, the experience of the First Federal Republic demonstrated that federalism weakened the nation. By 1835 many had reached the same conclusion, and the change to centralism did indeed reflect Mexican public opinion at a time when federalism had lost its charm. Over four hundred *pronunciamientos* were written between May and October 1835. After a summer of heated deliberations, Congress pushed forward the resolution whereby on 23 October 1835, the federalist Constitution was abolished, a Constituent Congress was called for, and a centralist constitution was eventually drafted and approved a year later (29 December 1836).[7]

Santa Anna was not lying when he stated in 1837 that "the abolition of the old system [the 1824 Constitution] was not an endeavor I influenced."[8] Although friends of his such as Tornel and Bocanegra had renounced their federalist credentials, he remained unconvinced and was notably ambivalent about the entire issue during the year in which federalism was abandoned. Having a veracruzano like Tornel at the head of the ministry of war probably dampened his possible opposition to the proposed change. Nevertheless, once more, we have an instance of policy being determined by the legislative branch of government, in which Santa Anna did not play a noticeable role. Moreover, he never took to the centralist 1836 Constitution with its novel Supreme Conservative Power. As he noted in 1841, it "was not the one the *pronunciamien-*

tos of that period were calling for, nor was it certainly that which the country needed at the time."[9] The change to centralism was the spark that ignited the province of Texas.

This is not the place to offer a comprehensive analysis of the causes of the Texan revolution of 1835–36. Nevertheless it is worth noting that the view espoused here is not the popular Texan historiographical standpoint interpreting U.S. expansionism in Texas in terms of "settlements" established in an empty wilderness by freedom-loving and self-reliant pioneers who moved into a "frontier" that was there for the taking. Nor do I endorse the view that these U.S. immigrants brought with them "Anglo-American democracy . . . in triumph over inferior races." The more scholarly interpretation of New Western Historiography, which in recent years has moved toward depicting this "settlement" as a "conquest," the pioneers as "profit-driven entrepreneurs," and the "wilderness" as "a land already occupied by indigenous peoples with cultures of their own" or, for that matter, the Mexican nation, is more in line with the interpretation presented here.[10] Given that this is a biography of Santa Anna it is important, whether we agree with him or not, to appreciate his understanding of the conflict, in order to come to grips with the choices he made and the actions he took. Therefore, what follows is an interpretation of the Texan revolution that, inevitably, privileges the Mexican point of view and, in particular, Santa Anna's own standpoint.[11]

From the Mexican perspective it can be argued that an extremely liberal law of colonization, paired with the fact that distance prevented the government from controlling the influx of Anglo-American settlers who came to occupy Texas, resulted in there being nine Americans for every Mexican in the region by 1828. These settlers were not inclined to integrate into Mexican society. To quote Tornel, "for the colonists of Texas, the name *Mexican* is and has been an execrable name and there has not been insult or violation that our compatriots have not suffered finding themselves reduced to being treated as foreigners in their own country." The realization that this could result in the loss of Texas to the United States led the Bustamante administration (1830–32) to issue the law of 6 April 1830, which forbade U.S. citizens from emigrating to Texas. It was a law that was impossible to enforce, considering the state of communications at the time. In a similar vein, Santa Anna's government declared void a decree passed on 14 March 1835 by the State of Texas and Coahuila, legalizing the colonization of uncultivated land in the province. The aversion toward the Mexican government felt by most American Texans (who objected to learning Spanish, abiding by Mexican law, becoming Roman Catholics, etc.) was further exacerbated by the 1829 abolition of slavery. As long as the federal 1824 Constitution was in place slavery was allowed to continue under Texan law. The overthrow of federalism in 1835 finally prompted the Texans to revolt, given that a centralist state would tighten the Mexicans' grip over the distant and increasingly U.S.-populated secessionist province with uniform laws and taxes. However, the fact that the imposition of a centralist state would result in the abolition of slavery in Texas remains one of the main, yet often downplayed, reasons why the Texans rose up in arms.[12]

Santa Anna was under no obligation to lead the Texan campaign in person. As he noted himself, the Constitution provided him with a decorous way of excusing himself from entering the fray. Nevertheless, he chose to leave his old escocés friend from Veracruz, Miguel Barragán, in charge of the executive and lead the government forces into battle in the remote province of Texas. To quote Santa Anna: "I preferred the hazards of war to the seductive and sought-after life of the Palace."[13]

He returned to Mexico City on 17 November 1835, and from there departed to San Luis Potosí on the 26th to organize the expeditionary army, wearing the green frock-coat that was later to become associated with him. He prepared for war despite the fact that one rumor alleged he had been involved "in a scheme to transfer Texas to the United States in return for five million dollars and a personal bribe of half a million dollars."[14] U.S. Consul W. S. Parott, in his report of 14 December 1835, noted that Santa Anna was threatening to attack the United States. Santa Anna told the French and British ambassadors in Mexico City that if he found that the U.S. government was backing the rebellion in Texas, "he would continue the march of his army to Washington and place upon its *Capitol* the Mexican *Flag*."[15] The man who, according to one rumor, was willing to sell off chunks of his country, was the same man who, according to another source, was prepared to invade the United States.

Raising funds to finance the military expedition to Texas was to prove difficult. Santa Anna reached San Luis Potosí on 5 December and was haunted by the memories of the reception he had been awarded there in 1823. For five whole days the *potosinos* found ways to avoid providing his troops with either funds or food. He was able to force a 10,000-peso loan on the town council only by guaranteeing its repayment with his own funds. Given the desperate circumstances of the army and the urgency of the situation, the more substantial loan he negotiated with Cayetano Rubio and Juan M. Errazu, of 400,000 pesos—half of which was paid in cash, the other half in IOUS—was attained only because he was prepared to accept the steep interest rates they demanded in return. He recognized that the terms of the loan were "disadvantageous for the Nation" but could not see what other choice he had. It was only after the funds had been given to him and the expedition was well under way that, despite the cabinet's approval of the loan, it was rejected by Congress.[16]

The army Santa Anna found in San Luis Potosí was seriously lacking. It had neither surgeons or medical assistants. The armament was deficient, mainly made up of rifles that dated from the War of Independence. The men were inexperienced. Of the 3,500 men he managed to concentrate in Saltillo by January 1836, 2,000 were new recruits in need of instruction. He was not amused and, according to Vicente Filisola, spent much of the time devoted to organizing his expeditionary army in a filthy mood.[17]

While he organized his army in San Luis Potosí, his former comrade in arms and friend, the Cuban José Antonio Mejía, having converted to the Texan cause, led an unsuccessful expedition from New Orleans to Tampico, where he was repulsed on 15 November. Mejía's action was consistent with that of other federalists, such as Gómez Farías, who supported the Texan uprising in its initial stages from his exile in New Orleans. Both Mejía and Gómez Farías saw the imposition of a centralist political system as unacceptable. Nevertheless, once they became aware that the Texan revolt had independence as its main aim, both men withdrew their support. Notwithstanding Mejía's reluctance to support the Texan revolt to the end, his involvement in the failed expedition to Tampico marked the end of his long-standing friendship with Santa Anna, who never forgave him for this act of disloyalty.[18]

Against all odds, Santa Anna armed and clothed a 6,111-strong force, which he led from San Luis Potosí to San Antonio de Béxar in the winter of 1835–36. Mobilizing this army, accompanied by their wives and offspring (a total of 2,500 women and children) was a logistical nightmare. They carried out this feat, however, taking with them the necessary military equipment and ensuring that they had an adequate supply of food and water to cross more than sixteen hundred kilometers of hostile territory, in the coldest months of the year. There were eight hundred mules, two hundred carts pulled by oxen, and four wagons. They had to take the longer route so that the animals could find food along the way, and had to cross rivers such as the Bravo (Río Grande) and the Nueces, which entailed abandoning carts, oxen, and munitions. Illness, hunger, and the cold took their toll on Santa Anna's army, with more than four hundred men dying during the journey. Despite the ordeal, there is a sense that Santa Anna's exertions inspired them to follow him. According to Mariano Arista, Santa Anna always led from the front, riding ahead of his army with an escort of about thirty dragoons, and thus inspired confidence in his men. According to one historian, he always led from the front because he had apparently seen a portrait of Napoleon where the great warrior was depicted riding heroically ahead of his troops.[19]

Santa Anna's army occupied San Antonio at 3:00 P.M. on 23 February. One wonders what memories flitted across his mind, finding himself in the old haunts from his Arredondo days. Although the Texan rebels had found the time to retreat to the fortified Franciscan mission of El Alamo, adjoining the town, they had been taken by surprise, as nobody had expected Santa Anna to turn up in San Antonio so soon. While the Texans at the Alamo took potshots at the Mexican forces, Santa Anna had his forces take up their positions in and around San Antonio. He was determined to assault the Alamo and continue his operations north, occupying all the fortifications they found on the way. He was confident that they could reach the Sabina (Sabine) River, which separated Mexico from the United States, before the rainy season began.[20]

He did not want to waste time on placing the fortification under siege. He did not have enough men to leave troops behind besieging the Alamo while the rest pressed ahead to engage General Samuel Houston's army and capture the newly formed Texan government. Although he recognized that the Alamo was not a strategically important objective, he could not ignore it. The defenders of the Alamo could cut off his army's retreat and disrupt their lengthy line of supplies. Although an assault on the fortification would be costly, there seemed to be no other option. Giving the Texans one last chance, Santa Anna sent Colonel Juan Nepomuceno Almonte with his offer of allowing the men at the Alamo to walk away free as long as they promised never again to take up arms against the Mexican nation. A refusal of this generous offer would be equivalent to passing their own death sentence. Colonel William Barret Travis replied by opening fire on the Mexican forces and, to quote Santa Anna, in so doing, sealed the fate of those obstinate men.[21]

Mirroring his tactics at Tampico in 1829, the assault on the Alamo started at five in the morning of 6 March 1836 and lasted for an hour and a half. It is clear that he valued the glory attained in a victorious dramatic assault more highly than keeping the number of casualties to a minimum. He divided his army into four columns. The attack was as relentless as the defense of the mission was hard-fought. Santa Anna was forced to throw in the reserve as well. The intensity of the gunfire lit up the Alamo from inside. With Travis having refused to surrender, Santa Anna ordered "*degüello*" (fire and death), and no quarter was given. All of the 183 men who chose to reject the offer of an amnesty died. The only people whose lives were spared were three women, two children, and a Negro slave. The Mexican forces probably suffered far more casualties than the seventy dead and three hundred wounded Santa Anna reported having lost in the battle.[22]

The excitement of war and the sight of a beautiful woman apparently aroused Santa Anna's notoriously insatiable sexual desire. While he was in San Antonio he allegedly set up a bogus wedding so that he could bed a young woman who would not sleep with the *señor presidente* if she was not his wife. He had General Manuel Fernández Castrillón act as one of his witnesses, made an aide dress up as a priest, and went through with the charade. According to one source, having accomplished his mission, he then dispatched the woman to Mexico City, where she was "given" to an officer who was promoted to colonel in exchange for marrying her.[23] According to biographer Wilfrid Callcott, on the other hand, "she was duly installed as [Santa Anna's] mistress in a very good dwelling just a few doors from the public square of Jalapa, where legend still has it that she lived, childless, for many years."[24]

Following this victory, Santa Anna decided to divide his army to advance on three different fronts, leaving one division behind in San Antonio. The sooner they attacked the remaining Texan forces, the more definitive would be the resulting victory. He did not want to allow the Texans, their morale low after the news of the Alamo had spread, to regroup. He left General Juan José Andrade in San Antonio to cover their retreat and their line of communications. He sent General José Urrea, at the head of one division, to his right, to take Goliad, Cópano, and the Atlantic coastline of the province as far as Brazoria. Urrea's orders were to rejoin Santa Anna's column at San Felipe de Austin. He dispatched General Antonio Gaona, at the head of a second division, to his left, to cover a similar stretch of territory, as far as Bastrop, and from there to Nacogdoches. Gaona also had orders to meet up with Santa Anna at San Felipe de Austin. Santa Anna led the main bulk of the expeditionary army between Urrea's and Gaona's areas of operations.[25]

He claimed that "by dividing my army into three sections, my objective was none other than to speed up its march forward, protect it from the guerrillas, guard our flanks, facilitate our retreat, ensure food reached us from the ports, and destroy the enemy . . .; all of these aims were accomplished until we reached the River Brazos, when the army should have become reunited." The initial results were favorable to the government forces. Urrea's eastern march attained a stream of victories. It was to be the fate of 445 of his prisoners, however, taken at the actions of Llano or Encinal del Perdido, Guadalupe Victoria, and Goliad, that would be remembered, rather than Urrea's military prowess. All 445 were executed on 27 March 1836.[26]

The mass executions of Goliad were to haunt Santa Anna for many years. He argued that he was obeying orders and that the prisoners were not Mexicans. They were pirates and bandits, foreign filibusters causing trouble in a country that was not theirs. The so-called Tornel Decree (30 December 1835) made it clear that "speculators and adventurers," "foreigners that disembark in one of the ports of the Republic or enter it, armed and with the intention of attacking our territory, will be treated and punished like pirates" and were to suffer the death penalty. To quote Santa Anna, who was adamant that he could not be accused of having treated the prisoners arbitrarily: "Law decrees and it is not the magistrate's responsibility to examine it, but to apply it. . . . The prisoners of Goliad were condemned by the law." As he wrote to Urrea at the time:

> Who gives me powers to override what the National Government has ordered in such categorical terms, pardoning delinquents of the caliber of these foreigners? Under which flag do they make war on the entire Republic, murdering our detachments treacherously, burning our villages, attacking the properties of the peaceful citizens, and attempting to rob a large chunk of our territory? And you believe that the indignation of the country should fall upon me, as it indeed would, were I to protect these outlaws? You can evidently tell that this is no war among brothers like the ones we have unfortunately had to suffer. But it is not a war between nations either, in which . . . prisoners are respected and even exchanged. These foreigners are bandits that have attacked the territory of the Republic to steal a part of it . . . ; that is why the Supreme Government has declared, with reason, that they are pirates, and orders that they are treated and punished as such.

The legalistic validity of his argument notwithstanding, the shock caused by the killings was not easily overcome.[27]

Santa Anna felt impelled in 1837 to demand an inquiry by the government to clear his name of any wrongdoing. According to a letter he wrote on 13 May 1837, one of the greatest causes of irritation to him was the assertion that James W. Fannin and his men were executed after they surrendered on the understanding that their lives would be spared. He claimed that there was no evidence Urrea had negotiated Fannin's surrender (an action Urrea was not authorized to undertake). Moreover, had such an agreement been signed, Santa Anna had never been informed of it. In a bid to clear his name of the accusation of having applied the law in "a cruel and inhuman fashion," he demanded that Urrea, Colonels Juan Morales and Mariano Salas, and Lieutenant Colonel Juan José Holsinger declare whether they had agreed to spare the prisoners' lives, and if so, whether Santa Anna had been informed of this. In the inquiry that was subsequently held, Urrea's statement cleared Santa Anna of applying the Tornel Decree with the knowledge that Fannin's men had surrendered believing they would not face the firing squad. However, he made it known that he had suggested their lives be spared and that Santa Anna would have none of it. Santa Anna thus cleared his name to the extent that the mass execution of Texans was consistent with the supreme government's decree of 30 December 1835, and there was no evidence that Urrea had agreed to spare the Texans' lives when they surrendered. However, the Goliad massacre remained a blot on his career. Lieutenant Colonel José Nicolás de la Portilla and Urrea were traumatized by the experience of implementing this order.[28]

Santa Anna's main column reached San Felipe de Austin on 7 April. Here he was informed that Houston was camped in a wood near Gross's Pass, that his men numbered no more than eight hundred, and that he intended to retreat to the Trinidad (Trinity) River if Santa Anna's forces crossed the Brazos. He looked for ways of getting his army across the river that day but was unable to do so. On the 8th he ordered two barges to be built, but as wood was difficult to find and they had few carpenters, it could take as many as fifteen days to complete them. He headed off with five hundred men to reconnoiter the area to see if he could find an easier point to cross the Brazos, leaving Ramírez y Sesma and Filisola behind in San Felipe while the men set about making the two barges.[29]

He spent three days exploring the banks of the river, marching all day, sleeping rough at night. He came across a rebel stronghold at Thompson's Pass and attacked it, obtaining a quick victory, a barge, and two canoes. A messenger was dispatched to order Ramírez y Sesma to join Santa Anna at Thompson's Pass, which he did on the 13th, leaving Filisola behind in San Felipe. Santa Anna was troubled that he had not yet heard from Gaona, who he was hoping would have reached San Felipe de Austin by then. However, news that Harrisburg was only sixteen kilometers away and that the rebel Texan government was there absorbed his attention. Were he to capture the Texan government, the rebellion would be speedily brought to an end.[30]

Displaying his characteristic recklessness and impatience, he left Ramírez y Sesma behind at Thompson's Pass and led his men into a burning Harrisburg on the night of the 15th. News of his proximity had reached the Texan government, and they had fled that afternoon in a steamboat, heading for Galveston Island. Before leaving they had set fire to the place. The few inhabitants who chose to stay behind were questioned about the government's intentions and Houston's position. By all accounts Houston was still at Gross's Pass with eight hundred men. Santa Anna sent Almonte with fifty of his dragoons to find out whether Houston was camped where they had been told. The following day Almonte returned with news that Houston was heading toward Lynchburg Ferry (then Lynchburg Pass). With the Texan government having escaped him, Santa Anna decided to make a dash there.[31]

His disregard for Houston's military abilities and his overconfidence at the time must be noted. He had with him one cannon, seven hundred infantry troops, and fifty cavalry. He knew Houston had around eight hundred men. Given the importance of numerical power in any military conflict, his willingness to take on Houston without reinforcing his army shows that he thought his abilities and those of his men far surpassed those of Houston's "army of pirates." The triumphs of the Alamo and Goliad had made him overconfident. The experience of the Zacatecas campaign was there to justify the high regard he had for himself and his regular troops. His poor regard for improvised militias (when he was not leading them himself) was representative of a view commonly held among high-ranking officers in the regular army. Tornel, as minister of war, was one to profess that "the superiority of a disciplined and hardened army over irregular masses is as clear as that of light over darkness, of science over ignorance." Santa Anna's underestimation of Houston's military power was understandable, although misguided, and it was ultimately to prove incredibly costly.[32]

He was at New Washington when he received Almonte's intelligence on the afternoon of the 18th. In the early hours of the 19th he sent Captain Marcos Barragán with some dragoons to reconnoiter Houston's position. Barragán returned the next day with news that Houston was close to reaching Lynchburg. Santa Anna's delight could not be contained. They were only days, perhaps hours, away from confronting the last armed rebel force left in Texas, and the end of the exhausting pursuit was in sight. He immediately set his army in motion and caught up with Houston the evening of the same day, 20 April 1836.

Houston had positioned his troops in some thick woods by the riverbank of Buffalo Bayou, where the San Jacinto River merges with it to flow into Galveston Bay. According to Santa Anna's calculations, Houston had only two choices: to come out and fight or to retreat by wading into the river. His enthusiasm spread to the troops, and they opened fire on the Texans. Houston kept a cool head. The Texans returned the fire, but they did not abandon their sheltered position. Santa Anna then chose where to set up his camp. He decided to move about a kilometer and a half away from the enemy, onto a slight promontory that he considered would give his forces an advantage were Houston to attack them. A flying detachment of around a hundred horsemen came out of the woods to harass Santa Anna's escort but were easily repulsed. It was about five in the evening by then. It looked as if Houston was not going to launch an attack just yet, and Santa Anna's troops were hungry and in need of rest. Despite allowing his men to take it in turns to eat and sleep, the night was spent on high alert. Santa Anna made it a point to stay up himself, checking that the sentries were in their places.[33]

At nine on the morning of 21 April, General Cos arrived with reinforcements. There were four hundred of them. They were all recruits who had been in the army for just over three months. Levied in San Luis Potosí and Saltillo, these were not the "five hundred *chosen* infantrymen" he had asked for. They were exhausted. Cos and his men had marched as fast as they could in order to reach Santa Anna in time, and if they did not eat or rest, they would be in no shape to fight. Santa Anna relented to Cos's pleas, and for the next three hours Cos's recruits ate and slept. Santa Anna burned his energy ensuring that the sentries were in place and the defenses were ready for action. He even rode out with two cavalry pickets and a number of aides to explore the enemy positions during that morning. Lunchtime came and there was still no sign of an attack. It looked as if Houston could not make up his mind what to do next. Santa

Anna suspected he was probably too afraid to engage them in combat. But retreating into the river was not an option. Sooner or later a clash of arms was inevitable. Miguel Aguirre's men, a subgroup of Santa Anna's expeditionary army, were now the ones who wanted to get a bite to eat. Santa Anna gave way to their demands. He was exhausted himself. Having been up all night, he needed a rest as well.[34]

He advised General Manuel Fernández Castrillón he was going to try and get some sleep, giving strict orders to ensure that all the sentries remained extra-vigilant and to wake him up at the first sign of any enemy movement. Santa Anna intended to catnap rather than settle down for a siesta. Fernández Castrillón was to wake him the moment Aguirre's men finished their lunch. With these dispositions in place, he found a shady spot under the trees and fell fast asleep. The next thing he knew was that Houston's army was upon them, cutting down the Mexicans to the bloodcurdling cry of "Remember the Alamo! Remember Goliad!" He dashed to where the Aldama, Guerrero, and Matamoros battalions were positioned and started yelling orders to them. But it was of no use. The young recruits appeared to be dumbstruck with fear. They were not even returning the Texans' fire. His orders had not been obeyed. Most of the troops had followed his example and succumbed to their accumulated exhaustion by taking a siesta. Fernández Castrillón had decided to shave, wash, and get changed and did not inspect the sentry posts. He was chatting with some of the other officers when they came under attack.[35] Houston, on seeing that almost the entire Mexican camp had lowered its guard, had seized the moment. He had led his men stealthily as close to the enemy as possible, urging silence, restraining his men from giving away their advance too soon. Only once he was within a few meters of the Mexicans did he initiate the surprise attack that was ultimately to seal the independence of Texas.

Santa Anna could not believe his eyes as he surveyed the chaos surrounding him. His entire army was being savaged before him, and there was nothing he could do to reverse the situation. The Texans were routing them. At this point Colonel Juan Bringas's batman spotted him standing hopelessly in the middle of the fray and offered Santa Anna his master's horse. Santa Anna, the perennial survivor, did not think twice. In the hope that if he escaped he could reach Filisola's division at

Thompson's Pass and initiate a counterattack, he rode past the enemy lines and outran the horsemen who went after him.

However, his escape route was cut off. The bridge he was planning on crossing had been burned down. His horse could not keep up the pace and collapsed. With his pursuers not far behind, he was reduced to hiding among some pine trees. Once night fell, he eluded his trackers, wading across the river with the water coming up to his chest. Drenched and freezing in the middle of the night, he was lucky to come across an abandoned farmhouse. There he found some dry clothes and changed, taking off his uniform but keeping his "fine linen bosom shirt, and sharp pointed shoes," as well as a very distinctive diamond shirt stud. The next morning, close to midday, two Texan scouts found him. Not recognizing him, they asked whether he had seen General Santa Anna, and he replied that Santa Anna was farther ahead. They took him prisoner nonetheless and marched him back to Houston's camp.[36]

Santa Anna summarized the reasons for the defeat of San Jacinto as follows. There were too many recruits and not enough veterans. General Martín Perfecto de Cos's men were unable to respond to the unexpected Texan attack because they were inexperienced and panicked. The reinforcements he had asked for never materialized. Of the five hundred men who could have been with Cos, one hundred were sent (four hundred, according to his 11 March 1837 account); and Filisola never left his position by the banks of the Brazos. A letter giving away Santa Anna's position had been intercepted, after he had expressly ordered that no such communications should be dispatched to him. Gaona did not join the expeditionary army at San Felipe de Austin as he had been instructed to do, depriving Santa Anna of much needed troops. Cos's men and Santa Anna's escort were hungry and exhausted. They needed to rest. This in itself would not have presented a problem had his orders that the sentries posted around the camp remain awake and alert been obeyed. He was not prepared to accept that he had erred in his leadership of the expeditionary army.[37]

This was not a simple domestic revolt, even though the government attempted to treat it as such. In his 1837 historical interpretation of the conflict, Tornel would make the point that they were up against the might of the United States. The eventual U.S. annexation of Texas would prove his assessment correct. Santa Anna was not impervious to the fact that he was fighting foreigners. According to his account of the revolt, it was not the locals who were up in arms against the national government. The rebels were predominantly U.S. citizens who had brought their troops with them from New Orleans. He noted that Travis's, Fannin's, Grant's, and even Houston's men were mainly U.S. citizens who had moved to Texas to fight the Mexican government. They did not belong to any colonization enterprise.[38]

Santa Anna and Tornel had a point. Of the fifty-five men who signed the 7 November 1835 Declaration of War against Santa Anna's centralist institutions, Lorenzo de Zavala was the only Mexican signatory. Of the fifty-eight men who signed the subsequent Texan declaration of independence, on 2 March 1836, only two were actually from Texas: José Antonio Navarro and Francisco Ruiz. Of the rebels who defended the Alamo, only a handful had been born in Texas. The great majority were settlers of U.S.-European extraction, backed financially by the Galveston Bay and Texas Land Company and other land speculators based in New York and New Orleans. Samuel Houston was from Virginia. The first time he set foot in Texas was in 1833. He was not an aggrieved Texan, as such. James W. Fannin was a slave trader from Georgia who first went to Texas in 1834, bringing with him fourteen slaves from Cuba. James Bowie was from Kentucky. He was also a slave trader. Together with his brothers John and Bezin he had made a small fortune of seventy-five thousand dollars by introducing slaves in the United States. He was also a newcomer to Texas, having moved to Saltillo in 1830, where he met and married Úrsula Veramendi, the daughter of the vice-governor of Coahuila and Texas.[39]

The issue of slavery must not be downplayed. To quote from a dispatch Santa Anna wrote in Villa de Guerrero, on 16 February 1836, "there exists in Texas a considerable number of slaves, introduced here by their owners under certain legal pretexts; but who, according to our laws, should be free. Will we tolerate for much longer that these poor people suffer the pain of the chains in a country whose kind laws protect man's liberty without making distinctions of color or race?" In a letter he wrote to Tornel, it was clear that he was aware that in quelling the Texan revolt, he would be responsible for liberating all the slaves who had been kept there in defiance of the 1829 law that abolished slavery in the republic. With the federal Constitution in place, the Texan slave owners had found legal ways of avoiding the implementation of this federal decree. After the demise of the 1824 charter, there were no longer any legal loopholes whereby slaves could be legitimately kept in Texas. From where Santa Anna was standing, this was one of the prime causes of the revolt. The U.S.-born Texan slave owners were not prepared to give up this particular "commodity": "Given that the laws of the Republic prohibit slavery . . . it is our duty to ensure they are everywhere respected."[40]

This was also the view in the northern states of the United States. For many U.S. northerners, the Texan war of independence had as its sole purpose to grab "bigger pens to cram slaves in." A number of eminent U.S. intellectuals and politicians, such as John Calhoun and Abraham Lincoln, were opposed to the U.S. annexation of Texas on the grounds that it would strengthen the slaveholding states of the South. R. M. Williamson's incendiary address before a secessionist assembly in San Felipe de Austin, on 4 July 1835, certainly made a point of stressing that Santa Anna was going to "compel you into obedience to the new form of Government; to compel you to give up your arms; to compel you to have your country garrisoned; to compel you to liberate your slaves." In the mind of Carlos María de Bustamante, the Texans' determination to retain their slaves was "the sole and only motive why Texas . . . sought to separate itself from Mexico."[41]

When Santa Anna was captured on the morning of 22 April, his captors, unaware of who he was, took him back to where the rest of the prisoners were being held. One of them was intrigued by Santa Anna's "very splendid" shirt, but his suspicions were allayed by the prisoner's admission that he was Santa Anna's aide. It was the captive Mexicans' welcoming shouts of "El Presidente! El Presidente!" and the way many of them stood to attention on seeing him arrive that gave away his true identity. He was then taken to see General Houston, who had been wounded in battle. According to Colonel John Forbes, "the prisoner was dignified and impassive while the other Mexican officers were trembling for their own safety."[42]

On hearing of Santa Anna's captivity, Urrea decided to use the pretext of visiting his commander to ensure that he was well to evaluate the strength and state of the enemy army. The Texans refused to see him, allowing General Adrián Woll to go instead. Santa Anna claims it was following his interview with Woll that he realized all was lost. News of his capture had resulted in mayhem. The troops remaining in the field had retreated instead of attacking the enemy. One Mariano Garfias visited Santa Anna at the time and broke into tears when the captive caudillo embraced him. While Garfias was speechless with distress, Santa Anna "retained all his serenity with his characteristic fortitude of spirit."[43]

In captivity, Santa Anna controversially ordered Filisola and Urrea to retreat and signed two treaties with his captors (one public, one private) on 14 May, both of which became known as the Treaty of Velasco. In the public peace treaty he agreed to end the hostilities and evacuate the Mexican troops south of the Río Grande. In the private and confidential treaty he agreed to try to persuade the Mexican government to receive a Texan commission so that the independence of Texas was recognized. In exchange, his captors agreed to guarantee his release and reembarkation for Veracruz.[44]

It is important to evaluate the Treaty of Velasco while bearing in mind Santa Anna's past tricks. We need to remember that this was the man who had tried to con the Spanish commander in San Juan de Ulúa into believing that he was surrendering Veracruz to him in October 1822. This was the general who had had his friends write to Echávarri during the 1823 siege of Veracruz to tell him that they were ready to betray him, as long as he sent in his troops by the Escuela Práctica entrance, in January 1823. He was the general who allegedly dressed up as a monk in Oaxaca, in 1828, to capture Calderón, and who succeeded in getting out of Tampico in August 1829 by getting Mejía to pretend reinforcements had arrived from the capital. His aim was to deceive the Texans and come up trumps. The general of tricks was at his most ingenious. The wording of the treaty exemplifies this. He did not actually commit himself to doing anything other than promise to allow a Texan commission to make their case to the Mexican government. He did not actually recognize Texan independence. Moreover, he negotiated with the Texans throughout on the premise that as a prisoner, he was no longer in a position to act freely, and anything he said or signed would not be validated by Congress. The moment he had been made captive he had ceased to be president of the republic.

Even then, he did not acknowledge the Texans' demand for independence. The original treaty he was presented with had to be significantly altered before he signed it. He used all his powers of persuasion to come up with a treaty in which he did not commit himself to anything binding. As an example, article 4 in the original draft, stating that Santa Anna solemnly recognized the independence of Texas as Head of the Mexican Nation, had to be dropped. He was quite proud of his handling of the situation. The Texan directorate wanted independence to be recognized there and then, with a document that sealed its borders. He did not give in to them. Instead he found a "decorous" way out, which did not tie or bind the nation to recognizing the Texans' demands.[45]

What he did do was dispatch orders for Filisola and his men to retreat south of the Río Grande. This would be held against him. Nevertheless, he was right in stating, in his own defense, that Filisola should have had the astuteness to know that he was under no obligation to obey a captive superior. A close inspection of Santa Anna's letter to Filisola does substantiate his claim that between the lines, he was urging Filisola to reorganize what was left of the expeditionary army in order to bring about a counteroffensive. Pressurized by his captors into ordering his troops to retreat, he complied in the first part of the letter with their demands. Had Santa Anna limited himself to ordering his men's retreat, it could be confidently stated that he was ready to sign anything in order to save his skin. However, the second half of the letter contained indications of how Filisola could replenish his army: "Your Excellency may dispose of the funds that have arrived in Matamoros as well as of the supplies that must exist at this point in order to maintain the army that is now most certainly under your command, and in Victoria, where moreover, you will find 20,000 pesos." The emphatic confirmation that Filisola was now solely in charge of the expeditionary army can definitely be read as an order to Filisola to assume control of the government forces in the field and act independently of him. By stating unequivocally that Filisola was "most certainly" in command, Santa Anna was saying that *he himself most certainly was not*. The fact that this assertion was included with some clues as to where the Mexican forces could regroup, and how they could finance a counteroffensive, does give credence to the notion that he was trying to keep the struggle going from the difficult position of his captivity.[46]

It is perhaps not surprising then, that Santa Anna subsequently accused Filisola, Gaona, Urrea and Ramírez Sesma of committing the ignominy of not turning their guns against Texas. He asked, poignantly, "for the Mexican people to love their country, and know how to defend her with heroism, do they really need *me* to tell them to do so?"[47] As he would recall in 1849, "if General Vicente Filisola, with the army that was left under his orders, as second-in-command, initiated the retreat to Matamoros the moment he heard of the debacle of San Jacinto, out of his own volition, instead of looking for the enemy, who was nearby, it is to his excellency that we must attribute the precipitated abandonment of Texas."[48]

The fact that Filisola gave priority to ensuring the caudillo's life was not jeopardized is confirmed in the letter he addressed to Santa Anna on 28 April, in which he admitted to having toyed with the idea of renewing the offensive but said had chosen not to do so: "Wishing to prove to you how much I appreciate your person, as well as that of the prisoners . . . I will retreat beyond the Colorado and cease all hostilities. . . . I cease all hostilities despite my responsibility to the Supreme Government, with due consideration given to the peace of the Republic, and the person of Your Excellency."[49]

Tornel's secret orders to Filisola to make sure that Santa Anna came to no harm, paired with his staff's own reluctance to take the initiative, certainly point toward there having been an excessive dependency on the part of the key high-ranking officers in the campaign. When news reached Mexico City that Santa Anna had been taken prisoner, Tornel argued publicly, on 20 May, that the war must go on. Privately he wrote to Filisola, ordering him to act "with 'extreme prudence,' in order not to endanger in any way the life of the illustrious General Santa Anna." Tornel found himself in the difficult situation of having to act in accordance with the nation's needs while at the same time hoping to save Santa Anna's person and image. The adoration Mexicans felt for Santa Anna and the dependency they had forged, relying on his presence to feel confident, was in part to blame for the approach of Tornel and the other generals to his captivity. Saving him was more important to them than securing a victory over the Texan forces by launching a major counteroffensive. In retrospect, Santa Anna would find a degree of consolation in noting that a number of his contemporaries compared his Texan misadventure with Napoleon's Russian campaign of 1812. In so doing, both his critics and supporters inadvertently and deliberately adorned the narrative of his actions with Napoleonic motifs, which gave the events a status that it could be argued they did not deserve.[50]

After the battle of San Jacinto, Santa Anna was incarcerated with his aide and interpreter Juan Nepomuceno Almonte, the illegitimate son of the War of Independence patriot hero José María Morelos; his brother-in-law Gabriel Nuñez; and his Cuban secretary Ramón Martínez Caro.[51] Santa Anna did make it as far as boarding the *Invincible* on 1 June and was persuaded that he had duped the Texans with the Treaty of Velasco. With a definite sense of irony, he wrote the address with which he intended to bid farewell to the Texans who were prepared to let him return to Veracruz in exchange for some very feeble assurances: "Friends! I have seen how brave you are in battle, how generous you are in its aftermath. You may count upon my friendship forever and you will never regret having dispensed these considerations upon me. In returning to my place of birth thanks to your generosity, please admit this most sincere farewell."[52]

His escape to freedom was not to be. On 1 June 1836 Thomas J. Green at the head of 130 volunteers from New Orleans arrived in Velasco baying for Santa Anna's blood.[53] They ordered the captain of the *Invincible* to hand the prisoner over to them. A crowd soon gathered along the waterfront, and Santa Anna realized that if he were handed over to Green and the jeering populace he was going to be humiliated and made to suffer. He wasted no time in writing to President Burnet of Texas, resolved to die: "I ask you to grant me the one wish of having me shot aboard this ship; there is no scarcity of soldiers to execute such an order, and I will not leave this boat unless I am dead." He was granted protection instead and avoided being stoned to death there and then, but his hopes that his captivity was over were dashed. He was made to disembark and locked up in a cell in Velasco. According to some accounts he was made to wave a Texan flag as he came out of the boat.[54]

Livid, he wrote a lengthy protest letter to Burnet on the 9th, expressing his anger that the Treaty of Velasco had been breached and his
disgust at his treatment. As agreed in article 9 of the public treaty all
Mexican prisoners had been released, and yet he was still locked up.
He pointed out that the critical condition upon which the entire treaty
rested, namely that Santa Anna must be returned free to Veracruz, had
been completely ignored. He was aggrieved that Burnet could have let
him be subjected to the kind of torment Green and the rabble put him
through, after Filisola had done exactly what they wanted him to do.
He deplored Burnet's weakness in letting the people make a spectacle
of him. He described as intolerable the abysmal conditions he was expected to put up with, surrounded by highly objectionable guards, and
all the privations he was to survive.[55]

Santa Anna's complaints fell upon deaf ears. With Houston away in
New Orleans he was left at the mercy of General Rusk, who had no
qualms about making the Mexican suffer for what he had done. He
was regularly insulted by his Texan captors, who enjoyed themselves
firing shots into his cell from the street outside. On 27 June one aggressor took a shot at him and came close to striking Almonte and Núñez.
When Santa Anna's secretary, Martínez Caro, told the Texan authorities that the caudillo was planning to escape, they locked him up in a
cell in Orazimba, where, on 17 August, he was actually chained with
his interpreter Almonte to a heavy lead ball. Displaying a certain heroic
sangfroid, Santa Anna claimed he did not look upon death with fear. It
was the sadness of never seeing his wife and children again, and that
Mexico's troubles were far from over, that pained him. Looking back
at his ordeal in 1837, Santa Anna could not help noting that whatever
he signed or agreed to in the Treaty of Velasco was invalidated by the
Texans' refusal to allow him to return to Veracruz.[56]

Stephen Austin, with whom Santa Anna had been acquainted for
several years and with whom he maintained a cordial relationship,
proposed to him to write to President Andrew Jackson of the United
States. Austin's suggestion was not entirely altruistic. He wanted the
U.S. government to serve as the official guarantor of Texan sovereignty.
Austin was seeking the means whereby any subsequent direct U.S. intervention in Texas could be carried out legitimately. If the president of

Mexico agreed to invite the U.S. government to participate in the Texan peace process, this in turn would allow the United States to take any action deemed necessary thereafter, should Mexico break any agreements made.[57]

In the letter Santa Anna addressed to President Jackson he did acknowledge that the possibility of recognizing Texan independence might bring about a peaceful conclusion to the region's problems. In what must have struck him as his last and only chance of release, he was no longer worried about whether there could be a clever way of appearing to promise something when, in fact, he was not doing so. He no longer had the energy to be his ingeniously deceptive self. The Mexican troops had withdrawn. His captors had not respected the Treaty of Velasco. He was prepared to put in writing the inadmissible: "Let us establish mutual relations so that your nation and the Mexican one may seal a bond of friendship, and together may find an amicable way of giving stability to . . . [the Texan] people who wish to figure in the political world, and which may do so over the next few years under the protection of [our] two nations." In his 1837 *Manifiesto*, Santa Anna claimed that the letter was written at a particularly difficult time for him. Having come so close to being executed, he felt that to have ventured a defiant stance would have been futile. Again the stress in his defense was that nothing was ever formally approved or agreed to in the letter. There was nothing binding, and it was unfair to try and read it, out of context, as if there were. It was his ticket to freedom.[58]

President Jackson was more than aware that "as long as you are a prisoner, no act of yours will be regarded as binding by the Mexican authorities." However, he was prepared to intercede for Santa Anna, for which the caudillo would be sincerely grateful. He was therefore released after seven months of captivity. Burnet released him from his chains in the second week of October and allowed him to walk free, a month later, under the understanding that he would pay Jackson a visit in Washington before returning to Mexico. Jackson's involvement in the whole affair merits some more attention.[59]

According to Jackson's biographer, Robert V. Remini, "the President had long coveted Texas as an essential component of his dream of empire. . . . Jackson's paramount objective with respect to Texas—indeed,

his only objective—was its acquisition." He sent Colonel Anthony
Butler to Mexico City as Joel Poinsett's successor with instructions to
negotiate the purchase of Texas, and Jackson became increasingly de-
spondent as a result of Butler's failure to fulfil his promise of "uniting T—— to our country before I am done with the Subject or I will
forfeit my head." Butler went on to recommend that Jackson authorize
dispatching troops to the province and seizing it as well as bribing
Mexican officials to attain their aim. Jackson distanced himself from
Butler's dealings, in particular his attempts to bribe a number of Mexicans, including Santa Anna. Nevertheless, as he noted in one letter, "All
the U.S. is interested in is the unencumbered cession [of Texas]." The
issue, as expressed by the secretary of state, John Forsyth, was "the annexation of Texas to the U. States was a favorite measure of Gen'l Jackson whenever it could be done with propriety." Achieving this aim "with
propriety," without being seen as the perpetrator of a dishonorable act
of aggression, was where the main problem lay. With Santa Anna in
captivity, it is evident that Jackson saw a possible peaceful means to
accomplishing his dream of annexing Texas. If Santa Anna could be
persuaded to use his influence to bring about such an aim peacefully, it
was certainly worth a try. When Santa Anna finally met Jackson in January 1837, the U.S. president proposed extending his country's border to
include Texas and northern California, offering three and a half million
U.S. dollars as compensation.[60]

In mid-November 1836 Santa Anna set off for Washington together
with Almonte, whom he would later commend for being his faithful
companion and interpreter during his captivity. Also with him were
Colonels Bernard Bee and George Hockley and a small escort. The journey to the capital of the United States took him across the Brazos to
the Sabine, overland to Plaquemine, Louisiana, and up the Mississippi,
which they then navigated for twenty days on the paddle wheeler *Tennes-
see*. They passed Natchez and went up the Ohio River until they reached
Louisville, Kentucky, on Christmas day. Much to Santa Anna's delight,
he was given a hero's welcome, celebrated as a "hero of human liberty"
by groups of northerners who opposed what they considered to be a
conspiracy of the slave states to add Texas to the Union. From Louisville they made their way to Washington by land, across the snow-cov-

ered countryside of Kentucky. The cold apparently affected Santa Anna badly, and he had to be attended by a doctor at Lexington. On 5 January 1837 the group resumed its journey. They passed through Wheeling (in the present-day state of West Virginia) and stopped in Frederick, Maryland, where it is alleged that he had the opportunity to meet his future adversary during the Mexican-American War, General Winfield Scott. However, no evidence has been found to support this.[61]

Santa Anna's party arrived in Washington on 17 January 1837. President Jackson was extremely pleasant to him. He held a private interview with Santa Anna and invited him to dinner with a group of select guests. No official record of the private conversation was kept. According to Waddy Thompson, who was present, Santa Anna proposed to cede Texas to the United States for a "fair" consideration. According to Santa Anna, when the subject of Texan independence was broached, he replied: "That question can only be resolved by the Mexican Congress." Whether he was prepared to sell Texas to the United States at the time cannot be proven. Jackson was clearly aware that he was not in a position to do so, even if he had been willing. In the end, we are left with speculative accounts that accept either Thompson's or Santa Anna's version of the events, depending on the historian's particular agenda. In factual terms, no sale of the region took place, and once Santa Anna returned to the presidency in 1841, he made the reconquest of the province one of his government's priorities. Following their two encounters Jackson placed the corvette *Pioneer* at Santa Anna's disposal, and he made his way back to Veracruz, having been away from home for over fourteen months. Although many must have thought Santa Anna would never recover from the debacle of San Jacinto, his political and military career was far from over.[62]

9. The Landowner President, 1837–1841

Despite Santa Anna's spectacular fall from grace, the Mexican government remained fearful of his influence. On receiving news that Santa Anna was making his way back to Veracruz, Antonio de Castro, commander general of the Veracruz garrison, had set in motion a series of precautionary measures. His response to those who had asked him how they were meant to welcome Santa Anna had been to tell them that the caudillo was coming as nothing more than a general. The commander general intended to place the garrison on alert and ask the caudillo to make his way to the capital so that he could be questioned about his conduct during the Texan campaign. Castro was determined not to let him stop either in Veracruz or at his hacienda, for fear that he would start a new revolution the moment he was given the chance. As Santa Anna made his way back home, exhausted and demoralized, yearning to be reunited with his family, the last thing on his mind was starting another revolution.[1]

Tornel was one of the few santanistas left in the government who was delighted to hear of Santa Anna's freedom in January 1837. On 11 January 1837 he ordered with "inexplicable pleasure" that the different authorities should arrange for the celebrations such news merited and that the decree of 20 March 1836, whereby a black bow had been attached to all Mexican flags, was lifted; bows could now be taken off. A month later Tornel circulated copies of the issue of the *Diario del Gobierno* containing all the relevant documents demonstrating that Santa Anna had returned safely and that he had not "entered into any commitments of any description that would prejudice the rights of the Nation." Worthy of note is that the reception Santa Anna received on his arrival in Veracruz was not frosty in the least, as described in a number of studies. On the contrary, the people of Veracruz welcomed their local hero with "innumerable mani- festations of happiness." Only a year after the Texan debacle, the *jarochos* were ready to forgive Santa Anna and forget his recent failures. For Santa Anna, this homecoming must have been profoundly emotional. Against his expectations he had made it back home, and the dingy, stifling cell in Orazimba was now just a memory. On the horizon the familiar peak of Orizaba reached up into the intense blue sky, welcoming him back to Veracruz. Before him his people were on the wharf, "a crowd, as far as the eye could reach, of all ages and sexes of Vera Cruzians . . . assembled to witness his Excellency's arrival."[2]

He returned to a country that was, in many senses, more divided than it had been when he had set out. However, he was neither in a position nor willing to return to the political stage. Following his Texan ordeal he retired to the "pleasant enclosure" of Manga de Clavo, pleased to be "incorporated into [his] family" once more. He claimed he "blessed [his] solitude and happily dedicated himself to the occupations of [his] domestic home . . . an oasis in the desert for a tired pilgrim." Needing to recover from the humiliating defeat of San Jacinto, his long stretch of captivity, and his trip to Washington, Santa Anna appeared to be genuinely determined not to return to the political arena. Far from the clamor of war and the bickering of the National Palace, he could spend entire days riding the length of his haciendas, spending time with his wife (his son Manuel was born a year later), and resting in a hammock in the lulling heat of the tropical afternoons of Veracruz.[3]

Santa Anna's adventures of the previous two years posed a number of problems to the minister of finance, in particular that of calculat- ing what the caudillo was owed in terms of his salary. In a letter José María Cervantes wrote to the minister of war, on 2 April 1837, he asked whether Santa Anna should be paid for the period of time he was in captivity. He also wanted to know whether the salary he was owed was that of president of the republic or whether he had ceased to be presi- dent upon his capture, in which case his salary would be that of general of division. And now that he was back, what salary, if any, should he receive? The correspondence Cervantes's queries generated was both extensive and all too often unclear. From what can be gathered, Santa Anna did eventually get his salary as general reinstated but was not given any back pay for his time in captivity.[4]

While the divisions in the political class grew increasingly acrimonious under General Anastasio Bustamante's newly elected government (1837–41), the French government demanded the immediate payment of 600,000 pesos in compensation for the damages that had been inflicted on a number of French shops (including a bakery—hence the name the conflict was given: the French Pastry War) during the 1828 Parián riot. Given that the Mexican government was not in a position to pay the extortionate amount the French government was demanding, and did not believe that the demands were justified, Bustamante's government became involved in an international conflict that resulted in particularly damaging consequences for the republic's economy. The French sent their fleet to the Gulf of Mexico and blockaded the key ports of Tampico and Veracruz for over a year. Since the Mexican government refused to pay the sum of money demanded, the blockade escalated into a war, with the bombardment of Veracruz on 27 November 1838.

Little is known of Santa Anna's activities during this period. For the greater part of nineteen months he stayed away from politics and the army. No correspondence has been found that may point to him having conspired against the government or plotted a comeback. There are not even letters showing that he took any interest in national events. Beyond writing his account of the Texan campaign and demanding an inquiry into the Goliad massacre, Santa Anna disappeared from the public scene and dedicated himself to running his haciendas. Far from the corridors of power and from the excitement of the battlefield, he gave himself over to the pleasures of the life of the hacendado and started to buy the lands that spread around Manga de Clavo.[5]

However, when the sound of cannon fire reached Manga de Clavo, on 27 November 1838, he could not help but saddle his horse and return to the theater of war. He claimed he felt it was his obligation to place himself at the nation's service. He offered his services to his longtime foe Manuel Rincón, stating that he wanted to "run the same risks as his old companions in arms," and he presented himself in Veracruz before the bombardment was over.[6]

Rincón acquiesced. He instructed Santa Anna to inspect San Juan de
Ulúa and assess how much damage the French had inflicted upon the
fortress, in order to establish whether it was worth defending. Santa
Anna, having seen the poor condition of San Juan de Ulúa, recommended capitulation of the fortress. On 28 November Rincón set in
motion arrangements to surrender San Juan de Ulúa. Receiving no further instructions from Rincón, Santa Anna retired to Manga de Clavo.
Unbeknownst to him, news of Rincón's surrender of San Juan de Ulúa
sent President Bustamante into a paroxysm of fury. The government
immediately repudiated the capitulation and, surprisingly, opted to replace Rincón with Santa Anna. In a particularly striking scene, considering how recently Santa Anna had been defeated in Texas, the galleries
of the chamber of deputies burst into cheers and applause when the
appointment was announced. Congress thundered to cries of "He's the
man we want! He's the savior of the country!" The memory of his triumph of Tampico evidently carried more weight than that of his more
recent defeat at San Jacinto.[7]

Once orders reached Santa Anna that he was to replace Rincón, he
summoned General Mariano Arista, who had been sent to the region
with reinforcements. He also ordered the commander stationed in Puente Nacional to move to the hacienda de Santa Fe on the city outskirts.
He returned to Veracruz and sent a letter to the French rear admiral, informing him of the Mexican government's rejection of the agreements
of 28 November and that they were at war with the French government.
The reply from the French commander reached Santa Anna at six in
the evening on 4 December, "full of arrogance," making it known that
the Mexicans were committing a dreadful mistake. Veracruz would be
razed to the ground.[8]

At eight the same evening, the British consul visited Santa Anna. He
had been on board Monsieur Baudin's corvette and wanted to let Santa
Anna know that the French admiral did not actually want to open fire
on the port. Santa Anna was not convinced. He visited the fortifications, ensured that the troops garrisoned in the port were ready for an
offensive, and gave them words of encouragement. At ten that night
Arista arrived in Veracruz with his division. Arista and Santa Anna had
a lot to discuss. From what can be gathered from Santa Anna's mem-

orable dispatch of 5 December, the two men argued until two in the morning. One can only imagine what was said, the memories that were summoned late into the night, recollections of times when they had fought together—Tulancingo (1827), Perote and Oaxaca (1828), Tampico (1829); of Arista's profound admiration for Santa Anna, which had led him to call for his hero to be made dictator in 1833; and then there had been the brutal pursuit of that summer, which had concluded with Santa Anna defeating and humiliating Arista at Guanajuato. Tired and "unfortunately at odds with one another," the two men retired to their quarters in a house in downtown Veracruz at two in the morning.[9]

At half past five on the morning of 5 December 1838, Baudin sent three thousand troops into Veracruz, under the cover of thick fog. In what amounted to a three-pronged attack, his men took the bastions of Santiago and Concepción, while Prince Philippe de Joinville, the king's son, led a detachment into Veracruz, sending a platoon to find Santa Anna and take him prisoner. The quiet of dawn was soon broken by the crackling thunder of gunshots. Santa Anna leaped out of bed and ran out into the street, where he joined his retreating guards, taking cover behind their wall of fire. According to some accounts he ran past the French guards as they made their way into his house. According to another, he escaped by clambering away on the rooftops. Arista, less fortunate, was taken prisoner.[10]

Santa Anna managed to reach the barracks where most of his troops were stationed, and with characteristic energy he rallied the men and set in motion the counterattack. What happened next is still a matter of controversy. According to his critics the French troops had already started to return to their ships when his counteroffensive was launched. (What they do not make clear is why the French were returning to their ships. What was the purpose of entering Veracruz if all they wanted to do was evacuate the place?) In this reading of events, Santa Anna never actually repulsed the invaders because they were leaving the port when he attacked them. There are also critics who claim that Santa Anna was running away when his horse and leg were hit by a cannonball. However, according to the dispatch issued by Baudin, it was the Mexican counterattack that forced the French troops to evacuate Veracruz in haste.[11]

Bearing in mind the extraordinary impact that Santa Anna's personal account of the conflict had on his contemporaries, effectively enabling him to return to the presidency in 1839, it is worth noting his version of events. Whether he is entirely truthful about certain details of the clash that took place that morning is superfluous, in the sense that his account was the one the majority of Mexicans chose to accept at the time, which allowed him to regain his former glorious reputation and overcome the recent memory of the Texan debacle. It was no doubt the account Joaquín M. Alcalde, Santa Anna's defense lawyer in his 1867 court-martial, believed. Alcalde was only five years old at the time of the French attack, but like so many Veracruzans, he was no doubt brought up to believe that thanks to Santa Anna's valor, the French invaders were repulsed that glorious 5th of December. It is certainly the case that the French abandoned the port and that Santa Anna came close to dying in the fray. The French retreat allowed Santa Anna to claim until his death that he was responsible for repulsing their occupation of Veracruz. Dictating the dispatch of the battle at two in the afternoon, from what Santa Anna thought was his deathbed, he stated:

> At the head of my column I had the honor of repulsing the invaders, notwithstanding that we had been taken by surprise, forcing them with our bayonets to reembark, seizing on the very wharf their eight piece [cannon], which will serve as a monument to the valor of our men. We won! Yes, we won! The Mexican arms achieved a glorious triumph here, and triumphant is the Mexican flag: I was wounded in this last effort, and it will probably be the last victory I offer my mother country.[12]

Santa Anna had indeed been badly wounded. The French fired their cannon at him and took the horse from under his legs. The horse died instantly. Santa Anna's left leg was full of shrapnel.

After the French troops returned to their ships, Baudin retaliated by unleashing the full weight of his cannon power upon the battered walls of Veracruz. Humiliated, in Santa Anna's mind, by the unquestionable heroism of the Mexican force, Baudin vented his displeasure by pounding the port. However, most of the porteños were not exposed to this

bombardment, Santa Anna having had the foresight to order the evacuation of the city in the immediate aftermath of the battle. Lying agonizing
yet happy at the day's results, he estimated that only twenty-five Mexicans had died (among whom he included himself!). The French had left
behind over a hundred dead, scattered in the streets of Veracruz.[13]

It was then, as he finished dictating his dispatch, that he launched
into what was to become one of the most effective and influential rhetorical passages of his life. Although long, Santa Anna's infamous farewell to his people is worth quoting in full. It contains all the trademarks
of his political creed and epitomizes how he wanted to be seen by his
contemporaries and posterity. The allusion to the destruction caused
by factionalism and party politics; the depiction of himself as a selfless
patriot and arbitrator, a cut above the partisan and misguided politicians of the day; the [false] modesty; the military values; the taste for
the melodramatic—all are vintage Santa Anna.

> As my existence draws to an end I cannot but manifest the
> satisfaction that also accompanies me of having witnessed
> the beginnings of a reconciliation among the Mexican peo-
> ple. I gave General Arista my last embrace, with whom I was
> unfortunately at odds, and from here I address this embrace
> to His Excellency the President of the Republic as a measure
> of my gratitude for having honored me [with this commis-
> sion] at a time of danger: I offer it as well to all of my compa-
> triots, and I urge them, in the name of our mother country,
> which is in so much danger, to put aside their resentments,
> to join together to form an impenetrable wall French bold-
> ness will crash against.
>
> I also ask of the government, that my body may be buried
> in these very sand dunes, so that my comrades in arms know
> that this is the line of battle I leave marked for them: that
> from today onward the Mexicans' most unjust enemies may
> not dare place the filthy soles of their feet on our territory. As
> well, I demand from my compatriots not to stain our victory
> by attacking helpless Frenchmen, who reside among us,
> their lives guaranteed by our laws, so that we may be forever

presented as magnanimous and just, as well as brave in the defense of our sacrosanct rights.

All Mexicans, forgetting my political errors, do not deny me the only title I wish to donate to my children: that of [having been] a *Good Mexican*.[14]

On the 6th his left leg was amputated. The shrapnel was impossible to extricate and gangrene was inevitable. His right hand had also been badly wounded. The inexperienced medical practitioners who cut off his leg below the knee botched the operation, not leaving enough skin to cover three centimeters of bone that protruded jaggedly beneath the joint. They were forced to overstretch the skin in order to seal the wound. In years to come he would complain repeatedly of the pain this caused him, with his badly stitched wound having a tendency to open up and bleed.[15]

By the 13th, convalescing in Los Pozitos, he felt well enough to write to the minister of war to inform him of the success of the operation ("my doctors tell me that my life is no longer at risk") and of his intentions. He felt a "remarkable relief" in his right hand, which had also been badly splintered with shrapnel. He intended to retire to Manga de Clavo, five leagues away, in order to recover from his ordeal. He hastened to add that "regardless of having half a leg less, I will continue to serve [my country] where possible in whatever events may follow in the declared war against France. . . . On the glorious 5th . . . [the French] suffered a cruel disappointment."[16] Santa Anna would look back in 1874, having suffered nearly twenty years in exile bearing the heavy load of the accusation of treason, and claim that he wished he had died then, "with glory."[17] It is almost certain that had he died in 1838, after publishing the famous dispatch of 5 December 1838, there would today be streets, squares, and schools named after him in every single town in Mexico.

Nevertheless, at the time, Santa Anna's performance in Veracruz, his emotional dispatch, and the fact that he had come close to death in the name of the mother country all contributed to his political recuperation after the Texan disaster. The pariah of San Jacinto had managed somewhat incredibly to blot out, at least temporarily, the memory of the tragic events of 1836. He was awarded a "great cross and a plaque" for his action of Veracruz. The cross, made to be worn on the chest attached to a red and white band, had four arms of gold, each forming a triangle, like the rays of the sun. On the top a crown of laurels was placed, and in the center of the cross, the words "Triumphed in Veracruz on 5 December 1838" were inscribed in gold. As for his amputated leg, he had it buried at Manga de Clavo. Its remains would subsequently be exhumed and buried in the cemetery of Santa Paula, in Mexico City, on 27 September 1842.[18]

There was willingness on the part of the political class, and the populace, to forgive him for what had happened in Texas and to overlook the negotiations he appeared to have entered into there. Needless to say, it is this willingness that has repeatedly baffled historians. How did Santa Anna succeed in making extraordinary comebacks like this one? It would not be farfetched to think that following the debacle of San Jacinto, Santa Anna's political career was over. How did he find ways of rising from the ashes, like a Phoenix, time and again?

Evidently he was an immensely skillful politician, able to play off rival factions and generals against each other and to turn their disputes to his advantage. He had learned that in the context of the fraught and bitter political disputes of the early national period, the best way to overcome party factionalism was to appear to be above partisan interests, to be beholden to no faction, and to appear to assume power reluctantly. He repeatedly criticized those politicians who placed their faction's interests before those of the country. He consistently projected himself as an arbitrator and a mediator. When he was invited to intervene, time and again, he made a point of stressing that he accepted for the good of the nation. He stressed that he was not a legislator and that he preferred retiring to his haciendas. It was a discourse that clearly resonated with his contemporaries as the political class in the capital failed to establish a long-lasting and stable political system.

Santa Anna also understood the importance of propaganda in a way that none of his antagonists did. With Tornel by his side, pamphlets and rituals, pieces of oratory, and fiestas had gone hand in hand, giving him a mythical status that none of his contemporaries enjoyed. For most Mexicans he was known as the Liberator of Veracruz, the Founder of the Republic, the Hero of Tampico. He was now the Hero of Veracruz as well, a great, courageous, and selfless warrior who had been prepared to die for his mother country, who wanted to be remembered as a *good Mexican*, who had lost a leg in battle. Santa Anna and Tornel had found the way to convert his campaigns into the stuff of epic legend. Questionable triumphs became dazzling victories. Objectively, Santa Anna also had the gift of appearing at just the right moment, when the Mexican people had had enough of a particular ruler or government and wanted peace and stability, and when lesser generals floundered against foreign or domestic aggressors. In this sense, his reading of the popular mood was shrewd and timely.

He had physical magnetism and presence. He inspired those around him. He impressed even his enemies with his dynamism, his ability to work or march for hours on end without tiring, his impressive intelligence. And the context was one that lent itself to charismatic domination, to the emergence of messianic leaders. As Max Weber argued so persuasively, "Charismatic domination in the 'pure' sense . . . is always the offspring of unusual circumstances—either external, especially political or economic, or internal and spiritual, especially religious, or both together. . . . It arises from the excitement felt by all members of a human group in an extraordinary situation and from devotion to heroic qualities of whatever kind."[19] Just as many other Spanish American caudillos were natural leaders in a time of unusual circumstances and critical emergencies, Santa Anna was the providential figure whom people in Mexico were predisposed to trust, rather than relying on the impersonal bureaucracy of legal authority of the day. General relief was therefore palpable when a warrior on horseback like him returned to the political arena with clear aims. He was a necessary gendarme, a strongman who represented authority and order. He was also a pragmatist and a master of reconciliation. The Mexican people, or at least enough of them to make Santa Anna's repeated rise to power possible, admired his sureness of touch and did not care much about constitutional niceties. Historical necessity, it would appear, had created Santa Anna.

It is evident that his victories still carried more weight than his defeats, especially after the battle of 5 December. People wanted to believe that he had it in him to redeem the country. In their time of need they wanted a hero. On 23 January 1839, the Supreme Conservative Power (a moderating power of five members created in the 1836 Constitution) decided to appoint him interim president in order to allow Bustamante to go to Tamaulipas to confront a federalist revolt that had erupted, led by Generals José Urrea and José Antonio Mejía, both former comrades in arms of Santa Anna's.[20]

Anastasio Bustamante's second term in office had not been significantly easier than his first (1830–32). If anything, it had been worse. The appalling state of the country's economy, the defeat in Texas, the divisions between moderate and radical federalists and centralists and the conspiracies they had woven, and the French blockade had together resulted in two extremely difficult years for Don Anastasio. To make matters worse, Bustamante's ability to respond to the multiple crises that affected his government was particularly limited. This was not so much because of his allegedly indecisive nature but because there was little he could do while respecting the 1836 Constitution. Power lay with Congress and the Supreme Conservative Power, not with the executive.[21]

By January 1839 the Mexican government was dealing with the French navy and a radical federalist revolution in the northeast. On 16 December 1838, in Santa Anna de Tamaulipas (Tampico), General José Urrea launched a federalist *pronunciamiento* that attracted significant support from other federalist strongholds. Bustamante saw the rebellion as an opportunity to counter Santa Anna's unexpected resurrection as a national hero following the events of 5 December. He was determined to prove himself an equally dynamic president by leading the army that would crush the rebels.

Santa Anna arrived in the capital on a litter on 17 February and was given a rapturous reception. A month later, on 19 March, Bustamante finally departed for Tampico and Santa Anna became president for a second time. He tried to give his government a sturdier sense of direction than it had enjoyed under Bustamante. In order to do this he had to adopt extra-constitutional measures. In the four months he was acting president, without seeking permission from the Supreme Conservative Power, he tried to have the 1836 Constitution reformed; he signed the peace treaty with France that brought an end to the French Pastry War,

General Santa Anna, President of Mexico "on several occasions," ca. 1841. Courtesy of Nettie Lee Benson Latin American Collection, University of Texas at Austin.

paying the French government 600,000 pesos; he imposed tough sanctions on journalists and newspapers who were deemed subversive (by the law of 8 April); he contracted a loan of 130,000 pounds with a British firm at a highly disadvantageous rate; and he left the capital to crush Mejía's revolt. Each one of these measures resulted in controversy. Moreover, although he favored a "moderate and just freedom that excludes both license and detestable arbitrariness," this middle-ground stance failed to unite the divided factions. His behavior during his short time in power convinced the centralists in the Supreme Conservative Power and

Congress that it was better to support the submissive Bustamante, since he at least observed the Constitution and respected Congress. Having said this, Michael Costeloe's interpretation of his brief spell in power still rings true: "Santa Anna used his interim presidency very astutely to restore and enhance his reputation, above all with the army. He had done in a few weeks what Bustamante had failed to do in two years. He had silenced the radical press, publicly but obtusely backed constitutional reform and defeated the main federalist revolt."[22]

The clearest example of the way he succeeded in presenting himself as a man of action was the manner in which he crushed Mejía's rebellion. On 30 April, in a litter, he left Mexico City at the head of an army led by Generals Valencia and Tornel. They reached Puebla hours before a federalist *pronunciamiento* in favor of Urrea and Mejía's revolt erupted and, in doing so, prevented it from taking place. From Puebla they proceeded to Acajete on the Puebla-Veracruz border and confronted Mejía's rebel forces, which had made their way into Puebla from Tamaulipas. The battle of Acajete took place on 3 May, and the government forces routed Mejía's troops. It was another bloody affair, with a death toll of around six hundred men. A number of sources point to the fact that Generals Valencia and Tornel played a crucial role in determining Santa Anna's victory. Mejía was taken prisoner. In what had become an uncommon practice in these civil conflicts, the order was issued for Mejía to be executed along with all the other officers taken prisoner. The evidence suggests that it was Tornel, who had an unquestionable ruthless streak, who gave the order. Tornel had his own motives. Mejía had served, albeit briefly, as Tornel's secretary in Baltimore in 1831, during the months when Tornel served as Mexican minister plenipotentiary in the United States. The two men had fallen out seriously at the time, after Mejía left his post and became involved with Lorenzo de Zavala in selling large areas of Texas to U.S. settlers, breaking the law of 6 April 1830. One can but imagine what Santa Anna's thoughts on the matter were.[23]

Mejía had been one of his closest comrades in arms. He had accompanied Santa Anna in Perote and Oaxaca in 1828; had been beside him at Tampico in 1829; and he had backed Santa Anna's 1832 revolt from Tampico. However, their paths had taken very different courses thereafter. Mejía's activities as a land speculator in Texas had led him to support the Texan revolt in 1835. A radical federalist, like Valentín Gómez Farías, he had supported the Texan revolt but had not gone as far as supporting the bid for independence. From Mejía's perspective it had been Santa Anna who had abandoned their cause by turning against Gómez Farías and endorsing the move to replace the 1824 charter with a centralist constitution. Mejía's sailing from New Orleans to Tampico in 1835 with the intention of spreading the revolution was a clear expression of the political divide that had grown between the two men. Santa Anna had not forgiven him for this lack of loyalty. The fact that Mejía had unexpectedly acted as one of Santa Anna's lawyer's witnesses in New Orleans, in his bid to regain a diamond stickpin that was stolen during his captivity in Texas, did not influence the decision to have him executed. When Tornel ordered that Mejía be given only three hours of grace before being shot, Santa Anna, in all likelihood, approved. Mejía was convinced that it was Santa Anna who had sentenced him to death. It is alleged that when he heard of the order he replied: "Had Santa Anna fallen into my power, I would not have given him more than three minutes."[24]

Santa Anna returned to the capital on 8 May and received a hero's welcome. Despite the popular appeal of Santa Anna's actions, the members of the Supreme Conservative Power were becoming increasingly concerned about his apparent lack of respect toward them. Santa Anna, confronted with the country's growing problems and a possible confrontation with Bustamante on his return to the capital having defeated Urrea's rebel forces, opted to leave Mexico City. Claiming bad health, he sought permission to retire to Manga de Clavo, and this was granted. He made Nicolás Bravo interim president and left Mexico City on 11 July, nine days before Bustamante returned from Tampico. Back in his bailiwick, Santa Anna held the post of commander general of the garrison of Veracruz until October, when Bustamante replaced him with Guadalupe Victoria.[25]

During the four years that passed between his return from the United States and his involvement in the Triangular Revolt of 1841, Santa Anna spent what amounted to less than nine months involved in national politics, including fighting the French in December 1838, serving as acting president in the first half of 1839, and confronting the federalist rebels led by his old friend Mejía. The greater part of this four-year period was spent on his hacienda, taking care of his family and his properties. A closer look at his activities away from the theater of events allows us to see him as a dedicated hacendado and a caring father. It was during these years (1837–42) that he purchased the properties that, together, would make him the owner of all the land stretching out from either side of the main road connecting the port of Veracruz to Xalapa. Considering that he was the son of a second-rate bureaucrat, there must have been times when he paused to marvel at the extent of his acquisitions. The land surrounding the route his family had once used to travel between the port and Xalapa now belonged entirely to him.

Prior to 1839 he had acquired the haciendas Manga de Clavo, Paso de Varas, and part of that of Santa Fe. His land already sprawled around the port of Veracruz, reaching Boca del Callado and Boca del Río. Following his retirement from public life in July 1839, he seriously dedicated himself to acquiring more land. On 24 September 1839 he expanded Manga de Clavo by purchasing a property that belonged to the haciendas of San Juan Bautista Acanonica and Santa Fe. On the 7th of November he added Tenespa to his spreading domain. Following his return to power in 1841, he was able to consolidate the acquisitions he had made in 1839 with the purchase of the haciendas of El Jobo (which had belonged to Guadalupe Victoria), El Encero, La Palma, and another part of Santa Fe in 1842. To these purchases he added those of the haciendas of Los Ojuelos (1843) and Boca del Monte (1844) as well as that of the rancho of Chipila y el Huaje (1842).[26]

If we focus on the time and energy he dedicated to running these haciendas, renting out parts of them with extremely detailed instructions about what could and could not be grown, it is possible to think of Santa Anna, first and foremost, as a hacendado. It is certainly worth bearing in mind that he was as much a powerful landowner as he was a general and a politician. In becoming the region's most influential hacendado, he transformed his relationship with the people of Veracruz as their leading military chieftain and hero into one in which he became the province's main provider of employment, produce, and patronage. The fact that these different aspects of his career merged in

Veracruz gave his influence in the region a weight enjoyed by no other veracruzano. By the mid-1840s he owned most of the land between the port and Xalapa. His cattle, worth 315,244 pesos in 1844, provided both the port and the provincial capital with most of their beef. There was a dependency on the produce of his land that made his contribution to the local economy all-important. He was also dedicated to making the most of his properties, actively taking every available opportunity to ensure their efficient maintenance.[27]

Although few testimonies have survived of the way he ran his properties, we can make an educated guess. The extremely detailed instructions he gave the tenants who rented parts of his haciendas demonstrate his personal knowledge of the land and his awareness of what should be grown or raised in specific areas. The activities in which he engaged in Medellín, Xamapa, San Diego, and Tamarindo in 1819–20 serve to remind us of the energy he could channel into organizing the communities that lived under his patronage. Likewise, the professions of gratitude that were left behind by the people who worked for him at his hacienda in Colombia in 1858 are also helpful in illustrating the activities Santa Anna enjoyed as a hacendado and a *patrón*. He created jobs and looked after the community's interests, built cemeteries, and helped people build their houses and rebuild their churches. He indicated whether his tenants could grow sugar cane, how many head of cattle they were allowed to look after, and where he expected them to plant their beans or lay down their chicken coops. If he spent far more time in Veracruz than he did in Mexico City, this was probably because he was a committed hacendado. Far from the dirty, busy streets of the sprawling capital he could sit on the veranda and contemplate the rolling green hills of his lands spread before him, all the way from Xalapa down to the deep blue sea.[28]

He was also a father who expressed his love for his children, both legitimate and illegitimate, in numerous ways. He demonstrated his affection by giving his children properties, allowing them to live on his lands with their partners, permitting his illegitimate children to carry his surname and ensuring that none of them went lacking. His children were to reciprocate his love by accompanying him in exile and standing up for him in the public arena. Santa Anna fathered four (perhaps five) legitimate children with his first wife, Inés García (Guadalupe, María del Carmen, Manuel, and Antonio). In his last will (29 October 1874) he acknowledged four of his illegitimate children (Paula, Merced, Petra, and José).

To his daughter Guadalupe, born in 1829, he gave a house in Veracruz, Calle del Vicario number 692, worth six thousand pesos, to show her "the great love he feels for her."[29] After she married his nephew, Francisco de Paula Castro (son of his sister Francisca and her second husband Lic. José Agustín de Castro), Santa Anna ensured that they started life together on a good footing.[30] He gave them forty thousand pesos on their marriage and allowed them to settle at El Encero. He demonstrated the high regard in which he held his nephew and son-in-law Francisco by appointing the young man as his legal representative, awarding him full powers of attorney, during his early exiles. Guadalupe and Francisco reciprocated his affection by looking after his affairs during his many absences and by defending him publicly on several occasions. Following the triumph of the *juarista* camp in 1867, once it became clear that there was little they could do to recover his confiscated properties, Guadalupe and Francisco joined him in exile for several years. When he returned to Mexico in 1874, it was Guadalupe and Francisco who ensured that he was looked after, giving him a monthly allowance of one hundred and fifty pesos. Guadalupe and Francisco had five children (Aurelia, Francisca, Inés, Pedro, and Agustín), and their descendants live in Mexico City to this day.[31]

With his daughter María del Carmen, born in 1834, he was equally generous. When she married Carlos Maillard, Santa Anna gave them fifty thousand pesos as their wedding present and also gave them the hacienda Boca del Monte. María del Carmen, Carlos, and their daughter María Carolina Maillard López de Santa Anna, would accompany Santa Anna during his long exiles. From what I have been able to gather, María del Carmen died while still young, when they were abroad. When Santa Anna returned to Mexico in 1874, he was accompanied by his son-in-law Carlos and his granddaughter María Carolina.[32]

With his son Manuel, born in 1838, he was again magnanimous. Unfortunately for Manuel, it was only as a child that he was able to enjoy the formidable fortune Santa Anna amassed at the height of his career.

By the time he was twenty-one he was accompanying his father in exile and was to spend the greater part of his life thus as they moved between a number of Caribbean islands, Colombia, and the United States. In Santa Anna's final will, Manuel and his siblings were to inherit haciendas such as Manga de Clavo, Paso de Varas, and El Encero, but they were unable to overcome the laws put in place by Benito Juárez. The properties had long since been confiscated, parceled up, put up for auction, and sold.[33]

With his illegitimate children he was also kind and considerate. He allowed his daughter Merced and her husband José Arrillaga to live in Manga de Clavo, and after Doña Inés died, he empowered his son-in-law José to manage this hacienda for him as well as Paso de Varas. He allowed his illegitimate daughter Agustina López de Santa Anna to live with her husband, Lieutenant Colonel Pedro Pablo Cortez, at the hacienda de Los Ojuelos, which he bought in 1843. In his last will he requested that the four illegitimate children he recognized (Paula, Merced, Petra, and Colonel José María López de Santa Anna) were included in the inheritance "with the rights they are granted by the current Civil Code." All of them, including the children he did not recognize, were his loyal supporters and defenders. For instance, his son Colonel Ángel López de Santa Anna accompanied him during his brief visit to Mexico in 1864 and went with him into exile in his house on the Caribbean island of St. Thomas. Colonel José María López de Santa Anna went as far as starting a revolt in Xalapa in 1844, to defend his father's cause, once news reached him that Santa Anna had been deposed following the so-called Revolution of the Three Hours (6 December 1844). His children's loyalty suggests that at the very least, they respected him deeply. By all indications his relationship with his children, both legitimate and illegitimate, mirrored that which he established with the people of Veracruz, of a caring father figure.[34]

At the end of 1839 Santa Anna toyed with the idea of traveling to Colombia. On 30 December he wrote to President Bustamante and asked to be issued with a passport in order to do so. The existing documents concerning this passing fancy do not, unfortunately, offer any clues as to its origins. In a letter dated 27 January 1840 he requested financial assistance for his intended journey and again asked for his passport to be issued. In a subsequent letter, of 12 February 1840, he specified that he needed fifty thousand pesos to cover his travel expenses. It is difficult to guess what he was hoping to find in Colombia. It could be that disappointment at his treatment following the Texan debacle led to a desire to start a new life elsewhere. The political labyrinth he had found in the capital in the first half of 1839 may well have persuaded him that it was impossible to govern the country. What is certain is that the intended journey confirms that he did not harbor any ambitions of overthrowing Bustamante at the time.[35]

The authorization for him to leave never came, and he spent the greater part of two years running his sprawling haciendas, entertaining personages on their way to the capital, such as the Calderón de la Barcas, and maintaining a marked distance from the political shenanigans in Mexico City. The only occasion when he felt impelled to leave Manga de Clavo was when his former comrades and adversaries, Gómez Farías and Urrea, stormed the National Palace on 15 July 1840, taking President Bustamante prisoner and launched a federalist *pronunciamiento* with the aim of restoring the 1824 Constitution. Santa Anna was summoned to the capital to rescue the government, and he got as far as mobilizing the local troops to Perote. However, order was restored in Mexico City by the end of the month, thanks in part to General Valencia's exertions, and his services were not required, enabling him to return to his country retreat. It is difficult to tell whether he was yearning to return to the corridors of power at the time. There is no evidence that he was involved in any political activity at this stage. The time was not right. A year later, however, the growing dissatisfaction with Bustamante's government had become far more widespread.[36]

The clearest example of the extent of the disillusionment of Mexico's political class after two decades of unstable independent life is to be found in José María Gutiérrez Estrada's controversial 1840 monarchist proposal. Gutiérrez Estrada, "a man of progress," according to Mora, argued in the aftermath of the 15 July Revolution that nobody would proclaim, in a different context, the advantages of a republic more "cordially" than he.[37] However, the "sad experience" of Mexico demonstrated that it could not be, for the time being, that privileged country: "We have experimented with all the possible forms a republic can adopt: democratic, oligarchic, military, demagogic and anarchic; to the extent that all of the parties, and always to the detriment of the nation's honor and happiness, have tried every conceivable republican system [to no avail]." The 1824 Constitution had been a failure, and to reintroduce it would lead to "the most abject state of social dissolution." The 1836 Constitution was no better. The only solution left was to impose a constitutional monarchy. For Gutiérrez Estrada the "monarchical system . . . was more suited to the character, customs, and traditions of a people who had been governed by a monarch since the foundation of their society." Given that the experience of Iturbide's reign had demonstrated the futility of forging an entirely new Mexican dynasty, Gutiérrez Estrada proposed "a *real* monarchist experiment, with a *foreign prince.*"[38]

Although Gutiérrez Estrada's 1840 monarchist proposal did not inspire much enthusiasm at the time, it did reflect the sense of profound disillusion that had come to characterize Mexican politics after two decades of instability. By 1841 many santanistas had come around to sharing Gutiérrez Estrada's sentiments. In September 1840, Tornel had used the opportunity of giving that year's Independence Day oration to give vent to his spleen in the capital's Alameda square. Although the santanistas remained committed republicans, and their populist patriotism prevented them from wanting to invite a European prince to take the Mexican throne, they had started to consider the possibility of imposing a brief "enlightened" dictatorship that could restore order to the country and give the political class time to find a constitution that was more suited to the needs and customs of the Mexican people.[39]

The many failings of Bustamante's 1837–41 government were finally beginning to grate. The centralists' dream that Bustamante would be able to give the government formed in 1837 the kind of vigor that had become associated with his 1830–32 administration had never materialized. The expectation that he would bring order and stability to Mexico was far from fulfilled. The hope that he would bring about the reconquest of Texas had been frustrated, and the belief that he would be capable of placing the country's economy on a sound footing had been disappointed. During the three years of Bustamante's presidency Mexico had suffered a stream of rebellions, including the bloody federalist revolts of 1839 and 1840, the latter having taken place in the very heart of the capital. The plan to send an expeditionary army to Texas had not been carried out, and what was worse, Tabasco and Yucatán had been up in arms since 1840 and little was being done to quell their respective rebellions. Likewise, in the northern provinces, scant assistance was being offered to those communities exposed to the devastation caused by Indian raids. The war with France had done little to enhance the government's prestige, and Bustamante was blamed for what was perceived as the eventual pathetic capitulation to the aggressor's demands. His hands tied by the 1836 Constitution, there was very little Bustamante could do to reverse his government's misfortunes.

Bustamante's government had been unable to solve the perennial financial crises that crippled the country. In terms of factional politics, he had lost the support of the party of order and the centralists since he had flirted with the moderate federalists in 1838 and had shown himself indecisive during both the conflict with France and in relation to the federalist rebels of 1839. The fact that he was taken prisoner in the National Palace in 1840 was seen by many as proof that he was weak as well. He was hated by the radical federalists, who had seen his government crush all the rebellions they had organized, including the 1840 coup in the capital. The moderates felt betrayed after they had been led to believe that they would play an active part in his government and that he would bring back an amended version of the 1824 Constitution. In brief, the majority of the political class was against him. Sooner or later a new revolt was bound to get under way, and on this occasion, Santa Anna was prepared to saddle his horse. Almost ten years after he had last rebelled against the government (Bustamante's previous government, at that) in January 1832, Santa Anna once more abandoned the quiet life of Manga de Clavo to participate in the political life of the republic.

He was much sought after by the different interested parties. In what was already characteristic of his involvement in previous *pronunciamientos*, he was invited by others to take action, and when he did so, he stressed that he was intervening as a mediator rather than as the instigator of the rebellion. In this instance, he started to express his discontent eight months before he actually revolted. In February 1841, the cotton growers of Veracruz sent a delegation to see him at Manga de Clavo. Their interests were threatened by the British imports that had been introduced in Tampico. They were hoping he would use his "patriotism" to support their cause, ensuring that the government fulfilled its protectionist policies, despite the fact that he was not part of the government. He obliged by writing a public letter to Bustamante in which he demanded that the president put a stop to foreign imports. Tornel, in turn, took it upon himself to represent the interests of the tobacco growers of Xalapa and Orizaba and published an equally incensed pamphlet.[40]

With the province of Yucatán up in arms, Bustamante responded by appointing Santa Anna head of the expeditionary army that was to be sent to quell the uprising. Santa Anna was not prepared to comply. No doubt he remembered the difficult time he had endured there back in 1824. To be posted to Yucatán at this juncture would amount to being sent into exile. He would be too far from the capital to play a part in the imminent revolution. Nevertheless, he did not refuse to go. Instead he simply took his time getting prepared for the expedition. It was at this stage that another aggrieved party sent a delegate to persuade him to come to their aid: the merchant lobby.[41]

An English gentleman by the name of Francisco Morphy visited Santa Anna at Manga de Clavo twice and then went to see General Mariano Paredes y Arrillaga in Guadalajara. Representing the interests of foreign (and in particular British) merchants, Morphy asked Santa Anna and Paredes y Arrillaga to put pressure on the government to remove all taxes on foreign imports. Santa Anna obliged him by writing another letter to Bustamante demanding, on this occasion, that he abolished the levies on foreign merchandise. In coming to the aid of Morphy's merchants and the veracruzano cotton growers, Santa Anna was, in essence, defending opposed interests. The former wanted free market economics, while the latter favored protectionist policies. What they had in common was their opposition to Bustamante and to the taxes that were crippling them. Santa Anna was prepared to uphold their claims on the basis that they could help him bring down Bustamante. There is little doubt that once the rebellion erupted, Santa Anna and Paredes y Arrillaga had the full financial backing of what were particu-

larly influential lobbies: the foreign merchant community and the tobacco and cotton lobbies of Veracruz. To be fair, as is seen in the following chapter, Santa Anna's minister of finance, Ignacio Trigueros,
would try to accomplish the near impossible aim of pleasing these two
opposed economic groups once the santanistas came to power.[42]

August 1841 saw the advent of what has been described as the Triangular Revolt. The first player to move into action was the profoundly
reactionary, elitist, and hard-drinking General Mariano Paredes y Arrillaga, who launched his pronunciamiento of Guadalajara on 8 August. In
his plan, Paredes y Arrillaga called for the creation of a new congress,
the sole purpose of which would be to reform the 1836 charter. He also
demanded that the Supreme Conservative Power name one individual
who would be given extraordinary powers to oversee the peaceful transition from the current government to the new one.[43]

Santa Anna, albeit abstaining from committing himself to supporting Paredes y Arrillaga's revolt in Jalisco, made his views on Bustamante's regime known in a letter he wrote to Juan Nepomuceno Almonte
on 24 August 1841. He accused Bustamante of destroying the intent of
the 1824 Constitution, crushing the hopes that had been placed in the
1836 charter, of being unable to pacify the departments, of not defending the country's coast, of overtaxing the people, and of doing nothing
to regain Texas. He was unequivocal in presenting Paredes y Arrillaga
as an honorable man with good intentions. Following a similar path to
that which he had taken in 1832, he offered to mediate between Paredes
y Arrillaga and the government. The following day a crowd of jarochos
gathered in the main square of Veracruz and forced the town council
to call an emergency meeting in which it was resolved that all taxes on
foreign imports would be abolished and that the tobacco monopoly
was to be dismantled in the region. Over the next two days the town
councils of Xalapa, Orizaba, and Córdoba backed the demands made
in Veracruz on the night of the 25th. They all called for Santa Anna to
defend their cause. Then, on 27 August, Santa Anna gave orders preventing the customs house in the port from sending any more money
to Mexico City and made his way to Perote where fifteen hundred men
were waiting for him.[44]

From Perote Santa Anna wrote another lengthy letter to Almonte so that Almonte could acquaint the president with his concerns and the reason why he had moved to the Fortress of San Carlos. He was returning to the political scene "not to perturb society" but "as a peaceful mediator." He reiterated the views he had expressed in his letter of 24 August. True to form, he claimed that many were those who said "no more [political] parties." What was required was patriotic unity. In the present circumstances, "without commerce . . ., without agriculture, without an economy, without an army, without laws that may protect the growth of our people and industry, without a government, in the end, our perdition is not uncertain." He stressed that the revolt in Jalisco was not an isolated cry in the wilderness. It was the "penetrating cry of a generous people tired of suffering." He urged Bustamante to listen.[45]

Much to Bustamante's horror, his faithful aide General Valencia, who had played such an important role in quelling the revolt by Urrea and Gómez Farías the previous summer, took the Ciudadela barracks in the capital on 31 August and launched the *pronunciamiento* of 4 September. Valencia stated that his aims were to obey the will of the people and that this had been eloquently expressed in the *pronunciamiento* of Guadalajara. Valencia proclaimed that the people did not want a tyrant, and he went on to stress the need to forge a new constituent congress. Unlike Paredes y Arrillaga, who believed the Supreme Conservative Power should name a provisional president, Valencia believed such an individual should be chosen by a popular junta. After much deliberation, the Supreme Conservative Power finally gave Bustamante emergency powers, and he immediately set about organizing the defense of the government, declaring the capital to be in a state of siege.[46]

On 9 September, from the Fortress of San Carlos in Perote, Santa Anna made his own revolutionary plan known and started his march toward the capital. In the open letter addressed to Bustamante in the form of a published pamphlet on 13 September, including a copy of his Plan of Perote of the 9th, he justified his decision to take up arms against the government. He claimed that the 1836 Constitution had never been in accordance with his principles or those that inspired the plans that brought about the end of the radical government of 1833. By wresting all power away from the executive, the new constitution made governing Mexico at a time of conflict a near impossibility. The urgent responses required to organize an army, tackle the country's significant diplomatic problems with France, and reform the country's financial and judicial systems were simply not possible under the Seven Laws. With adventurers still running amok in Texas, and with Tabasco and Yucatán in flames, it was about time the government became "strong and vigorous." Texas was waiting to be reconquered. The constitution needed to be reformed. Tabasco and Yucatán had to be brought back into the fold. He reminded Bustamante that he had offered to mediate between him and the rebels. He criticized the president for ignoring his letters. He had been given no choice but to join the revolutionary movement. Proving his point that the 1836 Constitution did not work, he accused the Supreme Conservative Power, of all institutions, of being in breach of article 18 of the 1836 charter for having given Bustamante emergency powers. As was expressed in the actual Plan of Perote of 9 September, Santa Anna was demanding the removal of Bustamante as the head of the executive, that General Valencia's Plan of 4 September be endorsed, and that all Mexicans should leave aside their factional differences and join in a "conciliatory embrace."[47]

Despite Bustamante's attempts to resist the revolt, it became evident that he was alone as Paredes y Arrillaga and Santa Anna's respective forces made their way to the capital to join Valencia. By 27 September, the three rebel forces converged in the Archbishop's Palace in Tacubaya, on the outskirts of Mexico City. Having succeeded in forcing Bustamante to accept a truce, Paredes y Arrillaga, Valencia, and Santa Anna thrashed out what was to become the Bases de Tacubaya. With this plan, promulgated on 29 September, a temporary dictatorship was to be established with the objective of calling a new Congress to devise a new constitution. Despite the ambitions of Paredes y Arrillaga and Valencia, Santa Anna managed to persuade them to let him take the lead once more.

In a final and desperate bid to rally support for his cause, Bustamante proclaimed the restoration of the federalist charter on 30 September. Hoping this would inspire the moderate and radical federalists to come to his aid, Bustamante reorganized his defenses, and between 2 and 4 October the capital was exposed once more to the horrors of war.

Cannons once again pounded the city center and there were bloody street fights. In the end Bustamante was forced to face the inevitable. He finally met with Santa Anna on 5 October at Punta del Río, outside Mexico City, and they formally agreed the following day to end all hostilities, with Bustamante accepting the Bases de Tacubaya and agreeing to be replaced by Santa Anna as provisional president.[48]

On 7 October Santa Anna marched into a battered, tired, and distrustful Mexico City. The repeated revolts and the short lifespan of most of the presidencies that had succeeded Guadalupe Victoria's record-setting full four-year term in office were beginning to take their toll on people's patience and faith in politics. It is possible to appreciate from the observations of Fanny Calderón de la Barca and Carlos María de Bustamante that the populace was no longer in the mood to cheer and welcome yet another new political dawn. According to Doña Fanny, "not a solitary *viva* was heard." According to Don Carlos María there was hardly anybody in the streets, the Church was poorly lit, and Santa Anna did not even go to the cathedral to attend the *Te Deum* that was sung in his honor. The following morning the expression on "the faces of the inhabitants of Mexico City, victors and vanquished, [was] one of mourning." Unperturbed by the population's ostensible lack of enthusiasm for his return to power, Santa Anna went ahead with the investiture ceremony on 10 October 1841 and initiated what would be his longest and most successful term in office.[49]

Part 4
A Road Paved with Good Intentions, 1841–1848

The road to hell is paved with good intentions.

Proverb

10. The *Santanista* Project, 1841–1844

The British minister plenipotentiary, Richard Pakenham, summarized the implications of the Bases de Tacubaya as follows: "[For] at least a year, General Santa Anna will, according to the plan proclaimed by him and his adherents, be invested with almost absolute power." He noted that unlike in the previous revolts Santa Anna had led, "his success has been most rapid—I might almost say unopposed." He also pointed out that "persons of every party and of the most opposite political opinions have supported his undertaking, apparently from the impression that any change from the order of things previously existing would be for the better." The Bases de Tacubaya caused little discontent. The *pronunciamientos* that were launched to oppose them were exceptional. In the south, Nicolás Bravo and Juan Álvarez joined forces and issued the Plan of Chilpancingo against "the odious tyrannical dictatorship" that was being ushered in. However, their voice of dissent did not stir the wave of support they expected. The government Santa Anna forged was able to administer the republic for three years without having to quell *pronunciamientos* on a regular basis.[1]

The result of the Triangular Revolt was the creation of a temporary dictatorship intended to restore order while a new constituent Congress was formed. Santa Anna, who for once opted to stay in the capital, was still in fine form at forty-seven. According to U.S. Minister Plenipotentiary Waddy Thompson, he "was about five feet ten inches high, with a finely proportioned person. His complexion is olive cast," and Thompson had never seen "a more striking and finely formed head and face."[2] For an entire year, from 10 October 1841 to 26 October 1842, he led his

government. It was the longest spell he had spent in the capital while
serving as president. Although eventually he could not resist the temp-
tation to leave, especially when faced with yet another uncooperative
Congress, he did return six months later, and remained in Mexico City
for a further seven months (4 March–4 October 1843). His presence in
the capital meant that he was able to oversee the drafting of the 1843
Constitution by the Junta de Notables (Junta of worthies) that replaced
the awkward Congress of '42. As a result the constitution that was presented to him was to his liking. He was also present at the inauguration of the Bases Orgánicas, duly approved on 8 June 1843, and was
ceremoniously sworn in on the 12th; and he was in Mexico City for the
primary and secondary elections (13 August and 4 September, respectively) that were organized as stipulated by the new Constitution. To
ensure that regardless of the electoral results, these could not damage
the santanista project, he reserved the right to nominate one third of
the members of the Senate. However, even then he was unable to stay
away from his lands for longer than eight months. He did not wait for
the results but returned to Veracruz on 5 October, this time leaving a
close friend, General Valentín Canalizo, as acting president. He was at
El Encero when he heard that he had won the presidential elections. Although the Bases Orgánicas specified that he was to begin his five-year
term as constitutional president on 1 February 1844, he did not return
to the capital until June. Old habits die hard.[3]

The santanista government formed in 1841 was one of the most stable
governments of independent Mexico. The four santanistas Santa Anna
appointed to run the ministries of relations (José María Bocanegra),
justice (Pedro Vélez), war (José María Tornel), and finance (Ignacio
Trigueros) remained, with a few minor spells of absence, at the head of
their respective ministries for the greater part of this period (1841–44).
The only significant upset occurred because of a lack of preparation
for the congressional elections of 1842, due to the government's many
other pressing concerns, which resulted, much to Santa Anna's dismay, in the election to the Constituent Congress on 6 March of a majority of renowned federalist deputies. This problem, however, was simply
overcome in the winter of 1842–43, when Santa Anna characteristically
returned to Veracruz, claiming ill health, and appointed General Nico-

lás Bravo acting president, leaving to him the unsavory task of clos-
ing down Congress on 19 December. After the Constituent Congress of
1842 was replaced with a handpicked santanista-traditionalist-central-
ist Junta of Notables on 2 January 1843, Bravo resigned toward the end
of February 1843, and Santa Anna returned to the capital with a more
receptive legislative branch in place.[4]

The Bases de Tacubaya allowed Santa Anna to impose order in the
country and create a stable context in which to forge a new and liberal
constitution. From his point of view, "without order there can be no
laws, and without laws, there can be no freedom."[5] On becoming president he pledged to direct all his efforts toward the glorification of the
nation, ensuring that there was harmony among Mexico's children and
the establishment of progressive principles worthy of this brave new
age.[6] His pride in the role he played in restoring order to the country
and giving it a new constitutional direction in which a popular representative republican system was forged was shared by his ministers.
Tornel, in his 1844 annual ministerial report, was proud of the progress
achieved during the three years the santanistas had been in power: the
1841 political plan, which "was ardently received by the nation," had already "provided [the nation] with so many hopes of a blissful future."[7]

The success of Santa Anna's government, according to the santanistas, was due initially to the Bases de Tacubaya but above all to the
1843 Constitution: the Bases Orgánicas (12 June 1843). The Bases de
Tacubaya created the peaceful conditions that made possible the drafting of a liberal and pragmatic constitution reflecting the customs of the
nation (after the 1842 Congress was closed). As Santa Anna stressed
on 13 June 1843 during the inauguration of this constitution, this was a
charter that was to facilitate popular elections, provide order, and guarantee the people's rights. It paid attention to the country's customs; it
made use of the lessons learned from the previous constitutional ex-
periments they had endured; and although it ensured that the different powers (executive, legislative, and judicial) remained separate, it
gave the executive power the necessary resources to make its "energetic
hand" firm in the name of progress.[8]

The Bases Orgánicas consolidated a centralist republic. This was
in line with what had been santanista political thought since 1834.

Although Santa Anna had remained ambivalent over his colleagues' adoption of the centralist cause in the mid-1830s, by 1841 he had come around to accepting their logic. In his own words: "It is good for a country made up of weak heterogeneous parts to become confederated into a strong united whole; but it is an inversion of the simplest of principles to break up a strong homogeneous whole into many weak members." As his government took on the major tasks of reconquering Texas and bringing an end to the secessionist revolt in Yucatán (1840–43), Santa Anna stressed that "we cannot allow to exist among us local interests that are contrary to the general interest [of the nation]." Aware of the growing threat posed by the United States, he had finally become a staunch centralist, convinced that a strong united front was the only means to surviving the horrors of a war against the Colossus of the North. His centralism in 1841–44 coincided as well with a period in which the santanistas were in power. The key ministers of war and finance were also veracruzanos.[9]

The 1843 charter endorsed the usual division of powers, abandoning the fourth power (the Supremo Poder Conservador) created in the 1836 Constitution. The government was to be elected, and thus the electoral system had to be both popular and representative. However, suffrage was further restricted in the 1843 charter. Only men who earned over two hundred pesos a year (one hundred more than under the 1836 charter) could vote. The reduction in the franchise was significant when it is remembered that up to 75 percent of the adult male population participated in the elections of the 1820s. Having said this, the suffrage enshrined in the 1843 charter remained higher than that of Britain, where only 4.2 percent of the adult population could vote at the time. Congress was to continue to have two chambers, one of deputies and one of senators. However, the Bases Orgánicas ensured that only the elite could become members of the Senate: only large landowners, mine owners, proprietors/merchants, and industrialists whose property was worth over forty thousand pesos could become senators. Generals, bishops, governors, and former senators could also aspire to join the upper house. The Executive had greater powers than those it had been awarded in the 1824 and 1836 Constitutions. The president was still accountable to Congress but was free to take a number of critical

decisions without first obtaining the approval of the legislative chambers. Freedom of the press was permitted but controlled. The Constitution explicitly forbade the publication of literary or journalistic texts
that attacked the Catholic faith. Roman Catholicism was, once more,
formally described as the official religion of the state. The military and
ecclesiastical *fueros* were also explicitly guaranteed.[10]

The santanistas' belief, by 1843, in the further limitation of suffrage
stemmed from their fear of the political participation of the masses—a
fear that had its origins in the 1828 Parián Riot. This classist resolution to keep the majority out of politics was shared by traditionalists,
moderates, and even some radicals. To quote Santa Anna: "Our people,
because of their [poor] education, still need to be led by the hand like
a child; although it goes without saying that he who leads them must
have good intentions."[11]

However, this somewhat negative view of the masses was counter-
balanced by a passionate conviction in educating the people. The Bases
Orgánicas stated that in seven years it was to be hoped that suffrage
would be opened up to anybody who could read and write, regardless
of their financial situation. The educational reforms carried out by the
santanista government from 1841 to 1844 were truly extraordinary. As
an example, by 1845 there were 2,200 children registered in 56 schools
in Zacatecas, and in Puebla there were 3,260 children attending 38
schools. In the state of Mexico alone there were 46,698 children going to 960 schools. Compared to the number of schools that had been
in operation only a decade earlier, these figures were truly astounding.
This educational revolution was possible thanks to the decree of 26
October 1842, which converted the Compañía Lancasteriana into the
Dirección General de Instrucción Primaria. Tornel, who served as president of the Compañía Lancasteriana from 1840 to 1847, played a key
role in directing this extensive educational reform.[12]

It is important to stress here that although Tornel and the santanistas' educational reforms displayed their enlightened and liberal values,
they were also an expression of a populist tendency within *santanismo*
that was not common among the other political factions. Spectacular
reforms such as the educational ones carried out by the santanistas between 1841 and 1844 undoubtedly had a major impact in transforming

the populist and popular Santa Anna into the much revered patriarchal figure he became in the eyes of the urban masses. The santanistas ensured they had the support of the populace by flamboyantly promoting free education.

Santa Anna had already shown a commitment to promoting education as acting governor of Veracruz in the late 1820s. He was outspoken in stressing that improving primary and secondary education was one of his government's priorities. In a list he drafted noting what he had worked to achieve between 1841 and 1844, the organization of a healthy educational system came third out of the nine areas he considered needed to be developed. His government's achievements in the field of education were aptly detailed in the 1844 report of the minister of justice and education, Manuel Baranda. In historian Anne Staples's view, Baranda's report was one of the most complete and sophisticated of the nineteenth century. Baranda's conclusions were indeed a tribute to one of the most remarkable success stories of Santa Anna's government: "The state of most of our schools is brilliant, especially those this Directorate established. Not only are the basics considered essential in any popular education learned there; a whole range of other subjects are offered . . . religion, mathematics, history."[13]

The fact that Santa Anna was equally dedicated to serving as the patron of a number of important welfare and charitable establishments, such as the Mexico City Poor House, must be seen as a parallel expression of his populism. According to historian Silvia Marina Arrom, "the dramatic recovery of the Poor House under Santa Anna's presidency reflected a broad effort to improve the delivery of public services. . . . The positive experience of the Poor House during three of his early administrations—1841–42 and 1843–44 as well as 1833–34 . . .—suggests that this much maligned figure may be due for a reassessment."[14]

Representative of Santa Anna's populism was his willingness to give away land to the people living and working on his estates. He did not forget the lessons he had learned as a royalist land reform administrator in 1819–21. Helping homeless families settle in the communities of Medellín, Xamapa, San Diego, and Tamarindo had proven a successful way of pacifying the region. As an example, toward the end of Santa Anna's 1841–44 term in office, he granted the people of the village of Apasapa in Veracruz a farm (*fundo legal*) of twelve hundred *varas*, which included the lands of Arrieles, Pueblo Viejo, Mapastla, and El Riego. Henceforth, the lands specified in his donation of 2 November 1844 were to belong to the people of Apasapa. He claimed he had been moved to make this donation after seeing the dire straits in which these people found themselves. The people of Apasapa gave him their "most expressive thanks" for this generous gift. His ability to win the hearts of the popular classes in Veracruz through actions such as the Apasapa donation and those in the capital and elsewhere by endorsing a dramatic literacy campaign cannot be underestimated.[15]

Together with Santa Anna's populist policies, another fundamental characteristic of his 1841–44 government was its determination to strengthen the regular army and its commitment to guaranteeing army privileges. On a national level the military was his most important clientele. One of the beliefs that differentiated the santanistas from the other factions was their dedication to enlarging the regular army. Unlike the conservatives of the late 1840s, the santanistas believed that the needs of the army were more important than those of the Church or those of the hacendados—as was captured in one critical and cynical slogan of the time: "The Nation for the Army; the Army for Santa Anna." By 1844 the figures given in Tornel's ministerial report were proof in themselves of how the santanistas had reduced the militias and enlarged the regular army during the three years they had been in power: there were 20,348 permanent troops and 6,372 civic militias. Tornel was still hoping in 1844 to increase the regular army to 32,263 men.[16]

Tornel's militarism, like that of the santanistas in general, went beyond the purely pragmatic belief that the army deserved to be fully supported because it was the only institution that could realistically guarantee peace and independence. For Tornel, the army was not simply "an isolated or passive institution" but was representative of the nation per se: "Its history is that of the politics of the people to whom it belongs." From this he deduced that "to know the army . . . it is essential that you become acquainted with the country . . . and do not distinguish its physiognomy from that of the nation itself." As I have noted elsewhere, santanista militarism represented an early version of that militaristic ideology that, at the beginning of the twentieth century, became common in most of Latin America—what Brian Loveman and Thomas Davies defined as "the politics of antipolitics."[17]

While it is true, as one historian noted, that "the duration of the governments depended on the loyalty of the army and this depended on a regular pay and the concession of multiple privileges," and that in comparative terms Santa Anna's success can be understood in that "he always gave everything to the army," it would be wrong to forget the ideological weight the santanistas allocated to their consistent support of the regular army. Their military ideology represented a political platform that claimed to be anti-parties. The santanistas projected the notion that they were interested only in the well-being of the nation and that, as a result, they were detached from the squabbling and the damaging divisive feuding of party politics. Santa Anna did not participate in corrosive party or parliamentary conflicts. If he and his men intervened in politics it was because they had no other choice, because it was what the nation expected from them when the political parties had brought the country to yet another dead end.[18]

Santa Anna was already cultivating this brand of political thought in the 1820s. He repeatedly presented himself as not belonging to a particular party and as being a soldier, first and foremost. He claimed he was an arbitrator, a mediator, a guarantor of peace and order, a republican, a liberator, and a selfless patriot who was prepared to defend the mother country against all foreign aggressions. His depiction of himself and, by association, of the army as the defenders of an antipolitical and patriotic movement played a critical part in turning the regular army into a santanista institution.

While there was never any ambiguity about the santanistas' commitment to supporting the regular army, the same cannot be said about their attitude toward the Church. Regardless of santanista discourse, they demanded a series of loans and found different ways to ensure that the Church financed the resurrection of the army. The santanistas were like most factions in the way that they were intolerant Roman Catholics; they were like the traditionalist-conservatives in the way that they paid lip service to defending Church privileges; but they were like the radicals in the way that they actually believed in expropriating Church property if the financial needs of the state and the army demanded such a measure. Santa Anna's approach to the Church during his 1841–44 government was characterized precisely by this conditional arrangement. The 1843 Constitution protected the Church's *fueros*, and Santa Anna decreed that the Jesuits expelled from Mexico since 1767 could return as well as the Sisters of Charity. On the other hand, he confiscated a number of Church properties, including the Pious Fund of the California missions. He also asked for five hundred thousand pesos from the archbishop of Mexico. The archbishop agreed to give him two-fifths of that sum.[19]

Ignacio Trigueros's economic reforms during his term as minister of finance (1841–44) illustrate only too well the extent to which the santanistas were pragmatic in terms of their economic policies. Trigueros's down-to-earth veracruzano approach mirrored the way that the santanistas and the Church struck a pragmatic relationship whereby they conditionally supported each other. Trigueros initiated his term in office by ensuring that all of those institutions, lobbies, and individuals that had backed the 1841 Triangular Revolt were given their reward. Vast sums of money were injected into the army. The tobacco contractors, whose acquisition of the tobacco monopoly under Bustamante had not been as profitable as they had hoped, were released from the contract. The entrepreneur and conspirator Francisco Morphy made a killing, acting as an intermediary in the negotiations that led to the dissolution of the monopoly on 12 November. Morphy was given preferential treatment again when Trigueros abolished the use of the much abused copper coins, by receiving the exclusive contract to buy all the old coins once they went out of circulation. The tobacco planters of Veracruz were also rewarded when, on 20 December, the import of foreign tobacco was forbidden. Likewise, the cotton lobby was included among the clientele that benefited from Santa Anna and Trigueros's early legislative spree, when it was determined that all seized contraband cotton, previously sold at public auction, was to be burned immediately.[20]

In terms of economic policy, Trigueros carried out a rather complex balancing act between free market economics and committed protectionism in an attempt to answer the opposed needs of the key states of Puebla and Veracruz. Above all, he was particularly thorough in seeking ways of either raising existing taxes or inventing new ones. He imposed a whole range of new taxes on "urban properties, rustic properties, industrial establishments, . . . salaries, professions . . . , luxury items, and a monthly direct tax of half a real." The amortization tax went up 15 percent; indirect taxes were imposed on the sale of cart wheels, the use of outside drainpipes, and postal services; direct taxes were extended to include a monthly contribution (to be paid in advance) from all the established businesses in the country, the notorious *alcabala* (a direct tax on any form of sale); and on 20 April 1843 the richest proprietors of the nation were forced to pay an emergency tax that in just nine days raised a total of 270,000 pesos. There was also a strong push to promote the growth of Mexico's nascent industry, and the Banco de Avío was replaced with a new Junta de Industria.[21]

The santanistas succeeded in raising both in 1843 and 1844 the highest income for this period through taxation (19,602,180 pesos in 1843 and 20,592,058 pesos in 1844). If the santanista economic project failed, this was because such a tax system, in order to function properly, required a well-organized and efficient collection system, which did not exist at the time. The spectacular rise in taxes was unfortunately outweighed by an even more dramatic rise in expenses, which meant that the nation's deficit continued to increase regardless of the large sums raised through taxation. The fact that Santa Anna and his cronies became significantly wealthier during these years, with all of them acquiring a number of magnificent haciendas, contributed to the tide of discontent that ultimately brought down the government in 1844. The provincial middle-class boy that Santa Anna had once been became what one historian described as "in modern terms a multimillionaire, owning according to his own account 483,000 acres in the department of Veracruz." Santa Anna would be at pains to demonstrate that he owed his wealth to twenty years of running a hacienda and the careful investment of his salaries as general and president. Understandably, nobody believed him. While his financial situation had benefited from marrying María Inés de la Paz García, the profits his lands had brought him, and the salaries he had earned as a high-ranking officer and president—the sheer scale of his wealth, acquired over a relatively recent period—would appear to demonstrate that like so many other Mexican presidents, he had helped himself to the national treasury.[22]

Not surprisingly, once the santanistas consolidated their hold on power in 1841, they exercised some censorship over publications that criticized their administration or that, in their view, abused that freedom of the press in which they theoretically believed. On 14 January 1843 the law of 8 April 1839 was reinstated; previously passed under Santa Anna's 1839 interim presidency, it fined heavily those editors or printers who were found guilty of disturbing the public peace with their publications in the Department of Mexico. On 16 January it was given national status, applying to the entire republic. Consequently, newspapers such as El Cosmopolita, El Restaurador, and El Voto Nacional closed down. However, although the santanistas became increasingly heavy-handed with those newspapers that were critical of their politics and policies, they did not indulge in the kind of repression that characterized other regimes at the time. Santa Anna did not have the equivalent of Argentine Juan Manuel de Rosas' paramilitary thugs la mazorca (más horca: more hanging) to intimidate the opposition.[23]

While the main principles of santanismo shared to varying degrees a number of aspects defended by the other political factions of the period (e.g., the populist tendencies of the radical federalists, the moderates' belief in reforming the country gradually, or the centralist values of the nascent conservative movement), there were two particularly salient characteristics of their ideology that distinguished their proposal from the rest. The first, as has been seen, was their rampant militarism, tied in with a deep-rooted disrespect for party politics. The second, and probably the more obvious, was their complete faith in the abilities of General Antonio López de Santa Anna. Valentín Gómez Farías became the visible leader of the radical federalists. Manuel Gómez Pedraza became that of the moderates. Anastasio Bustamante and Nicolás Bravo represented the centralist traditionalists at different junctures. But none of these factions saw in these individuals anything other than the preferred leader of the moment. Gómez Pedraza was in fact superseded by José Joaquín de Herrera and, by the end of the decade, by that former santanista zealot Mariano Arista. The radicals relied on other politicians and intellectuals to further their cause. For the moderates, the thinker and politician Mariano Otero was probably more influential than any of the politicians who led his party. With the santanistas this approach was difficult to conceive of. They did uphold a whole series of coherent political ideas. However, all of these ultimately revolved around the belief that there was only one Mexican talented enough to govern the country, and this was Santa Anna.

The most blatant expression of this dimension of *santanismo* was the personality cult that was forged around Santa Anna during the 1841–44 government. This entailed the hosting of regular fiestas and poetry recitals in his honor. It involved placing his portrait in all public buildings, erecting statues of him in main squares throughout the republic, and naming streets and theaters after him. The remains of Santa Anna's amputated leg were disinterred from Manga de Clavo and transported in a glass case, like a saint's relics, to the capital in the late summer of 1842. On the anniversary of the date Iturbide liberated Mexico City, 27 September 1821, Santa Anna's leg was ceremoniously buried in a magnificent monument that was erected for the purpose in the cemetery of Santa Paula. A new theater was erected in the capital that seated eight thousand people, called the Gran Teatro de Santa Anna. Toward the end of the regime, he unveiled during the celebration of his saint's day, 13 June 1844, a statue of himself looking heroic, pointing toward the north, giving it to be understood that he was resolved to reconquer Texas. By then, though, with his popularity on the wane, there were those who said he was pointing to the national treasury, yearning to steal more taxpayers' money.[24]

Santa Anna would look back on his 1841–43 government with a sense of achievement. While the Bases de Tacubaya were in place, he recalled that peace and order had been preserved. The first railway in Mexico was started between Veracruz and the interior. The customs house and the wharf in Veracruz were improved. The old Parián market in Mexico City was destroyed and replaced with the vast main square known thereafter as the Zócalo. The controversial and problematic copper coin was abolished. Foreign relations were advanced, and Mexico's territory expanded with the annexation of Soconusco (which, having belonged to Guatemala following independence, was thus integrated into Chiapas). Carlos María de Bustamante, one of Santa Anna's fiercest critics by this time, was prepared to admit that "Santa Anna's enemies multiplied [because of his reforms], even though he acted with upright intentions."[25]

Santa Anna's government, as might have been expected after what the caudillo had said about Bustamante's pathetic attempts to reconquer Texas, turned this into one of his administration's main objectives. There is no doubt that such a stance met with the support of most of the population. However, it was a stance that caused significant tension, not only with the U.S. government but also with the British diplomatic corps in Mexico, especially after Queen Victoria's government officially recognized the independence of Texas. General Tornel, whom Pakenham described as "the member of the government who possesses most influence with the president," went to see him to tell him "in strong words" what he thought of the British recognition of Texan independence. Pakenham had no choice but to tell his superiors in London that their hope that he could persuade the Mexican government to recognize the independence of Texas would not be fulfilled. In part, he claimed this was because the government, being "a military government," needed "a plausible excuse for a large military establishment; and this excuse the present government find in the projected reconquest of Texas." In part, Pakenham also admitted that were was "a question of national pride or conceit, a sore subject with almost every Mexican; and that it would try the strength and popularity of any administration, however enlightened and disinterested, that should recommend the final relinquishment of what is still considered a part of the national domain."[26]

Although Pakenham appreciated the Mexican government's position regarding the recognition of the independence of Texas, he still proposed that it should do so, for this would create a buffer state between Mexico and the increasingly hostile United States. Pakenham also warned the Mexican government that if it persevered with its intention of reconquering the province it ran the risk of pushing the Texans into seeking annexation by the United States. Bocanegra replied to Pakenham that the government could not and would not change its line of conduct on this matter. The war against Texas would be carried out until Mexico's rights over that part of its territory were reinstated.[27]

Santa Anna set in motion the reconquest of Texas from the moment he returned to power. In early December 1841 orders were dispatched to General Mariano Arista in Monterrey to renew hostilities with Texas.

Although the results the Mexican forces were to obtain between 1841 and 1844 were not significant, they served the purpose of confirming that Santa Anna's determination to reconquer Texas was sincere. Colonel Rafael Vásquez with four hundred men took San Antonio de Béxar from 5 to 8 March 1842 but returned to Mexico after capturing the town. Captain Ramón Valera led another detachment into the province. Although his men failed to take Goliad and Refugio, they did defeat three hundred Lipan Apache and Tancahue Indians on the Santa Gertrudis River. Colonel Antonio Canales succeeded in defeating a Texan detachment in Lipantitlán on 7 July 1842 and frustrated the Texans' intention of mounting a counteroffensive that went as far south as Matamoros. General Adrián Woll took San Antonio de Béxar again on 10 September 1842, captured a significant number of prisoners who were subsequently sent to Mexico City, and took on the Texan forces sent to liberate San Antonio at the battle of Salado Creek of 18 September, leading the onslaught that became known as Dawson's Massacre. In response, the Texan government attempted to punish the Mexican incursions by sending their own war parties into Mexico. These attacks were even less successful than the Mexican incursions. The Texan raid of Santa Fe in New Mexico resulted in more Texans being made prisoner and sent to Perote. On 25 December 1842 General Pedro de Ampudia repulsed a Texan attack on Mier and captured around two hundred men, who were dispatched to Mexico City.[28]

Santa Anna was magnanimous with some prisoners, but his resolve to punish the Texan rebels remained undiminished. On his saint's day, 13 June 1842, he freed the Santa Fe prisoners and those seized by Vásquez, and told them to "make public the fact that the Mexican people are as generous toward the defeated as brave on the battlefield." However, when 114 Texan prisoners seized in the battle of Mier escaped from prison and were subsequently recaptured, his initial response was to have them all executed. In the end, the intervention of Pakenham led Santa Anna to moderate his original order. Nevertheless, one in every ten of these prisoners was executed.[29]

His commitment to reconquering Texas found expression, as well, in the way that he rejected a Texan attempt to bribe him into recognizing the province's independence. One James Hamilton wrote to him on

13 January 1842, offering to pay the Mexican government five million dollars, implying that two hundred thousand dollars would be paid to Santa Anna for the favor. His reply on 18 February was full of indignation: "[It] is an insult and infamy unworthy of a gentleman." But with the passing of time, it became increasingly evident that the reconquest of Texas was an impossible dream. Santa Anna maintained in public a commitment to leading a merciless war against Texas, but he started to show signs of being prepared to listen to proposals for a peaceful solution. He freed Texan Lieutenant Governor James W. Robinson and talked the situation over with him at Manga de Clavo. An armistice was approved in September 1843 precisely for this purpose, even though no agreements were made.[30]

It was only at the very end of his 1841–44 spell in power that he realized his government had little choice but to recognize the independence of Texas. After three years of attempting to reconquer the province, it remained independent. The United States government's expansionist ideals were becoming more obvious, and there was a real danger that Texas would be annexed into the Union. Political divisions were once more tearing the country apart, making any attempt to regain Texas unrealistic. If a major expedition was miraculously launched against Texas, at this late stage there was every probability that the United States would become involved, turning what would have been a domestic conflict into an international war. The British recommendation that Mexico recognize Texan independence, first mooted by Pakenham in 1842, suddenly made a lot of sense, especially given that it now came with an offer of military support should the United States attempt to seize the estranged province and any other northern province of Mexico.

Charles Bankhead, the British minister plenipotentiary, went to meet Santa Anna at Guadalupe, on his way to Querétaro to lead the government's army against the rebels in Guadalajara in November 1844. Santa Anna told Bankhead he was ready to consider ways of recognizing Texan independence, "without compromising the *amour propre* of Mexico." The boundaries of the Lone Star Republic needed to be reduced, with its territory stretching from the Colorado River (rather than the Bravo) to the River Sabina; an indemnity would be required; the British and French governments would have to guarantee that the Texan Republic respected the boundaries outlined in the treaty, and they would also have to agree to guarantee that Mexico's other borders with the United States were safeguarded. If the United States annexed Texas, Britain and France would be obliged to send troops to assist Mexico in its war against the government in Washington. One cannot help wondering what would have happened had this treaty ever been signed.[31]

A character who played a surprising role in the liberation of the Texan prisoners held in Perote was Santa Anna's wife, Inés. For the last two years of the 1841–44 government she was recurrently ill. Whether it was her illness, publicly lamented by the authorities, that led to Santa Anna spending ever less time in the capital is difficult to tell. When the U.S. minister plenipotentiary took up his post in 1842, he found Mexico City praying for Inés to get well. He observed a "magnificent procession of all the dignitaries of the church, headed by the archbishop, and numbering altogether more than twenty-thousand persons; among whom . . . were all the highest officers of the church, the army and the government." Inés's health did improve, at least enough for her to live for another two years. However, coinciding with what was the beginning of the end of Santa Anna's 1841–44 period in power, on 23 August 1844, Inés García de López de Santa Anna finally passed away at nine minutes to one in the morning, while staying in Puebla.[32]

The City of Angels, Mexico City, Xalapa, and subsequently most of the main cities of the republic pronounced themselves in mourning. In the capital the church bells started to toll for her at six in the evening on the 26th. The entire political class, including the members of the town council, were summoned to the National Palace at half past five so that they could start the solemn procession to the cathedral, where a service was held in her honor. The public ceremonies organized for Doña Inés included a whole day of prayer, which was inaugurated with another grand procession at half past eight in the morning on the 27th, followed by a funereal oration read by the canon and master Manuel Moreno y Juve.[33]

Although Santa Anna's infidelities were well-known at the time, few people were expecting him to start looking for a spouse so soon after Inés's death. Even in the case of Santa Anna, it was assumed that he would observe the customary period of mourning before seeking a new match. Santa Anna, however, had other ideas. According to one source he approached the father of one Concepción Velasco with a proposal within days of the funeral. Apparently horrified, the father prevented Santa Anna from tying the knot by marrying Señorita Concepción off to one of his nephews the day after he heard that Santa Anna was going to propose to her formally. Thwarted by Velasco's quick thinking, Santa Anna's set his sights on the young Dolores Tosta, not so much because she was beautiful (which she was) but because she was "the daughter of very rich entrepreneurs."[34]

Given that we do not have written evidence of Dolores's views on the marriage, we can only imagine what it must have been like for this fifteen-year-old girl to have been told out of the blue that she was to be married to a fifty-year-old, one-legged president. The wedding ceremony was on 3 October 1844, barely a month after the capital had so publicly mourned the death of her future husband's previous wife; Dolores gave her hand to Juan de Dios Cañedo, since Santa Anna could not be present, in the presence of the acting president, Valentín Canalizo, who served as best man. The thought of the young Dolores making her way to Xalapa to meet her famous husband that October conjures up the image of a powerless individual who must have felt some apprehension, knowing that she would have to get on with three stepchildren, two of whom were of a similar age to her, and that she would be expected to consummate the marriage with the somewhat mature general.[35]

However, what emerges from the few insights we have into Dolores's life is that she soon acquired a significant degree of control in determining where she lived and what kind of lifestyle suited her best. Despite the fact that in 1842 Santa Anna had bought the vast hacienda of El Encero, on the outskirts of Xalapa, Dolores did not settle there. Instead she returned to the capital, where she remained most of her life, even when her husband was in exile. She did not like country life, and Santa Anna was not in a position to force her to stay there. She moved into the house Santa Anna bought her in Mexico City, number 6 Calle Vergara (Calle Bolívar today) and made that her home until she died in 1886. Considering her husband's evident potency, the fact that she remained childless gives rise to speculation on the nature of the marriage or on her fertility.[36]

The few insights we have about her life suggest that "la flor de México" (Mexico's flower), as she became known, made the most of her husband's wealth and absence. On getting married Santa Anna gave Dolores 14,000 pesos' worth of jewels and presents as well as a pledge of 50,000 pesos (it being customary to offer 10 percent of the husband's property), all of which was deposited with Embil y Compañía in Havana. By the time Santa Anna died, according to Santa Anna's aide Colonel Manuel María Giménez, she owned "two good-sized properties in Mexico City and more than 150,000 pesos in jewels, all of which was hers thanks to her husband's generosity"; he provided her with a monthly allowance of 200 pesos for most of their married life, giving her 8,000 pesos in U.S. gold coins when he went into exile in 1864. Rumors abound that she enjoyed throwing extravagant parties and lived life to the full regardless of whether her husband was away at war or in exile. As historian Sara Sefchovich reminds us, "the señora loved fiestas and soirées and often organized them, sparing no costs, not caring about what could be happening to the country. If one is to believe the gossip of the time, she went on doing her thing even when there were uprisings against her husband." Juan Cordero's famous 1855 portrait of her, at the age of twenty-six, standing by a window in the National Palace, depicts her not only as a beautiful and serene young lady but also as one who clearly enjoyed displaying the latest fashions, with a distinct taste for expensive jewelry. She apparently shared that love of elaborate clothing that Fanny Calderón de la Barca found so striking in the ladies of the capital, with their dresses of rich velvet or satin, heavily embroidered with flowers of silk, mantillas, diamond earrings of extraordinary size, diamond rings "like little watches," gold chains "going three times round the neck, and touching the knees," necklaces of pear pearls "valued at twenty thousand dollars," splendid diamond brooches, sévignés, and parures.[37]

Ultimately, the impression we are left with is of a woman who made the most of her circumstances. Forced into marriage as a teenager and expected to spend the rest of her life as the wife of a man more than old enough to be her father, Dolores was nonetheless able to find ways of enjoying herself. She proved to have a noteworthy degree of independence in her decision not to live with Santa Anna for long periods of time when he was forced into exile, and she did not feel compelled to follow him wherever he went. Her decision to stay in Mexico City rather than move to Veracruz was respected, and she took advantage of her husband's wealth, finding pleasure in living the good life in the capital. She dutifully stood by her husband at a number of crucial junctures, such as his exile in 1855 or during his 1867 court-martial, when she even went to plead with President Benito Juárez to grant her husband a pardon. And she did look after the caudillo during the last two years of his life when in 1874 President Sebastián Lerdo de Tejada granted him permission at the age of eighty to return to Mexico, and he moved into her house on the Calle Vergara. According to one source, by then Dolores, having reached the age of forty-six, felt so sorry for the forgotten and vilified old man that she paid people from the street to visit him and tell him that the country still needed him. Yet she apparently refused to part with any of her money to help Santa Anna when he returned from exile and found that the government would not give him his pension. While his daughter Guadalupe gave him 150 pesos a month, and his illegitimate son José contributed 50 pesos, Dolores "answered in unequivocal terms that she would give him nothing, for she did not want to end up pesoless by contributing to her husband's extravagance."[38]

It would appear that Santa Anna and his second wife were never close. He was closer to her relatives than he was to her. According to one biographer, it was with her brother, Bonifacio Tosta, that the octogenarian general conversed most freely in the last two years of his life. Research also shows that while Dolores stayed behind in the capital, her stepfather, Luis Vidal y Rivas, accompanied Santa Anna into exile, enduring incarceration in San Juan de Ulúa together with the caudillo in 1867 as a result.[39]

In brief, although the context in which Dolores was forced to marry Santa Anna would lead us to believe that she subsequently spent the following thirty-two years condemned to live her life with a man she did not love, the reality would appear to be somewhat different. Relatively speaking, Dolores enjoyed a significant degree of independence. The fact that Santa Anna's loyal field-marshal and friend Colonel Manuel María Giménez described Dolores as having been the caudillo's "evil star in life . . . [and] after he died" may be taken as evidence in itself of the fact that she was not a submissive and subservient wife.[40]

Doña Inés's death and Santa Anna's marriage to Dolores may be seen as representative of a critical turning point in his life. The passing away of the woman who had stood by Santa Anna from the mid-1820s up until the end of his fourth presidency was in a strange way emblematic of the end of a series of close ties, alliances, and allegiances that the caudillo had developed while Doña Inés was alive. With her, many of the bonds that had kept Santa Anna's most loyal supporters together were also buried. Evidently there was no direct relation between Doña Inés's death and the figurative death of the project of the santanista generation of 1841. However, one event and the other took place at about the same time. The decline in Doña Inés's health uncannily mirrored that of the 1841–44 santanista administration.

Considering the pride and confidence Santa Anna's four ministers (Tornel, Bocanegra, Trigueros, and Baranda) exuded in the reports they presented to Congress in January 1844, the complete breakdown of the santanista leadership that was to take place in the following months was dramatic and remains difficult to understand. Tornel, Bocanegra, and Trigueros all decided to resign in circumstances that point to there having emerged a serious conflict of interests between Santa Anna and the santanista intelligentsia. The evidence would appear to suggest that there were personal and political reasons for the schism.

Tornel was the first to enter into a bitter dispute with Santa Anna. In a matter of months, a friendship that spanned two decades was in ruins. Santa Anna appeared to turn suddenly on the man who had consistently supported him as his informer in the capital, his panegyrist, his arch-conspirator and master of intrigue, his political thinker, and his pillar of support at the head of the armed forces. According to Carlos María de Bustamante, Santa Anna turned against his ever-loyal advisor and propagandist because Tornel gave himself certain presidential airs when he presented himself in Puebla in April 1844, having gone there to buy some haciendas in San Martín Tesmelucam. The main plaza of Puebla filled with a jubilant crowd who cheered him and celebrated his arrival by waving flags and throwing flowers, and the local authorities welcomed Tornel by offering him a guard of honor to accompany him during his visit. In Bustamante's words, Santa Anna was livid on hearing about this event and immediately asked Tornel to resign because "he is very jealous of his authority and will not admit any rivals."[41]

There could have been personal reasons for this rupture. Following the death of his wife, María Agustina Díez Bonilla, in October 1843, Tornel in March 1844 had married the actress Catarina Silva, with whom he had been having a notorious affair since 1839. Santa Anna might have been jealous of Tornel's relationship with the actress, and their marriage could have been the final straw that led the caudillo to order Tornel's resignation. However, the fact that Bocanegra and Trigueros also resigned suggests that there must have been other reasons for the schism—reasons that must have been of a more general nature, more political and less personal.[42]

From Tornel's perspective, Santa Anna's reluctance to remain in the capital and exercise power must have been one of his hero's most frustrating traits. For a man who clearly believed by 1841 that Mexico needed a strong energetic leader to hold the country together, Santa Anna's taste for packing his bags and returning to Veracruz whenever he had the chance must have started to grate after a while. At least for the first year the Bases de Tacubaya had been in place, the caudillo had stayed put and given the country the kind of forceful leadership Tornel believed it needed. However, thereafter, Santa Anna had spent less and less time in the capital. Had Bravo not resigned in February 1843, Santa Anna would not have left El Encero. According to some sources, the caudillo had become infatuated with his own sense of importance. It was as if he had come to believe that he was too important to be expected to look after the daily affairs of the nation.[43]

It may also be possible that Santa Anna was not lying on the numerous occasions when he stated that his preferred occupation was to look after his haciendas in the company of his family, and that he saw himself as an arbitrator and a mediator rather than as a political leader. His reluctance to consolidate his hold on power by remaining in the capital could be interpreted as evidence that he did not aspire to having absolute power or want to forge a permanent dictatorship. He clearly enjoyed the benefits of power, sacking the treasury just as many of his predecessors and successors did. He was flattered by the tributes and the festivities. However, the evidence points to the fact that although he liked to don the title of president, he did not enjoy *serving* as one. It was his followers who wanted him to be the hands-on ruler he was never prepared to be, at least not for any extended period of time.

After Santa Anna left the capital again in October 1843, Tornel actually plucked up the courage to write to him, several months later, to complain about his absence. On Santa Anna's being elected president, with the Bases Orgánicas in place, Tornel hoped that Santa Anna would return to the capital and give the government the strong sense of direction it required. The 1843 Constitution had been designed precisely so that the Executive could play a more active role than before. And yet, Santa Anna appeared to be happy to let his friend Canalizo stand in for him. Tornel noted that the situation was worsening, criticism of the government was mounting, and the word on everybody's lips was that Santa Anna was wasting his time on cockfighting when the country needed him to be taking action. Santa Anna replied: "Every man can enjoy himself as he pleases, provided he maintains a proper dignity and does his gambling with gentlemen and, as I do, for entertainment and not for speculation; entertainment is very necessary for a man isolated in the country as I am where the spectacles, dances and promenades of the capital do not take place." He was avoiding the issue. He was probably irritated as well by Tornel's impertinence.[44]

Not long after Tornel urged Santa Anna to return to the capital, Santa Anna demanded his resignation. Tornel, still loyal, did as he was told and resigned, claiming he was ill, and did not challenge Santa Anna as he had done with Bustamante, who had asked him to resign in the summer of 1839. It was not long before Bocanegra and Trigueros followed in his steps. Bocanegra alleged in his letter of resignation of 16 August 1844 that ill health prevented him from continuing at the head of his ministry. In his memoirs, however, he noted that one of the reasons he had opted to resign was "the awful political outcomes he feared [were about to erupt] . . . against the well-being of the Republic." Santa Anna's reply to Bocanegra's resignation suggests that he knew perfectly well that health was an excuse, not the real cause of his desertion. He begged Bocanegra not to abandon him and hinted that he was aware that an ideological schism was developing between him

and his ministers: "I do not ignore your powerful reasons for wanting
to abandon such an arduous and complicated post; but men who love
their mother country and who are, like yourself, useful to her, commit
an unforgivable fault by abandoning her when she most needs them."
Trigueros handed in his resignation two months later.[45]

Despite the divisions that were beginning to undermine Santa Anna's
government, there were still santanistas who were prepared to voice
their zealous admiration of the caudillo. For example, the commander
general of Veracruz, Benito Quijano, not only wrote to the minister of
war to celebrate Santa Anna's return to Mexico City in the spring of
1844; he went as far as publishing a pamphlet in which he enthusiastically claimed that "with the reins of government in the expert and vigorous hands of the Hero of Tampico and Veracruz, it can be predicted,
without hallucinating, that the Republic will not suffer any disorder,
will not tolerate any injustice, will not be humiliated. Internal peace will
be preserved and Texas will be regained."[46]

Those who sustained such views were clearly deceiving themselves.
By the time Santa Anna returned to Mexico City his government had
entered a crisis from which it would be unable to recover. Although the
glowing ministerial reports of January 1844 were a truthful reflection
of the achievements of the 1841–44 santanista experiment, they failed
to note the administration's failures. And these had been mounting
since Santa Anna had returned to Veracruz in October 1843. It can be
deduced from the letter Tornel addressed Santa Anna in the buildup to
their estrangement that for the santanista intelligentsia, the problems
they had been forced to confront had been made all the worse because
of the president's absence. Without Santa Anna at the head of the nation, the government's authority was visibly weakened. Given that a
number of santanista reforms were unpopular, Santa Anna's absence
proved fatal. The man santanistas like Tornel believed had the ability to
muster the country's support in the most adverse of circumstances was
simply not around to assist his team in implementing an increasingly
challenging political project.

The abolition of copper coinage was a necessity, and although in the
long term Trigueros was right to pursue such a policy, the short-term
impact of the reform was disastrous. Without the means or infrastruc-

ture to gather all the redundant coinage or the ready cash to reimburse
the popular classes, the reform proved deeply unsettling and unpopular. The formidable effort that was put into forging a modern tax system upset the majority of the population, including the Church and the
elite. It was also severely undermined by the government's exorbitant
expenditure. The extraordinary fortune Santa Anna amassed at the time
stank of corruption. Furthermore, the much-trumpeted reconquest of
Texas had ultimately consisted of little more than a few skirmishes.
The santanistas' attempt to reconcile free market and protectionist interests, although initially successful, ended up alienating the different
lobbies that financed the 1841 revolt. The santanista project, as represented by the 1843 Constitution, could not work if the strong president
was not there to perform his role and Congress was, once more, dominated by the opposition. Tornel and his fellow ministers paid the price
for relying on Santa Anna's presence to execute their plans. And they
paid the price for not abandoning their faith in upholding a representative republican political system. Despite limiting the suffrage and creating a context in which Santa Anna could fill the Senate with his supporters, the 1843 Constitution brought to life a system that continued
to rely on elections, which could not be completely fixed. The santanista leadership found itself in a situation where it could control neither
Congress nor its leader—a leader who seemed to be in a world of his
own, uninterested in power or, perhaps, the mechanisms of power. By
the spring of 1844 Congress was very much in the hands of those radical and moderate federalists they had tried to keep out when they closed
down Congress in December 1842.

At odds with the santanista intelligentsia, Santa Anna tried to force
Congress into granting him extraordinary powers and raising four million pesos so that he could organize a 30,000-strong army to reconquer Texas in the summer of 1844. Having received a messenger from
the United States in May with confirmation that the U.S. annexation
of Texas was imminent, he felt justified in making this request. It is
clear, as noted by one historian, that this was an issue he could use
"to deflect attention from the domestic situation and which would enable him to return to restore order and assert his authority."[47] However, Santa Anna's attempts to get Congress to agree to his demands

were not successful; "excessive spending and venality [had] proved too much."[48] Although several measures were approved aimed at raising funds and preparing an expeditionary army, these did not come close to tallying with his exorbitant demands. Following Doña Inés's death, he found a pretext to retire to his hacienda once more. The closure of Congress in December 1842 was still too recent to have been forgotten, and many suspected that the caudillo was planning to repeat the experience of two years earlier, with Canalizo being expected to do the dirty deed on this occasion. Without Tornel and the santanista leadership at his service in the capital, and with a hostile Congress growing increasingly confident and belligerent in his absence, the caudillo, as noted by Wilfrid Callcott, was "'at sea.' He did not know just what to do, or how to do it."[49]

On 2 November 1844 General Mariano Paredes y Arrillaga launched the *pronunciamiento* of Guadalajara. Paredes y Arrillaga had grown increasingly bitter since 1841, when having initiated the Triangular Revolt, he had ended up serving as a stepping-stone for Santa Anna. His frustration, paired with the humiliation he had suffered at the hands of Santa Anna over a drinking incident in 1843, led him to start a revolt in Guadalajara that served the aspirations of the moderates. Santa Anna returned to Mexico City on 18 November and set off to quell Paredes y Arrillaga's revolt in person three days later. While Santa Anna found himself being rejected by the authorities in Querétaro, his acting president tried to dissolve Congress on the 29th. The 1841–44 government was in its final throes.

11. Our Man in Havana, 1844–1846

Charles Bankhead, who replaced Richard Pakenham as British minister plenipotentiary in Mexico, was aware that circumstances had changed significantly over the preceding year. Although he believed the caudillo would quell Paredes y Arrillaga's revolt, he could not help noting that "the prestige heretofor attached to General Santa Anna's name has of late been much damaged for even with the apathy naturally belonging to this people, they now begin to express themselves loudly in opposition to the wholesale corruption that has distinguished General Santa Anna's administration."[1]

Santa Anna believed that Paredes y Arrillaga's prime motivation was revenge. Paredes y Arrillaga was hoping to avenge the humiliation he had undergone a year earlier, when he was sacked from his military and political posts in the capital for drunken behavior. Aware that the situation in the capital was fast deteriorating and that his popularity was on the wane, Santa Anna likely viewed Paredes y Arrillaga's uprising as an opportunity to salvage his presidency. His military victories had always raised his profile and his popularity in the political life of the republic. The action of Veracruz of 5 December 1838, for example, had helped him recover from the disastrous Texan campaign. If he could crush Paredes y Arrillaga's revolt, it was possible that he could recoup his former popularity. The army was still loyal to him. He thus chose to confront Paredes y Arrillaga in person.[2]

As he went after Paredes y Arrillaga's forces toward the end of November, he was confident he would succeed in bringing the *pronunciamiento* to an end. He even gloated over his adversary's retreat: "Everywhere along the way you can see the abandoned gear and munitions of [his] deserters." But Santa Anna's confidence was misplaced. With Tornel no longer around to keep him posted of developments in the capital, Santa Anna had not grasped the extent of his unpopularity. As was noted by Bankhead, the whole nation appeared to be calling for an end to his government: his "total disregard of public opinion and interests—and a systematic determination to feed on the resources of the country for his own benefit, and that of the persons surrounding him," reached such extremes that "even Mexican laxity of principle could no longer endure [it]."[3]

In the late morning of 6 December 1844 the troops garrisoned in the Ciudadela barracks pronounced themselves against him. By 2:00 P.M. José Joaquín de Herrera at the head of a number of deputies wrote to Canalizo demanding that he restore constitutional order. Canalizo offered to resign, in response, as long as his life was spared. By 3:00 P.M. the "three-hour revolution" was over, and not a gunshot had been fired. The deputies made their way to Congress, and by half past four when they reopened the building, news had spread around the capital that Santa Anna was on his way out. The populace took to the streets and in the following hours vented their accumulated hatred of the caudillo by pulling down his bronze statue in the Plaza del Volador. Other statues and portraits were destroyed and defaced. One crowd broke into the cemetery of Santa Paula and dug up Santa Anna's buried leg. It was dragged along the streets as people howled "Death to the Cripple! Long live Congress!"[4]

On hearing of the events in the capital, Santa Anna's initial reaction was one of utmost indignation. What appears to have hurt him the most was the treatment that had been given to the remains of his amputated leg. He was to claim, many years later, that on hearing this shocking piece of news he decided there and then to leave Mexico. However, the correspondence of the time tells another story. He was not prepared to let the triumphant rebels get away with their actions. He wrote a strongly worded letter to Herrera telling him that under no circumstances could he call himself president, as Santa Anna was himself the constitutional president, and that to depose him in this manner was illegal. He threatened to bring his army into Mexico City and bring about his own restoration by force: "Your position is truly difficult. I am . . . the magistrate

who has the laws on his side and the means to sustain them." Did the
two men remember their first encounter in Orizaba, twenty-three years
earlier, when Herrera persuaded Santa Anna to join the Army of the
Three Guarantees? One can only speculate over whether the memories
of their joint campaign in Córdoba and Santa Anna's subsequent decision to go it alone in Veracruz haunted them, in the still of the night, as
they prepared to confront each other that winter.[5]

It soon became apparent that Santa Anna was not in a position to attack the capital. Generals Bravo and Valencia, both of whom had also
come to feel ill-treated by the caudillo, offered to defend Mexico City at
the head of eight thousand men. Paredes y Arrillaga continued to have
four thousand men up in arms in Jalisco, and Juan Álvarez voiced his
determination to lead his southern army against the deposed president.
Santa Anna moved his forces to Puebla and, on finding that its garrison
was not prepared to support him, gave vent to his anger and frustration
by placing the City of Angels under siege. From 1 to 10 January 1845, his
forces battled with the troops garrisoned in Puebla. Although the fighting did spread into the city on a number of occasions, with Santa Anna's men taking a convent and several houses, including a baker's near
the main square, it finally dawned on the caudillo that he was alone,
and that the winds of change favored Herrera's movement.[6]

On 10 January 1845 he decided to accept the inevitable. He wrote to
the new revolutionary government to inform them that he was abandoning the struggle and retiring to Amozoc, where he intended to leave
the army he had with him under the orders of General Juan Morales. He
thereby renounced the presidency and noted that all he wished was to
leave Mexico and go into exile. He was to make his way to Veracruz and
from there head for foreign lands, where he hoped the bitterness of his
heart would be sweetened with the passing of time.[7]

When he reached Las Vigas, near Xalapa, he wrote to General José
Rincón to ask for permission to make his way to his estates and from
there to Veracruz, from where he intended to go into exile. His old enemy took pleasure in denying him any such safe conduct, stating that
he was a criminal and a fugitive and expressing determination to have
him captured. Santa Anna decided to proceed with his journey anyway
and took the less frequented route to El Encero, via the mountain town

of Xico. It was here, according to a number of biographies, that he endured a particularly bizarre and humiliating experience. According to the legend, a group of Indians recognized him, captured him, and then, for a laugh, decided to cook him alive. They wrapped him up in banana leaves, spiced him with chiles and other condiments, and placed him like a *tamal* in a large cauldron full of water. It was only because the village priest heard about what was happening and rushed over to call an end to the prank that Santa Anna was spared from losing his life in what would have been one of the most bizarre executions in history. An early mention of this episode may be found in Villa-Amor's biography of Santa Anna, first published in 1849. Villa-Amor naturally lamented that the "unfortunate" intervention of the village priest had prevented Santa Anna from dying in such a "sublime and unique way."[8] However, although the anecdote is wonderfully picturesque, it is not backed by the documents of his capture.[9]

By all official accounts, Santa Anna was seen traveling with five servants on the outskirts of Xico on the evening of 15 January 1845. He was immediately recognized and arrested by a group of villagers who belonged to the civilian-based militia known as the Defenders of Xico. He asked their captain, Amado Rodríguez, to escort him to his hacienda of El Encero, where he claimed he was to be sent his passport and allowed to go into exile. Rodríguez, having read the orders that had been issued by the government, did not acquiesce to the caudillo's request. Instead he allowed the prisoner to get some rest, spending the night locked up in the local prison, and marched him down to Xalapa at six the following morning to deliver him to the authorities. Much to Santa Anna's disgust a crowd gathered to see him arrive in Xalapa on the afternoon of the 16th, and he claimed that this humiliating treatment would not have been awarded even to a Texan outlaw. Although he had a house in Xalapa where he could have stayed, he was made to spend the night locked up in the town council building, where guards were posted even inside his room. He was allowed no butler and no privacy whatsoever and could not sleep because the sentries were so noisy. He claimed in outrage that his Texan captors had treated him better in 1836. He was also indignant that the government had called him a tyrant, totally rejecting their accusation.[10]

He spent four days locked up in an improvised cell in the town council offices and was taunted and abused by his old enemy, General José Rincón. Writing his memoirs thirty years later, Santa Anna avenged Rincón's treatment and their lifelong animosity by gleefully noting that his longstanding foe had died just over a year after the events of his capture, as the caudillo made his way back to the capital to resume the presidency: "He died as the people of Xalapa went out into the streets to celebrate my return to the mother country."[11]

Fearing that the government would set about seizing all his assets, he wasted no time in attempting to ensure that the money he had deposited in Xalapa with Dionisio J. de Velasco, Ramón Muñoz, and Manuel de Viya y Cosío was transferred to the British house of Manning, Mackintosh and Company. The logic behind this immediate decision was that if his funds were held by a British company, the Mexican government would not be able to touch them. However, his letters were seized and the government was able to freeze his assets before they could be placed under the protection of the Union Jack. Furthermore, in a bid to prove that Santa Anna was not only a despot but also a thief, the minister of war, Pedro García Conde, leaked the caudillo's letters to the press. This in turn led to much speculation about the immense fortune Santa Anna had amassed by embezzling government funds. Santa Anna protested about the confiscation, defended his right to protect his family's estate, and defiantly challenged anyone who could prove that he had stolen any money to speak out.[12]

He was then escorted back up the mountain to Perote, where he was locked up in the Fortress of San Carlos. From Perote he petitioned the government to allow him to go into exile. He also protested about his treatment. He made a point of emphasizing that he was the constitutional president of the republic and that his incarceration was not only cruel; it was illegal. He had been overthrown by a revolutionary movement that lacked legitimacy. He was a citizen of the republic, and yet he appeared to have no rights. After a month in prison he remained in the dark as to why he was being held captive. All his properties and assets, moreover, had been confiscated. Even his wife Dolores's clothes had been expropriated, together with his children's properties. Furthermore, the government refused to repay him the eighty-nine thousand pesos he was owed, which he had spent on the army while in office. The government was not even prepared to cover the cost of his food in prison. The young Dolores, who had gone to Perote to accompany him in his time of need, was also being deprived of sustenance. Considering the wages he was owed as former president and as a general, and a loan of twenty-eight thousand pesos he could reclaim from the town council of Veracruz, he reiterated that it was obscene that he was being made to pay for his food, especially after the government had seized his assets. He had "no power, no freedom, no goods, in brief, not even the right a bandit has of being considered innocent until proven guilty." All he wanted was to leave Mexico. He was happy to renounce the presidency. He still hoped the government would have a sufficient sense of decency to let him go rather than give the international community good reason to believe that in Mexico injustice and indignity prevailed.[13]

Not everybody wanted to see Santa Anna suffer. Ignacio Inclán, who as commander general of Puebla had withstood Santa Anna's siege of the city, was prepared to intercede on the caudillo's behalf, writing petitions to the government, urging it to be lenient with an "illustrious" man who had governed and spilled his blood for their country. According to the British minister plenipotentiary, "Notwithstanding his great unpopularity and the contemptible manner in which he has conducted himself ever since he became aware of the existence of the Revolution, there exists here a strong feeling that his life may at all events be spared." Proof of this was that "the Congress are much puzzled to know what to do with him." The fact remained that Santa Anna's knowledge "of his countrymen was unbounded, and he might have ruled them for his own and their advantage." Had he even "shown in latter times some compunction for the real wants and interests of his country . . . , he might have been one of the most powerful men that any of these republics have produced." While recent events demonstrated that he had brought about his own downfall by surrounding himself of "mercenary individuals" and by allowing "rapacity and corruption" to dictate his actions, nobody could forget his legendary talents.[14]

On 24 February 1845 the charges that were made against him were finally given the formal approval of the Chamber of Deputies. He was accused of attacking the political system established in the 1843 Constitution, of dissolving the state legislature of Querétaro in December 1844, of arresting its officials and suspending its governor, of cooperating with Canalizo in the issuing of the decree of 29 November 1844 whereby the acting president tried to close down Congress, and of leading an armed rebellion against the reestablished constitutional government. Notwithstanding the government's ostensible resolve to see him tried and brought to justice, the caudillo was still capable of using a trial to his advantage.

Herrera's government was also embroiled in deeply unsettling problems of its own making. The tenuous radical-moderate alliance that had contributed to Santa Anna's fall became fractured almost the day after Herrera became president. Herrera's moderate-led cabinet hesitated over replacing the centralist 1843 Constitution with the federalist 1824 charter. The fear of a war with the United States was strong enough for the moderates to believe it preferable to retain the 1843 charter, despite their federalist ideals. The puros, in contrast, believed that only if the 1824 Constitution were brought back would the people rally behind the government against the United States. They soon became incensed, as well, with Herrera's reluctance to replace the large regular army with civic militias. Moreover, Herrera's inner circle started to consider the possibility of recognizing the independence of Texas. They severed diplomatic relations with the United States after the U.S. Congress voted in favor of the annexation of Texas on 6 March 1845, but they sought a peaceful solution to the inevitable conflict at all costs. Facing fast-mounting internal problems, Herrera's government clearly did not have the time or inclination to complicate them further by giving Santa Anna a highly publicized trial in which the caudillo would make the most of the opportunity to present himself as a martyr and point out the government's increasingly obvious failures.[15]

After Santa Anna had spent five months in captivity, the government decided to release him, and on 24 May 1845 a general amnesty was offered to all his "rebels." Although Santa Anna was not officially granted this amnesty, it was agreed that the indictment against him would be dropped providing he left the country "at once and forever." He was allowed to keep his property. Remarkably, it was determined that he would also continue to receive half-pay as general. Fearing that such a decision could well be controversial, given the amount of popular discontent he had generated toward the end of his period in office, Pedro García Conde's first intimation that the Chamber of Deputies had voted to grant Santa Anna this conditional pardon was written in secret. His release and immediate departure to the coast from where he was expected to leave on a British packet were to be undertaken as swiftly and as unobtrusively as possible. In order that his departure did not lead to any disturbances on the part of Santa Anna's *jarocho* supporters, it was also determined that he would leave the republic from La Antigua rather than from either Veracruz or Tampico.[16]

Once these orders were released they were diligently put into effect. By 29 May Santa Anna and Dolores were ready to embark on the *Midway*, and they were prevented from doing so only by the delay in the arrival of their luggage. Santa Anna pleaded for permission to leave with their savings and their possessions as they were condemned to spend the rest of their lives in foreign lands. Ignacio Inclán, who escorted Santa Anna, Dolores, and his seven-year-old son Manuel to the coast, acquiesced, and they finally departed on 2 June 1845 with thirty-seven items of luggage. Dreading that he might try to make a surprise comeback by disembarking farther up the coast, Mariano Arista set about guarding it, determined to "turn this baneful man to ashes" should he try to pull off such a stunt. Santa Anna did not harbor any such intentions, however. At least, not yet.[17]

Santa Anna, the seventeen-year-old Dolores, and Manuel arrived in Havana five days after leaving La Antigua and were welcomed ashore by the Spanish captain general, General Leopoldo O'Donnell. O'Donnell and Santa Anna got on extremely well, and the Spanish commander encouraged the Mexican caudillo to take up residence on the island. Although no record of Santa Anna and O'Donnell's conversations has survived the passing of time, it remains interesting that these two generals and politicians, both of whom played such an important role in their respective countries and whose principles and careers were so similar, established such a good rapport.[18]

Carefully observed by the United States consul in Havana, the caudillo spent the first days of his new life as an exile "confined to the cockpit" and looking out for "the arrival of a steamer or other vessel from

Vera Cruz." For the greater part of the fourteen months he spent in Havana (June 1845–August 1846), it appears that little changed. He spent his days frequenting the local cockpits and hanging around the waterfront waiting for latest batch of news to arrive from Mexico. It was not long before he started to plot his return. Two extremely unlikely and very different forces were to provoke his political comeback. One was the radical puros led by Gómez Farías; the other was President James K. Polk's U.S. government.[19]

Extraordinary as it may seem, a number of radicals, disgruntled with Herrera's moderate government, started investigating the possibility of obtaining Santa Anna's support for their cause even prior to his exile. In a letter Manuel Crescencio Rejón wrote to Gómez Farías on 13 February 1845, he mooted the possibility—which for the moment had to be kept "a profound secret"—"of seeking the aid of *don* Antonio" to further their federalist ideal. Once Santa Anna settled in Havana, Rejón concerned himself with securing the caudillo's backing. In a letter he addressed to Gómez Farías as early as 7 July 1845, he made it known that Santa Anna was tired of politics and did not covet the presidency at all. However, he was willing to lead the army if Gómez Farías was prepared to look after the government. Santa Anna allegedly claimed the escoceses were his real enemies, the *hombres de bien* he had fought against in 1828, 1832, and 1841. He would help Gómez Farías on condition that his contribution was limited to that of soldier and that once peace was restored he could look after his land in Veracruz. At the time, Rejón's ideas seemed remote and unlikely. A year later there was every possibility that they could be realized.[20]

Herrera's government failed to bring any significant relief to the discord that had come to characterize Mexican politics. Its reputation was further damaged by its pragmatic approach to the unresolved issue of Texas. Herrera's cabinet came to the conclusion by the middle of 1845 that Mexico would never succeed in reconquering Texas. Confronted with the increasingly aggressive expansionism of the U.S. government, they felt it made sense to discuss the British suggestion, first offered secretly to Santa Anna, of recognizing the independence of Texas in exchange for the guarantee that the British government would prevent the United States from annexing the northern states of California, Ari-

zona, and New Mexico. The moment Herrera's government's willingness to consider recognizing the independence of Texas became public
knowledge, the opposition exploited the president's perceived weakness and lack of patriotism for all it was worth.

Herrera's readiness to consider the British offer was frustrated by the
constitutional limitations placed upon the Executive, which prevented
the president from negotiating any territorial cessions. It also came
too late. On 15 July 1845 the Texan government voted to become a part
of the United States of America. Although the formal U.S. annexation
of Texas was not officially ratified until 29 December 1845, everybody
knew by the middle of the summer that it was a fait accompli. While the
opposition forces—puros, centralists, santanistas, and an emerging
faction of monarchists—accused the government of being weak and
indecisive and clamored for war, Herrera tried unsuccessfully to find a
peaceful solution.

His cabinet agreed to receive a U.S. envoy, John Slidell, in the fall
of 1845, as long as he was precisely that: an envoy and not a minister
plenipotentiary. To have welcomed a minister plenipotentiary would
have amounted to renewing full diplomatic relations with the United
States, something the Mexican government was not prepared to do as
long as Mexico received no compensation for the loss of Texas. It would
have weakened Mexico's position in the negotiations. President James
K. Polk, working on an entirely different premise, sent Slidell to Mexico with instructions to ensure that its government compensated the
United States for its citizens' claims against Mexican depredations on
the disputed Texan boundary. Aware that the Mexican treasury did not
have the funds to meet such claims, Polk hoped that Herrera's government might be prepared to recognize the Texan boundary in exchange
for the dropping of the U.S. claims. Slidell also had orders to offer to
purchase California for twenty-five million dollars. When the objective
of Slidell's visit became known, Herrera's cabinet refused to see him,
on 16 December, claiming he did not have the appropriate credentials.
At last the government appeared to show some sense of national pride.
It was too late, however. On 14 December 1845, third-time-lucky Paredes y Arrillaga launched the *pronunciamiento* of San Luis Potosí at the
head of the army formed to reconquer Texas and brought down Her-

rera's administration. In Washington on 13 January 1846, the day after
President Polk heard of Slidell's rejection, Polk ordered General Zachary Taylor, based on the southern bank of the River Nueces in Texas, to
move his forces south to the Río Grande (Bravo) and occupy the area
under dispute.[21]

Symptomatic of the last years of the stage of profound disillusion,
despite facing an unavoidable war with the United States, the traditionalist centralist factions that rallied behind Paredes y Arrillaga's
dictatorship found themselves becoming increasingly divided at a time
when unity was all-important. With the outbreak of war imminent, a
growing faction of monarchists, encouraged by the Spanish minister
plenipotentiary, Salvador Bermúdez de Castro, tried to persuade General Paredes y Arrillaga to prepare the ground for the crowning of a
European prince in Mexico. Gutiérrez Estrada's views, first publicized
in 1840, had gained significant support in some quarters. Experience
demonstrated that Mexicans were unable to govern themselves and a
monarchy was perceived as a system that suited Mexico's political customs and traditions. There was, however, the more pragmatic fact that
if Mexico's destiny could be linked to that of a European power, there
was hope that the country would have a strong enough ally to fend off
any U.S. aggression. Notwithstanding the persuasiveness of such an
argument at a time when desperate measures were called for, the majority's republicanism thwarted the monarchist plot of 1846. Paredes
y Arrillaga's perceived monarchist sympathies lost him the support of
most of the factions, who remained deeply republican. A number of
federalist santanista republican revolts broke out in Mazatlán (5 February and 6 May) and Guerrero (15 April). As Paredes y Arrillaga divided his army to quell the uprisings and defend the northern border,
war commenced on 25 April 1846. Mexican forces operating in Mexico
opened fire on Taylor's forces as they advanced to the Río Bravo. It was
the excuse Polk was looking for. On 11 May 1846, President Polk declared war on Mexico, stating that "American blood" had been shed on
"American soil."[22]

Santa Anna was kept informed of these developments. Although he
refrained from publicly expressing his views on what was happening
in Mexico during his first year in Cuba, he could not resist having a

pamphlet published in order to defend himself from the accusation that he had started to harbor monarchist sympathies. The pamphlet contained a subtle yet noteworthy profession of principles. He denied having sought the cooperation of the Spanish, British, and French governments to impose a European prince on the Mexican throne. He also denied that he had entered negotiations with the British government in a bid to give the Californias to the United Kingdom. He stressed that he was a die-hard republican, that he was obstinate in sustaining the view that the nation's territory should not be broken up under any circumstances, and that he had come around to viewing a popular (radical) government as the only way to save Mexico from foreign domination. He was publicly distancing himself from Paredes y Arrillaga's monarchist faction and from Herrera's *moderados*, who had looked into the possibility of recognizing the independence of Texas in exchange for a United Kingdom pledge to protect the rest of Mexico's border. He had come to believe that Gómez Farías's puros were the faction that stood the greatest chance of overthrowing Paredes y Arrillaga and was making his sympathies known.[23]

It was his sister Francisca who organized the circulation of Santa Anna's May 1846 pamphlet in the capital, having her two servants, Hilario Pérez and Juan López, post copies of it on walls in the city. They were caught in the act of plastering up one of these pamphlets on a street corner, and Doña Francisca, who had spent most of the summer of 1832 in prison for conspiring to bring her brother back to power in the capital, found herself once again under investigation for illicit political activities. On 8 July 1846 she was interrogated. As can be seen in the transcription of her replies, Doña Francisca was a forceful character, like her brother. Asked whether she was aware of the contents of the pamphlet, she replied: "They contain a manifesto by [my] brother, General Santa Anna, to his fellow citizens in which he tries to vindicate himself from the accusation that he is a monarchist. He mentions the publications that have said this in the manifesto." Questioned as to why she had arranged for this pamphlet to be stuck on the city walls, she retorted: "To publicize my brother's vindication. I am interested in his honor, because of who he is, but also because of the family ties that unite us." Showing the utmost disdain for her interrogators, Doña

Francisca went on to say that she was not aware that by circulating the pamphlet she was committing a crime, let alone doing anything vaguely wrong. On this occasion, events in the capital meant that her trial never took place.[24]

Against the backdrop of the war, and with the puro proposal gaining popularity on the back of Herrera and Paredes y Arrillaga's governments' failed attempts to impose order and settle the dispute with Texas and the United States, Santa Anna's name once again began to be fondly recalled. One newspaper that became dedicated to heralding the need for his return was La Reforma. As it stressed in one of its editorials:

> [Santa Anna's] private conversations and letters speak the language of disillusionment, and make manifest his repentance at having abandoned the people, whom he is now willing to support until his death. Come, then, he who had the courage to lead our troops to the Sabine [River]; he who lost a limb fighting a foreign enemy in Veracruz; he who affirmed [our] independence and conquered trophies of glory on the Pánuco's edges that constitute our pride. Come and help us defend the right of universal suffrage and the dogma of popular sovereignty which have been trampled upon by the present administration. Come and save us from the monarchist Congress. Come and save our nationality and sustain the independence of our politics from any foreign influence. Come, in short, and be reconciled with the nation and the army, as Napoleon reconciled himself with France when he returned from the island of Elba.[25]

The puros and the moderates, federalists alike, began to overcome their differences in order to bring down Paredes y Arrillaga's government. Both also saw the logic of including Santa Anna in their plans.

Considering the principles for which he stood between 1841 and 1844, it is difficult to see how he could possibly have become a radical federalist again. How could the man who had brought down the Gómez Farías administration of 1833–34 be prepared to rejoin forces with him? How could the caudillo who had come to believe in the need to guide the Mexican people by the hand have regained his belief in the virtues of universal male suffrage espoused by the 1824 Constitution? The truth is that he needed the puros as much as they needed him. Understandably intent on returning to Mexico, and estranged from the santanista leadership, he had little choice but to join forces with Gómez Farías. This does not mean that he was not sincere when he stressed that he was disillusioned with politics or that all he wanted to do was lead the Mexican Army against the U.S. aggressors. As events would show, he did not show any inclination to remain in Mexico City and govern the country when he returned in the summer of 1846. He channeled all his energy into fighting the invaders. One suspects that what he wanted was to be a hero again. He wanted to recoup his prestige as the patriot who founded the republic, who repulsed Barradas's 1829 expedition, who lost his leg fighting the French in 1838. The shady dealings he entered into with President Polk's intermediaries must be understood along similar lines. In the same way that joining forces with such an unlikely ally as Gómez Farías was a way of ensuring his return to Mexico in the fraught context of 1845–46, so tricking the U.S. president into believing that he would bring about a peaceful cession of the territories coveted by the U.S. government was a way of ensuring he would be allowed to return to the republic past the U.S. navy's blockade of Mexico's Atlantic coast.

During Santa Anna's exile in Havana he was notoriously visited by a number of secret emissaries sent to see him by the President Polk. Polk had won the 1844 elections on an aggressive platform that had made the annexation of Texas the main focus of his campaign. He was prepared to use any means to achieve this goal. The U.S. consul in Havana, R. B. Campbell, was the first to look into a way of gaining Santa Anna's favor. He invited the caudillo to the consulate celebrations of 4 July 1845, but Santa Anna declined. As Campbell did not speak Spanish and Santa Anna did not speak English, other agents became involved in the negotiations that ensued.[26]

The first individual to serve as an intermediary between the U.S. president and the exiled caudillo was a U.S. citizen of Spanish birth, Colonel Alejandro José Atocha. Atocha claimed to be a friend of Santa Anna's, having rented a piece of land from the caudillo, the Paso de San Juan in Manga de Clavo, at eight thousand pesos per annum for a period of nine years (1844–53). From what may be gathered from Polk's diary, Atocha first visited him in June 1845. Whether they discussed the possibility of using Santa Anna in President Polk's aim to fulfill the United States' Manifest Destiny, as journalist John L. O'Sullivan termed the country's mission to take possession of the entire North American continent, is not known. However, when he saw Atocha again, on Friday 13 February 1846, Polk did annotate the content of their discussions. Atocha told Polk that since their meeting in June he had visited Santa Anna in exile at Havana. He urged Polk to treat the conversation confidentially and claimed to represent Santa Anna. He told Polk: "Santa Anna was in constant communication with his friends in Mexico, and received by every vessel that left Veracruz hundreds of letters." Atocha said there was reason to believe that Santa Anna "might soon be in power again in Mexico" and that the general

> was in favor of a treaty with the United States, and that in adjusting a boundary between the two countries the Del Norte should be the western Texas line, and the Colorado of the West down through the Bay of San Francisco to the sea should be the Mexican line on the north, and that Mexico should cede all east and north of these natural boundaries to the United States for a pecuniary consideration, and mentioned thirty millions of dollars as the sum. This sum he said Santa Anna believed would pay the most pressing debts of Mexico, support the army until the condition of the finances could be improved, and enable the government to be placed on a permanent footing.

Atocha then said Santa Anna was surprised that the United States naval force had been withdrawn from Veracruz and "that General Taylor's army was kept at Corpus Christi instead of being stationed on the Del Norte." Atocha added "his own opinion" that "the United States would never be able to treat with Mexico, without the presence of an imposing force by land and sea." Polk made a point of noting that "Col. Atocha did not say that he was sent by Santa Anna to hold this conversation with me, but I think it probable he was so." The following day, after Atocha visited Polk again, the president wrote in his diary that Atocha stressed that for any negotiation to be possible, the Mexican government would have to be seen to have little choice in the matter, otherwise "there would be another revolution by which they would be overthrown. He said they must appear to be forced to agree to such a proposition." In order to do this, Atocha suggested Taylor's force should leave Corpus Christi and move to the Bravo (Río Grande). The U.S. Navy should step up its blockade of Veracruz. This would put significant pressure on the Mexican government. He said: "The last words which General Santa Anna said to him when he was leaving Havana a month ago was, 'when you see the President, tell him to take strong measures, and such a treaty can be made and I will sustain it.'" Although Polk felt that Colonel Atocha was "a person to whom I would not give my confidence," the possibility of obtaining a peaceful cession was too good to be missed. It would become clear a year later that Santa Anna's real intention was to fight the U.S. Army to the end, and Polk recognized with bitterness that Atocha was "a great scoundrel."[27]

At the time, Polk pursued the route opened up by Atocha's suggestions. Suspecting Atocha to be the fraudulent trickster that he was, Polk decided to send an agent of his own to meet Santa Anna: Commander Alexander Slidell Mackenzie (John Slidell's brother). Mackenzie arrived in Havana on 5 July 1846 and went to see Santa Anna the following day. Their rendezvous lasted three hours. Mackenzie told Santa Anna that Polk would like to see the caudillo in power in Mexico and had "given orders to the squadron blockading the Mexican ports, to allow General Santa Anna freely to return to his country." Polk was willing to reach a peaceful settlement with whatever government Santa Anna might forge. Polk was prepared to offer an "ample consideration in ready money" for the territory he wanted Mexico to cede to the United States. Santa Anna appeared to be receptive to Mackenzie's proposals. He replied that the government he would like to lead would support "republican principles" and "an entirely liberal constitution." If the United States were prepared to "promote his patriotic desires, he offer[ed] to respond with such a peace as has been described." In what the Americans initially interpreted as proof of his sincerity, he went on to give Mackenzie a number of tips as to the best way the U.S. Army should conduct its offensive on Mexico. He recommended that General

Taylor advance to Saltillo rather than remain in Monterrey and from there progress to San Luis Potosí. He also suggested that a different force be sent against Veracruz and San Juan de Ulúa.[28]

One of the results of the MacKenzie–Santa Anna interview was that on 4 August, Polk asked the Senate for two million dollars "to be used in negotiating a treaty with Mexico, the sum to be used, if necessary, as a payment before the Senate ratified the treaty." Charles Bankhead had little doubt that "some understanding took place at the Havana between General Santa Anna and the American Consul," and that when on 8 August 1846 President Polk "asked the sum of two millions of dollars from Congress, for the purpose of satisfying any unforeseen expenses which might arise in the settlement of differences with Mexico," it was more than likely that "a portion of this vote was destined to be applied towards the success of the alleged arrangements entered into at the Havana." For Bankhead, proof that there was a "special arrangement" between the U.S. government and Santa Anna was that a Spaniard by the name of Atocha was known to have accompanied Santa Anna to Havana, visited the United States, returned, accompanied the caudillo back to Xalapa, and since left.[29]

The British press of the time interpreted the rumor of the Cuban meeting along similar lines. The *Manchester Guardian* stated on 16 September 1846: "The probability seems to be, that there is an understanding between [Santa Anna] and the American government; and we should not be surprised to hear that he has been furnished from Washington with the funds which have doubtless been used to corrupt the Mexican troops. In that case, most probably, the price of his restoration to power will be a treaty of peace, advantageous to the United States."[30] The private and confidential order of 13 May 1846, which stated that "If Santa Anna endeavors to enter the Mexican ports, you will allow him to pass freely," was respected when Santa Anna finally made his return to Mexico in August. The U.S. naval officer who boarded the British ship that returned Santa Anna to Veracruz "allowed him [Santa Anna] to enter without molestation."[31]

Polk was to claim later, on 8 December 1846, that his main objective had been to weaken the enemy by allowing Santa Anna to enter the republic, since it was obvious that the caudillo would foster internal divisions. Santa Anna was to deny all knowledge of the meetings or the transactions that took place. However, he made good use of Polk's ingenuousness. He was not Polk's Trojan horse. On the contrary, he pocketed whatever money Polk passed to him and set about working hard to organize his country's defense. When General Winfield Scott noted in May 1847 that the U.S. government had been wrong to believe Santa Anna, and that had they known his true intentions, they would not have made the mistake of allowing him to return to Mexico, Santa Anna gloated over his enemies' naïveté: "The United States were deceived in believing that I would be capable of betraying my mother country. Before such a thing could happen, I would rather be burnt on a pyre and that my ashes were spread in such a way that not one atom was left."[32]

12. The Mexican-American War, 1846–1848

Santa Anna disembarked in Veracruz on 16 August 1846. Yet again, his supposed betrayals and military failings appear to have been forgotten and there appears to have been a willingness on the part of many Mexicans to believe that he would save the day. As was expressed in one pamphlet: "The most illustrious of its children [is] home again; he who has saved us always during the great conflicts. . . . The courageous and great Santa Anna is in Veracruz. God has saved Mexico." On the 19th, just over a year after he had been ushered out of the republic, and less than two years after an angry mob had disinterred his leg in the capital, the cathedral bells peeled and its choir sang a *Te Deum* to celebrate his safe arrival. Santa Anna could not help noticing this extraordinary change himself: "What a transformation!"[1]

Villa-Amor was one of many who could not understand how Santa Anna had achieved this resurrection, considering the series of events that had previously unfolded. The "most corrupt of all Mexicans" was back. He attributed it to fear and ignorance and described it as shameful that although everybody knew about his treacherous deeds, nobody was prepared to prevent his return to Mexico City. There was certainly something odd about the political statements Santa Anna made on returning to Mexico. Little of what he said sounded as if it was coming from him. He issued a manifesto on disembarking in Veracruz that espoused the need to reinstate the 1824 Constitution while a new constitution was forged. A number of the points he made were consistent with his past political statements. However, there were also obscure passages in his text about issues of inequality and democratic practices that did not read like his own.[2]

The fear harbored by a number of radicals, who had not forgotten the experience of the 1833–34 administration, was that he was waiting for any excuse to proclaim himself dictator. As was expressed in an anonymous letter of the time, "Genuine liberals cannot believe that the union between General Santa Anna and yourself [Gómez Farías] and the federation is in good faith." It was a fear that made itself apparent on a number of occasions. Anything that Santa Anna did or said was immediately interpreted as containing proof of his ill-disguised sinister intentions.[3]

The British minister plenipotentiary did not believe Santa Anna had become a radical puro. Despite what he considered to be a very gifted performance when he went to pay his respects, Bankhead was not taken in by the caudillo's defense of the voice of the people, U.S. institutions, free trade, free emigration, and religious tolerance. On the other hand, the U.S. consul in Mexico City, John Black, was prepared to believe in Santa Anna's conversion to the puros' cause, only because Gómez Farías "honestly thinks Santa Anna has truly repented of all his political sins and errors, and that he is politically a regenerated man, and only wants an opportunity to atone for his past misdeeds . . . no one has had a better chance to know Santa Anna than [Gómez Farías]."[4]

Santa Anna may not have been a radical, but there is ample evidence that he was committed to avoiding the political shenanigans of the capital and dedicating himself to organizing Mexico's war effort. Again, he claimed not to have come to govern, but to fight. Following his return to Veracruz, a month lapsed before he made his way back to the capital on 14 September. He allowed the politicians their space, and when Gómez Farías sent the former santanista minister Manuel Baranda to urge the caudillo to make his way to Mexico City "to assume the presidency as soon as he arrived," he replied that it would be "most degrading" for him to serve as president when "duty called him to fight the enemies of the republic." When he did arrive in the capital, his actions were limited to implementing Gómez Farías's scheme of establishing a Council of State. It was this council's responsibility to oversee the reintroduction of the 1824 federal Constitution, with its corresponding organization of elections, serving as a caretaker government in the meantime. Gómez Farías became the president of the Council of State under the provisional presidency of General Mariano Salas, the chieftain who had led the coup in the capital of 4 August 1846 that had brought down Paredes y Arrillaga's regime.[5]

The Council of State and Salas's interim government were riddled with in-fighting. Despite Santa Anna's move to "showcase Mexico's newly fashioned domestic harmony" by inviting members of different political factions to join the council, moderates, puros and santanistas were at one another's throats from the outset. Santa Anna did not have the energy to end the feuding by becoming the dictator many suspected he aspired to be. Instead, he set off to San Luis Potosí on 28 September. He made a point of remaining on the margins of the factionalist disputes that undermined the government. He did not remove Salas from the presidency as Gómez Farías would have liked him to do. Neither did he marginalize Gómez Farías. Instead "he refused to govern [the country] and urged Gómez Farías to find a way of uniting the factions."[6]

It was while he was organizing an expeditionary army in San Luis Potosí, with the hope that it would recover the northern posts lost at the battles of Palo Alto, Resaca de la Palma, and Monterrey (8–9 May and 20–24 September 1846) that elections were held. Santa Anna and Gómez Farías, in a repeat of the 1833 elections, were elected president and vice president, respectively, on 23 December 1846. Santa Anna, as promised, did not return to Mexico City to take up his post as president and allowed Gómez Farías to lead the country as vice president. His sole concern was to organize an army that could confront General Zachary Taylor's forces in the north. This was why he had been prepared to enter into shady deals with President Polk's emissaries. This was why he was ready to join forces with Gómez Farías. He believed that he was the only person who could lead a successful campaign against the invaders. He was not interested at the time in who was in power. All he wanted was to "fight . . . [and] defend with ardor and enthusiasm the independence of the republic." As long as Gómez Farías fulfilled his part of the deal—raising funds for the army—Santa Anna did not care whether radicals or moderates were in charge of the government.[7]

He certainly backed Gómez Farías's drive to finance the much needed resurrection of the army with Church funds. The Church was the only institution that had the money to salvage the situation. In the

Santa Anna, the Warrior President, ca. 1847. Courtesy of Nettie Lee Benson Latin American Collection, University of Texas at Austin.

many letters he wrote to the minister of war during the war, the dire straits of the army were a recurrent theme. The reintroduction of the federal Constitution did not help in this sense. Many reconstituted states made the most of their newly acquired sovereignty, refusing to send men, arms, and funds. The governor of Zacatecas, who had not forgiven Santa Anna for his assault on the city in 1835, stated that he would rather the Americans won the war than that the caudillo and his army triumph. In his despair Santa Anna actually urged Gómez Farías to assume dictatorial powers in the same way that Vicente Guerrero had done in 1829. Having a federal Constitution in place was no justification for the states to avoid helping the national government when the country's independence was at stake. He even wrote a forceful letter to Congress telling them that if they failed to support the army with the resources it urgently required, he would refuse to be held responsible for the inevitable defeat to which they were condemning it.[8]

Santa Anna supported Gómez Farías's move to force a loan of twenty million pesos from the Church. As he noted on 2 January 1847:

> At the moment I am desperate because it's the second day of the month, and every commander is frantically seeking food for his soldiers. . . . A loan of twenty million, that is all, mortgaging church assets, that is what our Congress must address. . . . I had my worries, and for ten years I have resisted with all of my might authorizing such a measure against Church wealth. I even assured my cabinet on numerous occasions that I would rather have my hand cut off than sign a decree that might dispose of these assets. . . . I do not oppose this measure [anymore] . . ., if this is Congress's will, I will support it.[9]

When news reached him that the decree authorizing the Executive Power to confiscate up to fifteen million pesos by mortgaging or selling unused Church properties had been passed by Congress on 11 January 1847, he immediately wrote to the minister of war to celebrate such a move. He called it "the only way of saving our national independence." The law was proof of Congress's patriotism. He went as far as stating that he considered the application of "repressive laws" acceptable if these were necessary to ensure that the funds were obtained.[10]

Santa Anna's army in San Luis Potosí was poorly resourced. Entire regiments, such as the Sixth, had neither clothes nor weapons. Nevertheless, he came to the conclusion that there was nothing worse than inactivity. The longer they took to move into action, the more the United States would consolidate control of the northern provinces. The Mexicans would lose hope if their government did not act decisively. Rumors that he was planning to use the army in San Luis Potosí to take on the government in a repeat of Paredes y Arrillaga's revolt of 14 December 1845 also needed to be silenced. A surprise attack on Taylor's positions could only result in a resounding victory for Mexico, and that was urgently needed at present.[11]

He harangued his men in San Luis Potosí on 27 January 1847, on the morning of their departure to Saltillo. He could not hide the lack of resources that afflicted his expeditionary army from his men, so he had little choice but to equate his troops' suffering with their valor, presenting their ability to endure hunger as proof of their strength. Behind the scenes, he was disgusted that the government had failed to secure any funds for this expedition. In public, he gave his troops a speech about privation and heroism so that they followed him across the desert. In private he was more frank about the situation to the minister of war. Having reached Matehuala on 7 February 1847, he made a point of protesting about his troops' hardships. Not having received one peso from the government in more than a month and a half, their condition was abysmal. He wanted to know if the vice president thought it was just to deprive of any supplies those men who were to sacrifice their lives to defend Mexico's independence. He had no choice but to fund part of the expedition from his own pocket, mortgaging all his properties as well as those of his children. In his memoirs, he pointed out for posterity that he had armed and dressed 18,000 men, thanks to the 500,000 pesos he raised.[12]

On this occasion, he initially had 64 chiefs, 433 officers, and 5,298 soldiers, as recorded in October 1846. By the time he decided to head north, he had 20,910 men. However, not all of them were present at the battle of Angostura–Buena Vista of 22–23 February 1847. Desertions, losses caused by the long march north, and the reallocation of some of the troops to other spheres of action resulted in his having 15,152 men at his disposition when he reviewed his troops at la Encarnación on 19 February 1847.[13]

News of Taylor's proximity reached him on 17 February 1847. His scouts told him that Taylor's forces numbered between seven thousand and eight thousand, that he had twenty pieces of artillery, and that he was only twenty leagues away, camped at the hacienda of Agua Nueva. Santa Anna was confident that his larger army would crush Taylor. His plan was to attack on the 21st—his birthday; had he feared being defeated, it is unlikely that he would have chosen such a date for launching the offensive. However, Santa Anna's position became known to Taylor, who abandoned Agua Nueva, where he could be flanked, and retreated to the foothills of Buena Vista, where he fortified himself. Given that there were between four and five Mexicans for every U.S. soldier, Taylor was aware that to attain a military victory it was essential to use the terrain to his advantage. The position he chose to wait for a Mexican offensive was perfect. Working with a gully that grew narrower as the foothills ascended Buena Vista, hence its name la Angostura (The Narrowness), Taylor could parapet his forces behind privileged vantage points and natural trenches. To his right the terrain was so uneven that he was convinced it would prevent the Mexican artillery from getting close enough to harm his troops. To his left there were too many ravines for the Mexican cavalry to be of any use. If Santa Anna decided to attack, he would have to make exclusive use of his infantry, and although this far outnumbered Taylor's forces, many Mexican soldiers would have to die before they could reach the fortified U.S. positions.[14]

The battle of Angostura–Buena Vista was fought over two days (22–23 February 1847). Santa Anna initiated this particularly gruesome clash of arms the day after his fifty-third birthday. In his dispatch he recognized that Taylor had succeeded in fortifying his troops in a notably strong position. Nevertheless, "neither the rough mountain terrain, neither the strength of their positions, nor the advantages these gave them, however many these may have been, could stop the Mexican soldier when he fights to defend his country's rights." Santa Anna described the two-day bloodbath as having been fought by both sides with "rage and despair." He noted that his horse had been shot from under him during the fray and that all of the action had caused the wound on his mutilated leg to open up again. The Mexican forces succeeded in seizing two enemy flags, three pieces of artillery, and four carts. He estimated that around two thousand U.S. soldiers had died and either deliberately downplayed the human loss among his men or deceived himself into believing that not more than a thousand Mexicans had died. According to other official figures, put together at the end of the battle, Santa Anna's army of 15,000–20,000 had shrunk to a total of 93 chiefs, 769 officers, and 9,043 men. More recent sources list Mexican losses as follows: 591 killed, 1,037 wounded, and 1,854 missing; or "more than 3,400 dead."[15]

After two long days of continuous fighting Santa Anna admitted that the outcome of the clash remained undetermined. The enemy's strong position had prevented them from being routed. He was persuaded that Taylor's men would succumb once the fighting was renewed. However, after forty hours of relentless combat, his men needed some respite. They were exhausted and hungry, had no rice, no bread, and no biscuits. In the last few days all they had had to eat was meat. Before daybreak, on 24 February, he decided to retreat with his troops to Agua Nueva so that his men could eat and rest. He was determined to renew the offensive once the wounded were taken care of and his troops had been given some time to garner their strength. On 26 February, however, following a meeting with his staff, he decided to withdraw to San Luis Potosí. He realized there was little to be gained by launching another major offensive against Taylor's forces.[16]

By the time he reached San Luis Potosí on 9 March 1847, he only had around five thousand men with him. About fifteen thousand men had died between January and March 1847, during the expedition to Saltillo, on the way back, or at the battle of Angostura–Buena Vista. As he made his way back to San Luis Potosí (and not while he was on the plains of Angostura, as he would recall in his memoirs), news reached him that a revolt had erupted in Mexico City on 27 February and that his presence was urgently required to restore order in the capital. On 6 March he wrote to Gómez Farías from Matehuala to tell him that he was "profoundly affected by the scandal." He promised to send four thousand soldiers to back the government. Informed at the same time of General Winfield Scott's imminent landing in Veracruz (9 March) he urged Gómez Farías to reinforce the port's defenses.[17]

While Santa Anna he had been engaging Taylor's army in battle, the moderate liberals had been busy conspiring to bring down Gómez Farías and put an end to the hold the radicals had on the government. It is evident that for most of the moderados, forcing a change of government was the main priority, whatever the consequences. The notion that it might have been better to wait, that it made sense to put aside their political differences temporarily and stand by the government in a show of patriotic unity while the war raged on, evidently carried no weight.

Between 27 February and 8 March the streets of the capital were transformed into a bloody battlefield. The government's regular troops and puro militias resorted to violence to defend Gómez Farías's policies against the upper-middle-class moderado militias who chose to turn against the government rather than reinforce Veracruz's defenses.

The Revolt of the Polkos, as it became known—according to some because the well-to-do moderado rebels danced the trendy polkas of the day, and according to others because the revolt favored Mr. Polk's war effort—was extremely disruptive. In their original plan, comprising thirteen articles, they demanded the resignation of Santa Anna and Gómez Farías, the dissolution of Congress, and new federal and state elections. Article 12 critically demanded the abolition of the law of 11 January concerning the confiscation of Church properties. With the financial backing of the Church, whose higher clergy would appear to have been more concerned with looking after their institution's wealth than with defending Mexico, the polkos proved highly resilient in the face of government reprisals and ultimately undermined Gómez Farías's government beyond salvage.[18]

Initially Santa Anna sent a number of letters from San Luis Potosí confirming that he fully backed Gómez Farías's government and urging the acting president to be tough on the rebels. However, neither side seemed able to gain the upper hand. With it becoming apparent that public opinion was beginning to turn against the rebels, on 8 March, the polkos took back their original plan of 27 February and replaced it with a single-article pronunciamiento that limited itself to demanding Gómez Farías's removal from office.[19]

The leading luminaries of the moderado party now saw in Santa Anna, just as the puros had six months earlier, the providential leader who could bring an end to the nation's crises. It is clear that they had not believed his radical-republican act of the summer of '46, otherwise they would not have sought his help at this juncture. On 10 March 1847 forty-one moderates, including such prominent politicians as José María Lafragua, Pedro María Anaya, José Joaquín Herrera, Ramón Gamboa, Ignacio Comonfort, Mariano Otero, and Mariano Riva Palacio, signed a petition that begged Santa Anna to return to the capital to assume the presidency and save their country.[20]

Street fighting continued in the capital between the warring factions despite the changes in the moderates' demands. Nobody seemed to care that Scott's forces had launched a major offensive on Veracruz. As Santa Anna would reply to his critics in 1849, how could they accuse him of treason when he was the one who had gone to fight the invaders? What did his critics have to say about "the scandalous rebellion that shook the capital of the Republic to overthrow the supreme authority [of the Republic] and sink us in anarchy"? In what sense were the polkos' actions patriotic?[21]

He reached the outskirts of the capital on 21 March and finally, on the 23rd, a truce was declared. Puros and polkos sent their representatives to see him, and the caudillo was forced to arbitrate once more between Mexico's feuding parties. Although he had backed Gómez Farías's drive to finance the army with Church funds, it became obvious to him that retaining the vice president would be more disruptive than dispensing with him in the light of almost a month of violent clashes in the capital. He who had fully supported the 11 January decree, to quote one historian, "now abandoned it and Gómez Farías, both because of political expediency and to some extent because of his government's desperate need for money to prosecute the war." A compromise was reached. The Church agreed to lend the government between one and a half and two million pesos in cash. Santa Anna agreed, as president, to remove Gómez Farías and the post of vice president; to name a moderado, General Pedro María Anaya, acting president, while he set off to organize the Mexican defense of Xalapa, Córdoba, and Orizaba; and to nullify the 11 January anti-clerical legislation.[22]

There was a marked sense of exasperation in the manifesto he circulated after he returned to the capital. He wanted to dedicate himself to fighting the invaders; he clearly did not want to waste time sorting out the political mess in the capital. The events in the capital epitomized everything he hated about political factionalism. While he had put together an army and marched north to confront the invaders, poorly resourced, and seen around fifteen thousand men die to defend Mexico, the political class in the capital had been incapable of putting aside their differences. They had bickered, plotted, and counterplotted, ultimately creating a situation where no clearly defined government existed. In the meantime, the U.S. Army, led by General Winfield Scott, had captured Veracruz (29 March). He did not mince his words on hearing of the fall of the port: "However shameful it may be to admit this, we have brought this disgraceful tragedy upon ourselves through our interminable in-fighting."[23]

Coinciding with his brief return to the capital in March, he met with Tornel. After three years of estrangement the two men overcame their differences and somehow reestablished their old friendship, which had been severely damaged by the caudillo's forcing Tornel to resign in 1844 and then ordering his banishment from the capital in September–October 1846, because Tornel had served as Paredes y Arrillaga's minister of war during Santa Anna's Cuban exile and had not renounced his centralism. Regardless of their longstanding personal ties, however, politics was also on the agenda. Considering the dislike Tornel felt for Gómez Farías, it is feasible that he persuaded Santa Anna to drop his association with the puro federalists. The way Santa Anna turned against Gómez Farías would certainly appear to suggest that Tornel had some influence on his actions. In moderate José Fernando Ramírez's words, Santa Anna turned against the Gómez Farías administration because Tornel "perverted him with ideas that were entirely contrary [to what was expected], convincing him to march to take over the government because *his personal security and the salvation of the republic depended upon this step*." Tornel went on to create a santanista league to consolidate their power over the federalists, silencing the moderate and radical enemies of the president as he set off to fight the invaders at Cerro Gordo.[24]

Having temporarily restored peace in Mexico City, Santa Anna left the capital on 3 April. As his coach made its way out of Mexico City the crowd could distinctly hear the caudillo hoarsely calling out to them, time and again, "Union, Mexicans, union, union!" He reached his hacienda of El Encero on the 5th and set about organizing a new army with which he could halt Scott's ascent from Veracruz to the Altiplano. He could feed his troops with his cattle and the produce of his land. This solved one problem. However, they also needed to be armed. Political divisions continued to cripple the government as moderates, puros, and a reinvented faction of santanistas vied for power. Santa Anna in El Encero, and Gaona in Perote, both wrote to the minister of war, on 7 and 8 April, begging the garrisons in Puebla and Mexico City to supply their eastern army with gunpowder. They had no funds, and neither the state legislature of Veracruz nor the town council of Xalapa had any money left to assist them. Santa Anna had no option but to pay 560 pesos from his own pocket to cover the cost of the materials they needed to make their ammunition. The men responsible for holding onto Puente Nacional had been forced to retreat, having run out of supplies.[25]

His consolation was that he could choose the terrain where they would wait for Scott's army. He knew the land well. He would be fighting quite literally on home ground, on a route he had traveled countless times. He had grown up in the region and fought there as a royalist, an insurgent, and a federalist rebel. Confident in his knowledge of the region, he ignored the recommendations of the commander of engineers, Lieutenant Colonel Manuel Robles Pezuela, and chose to fortify Cerro Gordo, also known at the time as El Telégrafo. Robles Pezuela believed that Corral Falso, farther up the slope and nearer Xalapa, was a better location, as its fields would allow Santa Anna to make better use of the cavalry. Santa Anna, who subsequently denied that any such suggestion was made, clearly thought he knew best.[26]

While it is true that the chaparral, ravines, and steep slopes that surround Cerro Gordo limited the impact the cavalry could have on the battle, the choice of Cerro Gordo was not as foolish as Santa Anna's critics later made it out to be. Cerro Gordo (Fat Hill) lies at the top of the long and steep slope where the tropical yellow-fever-infested hotlands of the coast are finally left behind. It towers over the area, affording those who climb it a spectacular view of the densely vegetated slopes below and the Gulf of Mexico in the distance. It is a natural vantage point and one that is not easily accessible because of its height and the thick vegetation that grows on and around it. To its right as one faces the Gulf of Mexico is the Xalapa-Veracruz road, which meanders down to Plan del Río, alongside the Río Azul (Blue River), dropping from 500 to 300 meters above sea level. To its left is a smaller promontory, Cerro Chato (Small Hill), which was then known as the Atalaya. If Santa Anna succeeded in adequately fortifying his positions on and around Cerro Gordo, there is no denying that Scott was going to have a hard time breaking through his defenses.[27]

After his usual frantic endeavors, he fortified Cerro Gordo with around 9,000 men and 40 pieces of artillery. Under his command he had the 4,000 "veterans" who had seen action in Angostura, General Valentín Canalizo's 2,000-strong cavalry, and 3,000 new recruits, many of whom belonged to the militia units known as the *guardias nacionales*.

Scott's expeditionary army numbered a similar figure, which in turn meant that with the advantages the terrain afforded him, Santa Anna stood a good chance of halting the Americans' advance. If the Americans were made to stall in Plan del Río (rather than at Cerro Gordo, which is where they would have camped had Santa Anna waited for them at Corral Falso, as recommended by Robles Pezuela), Santa Anna would succeed in keeping "the Americans in the yellow-fever zone."[28]

With it becoming increasingly obvious that Scott would attempt to ascend the Cerro Gordo Pass, Santa Anna wasted no time in fortifying Cerro Gordo. It was as he distributed his men and prepared for battle that Robles Pezuela questioned his tactics again. According to the engineer, the Cerro de la Atalaya (Cerro Chico) had not been given the attention it deserved. It was imperative that more men and heavy artillery were mobilized to the Atalaya hill to ensure that the Americans did not flank the main bulk of the Mexican army by seizing this badly defended left-hand position. Santa Anna told Robles Pezuela that as the Cerro Gordo (Telégrafo) was on higher ground, were the Americans to take Atalaya (Cerro Chico), they would not be able to cause his men much trouble. He did not see how the Americans could take Cerro Chico anyway. It was above a particularly impenetrable forest and above a very steep ravine: "Not even a rabbit could reach it." If the Americans took it, the Mexicans would fell them with the batteries on Cerro Gordo.[29]

At twelve noon on 17 April 1847, Scott launched his first attack. The first clash of arms lasted four hours and was extremely intense. Both sides suffered significant losses. Nevertheless, Santa Anna's men held their ground. While it became clear that some U.S. forces were attempting to take the Atalaya hill, these were kept at bay by Mexican fire for the greater part of the day. As night fell, convinced that Scott would try to storm Cerro Gordo again the following morning, Santa Anna reinforced his positions on the main hill. He claimed later that the precarious situation of the Atalaya did not escape him, having seen the U.S. attempts to seize it that day, and that he went in person before the crack of dawn, in the early hours of the 18th, and placed five battery pieces there. He was lying. After a long day's combat, in the late evening of the 17th, General James Shields's brigade succeeded in taking the Atalaya. Moreover, under the cover of darkness, the U.S. forces were able to drag several artillery pieces up onto it. Santa Anna, convinced that the main attack would develop along his front and right flanks, did not pay the necessary attention to the developments on the Atalaya.[30]

When the battle recommenced on the morning of 18 April, his positions on Cerro Gordo found themselves pounded by cannon fire from the Atalaya. Under the cover of this heavy cannonade, General David E. Twiggs and Colonel William S. Harney's men were able to flank the Mexican forces from the left. At the same time a full frontal attack on Cerro Gordo was launched by General Gideon Pillow, on the back of an unexpected incursion on the Mexican right flank led by General Bennet Riley. The battle was carnage, with man to man fighting. Santa Anna not only lost between one thousand and three thousand men; some of his old veracruzano comrades in arms died in the fray. One of these was General Ciriaco Vázquez. Once it became clear that the U.S. forces were on the verge of cutting off the Mexican army's retreat, Santa Anna withdrew from Cerro Gordo, and those who stayed surrendered after "three hours of appalling violence." It was an unmitigated disaster. As expressed by José Fernando Ramírez in a letter he penned to Francisco Elorriaga on 25 April 1847: "Our ill-fortune in Cerro Gordo has been a defeat that is both complete and shameful; everything has been lost, nothing saved, absolutely nothing; not even hope."[31]

Following the battle of Cerro Gordo, Scott's army was able to progress to Xalapa, and from there on to Puebla, without meeting any significant opposition. Santa Anna claimed that much to his dismay, neither in Orizaba nor in Puebla did he find the people prepared or willing to fight for their mother country: "There was neither the enthusiasm or the patriotism I was hoping to find; they were all resigned to receive the invader . . . the idea of resistance was not sustained by anybody [among the civilian population]." It was as he retreated back to the capital, defeated and disheartened, that news reached him that there were politicians who had had the nerve to accuse him of being exclusively interested in self-aggrandizement. He could not contain his disbelief. How could there be people prepared to bicker over his dictatorial tendencies and his badly disguised ambition when he was risking his life trying to repulse the invaders? In an angry letter to the minister of war from Ayotla, on the outskirts of the capital, he protested that since he had returned to Mexico he had spent his life campaigning against the foreign intruders. He had given thought to the presidency only when the majority of the country's deputies had urged him to put an end to the civil war that had exploded in the very heart of Mexico. Close to despair in the wake of the defeat of Cerro Gordo, his self-esteem having reached rock-bottom, he wrote to Congress to offer his resignation on 18 May.[32]

It was at this point that many of the santanistas who had been estranged from him since the summer of 1844 rallied behind their leader. Just as Santa Anna announced in exasperation to Congress that he was willing to resign, he was visited in Ayotla by none other than his old friend Tornel. Tornel dissuaded him from letting the moderates determine what happened next. Urging him to be strong, Tornel convinced Santa Anna that he should take hold of the government the moment he got back to the capital and place the santanistas of the early 1840s in key positions of power. Following Tornel's advice, Santa Anna returned to Mexico City, called a military junta, and broke with the moderates in the same way that he had broken with the puros the previous month. Many of the men who had worked for the 1841–44 administration regained their former influence. Tornel, Trigueros, and Baranda were three former santanista ministers who started to make their mark on the government. Mustering the courage to fight on, Santa Anna reorganized yet another new army with which to confront the invaders, this time in the heart of the republic.[33]

On 20 May 1847 an extraordinary meeting was held in Mexico City attended by nearly all the generals based in the area. The purpose of the meeting was to decide whether they should surrender. The minutes of the meeting, held in the Archive of the Mexican Ministry of Defense, provide a rare and insightful account of what the Mexican high command thought of the war at the time. It is an important document given that it contains the reasons used by Mexico's top brass to explain the U.S. victories up until the end of May 1847.[34]

They were all aware of their appalling situation. Scott's army had occupied Puebla (15 May) and it would not be long before he advanced to the capital. They were also aware that it continued to be extremely difficult to present the invading army with a united front. A number of generals lamented the irreparable damage that factionalism had inflicted upon Mexico in its time of need. They could not believe that even now, with the U.S. forces only kilometers away from the capital, there were still parties who were prepared to plot against each other. The memory of the recent Revolt of the Polkos was clearly on the generals' minds. Contempt was expressed for "the parties that unfortunately divide the country, and that instead of proclaiming a reconciliation and a tight union of all the Mexican people, as they should, persevere, on the contrary, in destroying one another, incessantly promoting civil wars." In a similar vein, the junta noted its disgust for the lack of support the army had received. How could there still be state legislatures that were refusing to send funds and men to save their country? How could the war be sustained with a bankrupt treasury? The army had not been given the kind of resources it needed, and this was unlikely to be rectified now. The absence of a generalized national spirit troubled the generals. The parties were more interested in discrediting the country's officers than in defending their country. The press was more concerned with spreading a message of doom and gloom than in rallying behind the army. Santa Anna then stressed that if the generals present felt that he stood in the way of victory, he was willing to resign. The generals rejected his offer. Despite being acutely aware of the imminent danger facing the capital and, by default, Mexico, when it came to voting on whether the war should continue, not one general voted against fighting. They voted unanimously in favor of channeling all of the country's energies into organizing the defense of Mexico City.[35]

Following the generals' decision to dedicate themselves to forming a strong army in the Valley of Mexico, Santa Anna entered into a new round of secret negotiations with Polk's emissaries. Back in April 1846 Polk had asked Congress for a million dollars so that he "might be able to settle our Mexican difficulty speedily." After Scott captured Puebla (15 May), conscious that the march to Mexico City was proving bloodier and more difficult than he expected, he decided to make use of the "secret service funds" Polk had entrusted to himself and Nicholas P. Trist to "overcome the resistance of members of [the Mexican] Congress." With the U.S. forces preparing to leave Puebla and start the march to the capital, Santa Anna found a way of contacting Scott in the last week of June. British residents were employed as go-betweens, and money changed hands again. By all accounts, Santa Anna pocketed another significant sum, reported to have been ten thousand dollars, delivered on 12 July, to "persuade" his government to accept Scott's terms. Santa Anna's proposition was as follows: if Scott's army remained in Puebla and paid him ten thousand dollars immediately and a million dollars when negotiations were over, he would ensure that talks could commence. Of course, the caudillo, by taking the money without having any intention of fulfilling his part of the deal, proved as infuriatingly frustrating as ever for Polk, who indignantly denied all knowledge of the transactions thereafter, and for Scott, who faced an official investigation in 1848.[36]

It is not difficult to imagine that Santa Anna reveled in this piece of trickery. He gave himself a little more time to organize the defense of the Valley of Mexico and made an excellent deal in the meantime, lining his pockets nicely. Had the Americans not learned from their earlier mistakes? Did they really think he would make life easier for them? He was back to his good old ingeniously deceitful self; the general of tricks. With no news forthcoming from him once the money changed hands, Scott finally decided to start the climb into the Valley of Mexico on 7 August 1847. Santa Anna did what he could, in the month he stole from the invading army, to organize the capital's defenses. As he put it himself, "the invader lost three months waiting for reinforcements, and I made the most of this time [to prepare for the forthcoming campaign]."[37]

He concentrated on recruiting more men, seeking the means to feed, dress, and arm them, fortifying strategic points in and around the capital, and giving his army a sense of pride and purpose. He also strove to drill into the populace of the capital a sense that this was a war that affected them. They needed to be awakened from their ostensible apathy, made to realize that the enemy really was at the gates and that it was their obligation to defend their country. He exhorted the people of Mexico to rally to the defense of the capital. He called upon them to fight until death and urged them to draw on the memory of their glorious past. He reminded them of Hidalgo and Iturbide's heroic deeds and of his 1829 victory of Tampico.[38]

He also wrote a circular addressed to the invading soldiers, inviting them to desert. He pointed out that Mexico had caused them no offense and that it was a country with rich lands in which "all the races receive equal treatment, in which there is liberty and no slaves." If they were prepared to desert, he promised to recompense them with land and the possibility of living among the free Mexican people. The Mexican people remained uninterested in the preparations for war; something that would lead Mariano Otero to say that "there has not been, nor could there have been, a national spirit, for there is no nation." Scott's U.S. forces were too engrossed in their adventure to pay any heed to Santa Anna's invitation.[39]

On 11 August Scott's army arrived at the village of Ayotla, only twenty kilometers away from Mexico City. Santa Anna, thinking Scott would approach the capital from the east, placed the main bulk of his army in and around San Antonio. He made sure, all the same, that he deployed the 25,000 men he had succeeded in placing under arms along a number of strong points on the periphery of the capital. Scott's scouts were able to see that the San Antonio entrance into the city was heavily guarded, and provisions were made to explore the possibility of an advance along the south.[40]

Over the next two days Scott moved his army to San Agustín de las Cuevas, around thirteen kilometers away from the capital's southern city gates. Santa Anna responded to Scott's flanking movement by dispatching a large contingent of his army to fortified posts between Contreras and Churubusco. From Scott's perspective it became imperative to find a way through the lava field of El Pedregal in order to flank the Mexican line of defense. On 18 August, Captain Robert E. Lee found such a way. Major General Gideon J. Pillow's division set about building a road to enable the artillery to pass, and together with Brigadier General David E. Twiggs's division, they advanced along it, reaching the outskirts of Padierna on the afternoon of 19 August. It was then that General Gabriel Valencia, who had received instructions to defend the Mexican positions in Coyoacán, disobeyed Santa Anna's orders and impetuously decided to confront Pillow and Twiggs's divisions alone. Initially, Valencia's forces held out. However, the clash of arms was interrupted by a particularly heavy rainstorm.

Santa Anna claimed subsequently that he was horrified the moment he heard of Valencia's lack of discipline. He accused Valencia of being blind with ambition, of taking on the invading army without consulting his superiors. The consequences were to be fatal. He confronted the enemy six and a half kilometers south of where he was meant to be positioned, where the other generals assumed he was, and where he could have been assisted with reinforcements. He allowed the invaders to determine the time and place of the battle when he should have waited for the U.S. forces to weaken their line of supplies and communications by luring them farther away from the bulk of their army and closer to the Mexican defenses.

Santa Anna attempted to mobilize the forces he had under his command in San Angel to support Valencia. He dispatched Francisco Pérez at the head of three thousand men to Padierna. U.S. artillery fire prevented them from reaching Valencia, however. Those of Pérez's troops who did come close to reinforcing Valencia's men were mistaken for Americans and were killed by friendly fire. Having deployed a large force to aid Valencia, to no avail, Santa Anna ordered Valencia to spike his guns, destroy his ammunition, and retreat. Valencia ignored him. In a last desperate bid to salvage the situation, Santa Anna attempted to bolster Valencia's troops by reinforcing them with his own army. However, the heavy downpour prevented his force from reaching Valencia. By the time his division approached Padierna on the morning of the 20th, Valencia's army was retreating in disarray. At 3:00 A.M. the U.S. forces had found a concealed route along a hidden ravine that took them behind Valencia's defenses. At 6:00 A.M., when the fighting was renewed, Valencia's forces were routed, attacked from behind as well as from the front.[41]

Santa Anna was forced to withdraw to the fortified positions in Churubusco. Here the Mexican army presented the invaders with a spirited defense. They held onto the convent and bridge of Churubusco from nine in the morning to five in the evening. Santa Anna fought alongside Generals Manuel Rincón and Pedro María Anaya at the head of their respective divisions in the defense of Churubusco and supported them by allocating them the retreating forces based at San Antonio and Contreras. The San Patricio Battalion, made up of U.S. deserters (mainly

Catholics of Irish extraction), was also summoned to the defense of Churubusco. As the day went on, it became evident to Santa Anna that he needed to counter the rapidly increasing enemy presence to his rear. This led him to withdraw a few kilometers north of Churubusco at the head of the Fourth Light Cavalry unit. The so-called Mexican heroes of Churubusco he left behind fought on until they ran out of ammunition. Once this happened they had no choice but to surrender. The culmination of the actions of Padierna-Contreras and Churubusco (19–20 August 1847) resulted in a U.S. victory. However, it had been a costly affair for both sides. Santa Anna claimed that the battle of Churubusco was a victory of sorts for the Mexican army, and that the Mexicans' valiant defense of the convent and bridge forced Scott to ask him to accept an armistice.[42]

In reality, it was Santa Anna who called for a ceasefire. The Mexican losses had been significant. Santa Anna had lost almost a third of his force, approximately, ten thousand men, in the two battles. Following consultation with his ministers, it was agreed that a truce might give the Mexicans the chance to garner their strength and recover from the defeats of Padierna and Churubusco. Astute as ever, Santa Anna did not commit his proposal of an armistice to paper. Instead he sent a Mexican officer under a flag of truce to meet up with Scott and give the U.S. commander a verbal request to stop hostilities. Scott, either because he believed that peace was at hand or because his troops were also in much need of some respite, committed himself in writing, on 21 August, to formally requesting an armistice. Santa Anna was then able to claim that he was accepting the U.S. request for an armistice, which was proof in itself of how much Scott's army had suffered and how weak the enemy's position was. As may be evidenced in the minister of war's reply, wherein it was confirmed that "the president and general-in-chief [. . .] accepts the proposal to hold an armistice session," Santa Anna succeeded in getting the documents to back his claim that it was Scott, and not Santa Anna, who asked for an armistice.[43]

On 24 August the armistice was ratified, and on 1 September José Joaquín de Herrera, Ignacio Mora y Villamil, José Bernardo Couto, and Miguel Atristán met Polk's emissary, Nicholas Trist, in Atzcapotzalco. Trist proposed a treaty in which Texas, New Mexico, Alta and Baja California, and part of Sonora would be handed over to the United States "in perpetuity," as would exclusive rights to use and exploit the Isthmus of Tehuantepec. In exchange, the United States agreed to waive all claims for war reparations and to provide a cash settlement. The Mexican government categorically rejected Trist's proposal. Santa Anna noted his disdain in his memoirs. The pretensions of the Washington government were scandalous. Neither he nor his commission was going to agree to such an insulting treaty.[44]

It was in the middle of the armistice—while Santa Anna set about breaking its terms on multiple accounts, principally to prepare the defense of the capital—that on 27 August 1847 in Congress, deputy Ramón Gamboa accused Santa Anna of treason. Santa Anna's disbelief would be as great almost thirty years later as it was when he first heard of Gamboa's attack: "Accusations of treason against the only caudillo who was fighting resolved, sacrificing everything, from one end of the Republic to the other!" What could possess any Mexican in his right mind to call for an investigation of their leading general when the invading army was literally at the city gates? For Santa Anna, Gamboa's behavior epitomized the lack of patriotism of much of Mexico's political class. Gamboa, like so many others, was more interested in gaining political ground by making clever allegations in Congress than by fighting side by side with his fellow Mexicans. Nevertheless, Gamboa's accusations, developed further on 17 November 1847, would prove remarkably influential in determining much of the historiography's understanding of Santa Anna's actions during the Mexican-American War.[45]

With negotiations having broken down, the hostilities were renewed on 6 September. In the time Santa Anna had managed to secure thanks to the armistice, he realigned the city's defenses, repositioning his forces on and around the southern hill of Chapultepec. Given that the U.S. advance was coming from the south, this made plenty of sense. As ever, he was his usual energetic self as he rode around the south of the city, organizing its defenses. Guillermo Prieto provides us with a vivid portrait of his behavior at the time: "You could see Santa Anna constantly crossing the street[s], now ordering a march, now reconnoitering an incredibly dangerous post, showing fearless valor, now quarreling with some muleteers, now shouting and fighting some cart-drivers, now making deals and holding meetings full of interruptions with his staff and employees."[46]

On 8 September the battles of Casa Mata and Molino del Rey were fought. Having heard that Molino del Rey was where the Mexicans kept a factory for casting cannon, Scott sent General William Worth at the head of 3,400 men to take it. Molino del Rey was to prove the most costly battle of the campaign for the U.S. invading army. U.S. casualties rose to 800 men, and their eventual victory proved empty since there were no cannon there. For Santa Anna the battle would have had a different outcome had General Juan Álvarez committed his 4,000-strong cavalry to backing up General Antonio León's artillery fire. Instead, Santa Anna claimed Álvarez did little but contemplate the clash of arms from afar, like a spectator. Like that of Santa Anna and so many other high-ranking officers, Álvarez's conduct would subsequently be investigated.[47]

As the U.S. army approached the capital the chaos of war led to numerous misunderstandings and fatal blunders. One example of this was Santa Anna's unnecessary excursion to the gates of the Candelaria and San Lázaro on 13 September, after General Antonio Vizcaíno had sworn to him that the enemy was about to attack these points. The enemy was not there—but was in fact assaulting the Castle of Chapultepec on its way into the capital. After a day spent pounding the Castle of Chapultepec with a 2,000-round artillery bombardment (12 September), the U.S. forces assaulted Chapultepec, where the cadets of the Colegio Militar were based. Following an hour and a half of severe fighting, General Bravo surrendered at 9:30 A.M., and Scott's army was able to advance up to the capital's city gates of San Cosme and Belén.[48]

Santa Anna set about leading the defense of Belén. When a messenger rushed to tell him that San Cosme was about to fall, he left General Andrés Terrés in charge of the defense of Belén and made his way to assist the men fighting to save San Cosme. According to his memoirs, he succeeded in preventing the U.S. troops from taking San Cosme. However, the city gates of Belén, left open, fell to the invader after Terrés decided to abandon his position. Confirmation of this last piece of news was the arrival of U.S. troops in the proximity of the Ciudadela barracks. Santa Anna dedicated the next few hours to forcing these U.S.

troops back as far as Belén, where they barricaded themselves. He led two attacks against the forces that had occupied Belén but was unable to recover the lost gates. When General Terrés presented himself the caudillo exploded, tore off his epaulettes, and whipped him in the face with his horsewhip.[49]

That night the Mexican high command held a meeting in the Ciudadela barracks that lasted for three long hours. All the generals present took it in turns to make their views known. They all regretted the lack of enthusiasm and support they had received from the people. Only the soldiers had shown a disposition to fight. Without the support of the masses, Mexico City could not be saved. It would cause unnecessary deaths among the civilian population to try to defend the capital to the bitter end. The junta decided, unanimously, to abandon Mexico City at the head of the Mexican army and proceed to Guadalupe Hidalgo, leaving the capital in the hands of the governor of the federal district. Therefore, on 14 September the government decided to move out of the capital and head for Querétaro. Santa Anna, who had come to the conclusion that there was no point in defending Mexico City any longer, opted to take what remained of the army out of the capital and reorganize it, to continue the war.[50]

On 14 September 1847 Scott's U.S. army made its way into the center of Mexico City. On seeing the invading troops advance into the capital, the people of the capital, abandoned by the army, finally woke up to what was happening and tried to resist the U.S. soldiers. They fought against the soldiers with whatever they had at hand. But it was too little, too late. By the next day the National Palace was taken and the stars and stripes flag was raised in the Zócalo. Carlos María de Bustamante wrote in his diary on 15 September: "Today, 37 years ago, the happy voice of Dolores was heard. Today a wounded scream is heard all over the Republic . . . the Mexican Republic is finished, as is its independence and liberty . . . God, please let me ask you, have you done this so that the world can see in the full light of day how you punish a people who have not made good use of their independence?"[51]

Santa Anna did not consider the U.S. capture of Mexico City to constitute the end of the war. He was determined to keep fighting. He asked the government to send him funds and munitions and made his way to

Puebla. Despite his worthy intentions, he did not have the men or resources to develop a guerrilla-based war of attrition against the invaders. On 22 September he reached the outskirts of Puebla at the head of four thousand men and six pieces of artillery with the intention of harassing the U.S. fortified positions of Loreto, Guadalupe, San José, and San Juan de Dios and of attacking a U.S. convoy that was expected from Xalapa. However, massive desertions in his army soon started to make themselves felt. In a matter of four days, Santa Anna lost five hundred men. Although Juan Álvarez joined him at the head of his own depleted troops, willing to carry out an attack on the U.S. forces in the area, the two men were aware that their men were demoralized and looking for the right moment to leave. Álvarez and Santa Anna decided that the best course of action was for Santa Anna to head south for Oaxaca, where he could reorganize his army and replenish it with the troops held in that State. Once their army was reinforced, they believed it would be possible to renew the war against the forces of occupation, launching a counteroffensive from the south.[52]

Before heading south, Santa Anna tried nonetheless to persevere with his original plan near Nopalucan. However, he was forced to retreat to the outskirts of Huamantla on 8 October. In two weeks his army had been reduced from four thousand men to just one thousand. On the 10th he attacked the U.S. troops stationed in Huamantla. He claimed his force killed around one hundred of them during the assault and that twenty-four American soldiers surrendered. From there he pursued a U.S. convoy through Acajete and Amozoc but failed to prevent it from entering Puebla. He returned to Huamantla still determined to "seek the enemy and continue to harry him, as best I can." However, help was not forthcoming, and finally "such was [his] despair that [he] resolved to retreat to Oaxaca."[53]

In the days following the action of Huamantla, the Mexican government that was formed in Toluca following the army's departure from the capital relieved him of all command. Manuel de la Peña y Peña, the president of the Supreme Court of Justice who became president of the republic by default following Santa Anna's resignation on 16 September, backed the newly formed cabinet's decision to prevent Santa Anna from derailing the peace treaty they took it upon themselves to negotiate. Devastated, Santa Anna wrote several letters of protest to the government, urging them not to surrender, but his words were of no avail. Intent on persevering with the struggle, he made his way to Oaxaca as Álvarez and he had planned. However, his intention to reorganize a new army was foiled when, on entering the southern state, he was informed that Benito Juárez, then governor of Oaxaca, had ordered that he was to be denied access to Oaxaca. All the disgust and bitterness he felt at the time is captured in the letter he wrote to the government asking for permission to go into exile. He had been called back to power from exile in 1846 by the Mexican people, and he had given up the pleasures of his retirement to fulfill his patriotic duties, making whatever sacrifices were necessary. He lamented that fate had not been on Mexico's side on this occasion. There was little he could do about this now. However, he was not prepared to accept the accusation a number of "bastards" were bandying about in the press that he was a "traitor." He could not understand how people could say such a thing when his own properties had been ruined by the invaders, when he had paid for his soldiers' salaries out of his own pocket and had not been refunded by the treasury, when he had risked his life on the battlefield, and when rather than accept a degrading peace, he had chosen to keep fighting. He was furious with the government for ordering him to put down his arms, for not having supported him when he tried to keep the campaign going in Puebla, for having abandoned him. He could not believe that if he stayed in Mexico he would have to witness the signing of a humiliating peace treaty. Given that the government did not deem his services necessary, he asked to be allowed to leave Mexico.[54]

His situation took a turn for the worse on 22 January 1848, when General Joseph Lane, at the head of four hundred U.S. dragoons, entered Tehuacán, where they had been informed they would find Santa Anna with his wife and son. General Scott had issued the order to capture Santa Anna at all costs. Just two hours before the American forces fell upon Tehuacán, Santa Anna was woken up in the middle of the night and told that they were approaching. Although he and his family managed to escape, his pursuers broke into his quarters and destroyed all his luggage, stealing the wrought silver he had with him, two walking sticks, and a new uniform, among other valuables. He hid in Teotitlán del Campo until Lane left, then returned to Tehuacán and from there moved on to Coscatlán. With no weapons or troops to fight against the invaders, he was at the mercy of "Mexican bastards and the invaders . . .: the ones call me traitor, the others an obstacle to peace." He wanted protection. He wanted guarantees.[55]

On 2 February 1848 the peace treaty of Guadalupe Hidalgo was signed. The moderate Mexican government of Manuel de la Peña y Peña committed itself to signing away half of the country's territory to the United States. The United States government agreed to furnish the Mexican Republic with fifteen million dollars. Santa Anna was to describe the treaty as one "of eternal shame and bitter regret for every good Mexican." He and his family finally left Mexico in March 1848. They headed first for Jamaica, where they were to spend the following two years in Kingston. Thereafter, urged to move to a Spanish-speaking country by his family, who found it difficult to settle in the British Caribbean colony, Santa Anna and his entourage moved on to Turbaco, in Colombia, where they were to spend the next three years, from April 1850 to April 1853.[56]

The experience of the Mexican-American War was devastating for most Mexicans. Coming to terms with the defeat and the resulting loss of half of the country was to prove difficult. In political terms, Mexico entered a stage of despair. For many politicians, the debacle pointed to the unpalatable truth that the Mexican people did not know how to govern themselves. In the painful process that ensued in which Mexico's political class tried to understand what had happened, the easiest option was to blame particular individuals for what had gone wrong. Most of the generals who fought the war were investigated at one point or another between 1848 and 1850. To note some examples: Mariano Arista faced a court-martial for losing the battles of Palo Alto and Resaca de Guerrero; Generals Manuel Andrade and José María Jauregui were accused of cowardice for their behavior during the Battle of Molino del Rey (8 September 1847); Generals Nicolás Bravo and Andrés Terrés were investigated for having allegedly allowed themselves to be taken prisoner outside the battlefield.[57]

Santa Anna was the obvious candidate to carry the blame for the tragedy. To this day the hegemonic view in Mexico is that the war was lost because he allowed the invading army to win. He was, of course, the perfect scapegoat. As if the entire fate of a war could depend on the actions of one individual, Santa Anna's critics blamed him squarely for the defeat. The numerous, complex factors that had contributed to the defeat were swept under the carpet. The pain of the loss, still felt by many Mexicans to this day, would make coming to terms with the debacle of 1847 a soul-destroying process. Claiming Santa Anna was solely responsible for this devastating defeat hurt less than sharing the blame.[58]

It was within this context of despair that Ramón Gamboa's accusation against Santa Anna was made. He first accused Santa Anna of being a traitor on 27 August 1847, during the armistice. Two years later he developed his original accusation into what became a lengthy study of the caudillo's many acts of treason, completed on 15 July 1849. Gamboa's charges against Santa Anna were to prove remarkably influential. That there are still people today who believe that Santa Anna was a despicable traitor, who deliberately lost the war, we owe in no small measure to Gamboa's compelling interpretation. He believed that the Santa Anna's dealings with Polk's emissaries entailed losing the war on purpose for a significant sum of money, and that he facilitated the conditions for a triumphant U.S. invasion.[59]

Gamboa's thesis was supported by Carlos María de Bustamante, who, in his equally influential and emotive account of the invasion, blamed the federal Constitution, Gómez Farías's puros, and above all Santa Anna's act of treason: "We can only conclude that either this man is entirely mad or that he has come here to conclude the final act of his betrayal, taking our money, dispersing our army, and leaving the way from Veracruz to the capital open for ten U.S. regiments to come in." It is not difficult to appreciate how Gamboa and Bustamante came to interpret Santa Anna's tricks and military failures as proof of some incredibly elaborate master plan. To quote one historian: Santa Anna "was more machiavellian than Machiavelli."[60]

Yet, as has been seen throughout these pages, what Gamboa, Bustamante, and their followers interpreted as an extremely cunning and treacherous plan, executed with amazing aplomb, was nothing more than a litany of errors. To believe that Santa Anna fought in Angostura–Buena Vista and Cerro Gordo with a mind to losing is absurd, considering the documents to hand. As increasing numbers of studies have shown, he did not lose the war deliberately. As was stressed by one biographer, "no one can doubt the sincerity of his effort who reads the accounts of the northern campaign." To suggest otherwise is to ignore the evidence.[61]

Mexico lost the war for many reasons that can only be hinted at here. It was an unequal contest. The population of the United States was already nearing twenty million by the mid-1840s; Mexico's did not rise to more than seven. With the population concentrated mainly on the east, the United States had not had to contend with the same problems as Mexico had, having to overcome the strains placed by a vast territory characterized by its geographical diversity and particularly poor communications. The Mexican population was divided by issues of race and ethnicity that were not yet present in the United States. Although there was no slavery, the social, racial, and regional inequalities made the concept of nationhood a difficult one to grasp. Following its achievement of independence, the United States had benefited from over two decades of peace. With the eruption of the 1789 French Revolution and the Napoleonic Wars serving as a major distraction, the United States had been able to consolidate a stable political system and establish deep-rooted political traditions.

Mexico, in contrast, had had to contend from the outset with Spanish and French military interventions and a hostile international community. The founders of the U.S. Constitution were able to use the experience that a comparatively more autonomous colonial system had afforded them. Their Mexican counterparts were to a greater extent starting from scratch. Mexico also became independent after a brutally devastating eleven-year civil war. The American War of Independence had only lasted six years, and half a century had passed since then, enabling the United States to develop a vibrant economy. Mexico had no economy to speak of. Its treasury was bankrupt. After two decades of constitutional strife and instability, the authority of the Mexican government continued to be challenged by force, even as an invading army landed on its beaches. Although deeply polarized and divided, as would be evidenced two decades later, the majority of the U.S. population was united in the 1840s by hunger for land and expansion, a common belief in their country's Manifest Destiny. Mexico could not have been more divided.

As became evident once the 1824 federal Constitution was reinstated in 1846, not all of its state legislatures responded to the federal government's desperate call for funds and men. The country's political parties reflected Mexican society's polarities, finding it impossible to reach consensus even when the enemy was at the gates. Two decades of repeated armed rebellions meant that the Mexican military commanders, most of whom had fought against each other at some stage, found it difficult to follow each other's orders or come to each other's help. The armies they organized, having to force men to fight through levies and impressment, were not only poorly resourced but lacked discipline, training and a hunger for victory. The U.S. forces were made up of eager volunteers and an army that had all the makings of a professional force. Their weapons were also significantly more powerful and accurate. Many Mexican troops were still having to make do with guns that dated from the War of Independence.

Mexico was up against a country that had political stability and economic resources. Painful as it was to accept, moreover, its population did not seem to have any sense of nationhood. For the great majority, the war only provoked a patriotic reaction when they saw the invading army with their own eyes. Even then, the great mass of the population viewed the intervention with indifference. All this explains why President Manuel de la Peña y Peña believed that the 1848 Treaty of Guadalupe Hidalgo was a triumph of sorts. His people deserved praise for having saved at least half of their national territory and for not having lost it all to the United States. In the light of these ideas, it is possible to suggest that although Santa Anna was soundly defeated as commander general of the Mexican forces, he deserves credit for his desperate and valiant year-long defense of his country.[62]

With Mexico beaten and Santa Anna forced into exile, accused of being a traitor, a turncoat, and a tyrant, most people must have thought this was the end of the caudillo's career. Extraordinary as it may be, the Spanish minister plenipotentiary, Salvador Bermúdez de Castro, was not so sure. As he wrote somewhat prophetically in the summer of

1847, Santa Anna would most certainly be back: "The man who has just lost two battles and two armies cannot be popular or head a nation. But since all of his rivals are more ignorant than he and more inept, since they do not know how to inspire obedience . . . and lack the profound knowledge Santa Anna has acquired of his countrymen, it is certain that they will let him be president again."[63]

Part 5
The Autumn of the Patriarch, 1849–1876

By virtue of the authority vested in me by my own right and
and the help of Peachey, I declare myself Grand-Master of all
Freemasonry in Kafiristan in this the Mother Lodge o' the
country, and King of Kafiristan equally with Peachey!
Rudyard Kipling, The Man Who Would Be King

I have liv'd long enough: my way of life
Is fallen into the sere, the yellow leaf;
And that which should accompany old age,
As honour, love, obedience, troops of friends,
I must not look to have; but in their stead,
Curses, not loud, but deep, mouth-honour, breath,
Which the poor heart would fain deny, and dare not.
William Shakespeare, Macbeth

13. The Man Who Would Be King, 1849–1855

Toward the end of Simón Bolívar's life, the liberator of the present-day countries of Venezuela, Colombia, Panama, Ecuador, Peru, and Bolivia had come to despair of his people's ability to forge a stable and representative political system. The nature of the countries' population, their lack of political experience, and the propensity of their congresses to tie "the hands and even the heads of its men of state" meant that "no form of government is so weak as the democratic." They were "far from emulating the happy times of Athens and Rome"; they could not compare themselves "in any way to anything European." Given that their race was "of the most unwholesome sort," they were not in a position to "place laws above heroes and principles above men." If they attempted to do so, they would witness again "the beautiful ideal of a Haiti and see a breed of new Robespierres become the worthy magistrates of this fearful liberty." In brief, "our America can only be ruled through a well-managed, shrewd despotism." On 9 November 1830, two months before his death and while he was preparing to go into exile, an ailing Bolívar wrote one of the bleakest texts penned by a Latin American liberator:

> You know that I have been in a position of power for twenty years, and from these I have only been able to draw a few uncertain conclusions: 1. America is ungovernable for us; 2. He who serves in a revolution ploughs the sea; 3. The only thing you can do in America is emigrate; 4. This country [Gran Colombia] will fall infallibly into the hands of a wild multitude,

and then go on to be governed by minor and imperceptible
tyrants of all races and colors; 5. Devoured by all possible
crimes and extinguished by their ferocity, the Europeans will
not lower themselves to conquer us; 6. If it were possible for
a part of the world to return to its original state of primitive
chaos, this would be the last period of history in America.

Bolívar's despair was to be echoed in the writings of his Mexican contemporaries.[1]

Manuel de Mier y Terán's suicide in July 1832, on the very spot where
Iturbide had been executed, was probably the most striking as well
as the earliest expression of a parallel Mexican despair. Mier y Terán
had inspected Texas in 1828 and had realized that it was only a matter
of time before the province was lost. He had fought alongside Santa
Anna against Barradas's Spanish expedition in 1829 and had then been
encouraged to replace Anastasio Bustamante as president. Many perceived Mier y Terán as one of Mexico's most gifted and intelligent general-politicians. He was also extremely sensitive and deeply affected by
the fading into thin air of the hopes of the early 1820s. José María Luis
Mora had no doubts about the motive that inspired Mier y Terán to drive
his sword into his chest: "the political state of the country."[2]

José María Gutiérrez Estrada's 1840 monarchist proposal was also
an expression of despair. They had tried every possible form of government and all had failed. The history of the first national decades was
written in blood. The only outcomes of independence had been penury,
civil war, tyranny, and loss. Whether they had adopted a federalist or
centralist constitution, the result had always been anarchy. For Gutiérrez Estrada it was clear that they needed a European prince to save them.
As was noted in an 1849 calendar: "For war? We aren't [any good]. For
governing? We don't know how. Thus why do we exist?"[3]

The war with the United States had amply demonstrated the extent
of their failure. So many deaths, so much destruction, and half of Mexico's national territory had been irrevocably lost. The first three decades
of independent life had been a long, painful haul that could possibly
culminate in the eradication of the entire Mexican nation. There were
those like Lucas Alamán who feared that it was only a matter of time

before the United States moved in and took the rest. If Mexico's political class failed to get their act together the complete disintegration of the republic would be unavoidable. As Tornel argued in the history of the early national period that he compiled during these years, "there is a threat of new misfortunes, and even of a definitive and tragic cataclysm that may bring an end to our political existence, the glory of our race, our language and the religion of our forebears." Tornel wrote a history of Mexico precisely so that there was a record of "everything that we are, everything that we have, everything that we are worth, . . . and of the great injustice that led the Mexican nation to become a tragic victim."[4]

Following the 1846–48 war, Mexico entered a stage of despair. Besides the humiliation and trauma of the defeat, class and ethnic tensions erupted in a wide range of agrarian revolts. One of the more violent of these was the Caste War fought in Yucatán (1847–52). Unlike all the previous creole-led secessionist revolts that had taken place there prior to 1847, the Caste War was a devastating racial, social, and political revolution in which the Maya almost succeeded in driving the white minority out of Yucatán. Other agrarian and indigenous revolts surfaced in the central Sierra Gorda and in the southern present-day states of Oaxaca, Guerrero, and Morelos, reaching the State of Mexico in 1849. The Mexican political class—regardless of their factional allegiances—became convinced that they were about to suffer an even worse revolution than the French one of 1848, especially given that the agrarian revolts had an additional racial dimension absent in France.[5]

During the moderate presidencies of José Joaquín de Herrera (June 1848–January 1851) and Mariano Arista (January 1851–January 1853) the different factions organized themselves into more formal parties. The year 1849 witnessed the creation of the Conservative party, the Moderate party, the Puro party, and José María Tornel and Juan Suárez y Navarro's Santanista party. Tornel's santanista proposals had evolved to the extent that he had ceased to believe in constitutional projects, in the need for a Congress, or in the need for elections. The despair of the 1848 loss caused him to advocate the creation of a dictatorship that would benefit from having a small council of enlightened individuals to advise its executive and control it. In some respects santanista political thought had evolved in such a way that it shared many of Alamán's conservative principles. They supported the Roman Catholic faith in that it represented one of the fundamental defining characteristics of Mexican nationality and identity—what Alamán described as "the only tie left that unites the Mexican people." They also believed in creating a strong centralist state with a large army and a modern system of taxation. Where they differed from the conservatives was over the santanistas' republicanism and their populist tendencies.[6]

By the end of the 1840s the santanistas had come to see a dictatorship as the only means of establishing long-lasting order, peace, and stability. As was voiced in the Santanista party newspaper, La Palanca, Congress was one of the main culprits of their previous disasters: "Mexico needs a government in which strength may be concentrated and which occupies only a handful of men, a government that thinks, [in a system] in which the majority are not expected to participate in public matters." A weak representative system had brought with it disunity and the loss of "half our territory . . . *the wasted legacy of our elders.*" La Palanca presented the people as a sick man. One of the lessons they needed to learn after three disastrous decades was that this "sick man," while aware of his illness, had not known how to cure himself and had been ill advised and had chosen the wrong doctors. The "sick man" needed a dictatorship: "not just a doctor, but a guardian who ensures the prescribed medicine is taken." The man they wanted to name dictator was, not surprisingly, Santa Anna.[7]

Predictably, the Santanista party presented itself as a national movement rather than as a political party. La Palanca claimed that it was natural, therefore, that the Santanista party included men who had previously been monarchists, puros, and moderates. The santanistas represented a national patriotic movement. They were opposed to "party hatreds" and ardently desired "UNION NATIONALITY." They wanted to create a government in which Santa Anna could rule "our destinies" with a "wide base, in which there may be space for all the factions." This would be possible because a santanista government would not represent "a faction but the people."[8]

However, although Tornel and Suárez y Navarro kept the santanista flag flying in the daily editorials of La Palanca up until November 1850, also publishing historical treatises that glorified Santa Anna's role and influence in Mexico's recent past, the time was not yet right for the santanistas to stage a successful comeback. Only in 1853, after three more years of instability, did it become possible for Tornel and the santanistas, in tandem with the Conservative party, to organize the return of the caudillo.[9]

Such was the failure of Mariano Arista's moderate government to bring any respite to postwar Mexico that conservatives and puros found themselves eventually joining forces in a very unlikely alliance. They were united by their desire to bring down the *moderado* administration but by little else. Santa Anna appeared as a leader they could both use for their own ends. He had been absent from the political scene for long enough not to be associated with any of the warring factions, and his triumphs still appeared to count for more than his failures. There was simply no other leader equally acceptable to santanistas, puros, *and* conservatives.

The movement to stage his return started in Jalisco, on 26 July 1852, when the moderate governor of the state, Jesús López Portillo, was deposed by José María Blancarte's *pronunciamiento*. In his Plan of Guadalajara he demanded Arista's resignation, pledged to retain a federalist system, called for a temporary dictatorship, and asked for a new constituent congress to be formed. This regional outburst was soon supported by a number of *pronunciamientos* staged in the states of Mexico, Coahuila, and Oaxaca. The santanista Juan Suárez y Navarro persuaded Blancarte to issue a second plan, in which it was noted that "the nation invites General Santa Anna to return to the Republic to co-operate with . . . re-establishing order and peace."[10]

Arista soon realized that his was a lost cause. He resigned on 5 January 1853 after Congress refused to give him emergency powers. He was replaced by Juan Bautista Ceballos, who in turn resigned a month later, on 8 February, unwilling to be part of the so-called Agreements of Arroyo Zarco, ratified by the rebels in the first week of February, whereby it was agreed that the temporary president would be awarded extraordinary powers for a year. Thereafter a constituent congress would be convoked and a republican, representative, and popular *magna carta* would be drafted. In the immediate future, the governors of the republic were asked to elect the man who should lead this one-year dictatorship, and it was agreed that this man would then name the twenty-one individuals who would form his State Council.[11]

General Manuel María Lombardini, a die-hard santanista who had accompanied the caudillo during the northern campaign and participated in the battle of Angostura–Buena Vista, stepped in following Ceballos' resignation with the sole objective of preparing the ground for Santa Anna's return. He proved to be remarkably adept at his job. Under his supervision, when the votes of all twenty-three states were counted on 17 March 1853, Santa Anna secured a comfortable majority, with eighteen ballots cast in his favor. Lombardini also passed a law permitting Santa Anna to "wear any foreign orders he possessed or might acquire," named him captain general of the army, and saw to the approval of measures that paved the way for a massive celebration the day he returned from exile.[12]

Since April 1850 Santa Anna and his family had been living in Colombia. By all accounts he had enjoyed his time there, eventually settling down in Turbaco, a village eight kilometers from Cartagena de Indias, in a landscape bearing a great resemblance to his native Veracruz. He put aside his bitterness at the 1847 debacle, at the undignified manner in which he had left Mexico in 1848, and at the troubled year he had spent in Jamaica, where his relatives found coping with the language barrier as well as Anglo-Saxon customs particularly hard. Determined to make the most of his circumstances, he bought a number of properties in Cartagena. During the first year of his family's Colombian stay, he bought and lived in a house in the Calle del Cuartel and purchased a further three properties in the main square of Cartagena, for less than seventeen hundred pesos. He acquired three more houses in the Calle de Lozano and in the Calle de la Puerta del Colegio, which he then sold on for a quick profit. His most prized property in Cartagena, however, was the "house of tiles" (*casa de tejas*) he built on a plot of land once belonging to the archbishop and viceroy Caballero y Góngora, in what is today the Calle República de México.

Having spent the first year of his Colombian exile in Cartagena, he was then tempted to buy the run-down hacienda of La Rosita, in Turbaco, that had once belonged to Simón Bolívar. He found the bronze rings from which the Liberator used to hang his hammock and en-sured that they were left untouched so that he could rest in the very same place as Bolívar had. He channeled his energy into regenerating the local economy of Turbaco, transforming the sleepy, depressed vil-lage, along with La Rosita, into a thriving community. He introduced the planting of sugar cane and tobacco in Turbaco. He was also respon-sible for overseeing the establishment of a sugar mill and a cemetery. He brought cattle into the area and created jobs. He put to good use his experience from his days at the head of the communities of San Di-ego, Tamarindo, Xamapa, and Medellín and inspired the inhabitants of Turbaco to improve their houses and living conditions. He even led the reconstruction of the local church. He was clearly happy in La Rosita. His illegitimate son Ángel fathered two Colombian children with two different women, María de los Ángeles (born on 27 August 1851) and María de las Mercedes (born on 5 December 1851). According to one source Santa Anna was himself not immune to the charm of the *colom-bianas* and fathered several illegitimate children there.[13]

During his exile he continued to receive his salary as general. He was also sent the money acquired by his son-in-law, Francisco de Paula Castro, through the rent of the numerous ranches belonging to his Veracruzan haciendas (Dos Ríos, Ojuelos, Paso de San Juan, Plan del Río, Miradores, etc.). It must be presumed that during his exile it was not just his family with whom he was corresponding. In all likelihood Tornel and other santanistas kept in touch, informing him of events in Mexico. By the time he was invited to return to the republic, he must have had a clear idea of his chances of staging another triumphant re-turn.[14]

On 1 April 1853 news reached Mexico City by telegraph that he had disembarked in Veracruz. Immediately provisions were made for a *Te Deum* to be sung the following morning in the cathedral of Mexico City. Tornel was in Xalapa to initiate the festivities. The return of Santa Anna inspired a plethora of celebrations, demonstrations of allegiance, and poetic tributes. He was again Mexico's favorite arbitrator and the temp-tation of all the parties. All of the factions plotted and counterplotted on the eve of his arrival in Mexico City, in the hope that he would give preference to their men and ideas when appointing his State Council.

Between arriving in Veracruz on 1 April and riding into Mexico City on the 20th, he was visited at El Encero by a whole range of politicians, merchants, and officers, all determined to persuade him to endorse their projects. It was in this context that Lucas Alamán wrote his famous letter of 23 March 1853, outlining what he considered the main principles of the Conservative party, and that the radical liberal Miguel Lerdo de Tejada did the same for the puros on 18 April.[15]

True to form, Santa Anna stressed that he had not come to support the project of any particular party. He created a Cabinet that included conservatives, santanistas, and one alleged puro: Teodosio Lares. Great expectation surrounded Santa Anna, but the challenges he faced were great. The treasury was bankrupt. The northern states were experiencing an increase in Indian raids, and peasant unrest was on the rise. The threat of another caste war remained strong. The government was ridden with factionalism and its representatives lacked authority. The country's political institutions had lost the little prestige they had had. The political class was mistrusted. There was every indication that the United States was on the verge of launching a new offensive. He must have known this was not going to be an easy ride. He said little the day of his triumphant return to the capital, claiming he had a sore throat, and did not attend the sumptuous banquet General Lombardini hosted in his honor that same evening. According to some French observers, he struck them as looking worried and distant.[16]

Santa Anna's entourage worked toward giving the dictatorship a certain façade of constitutional legitimacy. As with the Bases de Tacubaya, this was not intended to be a permanent military dictatorship. He was being asked, once again, to restore peace and order in the republic so that a constituent congress could be formed and a new constitution drafted. Once this had been achieved, he was to abandon his emergency powers and retire to his haciendas.[17]

However, whereas in 1841 there had been a commitment on the part of the santanistas to fulfill these constitutional aspirations, even when the 1842 Constituent Congress was dissolved, the same cannot be said about their intentions in 1853. The experience of three decades of constitutional failure and the trauma of the 1846–48 war had led to the santanistas reneging on their past faith in representative politics. The men behind the 1853–55 dictatorship were committed to having Santa Anna govern the country for an indeterminate period of time. Although his exercise of extraordinary power was supposed to end on 6 February 1854, a *pronunciamiento* in Guadalajara on 17 November 1853 calling for Santa Anna's powers to be prorogued indefinitely was seconded by enough plans of allegiance for the State Council to determine, on 16 December, that he should continue in power. A year later, a referendum of sorts was organized and duly fixed on 1 December 1854, giving him the right to extend his dictatorial rule of the republic for a while longer, receiving 435,530 votes in favor, and 4,075 against. Santa Anna himself admitted that he could not foresee when Mexico would be ready for democracy, even though he wished "such a desirable day comes soon, so that I may be able to retire to my domestic home to conclude my days in peace."[18]

The measures adopted by the 1853–55 government to ensure that all opposition was silenced exceeded anything carried out by any of his previous administrations. It had become obvious to him that authority was no longer respected. He was committed to repressing all forms of subversive immorality, whether this entailed censoring the press or showing zero tolerance to bandits and rebels. In the first year of his government many renowned federalists were exiled, including such prominent figures as Mariano Arista, Benito Juárez, and Melchor Ocampo. The law of 25 April 1853 and those that followed in its wake imposed a particularly effective censorship of the press, leading to the closure of over forty newspapers. Books deemed to be subversive were banned and their authors persecuted. Plays deemed to uphold questionable values were prevented from being performed. Secret police forces were also formed to spy on the population, gather information, and track down pockets of subversion. People were made to carry passports. According to the decree of 1 August 1853, anybody suspected of conspiring against public order was court-martialed and executed if found guilty.[19]

The santanistas' traditional belief in imposing a strong government held firm. Their resolve to forge a powerful administration that could not be weakened by the regional impulses of the provinces and the infighting of political factionalism had become deeper and more urgent.

Santa Anna's flirtation with the puro federalists in 1846 was seen as an aberration. Santanistas like Tornel had espoused the logic of centralism in 1834 and had not looked back. Two days after the dictatorship was inaugurated, it was stipulated that the government would endorse a centralist model. Santa Anna had come around to believing that "the humiliation [of 1846–48] had its origins in these perverse [federalist] doctrines and the anarchic system established in the 1824 charter." It was clear to him that "as long as our national independence is under threat, in Mexico there can be only one government that rules." As a result, all state legislatures were closed down. So were the majority of town councils. All governors were made directly responsible to the president. Beneath them, individual justices of the peace were appointed. The use of the words "free, sovereign, and independent" to describe the states was formally forbidden. By September the term *state* was erased from the political vocabulary, and the provinces became known as departments.[20]

Linked to the santanistas' belief in forging a strong government, and with Tornel again at the head of the Ministry of War, every effort went into creating a large, strong army. Following the humiliation of the Mexican-American War, the need for a regular military force that was well dressed, well armed and adequately trained was seen as a key priority. With the threat of another war still present, there was a sense of urgency in creating an army that could repulse another invasion. Santa Anna made a point of stressing that he saw this as one of his main priorities, especially following the cuts in the army that had been inspired by Arista's moderate government.[21]

His determination to give the army the respect he believed it merited was not limited to increasing its numbers and providing it with modern weapons. He became equally concerned with dressing his troops accordingly. As one observer commented, "The army is being clothed in the most expensive manner, and in the enjoyment of all the colors of the rainbow." It also made sense to have a strong army to quell any pockets of rebellion. By February 1855, Santa Anna claimed he had succeeded in forging an army that had 45,000 well-armed and well-trained veterans. Although he had originally intended to create an army that had 91,499 men, he was pleased with the force that was reorganized under his government. While he would recall much of what was achieved during his dictatorship with pride, the improvements that were made in the army were what he remembered most warmly.[22]

In order to finance the formation of such a powerful army, there was a reprise of the santanistas' past policy of raising taxes and borrowing heavily. This state of affairs was captured in the anecdote Guillermo Prieto recorded in his memoirs, in which he claimed that Tornel one day turned around to the minister of finance, Antonio Haro y Tamariz, and said, "Our system of government consists basically of Señor Haro, minister of finance, looking for money, so that I can throw it away as minister of war." All existing taxes were retained. All abolished direct taxes on properties, industrial activities, salaries, and luxury items were reintroduced. The export tax on minted silver was raised. New export taxes were placed on dyewoods, livestock, and packing house products. The urban tariff known as the *alcabala* was restored, as was the poll tax. The tobacco monopoly was extended, affecting regions that had been relieved from its tributes since 1848. A value added tax was imposed on auctioned goods, and new levies were placed on *mezcal*, loans, mortgages, imported paper, public diversions, commercial enterprises, and properties. People were taxed for owning a dog and for each door or window they had looking out onto the street.[23]

With the conservatives intent on defending the privileged status of the Roman Catholic Church, the santanistas were able to draw on their former defense of the values of the Church as well as of its *fueros* to sustain a dictatorship that was outspoken in its religious agenda. On the one hand, this was a way of attempting to consolidate a sense of national pride and identity, which had been so patently absent during the 1846–48 war. As Santa Anna put it: "The mission I have taken it upon myself to lead extends to preserving the interests of our Religion and Race, handed down to us by our illustrious ancestors." The santanistas had always guaranteed Church and army *fueros*. Their anticlericalism had been an exclusively financial matter. The desperate need for ready cash had led them to support the radicals' measures of 1833–34 and 1847. In the end they had reversed the legislation that had most antagonized the higher clergy—but at a cost. Linked to the conservatives in 1853, the santanistas, although displaying their characteristic commit-

Gral. D.ⁿ Antonio López de Santa Anna; dos veces presidente de la república federal; dos en la central y dictador en 1841 y 1853, con el título de Alteza Serenísima en su última época gubernativa.

Lotog de la Y de Murguía é hijo.

"General Antonio López de Santa Anna, twice President of the Federal Republic, twice of the Central Republic, and Dictator in 1841 and 1853, bore the title of His Serene Highness in his last governmental period." Lithograph intriguingly presents the mature caudillo in civilian and republican clothes. Photo by Alfredo Ávila. Courtesy of Centro de Estudios de Historia de México Condumex, Mexico City.

ment to raising revenue through taxation, avoided alarming the Church with demands for loans. They backed this drive to give the 1853–55 regime a pronounced Catholic-nationalist feel by supporting the return of the Jesuits and ordering the restoration of most of the expropriated properties of the Society of Jesus. Santa Anna also made highly publicized visits to the Basilica of Tepeyac, to demonstrate his veneration of the very Mexican Virgin of Guadalupe.[24]

This stress on the cultural values of the Church came hand in hand with a push to renew what were considered to be autochthonous traditions. Determined to give Mexico a government that respected and indeed promoted the country's customs, in order to foment a unifying sense of patriotic pride throughout the republic, Santa Anna led a renaissance of Mexican political forms. Titles and orders that had their origins in the Mexican War of Independence were recovered. The title of *Su Alteza Serenísma* (His Serene Highness), first donned by the so-called Father of Independence, Miguel Hidalgo, was given to the caudillo by his State Council in December 1853. The Order of Guadalupe, originally created by the other Father of Independence, Agustín de Iturbide, was likewise rescued, and Santa Anna made sure he rewarded his followers by making them members of this privileged sect. It was part of this drive to give Mexican traditions a prominent place in 1850s society that significant attention was given to all aspects pertaining to the realm of ritual and ceremony. Legislation was put in place detailing what civil servants could wear and even how long their mustaches could be.[25]

Likewise, all parades and festivities were treated with extraordinary attention to detail. The instructions laid down for the clothes to be worn during the parade organized to celebrate the foundation of the Order of Guadalupe were over-elaborate and obsessive in their attention to detail. Santa Anna's decision to commission the composition of a national anthem dates from these years and is emblematic of his government's determination to give the country a unifying sense of national pride and identity.[26]

The santanistas' historic anti-parties/anti-politics political credo was incorporated into the administration's move to regenerate the country's "national spirit." Drawing on the views reiterated in *La Palanca*, there was no place for factionalism in Santa Anna's Mexico. They were all Mexicans. They were all Roman Catholics. What they believed in was "UNITY NATIONALITY"; as Santa Anna said himself, "My true program has been, is, and will be: 'THE CONSERVATION OF MEXICAN NATIONALITY AT ALL COSTS.'" For the country to prosper it was essential that all political differences be buried and that the enlightened men who governed the republic did so in the nation's name and not to promote the agenda of one particular party. To quote Santa Anna: "I exercise supreme power with all the independence with which I have always exercised it; never has my name sustained any one particular [party] banner, nor am I, thank heaven, stupid enough to allow myself to be led blindly by the inspiration of one party alone, whatever its name may be."[27]

Having said this, despite his profession of an anti-parties agenda, his dictatorship was rabidly anti-liberal. He blamed the liberals, whether they were puros or moderates, for bringing about the anarchy that had led to his return to power. Their federal constitution, their divided and divisive Congress, the belief in a freedom of the press that was systematically abused, their useless *guardia nacional* (civilian militias) and the multilayered judicial system they defended had exacerbated all of Mexico's troubles. Neither did he forgive Arista's government for "destroying the regular army," the very institution that had brought about Mexico's independence. He pointedly asked in 1855 what they had done while in power to think they could manage the country better than he. What had happened to the millions the United States government had given them following the end of the war? Why had it been necessary for him to return from exile and impose a dictatorship?[28]

The belief espoused by the French journalist Emile Girardin, incorporated in August Comte's positivist philosophy, stressing the need for "plenty of administration, no politics," which is so often associated with General Porfirio Díaz's government (1876–1910), found an early exponent in Santa Anna's 1853–55 dictatorship. The values of "order and progress" defended by Diaz and espoused by most liberal developmentalist (and often authoritarian) Latin American governments of the latter half of the nineteenth century were indeed present in Santa Anna's "peace and order." Contained in the decrees initially inspired by Minister Teodosio Lares was a drive to foster an economic revival in Mexico. The railway was given priority, and a plethora of concessions were given to a whole array of Mexican and foreign companies to develop railway lines from one end of the republic to the other. It is interesting to note that Alejandro Atocha, "the scoundrel" who fooled President Polk as Santa Anna's intermediary, was given the exclusive right to develop one particular railway line for a period of ninety-nine years. Although no proof has been found to substantiate this, it is highly likely that Santa Anna benefited from a bribe or two when granting these concessions.[29]

It was under the tenets of "peace and order" and progress that the dictatorship promoted the establishment of telegraph lines and a network of communications that included the purchase of new stagecoaches and steamboats. A renewed project to link the Atlantic and the Pacific through the Isthmus of Tehuantepec, by developing a canal and improving the roads across the region, was also given a new injection of life. Work was commenced to introduce gas streetlights in the big cities. Particular attention was given to the capital's waterworks in a push to make Mexico City more hygienic. As a reflection of the government's bid to figure among the modern and civilized countries of the day, a whole range of French quality goods became accessible in the capital's high streets. It was also possible to have one's portrait made in daguerreotype.[30]

Santa Anna was indeed proud of his government's "material improvements," and initially, the government's reforms were partially successful. The government was seen to make firm progress in stamping out banditry, improving the highways, stimulating education, reforming the judicial system, and promoting a whole range of "works of material improvement." In the field of education there was a reprise of the santanista populist drive of the 1841–44 administration. Charitable associations together with the Compañía Lancasteriana were encouraged to support a constellation of primary schools. Santa Anna played an active part in visiting some of these institutions. On one such occasion he was deeply moved when surrounded by three thousand "indigent" children. Predictably, he pledged to support all philanthropic organizations dedicated to giving an education to the needy. Awards were also created for "excellence in education" to encourage the professionals to take pride in their work (and, we suspect, to speak well of the government). Santa Anna is said to have actually designed the medal that was given to those headmasters and primary and secondary school teachers whose exertions in their field were deemed outstanding. It carried the initials "A.L.S." on the back, as a reminder of the paternalistic leader who had given all good teachers the recognition they deserved (Antonio López de Santa Anna). On balance, however, Santa Anna's educational reforms in 1853–55 proved far less effective than those implemented by his 1841–44 government. In part, this appears to have been the result of a marked lack of funds, especially after it was determined, for reasons that remain unclear, that Mexico's education service was to share its allocated fund with the judiciary.[31]

The cult of Santa Anna that had characterized in no small measure the santanista administration of 1841–44 was also rekindled and revamped during the dictatorship. His saint's day (13 June) and his victory of 11 September were inscribed in the national calendar of festivities. Statues of Santa Anna were erected once more throughout the republic. The theater of Santa Anna regained its original name. His portrait was hung in all government buildings.

Alongside the santanistas' faith in the benefits of a strong centralist authoritarian political system, there was a deeply entrenched pragmatism. The santanistas and the conservatives were not utopians. They liked to believe that their beliefs stemmed from an undiluted understanding of reality. Their worldview had its origins in empiricism, experience, and the actual state of society, and they had no patience with beautiful yet unpractical constitutions. Their defense of a dictatorship stemmed from the pragmatic belief that the Mexican people were insufficiently educated to sustain a successful democratic system. The foreign policy Santa Anna's government pursued in 1853–55 was also deeply pragmatic. The signing of the Treaty of La Mesilla and the government's rapprochement with Europe, in particular with France, Spain, and Britain, had their origins in the administration's acceptance of a number of crude realities. The cession of La Mesilla to the United States for an acceptable sum of money appeared to Santa Anna and his Cabinet to be the only way to avoid another war with the Colossus of the North. The quest for a European prince and the amicable relations that were rekindled between Mexico and the European delegations in the republic made sense as a means to guaranteeing that Mexico had strong and important allies should the United States attempt to annex even more Mexican territory.[32]

From the moment the dictatorship was inaugurated, a concerted effort was made to inform the governments of Spain, France, and Britain that it was imperative that they collaborated to maintain the balance of power in the Americas. Santa Anna's diplomats put forward an array of treaties in which reciprocal territorial guarantees could be set in place. Alamán, as minister of foreign relations, went as far as writing to Louis

Napoleon to invite him to lead a triple negotiation between France, Spain, and the United Kingdom with the main objective of protecting Mexico from U.S. expansionism. The idea that Louis Napoleon should assist the Mexican government in finding a European prince who could establish a long-lasting and stable Mexican dynasty was first expressed in this context. Santa Anna stressed that all monarchies were endangered by the rise of the United States, that Spain ran the risk of losing Cuba to the Americans, and that it was their obligation to commit themselves to assist Mexico in case of a U.S. invasion.[33]

Santa Anna's closet or reluctant monarchism manifested itself for the first time in this context. The idea of offering the Mexican throne to a European prince was an unquestionably pragmatic decision. It was also symptomatic of the stage of despair. As was recorded by the British ambassador at the time, Santa Anna's monarchist proposal was "the only means he sees of saving [Mexico] from falling into the hands of the Americans." Troubled by the U.S. government's "evident determination either by fair means or by foul to get the Mesilla valley," and fearful that the republic "was too weak to resist the attacks of the United States and must fall into their power," Santa Anna was desperate to secure the support of the "Great Powers of Europe." He was therefore ready to give Britain "his best assistance to any plan which they might propose." So determined was he to prevent the United States from annexing more Mexican territory that he was prepared to allow the Great Powers of Europe "to establish a monarchy here that he would resign his power into the hands of any Foreign prince who would be supported on his throne against the rapacity of the United States, in short that the Great Powers should act with respect to Mexico as they thought best for the preservation of her independence." He was, according to Doyle, "willing to assist in establishing a monarchy here or any form of government to save the country, . . . with a view of putting an effectual barrier to the rapacity of the United States and its citizens." Even after La Mesilla became part of the United States, the fear of losing more territory to the northern neighbor remained. This would lead him to send José María Gutiérrez Estrada in 1854 on a trip to Europe to seek a prince fit for the Mexican crown. It was a decision that would come back to haunt him thirteen years later.[34]

The Treaty of La Mesilla (also known as the Gadsden Purchase) was another example of Santa Anna's pragmatic approach during the 1850s. Rightly or wrongly, it was to become another blot on his career. According to the Treaty of Guadalupe Hidalgo, "commissioners were to be named by the two governments . . . to run the northern boundary line between the two republics." With this process in progress, the United States government allowed the governor of New Mexico, General William Carr Lane, in the spring of 1853, to take the valley of La Mesilla by force, under the pretence that its inhabitants had requested his help. La Mesilla was in Chihuahua, even though the U.S. authorities tried to justify their actions by claiming the boundary had not been clearly defined. On 18 May 1853, President Franklin Pierce's government actually claimed that La Mesilla was part of New Mexico. From the U.S. perspective, the discovery of gold in California meant that it was imperative to strengthen communications between the East Coast and the remote southwestern province. Developing a railway along La Mesilla was one way of gaining faster access to California. The other would be to build a canal across Central America.[35]

Coinciding with James Gadsden's arrival in Veracruz in August as U.S. minister plenipotentiary, alarming reports of a major mobilization of U.S. troops along the Chihuahua–New Mexico border began to circulate. By the time Gadsden arrived in Mexico City, Santa Anna feared the worst, especially as a minor skirmish had taken place between Mexican and U.S. troops. Between September and December, Santa Anna and Gadsden entered into a lengthy series of negotiations, with the United States government making it known that they were interested in more than just permission to build a railway along the disputed region. Santa Anna delayed the onset of formal conferences for as long as he could, while desperately seeking a way of securing European support. In the meantime, the ever-present threat of another U.S. intervention was heightened by William Walker's filibustering expedition to Baja California in November 1853. Having failed to obtain any formal guarantees from Spain, France, or Britain, Santa Anna finally met Gadsden on 10 December 1853. After twenty days of bartering, he signed the Treaty of La Mesilla on 30 December.[36]

In the treaty it was agreed that Mexico accepted the frontier limits established in the Treaty of Guadalupe Hidalgo, with the area of La Mesilla (109,574 square kilometers) becoming part of the United States. The United States government was no longer bound (as stipulated in the 1848 treaty) to prevent the Indians based in its territories from conducting raids into Mexico. In exchange the United States agreed to pay Mexico an indemnity of ten million pesos. Seven million were to be paid in advance; the remaining three once all the agreements had been ratified. The United States was also authorized to build a railway across the Isthmus of Tehuantepec, after the 5th of February 1854. Santa Anna was adamant that they had come out of the affair far better than he had dared hope "when so recently we feared to see ourselves involved in a disastrous war. . . . Yesterday we did not even have the means of subsistence, and the government, affected by a lack of resources, did not know what to do; and today we resemble the man who wins the lottery."[37]

He was to claim subsequently that he had been given little room to maneuver. In his mind, the United States government was preparing to launch a new military offensive if its demands were not accommodated. As he put it: "Without an army, without materiel, without a treasury, and in the middle of the horrors of anarchy, were we in a position to enter a war? Prudence and patriotism recommended we avoided [such a conflict]." He considered that given the circumstances they had done remarkably well. The area in itself was of little use to Mexico, he added, and Mexico could make good use of the money that was obtained through the transaction. To those liberales who made a big song and dance about the whole affair, he replied that it was quite rich coming from them. Had they not been the ones who had signed away half of the country's territory to the United States in the scandalous Treaty of Guadalupe Hidalgo? Who were they to question his patriotism or the wisdom of his decision to sell La Mesilla? Sometimes one had to "give in to necessity . . . make the sacrifices the situation warranted." He believed that in the given context, the signing of the treaty was the lesser of two evils. He was forced to think with his head rather than feel with his heart.[38]

Notwithstanding Santa Anna's arguable victory, according to biographer José Valadés, when the cartographer Antonio García Cubas showed him the map he drafted of Mexico in 1854, Santa Anna was not able to repress the expression of horror that came over his face. According to the anecdote, it was not until he saw García Cubas's map that he realized the extraordinary amount of land they had lost in one way or another to the United States.[39]

The expected financial gains resulting from the sale of La Mesilla never truly materialized either. They were squandered, in part through the corruption of the Mexican officials based in the United States, in part through Santa Anna's own wrongdoings. A number of sources claim he pocketed $600,000 of the U.S. indemnity "for losses suffered during the war with the United States." A significant portion of it was also lost in the repayment of the onerous loans the government had allowed itself to take, at disadvantageous rates, from the *agiotistas*, also known as the "vampires of the treasury." The bitterness expressed by many Mexicans over Santa Anna's sale of La Mesilla is easily understood. The fact that he had little choice in the matter was ignored, outweighed by the failure of the anticipated financial benefits of the sale to materialize. His patriotism was questioned and his negotiations with Gadsden, on the back of Gamboa's accusations, along with the memory of his defeats in Texas and during the Mexican-American War, inspired many to join the Revolution of Ayutla once it broke out. The suspicion that he was entering shady negotiations with his European counterparts in a bid to compromise Mexico's independence by imposing a foreign prince on the Mexican throne did not make matters any easier for him.[40]

Notwithstanding the less redeeming qualities of Santa Anna's authoritarian regime, the dictatorship commenced on a good footing. His abilities were recognized by somebody as unexpected as Karl Marx. In a letter he wrote to Friedrich Engels in 1854, despite describing the Mexican people as degenerate Spaniards, Marx noted that "the Spaniards have produced no talent comparable to that of Santa Anna." Echoing the first year after the Bases de Tacubaya were in place, the first six months of his 1850s dictatorship were characterized by the energy the government injected into kick-starting the country's economy while promoting order, progress, and a whole range of nationalistic values. Santa Anna established himself in the Palace of Tacubaya, in the south of the capital, and stayed put while the team he had selected to run the country got on with reforming Mexico.[41]

Tragically for Santa Anna, by September 1853 he had lost three of his most talented ministers. Lucas Alamán died on 2 June. Antonio Haro y Tamariz resigned as minister of finance on 5 August after it became obvious that Santa Anna would not tax the Church on this occasion. And Santa Anna's key ideologue, conspirator, and informer José María Tornel died on 11 September 1853. Without these gifted statesmen to restrain his exuberance and ensure that the government's purpose was not lost under the fast-growing thickets of flattery and adulation, Santa Anna's excesses soon became too great to be tolerated. The dictatorship's virtues were fast superseded by the brutal repression that came to characterize it, following the eruption of the Revolution of Ayutla of 1 March 1854.[42]

Two personal disputes in which Santa Anna became involved during his 1853–55 dictatorship reflect the extent of his tyranny and of his detachment from reality. Following Tornel's demise, he started to have problems in judging who his real supporters were. His punishment of Súarez y Navarro was an early example of this. The fact that he forgot to reward the army with the customary promotions they had come to expect at Christmas 1854 would be a far more damaging instance of his inconsistent treatment of his supporters and would prove fatal in provoking a number of high-ranking officers to join forces with the revolutionaries of Ayutla.[43]

In the case of Suárez y Navarro, Santa Anna not only refused to make him minister of war when Tornel died; he ordered Suárez y Navarro's arrest and had him escorted to Acapulco, from where he was to be sent into exile to Manila. Suárez y Navarro could hardly believe Santa Anna's refusal to appoint him minister, let alone being banished into exile. He had proven himself to be one of the most active santanistas in orchestrating the caudillo's return from exile. Súarez y Navarro had been one of the main editors and contributors of *La Palanca*. He was the author of the santanista *History of Mexico and General Antonio López de Santa Anna, 1821–1848*. He had been instrumental in converting Blancarte's *pronunciamiento* of Guadalajara of 1852 into a santanista affair. When Santa Anna returned these favors by naming Lino José Alcorta minister of war, Suárez y Navarro made his surprise known. Santa Anna retaliated by forcing him out of the country.[44]

The more notorious personal dispute Santa Anna was involved in during his last government was his clash with the Romantic Spanish playwright and poet José Zorrilla. Everything about the "Zorrilla affair" pointed to the fact that he had lost all sense of proportion and that his despotic tendencies, unrestrained, were entirely out of control. Here was one of the great Spanish writers of the time, adored in Mexico following the extraordinary success in 1844 of his memorable and lively version of the Don Juan story, Don Juan Tenorio. He arrived in Mexico City in January 1855 and was given a hero's welcome. Anybody who was somebody wanted to be seen next to this great living poet. He was wined and dined and a poetry recital he gave at the university was received with rapturous applause. Santa Anna's vanity could not stomach the fact that a poet, not even a soldier, and a Spaniard at that, could be given such privileged treatment by the Mexican elite. What was wrong with them? Did they not have any sense of dignity or patriotism? Using the pretext that some subversive verses published in El Siglo XIX could be attributed to Zorrilla, he ordered a formal inquiry into the matter.[45]

Zorrilla wrote a highly entertaining account of the scandal that ensued in his autobiographical Recuerdos del tiempo viejo (Memories of the old time, 1882). He acknowledged that Mexico in 1855 was a safe country to visit and that all bandits had been caught and executed, adding that this was because when Santa Anna ruled, only he was allowed to rob. Zorrilla did not doubt that his arrest stemmed from the fact that Santa Anna was very vain (vanidosísimo). He recognized that this was understandable given that his followers had given him reason to believe that he was a god. Zorrilla denied being the author of such dreadful verses. He actually went to visit His Serene Highness in person to defend himself and provided enough letters of recommendation from enough high-placed Spanish and French officials to be forgiven. For Zorrilla, this brush with Santa Anna was little more than a spicy anecdote he could add to his colorful autobiography. For many it demonstrated the tyrannical nature of Santa Anna's vanity. It was a cause for concern even to his loyalist supporters, who by February 1855 were becoming sparse. Regardless of the results of the farcical December 1854 referendum, the dictatorship was in its last throes.[46]

Santa Anna's regime entered a terminal crisis once the Revolution of

Ayutla erupted in March 1854. As was noted by Anselmo de la Portilla in his firsthand account of the revolution, although many Mexicans had come to accept the need for a dictatorship in 1853, a year later most had realized that Santa Anna's tyranny was not what was needed. What people were hoping would be a strong and enlightened government that would restore peace to the republic and facilitate the formation of a new constituent congress had turned out to be an unbearably repressive dictatorship.[47]

The Revolution of Ayutla was launched on 1 March 1854 with the *pronunciamiento* Colonel Florencio Villareal proclaimed in the small town in present-day Guerrero. Although it was initially too radical to gain the support of a number of key liberals, it was eventually endorsed a fortnight later by leaders such as Ignacio Comonfort, Juan Álvarez, and Tomás Moreno, after the original document was redrafted. It was the beginning of the end. By 1854 the dictatorship had succeeded in alienating just about everybody. Many conservatives felt betrayed by the fact that Santa Anna was doing little to pacify the increasing popular discontent, which was threatening to destroy their property. The extraordinary rise in taxes had proven profoundly unpopular with all sectors of society. The moderates and the radicals despised everything about the regime: its constitutional illegality, its repressive measures, and the government's preposterous levels of corruption. The sale of La Mesilla paired with the realization that the funds it was meant to generate had been squandered by the spring of 1854 turned even some of Santa Anna's most loyal supporters, such as Haro y Tamariz, into his enemies. The government's repression had also become intolerable, even for many of those *hombres de bien* who had initially welcomed the arrival of a strong regime. Although the Revolution of Ayutla was "very much a product of the South," its popular federalist agenda and the rebels' resilience succeeded in "emboldening opponents of the regime elsewhere."[48]

Santa Anna's initial response to news of the revolution was characteristic. Rather than dispatch one of his generals to crush the rebellion, he chose to lead the government army in person. Although his ministers did everything possible to dissuade him, he did not heed their pleas. On 16 March 1854 he left Mexico City at the head of a five-thousand-strong division and initiated his pacification of the South. The first stages of his march were one long series of celebrations. He made his way through Cuernavaca and Taxco with the "pageantry of a king and the pomp of a conquistador." He reached Iguala on the 27th, and his vanguard detachments forced the rebels to retreat after a clash at the Mescala River. The march to Chilpancingo unfolded without meeting any resistance. He stayed there for a week while some of his men progressed to Ometepec, succeeding in regaining two of the nine districts in Guerrero that had fallen into the rebels' hands. Having recovered from a minor indisposition, he led his army to the proximity of Acapulco, which he reached on 19 April, after defeating the rebels posted at El Coquillo along the banks of the Papagayo River.

It was during his march to Acapulco that the improbable anecdote was circulated in the press that a magnificent eagle had flown down and rested at his side, allowing only the dictator to stroke it. Despite the good fortune augured by his triumphant march to Acapulco and the willingness of Mexico's sacred king of birds to let itself be caressed by the caudillo's hand, the context was not one that favored his expeditionary army. Once they reached Acapulco, the rebels cut their line of communications with the capital, and for an entire month no news of Santa Anna's activities reached Mexico City. While the government became increasingly agitated by this state of affairs, Santa Anna discovered that the revolutionaries were better prepared than he had thought.[49]

Despite the weak condition of some of Acapulco's defenses, General Ignacio Comonfort had been fortifying the rebel positions in and around the castle of San Diego during the month and a half it had taken Santa Anna's troops to reach its city walls. Although Comonfort was outnumbered, having only nine hundred armed men with whom to resist the attack of Santa Anna's force of five thousand, the caudillo's division had been unable to bring sufficient pieces of artillery to breach Acapulco's defenses. The assault of Acapulco began at three in the morning of the 20th, and much to Santa Anna's disgust, after four hours of combat, Comonfort's rebels repulsed the attack. He then tried to buy Comonfort and Álvarez's surrender with a bribe, but both rebel leaders rejected the offer of money separately. On the 26th, he ordered the retreat of his expeditionary army back to the capital. It was a decision not dissimilar from that he took at Angostura–Buena Vista. On this occasion it became obvious to him that the rebels' fortified position in Acapulco was too strong for him to breach successfully. Neither did he have the time to place the port under siege. His army, in contrast, needed to restore its line of communications cut off by Álvarez's troops. The rebels had also ensured that all provisions in the vicinity had been duly appropriated or destroyed. And he was troubled by what could be happening in the capital during his absence.[50]

It was not a happy withdrawal. Santa Anna vented his anger by laying waste to the countryside as his army made its way back, indiscriminately burning a number of hamlets along the road back to Mexico City. The villages of Las Cruces, La Venta, Egido, Dos Arroyos, and Cacahuatepec were razed to the ground. All rebel prisoners were executed, and their corpses were drawn and quartered and hung from the trees. The return was not a smooth operation either. Rebel guerrilla forces harried his men along the way. On 30 April he was forced to fight the battle of El Peregrino, the most serious clash of arms of the campaign. He only narrowly escaped capture. Although the government army won the battle, in that it was able to proceed with its march back to the capital, it suffered major losses. The rebel chieftain, General Tomás Moreno, succeeded in wresting over 360 animals from Santa Anna's train. And although the remaining journey from El Peregrino to Chilpancingo took place without incident, his army endured another attack at the Pass of Mescala on 7 May. Although his men received a welcome worthy of a triumphant army when they returned to Mexico City on the 16th, Santa Anna's expedition to Acapulco had been a failure. More disturbing yet, while he had been to Acapulco and back, a whole range of garrisons and chieftains had joined the revolution, issuing pronunciamientos in the Sierra Gorda and Michoacán.[51]

During the following year other generals were sent to the areas of conflict, but to no avail. Santa Anna made a second incursion to the South in February 1855 but did not go beyond Iguala. His presence did nothing to persuade the rebels to lay down their arms. In response to the people's reluctance to help the government track down the insurgents, he decreed on 6 March that in and around Iguala all rebels were to be hung from the trees and all of their sources of subsistence, including villages, ranches, cattle, seeds, and fields were to be set on fire. His illegitimate son José López de Santa Anna took great relish in obeying his father's orders and left a trail of horror in his wake as he dedicated himself to executions and burned his way like "a bloody comet" through Michoacán.[52]

In a last and desperate bid to regain control of the situation, a sixty-one-year old Santa Anna went on the warpath again on 30 April 1855. On this occasion he led his army to Michoacán, where he had been led to believe he would find Comonfort. He entered Morelia on 9 May, and on the 13th proceeded to Zamora, which he reached on the 15th. The rebels in Michoacán retreated rather than engage in battle. As a result his expedition was successful to the extent that wherever he went, the revolutionaries ran away from him. But they did not surrender. Following his foray to and around Zamora he returned to Morelia. With the enemies on the retreat, he spent the following month playing cat and mouse with them, trying to catch them moving in and out of Morelia, coming and going in between a number of towns in the departments of Mexico, Morelia, and Pátzcuaro. In the end he decided to return to the capital on 2 June, leaving a strong contingent behind in Morelia. When he marched back into Mexico City on 8 June, "he could truthfully describe his campaign as a success; for the garrisons of northern Michoacán had been restored and reinforced, [and] the rebels had fled before him." However, the revolutionaries were still at large, and the Plan of Ayutla continued to gain support in other parts of the republic.[53]

Realizing that his was a lost cause, he chose to leave before the revolution triumphed. It was obvious that even his Cabinet had lost confidence in the dictatorship, as when he asked them on 25 June whether the time had come to draft a new constitution, their reply was a resounding "yes." Dolores Tosta left the capital on 29 July, and speculation abounded over whether her departure to Veracruz meant that Santa Anna was on the verge of resigning. Although the government publicly denied this, he left Mexico City on 9 August at 3:00 A.M. He named Generals Mariano Salas and Martín Carrera his successors and formally abdicated in a letter written at El Encero on 12 August 1855. On the 13th, the Mexico City garrison pronounced itself in favor of the Plan of Ayutla, and as it became apparent that the dictator was gone for

good, a jubilant crowd took to wrecking his family's and his supporters' properties in the capital in a day-long rampage.[54]

Back in his bailiwick of Veracruz, he was given a hero's welcome in
Xalapa on his way to the port. The *jarochos* came out in their hundreds
to receive first Doña Dolores and later Santa Anna, as if the events that
were tearing the rest of the country apart belonged to a remote land that
bore no relation to the caudillo's home province. On 16 August Santa
Anna, his wife, and a number of relatives boarded the *Iturbide* and went
into exile for a third time. Following his departure it took a while for the
rebels of Ayutla to settle their differences, divided as they were between
moderates and radicals. Notwithstanding these differences, the rebel
government that was temporarily formed in the capital decreed in September 1855 that all of Santa Anna's assets, including the haciendas of
El Encero, Paso de Varas, and Boca del Monte, were to be confiscated to
recoup the money lost in the sale of La Mesilla.[55]

Having twice gone into exile and twice succeeded in returning, Santa
Anna must have suspected that it would only be a matter of time before
the chance for him to make yet another extraordinary comeback surfaced. However, as he was to discover to his dismay over the following
nineteen long years, times had changed. The Liberator of Veracruz, the
Founder of the Republic, the Hero of Tampico, the mutilated warrior
of '38, six-times president General Antonio López de Santa Anna was
to become a pariah, repeatedly accused of treason, rejected by liberals
and conservatives alike, remembered as a sanguinary tyrant, an opportunistic and cynical turncoat, a cowardly traitor. In a sense, the 1853–55
dictatorship and the Revolution of Ayutla brought to an end an era in
modern Mexican history. The early national period, the age of proposals, drew to a close. The period known as that of the mid-century reform began.

Coinciding with the end of his dictatorship, a whole generation of
generals and politicians was dying, to be replaced by a new generation too young to have fought in the War of Independence and who did
not share their elders' fear of and/or respect for Santa Anna. As noted,
Alamán and Tornel died in 1853. So did Anastasio Bustamante. And
between 1854 and 1855, José Joaquín de Herrera, Nicolás Bravo, and
Mariano Arista joined them. Most of the influential men who had stood

by or against Santa Anna during the early national period were no longer around.[56] As Santa Anna set sail on the *Iturbide* he was one of the very few survivors of his generation. Valentín Gómez Farías and Juan Álvarez were the other two. Unlike Santa Anna, the twice vice president Gómez Farías would end his days on a high, honored by the radicals who forged the 1857 Constitution, which Gómez Farías had the honor to sign on 5 February 1857, accompanied by his sons Fermín and Benito. He died in 1858, before the civil war of the *Reforma* erupted, and he was honored in the press as having been a "Friend of the People," Mexico's "Patriarch of Democracy." Álvarez would die in 1867 after Benito Juárez succeeded in restoring the liberal republic.[57]

Santa Anna would have no such luck. As he looked back from the deck of the *Iturbide* at the coastline of Veracruz, with the majestic Peak of Orizaba on the horizon, unbeknownst to him he was saying goodbye not just to his homeland; he was parting from a way of life, a period of history. The next time he was to see San Juan de Ulúa and the port of his beloved Veracruz, Mexico was well into a new cycle in its history, and it held no place for the confused and rejected septuagenarian he had become.[58]

14. The General in His Labyrinth, 1856–1876

During the two decades Santa Anna spent in exile, Mexico underwent one of the most violent and significant periods of its history. The Revolution of Ayutla led to the establishment of a liberal government that was tragically (and violently) divided between radicals and moderates. The presidencies of Juan Álvarez (October–December 1855) and Ignacio Comonfort (December 1855–January 1858) saw the beginning of what was to become known as the mid-century reform. With Benito Júarez and Miguel Lerdo de Tejada heading the Ministry of Justice and Ecclesiastical Affairs and that of Finance respectively, the laws of 23 November 1855 and 25 June 1856 were passed, bringing an end to all *fueros*, curtailing Church and military power, and confiscating all corporate-owned properties. The radical federal 1857 Constitution was also initiated. Almost inevitably, the conservative backlash, when it came, was especially violent. Following *moderado* president Comonfort's coup d'état against his own Congress on 17 December 1857, conservative General Félix Zuloaga overthrew the government with the troops of the Mexico City garrison on 11 January 1858, and all hell broke loose. From January 1858 to January 1861 the Civil War of the Reform was fought, with the conservatives holding onto the capital while Juárez became the president of the displaced legitimate liberal government established in Veracruz. Although Juárez's camp succeeded, after three years, in re-taking the capital and winning the war, armed conflict soon broke out again, this time involving a European military intervention.

Coinciding with the eruption of the U.S. Civil War in April 1861 and nourished by a clique of conservative monarchist Mexican exiles, the idea of a Mexican adventure finally gathered momentum in the French imperial court. The Civil War represented an important distraction that would prevent the United States from intervening in a European military expedition to Mexico. The excuse to mount such an expedition had also arisen. On 17 July 1861, Juárez's radical liberal government decreed that all payments on the external debt would be suspended for a period of two years. Britain, France, and Spain reacted by signing the Tripartite Convention of London in October, agreeing to occupy the main Atlantic ports of Mexico to enforce debt payment. Britain and Spain soon realized that the French intended to use this as a pretext to enforce a change of regime. Therefore, in the spring of 1862, while Britain and Spain withdrew their forces, France embarked upon its costly and ultimately disastrous Mexican campaign. Mexico City was taken in June 1863, and in June 1864 the doomed Austrian Habsburg prince, Archduke Ferdinand Maximilian, was placed on the Mexican throne by Napoleon Bonaparte's nephew, Napoleon III, where he would remain until June 1867. Juárez persevered as the legitimate president of Mexico, fleeing from the imperial forces and leading the forces that waged an unremitting guerrilla war on Maximilian I. After three more bloody years and with the U.S. Civil War (1861–65) having ended, the French abandoned their puppet Maximilian and withdrew their forces. Supported by a handful of Mexican conservatives, Maximilian refused to leave Mexico and was executed outside Querétaro on 19 June 1867. Once Maximilian's government fell, Juárez was able to complete his term in office, being re-elected in 1871. He died in 1872 having inspired a whole range of profoundly influential reforms that succeeded in ending those colonial legacies that had survived the achievement of independence. Júarez was replaced by Sebastián Lerdo de Tejada (1872–76).[1]

Santa Anna's experience of the Civil War of the Reform (1858–61) and the War of the French Intervention (1862–67) would be from afar. His political involvement in the conservative backlash of 1858–60, the imposition of a European prince, and the fall of Maximilian I would be peripheral and barely significant. Much to his disgust, he was to discover that none of the factions trusted him any more; neither the conservatives who forged the empire nor the liberals who overthrew it.

He was to spend the last twenty years of his life in a hostile labyrinth, forced to endure the bitter taste of rejection.

In the late summer of 1855 he went back to La Rosita in Colombia and found that the people of Turbaco remembered him fondly. He dedicated himself to his hacienda again, and "for two years and seven months," as he would recall in his memoirs, he channeled all his energies into administrating his land. He was happy and was able to recover from what had been yet another "disappointment." Had he not become preoccupied about the outcome of the political turmoil that started to threaten Colombia's own conservative pro-clerical administration, with which he sympathized, he would no doubt have remained in Turbaco. Mariano Ospina Rodríguez's administration (1857–61) had a lot in common with Santa Anna's last government. Unnerved by the increasing threat posed by the Colombian liberals who wanted to destroy his property, he decided to sell La Rosita and move to the isle of Saint Thomas. He also wanted to be nearer Mexico after news reached him that the conservatives had succeeded in taking the capital. He was convinced that he still had it in him to make another comeback and that there was a large section of Mexican society who continued to adore him. Although he was to discover that he was deluding himself, there were still many Mexicans who thought highly of him. As the U.S. minister plenipotentiary in Mexico City noted in 1858, the majority of the population in the capital "agreed" that Santa Anna had been "the best ruler of the nation."[2]

As evidenced in the petitions signed by the people of Turbaco on 10 and 17 February 1858 on hearing of his departure, the caudillo had become as popular with the Colombian community he employed as he had been with the *jarochos* of his homeland. They thanked him publicly for having been such a caring "father and benefactor." They noted that their move from "miserable shacks and deserted plots of land" to "comfortable houses" had occurred thanks to him, as had the building of a cemetery, and that "by example [he had] inculcated in [them] a love of work," employing over a hundred proletarians who, until then, had lived in indigence. It was one of the last times that a community would be prepared to praise and thank him.[3]

For the five years between 1858 and 1863 he established himself on the Caribbean island of Saint Thomas in the Danish West Indies (today one of the Virgin Islands). Hardly any documents have been found that allow us to know what his life was like there. What we do know is that it was from here that he started to take an active interest in Mexican politics again. No longer involved in the running of a large hacienda, he had time to get involved in a conspiracy that he hoped would result in his return to Mexico. Much of what we know about his monarchical activities is based on the correspondence José María Gutiérrez Estada published subsequently to prove that Santa Anna had been involved in the move to bring a European prince to Mexico. It is possible that this correspondence was fabricated. During his 1867 court-martial Santa Anna denied having written these letters. However, they have a turn of phrase and an ideological coherence that force us to view them as Santa Anna's.

There was nothing surprising about this monarchist stance. In 1853 his despair had already driven him to seek help from the British minister plenipotentiary. By 1861, having witnessed from afar the turmoil of the *Reforma* and watched with disgust the rise of Benito Juárez's radical faction (which had carried out the breakup and sale of his confiscated properties), the monarchist proposal was even more appealing. It would guarantee independence from the threat of U.S. expansionism, and it would ultimately bring an end to four decades of political unrest and upheaval.[4]

His priorities were the restoration of order and the preservation of Mexican sovereignty. If this entailed bringing a European prince to Mexico and establishing a constitutional monarchy, so be it. The monarchic aspect of the question was the means to an end (peace, order, stability, and independence) rather than an end in itself. As he noted in the *Manifiesto* circulated following his arrival in Veracruz, during his short-lived return to Mexico in 1864: "Mexicans: How many disturbances, how many tragedies have been played out on our soil since I left you! . . . It is not the Conservative party that has invited the French Intervention to unfold on our beaches, but the errors and blindness of the reformists." The monarchist proposal and French Intervention were a desperate response to a desperate situation. It was the sad consequence of the extreme reformism of the *juaristas*: "It is unquestionable that the excesses of the dominant party provoked the armed intervention and that this came about at a time in which our society was in the middle of a great convulsion." He welcomed the empire as a step toward bringing an end to the chaos: "The people, tired of half a century of anarchy, false promises and beautiful theories, anxious to forge a paternal, just and enlightened government, proclaim with enthusiasm the reestablishment of the Empire."[5]

Monarchism, like dictatorship, was a distasteful medicine that they had to swallow because of past mistakes and their failure to forge a long-lasting constitutional republican order. Santa Anna admitted as much when he recalled the role he had played in bringing about the First Republic. Time had proven him wrong: "In our history I figure as the one who first proclaimed the Republic. I believed I was doing a great service to our mother country . . .. But once the illusions of youth had passed, faced with so many disasters caused by that system, I do not want to fool anybody; my conscience and my convictions tell me that my last word on the matter is [that what is needed is a] constitutional monarchy." The Mexican people had little choice but to celebrate the arrival of Maximilian, given that "without his assistance you would suffer under the barbarous and oppressive weight of the wildest of anarchies."[6]

Obviously he was also desperate to return from exile. This was the longest spell of time he had spent away from Veracruz, and in order to orchestrate his return, he was prepared to side with what he considered to be the strongest party. On 30 November 1861 he wrote to Gutiérrez Estrada to say that Archduke Ferdinand Maximilian could not be better suited for the job at hand. Notwithstanding this, he also asked Gutiérrez Estrada to keep his monarchism a secret. As ever, he was trying to keep his options open, should the monarchist plot fail. But he was arguably also asking Gutiérrez Estrada not to publicize his monarchist sympathies given that these were not sincere. He was offering his services in the hope of securing his return to Mexico and because he shared the conservatives' despair and belief in the need for strong government. However, he was not a proud or a committed monarchist, for otherwise he would not have hesitated to make it known.[7]

He was also looking for a role in the imperial venture. In the letter addressed to the future emperor on 22 December 1861, from his exile in St. Thomas, he offered his services to Maximilian: "My adherence to your august person has no limits." Consistent, nonetheless, with his Mexican patriotism, he placed Maximilian's proposed monarchy within a Mexican (Aztec) tradition. He also stressed that the nation's (his) adherence to such an initiative originated in a wish to make a final desperate attempt to solve Mexico's problems: "The immense majority of the Nation aspires to reestablish the Empire of the Montezumas with Your Imperial Highness at its head, persuaded that this is the only remedy that can cure the grave ills of society, the last anchor of our hope."[8]

By 1863 it became obvious that Santa Anna was hoping to play a major role in the plot that was unfolding. As was expressed in a letter he addressed to Gutiérrez Estrada on 25 March 1863, he was hoping to serve as the interim prime minister or regent who would go to Mexico ahead of the emperor and organize his reception. Gutiérrez Estrada went as far as ensuring, as a result, that Santa Anna was included in the planned provisional regency that was to govern the country until Maximilian arrived. According to one draft plan, he was to be president of this regency with an annual salary equal to that of his last presidency. He was also to be given the titles of duke of Veracruz and duke of Tampico, and he was to be the leader chosen to greet Maximilian upon his arrival in Veracruz and escort him to the capital.[9]

Although Santa Anna came extremely close to pulling off another miraculous return to power, it was not to be. Had he been successful in returning as regent, he would have achieved his lifelong dream of having the prestige of leadership without the burdens it implied. He would have greatly enjoyed the acclaim of the return, the hero's welcome along the route from Veracruz to Mexico City, the roaring of the cannons, the pealing of the church bells, the echoes of the *Te Deums*, and the sight of the troops parading in the streets. He would have been able to retire to his restored haciendas in Veracruz, leaving the daily burden of running the country in the able hands of Maximilian and his court. In so doing, he would have distanced himself sufficiently from Maximilian to be in a position to pronounce against him in later years if the imperial experiment were to fail. The manner in which he reminded the Mexican people of who he was in the 1864 *Manifiesto* expressed, without doubt, a yearning, on the part of the seventy-year-old caudillo, to relive the adoration with which he was once favored by his countrymen:

> He who addresses you today from this enclosure, the theater
> in another time of his glories, is that caudillo of Indepen-
> dence who in 1821 you heralded with frantic enthusiasm;
> the victor of Tampico, he who in going from one end to the
> other of our national territory, acquired the honor of giving
> his mother country glory and esteem, without economizing
> his blood, for which you favored him on so many occasions
> by voting for him, conferring upon him the supreme magis-
> tracy of the nation, covering him in medals. Welcome him,
> therefore, as your dear brother, without doubting his sincer-
> ity for an instant.[10]

However, over the years he had acquired a number of influential enemies. On this occasion, they had the upper hand. Juan Nepomuceno
Almonte, Santa Anna's interpreter during his Texan captivity, bore a
grudge against him for having favored Tornel over him as minister of
war back in 1853. He worked hard to prevent Santa Anna from returning. Despite Gutiérrez Estrada's exertions, Almonte succeeded in rear-
ranging the triumvirate intended to form the regency so that he would
be the dominant member, excluding Santa Anna. When Santa Anna
finally packed his bags and made the journey home in early 1864, there
were people in high places who were determined not to let him remain
in the country for long. Santa Anna's friend Colonel Manuel María Giménez, who went to Veracruz to welcome his hero in February 1864,
suspected that Almonte was planning to spoil the caudillo's return but
was unable to reach the port in time to warn Santa Anna and his supporters. It was made clear to Giménez and his colleagues that they had
to refrain from making a fuss about Santa Anna's return, since he was
told on leaving Mexico City: "If you, General Santa Anna's friends, on
his arrival in Veracruz, welcome him with public ovations, or if he pub-
lishes anything, like a proclamation or a manifesto, General [Achille]
Bazaine, by means of an order, will force him to re-embark immediately, for Santa Anna does not come back today to govern, nor to do as
he damn well pleases, [today] he comes back to obey."[11]

Santa Anna arrived in Veracruz on 27 February 1864, expecting a triumphant welcome and the opportunity of returning, albeit briefly, to

the corridors of power. That very day he wrote to the minister of war to express his satisfaction with the current state of affairs and to offer his services to the government. When Manuel María Giménez caught up with him Giménez found him in high spirits, evidently unaware that he would shortly be expelled from Mexico once more: "Few times have I seen Sr. Santa Anna in such a good mood nor as complacent as he was during the last days of his stay in Veracruz. His conversation was pleasant, and he was convinced a great future awaited the country under the reign of His Imperial Majesty Ferdinand Maximilian, whose arrival he looked forward to with all his heart." Having spent the previous nine years in exile, and with the *imperialistas* having restored his properties back to him, Santa Anna must have been overjoyed at the chance to visit old haunts, enjoy his favorite dishes, and inhale the familiar scent of his homeland.

By the time Giménez met up with the caudillo, the deed that would justify his expulsion and torment him three years later during his trial had already taken place. Before disembarking, a French officer had asked him to sign the following statement (in French) before being allowed on *terra firma*: "I declare on my honor to adhere to the intervention of the French and to recognize as the only legitimate government the monarchy proclaimed by the Assembly of Notables, with the title of Mexican Emperor, and with Prince Maximilian as Emperor of Mexico. I promise equally to abstain from all political demonstration and to do nothing, be it written or verbal, that would make my return to my country be other than as a simple citizen."[12]

Santa Anna was aware that the document entailed pledging his allegiance to the empire. What he was deliberately not told was that he was also pledging to abstain from any political activity. When on 12 March, his friend Giménez translated Bazaine's letter of 7 March to him, ordering his banishment, Santa Anna was confused. General Bazaine informed Santa Anna of Almonte's pointing out that he had broken the pledge he had made aboard the *Conway*, and told him Almonte was demanding his immediate departure. The newspaper El *Indicador* contained lengthy fragments of a manifesto he should never have published. He could no longer stay in Mexico. Santa Anna wrote back stating that he was unaware of having promised to remain silent, and while admitting to having written the *Manifiesto*, he denied having arranged for its publication. He claimed this was a mistake. He did not speak any French. He was aware of pledging his allegiance to the emperor but did not recall promising anything else. His plea had no effect, and he was forced to leave Mexico on the 12th.[13]

In the somewhat unreliable memoirs Santa Anna wrote subsequently, his version of these events was rather different. Whether it was because he wanted to ingratiate himself with the republican liberals in power or because this was how he liked to remember the events at the end of his life—having reverted to his original republicanism and now ashamed of his dalliance with the imperialists—he denied ever having supported the empire. He claimed that on arrival in Veracruz in February 1864, when he was asked to show his allegiance to the empire and its emperor, he replied: "To what Empire and Emperor are you referring?" Asked whether he knew about the intervention, he wrote that he had said: "I have heard something [about it]. Once I am on land I will find out more about the situation." He admitted that he was made to sign a page in a book, which he did in haste because his wife Dolores was feeling seasick. However, he denied ever having consciously recognized the empire. It was "the newspapers in the capital [that] announced my return with the appendage that: he has recognized the Intervention and the Empire." What he deemed important in his memoirs was that he was expelled by the French high command and that this happened because they could not help remembering that it had been he who had founded the republic in the first place. While his version of events is somewhat embellished, two points are worth noting about the regency's decision to prevent him from making any public statements on his return. The first is that the imperialists did not trust him despite all his letters to Gutiérrez Estrada; his monarchism was never accepted as sincere. The second is that they clearly continued to fear his influence. Despite his age and loss of prestige, the imperialists were afraid that he could still muster sufficient support to bring about yet another miraculous return to power, disturbing the projected enthronement of Archduke Ferdinand Maximilian.[14]

Rejected and forced into exile, this time by the imperialists, he soon renounced his monarchism and reverted to his original republicanism.

He made his way back to St. Thomas, stopping in Havana on the way, and by January 1865 was prepared to come out with a public statement condemning the empire. There was no looking back now. Over the next two years, he became more vociferous in his anti-imperialist statements. Moreover, after he was visited in January 1866 by the U.S. secretary of state, William H. Seward, he convinced himself that the U.S. government would support him in liberating Mexico from the French Intervention, preferring him as president to Juárez. Increasingly lost in a labyrinth of his own making, Santa Anna mistook Seward's courtesy visit, made while on holiday in the region, for an official invitation to return to the fray. Santa Anna was desperate to believe that he was being urged to intervene, as he had been twenty years earlier by Alexander Slidell Mackenzie. He also allowed himself to be deceived by a number of con-men, who sought him out in St. Thomas and persuaded him to part with most of his savings in order to bring about his heroic return to Mexico as the Restorer of the Republic. Darío Mazuera, a Colombian allegedly intent on writing Santa Anna's biography, construed an elaborate web of deceit with the threads of Santa Anna's vanity, his predisposition to believe in the possibility of a heroic return, and Seward's fortuitous visit. Together with a Venezuelan swindler, Abraham Báez, Mazuera persuaded an aging Santa Anna to finance their return trip to New York to prepare the grounds for his intervention. He gave them all the money they requested to buy arms and a ship (the *Georgia*) and to make preparations for his planned "U.S.-backed" liberating expedition. They also convinced him that Seward was prepared to put thirty million dollars toward his patriotic venture. He accepted as genuine the forged letters they showed him. He finally went to the United States in May 1866, where he allowed Báez to set up his home in Elizabethport, New Jersey, conning him one last time by asking him to advance an outrageous $2,400 for the rent. Less than a month after Santa Anna had established himself in Elizabethport, Mazuera and Báez disappeared. The owners of the ship he thought he had bought with forty thousand pesos came demanding payment for use of their vessel. The lawyers he hired to establish his innocence in the various financial ventures in which Mazuera had embroiled him cost him a further thirty thousand pesos. Isolated in New York, he was horrified to discover that Seward had never heard of, let alone met, Mazuera and that the U.S. government was fully behind Juárez. Santa Anna, bemused and affronted, left the expensive house at Elizabethport and moved to Staten Island. Not backed by the U.S. government as he had believed, he offered his services to Juárez's liberal government. However, the republicans, under Juárez's leadership, did not trust him.[15]

Coinciding with Santa Anna's initial overtures to Benito Juárez's representatives in the United States, Gutiérrez Estrada set about discrediting the general by printing his views on Santa Anna's actions together with copies of the caudillo's "monarchist" letters in *El Diario del Imperio*. Santa Anna was presented as a fraud, a turncoat, an opportunistic scoundrel, and an ungrateful traitor. To make matters worse, the *juaristas* in New York were adamant that they would have no dealings with him. Not only was he perceived as a fraud and a traitor; he was described as a liability, a tyrant, and a criminal who should be brought to justice. The Juarista Club in New York, presided over by Francisco Zarco, actually published a statement on 15 May 1866 that expressed in unequivocal terms the extent to which they despised him:

1. We do not see in Don Antonio López de Santa Anna anything other than the odious tyrant who betrayed our national independence, abusing public power.
2. We believe that his name alone would be enough to stain the noble and sacred cause defended by the Mexican people; making the consolidation of liberal institutions impossible, and ensuring all traitors were awarded impunity.
3. We believe that the Mexican people can have no faith in the word of a man who has always betrayed it; and that *were it to see him in our national territory, it would demand in the name of the law and public morality, and for the love of justice, to subject him to a trial and punish him exemplarily for high treason.*[16]

Gutiérrez Estrada's campaign was successful in damaging the general's reputation. Matías Romero, head of the Mexican Legation in the United States, told him as much when he wrote: "If you had not first requested the establishment of a monarchy in Mexico, when you were the Supreme Magistrate of the Nation, and if you had not recognized and supported the intervention the Emperor of the French brought about in our mother country, *as proven in the documents that have been published recently*, I do not believe that the Government of the Republic would have had any difficulty in accepting and employing your services." The republicans could not have him on their side when he had been the one to initiate the quest for a foreign prince.[17]

Santa Anna set out to demonstrate that he was a republican and to explain why he had temporarily erred and warmed to the monarchist ideal. He did this by writing a number of letters to Matías Romero and by publishing his Elizabethport *Manifiesto* of 5 June 1866. To begin with he had no doubts as to what he wanted to achieve by the spring of 1866. He had moved to the United States in order to return home. He could no longer remain passive when confronted with the "misfortunes of our mother country." Given that he had received letters from all over the country, "from old friends, and even political adversaries, from disappointed imperialists and relatively inactive republicans," asking him to intervene, the time had come for him to join the fray. He was convinced that he was the only person, considering his past record, who could bring an end to the intervention and an end to the divisions that had led to so many years of civil war: "I am called to give the necessary example of the subordinate soldier and the disinterested citizen, and to reconcile the national elements, so that the Nation as a whole acts as one man, under the direction of her First Magistrate, and that the triumph may be as we must desire it to be, one that is truly national." His intention was to cooperate with "the reestablishment of our constitutional republican government in the capital of Mexico, to see the people ready to be organized freely by their representatives, and on the following day to retire to my private life, and die respected and at peace in the bosom of my mother country." Alluding as ever to his glorious past, his main goal in life was to "fight once more for independence, and reestablish the Republic I was the first to proclaim in 1822." He wanted to "throw our oppressors beyond the seas; reestablish the Republic, and retire to my domestic home; there is no throne on earth that shines more for me than that retirement." These professions of faith were vintage Santa Anna. They represented a true *encore* of the kind of language, line of action, and promise of intent he had used throughout his life. At the age of seventy-two, having overcome the aberration that was his monarchist despair, he had recovered his characteristic voice as the great arbitrator of the early national period. Here he was, once more, pledging to come to the country's rescue, resolved to retire from politics once he had succeeded in reconciling the divided factions and facilitated the conditions for a constituent congress to meet and determine the way forward.[18]

He also revived his traditional santanista platform as the Mexican patriot who, above the pettiness of party politics, had served as the supreme arbitrator of the nation on all of those occasions when factionalism had torn the country apart. Only he could bring about a true reconciliation because he did not belong to any particular faction or party: "Today I am neither a conservative nor a liberal, I am a Mexican, that is all, and I open my arms to one and all of my compatriots." This, he claimed, was the main premise behind his actions throughout his career. His political changes had always been guided by his patriotism. Although his understanding of what was best for the country may have evolved in response to the way the events had unfolded, his patriotism remained as ardent as ever: "Never, not even for a second, have I ever ceased to be Mexican, WHATEVER MY OPINIONS MAY HAVE BEEN AT DIFFERENT STAGES, concerning the system of government best suited to my country. . . . The mother country was the main concern behind all of my actions."

Santa Anna believed: "Providence has so desired it to pass that my history has been the history of Mexico, since 1821 when I figured as one of the caudillos of Independence," and it had been he who had first proclaimed the republic on 2 December 1822. As he liked to remind Matías Romero, "If you take this conflict as the exception, remembering that I did not bring it upon our mother country but that it was our evil passions and domestic discord that did; there has not been one occasion in Mexico, since . . . 1821, when faced with war, that I have not been the first to serve her with my person and resources." It was with reference to his historic patriotism, to his impressive reputation as liberator and founder of the republic and to his past record as an arbitrator, a man of action, and a leader whose alleged inconsistency in fact reflected a tendency to seek what was best for Mexico rather than a particular party, that Santa Anna claimed he was the man to bring peace to his country. The republicans were still divided: "Juárez is a good patriot and [Jesús González] Ortega is an honorable son of Mexico: why are they divided? . . . Let all differences among the patriots end, let all of our hatred be saved for the foreign domination." He liked to think that he, at the age of seventy-two, was the providential figure who could save Mexico in its hour of need: "My precedents, my position in the so-called conservative party, and even my long absence from my country, make me, in my mind, the one who has been called forth to bring about a reconciliation, leading by example, offering my submission to the constitutional government as its sincere friend." Santa Anna stressed that the way forward was to put their past political party differences behind them. It was imperative to join forces to expel the invaders and restore the republic.[19]

He admitted to having endorsed the monarchist proposal and was prepared to explain why he had done so, having since realized the enormity of his mistake. Like so many other distinguished liberators, including José de San Martín and Simón Bolívar, he had been blinded by his despair. Following independence, "in Mexico as well as in other parts of Spanish America, many became disheartened to see the sad results produced by the attempts to forge new institutions; and many men of goodwill . . . became so disheartened . . . that they believed it to be their patriotic duty to establish a Monarchy." With hindsight, he could say that "a monarchy is impossible among us. The throne in Spanish America leads to the scaffold." However, at the time, like so many other illustrious leaders in Spanish America, he had come to view the monarchist proposal as the only means of rescuing a country in disarray. He asked whether it was such a crime that he had been among those who had deluded themselves in their despair:

> Bolívar, who indignantly rejected San Martín's idea, later defended a republican plan called BOLIVIANO, which was considered to be monarchic by many liberals. . . . I point out these facts . . . registered in the annals of Spanish Ameri-

can history and do so to ask today: could I not have honestly erred like so many other men of good principles and
recognized talent? How serious a crime, how unforgivable
is it that I, like so many others, may have despaired of our
Republic and accepted the idea of trying out a constitutional
monarchy, established [however] without my cooperation
and with a scepter I was never meant to carry?[20]

It becomes obvious that he was pained by the distrust of Juárez and
his followers. He could not understand how they could have such a
twisted view of his intentions. For instance, he was shocked at the suggestion that he was planning to orchestrate a conservative counterrevolution from within the ranks of the republican movement. He was angry
that they insisted on characterizing him as an imperialist. It hurt him
that his republicanism was questioned. He rejected the accusation that
he was only joining the republican bandwagon at a time when the intervention was in its last throes. He was offering his services now because
now was when the need for reconciliation was at its most pressing.

The accusation that irritated him most was that his long career in
politics actually proved that he was unreliable and untrustworthy. Toward the end of his life, this was probably the most depressing aspect
of his rejection. The younger generation of liberals appeared to have
misunderstood completely his lifelong dedication to Mexico, above and
beyond the divisive concerns of party politics. Here was a man who had
fought in the War of Independence and played a major role in liberating Veracruz, who had fought against the Spaniards again in 1829, who
had gone all the way to Texas to fight against the Texan rebels in 1836,
who had endured captivity in the United States, who had confronted
the French invaders in 1838 and lost a leg in battle, and who had led the
Mexican forces against the U.S. army on several fronts, financing his
troops out of his own pocket. To accuse him of a lack of patriotism was
probably the most wounding insult possible. He had not betrayed every
party because he had never, as a military man, placed party interests
before what was best for the nation (or what he deemed to be best for
the nation).[21]

Rejected by the republicans, he had no choice but to attempt to put his plan into effect on his own. In a desperate attempt to raise funds to finance his restoration of the republic, he became involved in a number of dubious transactions. With his financial situation in bad shape after Mazuera and Báez had succeeded in swindling him, the general issued a series of mortgage bonds that were guaranteed by "his" properties. Circulating the first of these bonds, as early as 8 June 1866, "In amounts of five hundred dollars each, the total mortgaged sum was $750,000 and was attached to Santa Anna's three pieces of property of 378 square miles in all. Each bond showed Santa Anna's portrait (in a business suit), and there were three sketches of the properties mortgaged—the "palaces" of Veracruz [Manga de Clavo], Turbaco, and St. Thomas."[22] He also appointed a Hungarian con-man, Gabor Naphegyi, as his attorney. Evidence of how the once sharp and canny Santa Anna was losing touch with reality is that he did not limit himself to naming Naphegyi his formal representative in the United States while he set about leading his own quixotic revolution. He went as far as signing before a New York notary that the said Naphegyi could, in his name, issue bonds to the sum of ten million dollars, redeemable in three to five years' time, at the banking house of C. Powell Creene, promising 7 percent interest. The general also empowered Naphegyi to negotiate on his behalf with the United States government the sale of any portion of land in which they might be interested.[23]

By the beginning of June 1867 Napoleon III's imperial Mexican adventure was at its end. Since January the defenders of the French Intervention and Emperor Maximilian I's Mexican court had been on the retreat. On 14 January Ramón Corona's republican forces recovered Guadalajara. On 25 January General Tomás Mejía's imperial troops had to abandon San Luis Potosí and were forced to flee to Querétaro. The remaining French troops started to pull out of Mexico. On 5 February Achille Bazaine, commander in chief of the French Expeditionary Force (1863–67), ordered his troops' evacuation of Mexico City. On 12 March following the republicans' capture of Morelia (18 February) and Benito Juárez's move to San Luis Potosí (21 February), Bazaine and the last French troops in Mexico left the port of Veracruz. Emperor Maximilian, ignoring Bazaine's advice to return to Europe, took refuge in Querétaro, where he entrenched himself together with the conservative generals Tomás Mejía and Miguel Miramón and their supporters. Although they resisted General Mariano Escobedo's siege for two months (14 March–15 May), Querétaro did eventually fall to the republicans, and all three men were taken prisoner. By June, Porfirio Díaz's republican forces were getting closer to Mexico City, having liberated Puebla (2–4 April). The emperor himself, the Austrian Habsburg Archduke Ferdinand Maximilian, along with his aides, Miramón and Mejía, found themselves on trial. They were charged under the Law for the Punishment of Crimes against the Nation (25 January 1862), the sentence for which was execution by firing squad. Found guilty, they were indeed all executed on 19 June, at 7:05 A.M., on the Cerro de las Campanas. It was only a matter of time now before the republic would be restored. On 21 June Díaz succeeded in entering Mexico City, and on 15 July, with the arrival of Juárez in the capital, the republic was officially restored.[24]

Only a few weeks prior to these events, with the dream of a republican restoration becoming feasible, on 3 June 1867 the *Virginia* reached the coast of Veracruz. Santa Anna had left New York on 6 May and was confident that he would be in a position to return to his mother country for good, since he was accompanied by his wife, Dolores Tosta, his brother-in-law Bonifacio Tosta, his son-in-law Carlos Maillard, his granddaughter, a butler, and his young wife's stepfather, his personal secretary Colonel Luis de Vidal y Rivas. Initially, everything suggested that his hopes would be fulfilled. During the three days following his arrival, he was visited on board by the leaders of the port, he attended a dinner at the garrison and prison of San Juan de Ulúa, and on hearing the news that Maximilian's fate appeared to be sealed in Querétaro, he advised them to proclaim the republic. The said leaders went away, deliberated, and then agreed to launch a *pronunciamiento* "in favor of the Republic, informing Santa Anna that at five in the evening [of 7 June 1867] a commission would board the *Virginia* to fetch him, so that his presence could give the *pronunciamiento* for the Republic all the solemnity it required." As would be subsequently verified in the sworn declarations of Santa Anna's secretary, Vidal y Rivas, and the Veracruzan *jefes* and authorities who pledged their support to him (Manuel Sánchez, Ángel Arzamendi, Vicente Sánchez, and Jorge Murcía), he had returned to restore a "moderate liberal Republic."[25]

However, before Santa Anna was able to set foot in his homeland, he was prevented from disembarking by a U.S. warship. At 3:30 on 7 June the commander of the *Tacony*, Commander F. A. Roe, boarded the *Virginia* and sequestered Santa Anna. Roe allegedly threatened to bombard Veracruz if Santa Anna did not promise to leave immediately. As was stated by the *Virginia*'s captain, John Deaken, and his crew, the people of Veracruz resented the Americans' actions, since Santa Anna was extremely popular there and everybody was looking forward to his proclaiming the republic. According to the interpreter's testimony (Eduardo Gottliett), when Santa Anna asked Roe why he had been made prisoner, Roe replied, "No, General, you are not a prisoner; I just don't want there to be a bloodbath in Veracruz." The U.S. commander wanted Santa Anna to deny publicly that he had been sent to liberate Veracruz by the U.S. government. Above all, Roe wanted him to leave. Santa Anna denied that he had ever claimed to represent the U.S. government. Roe was aware that following the news of Santa Anna's arrival in Veracruz, the port, in imperial hands, was refusing to surrender to the republican General Rafael Benavides. They would surrender only to Santa Anna. For the *juarista* camp the possibility of Santa Anna liberating Veracruz from the imperialists could lead to an extremely awkward situation.

To this confession Santa Anna responded: "And what is it to you whether Veracruz obeys one Mexican and not another?" As noted by one historian, Roe had "orders to prevent his landing since the United States had committed itself to the support of Juárez as the legal President of Mexico." Santa Anna was kept prisoner on the *Tacony* overnight, and was allowed to leave the following day (8 June), so long as he did not return to Veracruz and made his way to Sisal, Havana, or the United States. On 8 June, the *Virginia* left Veracruz and made its way to Sisal, in Yucatán, which it reached on the 11th. There Lieutenant Colonel Hilario Méndez, obeying Santa Anna, disembarked with documents which, according to the *juarista* interim governor of Yucatán, Agustín O'Horán, demonstrated that he had returned to Mexico "to complicate matters for the Republic."[26]

Determined to return to Mexico and reclaim a stake in national politics, Santa Anna finally set foot on Mexican soil in Sisal on 30 June. There he made a characteristic call for peace and reconciliation, placing his services as the formidable arbitrator of the past at the disposal of the yucatecos. He could not help reminding them that many years before, he had served as their governor: "You will remember that between 1824 and 1825 I had the honor to serve as the principal military and political authority of this peninsula. . . . Call an end to this hostility betwixt brothers. We are all Mexicans. . . . My mission among our brothers is purely that of bringing peace and concord."[27]

His hopes of pulling off another remarkable return were soon dashed. He was arrested on 14 July, escorted to Campeche, and taken from there to arrive on 30 July at the notorious prison of San Juan de Ulúa—where he had been wined and dined a month earlier! Veracruz had by then fallen to Benavides's republican forces (27 July). Juárez, informed by telegram of Santa Anna's arrest, ordered that he be put on trial, charged with the Law of 25 January 1862. To ensure that this order was obeyed, Juárez reiterated it in the telegrams he sent on 14 and 27 July and 29 August 1867.[28]

Santa Anna and his stepfather-in-law Vidal y Rivas were locked up in San Juan de Ulúa in separate cells and not allowed to communicate with anyone from outside. His brother-in-law, Bonifacio Tosta, and his son-in-law, Carlos Maillard, were placed in a prison in Veracruz. His wife Dolores, his granddaughter, and the maid were allowed to disembark, having first been checked to ensure that they were not carrying any incendiary papers. Santa Anna and Vidal y Rivas had no money or food and were starving. Santa Anna was also suffering from "dyspepsia, although the symptoms are not alarming," and was resigned to death. Even so, in a letter written to his son-in-law and nephew Francisco de Paula Castro, which Dolores managed to smuggle ashore, he appeared not to have weakened in his resolve to die fighting. He urged Francisco not to spare any money in helping his wife and himself in this time of need. He was determined to give his persecutors a hard time.[29]

Notwithstanding the prisoner's age and poor health, on 2 September 1867, he was formally charged with treason. A month of interrogations followed. Finally, between 7 and 10 October 1867 he was put on trial in a theater in Veracruz. The prosecution rested its case on the following points: He had invited a European prince originally (1853–55) and was thus blamed for having caused the intervention. He had recognized the empire and offered his services to the emperor in the letters he wrote to José María Gutiérrez Estrada (1861–63) and which Gutiérrez Estrada published in El Diario del Imperio (1866). He had recognized the empire and offered his services to the emperor when he returned to Mexico in February 1864 and signed a document that said as much before disembarking. He had intervened in the 1867 conflict, after he was strictly forbidden from doing so. Juárez explicitly stated that he should be charged according to the extreme Law of 25 January 1862. As was made clear by the chief prosecutor, Colonel José Guadalupe Alba, during his summing up on 7 October 1867, he was calling for Santa Anna to be sentenced to death.[30]

Santa Anna rejected "the charge of treason as a caudillo of Independence who has spilt his blood in her defense." His defense stressed the following "facts." The document Santa Anna had signed authorizing a Mexican commission headed by José María Gutiérrez Estrada to go to Europe to find a prince for Mexican throne was being given an importance it did not deserve. He could not recall signing it, and if he did sign it this must have been done inadvertently. He was probably tired at the time and not entirely aware of its contents, taken by surprise by his minister, Manuel Diez de Bonilla. It was certainly absurd to blame him for the French Intervention, when this took place eight years after this letter was signed. He had had ample opportunities during his dictatorship to impose a monarchy and did not do so. Moreover, it was going against the spirit of the law to charge him under a law formulated in 1862 for a crime he had allegedly committed eight years prior to its formulation.

The letters Gutiérrez Estrada published in 1866 and used as evidence that he was a monarchist were not his or had been tampered with to the extent that he did not recognize them as his. Gutiérrez Estrada had published them to undermine his attempt to support the republican cause. He challenged the prosecution to find the originals. Without these they could not prove he had written the letters and, therefore, could not prove he had ever supported the intervention. As for the document he signed in 1864, it was in French. He did not know he was signing his allegiance to the empire. Proof that he was not a supporter of the intervention rested in the fact that the French authorities ordered him to leave Mexico in March, less than a month after he had returned from exile. He returned in 1864 to see what the situation was like, not out of allegiance to Maximilian, and he definitely had not obeyed its government in any way. Santa Anna was the Founder of the Republic. He was the first Mexican caudillo to have risen in arms in 1822 to proclaim the republican ideal. He had been arrested while attempting to restore the Republic in Mexico. The accusation that he was a monarchist and a supporter of the intervention was therefore nonsensical. The trial was a farce orchestrated by his enemies.[31]

On the third day of the trial (9 October), the tribunal or court-martial board, comprising seven officers (Ignacio Pérez, Manuel L. Aguilar, Angel Terán, Epitacio Gómez, Francisco Guevara, José de J. Ferrer, and Ambrosio Larragoiti), deliberated behind closed doors and reached their verdict. This came as a surprise, considering the fate of Emperor Maximilian and Generals Miramón and Mejía. Not a single member of the board believed that the crime merited the punishment specified in the Law of 25 January 1862. They all agreed that instead, Santa Anna should be punished with eight years' exile. The board consented to punishing Santa Anna for sending Gutiérrez Estrada on a monarchic quest in 1854; for accepting the intervention in 1864; and for attempting to interfere in the republican struggle in 1867 after this had been forbidden to him by the president. They believed, however, that the Law of 25 January 1862 could not be used retroactively to punish a minor act of treason committed in 1854. They were also adamant that the letters Gutiérrez Estrada had published could not be taken as proof since the accused denied having written them, and no originals had been produced. They stated that it was not possible to prove Santa Anna's activities in 1867 had been unpatriotic. Finally, the board recorded that it had borne in mind Santa Anna's services to the nation, including the fact that he had been, after all, "the first caudillo to proclaim the Republic." According to Miguel Castellanos, the assessor responsible for ensuring a fair trial, the board's verdict was just. Juárez was furious when he found out that Santa Anna had not been sentenced to death. He punished the board with six months' imprisonment for not having obeyed him.[32]

Brokenhearted but still alive, Santa Anna left Veracruz on 1 November 1867. He had succeeded in dispelling some of the allegations made against him, and once again he had survived. However, the view that he had favored a foreign monarchist experiment in 1854 had been generally accepted. He may have escaped the death penalty, and his crime had been described as a minor breach of patriotic confidence (a *conato de infidencia*), but the accusation of treason nevertheless remained. That it was viewed as a minor crime was unimportant—the accusations of *vendepatrias* (country-seller) and monarchist traitor would stick.

A fundamental question in all of this is why Juárez was determined to have a repentant republican seventy-three-year-old Santa Anna tried and executed. Why was it so important to him that Santa Anna be tried according to the Law for the Punishment of Crimes against the Nation (so important that he had the board members imprisoned for not obeying his instructions)? Needless to say, the two men despised each other. Their mutual dislike was based on personal, racial, social, and ideological issues. According to Santa Anna's memoirs, Juárez's hatred toward him stemmed from the fact that at the age of twenty-two, Juárez had served Santa Anna as a waiter during the caudillo's stay in Oaxaca in late 1828: "He never forgave me for having waited upon me in Oaxaca in December 1828, barefoot," wearing Indian clothes in Manuel Embides's house. Santa Anna never forgave Juárez for being a Zapotec of humble origins who succeeded in rising to the presidency. He viewed Juárez as an Indian who did not deserve the power he eventually acquired, and Santa Anna liked to remind those around him that there was a time when Juárez had to be taught "to wear shoes, a jacket and a pair of trousers." He also hated Juárez for having refused him admittance into Oaxaca in March 1848, when he was escaping from his opponents in the wake of the 1847 debacle. According to his biographer Brian Hamnett, Juárez, serving then as governor of Oaxaca (1847–1852), "feared that the perennial adventurer would attempt to use Oaxaca as a base for rallying support for a return to power." With his position "highly vulnerable to military intervention," it was essential that he kept Santa Anna at bay. When Santa Anna came back to power in April 1853, he placed Juárez under surveillance, and then ordered via Tornel that he be banished from Oaxaca. Santa Anna had Juárez escorted to Tehuacán, Xalapa (where, in Juárez's words, "I remained 75 days, where General Santa Anna's government did not lose sight of me and did not leave me in peace"), Huamantla, and Veracruz; he was arrested, locked up in San Juan de Ulúa, and exiled from the republic to Havana on 5 October 1853. Thanks to Santa Anna, Juárez was forced to remain in exile in New Orleans for almost two years, until 20 June 1855. Santa Anna thus avenged the "barbarous pleasure" Juárez had taken in denying him asylum in 1848. Santa Anna obviously despised him for his politics as well, opposed as he was to the regular army, the Church, and large hacendados. Juárez belonged, after all, to the radical liberal faction that had overthrown his last government in 1855 and that was responsible for confiscating his lands.[33]

It is more than likely that Juárez bore a personal grudge against Santa Anna for his imprisonment and exile in 1853. However, as one would have expected from a man of such moral rectitude, his dislike for the caudillo was mainly a political issue. For Juárez, whose constitutional Puritanism and whose civilian-liberal-republican convictions were so deeply entrenched, Santa Anna represented the institutions and tendencies he hated most. He characterized Santa Anna as a debauched cynical opportunist devoid of integrity. If Santa Anna represented anything, it was "the clerical-military tyranny he led." Juárez blamed Santa Anna and the regular army for most of the instability and strife that had characterized the early national period. According to Juárez, there was, hardly anybody in the army who had striven to guarantee "the inviolability of the democratic institutions."[34]

Having said this, it would appear that in 1866 Juárez did not really believe Santa Anna posed a serious threat to his bid for power against the empire and the intervention. As he noted on hearing that the caudillo was frantically attempting to garner support for his cause in the United States: "Whatever his supporters do to make him acceptable to today's Mexican society, they will fail. This character, in politics, is a corpse nobody can bring back to life." So why, only a year later, was he so resolute in his determination to have Santa Anna tried and executed? It becomes evident, when one considers his intentions in having had Maximilian, Miramón, and Mejía executed, that there was a symbolic aspect to his actions.[35]

In the cases of both Maximilian and Mejía, Brian Hamnett has developed an extremely persuasive interpretation of what Juárez was hoping to achieve by having them executed. The same objections that were raised when Juárez ordered Santa Anna to be tried according to the Law of 25 January 1862 were made when he instructed Escobedo to convene a court-martial for the trial of Maximilian, Mejía, and Miramón. The defense stressed then that the Law of 1862 was too harsh, and that Article 23 of the 1857 Constitution prohibited the use of the death penalty for political offenses. Juárez's wishes were nevertheless respected. All three men were executed, and their deaths came to represent a very deliberate end to causes Juárez wanted to demonstrate no longer had a place in republican Mexico. In the case of Maximilian, Juárez ensured that he was executed so that Europe never considered intervening in Mexico again. In the case of Mejía, Hamnett stresses that "his death before the firing squad dealt a violent blow to the popular religious sentiment he had embodied and mobilised. . . . His execution testified to the importance the Liberal leadership saw in physically destroying him and symbolically blotting out the cause for which he stood." In the case of Miramón, it follows that Juárez wanted to terminate physically and symbolically the elitist criollo conservative Mexico he represented. With Santa Anna's death by firing squad, Juárez would have added what he perceived as a symbol of Mexican military dictatorship to his figurative pyre of dead political phenomena. If we are to believe Santa Anna, Juárez was so confident the caudillo would be sentenced to death that when his wife Dolores went to Mexico City to beg forgiveness, Juárez turned round to her and said: "Señora, you are too late."[36]

Santa Anna was not executed, however, and went on to outlive Juárez, who died on 9 July 1872. Unlike in the cases of Maximilian, Miramón, and Mejía, his heroic past impressed the court-martial board enough to ensure that Juárez's strict orders were ignored. Santa Anna was still popular in Veracruz; not entirely the political corpse Juárez had made him out to be. Almost inevitably, one is left with the question of what would have happened had Commander F. A. Roe not boarded the Virginia and prevented Santa Anna from going ashore and liberating the port. In all probability, the imperial forces in Veracruz would have joined Santa Anna's republican pronunciamiento, and both Benavides and Juárez would have found themselves in the awkward situation of either having to negotiate with him, since he had liberated Veracruz, or having to attack him. Given that Santa Anna had come with the apparent intention of establishing a moderate liberal republic, rather than a radical one, and since there is some evidence that he was in contact with Porfirio Díaz and Jesús González Ortega, two important leaders whose support of Juárez was tenuous, a frontal attack would have probably been out of the question, since it could possibly split the republican movement, leading to another civil war. One way or another, attacked or talked to, Santa Anna would once more have been a political force that could not be ignored.[37]

What is clear is that regardless of his less redeeming qualities, the years he had spent in exile, and the fact that he was now seventy-three years old, he still commanded sufficient respect in Veracruz to be considered a force that had to be dealt with. However, although he was not executed, he was punished with eight years' exile on account of being found guilty of an act of treason. It did not matter that this was described as a relatively minor offense. Thereafter the label of "traitor" would haunt him and become the standard view of him. Few were to remember that his monarchism was, in a strange way, patriotic. As he put it himself, to accuse him of having been a "traitor" was "calumny, slander, madness." There was no justice: "accusations of treason against the only caudillo who fought resolved from one end of the Republic to the other, sacrificing everything!"[38]

Forced into exile once more, he spent the following six and a half years in Havana, Puerto Plata, and Nassau. For reasons that remain unclear, he did not return to St. Thomas. He sold the three properties he had in the Danish colony and was forced to live off the proceeds (seventy-three thousand pesos) until he died. If he had amassed a fortune at the height of his career, this had by now most definitely been spent. The lands he had once owned in Veracruz were no longer his, even if he claimed they were. Juárez ordered all of Santa Anna's confiscated properties to be inventoried, and these were broken up and sold off to different individuals, so that by the time he returned, despite noting in his last will that haciendas such as Manga de Clavo, El Encero, Boca del Monte, and Paso de Ovejas were his, they had been turned into several smaller properties and had acquired new owners.[39]

According to his last will, at the time of Doña Inés's death in 1844,

Santa Anna's estate had been worth 1,300,000 pesos. From what may be gathered from a description he made of three of his haciendas in 1845, when he considered selling them to one Alberto Gutiérrez before going into exile for the first time, El Encero was worth 140,000 pesos, Manga de Clavo 250,000 pesos, and Paso de Varas 150,000 pesos. The three properties sprawled over much of central Veracruz. Together they boasted over 16,000 cattle and 3,000 horses. The sale of livestock for Manga de Clavo alone produced a yearly income of 20,000 pesos. According to documents held in Margarita O'Reilly Pavón's private collection, in 1844 Santa Anna's estate was estimated as being worth 853,459,28 pesos. It must have been galling to find himself, in his final years, not only forced to live abroad but also in what must have seemed to him dire straits.[40]

His wife Dolores was no longer with him, having chosen to stay behind in her house in Mexico City. He spent most of his time reminiscing, working on his memoirs. If there was one purpose he appeared to have set himself at the end of his life, it was to clear his name. His autobiography, published posthumously, formed part of this final push to restore his reputation as one of Mexico's most prominent caudillos of the early national period. In a similar vein, as pointed out by historian Robert Potash, his last will was "the repudiation of an aging individual of the accusations that had been made against his character."[41]

Santa Anna found himself gazing out at the Caribbean Sea of the Bahamas, walking stick in hand, yearning to return to Mexico, obsessed with having his patriotism recognized. This was the man who in 1838 had asked of all Mexicans, forgetting his political errors, not to deny him the only title he wished to bequeath to his children: that of having been a *Good Mexican*. If there was one thing the new generation of Mexicans who filled the corridors of power appeared to be intent on refusing him, it was precisely that. He was bereft of his family, his property, his country, and his fame as a patriot. As he noted in those memoirs he scribbled down in the solitude of Nassau, "When I close my eyes forever, I want to be judged as I have been and not as my antagonists would have me remembered." He lamented that the invading U.S. army had burned his archive at Manga de Clavo in 1847. Otherwise, he noted, he would have all the necessary documents at hand to do justice to his claims. For Santa Anna there could not have been a worse punishment than this unbearable loss of prestige.[42]

As he neared his eightieth birthday, having lived thirty years longer than most of his contemporaries, he still found that "the life of a man is short, very short." His recollections spanned six decades from when he joined the royalist army in Veracruz as a cadet: "years that have flown away with the speed of thought." All that he asked was that his good deeds be given the credit they deserved: his reputation as a soldier and a leader, his contribution to the conquest of independence, his proclamation of the republic and the readiness with which he was willing to risk his life repeatedly for the mother country. He believed he deserved the "title of good patriot."[43]

When Juárez's government decreed a general amnesty for all political opponents on 14 October 1870, Juárez made a point of specifically excepting Santa Anna, for "he was a traitor to his country." As may be seen in the letters that exchanged hands in the different offices of the Ministry of War in October 1871, despite Santa Anna's exclusion, several bureaucrats thought that the exiled caudillo could return to Mexico. Santa Anna made it known that he was willing to come back. Much to these officials' embarrassment and Santa Anna's chagrin, under Juárez, he did not have recourse to this piece of legislation.[44]

His indignation at Juárez's determination to prevent him from returning to Mexico found expression in a letter of protest he issued from Nassau. He asked when had he been a traitor? When had he offended Mexico even with his thoughts? He listed his patriotic deeds yet again, the battles he had fought, the leg he had lost. He asked with contempt where Juárez was when he fought in the War of Independence, when he repulsed the Spanish invaders in 1829, when he repulsed the French invaders in 1838. At the end of his life, the world no longer made any sense to him. Everything was upside down. A "dark Indian," a "hyena," "symbol of cruelty" presided over the republic. And its founder, the "Leading caudillo of the Republic" was condemned to live in exile, branded a traitor.[45]

It was only after Juárez died, and the xalapeño Sebastián Lerdo de Tejada stepped into his shoes, becoming president on 18 July 1872, that Santa Anna's return was made possible. Even then, another year and a half passed before the octogenarian general was finally included in the amnesty and allowed to come back. Few documents have been found that allow us to draft a more detailed account of Santa Anna's crepuscular years in Nassau. On 27 February 1874, however, he finally disembarked in Veracruz in the knowledge that after nineteen years of exile, he would be allowed to stay. By the time he returned he could barely see. Nobody recognized the old man. Long gone were the days when crowds had gathered along the wharf to see him. All those years ago, following the triumph of Tampico, he had been carried around the port on people's shoulders. He did not stay in the port for long. Probably pained at the thought that all his former lands from Veracruz to Xalapa had been confiscated, broken up, and sold, he avoided taking the Xalapa road to Mexico City. Instead he boarded a train on the very line that he had ordered to be built forty years earlier and made his way to the capital, stopping in Orizaba. At least here he had the opportunity to meet up with some who remembered him. He arrived in the capital's Buenavista Station on 7 March 1874 and found his wife Dolores, two generals, a grandson, and an old friend waiting for him. Everybody else went about their business in the noisy station, oblivious to who he was and to the thrilling deeds of his long past. He moved into his wife's house at number 9 Calle Vergara (number 14 Bolívar today).[46]

On 9 March 1874 he went to meet President Lerdo de Tejada at four o'clock in the afternoon. There is no record of the conversation between the two men. Not long afterward he wrote to Lerdo de Tejada to ask for the wages he was due. He claimed he could barely make ends meet. He stressed that he had not received his salary for nineteen years. He reminded the president that he merited this back payment, given that he had been mutilated fighting for Mexico in 1838. He also noted that all his properties had been confiscated, resulting in his having unjustly lost over half a million pesos. For someone who had repulsed the Spanish invasion of 1829 and who had founded the republic in 1822, he claimed it felt extremely harsh that his country's government was prepared to let him die in penury.

In the laconic rejection he received, it was noted that he was not entitled to any such back payment. By leaving Mexico in 1855 without being granted permission to do so, he had become a deserter and had lost his right to a salary. His attempts to be reintegrated in the republican forces were rejected in 1867. The Amnesty Law of 13 October 1870 explicitly stated that those who had recourse to it would not be able to claim the return of past salaries. From all this it was also clear that following the restoration of the liberal republic, the laws the conservative and imperial governments had approved during the War of the Reform in 1859 and the French Intervention in 1863—returning to Santa Anna his rank of general, his right to a salary, and his confiscated properties—were short-lived.[47]

Santa Anna made a point of paying his respects to the Virgin of Guadalupe in the Basilica of Tepeyac ten days after his arrival. He spent the next two years secluded in Dolores's company. He was accompanied by her brother Bonifacio and Colonel Manuel María Giménez and a few other loyal santanistas. These, however, could be counted on the fingers of one hand. Little is known of his last two years. Little attention was given to him. It would appear that he resigned himself to waiting for death in anonymity, condemned to penury and oblivion. In the early hours of 21 June 1876, he finally died in his sleep, having suffered a severe attack of diarrhea. He was eighty-two years old. The obituary that was published in El *Siglo XIX* summed up fairly accurately the misery of his final years:

> GENERAL SANTA ANNA—The last hours of his life inspire the saddest of reflections: the man who controlled millions, who acquired fortunes and honors, who exercised an unrestricted dictatorship, has died in the midst of the greatest want, abandoned by all except a few of his friends who remembered him in adversity. A relic of another epoch, our generation remembered him for the misfortunes he brought upon the republic, forgetting the really eminent services he rendered to the nation. He was as a tree, stricken in years, destitute of foliage, to whose boughs even such parasites as are usually found on dry and withered trees did not cling.[48]

Conclusion

"A Good Mexican"

Santa Anna's death marked the passing of an era. He was born when Mexico was still a colony. He was buried at the end of the midcentury watershed, as a triumphant and long-lasting liberal order was about to become firmly consolidated under the rule of General Porfirio Díaz (1876–1910). He was born into a period when a Spanish viceroy sat in Mexico City, obeying orders from Madrid, and died in one in which Mexico was an independent republic that had boasted a Zapotec president and was governed according to a radical liberal constitution. During Santa Anna's lifetime Mexico had become independent from Spain, and its political class had experimented with four different constitutions (1824, 1836, 1843, and 1857), two empires (1822–23 and 1864–67), and a number of dictatorial spells. Numerous civil conflicts had marked the passing of time. Mexico had been forced to fight four international wars and had been occupied by invading armies on two occasions. Mexico had also lost half of its territory to the United States. Astonishingly, Santa Anna had witnessed and participated in most of these events.

During his wake, from two in the afternoon on 21 June 1876 to nine in the morning on the 22nd, over eight thousand people paid their last respects to the caudillo as he lay in an open coffin in his widow's house on the Calle Vergara. His body was then transported to Guadalupe Hidalgo to be buried, and a procession of over forty carriages accompanied him on his last journey. The funeral oration was delivered by General Santiago Blanco, a veteran of the battles of Angostura–Buena Vista and Padierna, who had served in the Ministry of War during Santa

Anna's last government and had fought against the revolutionaries of Ayutla. He paid tribute to "one of the last heroes of Mexican independence," described Santa Anna as a "genius," praised him for his ability to raise "armies out of nothing," and made a point of stressing that Santa Anna had never sought to impose a tyrannical regime. With the death of the last surviving caudillo of the early national period an era drew to a close.[1]

The long and painful transition from colony to independent republic, from absolutist monarchical rule to constitutional government, from a corporatist-feudal society to one that privileged individualism, from tradition to modernity, unfolded during Santa Anna's lifetime. His career, his successes and his failures, his rises and falls and the choices he made were all reflections of the times in which he lived. His story mirrored the violent transformations Mexican society underwent from being Spain's "jewel in the crown" to becoming a modern nation-state. It was a story shared by almost every other Spanish American republic. In this sense, Santa Anna was not unique. At a time in which the convulsion of revolutionary change with its consequent vacuum of power and absence of clearly defined political institutions gave way to the emergence of caudillos throughout the region, Santa Anna was the Mexican version of a continental phenomenon.[2]

The explosion of constitutional and political ideals that came with independence continues to deserve more attention. An extensive range of ideological proposals was conjured up in a determined quest to find a legitimate constitutional framework that would provide the new nations with a representative political system that could both guarantee order and stability and ensure an improvement in basic living conditions in the region. The intensity that characterized the political debate, and the energy that went into finding solutions to the numerous problems encountered by the emergent political class, meant that this was as much an age of proposals, of political inquiry and experimentation, as it was one of revolts and dictatorship.[3]

Nevertheless, the post-independence context remains one that lent itself to the emergence of caudillos throughout Spanish America. The end of the colonial tie to traditional monarchical authority opened up a vacuum that was occupied by the military or regional strongmen or chieftains of the newly formed republics. Caudillos who came to power during these years were Juan Manuel de Rosas (1793–1877, Argentine Federation), Andrés de Santa Cruz (1792–1865, Bolivia and Peru), Francisco de Paula Santander (1792–1840, Colombia), Rafael Carrera (1814–65, Guatemala), Dr. Gaspar Rodríguez de Francia (1766–1840, Paraguay), Ramón Castilla (1797–1867, Peru), Fructuoso Rivera (1790–1854, Uruguay), and José Antonio Paez (1790–1873, Venezuela).[4]

The context was one of violent turmoil. There was a vacuum of power and a generalized uncertainty over which political institutions and figures represented legitimate authority. Most caudillos were the creatures of the revolutionary wars of independence. They were famous before they rose to power because of their heroic feats in the army. Unlike civilian politicians who might have been better suited for the presidency, the caudillos were national heroes even before they moved into the National Palace. The publicity they received served to keep them in the public mind as warriors of Napoleonic stature. The personality cults, perpetuated in fiestas and ceremonies, further enhanced their popular status. A tendency to put on populist performances allowed them to appear before the eyes of the majority as the people's true representatives. Their opportunism enabled them, moreover, to know when the mood of the country was opposed to the rampant reformism of a particular government, regardless of however forward thinking it may have been. They generously rewarded those who supported them and established successful patronage-clientelistic networks with the more influential sectors of society. This in turn meant that their governments were bound to favor the more traditionalist factions of their countries. Their despotic inclinations represented a promise of stability, a halt to what the hombres de bien feared most—social dissolution. Although in some cases this represented a use of repression from which the gente decente themselves shied away, they supported their strong governments if these guaranteed a return of order and stability.

Santa Anna was very much a product of his age. He was representative of the kind of leader that came to the fore in most of postrevolutionary nineteenth-century Spanish America. His political role cannot be understood without an appreciation of the extent to which caudillismo was among the prevalent political phenomena of the time and an understanding that he represented its Mexican version. Nevertheless, this should not detract from an effort to assess his individual contribution to nineteenth-century Mexico.

Since he shares with other caudillos like Páez and Rosas a regional power base from where he was able to make his bid for national power, it is essential that the implications of Santa Anna's relationship with Veracruz are fully understood. This was not just any region. The economic and political significance of Veracruz must be stressed. The port of Veracruz was the country's main commercial outlet to the world. Its customs houses were the richest in the new republic. It was the gateway to the Altiplano as well as to the outer world. He who controlled Veracruz, in a sense, controlled the country. By seizing its customs houses he could finance an ambitious revolt. By holding onto the port Santa Anna could hold the national government to ransom. Had he been the strongman of Jalisco or Oaxaca instead, it is possible that his impact upon national politics would have been far less significant.

Having spent much of his childhood in the port, Santa Anna benefited from immunity to yellow fever, a critical factor when it came to holding onto Veracruz during a siege. While control of Veracruz could lead to control of the national government, only a veracruzano or someone immune to yellow fever could realistically control the port. Circumstances were such that Santa Anna, as a jarocho, enjoyed an advantage that competing caudillos from other provinces lacked. He could control the one region in the republic that would force any national government based in Mexico City, regardless of its tendencies, to listen to him. He developed a symbiotic relationship with Veracruz and its people that made it possible for him to master what was probably the country's most influential region.

He achieved this by three very different yet interrelated means, namely as a soldier, as a hacendado, and as a politician. As a soldier he was forced to travel throughout the region, enabling him to become acquainted with its people, their way of life, their needs, and their customs. Starting as a cadet in the Fixed Infantry Regiment of Veracruz, he went on to become a particularly successful royalist pacifier-cum-land-reform-administrator. The part he played in helping set up the communities of Medellín, Xamapa, Tamarindo, and San Diego was extremely important in establishing him as one of the province's strongmen. The gratitude and respect he earned from the eight hundred families who came to populate these four communities would prove long lasting. His popularity as Veracruz's favorite son would gather momentum after he changed sides in 1821 and joined the Army of the Three Guarantees. He astutely linked his cause to that of the much-admired Guadalupe Victoria and became the indisputable Liberator of Veracruz. There was something about him, as well, that fired up the *jarochos*, for they followed him in their droves from very early on. He further consolidated his hold of the region by initiating in Veracruz the revolt that brought down Iturbide. The republic was thus founded in Veracruz, and by the time he repulsed Barradas's 1829 expedition, as a gifted military hero, he was the adored caudillo of the region. The people of Veracruz could bask in his glory. They were veracruzanos like him. The man "who humbled Spanish arrogance on the shores of the Pánuco" was one of them.

By becoming the region's most influential hacendado, he transformed his relationship with Veracruz as their leading military hero into one in which he became the province's main provider of employment, produce, and patronage. The fact that the combination of these two aspects of his career merged in Veracruz gave his influence in the region a weight that no other veracruzano enjoyed. By the mid-1840s he owned most of the land between the port and Xalapa. His cattle provided both the port and the provincial capital with most of their beef. There was a dependency on the produce of his land that made his contribution to the local economy all-important. He certainly took every possible opportunity to retire to his lands and ensure that they were well run.

If he spent far more time in Veracruz than he did in Mexico City, it was because he was a committed landowner. We can appreciate the kind of landowner he was from the extremely detailed instructions he gave the tenants who rented parts of his haciendas; from his activities in Medellín, Xamapa, San Diego, and Tamarindo in 1819–20; and from the professions of gratitude from the people of Turbaco. He created jobs, looked after the community's interests, built cemeteries, helped the people build their houses and rebuild their churches, and gave firm instructions to his tenants regarding which crops to grow, the number of cattle they were allowed to keep, and where he expected them to grow their beans or lay down their chicken coops. His wife, Doña Inés, was also a gifted administrator, and while she was alive Manga de Clavo, Paso de Varas, and El Encero thrived during his absences.

His populism, captured in donations such as the one he gave the village of Apasapa in 1844 or in his predisposition to mingle with the common folk of the area and relax with them at the cockfights he frequented, strengthened even further the bonds that he established with the *jarochos* as their hacendado. He was their hero and their largest landowner and employer, he was their very own Founder of the Republic, Hero of Tampico *and* their *patrón*. It is not surprising that he turned Veracruz into the springboard for several of his revolts. He had the full backing of the people of the region, who both admired him and depended upon him.

He sealed his hegemony in Veracruz in the sphere of politics both at a regional and at a national level. In Veracruz itself he consolidated his political grip by serving as commander general and *jefe político* of the province in 1821–22, by favoring the Provincial Deputation in 1823, and by serving as an amalgamationist governor at a time of great dissension between *yorkinos* and *escoceses* (1827–29). His national yorkino sympathies and his regional escocés allegiances enabled him to perform a particularly skillful balancing act in Veracruz that confirmed him as the province's most respected leader. He was capable of maintaining a close friendship with escocés governor Miguel Barragán while having yorkino president Vicente Guerrero as his eldest daughter's godfather. Once he went on to play a major part in national politics, he remained committed to protecting Veracruz's interests, and the region's people—its cotton and tobacco planters, its merchants and its soldiers—returned his patronage with their unswerving support.

His federalism was undoubtedly tied to Veracruz's fortunes and his determination to protect his bailiwick. His initial endorsement of centralism in 1835 was hesitant and came only after he tried to ensure through the appointment of veracruzanos in prominent political positions that his region's interests were not forgotten. By 1841 he had become a centralist—even though he linked up with the federalists in 1846—but again there was a veracruzano feel to the government he forged, with the two all-important ministries of War and Finance being run by fellow *jarochos*: Tornel and Trigueros.

His success as caudillo of Veracruz was perhaps his most enduring achievement. Veracruz, unlike the other regions of the republic, never entirely gave up on him. He was given a hero's send-off in 1855, with most veracruzanos convinced that he would be back. Had it not been for the intervention of the U.S.S. *Tacony* in 1867, Veracruz would have welcomed him back with open arms as the Restorer of the Republic. Had his court-martial taken place anywhere other than Veracruz, it is also probable that Juárez's wishes to have him executed would have been respected. It is no coincidence that it was a xalapeño, Sebastián Lerdo de Tejada, who finally allowed him to return from exile in 1874. To this day, if there is one part of Mexico where people are still ready to give Santa Anna the benefit of the doubt, despite the national curriculum's heavy-handed condemnation of him, it is Veracruz.

If Veracruz was one of his main passions, the other was the army. Only by fully appreciating his relationship with the army—his lifelong dedication to this institution, the time he spent serving the armed forces, and the military values he fully espoused and represented—can we begin to understand the beliefs he sustained and his motivation. As he recognized himself in 1858, "Never have I had the presumption of considering myself a perfect man; on the contrary, I have always confessed my inadequateness for the fulfillment of the First Magistracy. My education has been purely military, and those years that should have been devoted to the sciences, I spent them in the barracks and in the camps."[5]

He was a soldier first and a politician second. As a soldier he intervened in politics as an arbitrator. His politics and his political behavior were marked by his military outlook on life, his time spent in the barracks or on the way to battle. The army provided him, a provincial middle-class criollo, with the opportunity to climb the social ladder in a way that no other profession would have. Despite the massive wealth he accumulated at the height of his career, however, we should not forget that for the creole elite in the capital he remained a parvenu and that this in turn may explain his dislike for Mexico City, and the ambivalent attitude toward him on the part of the *hombres de bien*. Given that his army career was what enabled him to become Mexico's most powerful caudillo, he owed everything to the military profession. He felt a special affinity toward the army and his fellow soldiers, an affinity expressed in the privileges awarded to this favored institution under each of his governments.

In the same way that he developed a symbiotic relationship with Veracruz, he developed an equally tight-knit relationship with the army. In power, the army was his main clientele. Given the power the army could wield to protect or overthrow a particular government, this was the most important clientele a caudillo could have. Through the exertions of his minister of war, José María Tornel, he succeeded in transforming the army into a santanista institution, and in so doing secured the kind of support that would allow him to acquire the dominance he enjoyed during the early national period. He had the power to mobilize troops against a particular government or ensure their undying support in a way that no other general of the period could. Given that his hegemony in Veracruz allowed him to hold the government to ransom if necessary, the added advantage of being the army's favorite general made him into a particularly strong player when it came to influencing the politics of the nascent republic.

His status as the army's idol was guaranteed by his plowing of funds into the forces whenever he was in power and by his showering of promotions upon his men. However, he also earned their respect and loyalty through his military exploits, his leadership skills, and his nationalist antipolitics. He participated in more battles than any other high-ranking officer during this period. His victories in Veracruz during the last year of the War of Independence and his clashes against Spaniards and government forces between 1822 and 1832 gave him a prestigious reputation as a man of action enjoyed by none of his contemporaries. He was the Liberator of Veracruz, the Hero of Tampico. Although he lost the battles of Tolome (1832), San Jacinto (1836), Cerro Gordo (1847), and the Campaign of the Valley of Mexico (1847), he won the battles of El Palmar and Rancho de Posadas (1832), Guanajuato (1833), Guadalupe (Zacatecas, 1835), the Alamo (1836), Veracruz (1838), and Acajete (1839) and came close to obtaining a victory at Angostura–Buena Vista (1847). His miraculous comebacks and his ability to raise armies during times of crisis point to the fact that for the majority of his contemporaries, his military triumphs outweighed his defeats. In this sense, we cannot underestimate the extent to which he benefited from Tornel's services as his leading propagandist. With a panegyrist like Tornel at work, Santa Anna's triumphs were publicized to great effect. His defeats were simply not given the same kind of coverage. His contemporaries in the army did not have a comparably gifted writer to wax lyrical about their exploits.

Furthermore, nobody could accuse him of sitting in a pleasantly ventilated room in the National Palace while Mexico's sons went to war. If he won the army over, this was in great part due to his willingness, indeed enthusiasm, to enter the fray; to his preference to be leading his soldiers into battle rather than waiting idly among the comforts of Mexico City. He was the first to volunteer to lead the troops regardless of whether the political class expected him to remain in the capital, whether he was the country's president, or whether he was living in retirement on his haciendas. His amputated leg did not prevent him from leading the campaign against Mejía in 1839 or against the U.S. invaders in 1847. It would serve him to remind his countrymen that he was prepared to risk his life for Mexico, which undoubtedly impressed his troops.

He led by example and gained his men's admiration as a result. There is no denying that he possessed natural gifts marking him out as a born military commander. These included an extraordinary capacity for work, often on little sleep, and a disposition to endure hunger and hardships alongside his men. He also had a personal presence that struck awe in those who met him. As a politician he could be charming and seductive, captivating his listeners with his eyes and the Veracruzan music of his voice. As a military leader he was forceful and inspiring. He had a unique ability to inspire his own troops to feats of courage and fearless loyalty to him.

As a strategist he earns a mixed verdict. With Arredondo as his mentor, he could be reckless and ruthless. The outcome of such an approach could go either way. In most cases it involved a high death toll. He was also averse to listening to his fellow commanders or to allowing them to take the initiative, and for this he paid the price, notably in 1847. His own lack of respect for his Texan opponents in 1836 proved disastrous at San Jacinto. It follows from this that his triumphs were not so much the result of brilliant strategies (although these were highly imaginative in a couple of instances) as of stubborn courage and fearlessness. However, as already noted, in the end this was irrelevant, given that his contemporaries were prepared to overlook his defeats until his exile in 1855.

Finally, through Tornel's exertions, he gave the army a raison d'être and an esprit de corps that were ideologically charged, which resulted in their symbiotic relationship having a depth and a meaning that went beyond a simple question of mutual back-scratching. Under Santa Anna the army became the most privileged institution in society because, as he reminded its members, it was thanks to them that Mexico was independent. Mexicans had a nationality because they had a strong army. It followed from this that to attack the army was to attack Mexico. He gave soldiers a pride in being part of this special and honorable military brotherhood that made them feel good. They were rewarded with promotions, pay rises, pensions, and prestige. Beside the army, the needs of the Church were undoubtedly secondary. Santa Anna was a practicing Roman Catholic, a *guadalupano* (adorer of the very Mexican Virgin of Guadalupe), and in later years, as a reluctant conservative-monarchist, he defended Church privileges. However, with the exception of his last government (1853–55), it was always the case that the Church was expected to help finance the regeneration of the army, whether this was carried out through confrontation (allowing the radicals to confiscate Church properties and assets) or negotiation (in exchange for *not* allowing the radicals to confiscate Church properties and assets).

His antipolitics stance was, therefore, a natural political development. The army's sole concern was the mother country. It was a pure concern, clean, honorable, and praiseworthy. The army was not there to participate in the dirty world of politics. If the army was dragged into the cesspit of national politics this could only be because the political class had reached a dead end and it was necessary to restore order before society was overtaken by the forces of chaos. Regardless of the fact that in reality, most general-politicians were as much part of the factional disputes of the period as their civilian friends and foes, the santanista militaristic antiparties/antipolitics discourse was extremely effective in giving military political intervention a particular moral rectitude. For a civilian politician like Mora, Santa Anna's antipolitics may well have appeared as empty propaganda. For the high-ranking officers who followed him it did not.

The santanistas' antiparties/antipolitics agenda was shared by most military men of the period, regardless of their nationality. The Duke of Wellington, to take one notorious example, was also averse to the antics of political parties. As his biographer Richard Holmes reminds us, in 1809 "[Wellington] opined that 'the Spirit of Party in England' was to blame for 'all the misfortunes of the present reign.'" In a similar vein, on another occasion he "made it clear that he was not a party man [and] . . . believed that 'factious opposition to the government' was 'highly injurious to the interests of the country.'" In this sense Santa Anna's politics were first and foremost those of a military man, which accounts for his view of himself as having been above party politics, *au-dessus de la mêlée*, an arbitrator whose actions were characterized by their selfless patriotism. It also explains his impatience with constitutional procedures and the endless discussions of Congress. Even Wellington, as a military commander accustomed to giving orders and having these obeyed, found the nature of democracy highly frustrating when he became prime minister: "They agree to what I say in the morning and then in the evening they start up with some crochet which deranges the whole plan. I have not been used to that in the early part of my life. I have been accustomed to carry on things in quite a different manner: I assembled my officers and laid down my plan, and it was carried into effect without more words."[6] Given Santa Anna's military background, it is surprising he did not close down Congress more often.

As a politician Santa Anna was as much a pragmatist, an opportunist, and a schemer as the rest of his political allies and opponents. It went with the job. He was not always honest, nor was he true to his conscience at all times. Circumstances dictated many of his decisions, which sometimes went against his better judgment or his true desires. Many of his political alliances were uncomfortable ones, as witnessed in his calling for the return of Manuel Gómez Pedraza in 1832, working with Gómez Farías in 1833–34 and again in 1846–47, or working with the centralists who came to the fore in 1834–35 and 1839. The only governments controlled from their inception mainly by santanistas who thought like him were those of 1841–44 and 1853–55. Even then, internal divisions ultimately led to the collapse of both. It was inevitable that political expediency determined both likely and unlikely alliances.

Nevertheless, the experience of the first national decades affected him in the same way that they did the entire Mexican political class, as the hopes of the 1820s degenerated into the despair of the 1840s. To ignore how events forced Mexico's politicians, including Santa Anna, to change tack, look for a different alternative, and abandon their original proposal, or to claim that they were all cynical turncoats, does not do justice to the complexity of the period. The failure of the different governments and political systems with which Mexico experimented in order to consolidate long-lasting stability and prosperity made everybody rethink their initial ideas as to what was the best way forward. Santa Anna changed sides, but then so did everyone else. His political ideas and allegiances evolved in tune with Mexico's cycles of disenchantment, profound disillusion, and despair.

He was an iturbidista before Iturbide closed down Congress and succeeded in alienating most of his supporters. An admirer and a close friend of Guadalupe Victoria's, he became a republican and a federalist, and his actions in Veracruz mirrored those of Victoria in the capital as he attempted to pursue a near impossible course that could accommodate the interests of yorkinos and escoceses. Ultimately he sided with Vicente Guerrero's faction and the yorkinos, although he was always distrustful and wary of the radicals and the extremists in the movement. When Guerrero was overthrown, Santa Anna did not join Bustamante's triumphant faction, although the invitation was there. He retired from politics and led the revolt that overthrew the administration of so-called party of order two years later. His liberal associations of the 1820s remained present as he linked up with Gómez Farías's men in 1833–34, although the upheavals of 1827–32 had started to undermine his confidence in federalism and the representative system forged under the 1824 Constitution. The extremism of the 1833–34 Congress and the reaction their anticlerical reforms provoked finally forced him to take action and turn against his former allies. However, the centralist factions that benefited from the Plan of Cuernavaca were not his own, and he was neither present at nor responsible for the dissolution of the 1824 charter or the drafting of the 1836 centralist constitution. He remained a half-hearted centralist until the Texan debacle of 1836 finally convinced him that the federalist model was to blame for some of the provinces' secessionist aspirations. By 1841 his faith in constitutionalism, while not altogether gone, had been severely weakened. If there was a government that was representative of a mature santanista ideology this was his 1841–44 administration, based upon the tenets of the 1841 Bases de Tacubaya and the 1843 Bases Orgánicas. Following their failure, his first exile, and the eruption of the Mexican-American War, he was prepared to link up first with the radical federalists, then with the moderate federalists, and finally with his former santanista comrades in a desperate bid to organize the country's defense against the U.S. invading army. Defeat and his despair led him to abandon all faith in representative politics and a federalist system. Like Simón Bolívar before him, he warmed to the idea of dictatorship and eventually became a reluctant monarchist, ready to accept as a lesser evil the imposition of a European prince on the Mexican throne. The abuses of the French Intervention and his deliberate exclusion from participating in the regency inspired him at the end of his life to recover his former moderate liberal and republican stance. However, by then, Juárez's liberal party was no longer prepared to accept his services.

His politics were characterized by a series of changes and transmutations. Notwithstanding, there were certain constants in his political actions that need to be stressed. These constants were a direct consequence of his military profile and perspective. His populist nationalism with its corresponding antiparties/antipolitics stance, present in all of his political interventions, stemmed from his affiliation to the armed forces. The same may be said of his repeated projection of himself as an arbitrator who sought to bring about reconciliation among the warring factions. It was as a high-ranking officer, distanced from the political shenanigans of the capital, that he intervened when the political class of the day came to an impasse. It was as a proud military hero who allegedly placed the country's interests before those of a particular faction that he pursued amalgamationist strategies where possible, inviting politicians from different factions to govern the country together. As a result, his politics were remarkably consistent throughout his lifetime. He always claimed to represent the "general will," "the will of the people," or "Mexico's best interests," all of which he believed to be ignored or oppressed by whichever government he revolted against; his motivation behind each of his forceful political interventions was the same. The government was not listening. Its policies were on the verge of causing the dissolution of society. It did not matter whether the governments he brought down belonged to one faction or another— he, the mediating general, was "above politics." To Santa Anna, the governments, individuals, and policies he challenged as a response to extreme contexts all needed to be corrected: Iturbide's tyranny in 1822, the Supreme Executive Power's centralist inclinations in 1823, Gómez Pedraza's aristocratic party's unjust electoral victory in 1828, Bustamante's repressive centralist ministry in 1832, Gómez Farías's unpopular reforms (on two occasions, 1834 and 1847), Bustamante's disastrous second government in 1841, Paredes y Arrillaga's ineffective dictatorship in 1846, and Arista's weak moderate administration in 1853.

Santa Anna's perennial quest for reconciliation with his propensity to figure as an impartial arbitrator was not new or unique. Napoleon Bonaparte was also one to project himself "as the great pacifier of all his subjects. . . . [Hoping] that if all groups rallied to his regime, the destructive political factionalism of the Revolutionary years would naturally give way to a loyal and orderly consensus, an aim which has sometimes been called his 'politics of amalgamation.'"[7] Santa Anna's constant political role as arbitrator was made credible by the way he repeatedly allowed new Constituent Congresses to seek a new constitutional solution to the present crisis and abandoned the presidential chair at the first chance. He did not play the card of arbitrator to become Mexico's *supremo*. He was not a Dr. Francia or a Rosas. Despite being repeatedly accused of craving absolute power and the imposition of a lifelong military dictatorship with him at its head, his lust for power was neither conventional nor, strictly speaking, political. He did not get his kicks out of governing his subjects.

A pertinent question here is whether he was actually interested in power. Did he live to rule? Was his life's main aim to become the supreme dictator of Mexico? The evidence would suggest otherwise. A study of his life not only gives credence to his claim that he saw himself as an arbitrator rather than as a ruler; it also demonstrates that he was not in power for a significant length of time during the early national period. In terms of actual time spent "governing" or actively presiding over the nation, he was the supreme magistrate of Mexico for a total of five and a half years. Even this figure is deceptive, given that the average spell of time he spent in power during one particular term in office did not tend to exceed six months. The only governments in which he stayed put, in relative terms, and dedicated himself to exercising power, were his 1841–44 and 1853–55 administrations. Apart from the few occasions when he made use of emergency powers and governed Mexico as a dictator (1834, 1841–43, 1853–55), his actions were restricted by the Constitution, the political class's policies, party divisions, and the impact on the country of the different conflicts in which he fought. When in power, he generally did not have carte blanche to rule as he pleased.

Whenever he was able to leave the capital he did so, either to be with his family and look after his haciendas or to go into battle. He did not show any inclination to exercise power on a permanent basis. His great ambition was to achieve recognition. Driven by a quest for military glory, he thrived on Te Deums, medals, fiestas, adulation, and demonstrations of public admiration. He intervened in politics as an arbitrator for the same reason: to serve and save the country but also so that people spoke highly of him. Happiness for Santa Anna was to be perceived as the Redeemer of the Mother Country, Mexico's favorite patriot, their adored benemérito de la patria en grado heroico. Power in itself, however, does not appear to have been his prime objective. When in power, he made the most of circumstances and notoriously lined his pockets by embezzling government funds. He tried to give the country a firm political direction by supporting one political proposal or another. In the end though, he repeatedly retreated to his private life. His consistent eagerness to offer his services on the battlefield can be explained partly because he was aware that his status depended on his military actions. He was not the power-crazed megalomaniac his critics made him out to be. If he was hooked on anything it was glory, not power.

Santa Anna said he wanted to be remembered as "a good Mexican." Throughout his military and political career he firmly reiterated his love of the mother country and his undying patriotism. His love of Mexico was his prime motivation, at the heart of all of his decisions. He fought from one end of the republic to the other for Mexico. He lost a leg for Mexico. He abandoned his happy retirement to arbitrate between the warring factions for Mexico. The question is, of course, whether such patriotic professions were genuine, or whether they were this scoundrel's last refuge, to paraphrase Samuel Johnson.

There is no denying that until the Mexican-American War, a clearly defined and widespread sense of nationhood was missing. Mexicans, overall, did not see themselves as Mexicans. The social, cultural, racial, ethnic, and geographic diversity of Mexico made it extremely difficult for there to be such a thing as Otero's "national spirit." For the majority of people who did not migrate and stayed put in the villages or towns of their birth, the very concept of Mexico as a country was abstract, diffuse, and ultimately meaningless. The people of Zacatecas refused to support the war effort in 1847 because they did not perceive the endangered capital of the republic as their concern. What could it mean to a peasant from Oaxaca that this or that government had risen or fallen in Mexico City? There were *jarochos* and *tapatíos*, Zapotecs and Maya, criollos and mestizos, hacendados and beggars. In what sense were they all Mexican? As Lucas Alamán pointed out in 1853, apart from the Spanish language and the Catholic faith, what else did they have in common? Was Santa Anna using a meaningless rhetorical turn of phrase to justify a more sinister motivation?

The answer to this question lies in his military background. It was as a soldier first and subsequently as a commander that he traveled extensively throughout the republic. More so than any other profession, the army's operations forced its members to see large parts of the country. Unlike that majority who did not know what there was beyond the *sierra*, the men who were conscripted into the army, together with their officers, did have to travel throughout the country, putting down or supporting rebellions and facing invading forces. Santa Anna got to see most of Mexico at one stage or another of his life. His operations took him from his native Veracruz to the provinces of Tamaulipas, San Luis

Potosí, Nuevo León, Texas, Puebla, Mexico, Hidalgo, Morelos, Guerrero, Oaxaca, Querétaro, Guanajuato, Zacatecas, Jalisco, Michoacán,
and Yucatán. Although he was a veracruzano, his career opened up to
him the whole of Mexico and, in so doing, gave him an empirical sense
of who his countrymen were, of the nature of his country's many land-
scapes—of what he was ultimately fighting for. His patriotism may not
have meant much to a civilian population with strong local or regional
affinities, but it must have had a singular resonance among his fellow
officers who, like him, did travel the length and breadth of the country
and risked their lives for that very nation they made their own. When he
stressed that he was driven by his love for his country, he was ignoring
many other motivations that were less altruistic and more personal (a
yearning for glory, a love of war, a need for revenge). However, there
was some truth in his assertions. Considering the numerous occasions
when he risked his life to defend Mexico, there must have been at least
a grain of genuine patriotism in his actions, however difficult accepting this may be for the generations brought up to believe that he was a
despicable traitor.

His personal corruption and alleged lack of principle differed little
from that of many other successful generals and politicians. Despite his
less endearing qualities, he succeeded in becoming the most famous
man in the country. The publicity given to his military victories certainly
served to keep him in the public mind as Mexico's greatest warrior. He
successfully created a personality cult that greatly increased his popularity, particularly in the army. His fame as liberator of Veracruz and
hero of Tampico had greater resonance in the collective psyche of his
contemporaries than did his defeats. His personal dynamism sharply
contrasted with the ostensible apathy and indecision of figures such as
Anastasio Bustamante. In this sense, he came across as a true man of
action, always ready to abandon the National Palace or the pleasures of
his retirement to lead the troops into battle, whether against domestic
rebels or foreign aggressors. It was because of this dynamism that he
also represented autocratic power and a promise of stability, a halt to
what the *hombres de bien* feared most—social dissolution.

In a context where representative politics were not working and
where the political class was seen by many as being remote, uncaring,

corrupt, self-serving, and cynical, Santa Anna's appeal was very strong. In a climate of mistrust and disrespect of politicians and party politics and of a generalized belief that it was the politicos with their Masonic affiliations and factionalist agenda who were responsible for repeatedly bringing the country to the verge of dissolution, it is hardly surprising that a military hero like Santa Anna could acquire such prominence. Not having been long enough in power to be tainted by the politicians' (mis)behavior, he was able to play the patriotic card both convincingly and with conviction. He was the officer who had fought for the good of the nation on repeated occasions while the *hombres de bien* bickered in the capital.

Similarly, the fact that the majority believed he was able to impose law and order in a society that was crippled by crime, banditry, and violence cannot be underestimated. When Mexicans spent (as many still do today) a significant amount of time taking precautions to avoid being mugged, assaulted, or kidnapped—living in fear, swapping after-dinner "horror stories" of attacks they, their relatives, or their friends had suffered—Santa Anna's appeal as Mexico's "necessary gendarme" was evidently great. As the one leader considered capable of restoring peace, order, and safety, his following, unsurprisingly, was massive.

The fact that he was a supreme manipulator, negotiator, and arbitrator is, of course, of great importance. He always generously rewarded those who supported him in the military, more so than did other generals. As we have seen, at a national level his most important clientele was the military. Likewise the merchant community and the cotton lobby benefited from his largesse and supported his rise to power financially. He was consistent in fulfilling his pledges to those who backed him. The support he received from the *jarochos* was also a key asset when he needed political and especially military backing. He targeted his patronage deliberately and consolidated a group of identifiable santanistas. He relied on the upper classes, the *hombres de bien* and the *gente de orden*, but was also capable of projecting himself to the masses as a man of the people.

He had his ears open to public opinion and knew when it was time to take advantage of his enemies' political difficulties. He succeeded in creating the notion that Mexico's troubles were to be blamed on the

political parties that divided the nation, producing a need for reconciliation. He also succeeded in convincing many that he was the great
arbitrator of the nation who intervened to protect the people against
misgovernment, whether it was under a radical, moderate, or traditionalist administration. In this sense he used and was used by the constitutional politicians of the "age of proposals." The fact that he did
not subscribe to any party-based ideology, believing himself superior
to all, meant that he came to be "the temptation of all parties." Most
factions and parties believed that they could use him to rise to power.
His charisma and the cult of his persona made him an indispensable
player. His absenteeism and his detachment from the party politics of
the capital also meant that he could return time and again, posing as
the great arbitrator of Mexico's divisions. This, in turn, made most parties believe that Santa Anna could be used for their own cause, as long
as he was kept happy, and so his support was sought by most of the
factions at one point or another.

   His loyal friend Tornel played a key role in orchestrating the caudillo's
repeated rise to power. He was Santa Anna's informer in the capital,
his leading propagandist, and his master intriguer. Without him Santa
Anna would not have been as well informed as he was about events in
the capital on the numerous occasions when he retired to his hacienda
or was away in exile. Likewise, he would not have acquired such notoriety and prestige, eventually being compared to Napoleon, recovering in
the process from such major disasters as the 1836 Texan campaign and
the 1847 debacle, had it not been for Tornel's eulogies to the caudillo.
It would have been very difficult for him, from Veracruz, to organize
the concerted *pronunciamientos* of 1834, 1841, and 1842 without the invaluable help of Tornel. Tornel also provided him and the santanistas
with their antiparties, antipolitics, nationalist ideology. It was Tornel,
as Santa Anna's minister of war, who ensured that the regular army
became a predominantly santanista institution, and he was equally
instrumental in giving *santanismo* a strong populist slant through his
exertions in the field of education. While Santa Anna appeared to be
mainly preoccupied with ensuring that he was in control of his home
province of Veracruz, it was Tornel who gave the caudillo a voice in national politics by consistently representing the caudillo's interests in

the capital (with the exception of their years of estrangement, 1844–47) and placing his verbal dexterity at Santa Anna's disposal.

The great irony or paradox of Santa Anna's success is that one of the main reasons he was able to rise to power on repeated occasions was also the cause of his repeated falls from grace: his absenteeism. Had he stayed put in the capital and governed the country with the iron fist his closest allies wanted him to use, he would have ceased to be the great arbitrator that he was. He would have been soiled by his involvement in power games, politics, and partisanship. However, by the same token, he would have been in a position to exert his power and influence in such a way that it is just possible some of his government's measures, in particular in 1841–44, would have been endowed with the authority and conviction they needed to be longer lasting than the rest. Instead, his repeated absences were responsible for the undoing of his governments. He was never there for long enough to consolidate his hold on power. He was not interested in doing so.

His 1833–35 presidency passed without him giving the country a direction that could rightly be described as his own. During the first half of his term in office, he spent the greater part of his time quelling a revolt that had as its aim to make him supreme dictator of the republic, while the acting president Valentín Gómez Farías and his radical Congress pressed ahead with a series of draconian anticlerical reforms. During the second half, he stayed in the capital for long enough to oversee the overhaul of Congress's reforms, but he was absent once the centralists took hold of the government, busy leading the troops that confronted the rebels first in Zacatecas and later in Texas. Likewise in 1839, his stint as General Bustamante's acting president did not last for longer than four months, and even then, he left Mexico City to confront José Antonio Mejía's federalist rebels in Acajete and found his hands tied by the Supreme Conservative Power. In 1846–47 he was simply not around to take charge of the executive, despite being the nation's president on paper. He led the defense of Mexico in the northern and eastern campaigns, as well as in the campaign of the Valley of Mexico. Even the two occasions when he remained in Mexico City for a respectable length of time to fulfill his duty as president in 1841–44 and 1853–55 were marred by his tendency to leave acting presidents in his place. His reluctance to govern was a key factor in the internal schism that brought down the santanista administration of 1841–44. The santanistas wanted him to rule Mexico. Santa Anna preferred to retire to his hacienda or lead his men into battle.

The greater part of Santa Anna's working life was spent either looking after his lands or preparing for war. Although he had a fine political sense that enabled him to use the different contexts to suit his own circumstances, he was not a politician. He did not spend his life in the National Palace chairing meetings with his ministers, attending sessions in Congress, negotiating draft reforms with the different lobbies and *camarillas* (informal political subgroups) who gathered in the corridors, or overseeing the development of his policies from their conception to their implementation. He was not dedicated to formulating a political project. He spent his time running his haciendas and preparing his troops for battle. When it came to the political scene, he was, as a soldier, consistent in acting the part of arbitrator. He was not one to linger in the capital after he had restored peace and order. Even in 1853–55 there is evidence that he was planning to return to El Encero in 1854 and was prevented from leaving an interim president behind because of the events in Ayutla. He was also looking into placing a European prince on the Mexican throne so that he could retire to his lands.

A study of his life shows that although Santa Anna made many highly questionable decisions and a series of disastrous mistakes, the claim that he was a "traitor" is a distorted misinterpretation of the events that led to the accusation. He did not recognize Texan independence in 1836. He did not lose the 1846–47 war on purpose. In both instances, the "general of tricks" tried ingeniously to deceive his Texan captors and President Polk's administration, respectively. The joke was intended to be on them, not on Mexico. The fact that Texas achieved its independence and the United States won the Mexican-American War seriously undermined Santa Anna's intentions. In the stark light of failure, what could have been the most cunning of plans became a despicable case of treason. But although one can understand how Santa Anna's transactions in Texas, Cuba, and Puebla backfired, and how it came to pass that defeat led the caudillo's critics to conclude that the Texan and 1847 debacles were all part of a carefully crafted secret Machiavellian plan, the truth was that he was hoping to steal time and use U.S. naïveté to serve his own purpose. Had Santa Anna succeeded in achieving the impossible—winning the Mexican-American War—the Treaty of Velasco and the meeting with Slidell Mackenzie would form part of his glorious narrative. They would be equated with so many other admirable, heroic military deeds based upon the principle of deceit. What Santa Anna did do was sign the Treaty of La Mesilla in 1853. For this action he may indeed be rightly accused of having been an unpatriotic *vendepatrias* (country-seller). However, the context was not one in which he had much space to maneuver. And it is the context, at all times, that we must keep in view.

In elaborating a final assessment of his life and career, we must judge him from the perspective of the context in which he moved, the context that led to his rise to prominence, the context he had to overcome. To compare him to a present-day politician of the Partido Revolucionario Institucional (PRI) may be suggestive, but it is ultimately unhelpful.[8] Santa Anna was a man of his time. He was a provincial middle-class criollo who benefited from being an army officer in a context of great turmoil, violence, and rupture. He became the strongman of Veracruz, one of the most important hacendados of the region, and succeeded in becoming Mexico's leading caudillo during the early national period. He fought with courage in numerous conflicts. He intervened on the political stage on repeated occasions, mainly as an arbitrator, siding with different factions at different stages. The fact that he continues to fascinate us stems without doubt from his remarkable ability to overcome spectacularly serious setbacks. His colorful and varied life continues to provide a good narrative. However, his legacy was not long lasting. Despite his early victories and the way the Mexican people venerated him, defeat and exile ultimately destroyed all the power and influence he came to acquire.

He was not a traitor. He was not a turncoat. He was not always a tyrant. Santa Anna was a general, a landowner, and a nineteenth-century caudillo who tried to prosper personally and help his country develop at a time of severe and repeated crises, as the colony that was New Spain gave way to a young, troubled, besieged and beleaguered Mexican nation. He may not deserve to have a square or even a back street in his native Xalapa named after him, but neither does he deserve to carry the full blame for everything that went wrong in Mexico following independence. His story, with all the contradictions, confusion, and pain that it entailed was one that reflected the traumas Mexico had to endure during the early national period to become a modern nation-state.

Chronology

1794	Birth of Santa Anna in Xalapa, Veracruz, 21 February
1794–1810	Santa Anna's childhood is spent in Xalapa, Teziutlán, and Veracruz
1808	Napoleonic occupation of Spain leads to replacement of Ferdinand VII with Joseph Bonaparte as king of Spain in May; Gabriel Yermo heads Spanish-led coup in Mexico City that prevents Viceroy José de Iturrigaray from setting up creole-dominated council in the capital, 15 September; Pedro Garibay is appointed acting viceroy
1810	Santa Anna joins the Fixed Infantry Regiment of Veracruz as a cadet, 6 July
August	New Viceroy Francisco Javier Venegas arrives from Spain

1810–1821 War of Independence

1810	
16 September	Grito de Dolores (War of Independence begins)

1811

17 January   Battle of Puente Calderón—leading to de-
                  feat, escape, capture, and execution of insur-
                  gent leader Miguel Hidalgo y Costilla, 31 July

13 March   Santa Anna is mobilized to Nuevo Santander
                  and the Provincias Internas de Oriente to
                  serve under Colonel Joaquín de Arredondo
                  y Mioño

29 August   Santa Anna participates in battle of Amolad-
                  eras and is wounded in one hand

1812

6 February   Santa Anna is promoted to lieutenant
18 March   Cádiz Constitution published
                  Santa Anna participates in pacification of
                  Sierra Gorda

8 October   Santa Anna is promoted to sublieutenant

1813

11 January   Félix María Calleja replaces Venegas as
                  viceroy

July   Santa Anna participates in Arredondo's
                  Texan campaign against Magee and Gutiér-
                  rez de Lara's expedition

18 August   Santa Anna participates in battle of Medina;
                  the rest of the year he spends in San Antonio
                  de Béxar, where he is disciplined for forging
                  his superiors' signatures to draw funds to
                  cover his gambling debts

October   Insurgent Congress of Chilpancingo is cre-
                  ated

6 November   Congress of Chilpancingo declares the inde-
                  pendence of Mexico

1814

Spring   Santa Anna is mobilized from San Antonio
                  to Monterrey

October	Congress of Chilpancingo issues Constitution of Apatzingán

1815

7 July	Santa Anna is promoted to royal lieutenant (*teniente por despacho real*)
November	Santa Anna returns to Veracruz
22 December	José María Morelos is executed

1816–17 Santa Anna serves under Governor José García Dávila as his aide

1816

1816	Juan Ruiz de Apodaca replaces Calleja as viceroy
29 December	Santa Anna is promoted to captain

1817–18 Santa Anna is ostracized in Veracruz following García Dávila's temporary departure.

1818–19 Santa Anna is reinstated as commander of the Realistas de Extramuros de Veracruz y Pueblo de la Boca del Río and is favored by Apodaca, who pardons him after he summarily executed an insurgent leader

1819–21 Santa Anna administers resettlement of amnestied insurgents in the villages of Medellín, Xamapa, San Diego, and Tamarindo and is successful in pacifying central Veracruz; Santa Anna is promoted to lieutenant of grenadiers, 17 January 1820; the Town Council of Veracruz accuses him of being despotic

1821

24 February	Royalist officer Agustín de Iturbide joins

	forces with insurgent leader Vicente Guerrero and launches the Plan of Iguala
29 March	Santa Anna defects to Army of the Three Guarantees in Orizaba
1 April	Santa Anna and José Joaquín de Herrera liberate Córdoba
7 April	Santa Anna is promoted to lieutenant colonel by the Spanish authorities before news reaches them of his defection; he is promoted to colonel in the Army of the Three Guarantees
25 April	Santa Anna liberates Alvarado
19–20 May	Santa Anna assists Herrera in defense of Córdoba
30 May	Santa Anna liberates Xalapa
7 July	Santa Anna attacks Veracruz but fails to liberate the port
24 August	Iturbide and Spanish Political Chief Juan de O'Donojú sign the Treaties of Córdoba
27 September	The Army of the Three Guarantees liberates Mexico City on Iturbide's birthday
7 October	Santa Anna liberates Perote
28 October	Santa Anna and Manuel Rincón liberate Veracruz; Iturbide replaces Santa Anna with Rincón as commander general of the province
Winter	Santa Anna visits Mexico City

1822–1823 First Empire

1822

February–May	Santa Anna is appointed commander of Xalapa garrison
19 May	Iturbide becomes Emperor Agustín I
16 August	Santa Anna is promoted to colonel *graduado* and *efectivo* (rank subcategories particular to the Mexican army)

26 August	Iturbide imprisons nineteen members of Congress
September–October	Santa Anna becomes political head and military commander of the Province of Veracruz
27 October	Santa Anna leads failed attempt to liberate island garrison of San Juan de Ulúa
31 October	Iturbide closes down Congress; on the same day Santa Anna is promoted to brigadier general
2 December	Santa Anna revolts in Veracruz, calling for the imposition of a republic

1823

1 February	Plan of Casa Mata
2 February	Santa Anna joins the Plan of Casa Mata
19 March	Iturbide abdicates
March–June	Santa Anna, following Guadalupe Victoria's instructions, mobilizes his troops to Tampico and from there to San Luis Potosí

1823–1824 The Triumvirate

Constituent Congress drafts federal constitution under a triumvirate, the Supremo Poder Ejecutivo, made up of Generals Guadalupe Victoria, Nicolás Bravo, and Pedro Celestino Negrete

1823

5 June	Santa Anna launches federalist uprising with his Plan of San Luis Potosí; Constituent Congress endorses federalist ideal and Santa Anna ends revolt in July
July 1823–March 1824	Santa Anna is escorted to Mexico City, where

he is put on trial for his revolt of San Luis
Potosí

1824–1835 First Federal Republic

1824

23 January   José María Lobato starts anti-Spanish revolt
in capital; Santa Anna offers to quell the uprising with Vicente Guerrero

March   Santa Anna is exonerated for his Plan of San
Luis Potosí and is subsequently appointed
military commander of State of Yucatán

May 1824–
April 1825   Santa Anna serves as military commander of
Yucatán; he is elected governor in July 1824

September   1824 Constitution is proclaimed; presidential elections are held, and Guadalupe Victoria is elected president

1824–29   Guadalupe Victoria is president

1825   Santa Anna returns from Yucatán, resigns
as director of engineers in the capital only
days after being appointed, and retreats to
Veracruz, where he marries María Inés de la
Paz García and buys his hacienda Manga de
Clavo
Masonic Rite of York is established in Mexico

1825–27   Santa Anna lives in retirement in Manga de
Clavo

1826   Congressional elections (August–October)
result in a landslide victory for the *yorkinos*

1827

19 January   Arenas Conspiracy dismantled

10 May	First expulsion laws
July–August	José Antonio Rincón leads *yorkino* revolt in port; Santa Anna abandons his retirement to quell the uprising
September	Santa Anna appointed vice-governor of Veracruz
20 December	Second set of expulsion laws
23 December	Plan of Montaño
	General Nicolás Bravo joins Montaño's revolt

1828

January	Santa Anna mobilizes his troops in support of the government and joins Guerrero at Tulancingo
7 January	Battle of Tulancingo: *Escoceses* are defeated
January–September	Santa Anna serves as acting governor of Veracruz
September	The moderate General Manuel Gómez Pedraza wins presidential elections
12 September	Santa Anna revolts in Perote, proclaiming Vicente Guerrero president
September 1828–January 1829	Santa Anna is pursued by Manuel Rincón and José María Calderón to Oaxaca, where he holds out until Gómez Pedraza's faction is defeated in the capital
30 November	Revolt of La Acordada
4 December	Raid of the Parián market
27 December	Manuel Gómez Pedraza escapes and goes into exile

1829 Vicente Guerrero, president

February–July	Santa Anna serves as governor of Veracruz
26 July	Isidro Barradas's expedition lands in Tampico to reconquer Mexico for Spain
29 July	Santa Anna is promoted to division general (*general de división*)

11 September	Santa Anna defeats the Barradas expedition
16 September	Slavery is abolished in Mexico
4 December	General Anastasio Bustamante leads the Plan of Xalapa
31 December	Bustamante takes Mexico City; Santa Anna retires to Manga de Clavo after attempting to defend Guerrero's faction, and remains there for the next two years
1830–32	Anastasio Bustamante, president (Also known as the Alamán Administration)
1830	Armed resistance begins in the South
1831 14 February	Vicente Guerrero is executed
1832 2 January	Santa Anna comes out of his retirement and endorses Plan of Veracruz
3 March	Battle of Tolome: government troops achieve initial victory against Santa Anna
March	Other federalist revolts second Santa Anna's uprising in Zacatecas, Aguascalientes, Jalisco, and Tampico
18 September	Battle of El Gallinero: government troops win again
29 September	Santa Anna wins battle of El Palmar
October	Santa Anna takes Puebla and moves to capital
6 December	Battle of Rancho de Posadas
December	Treaty of Zavaleta ends the 1832 Civil War and Bustamante's regime
1833 January	Manuel Gómez Pedraza, president (as agreed in Zavaleta, Gómez Pedraza re-

| | turns to complete his interrupted term in office while elections are held, and Santa Anna is voted president) |
| 1 April | Santa Anna, president; however, he does not take up the post, leaving Vice President Valentín Gómez Farías in charge |

1833–34	Gómez Farías's "radical" administration
June–October	Santa Anna dedicates himself to quelling revolt aimed at making him dictator
	Cholera epidemic hits the capital
November	Santa Anna returns to Mexico City but does not stay long and retires to Manga de Clavo

1834	
24 April	Santa Anna returns to the capital to serve as president
25 May	Plan of Cuernavaca starts a series of revolts against the reforms of the Gómez Farías administration; Santa Anna intervenes and annuls most of the reforms

1835	
January	Gómez Farías is stripped of his vice-presidential office
27 January	Santa Anna abandons the capital and leaves Miguel Barragán in charge

| **1835–36** | Santa Anna is president; however, he is largely absent |
| 28 January | Santa Anna departs the capital, leaving Miguel Barragán as acting president |

| **1835** | |
| 23 October | The federal Constitution is replaced by a centralist one |

1835–1846 The First Central Republic

1835

February	Federalist revolt against the rise of the centralists erupts in Zacatecas
April	Santa Anna abandons retirement to crush revolt
11 May	Santa Anna defeats rebels in the battle of Guadalupe, outside Zacatecas; he is named *Benemérito de la patria* (Hero of the mother country) as a result
22 June	Revolt in Texas begins
November–January	Santa Anna organizes expeditionary army in San Luis Potosí

1836

27 February	José Justo Corro, president (following Barragán's death)
6 March	Battle of El Alamo
27 March	Mass execution of Goliad
21 April	Battle of San Jacinto (Santa Anna is taken prisoner on 22nd)
14 May	Treaty of Velasco (includes a public and a secret treaty)
June–November	Despite agreements signed in Velasco, Santa Anna spends seven months in prison
November	Santa Anna is freed under the condition that he will visit President Andrew Jackson in Washington
29 December	The 1836 Constitution consolidates a centralist political system, limits suffrage, and creates a novel arbitrating body: the Supreme Conservative Power

1837

January	SantaAnna meets President Jackson

| February | Santa Anna returns from the United States in disgrace and retires to Manga de Clavo |
| April | Anastasio Bustamante, president (after winning elections) |

1837–1841 Anastasio Bustamante, president

1838

March	French fleet starts blockade of port of Veracruz
27 November	French Pastry War begins with the bombardment of Veracruz; Santa Anna rides to the port and offers his services
5 December	Santa Anna forces the French to retreat and is badly wounded in one leg; his left leg is amputated

1839

April	José Antonio Mejía and José Urrea start federalist revolt in Tamaulipas
March–July	Santa Anna acts as interim president
3 May	Battle of Acajete: Santa Anna defeats rebels Mejía is executed
July 1839–August 1840	Santa Anna retires to Manga de Clavo

1840

15 July	Federalist revolt in the capital; Bustamante is taken prisoner in the National Palace; Santa Anna starts to mobilize his men in order to defend the government
27 July	Revolt ends before Santa Anna reaches capital, and Bustamante is restored to power
October	José María Gutiérrez Estrada publishes his notorious defense of monarchism

1841–1843	Santa Anna, president (according to the Bases de Tacubaya)

1841

August–October	Triangular Revolt overthrows Bustamante's regime
October 1841	Bases de Tacubaya approved; they award Santa Anna "almost absolute power" so that he can restore order while a new Constituent Congress is elected

1842

April	Constituent Congress is elected; federalists are dominant and press ahead with drafting a new federalist constitution
May	Santa Anna buys hacienda El Encero
October	Santa Anna retires to Manga de Clavo and appoints Nicolás Bravo interim president
19 December	Congress is closed down

1843

January	A handpicked Junta de Notables is brought together to draft a new centralist constitution
March	Santa Anna returns to capital to serve as resident
8 June	Bases Orgánicas: Ultimate santanista constitution is accepted and sworn in on the 13th

1843–44	Santa Anna, president (according to the Bases Orgánicas)

1843

Summer	Santa Anna is elected president; however, he retires to his hacienda in October, leaves Valentín Canalizo in charge, and does not await the results

October 1843–	
June 1844	Santa Anna lives in retirement in El Encero

1844

June	Santa Anna returns to Mexico City and is sworn in as constitutional president
August	María Inés de la Paz García dies in Puebla
September	Santa Anna retires to El Encero
October	Santa Anna marries his second wife, Dolores Tosta
2 November	Mariano Paredes y Arrillaga rebels against the government in Guadalajara; Santa Anna abandons his retirement to quell the revolt
6 December	While Santa Anna is in Querétaro, the Revolution of the Three Hours overthrows Santa Anna's regime in Mexico City
December 1844–	
January 1845	Santa Anna initially refuses to accept defeat; he mobilizes his troops to Puebla, which he places under siege before accepting the inevitable

1845 — José Joaquín Herrera, president

January	Santa Anna decides to leave Mexico but is taken prisoner in Xico and imprisoned in Xalapa and then in Perote; his properties and assets are confiscated by the government; after several months of discussions, Herrera's government chooses to let him go
June	Santa Anna goes into exile in Cuba, where he enters into a number of shady deals with U.S. envoys
7 June	Gómez Farías leads unsuccessful radical revolt
14 December	General Mariano Paredes y Arrillaga's revolt begins in San Luis Potosí

1846	Paredes y Arrillaga's dictatorship
April	War with the United States begins
6 August	Federalist revolt overthrows Paredes y Arrillaga and replaces the Centralist Republic with the Second Federal Republic; Santa Anna returns invited by the federalists and after U.S. navy allows him past the blockade
August	José Mariano Salas, temporary president while elections are held
November	Santa Anna returns to San Luis Potosí, where he organizes an expeditionary army with which to confront General Zachary Taylor's invading forces in the north of the country

1846–1853 Second Federal Republic

1846	
December	Santa Anna, president; however, due to the war with the United States, Valentín Gómez Farías acts as president again
1847	
11 January	Decree expropriating Church property worth 15 million pesos is approved by Congress
January–February	Santa Anna leads Mexican army to proximity of Saltillo
February	Revolt of *Los Polkos*
23 February	Battle of Angostura–Buena Vista; Santa Anna retreats after two days of fighting
9 March	General Winfield Scott arrives in Veracruz
March	Santa Anna retreats back to the capital to pacify Mexico City
21 March	Santa Anna ends Gómez Farías's administration again and departs soon after to confront Scott's invading army in Veracruz,

	appointing Pedro María Anaya as acting president
18 April	Battle of Cerro Gordo: Santa Anna is defeated and retreats to Mexico City
August	Caste War begins in Yucatán
11 August	Scott reaches Valley of Mexico
20 August	Battles of Padierna and Churubusco
24 August	Scott and Santa Anna agree to an armistice
6 September	Hostilities are renewed
8 September	Battles of Casa Mata and Molino del Rey
12 September	Battle of Chapultepec
14 September	Government leaves Mexico City to become established in Querétaro; Santa Anna leaves at the head of the army determined to continue the struggle from Puebla
15 September	The U.S. Army takes Mexico City
September	Manuel de la Peña y Peña, president, forms new government in Querétaro

1848

2 February	Treaty of Guadalupe Hidalgo grants half of Mexico's national territory to the United States
March	Santa Anna leaves Mexico and goes into exile, first in Kingston, Jamaica (1848–50) and later in Turbaco, Colombia (1850–53); José Joaquín de Herrera is elected president; Conservative party is formed; Santanista party is formed

1850–1853

Mariano Arista, president

1852

26 July	Plan of Blancarte
14 December	*Pronunciamiento* of Durango
23 December	*Pronunciamiento* of Chihuahua

28 December	*Pronunciamiento* of Veracruz

1853

January–February	Arista resigns and is replaced by Juan Bautista Ceballos, president, who also resigns
February–April	The *santanista* Manuel María Lombardini becomes president
April	Santa Anna returns from exile and is proclaimed dictator

1853–1855 Santa Anna's Dictatorship

1853

1 August	Law of Conspirators
16 December	State Council extends Santa Anna's term in office for another year; State Council also determines that he should carry the title of His Serene Highness
30 December	Santa Anna signs Treaty of La Mesilla (also known as Gadsden Purchase), selling La Mesilla (109,574 square kilometers) to the United States for 10 million pesos

1854

1 March	Revolution of Ayutla begins
March–May	Santa Anna leads government troops to Acapulco to quell the rebellion; after failing to breach Ignacio Comonfort's fortifications, he returns to the capital empty-handed
1 July	Santa Anna addresses letter to the powers of Europe offering the Mexican throne to a European prince; Gutiérrez Estrada is sent to Europe to bring about this plan

1855

2 February	Santa Anna is allowed to extend his dictato-

	rial rule for a while longer, having received 435,530 votes in favor
April–June	Santa Anna leads government troops against rebels in Michoacán but fails to defeat them
8 August	Santa Anna leaves capital and on the 16th goes into exile
1855–1864	Santa Anna in exile, first in Turbaco, Colombia, and subsequently in St. Thomas

1855–1876 Reform Period

1855
4 October	Juan Álvarez, president
23 November	Ley Juárez
Dec 1855–Jan 1858	Ignacio Comonfort, president

1856
25 June	Ley Lerdo

1857
5 February	Federal Constitution published
17 December	Coup d'état of Tacubaya

1858–1860	Civil War of the Reform

1858
11 January	Félix Zuloaga, president of rebel conservative government (Mexico City)
4 May	Juárez becomes president of "legitimate" government on the move (Veracruz)

1859
31 January	Miguel Miramón, conservative president

1860
25 December	Liberal forces recover Mexico City

1861

| March | Benito Juárez, president after winning elections |
| 17 July | Government suspends payment on foreign debt |

1862–1867   The French Intervention

1862

| 7 January | Allied fleets land in Veracruz (Britain, France, and Spain) |
| 5 May | Mexican army succeeds in defeating the French at the Battle of Puebla |

1863

19 May	French take Puebla
9 June	Juárez's government flees to San Luis Potosí
10 June	French take Mexico City
18 June	Regency Council is formed with Juan Nepomuceno Almonte, Bishop Pelagio Antonio de Labastida, and Mariano Salas
3 October	Maximilian accepts the throne at Miramar (Europe)

1864

January	Juárez's government flees to the north
27 February	Santa Anna returns to Veracruz expecting to participate in the Regency Council
12 March	Santa Anna is ordered to leave Mexico by the imperial government and returns to St. Thomas
10 April	Maximilian formally accepts Mexican crown
28 May	Maximilian and Carlota arrive in Veracruz
12 June	Maximilian and Carlota in Mexico City
12 October	Juárez's government flees to Chihuahua

1865

14 August	Juárez's government flees to Paso del Norte
5 September	Maximilian's Colonization Law

1866

January	Napoleon III orders phased withdrawal of French troops; Santa Anna meets William H. Seward in St. Thomas and deludes himself into believing the U.S. government will assist him in liberating Mexico
May	Tricked by con-men, Santa Anna arrives in New York, only to find that the U.S. government is not behind him; the Juarista Club in the United States refuses to see him and Juárez forbids him from joining the republicans
17 June	Juárez returns to Chihuahua City
26 June	Imperial decree reaffirms corporate ownership of land
14 August	Republicans recover Hermosillo
27 August	State of Guerrero under republican siege
September	Last stage of French withdrawal begins
October	Maximilian considers abdication in Orizaba
30 November	Maximilian decides to remain in Mexico
26 December	Juárez arrives in Durango

1867

14 January	Mexican junta sustains the empire by 1 vote
14 January	Republicans recover Guadalajara
25 January	Imperial forces abandon San Luis Potosí
5 February	French troops order evacuation of Mexico City
18 February	Republicans take Morelia
21 February	Juárez arrives in San Luis Potosí
12 March	Last French troops leave Veracruz
14 March	Republicans start siege of Querétaro

4 April	Porfirio Díaz takes Puebla
15 May	Querétaro is taken; Maximilian, Mejía, and Miramón are captured
3 June	Santa Anna reaches shores of Veracruz and plans liberation of port
7 June	Santa Anna is prevented from landing and restoring the republic there by U.S.S. *Tacony*; he is ordered to sail to Yucatán
19 June	Maximilian, Mejía, and Miramón are executed
21 June	Porfirio Díaz enters Mexico City
30 June	Santa Anna disembarks in Sisal (Yucatán)

1867–1876 The Restored Republic

1867

14 July	Santa Anna is arrested and taken to prison island of San Juan de Ulúa
15 July	Juárez arrives in Mexico City
October	Juárez, president after winning elections
7–10 October	Court-martial of Santa Anna takes place in main theater of Veracruz; he is punished with eight years' exile
1 November	Santa Anna goes into exile once more—spending the next six years (1867–74) in Havana, Puerto Plata, and Nassau
8 December	Juárez surrenders extraordinary powers to Congress

1868

| 8 May | Juárez obtains further extraordinary powers |

1870

| September | Gran Círculo de Obreros de México is formed |

1871

February	Anti-Juarista rebellions in Nuevo León, Zacatecas, and Durango
June	Anti-Juárez rebellion in Tampico is quelled
12 October	Juárez reelected president
8 November	Porfirio Díaz stages failed revolt of La Noria
21 November	Anti-Juárez revolt in Puebla begins

1872

29 February	Government troops retake Aguascalientes
2 March	Government troops retake Zacatecas
5 March	Government troops start siege of Puebla
17 May	Congress extends Juárez's extraordinary powers
9 July	Government troops retake Monterrey and end rebellion in Nuevo León
9 July	Juárez dies
18 July	Sebastián Lerdo de Tejada, president
Autumn	Lerdo offers general amnesty to rebels
	Senate is created and Congress ceases to be unicameral as stipulated in the 1857 Constitution
27 February	Santa Anna returns to Mexico at age eighty

1875

	Cristero revolt starts in Michoacán and Jalisco
	Law authorizes foreigners to purchase land

1876

21 June	Santa Anna dies
	Lerdo de Tejada reelected president; he is accused of electoral fraud; Porfirio Díaz launches the Revolution of Tuxtepec
23 November	Díaz takes Mexico City and becomes president

Notes

Abbreviations

AHAGEV   Archivo Histórico del Archivo General del Estado de
Veracruz

AHMV   Archivo Histórico Municipal de Veracruz

AHMX   Archivo Histórico Municipal de Xalapa

AHSDN   Archivo Histórico de la Secretaría de la Defensa de la
Nación, Mexico City

AMGCV   Archivo Misceláneo General de la Catedral de Veracruz

ANBUV   Archivo de Notarías de la Biblioteca de la Universidad
Veracruzana

BLAC   Nettie Lee Benson Latin American Collection, University
of Texas at Austin

PRO   Public Record Office, London

f., ff.   folio, folios

Proceso   *Proceso del ex general Antonio López de Santa Anna, acusándole de infidencia
a la patria*

Introduction

1. *Proceso del ex general Antonio López de Santa Anna, acusándole de infidencia a la patria* (Veracruz: Imprenta de David, 1867), reproduced by Secretaría de Guerra y Marina (Mexico City: Talleres Gráficos de la Nación, 1926), "Confesión con cargos del acusado,"140.

2. Villa-Amor, *Biografía del general Santa Anna*, 3.

3. The fact that a national hero such as Benito Juárez was prepared to grant the United States the rights to transit the planned Tehuantepec Canal from the Pacific to the Atlantic in perpetuity, as well as several other routes from Guaymas to Nogales and Camargo-Matamoros to Mazatlán, as was stipulated in the McLane-Ocampo Treaty (14 December 1859), is conveniently downplayed or ignored.

4. Serna, *El seductor de la patria*, 503.

5. This chronological interpretation of the evolution of Mexican political thought, which highlights how ideas changed as the hope of the 1820s degenerated into the despair of the 1840s, is one I have developed in several studies, including Fowler, *Mexico in the Age of Proposals, 1821–1853*. Also see Vázquez, *Don Antonio López de Santa Anna: Mito y enigma*, 13.

6. Mora, *Obras sueltas*, 48, 129, 139, 154, 158, 159 (emphasis in original).

7. Costeloe, *The Central Republic, 1835–1846*, 214.

8. Those who count each time he returned to the capital to serve as president come up with the figure of *eleven* times president: 1. 16 May–3 June 1833; 2. 18 June–5 July 1833; 3. 27 October–15 December 1833; 4. 24 April 1834–27 January 1835; 5. 20 March–10 July 1839; 6. 10 October 1841–26 October 1842; 7. 4 March–4 October 1843; 8. 4 June–12 September 1844; 9. 21 March–2 April 1847; 10. 20 May–16 September 1847; 11. 20 April 1853–12 August 1855. However, he did not serve eleven different presidential terms. Santa Anna was in reality president on six different occasions: 1833–36, 1839, 1841–43, 1843–44, 1846–47, and 1853–55, and this is making a distinction between his mandate under the Bases de Tacubaya (6 October 1841) and the Bases Orgánicas (8 June 1843), because otherwise we could actually state that he was president only five times.

9. Vázquez, *Don Antonio López de Santa Anna*, 12.

10. See Fowler and Ortiz Escamilla, "La revuelta del 2 de diciembre de 1822."

11. Zárate Toscano, "Héroes y fiestas en el México decimonónico: La insistencia de Santa Anna"; María del Carmen Vázquez Mantecón, *La palabra del poder: Vida pública de José María Tornel*, 75; for Tornel also see Fowler, *Tornel and Santa Anna, the Writer and the Caudillo*. For Santa Anna's critics, the fact that he only had one leg gave them the opportunity to find different (and cruel) ways of ridiculing him. The longest-lasting nickname that emerged from the many jibes Santa Anna's leg inspired was that of *Quince uñas* (Fifteen claws). Having lost five of his "claws" with the leg that was amputated, he became known to those who despised him as "*Quince uñas.*" Leopoldo Zamora Plowes's classic novel about Santa Anna is entitled *Quince uñas y Casanova aventureros*.

12. William Parish Robertson, *A Visit to Mexico* (London, 1853), 271. Reference passed on to me by Michael Costeloe, private communication, 5 July 2002.

13. Percy Doyle to Lord John Russell, Mexico City, 4 March 1853, Foreign Office Papers FO50/259, folios 48–51, Public Record Office, London (hereafter cited as PRO).

14. Archer, "The Young Antonio López de Santa Anna," 4.

15. Calderón de la Barca, *Life in Mexico*, 32.

16. Calderón de la Barca, *Life in Mexico*, 443–44, 345.

17. See Costeloe, *The Central Republic*, 186–87.

18. Santa Anna's biographers include the following, in alphabetical order: Juan Gualberto Amaya, W. H. Callcott, Fernando Díaz Díaz, Carmen Flores Mena, José Fuentes Mares, Enrique González Pedrero, Frank C. Hanighen, Oakah L. Jones, Jr., Rafael F. Muñoz, Leonardo Pasquel, Manuel Rivera Cambas, Robert L. Scheina, Alfonso Trueba, Josefina Zoraida Vázquez, and Agustín Yáñez. Other monographs on specific

periods or aspects of Santa Anna's career include those written by Richard A. Johnson, Carlos R. Menéndez, José C. Valadés, Jorge Veraza Urtuzuástegui, and Carmen Vázquez Mantecón. See the bibliography for full references. Likewise see the bibliography for the complete references of the works by those historians who have contributed to this reevaluation and revision of the "forgotten decades."

19. Lucas Alamán to Santa Anna, Mexico City, 17 March 1853, reprinted in Lira (ed.), *Lucas Alamán*, 354.

20. Lynch, *Caudillos in Spanish America*, 335.

21. Full references for my work on the period are in the bibliography.

1. Between the Volcano and the Sea

1. Xalapa and Jalapa are both acceptable ways of spelling the city's name. For reasons of consistency and in line with the spelling favored by xalapeños today, I have chosen Xalapa.

2. Antonio López de Santa Anna, "Protesta," Nassau, 23 November 1870, in Genaro García (ed.), *Documentos inéditos o muy raros para la historia de México*, Vol. 59: *Antonio López de Santa Anna*, 78.

3. Verdict, in *Proceso del ex general Antonio López de Santa Anna, acusándole de infidencia a la patria*, 170.

4. Archivo Eclesiástico de la Parroquia del Sagrario, Iglesia del Sagrado Corazón, Xalapa (Veracruz), Caja [Bautizos] no. 7, vol. 21 (1792–1818), folio 9. Folios are hereafter abbreviated as f., ff.

5. Quoted in Gregory, *Brute New World*, 136.

6. Humboldt, *Essai politique sur le Royaume de la Nouvelle-Espagne*, 1:40.

7. Thompson, *Recollections of Mexico*, 13.

8. Humboldt, *Essai politique*, 2:771; and 1:40.

9. See Siemens, *Between the Summit and the Sea*, 176–87, for an analysis of a number of key nineteenth-century travelers' descriptions of Xalapa.

10. Calderón de la Barca, *Life in Mexico*, 38.

11. Siemens, *Between the Summit and the Sea*, 176–77; Humboldt, *Essai politique*, 1:281, 2:685–88; Carrera Stampa, "Las ferias novohispanas"; Real Díaz, *Las ferias de Jalapa*; and Rivera Cambas, *Historia antigua y moderna de Jalapa y de las revoluciones del Estado de Veracruz*, 1:140–47.

12. "Registro de protocolos de instrumentos públicos, otorgados ante el escribano nacional don José Ignacio Jiménez Pérez en 1824 [Xalapa], 20 September 1824, f. 46, Archivo de Notarías de la Biblioteca de la Universidad Veracruzana (hereafter cited as ANBUV); Minutes of the Town Council Meeting of 11 November 1822, "Libro de acuerdos del ilustre ayuntamiento de esta villa de Jalapa perteneciente al año de 1822," vol. 33, ff. 83–85, in Archivo Histórico Municipal de Xalapa (hereafter cited as AHMX, with volume and folio numbers); "Protocolo otorgado en el año de 1841 [Xalapa]," Power of attorney, 24 March 1841, ff. 77–78; and Fowler, "Las propiedades veracruzanas de Santa Anna," 66. Although the deeds for Manuel López de Santa Anna's property have

not been found, we know that he lived in Xalapa, where he became the military commander of the town (Town Council of Xalapa to Military Commander Manuel López de Santa Anna, 7 May 1824, AHMX, "Libro de acuerdos del ilustre ayuntamiento constitucional de la villa de Jalapa para el año de 1824," vol. 35, f. 409).

13. Minutes of the Town Council of Xalapa, 24 August 1846, AHMX, "Libro de acuerdos del muy ilustre ayuntamiento de la ciudad de Jalapa, del año de 1846," vol. 58, ff. 137–41. The defense archives contain four letters by Santa Anna, dated in Xalapa, 18 January 1845, asking Velasco, Muñoz, and Viya y Cosío to place his savings (the figure of $28,000 is mentioned) with Manning, MacKintosh and Company; see Exp. XI/III/1-116 [1-15], vol. IV, ff. 986–89, Archivo Histórico de la Secretaría de la Defensa de la Nación, Mexico City (hereafter cited as AHSDN). Also see Fowler, "Fiestas santanistas," 430–31; Callcott, Santa Anna, 216; and Fowler, "Las propiedades veracruzanas de Santa Anna," 64–65. For the financial backing Santa Anna received from members of the Xalapan elite see Minutes of the Meetings of the Town Council of Xalapa, 15 September and 3 October 1828, AHMX, "Libro de acuerdos del ilustre ayuntamiento constitucional de la villa de Jalapa para el año del señor de 1828," vol. 39, ff. 109, 113–16; and Costeloe, "The Triangular Revolt in Mexico"; for the relationship Santa Anna forged with the Xalapan industrialists responsible for the textile boom of the 1830s–40s see Chávez Orozco and Florescano, Agricultura e industria textil de Veracruz; León Fuentes, "Los antagonismos empresariales de Xalapa"; and Fowler, "Joseph Welsh: A British Santanista," 53–54.

14. Valadés, México, Santa Anna y la guerra de Texas, 31, 35; and González Pedrero, País de un solo hombre, 1:14. The quote is taken from a letter: Santa Anna to the town council of Veracruz, 12 August 1821. He repeated this assertion in his letters to the town council of Veracruz of 12 and 20 October 1821. Quoted in Trens, "Santa Anna, realista," 3. Also see Arroyo Cabrera, "¿Don Antonio López de Santa Anna."

15. Latrobe, The Rambler in Mexico, 300–1.

16. For the strategic and regional importance of yellow fever see chapters 2 and 3 ("Strategic Veracruz" and "The Port Versus the Viceroys") in Archer, The Army in Bourbon Mexico, 1760–1810, 38–79; also see chapter 4 ("Guardian Dragon") in Siemens, Between the Summit and the Sea, 82–94. As well, see Earle, "'A Grave for Europeans'?" 371.

17. Calderón de la Barca, Life in Mexico, 25.

18. Siemens, Between the Summit and the Sea, 77; according to Archer, between 1810 and 1818 the population in the port declined by 40 percent, from 15,000 in 1810 to 12,075 in 1812 and 8,934 in 1818 ("The Young Antonio López de Santa Anna," 6). Also see Chávez Orozco and Florescano, "La herencia colonial," 48–50.

19. For the Afro-Mexican population see Aguirre Beltrán, La población negra de México.

20. Calderón de la Barca, Life in Mexico, 24–25.

21. See Siemens's chapter on "The Macabre Port," Between the Summit and the Sea, 57–81; Chávez Orozco and Florescano, "La herencia colonial," 48–50.

22. Calderón de la Barca, Life in Mexico, 24, 26–27, 29.

23. Santa Anna to José García Dávila, outskirts of Veracruz, 30 June 1821, edited and

printed by José María Tornel in pamphlet *Sentimientos y heroismo del general de la provincia de Veracruz*, 2.

24. Vázquez, "Political Plans and Collaboration between Civilians and the Military," 23.

25. David A. Cole, "The Early Career of Antonio López de Santa Anna," Ph.D. diss., Christ Church, University of Oxford, 1977, 11. See "Diversos," año 1790, libro núm. 22, f. 168–83, in Archivo Histórico Municipal de Veracruz (hereafter cited as AHMV); Archivo Eclesiástico de la Parroquia del Sagrario, Iglesia del Sagrado Corazón, Xalapa (Veracruz), Caja [Bautizos] no. 7, vol. 21 (1792–1818), f. 9. For details on Santa Anna's father see "Acta de matrimonio" between Antonio López Santa Anna, pére, at the age of fifty-seven, with a twenty-three-year-old Dolores Zanso y Pintado, in *Matrimonios* 42 664, 3 June 1818, Archivo Misceláneo General de la Catedral de Veracruz (hereafter cited as as AMGCV). For speculative accounts of Santa Anna's origins see Valadés, *México, Santa Anna y la guerra de Texas*, 29–31; Callcott, *Santa Anna*, 4; Rivera Cambas, *Antonio López de Santa Anna*, 6; Jones, *Santa Anna*, 21.

26. Cole, "The Early Career," 11, makes reference to a Mateo López de Santa Anna found in Veracruz in 1744 ("Civil," vol. 65, exp. 8, Archivo General de la Nación, Mexico City, hereafter cited as AGN). He also located a probable relative, Juan Antonio López de Santa Anna, who owned a cigar store in Mexico City in 1772 ("The Early Career," 12 [AGN, "Tabacos," vol. 23]).

27. Callcott, *Santa Anna*, 4.

28. Acal does not figure as a Spanish surname in the *Base de datos de apellidos hispanos* (www.Idelpino.com/listasur.html) and is reminiscent of indigenous names from Chiapas, Yucatán and Central America (e.g., Acteal, Chahal, Chetumal, Corozal).

29. Cole, "The Early Career," 11–14, 31; Callcott, *Santa Anna*, 4; Valadés, *México, Santa Anna y la guerra de Texas*, 29–31; González Pedrero, *País de un solo hombre*, 1:13–14, 53; "Informaciones matrimoniales" Exp. 42 689, 22 May 1818, and "Matrimonios" Exp. 42 664, 3 June 1818, AMGCV.

30. For details of his career as *escribano*, see AHMV, Caja "Diversos," 1776/1802, vol. 103; for the correspondence that was generated by Don Ángel's protest in 1807, see "Expediente formado a Santa Anna. Veracruz, 1807,"AHMV, Caja 161, vol. 215, ff. 210–97 (and not ff. 253–97, as specified in the Archive's *Inventario*); also see Cole, "The Early Career," 13, and González Pedrero, *País de un solo hombre*, 1:14.

31. Valadés, *México, Santa Anna y la guerra de Texas*, 30.

32. See AGN, "Inquisición," exp. 14, ff. 168–94: (1797) "Relación de la causa que en este Santo Oficio pende a instancia del señor inquisidor fiscal contra don José López de Santa Anna, español de calidad, natural de la ciudad de Veracruz, de edad de 40 años cumplidos, presbítero, confesor y predicador, cura interino que ha sido en Medellín, y la Antigua Veracruz, preso en cárceles secretas por el delito de torpe solicitante, y cuya causa se halla en estado de definitiva." I thank Gabriel Torres for kindly forwarding me his transcript of the document.

33. Serna, *El seductor de la patria*, 29; "Denuncia hecha con motivo de suponerse en

ella que en casa de Da. Josefa Ximénez se profanó en un baile el Sto. Nombre de Dios (Xalapa, 1809)," AGN, "Inquisición," vol. 1414, exp. 3, ff. 328–37; González Pedrero, *País de un solo hombre*, 1:14; Valadés, *México, Santa Anna y la guerra de Texas*, 35; Yáñez, *Santa Anna*, 49–50.

34. See Archivo Eclesiástico de la Parroquia del Sagrario, Iglesia del Sagrado Corazón, Xalapa (Veracruz), Caja [Bautizos] no. 7, vol. 21 (1792–1818), 24 November 1799; ANBUV, "Protocolo otorgado en el año de 1841 [Xalapa]," Power of attorney, 24 March 1841, ff. 77–78; "Bautismos" Exp. 42 640, 3 October 1791, and "Matrimonios" Exp. 42 664," 6 March 1808, AMGCV; ANBUV, "Registro de instrumentos de este oficio público de la villa de Xalapa, para el año de 1820," Powers of attorney, 31 January 1820, ff. 23–26, and Powers of attorney, 15 September 1820, ff. 177–78; and copy of letter, Francisca López de Santa Anna to Town Council of Xalapa, Xalapa, 8 August 1820, AHMX, "Libro de acuerdos y demás documentos del año 1820," vol. 29, ff. 246–47. For her legal wrangles with her third husband, see AGN, "Ramo Civil," galería 4, Legajos: 154 1B (3 9), 1837, "Da. Francisca López de Santa Anna contra su esposo Sr. Coronel D. Ricardo Dromundo," and also 118 (38 17), 1839 EG; 118 (59), 1837; and 188 (38) 17, 1839. See also ANBUV, "Registro de instrumentos de este oficio público de la villa de Xalapa, para el año de 1820," Powers of attorney, 15 September 1820, ff. 177–78; Pablo Villavicencio y Varios Amigos de la Verdad, *Ya no muere fucilada*; AGN, "Indiferente de guerra," vol. 6, f. 5.; and Cole, "The Early Career," 31.

35. Lerdo de Tejada, *Apuntes históricos de la heróica ciudad de Veracruz*, 1:413; Arnold, *Burocracia y burócratas en México*, 161–65.

36. Villoro, *El proceso ideológico de la revolución*, 26–29.

37. Cole, "The Early Career," 13–14.

38. Fowler, *Latin America 1800–2000*, 40–41.

39. Tornel, *Respuesta del general José María Tornel y Mendívil*, 10. Also see Fowler, *Tornel and Santa Anna*, 173.

40. See Costeloe, "Mariano Arista y la élite de la ciudad de México, 1851–1852."

41. Rivera Cambas, *Historia antigua y moderna*, 2:103.

42. Rivera Cambas, *Historia antigua y moderna*, 2:103. Also see Callcott, *Santa Anna*, 4; and Jones, *Santa Anna*, 22.

43. Santa Anna, *Mi historia militar y política 1810–1874: Memorias inéditas* in García (ed.), *Documentos inéditos*, 59:5.

2. An Officer and a Gentleman

1. And not 9 June 1810, as Santa Anna himself recorded in his unreliable memoirs, *Mi historia militar y política*, 5. See AHSDN, Exp. XI/III/I-116 [1-15] vol. I, "Hoja de servicios [de Santa Anna]" December 1858 [signed by José María de la Cadena, Mexico City, 15 June 1859], ff. 17–19. Also Rivera Cambas, *Antonio López de Santa Anna*, 7; Callcott, *Santa Anna*, 5.

2. Blázquez Domínguez, *Veracruz: Una historia compartida*, 29.

3. Alamán, Historia de México, 1:379.

4. Torre, La independencia de México, 99.

5. Guardino, Peasants, Politics, and the Formation of Mexico's National State, 75; Blázquez Domínguez, Veracruz: Una historia compartida, 45.

6. See Suárez, Las Cortes de Cádiz; and Rodríguez O., The Independence of Spanish America, 75–106, 192–210.

7. As can be verified in his "Hoja de servicios" he went from being a cadet to a lieutenant colonel in the following steps: lieutenant (grado de teniente por el gobierno español), 6 February 1812; sublieutenant (subteniente por el gobierno español), 8 October 1812; royal lieutenant (grado de teniente por despacho real), 7 July 1815; graduate captain (capitán graduado por el gobierno español), 29 December 1816; lieutenant of grenadiers (teniente de granaderos por el gobierno español), 17 January 1820; and lieutenant colonel (grado de teniente coronel por el gobierno español), 7 April 1821. See AHSDN, Exp. XI/III/I-116 [1-15] vol. I, "Hoja de servicios [de Santa Anna]" December 1858 [signed by José María de la Cadena, Mexico City, 15 June 1859], ff. 17–19.

8. AHSDN, Exp. XI/III/I-116 [1-15] vol. I, "Hoja de servicios [de Santa Anna]" December 1812, f. 6.

9. See Archer, "Politicization of the Army of New Spain during the War of Independence, 1810–1821"; Cole, "The Early Career," 27.

10. Bustamante, Cuadro histórico de la revolución mexicana, 1:341; Jones, Santa Anna, 22.

11. Dispatch by Joaquín de Arredondo, Palmillas, 16 May 1811, quoted in Trens, "Santa Anna, realista," 6.

12. Quoted in Callcott, Santa Anna, 7–8; and Cole, "The Early Career," 28.

13. José Daicemberger to Cayetano Quintero, copied in Captain Cayetano Quintero's report to Colonel Arredondo, Hacienda de Amoladeras, 30 August 1811. The dispatch is reprinted in full in Trens, "Santa Anna, realista," 7–9. Also see Cole, "The Early Career," 28–29.

14. Callcott, Santa Anna, 8.

15. Cole, "The Early Career," 29, notes that in 1812, his promotion to sublieutenant listed him having fought in eight actions, receiving a light wound in one of them. Also see Callcott, Santa Anna, 9.

16. For an account of the Gutiérrez-Magee filibustering raid, see Warren, The Sword Was Their Passport, 1–95.

17. AHSDN, Exp. XI/III/I-116 [1-15] vol. I, "Hoja de servicios [de Santa Anna]" December 1817, f. 2. This action did not occur near the little town now called Medina (about 48 kilometers northwest of San Antonio) but about 28 kilometers south of San Antonio.

18. In contrast to Arredondo's policy of extermination, Colonel Ignacio Elizondo, charged with pursuing Toledo and those men who escaped with him, allowed the fifty filibusters he captured to go free (Warren, The Sword Was Their Passport, 69). Also see Garrett, Green Flag over Texas, 97–103; and Groneman, Battlefields of Texas, 10–13.

19. Mier y Terán, Texas by Terán, 45, 50, 66.

20. "Documento precioso para la biografía del general Santa Anna," Latin American Manuscripts, Num. 1685 [G 387], Nettie Lee Benson Latin American Collection, University of Texas at Austin (hereafter cited as BLAC); also see Callcott, Santa Anna, 12, 17; González Pedrero, País de un solo hombre, 1:37.

21. Archer, "The Young Antonio López de Santa Anna," 7.

22. González Pedrero, País de un solo hombre, 1:45; Cole, "The Early Career," 31–32.

23. Santa Anna to José García Dávila, outskirts of Veracruz, 30 June 1821, in the pamphlet Tornel produced, Sentimientos y heroismo del general de la provincia de Veracruz, 2 ("Yo siempre me he considerado como un hijo suyo"); and Santa Anna, Mi historia militar y política, 6 ("me quería como a un hijo").

24. Muñoz, Santa Anna, 23; Will Fowler, "Los placeres y pesares de Antonio López de Santa Anna (1794–1876)," in Gonzalbo Aizpuru and Zárate Toscano (eds.), Gozos y sufrimientos en la historia de México; Prieto, Memorias de mis tiempos, 39. Prieto tells us that the book in question was Casandra. Unfortunately he does not specify which Casandra this was. Therefore we cannot know whether the mention was intended to be ironic or whether it was simply accurate.

25. Archer, "The Young Antonio López de Santa Anna," 6–7, 9; Gaceta del Gobierno de México, 8 September 1816; José Dávila to Juan Ruiz de Apodaca, Veracruz, 9 September 1816, AGN, "Operaciones de guerra," vol. 260, ff. 208–9. Quote taken from Dávila to Apodaca, Veracruz, 26 September 1816, AGN, "Operaciones de guerra," vol. 256, f. 209:

26. For Santa Anna's actions against the rebels in the region during the month of October 1816, see Gaceta del Gobierno de México, 31 December 1816 and 2 January 1817. Also see Santa Anna to José Dávila, Boca del Río, 31 October 1816, BLAC, W. B. Stephens Collection, WBS-2870; Callcott, Santa Anna, 14; González Pedrero, País de un solo hombre, 1:49; and AHSDN, Exp. XI/III/I-116 [1-15] vol. I, "Hoja de servicios [de Santa Anna]" December 1817, f. 2, as well as "Hoja de servicios [de Santa Anna]" December 1858, ff. 17–19.

27. González Pedrero, País de un solo hombre, 1:52; Archer, "The Young Antonio López de Santa Anna," 11.

28. Santa Anna to Apodaca, 22 January, 6 March, and 13 June 1818; Santa Anna to Cincúnegui, 11 June 1818, all in AGN, "Operaciones de guerra," vol. 792, ff. 316–24.

29. Santa Anna to Cincúnegui, 11 June 1818; Cincúnegui to Santa Anna, 12 June 1818; Santa Anna to Llano, 13 June and 1 August 1818; Viceroy Apodaca to Santa Anna, 9 July and 2 September 1818, AGN, "Operaciones de guerra," vol. 792, ff. 317–32.

30. Santa Anna to Viceroy Apodaca, 1 August 1818, and Gaceta del Gobierno de México, 9 September 1818, AGN: "Operaciones de guerra," vol. 792, f. 330; Bustamante, Cuadro histórico de la revolución mexicana, 5:39; Archer, "The Young Antonio López de Santa Anna," 11; Callcott, Santa Anna, 14–15; González Pedrero, País de un solo hombre, 1:54.

31. Santa Anna to Apodaca, Extramuros, 4 December 1818, AGN, "Operaciones de Guerra," vol. 490, ff. 18–19, reprinted in Trens, "Santa Anna, realista," 12–14.

32. Pascual de Liñán to Conde de Venadito, Veracruz, 3 March 1819, AGN, "Operaciones de Guerra," vol. 490, f. 16.

33. Santa Anna to Field Marshall Pascual de Liñán, Campamento de Santa María, 13 and 16 January 1819, AGN, "Operaciones de Guerra," Vol. 495, ff. 84–85 and 32–34, reprinted in Trens, "Santa Anna, realista," 15–18.

34. Santa Anna to Field Marshall Pascual de Liñán, Medellín, 28 January and 3 February 1819, and San Diego, 23 February 1819, AGN, "Operaciones de Guerra," vol. 495, ff. 151–54, 165–70, reprinted in Trens, "Santa Anna, realista," 18–23.

35. Archer, "The Young Antonio López de Santa Anna," 10.

36. The three reports Santa Anna sent to Governor José García Dávila, detailing the success with which the insurgents of the area handed themselves in to him and went on to settle in the villages of Medellín, Jamapa, Soledad, Tamarindo, and San Diego, were published in the *Gaceta del Gobierno de México*, 28 June, 5 and 17 July 1820. Also see José Dávila to Viceroy Apodaca, Veracruz, 12 July 1820, copying Santa Anna's report of 4 July 1820, reprinted in full in Trens, "Santa Anna, realista," 24–28.

37. José Rivera in Xamapa, Manuel López de Santa Anna in San Diego, Rafael Villagómez in Medellín, and Miguel Rodríguez in Tamarindo.

38. Archer, "The Young Antonio López de Santa Anna," 14.

39. José García Dávila to Viceroy Apodaca, Veracruz, 12 July 1820, copying Santa Anna's report of 4 July 1820, reprinted in full in Trens, "Santa Anna, realista," 27.

40. A. Benavides et al. to Dávila, 5 January 1820, quoted in Cole, "The Early Career," 49; and in González Pedrero, *País de un solo hombre*, 1:58.

41. AHMV, Caja 117, vol. 157, ff. 69–72, contains letters dating from 1820 written by the town council of Veracruz complaining about Santa Anna's actions. Unfortunately, the condition of the documents is so bad that they are mostly illegible. See Manuel de Viya y Cosío to Town Council of Veracruz, Veracruz, 5 September 1820, and Viya y Cosío to Dávila, Veracruz, 9 September 1820, AHMV, Caja 130, vol. 174, ff. 58–60; and Minutes of Town Council of Veracruz, 9, 19 August, 6 and 13 September 1820, Caja 130, vol. 173, ff. 95–96, 103–4, 114–16, 118.

42. Muñoz, *Santa Anna*, 21.

43. Santa Anna, *Mi historia militar y política*, 12, 18.

44. Quoted in Archer, "The Young Antonio López de Santa Anna," 15.

45. Churchill, *My Early Life*, 82.

46. Santa Anna, *Mi historia militar y política*, 5.

47. Santa Anna, *Mi historia militar y política*, 5.

48. Prieto, *Memorias de mis tiempos*, 39.

49. Callcott, *Santa Anna*, 19.

50. Santa Anna, *Mi historia militar y política*, 6.

3. Liberator of Veracruz, Founder of the Republic

1. I would like to thank Juan Ortiz Escamilla for the ideas and documents he shared with me when we worked together to write "La revuelta del 2 de diciembre de 1822." See Iturbide to Guerrero, 10 January 1821, and Guerrero to Iturbide, 20 January 1821, in *Cartas de los señores generales D. Agustín de Iturbide y D. Vicente Guerrero*, 1–6.

2. Valadés, *México, Santa Anna y la guerra de Texas*, 41–42. The Plan of Iguala is reprinted in Torre, *La independencia de México*, 275–78.

3. *El Fénix de la Libertad*, 21 February 1833; Fowler, *Tornel and Santa Anna*, 18–24; ANBUV, "Registro de instrumentos de este oficio público de la villa de Xalapa, para el año de 1822," Powers of attorney, Xalapa, 28 March 1822.

4. José María Tornel y Mendívil, *Fastos militares de iniquidad*, 72–74; quote is taken from Santa Anna, *Mi historia militar y política*, 6.

5. Vázquez, "Iglesia, ejército y centralismo," 211. In a report by General Francisco Miranda, Ometepec, 13 September 1826, AHSDN: Exp. XI/III/I-93, he notes that the proclamation he read out on 18 March 1821 in favor of independence, on the outskirts of Tehuacán, was written by Tornel (as were all the others proclaimed in Veracruz and Puebla at the time); quote taken from Santa Anna to C. M. de Bustamante, 23 September 1827, BLAC, Hernández y Dávalos Papers, quoted in Cole, "The Early Career," 66.

6. González Pedrero, *País de un solo hombre*, 1:66–67.

7. AHSDN, Exp. III/1-33, "Hoja de servicio de José Joaquín de Herrera"; Alamán, *Historia de Méjico*, 5:176–77; Town Council of Orizaba to Viceroy, Orizaba, 7 March 1821, AGN: Gobernación, Legajo 1586, Exp. 1; José García Dávila to Conde de Venadito, 26 April 1821, AGN: "Operaciones de guerra," vol. 244, f. 260; quote taken from AHSDN, Exp. XI/481.3/174, ff. 9–10, Santa Anna to Iturbide, Alvarado, 25 April 1821; and see AHSDN, Exp. XI/481.3/174, ff. 55–60, Santa Anna to Iturbide, Xalapa, 23 June 1821.

8. Guadalupe Victoria, Campo de Santa Fe sobre Veracruz, 20 April 1821; reprinted in Bustamante, *Cuadro histórico*, 5:184–85.

9. Briseño Senosiain, Solares Robles, and Suárez de la Torre, *Guadalupe Victoria*, 38–41; Bustamante, *Cuadro histórico*, 5:184.

10. Callcott, *Santa Anna*, 22; Jones, *Santa Anna*, 29; Cole, "The Early Career," 72; Flaccus, "Guadalupe Victoria, Mexican Revolutionary Patriot," 150; AHSDN, Exp. XI/481.3/174: f. 32, José Joaquín de Herrera to Santa Anna, Córdoba, 25 May 1821; f. 33, Santa Anna to Herrera, Jalapa, 28 May 1821; f. 15, Santa Anna to Iturbide, Jalapa, 1 June 1821.

11. Minutes of Town Council meetings, all in AHMX, "Libro de acuerdos del ilustre ayuntamiento constitucional de la villa de Xalapa, para el año de 1821," vol. 32: 20 March 1821, ff. 35–36; 28 May 1821, ff. 57–58; 29 May 1821, ff. 58–59; and 30 May 1821, ff. 59–60. See also AHSDN, Exp. XI/481.3/109, f. 200, "Capitulación celebrada entre Juan de Obergoso y Antonio López de Santa Anna," Xalapa, 29 May 1821.

12. Minutes of Town Council Meetings of 1 and 2 June 1821, AHMX, 1821 "Libro de acuerdos," vol. 32, ff. 60–62. Also see minutes for 6 June 1821, ff. 62–63, and 8 June 1821, f. 65. For the record, the affluent xalapeños who carried the brunt of the loan were Juan Francisco de Abarroa, Francisco Lía, Juan Francisco Bárcena, Juan Lascuráin, Bernabé Elías, Rafael Pérez, Sebastián Aguirre, Antonio Medina, and Manuel Allen. Santa Anna never returned the 12,000-peso loan.

13. Minutes of Town Council Meeting of 6 June 1821, AHMX, 1821 "Libro de acuerdos," vol. 32, ff. 62–63. Santa Anna placed Joaquín Leño, a member of one of Xalapa's most distinguished families, at the head of the Xalapa garrison. He replaced Francisco

Montero as commander of the Dragoons Corps with Lieutenant José Velázquez. He made Juan Crisóstomo Gutiérrez responsible for the General Administration of the Province of Veracruz. In Córdoba he replaced Manuel Royo with Juan Bustamante de Echeagaray as Head of Customs. AHSDN, Exp. XI/481.3/174, f. 25, "Circular de Antonio López de Santa Anna," Xalapa, 1 June 1821; ff. 16 and 18, "Certificado de la averiguación realizada por Ignacio Menocal y Luis Fernández del Campo," Xalapa, 1 June 1821; f. 29, Santa Anna to Iturbide, Xalapa, 6 June 1821; f. 46, Santa Anna to Iturbide, Xalapa, 20 June 1821; f. 139, Santa Anna to Iturbide, Córdoba, 3 September 1821.

14. Following Santa Anna's departure, Diego Leño went on to ask separately for further funds to pay for his garrison's expenses. Minutes of Town Council Meetings of 13, 20, 23, 24, 27 July 1821, AHMX, 1821 "Libro de acuerdos," vol. 32, ff. 79–85; AHSDN, Exp. XI/481.3/174, f. 46, Santa Anna to Iturbide, Xalapa, 18 June 1821; Jones, Santa Anna, 31; Santa Anna to his soldiers, Campo del Encero, 24 June 1821, printed in Sentimientos y heroismo del general de la provincia de Veracruz, 3–4; Minutes of Town Council Meeting of 25 June 1821, AHMX, 1821 "Libro de acuerdos," vol. 32, ff. 68–69.

15. Santa Anna to the "Europeos habitantes de Veracruz, y personas que resistan la Independencia de la América Mejicana," Campo sobre Veracruz, 28 June 1821, and Santa Anna to the "Soldados de Marina y tripulaciones que guarnecen los baluartes de Veracruz," Campo imperial sobre Veracruz, 28 June 1821, both printed in Sentimientos y heroismo del general de la provincia de Veracruz, 4–7.

16. [José María Tornel], Introduction to Sentimientos y heroismo del general de la provincia de Veracruz, 1; Santa Anna to Field Marshall José García Dávila, Cuartel Imperial sobre Veracruz, 30 June 1821, Sentimientos, 2.

17. Gaceta del Gobierno de México, 24 July 1821.

18. [Tornel], Introduction to Sentimientos, 1; Jones, Santa Anna, 29; José García Dávila to Viceroy Apodaca, Veracruz, 8 July 1821, reprinted in Gaceta del Gobierno de México, 24 July 1821.

19. According to Callcott, Santa Anna then went to Puebla (Callcott, Santa Anna, 27). Santa Anna says as much in his 1823 pamphlet Manifiesto de Antonio López de Santa Anna, 5. Nevertheless, it is difficult to see how he could have traveled there and back since he was in Orizaba on 19 July; see Minutes of Town Council Meeting of 28 July 1821, AHMX, 1821 "Libro de acuerdos," vol. 32, ff. 35–36. See Alessio Robles (ed.), Archivo Histórico Militar Mexicano: La correspondencia de Agustín de Iturbide después de la Proclamación del Plan de Iguala, 2:148, 150–51; Minutes of Town Council Meetings of 13 and 15 August 1821, AHMX, 1821 "Libro de acuerdos," vol. 32, ff. 90–93, and see Santa Anna to Town Council of Xalapa, Perote, 12 August 1821, f. 243.

20. Treaties of Córdoba are reprinted in Torre, La independencia de México, 278–81; quote taken from Santa Anna, Mi historia militar y política, 7–8; Minutes of Town Council Meeting of 30 August 1821, AHMX, 1821 "Libro de acuerdos" vol. 32, ff. 99–100.

21. Minutes of Town Council Meeting of 10 September 1821, AHMX, 1821 "Libro de acuerdos," vol. 32, ff. 107–9; for letters from Santa Anna to Town Council of Xalapa, Cuartel general del Molino sobre Perote, 9, 10 and 15 September 1821, see ff. 253–59.

22. Minutes of Town Council Meeting of 28 September 1821, AHMX, 1821 "Libro de acuerdos," vol. 32, ff. 118–20.

23. Minutes of Town Council A.M. Meeting of 29 September 1821, f. 120, and second 29 September 1821 meeting, ff. 121–22.

24. Minutes of Town Council Meetings of 1 October 1821, ff. 122–23; 28 September 1821, ff. 118–20; and 20 December 1821, ff. 146–47.

25. Santa Anna to Town Council of Xalapa, Xalapa, 2 October 1821, AHMX, 1821 "Libro de acuerdos," vol. 32, ff. 269–70; Antonio López de Santa Anna, *Manifiesto que hace público el teniente coronel D. A. López de Santa Anna* (1821).

26. Santa Anna "Circular," Cuartel general del Molino sobre Perote, 9 September 1821, AHMX, 1821 "Libro de acuerdos," vol. 32, f. 253.

27. [Santa Anna], *Proclama del impávido teniente coronel D. Antonio López de Santana*, issued in the Fortress of San Carlos de Perote, 9 October 1821; copied and printed in Puebla by Tornel.

28. Minutes of Town Council Meeting of 16 October 1821, AHMV, Caja 136, vol. 181, ff. 234–35.

29. Minutes of Town Council Meeting of 21 October 1821, AHMV, Caja 136, vol. 181, ff. 238–40; Town Council of Veracruz to Iturbide, 27 October 1821, quoted in *Gaceta Imperial: Extraordinaria de México*, 2 November 1821, Condumex. And see AHSDN, Exp. 206: ff. 29–30, Manuel Rincón to Iturbide, Veracruz, 27 October 1821; f. 38, Iturbide to Manuel Rincón, Mexico City, 2 November 1821. See also Manuel Rincón to Iturbide, Veracruz, 14 November 1821, BLAC, Hernández y Dávalos Papers, 14-3.1463; Minutes of Town Council Meeting of 25 October 1821, AHMV, Caja 136, vol. 181, ff. 240–43.

30. AHSDN, Exp. 1372, ff. 1–5, Santa Anna to Iturbide, Xalapa, 18 June 1821; Exp. 206, ff. 29–30, Manuel Rincón to Iturbide, Veracruz, 27 October 1821; f. 38, Iturbide to Manuel Rincón, Mexico City, 2 November 1821. And see Minutes of Town Council Meeting of 27 October 1821, AHMV, Caja 136, vol. 181, ff. 243–45; Santa Anna to Town Council of Xalapa, Veracruz, 27 October 1821, AHMX 1821 "Libro de acuerdos," vol. 32, ff. 279–80: Santa Anna, *Proclama del sr. coronel D. Antonio López de Santa-Ana á los habitantes de Veracruz en la ocupación de aquella plaza* (1821).

31. Minutes of Town Council Meetings of 21 and 25 October 1821, AHMV, Caja 136, vol. 181, ff. 238–43.

32. Tornel, *Valor y constancia es nuestra divisa*, 1; *Sentimientos*, 1; Santa Anna, *Proclama . . . en la ocupación de aquella plaza*, 1 (issued in Campo de extramuros de Veracruz, 27 October 1821, and copied and introduced in Mexico City by Josef [sic] María Tornel); José María Tornel y Mendívil, *La aurora de México*, 1–2.

33. Manuel Rincón to Generalísimo de las Armas Imperiales [Iturbide], Veracruz, 14 November 1821, BLAC, Hernández y Dávalos Papers, 14-3.1463.

34. Minutes of Town Council Meetings of 13 and 20 November 1821, AHMX, 1821 "Libro de acuerdos," vol. 32, ff. 132–33, 135–36; Callcott, *Santa Anna*, 32, 37.

35. Minutes of Town Council Meetings of 12 and 20 March 1822, AHMX, "Libro de acuerdos del ilustre ayuntamiento de esta Villa de Jalapa, perteneciente al año de 1822,"

vol. 33, ff. 18–21; Copy of letter by Town Council of Xalapa to Captain General of the Province, Domingo Luaces, Xalapa, 20 March 1822, f. 152; and Minutes of Town Council Meeting of 10 May 1822, ff. 24–27.

36. Minutes of Town Council Meeting of 22 October 1822, AHMX, 1822 "Libro de acuerdos," vol. 33, ff. 77–79; and see correspondence in AHMV, Caja 139, vol. 184: José Govantes to Town Council of Veracruz, Veracruz, 29 and 30 September 1822, ff. 169, 171; Town Council of Veracruz to Govantes/Santa Anna, Veracruz, 30 September (two) and 10 October 1822, ff. 170, 174, 181; Town Hall of Veracruz to José Manuel de Herrera, Veracruz, no date, 10:00 PM, f. 175; José Manuel de Herrera to Town Hall of Veracruz, Mexico City, 6 October 1822, f. 178.

37. Santa Anna to Iturbide, Xalapa, 9 February 1822, BLAC, Hernández y Dávalos Papers, 15-1.1537; Briseño Senosiain, Solares Robles, and Suárez de la Torre, *Guadalupe Victoria*, 44–45.

38. The Provincial Deputation was a small elected junta responsible for the provincial government that had been reestablished following the restoration of the 1812 Constitution.

39. Minutes of Town Council Meetings of 7 January, 21 March, and 11 April 1823, AHMX, "Libro de acuerdos del ilustre ayuntamiento constitucional de la villa de Jalapa para el año de 1823," vol. 34, ff. 4–6, 34–35, 39–40.

40. See Santa Anna to Iturbide, Xalapa, 26 January 1822, Archivo Histórico del Instituto Nacional de Antropología e Historia, Colección Antigua, Tomo II, Doc. 10-2; Iturbide to Santa Anna, Mexico City, 16 February 1822, BLAC, Hernández y Dávalos Papers, 15-1. 1545; Santa Anna to Iturbide, Xalapa, 28 February 1822, BLAC, Mariano Riva Palacio Archive, 88; Santa Anna to Iturbide, Xalapa, 11 March and 1 April 1822, BLAC, Hernández y Dávalos Papers, 15-2.1714, 15-3.1752; and Santa Anna to Iturbide, Xalapa, 22 May 1822, *Documentos para la Historia de México*, Biblioteca Nacional, Colección Lafragua.

41. Santa Anna was promoted to brigadier general on 31 October 1822, according to AHSDN, Exp. XI/III/I-116 [1-15], vol. I, ff. 17–19, "Hoja de Servicios [de Santa Anna]," dated 15 June 1859. However, most other sources suggest that Iturbide made him general in May 1822 (Callcott, *Santa Anna*, 34; Jones, *Santa Anna*, 32).

42. Callcott, *Santa Anna*, 38–39; Jones, *Santa Anna*, 32; González Pedrero, *País de un solo hombre*, 1:203; Alamán, *Historia de México*, 5:387–88. Also see Alejo García Conde to Juan Cruz Cabañas, Mexico City, 1 January 1823, Condumex, and Cole, "The Early Career," 128–29.

43. To gain an impression of Santa Anna's disgust at the appointment of Echávarri, see Santa Anna to Iturbide, Veracruz, 5 October 1822, BLAC, W. B. Stephens Collection, WBS-1686; Jones, *Santa Anna*, 32; Santa Anna, *Mi historia militar y política*, 9. According to Joel Poinsett, not more than twenty-eight prisoners were taken. Poinsett, *Notes on Mexico*, 88; Santa Anna to the Town Council of Xalapa, 27 October 1822, AHMX, 1822 "Libro de acuerdos," vol. 33, ff. 290–91; María del Carmen Vázquez Mantecón, "La Jura de Obediencia al Emperador o el fin de la fiesta iturbidista," 22.

44. Memorias de Iturbide, Liorna, 27 September 1823, quoted in Gutiérrez Casillas, *Papeles de Agustín de Iturbide*, 246–47.

45. Poinsett, *Notes on Mexico*, 30.

46. Trueba, *Santa Anna*, 11.

47. Callcott, *Santa Anna*, 40–41; Jones, *Santa Anna*, 33.

48. Santa Anna, *Mi historia militar y política*, 9.

49. "Circular del gobierno expedida en Puebla el día 5 del corriente por el Excelentísimo Señor José Domínguez, Ministro de Justicia y Negocios Eclesiásticos," inserted in *Gaceta Extraordinaria del Gobierno Imperial de México*, 8 December 1822, Condumex, M.C. LXXII-2, carpeta 3-127.

50. Santa Anna, *Mi historia militar y política*, 9; T. E. Anna, *El imperio de Iturbide*, 168–69.

51. Santa Anna to Iturbide, Veracruz, 6 December 1822, BLAC, Hernández y Dávalos Papers, 15-7.2003.

52. Minutes of Town Council Meeting of 4 December 1822, AHMV, Caja 138, vol. 183, "Actas de Cabildo. 1822," ff. 187–88; Alejo García Conde to Juan Cruz Cabañas, Mexico City, 1 January 1823, Condumex.

53. *Gaceta del gobierno imperial de México*, 21 December 1822; AHSDN, Exp. 230, ff. 2–3, Colonel Ramón de Soto to SGM, Orizaba, 28 December 1822; Faustino de Capetillo to José Domínguez, Xalapa, 20 and 21 December 1822, BLAC, Hernández y Dávalos Papers, 15-7.2044; AHSDN, Exp. XI/III/I-116 [1-15], vol. II, ff. 284–85, Antonio López de Santa Anna, Mexico City, 11 September 1823, "Relación de las acciones particulares que tuvo la División de mi mando desde el 2 de diciembre de 1822, hasta la reinstalación del Soberano Congreso." Also see *Memorias de Iturbide*, Liorna, 27 September 1823, quoted in Gutiérrez Casillas, *Papeles de Agustín de Iturbide*, 246–47; Suárez y Navarro, *Historia de México y el general Antonio López de Santa Anna*, 1:25.

54. José Antonio de Echávarri to José Domínguez, Xalapa, 8 December 1822, and Govantes to un amigo, Xalapa, 8 December 1822, BLAC, Hernández y Dávalos Papers, 15-7.2014, 15-7.2017:; Condumex, M.C. LXXII-2, carpeta 3,144, news of which given in *Diario Redactor de México*, 4 January 1823.

55. Luis Cortázar to Francisco de Paula Alvarez, Santa Fe (Veracruz), 27 December 1822, BLAC, Hernández y Dávalos Papers, 15-7.2071.

56. José Antonio de Echávarri to José Domínguez, Xalapa, 9 December 1822, and Luis Cortázar to Francisco de Paula Alvarez, Santa Fe (Veracruz), 27 December 1822, BLAC, Hernández y Dávalos Papers, 15-7.2018, 15-7.2071; Condumex, M.C. LXXII-2, carpeta 3,144, *Diario Redactor de México*, 4 January 1823. José Antonio de Echávarri to Town Council of Veracruz, Campo sobre Veracruz, 27, 29, and 30 December 1822, and Town Council of Veracruz to Echávarri, Veracruz, 30 December 1822, AHMV, Caja 139, vol. 184, ff. 221–27.

57. According to Cole, "The Early Career," 143, Manuel was married in the cathedral of Veracruz on 26 December 1822; copy of reserved letter Crisanto de Castro and Bernardino de Junco to Echávarri, Veracruz, 9 January 1823, AHMV, Caja 144, vol. 189, f. 188. NB: The

date of the copy was the 9th. The original must have been written on 2 January; Echávarri to Town Council of Veracruz, Campo sobre Veracruz, 9 January 1823, ff. 183–87.

58. Echávarri to Francisco de Paula Álvarez, Campo frente a Veracruz, 11 January 1823, BLAC, Hernández y Dávalos Papers, 16-1.3109.

59. Alejo García Conde to Juan Cruz Cabañas, Mexico City, 1 January 1823, Condumex; Echávarri to Town Council of Veracruz, Campo sobre Veracruz, 11 January 1823, and copy of letter, Santa Anna to José María Lobato, Veracruz, 4 January 1823, AHMV, Caja 144, vol. 189, ff. 191–93.

60. Anna, El imperio de Iturbide, 168; the Plan of Veracruz (6 December 1822) and Plan of Casa Mata are reprinted in Jiménez Codinach (ed.), Planes en la Nación Mexicana, 1:139–44; also see Benson, La diputación provincial, 125–29.

61. AHSDN, Exp. XI/III/I-116 [1-15], vol. II, ff. 284–85, Antonio López de Santa Anna, Mexico City, 11 September 1823, "Relación de las acciones particulares que tuvo la División de mi mando desde el 2 de diciembre de 1822, hasta la reinstalación del Soberano Congreso."

62. Bocanegra, Memorias para la historia de México, 1:207.

63. Bustamante, Diario histórico de México, 1:134.

64. Proceso del ex general Antonio López de Santa Anna, acusándole de infidencia a la patria, 226.

65. Poinsett, Notes on Mexico, 20.

4. A Federalist on the Periphery

1. AHSDN, Exp. XI/III/1-116 [1-15], vol. II, ff. 284–85, Antonio López de Santa Anna, Mexico City, 11 September 1823, "Relación de las acciones particulares que tuvo la División de mi mando desde el 2 de diciembre de 1822, hasta la reinstalación del Soberano Congreso.".

2. For José Joaquín de Herrera see Cotner, The Military and Political Career of José Joaquín de Herrera, and Manzur Ocaña, Don José Joaquín de Herrera.

3. For the 1823–24 Constituent Congress see Quinlan, "Issues and Factions in the Constituent Congress, 1823–1824"; Tornel, Breve reseña histórica, 73; Santa Anna, Manifiesto de Antonio López de Santa Anna a sus conciudadanos (1823). Also see Muñoz, Santa Anna, 73; Díaz Díaz, Caudillos y caciques, 69.

4. The Ejército Protector de la Libertad consisted of 1,541 men (National Artillery: 69, Infantry Regiment Num. 1: 698, Infantry Regiment Num. 2: 506; Frontier Dragoons: 93; General's Escort: 74; Partidas sueltas: 101). See Plan del Brigadier Antonio López de Santa Anna en San Luis Potosí, AHMV, Caja 144, vol. 189, ff. 274–86, including on ff. 284–85 the 1823 Oficios dirigidos al Soberano Congreso y Supremo Poder Ejecutivo de la Nación, por el Ciudadano General Santana; que se imprime para que se imponga el Público de las sanas intenciones de este jefe, y acontecimientos que le mueven a suspender sus operaciones militares. For documents outlining the problems Santa Anna faced and caused during his stay in San Luis Potosí (1823), see "Causa formada al gral. Santa Anna por los sucesos de

S. Luis Potosí, en junio de 1823, fue absuelto," AGN, Archivo de Guerra, galería 5, vol. 458. Also see vol. 459, which includes: ff. 8–10, *Plan de San Luis Potosí* (San Luis Potosí: Imp. de Estrada, 5 June 1823); ff. 23–43, "Ocurrencias en San Luis Potosí ocasionadas del Plan que el Brigadier D. Antonio Santana proclamó en 5 de julio [sic]"; ff. 50–61, "Declaración del acusado" [4 August 1823]; f. 197, *Oficio que el ciudadano general Santana ha dirigido a la exma. Diputación de esta provincia, en contestación a las proposiciones que se le hacían para que entrase en consiliación con el ciudadano general Armijo, y que se imprime para satisfacción de los buenos ciudadanos* (San Luis Potosí: Imp. de Estrada, 1823). More specifically see Muro, *Historia de San Luis Potosí*, 1:350, 353; José Díaz de León to Lucas Alamán, San Luis Potosí, 30 May 1823, AGN, Archivo de Guerra, vol. 459, ff. 20–22; Callcott, *Santa Anna*, 49; Yáñez, *Santa Anna*, 96; AHSDN, Exp. XI/III/I-116 [1-15], vol. II, f. 281, Arrillaga (?) [illegible] to Minister of War, México City, 6 August 1823; and Valadés, *México, Santa Anna y la guerra de Texas*, 67.

5. Callcott, *Santa Anna*, 49–51; Valadés, *México, Santa Anna y la guerra de Texas*, 65. Invoking Jews would appear to be a matter of routine antisemitism.

6. Quoted in Yáñez, *Santa Anna*, 97.

7. Santa Anna, *Manifiesto* (1823), 11; Valadés, *México, Santa Anna y la guerra de Texas*, 64, 67.

8. Muñoz, *Santa Anna*, 74; Díaz Díaz, *Caudillos y caciques*, 70.

9. Plan del Brigadier Antonio López de Santa Anna en San Luis Potosí, AHMV, Caja 144, vol. 189, ff. 274–86, including on ff. 279–82 the 1823 *Plan de San Luis Potosí*. The articles of the plan as well as the concluding paragraph (albeit not the preamble), are reprinted in Bocanegra, *Memorias para la historia de México*, 1:256–58.

10. For a collection of documents on Santa Anna's San Luis Potosí revolt, and the trial he subsequently had to endure, see AGN, Archivo de Guerra, galería 5, vols. 458, 459. I thank Linda Arnold for kindly bringing these documents to my attention.

11. Callcott, *Santa Anna*, 51; Valadés, *México, Santa Anna y la guerra de Texas*, 65; Alamán to Santa Anna, Mexico City, 14 June 1823, AGN, Archivo de Guerra, vol. 459, f. 30; Cole, "The Early Career," 156–57; and see AHMV, Caja 144, vol. 189: f. 286, *Acta* [of suspension of the revolt] (San Luis Potosí: Imp. del Ciudadano Estrada, 1823); f. 283, *Impreso* by Santa Anna, 6 July 1823; and ff. 284–85, *Oficios dirigidos al Soberano Congreso y Supremo Poder Ejecutivo* (see note 4).

12. Valadés, *México, Santa Anna y la guerra de Texas*, 66–67; Jones, *Santa Anna*, 41; Yáñez, *Santa Anna*, 98; Cole, "The Early Career," 158; González Pedrero, *País de un solo hombre*, 1:265; Santa Anna, *Manifiesto* (1823); AHSDN, Exp. XI/III/I-116 [1-15], vol. 2, f. 277, Santa Anna to Minister of War, México City, 4 December 1823; f. 279 contains Minister of War's favorable reply.

13. "Sumaria de Ignacio Alvarado," AGN, Archivo de Guerra, vol. 458.

14. Fowler, *Tornel and Santa Anna*, 30.

15. Callcott, *Santa Anna*, 52; Jones, *Santa Anna*, 41; Valadés, *México, Santa Anna y la guerra de Texas*, 68; Yáñez, *Santa Anna*, 99; Díaz Díaz, *Caudillos y caciques*, 72; Muñoz, *Santa Anna*, 76. Quote taken from Anna, *Forging México*, 197.

16. The expulsion laws of 10 May and 20 December 1827 are reprinted in full in Tornel, *Breve reseña histórica*, 167–70; *El Correo de la Federación Mexicana*, 14 May 1827; Cole, "The Early Career," 162–63; Fowler, *Tornel and Santa Anna*, 47.

17. Jones, *Santa Anna*, 41.

18. Callcott, *Santa Anna*, 53; Jones, *Santa Anna*, 41. Valadés and González Pedrero confuse the date of his departure with that of his arrival, claiming Santa Anna disembarked in Campeche on 17 May (Valadés, *México, Santa Anna y la guerra de Texas*, 69; González Pedrero, *País de un solo hombre*, 1:306). Also see Molina Solís, *Historia de Yucatán desde la Independencia*, 1:21; Ancona, *Historia de Yucatán*, 3:207.

19. Fowler, *Mexico in the Age of Proposals*, 17–18.

20. Alamán, *Historia de Méjico*, 5:510.

21. Tenenbaum, *México en la época de los agiotistas*, 44; also see Costeloe, *Bonds and Bondholders*; Mateos, *Historia parlamentaria de los congresos mexicanos*, vol. 2, tomos 1–2.

22. AHSDN, Exp. XI/III/1-116 [1-15], vol. II: f. 336, Santa Anna to Minister of War, Campeche, 19 May 1824. Also see report of his arrival and reception in f. 333: *El Investigador o El Amante de la Razón (Periódico Instructivo de Campeche)*, 20 May 1824; f. 345: *El Comandante General del Estado Libre de Yucatán a sus habitantes* (Campeche: no publisher, 29 May 1824).

23. *El Investigador o El Amante de la Razón (Periódico Instructivo de Campeche)*, 20 May 1824. I have translated the term *patria* as mother country, rather than fatherland. *Patria* is a word that was taken from Greek into Latin, from where it entered Castilian intact, meaning "lineage," not necessarily "father." The *terra patria* thus meant the "the land of the lineage." The fact that *patria* did not directly mean father may account for the use of the feminine "la" article that precedes it in Spanish. By the nineteenth century, references to "la patria" were customarily accompanied with feminine imagery. I thank Dr. Kormi Anipa for his advice on this matter.

24. AHSDN, Exp. XI/III/1-116 [1-15], vol. II, ff. 340–41, Santa Anna to Minister of War, Campeche, 29 May 1824; ff. 342–43, Santa Anna to Minister of War, Campeche, 31 May 1824.

25. AHSDN, Exp. XI/III/1-116 [1-15], vol. II, f. 346, Santa Anna to Minister of War, Mérida, 10 June 1824; Santa Anna's report of Calkiní, 9 July 1824, is reprinted in Menéndez, *La huella del general don Antonio López de Santa Anna en Yucatán*, 219–26.

26. An example of his federalism was his reaction to news of Iturbide's execution on 19 July 1824. It was while Santa Anna was in Yucatán that Iturbide returned to Mexico, landing in Tampico, where he was captured and executed in Padilla. His executor, Felipe de la Garza, limited himself to carrying out the national government's directive. He did not think of the possibility of forgiving Iturbide by claiming, for instance, that the regional jurisdiction differed from the national one. Santa Anna claimed he was both shocked and disgusted and noted that he would have played his cards differently had the former emperor disembarked in Yucatán: "He was never my personal enemy. In Yucatán he would not have been shot" (Santa Anna, *Mi historia militar y política*, 11).

27. González Pedrero, *País de un solo hombre*, 1:307; Menéndez, *La huella del general*, 46;

González Pedrero dates Tarrazo's resignation on 6 July (*País de un solo hombre*, 1:325). Valadés dates Santa Anna's appointment as governor on 5 July (Valadés, *México, Santa Anna y la guerra de Texas*, 77). According to Muñoz, Tarrazo resigned in protest at the way Santa Anna rode roughshod over him, demanding forced contributions to cover the cost of repairing the city's fortifications (Muñoz, *Santa Anna*, 78). As Cole points out, Tarrazo was from Campeche and resigned because Santa Anna was undermining his determination to impose the federal declaration of war on Spain (Cole, "The Early Career," 173).

28. Menéndez, *La huella del general*, 55–57.

29. Santa Anna's "Cuban proposal," Mérida, 18 August 1824, is reprinted in González Pedrero, *País de un solo hombre*, 1:336–38; Bocanegra, *Memorias para la historia de México*, 1:387; Poinsett, *Notes on Mexico*, 17; Jones, *Santa Anna*, 43.

30. González Pedrero, *País de un solo hombre*, 1:341; Tornel, *Breve reseña histórica*, 77.

31. Callcott, *Santa Anna*, 53–54; González Pedrero, *País de un solo hombre*, 1:338–40; Solís Vicarte, *Las sociedades secretas en el primer gobierno republicano*, 73–83; Fowler, *Tornel and Santa Anna*, 48.

32. Menéndez, *La huella del general*, 80–84.

33. AHSDN, Exp. XI/III/1-116 [1-15], Vol. II: Santa Anna to Minister of War, Mérida, 13 July, 12 August, 2 September 1824, ff. 349, 351–52, 380–87; Santa Anna to Minister of War, Campeche, 28 October and 5 November 1824, 12 February 1825, ff. 390-395, 464-467; Alamán to Pablo Obregón, Mexico City, 3 August 1825, quoted in Chávez Orozco, *Un esfuerzo de México*, 9; Díaz Díaz, *Caudillos y caciques*, 73; Callcott, *Santa Anna*, 56; Jones, *Santa Anna*, 43; González Pedrero, *País de un solo hombre*, 1:327; Muñoz, *Santa Anna*, 81; Yáñez, *Santa Anna*, 101; *El Sol*, 10 April 1826.

5. Among the Jarochos

1. The files held in the Archivo Notarial del Archivo y Biblioteca Históricos de Veracruz start in 1844. The Archivo Notarial de la Biblioteca Central de la Universidad Veracruzana does not hold any documents from the legal offices of the port. The Archivo General de Notarías del Estado de Veracruz holds the records of the port notary Eduardo Fernández de Castro covering the years 1837–43. Therefore, while it was possible to trace the manner in which Santa Anna bought a series of neighboring *haciendas* and *ranchos* extending the size of Manga de Clavo, in particular, after 1839, it is still impossible to determine with precision the lands he acquired in 1825. For example, the deed for the purchase of the hacienda Paso de Varas has not yet been found, for which reason it must be presumed that he bought it before 1837. For details of the purchase of Manga de Clavo, see Callcott, *Santa Anna*, 56–57; Jones, *Santa Anna*, 44; González Pedrero, *País de un solo hombre*, 1:563; Potash, "Testamentos de Santa Anna," 429–30; and Díaz Díaz, *Caudillos y caciques*, 337. For the quoted travelers' descriptions see Calderón de la Barca, *Life in Mexico*, 31–33, and Thompson, *Recollections of Mexico*, 11–13.

2. Aviraneta e Ibargoyen, *Mis memorias íntimas*, 60. For a study on Aviraneta see Mé-

ndez Reyes, *Eugenio de Aviraneta*. For a study on Santa Anna's Veracruzan properties see Fowler, "Las propiedades veracruzanas de Santa Anna," 68–73.

3. According to Cole, Santa Anna offered his services to governor Barragán in October 1825 to assist with the final push to free San Juan de Ulúa. However, Barragán declined (Cole, "The Early Career," 199).

4. Calderón de la Barca, *Life in Mexico*, 33; Thompson, *Recollections of Mexico*, 231; Prieto, *Memorias de mis tiempos*, 233.

5. Arrendamiento, 8 August 1842, in ANBUV, "Registro de instrumentos públicos: Año de 1842" (Xalapa), ff. 300–2, provides details of how one of his ranches had a shop, a room, a kitchen, a stable, a chicken coop and fields for pasture. In Arrendamiento, 23 November 1842, in the same 1842 "Registro de instrumentos públicos," ff. 426–36, there is another example of the kind of activities that took place in Santa Anna's lands. In this case we can see that at the ranch of Chipila and El Huaje, rented to Soledad Duarte y Briseño, there were a house, offices, chicken coops, 200 cows, 43 mares, 8 colts, 13 horses, and 26 mules. In Arrendamiento, 30 October 1844, "Registro de instrumentos públicos: Año de 1844" (Xalapa), ff. 430–31, it is stipulated that Santa Anna had the right to stop at the ranch in Plan del Río if he was passing. The instructions contained in "Registro de instrumentos públicos: Año de 1847" (Xalapa), ff. 339–42, 28 December 1847, offer fascinating insight into the economic activities of Santa Anna's properties, with sugar cane planting and processing, cattle ranching, and woodcutting being among them. Equally interesting is the sense one obtains of Santa Anna having had strong ideas as to what activities could be done and where. For instance, he forbade the growing and processing of sugar cane in Plan del Río. He also forbade any cattle from being butchered anywhere other than in El Encero.

6. Marriages of convenience were the norm in early nineteenth-century provincial Mexico. Santa Anna later ensured that his eldest daughter Guadalupe married his nephew Francisco de Paula Castro when she was not even fifteen years old herself. In this way he made sure the amassed fortune of the López de Santa Annas stayed within the family.

7. ANBUV, "Protocolo de instrumentos públicos que pasaron ante el escribano don José Ignacio Jiménez en 1825"(Xalapa), ff. 288–89, Poder, 10 September 1825. For the authorization Santa Anna was given on 10 August 1825 to abandon service to marry Inés de la Paz García, daughter of Manuel García "español europeo" and María Jacinta Martínez "española originaria y vecina de este puerto (Alvarado)," see AHSDN, XI/III/1-116 [1-15], vol. III, ff. 501–18. Also see Potash, "Testamentos de Santa Anna," 429; Díaz Díaz, *Caudillos y caciques*, 337; Callcott, *Santa Anna*, 57; quote taken from Margaret Chowning, "Elite Families and Popular Politics in Early Nineteenth-Century Michoacán: The Strange Case of Juan José Codallos and the Censored Genealogy," *Americas* 55:1 (1998): 53.

8. Antonio died at the age of five. There is a rumor that Inés gave birth to a fifth child who was in some way disabled or physically impaired and was kept hidden from the world because Santa Anna and his first wife were ashamed of him or her. For de-

tails on his extramarital affairs and children see Sefchovich, *La suerte de la consorte*, 88; Callcott, *Santa Anna*, 184; Fowler, "Las propiedades veracruzanas de Santa Anna," 78; Villa-Amor, *Biografía del general Santa Anna*, 16. Santa Anna's 7 September 1844 will and his 29 October 1874 will are both reprinted in full in Potash, "Testamentos de Santa Anna," 430–34, and 434–40, respectively. Also see Zárate Toscano, "Los testamentos de los presidentes del siglo XIX," 256.

9. Quote taken from Callcott, *Santa Anna*, 57. For an evaluation of Inés's life with Santa Anna that highlights how she found subtle yet important ways of determining how she wanted to live, see Fowler, "All the President's Women." Also see Jones, *Santa Anna*, 44; Sefchovich, *La suerte de la consorte*, 87–88. For letters outlining Rincón's intention of expropriating the hacienda and President Guadalupe Victoria's reservations (Rincón went ahead without permission), see AHSDN, Exp. XI/481.3/432, ff. 2–3, José Rincón to Minister of War, Veracruz, 4 October 1828, and Unsigned [Minister of War] to Commander General of Veracruz [José Rincón], [México City], 8 October 1828. For Santa Anna's protest and the reply he was given in which the president denied that the government had ordered the confiscation of Manga de Clavo, see AHSDN, Exp. XI/III/1-116[1-15] vol. III, ff. 545, 550, Santa Anna to Minister of War, Xalapa, 12 February 1829, and Unsigned [President?—Minister of War?], México City, 18 February 1829.

10. Fowler, "Las propiedades veracruzanas de Santa Anna," 81, 86–87.

11. Calderón de la Barca, *Life in Mexico*, 32–33, 124–25.

12. Santa Anna to Inés García, Orazimba, Texas, 25 September 1836, BLAC, W. B. Stephens Collection, WBS-2081.

13. German travelers quoted in Vázquez Mantecón, "La prostitución de la sexualidad durante el siglo XIX mexicano," 40. Also see Arrom, *Las mujeres de la ciudad de México*, 297.

14. Thompson, *Recollections of Mexico*, 53; Minutes of the Town Council meetings of 26 August, 2 and 30 September, and 7 October 1844, AHMX, "Libro de acuerdos del muy ilustre ayuntamiento de la ciudad de Jalapa" [1844], vol. 56, ff. 111–18, 131–38. The "honras de la Exma. Señora Doña Inés García de Santa Anna" rose to 364 pesos 3 cuartillas reales; *La Excelentísima Señora Doña Inés García de Santa Anna*.

15. Mora, *Obras sueltas*, 7–8.

16. Tornel, *Breve reseña histórica*, 46; Fowler, *Mexico in the Age of Proposals*, 18–21, 42–45, 48–55.

17. Warren, *Vagrants and Citizens*, 80.

18. The *novenarios* were a breakaway Masonic society formed in 1827, made up of disillusioned *escoceses* and moderate liberals such as José María Luis Mora, who had become afraid of the excessive power the *yorkinos* had come to enjoy. See Fowler, *Mexico in the Age of Proposals*, 53–54. Also see Fowler, *The Mexican Press and the Collapse of Representative Government*; Blázquez Domínguez, *Políticos y comerciantes*, 35.

19. Costeloe, *La primera república federal*, 52; Fowler, *Tornel and Santa Anna*, 49–51.

20. Lucas Alamán claims Santa Anna became an escocés while he was in Yucatán (Alamán, *Historia de Méjico*, 5:481, n. 41). Manuel Villa-Amor, on the other hand, be-

lieves that Santa Anna joined the escoceses in 1822, becoming involved in the plot to bring down Iturbide as a result of this (Villa-Amor, *Biografía del general Santa-Anna*, 5, 7). Also see Tornel, *Breve reseña histórica*, 113; Costeloe, *La primera república federal*, 121; Callcott, *Santa Anna*, 61; Blázquez Domínguez, *Políticos y comerciantes*, 37. For documents confirming Santa Anna's appointment as vice-governor of Veracruz on 6 September 1827, see AHSDN, Exp. XI/III/1-116 [1-15], vol. III, ff. 526-30, Santa Anna to Minister of War, Xalapa, 23 September 1827; Santa Anna to Minister of War, Xalapa, 13 September 1827; President [Guadalupe Victoria] to Santa Anna, Mexico City, 18 September 1827; President [Guadalupe Victoria] to Santa Anna, Mexico City, 28 September 1827; and Governor Miguel Barragán's *Bando* (Xalapa, 7 September 1827).

21. Blázquez Domínguez, *Políticos y comerciantes*, 23. Blázquez Domínguez lists among the prominent *escoceses* of Veracruz the following politicians: José María Rodríguez Roa, Diego María de Alcalde, José Mariano Jáuregui, Manuel Facio, Manuel María Fernández, Joaquín de Herrasti y Alba, José Julián Tornel, and Nemesio and José Ignacio Iberri (*Políticos y comerciantes*, 35); and sees in them an evolutionary pattern whereby they were royalists before the Plan of Iguala, supporters of Iturbide, independence and the Empire subsequently; and republicans after Casa Mata, with a propensity to defend a centralist-pro-Spanish agenda.

22. Aviraneta, *Mis memorias íntimas*, 46; Tornel, *Breve reseña histórica*, 199.

23. Blázquez Domínguez, *Políticos y comerciantes*, 42, 47; Aviraneta, *Mis memorias íntimas*, 24.

24. For an account of these events see Costeloe, *La primera república federal*, 121–31; Blázquez Domínguez, *Políticos y comerciantes*, 31–76. Also see Esteva, *Exposición de las ocurrencias que motivaron la salida de Veracruz del Ciudadano José Ignacio Esteva*; *Correo de la Federación Mexicana*, 22 August 1827. Several copies of *El Veracruzano Libre* (28, 29 June, 1, 2, and 7 July 1827) are held in the AHSDN: Exp. XI/481.3/336, ff. 310–27. Its editorials were almost exclusively concerned at the time with disparaging the yorkinos and condemning José Antonio Rincón's arbitrary behavior. As evidenced in the issue of 29 June, *El Veracruzano Libre* also celebrated Santa Anna's heroic past. See also ff. 10–13, Barragán to Minister of War, Veracruz, 25 and 26 July 1827.

25. AHSDN, Exp. XI/481.3/336: Santa Anna to Minister of War, Xalapa, 31 July 1827, contains copy of Santa Anna to Barragán, Xalapa, 27 July 1827; Barragán to Minister of War, Veracruz, 30 and 31 July, 7 August 1827; José Rincón to Manuel Gómez Pedraza, Minister of War, Veracruz, 28 and (two) 31 July 1827, ff. 15–19, 27–30, 37–39, 51–52, 75–76, 90–96. And see Rincón, *Conducta que adopta la mayoría de la guarnición de esta plaza*.

26. AHSDN, Exp. XI/481.3/336: Barragán to Minister of War, 4 August 1827; Vicente Guerrero to Minister of War, 7, 16, and 29 August 1827, ff. 122–25, 135, 149. Also see Blázquez Domínguez, *Políticos y comerciantes*, 70, 112. She argues persuasively that had Santa Anna been involved in such a conspiracy, the escocés-dominated state legislature of 1828 would not have accepted Santa Anna's appointment as acting governor the way they did.

27. AHSDN, Exp. XI/III/1-116 [1-15], vol. III, ff. 532–34, Santa Anna to Minister of War, Veracruz, 11 August 1827; Exp. XI/481.3/336, ff. 202–6, Santa Anna to Guerrero, Veracruz, 29 August 1827.

28. AHSDN, Exp. XI/481.3/336, ff. 192–95, Santa Anna to Guerrero, Veracruz, 30 August 1827; Guerrero to Santa Anna, 1 September 1827, reprinted in *Correo de la Federación Mexicana*, 11 September 1827.

29. Archivo Histórico del Archivo General del Estado de Veracruz (hereafter cited as AHAGEV), *Colección de decretos correspondientes al año de 1827* (Xalapa: Tipografía del Gobierno del Estado), 212, 217–18. All the decrees contained in this volume may also be found in Blázquez Domínguez and Corzo Ramírez (eds.), *Colección de Leyes y Decretos de Veracruz*. Also see *Correo de la Federación Mexicana*, 18 September 1827; Blázquez Domínguez, *Políticos y comerciantes*, 75.

30. Muñoz, *Santa Anna*, 84; Aviraneta, *Mis memorias íntimas*, 58; Sims, *The Expulsion of Mexico's Spaniards*, 32. Also see Santa Anna to Cañedo, Veracruz, 13 May 1828, and Cañedo to Santa Anna, Mexico City, 21 May 1828, AGN, "Expulsión de españoles," vol. 6, ff. 281–83.

31. AHAGEV, *Colección de decretos correspondientes al año de 1827*, 220–21; Sims, *The Expulsion of Mexico's Spaniards*, 33; Fowler, *Tornel and Santa Anna*, 74–77.

32. The Plan of Montaño is reprinted in Tornel, *Breve reseña histórica*, 179.

33. Muñoz, *Santa Anna*, 85; Cole, "The Early Career," 237; Zavala, *Obras. El Historiador y el Representante Popular: Ensayo crítico*, 327, 338–40; Lerdo de Tejada, *Apuntes históricos de la heroica ciudad de Veracruz*, 2:302; Yáñez, *Santa Anna*, 103; Díaz Díaz, *Caudillos y caciques*, 77; Costeloe, *La primera república federal*, 144.

34. Santa Anna's letter to the Minister of War, Huamantla, 2 January 1828, is reprinted in Tornel, *Breve reseña histórica*, 198; also see Jones, *Santa Anna*, 46; Costeloe, *La primera república federal*, 145.

35. Costeloe, *La primera república federal*, 146; Blázquez Domínguez, *Políticos y comerciantes*, 105.

36. Callcott, *Santa Anna*, 66.

37. Callcott, *Santa Anna*, 5–7, 11; Blázquez Domínguez, *Políticos y comerciantes*, 80, 131.

38. Valadés, *México, Santa Anna y la guerra de Texas*, 82; Decrees of 28 January and 9 and 23 February 1828 established the dates for the celebration of fairs in Jalacingo, Papantla, and Córdoba (AHAGEV, *Colección de decretos correspondientes al año de 1828*, 12–13, 17–18, 20–21); Minutes of Town Council meetings of 23 and 29 February 1828, AHMX, "Libro de acuerdos del ilustre ayuntamiento constitucional de la villa de Jalapa para el año del señor de 1828," vol. 39, ff. 24–27; Decrees of 29 February, 21, 28, 29, 29 March, and 7 July 1828, AHAGEV, *Colección de decretos correspondientes al año de 1828*, 25–26, 39–40, 49–50, 58–59, 62–63, 80–83; Cole, "The Early Career," 243.

39. Minutes of Town Council Meetings, all in AHMX, 1828 "Libro de acuerdos," vol. 39: 11 April, ff. 36–38; 18 April 1828, ff. 43–45; 2 and 5 May, ff. 64–66; 10 May 1828, ff. 57–58; 9 and 11 June, ff. 52–55; and 19 July 1828, ff. 79–80. And see Decrees of 8 Feb-

ruary, 18 and 28 March 1828, AHAGEV, *Colección de decretos correspondientes al año de 1828* 15–16, 30–31, 48–49.

40. Fowler, "The Compañía Lancasteriana and the Élite"; Fowler, *Mexico in the Age of Proposals*, 238–40; Fowler, *Tornel and Santa Anna*, 218–30; *El Sol*, 13 November 1823; Decrees of 23 February, 20 March and 7 July 1828, AHAGEV, *Colección de decretos correspondientes al año de 1828*, pp. 22–23, 34–37, 80–83; Minutes of Town Council Meetings of 25 April, 30 May, 27 June, 4, 5, 24 July; and 1 August 1828, AHMX, 1828 "Libro de acuerdos," vol. 39, ff. 48–49, 62–64, 69–73, 81–85.

41. For example, he enthusiastically praised and thanked the town council of Xalapa, in April 1828, for raising 536 pesos to assist with the rebuilding of the brig *Guerrero* and for ensuring there was "buen orden y tranquilidad" in Xalapa. Minutes of Town Council meeting of 28 April 1828, AHMX, 1828 "Libro de acuerdos," vol. 39, ff. 49–50.

42. Quoted in Yáñez, *Santa Anna*, 104.

6. General of Tricks

1. Anna, *Forging Mexico*, 216; Zavala, *Viaje a los Estados Unidos del Norte de América*, in Zavala, *Obras* (1976), 11; Bocanegra, *Memorias para la historia de México*, 1:474.

2. *El Correo de la Federación Mexicana*, 11 September 1827; also see Blázquez Domínguez, *Políticos y comerciantes*, 73; Decree of 9 May 1828, AHAGEV, *Colección de decretos correspondientes al año de 1828*, 73–74; Santa Anna to Guerrero, 24 April 1828, noted in Costeloe, *La primera república federal*, 190; Aviraneta, *Memorias íntimas*, 134–35.

3. Blázquez Domínguez, *Políticos y comerciantes*, 134; the town council of Xalapa remained loyal to Santa Anna throughout the revolt of Perote; see Minutes of Town Council Meetings of 12, 14, 15 September, 3, 10, 18, 20, 24, 25, 29 October, 4, 14, 21, 29 November, 4, 13, 21, and 27 December 1828, all in AHMX, 1828 "Libro de acuerdos," vol. 39, ff. 106–9, 113–28, 132–48. Also see Callcott, *Santa Anna*, 64; Díaz Díaz, *Caudillos y caciques*, 78; Costeloe, *La primera república federal*, 192–93; Decree of 5 September 1828, AHAGEV, *Colección de decretos correspondientes al año de 1828*, 93; AHSDN, Exp. XI/481.3/423, f. 6, Justo de Berdejo to Minister of War, Puebla, 13 September 1828; Un ciudadano que no tomó la más mínima parte en aquellos acontecimientos, *Pronunciamiento de Perote por el general Antonio López de Santa Anna*; Bocanegra, *Memorias para la historia de México*, 1:474–75; Muñoz, *Santa Anna*, 86; Yáñez, *Santa Anna*, 106–8.

4. AHSDN, Exp. XI/481.3/423: f. 7, Ignacio de Mora to Minister of War, Xalapa, 12 September 1828; f. 12, Ignacio de Mora to Commander General of Puebla, Xalapa, 12 September 1828; ff. 98–99, 126–27, copy of dispatch by Joaquín Marroquí to Commander General of Puebla, Puebla, 15 September 1828, and original letter by Marroquí to Commander General of Puebla, Huamantla, 14 September 1828; Exp. XI/481.3/513, ff. 31–32, copy of letter, Pedro González to Minister of War, Hacienda del Molino, 1 October 1828. Also see Rivera Cambas, *Antonio López de Santa Anna*, 12.

5. Victoria, *El Presidente de los Estados Unidos Mejicanos a sus Conciudadanos*; Esteva, *José Ignacio Esteva, Secretario del Despacho de Hacienda*; Bocanegra, *Memorias para la historia de*

México, 1:475–76; *Voz de la Patria*, 3 and 28 July 1830; Tornel, *Manifestación del C. José María Tornel*, 6–7; Fowler, *Tornel and Santa Anna*, 90–94.

6. Quoted in Cole, "The Early Career," 267.

7. Muñoz, *Santa Anna*, 87; Rivera Cambas, *Antonio López de Santa Anna*, 13; Valadés, *México, Santa Anna y la guerra de Texas*, 84–87; Cole, "The Early Career," 271.

8. Rivera Cambas, *Antonio López de Santa Anna*, 14; AHSDN, Exp. XI/481.3/454, f. 2, Manuel Rincón's "Dispatch of Battle of Oaxaca, 14–15 November 1828," Oaxaca, 15 November 1828, reprinted in *Suplemento al Aguila Mexicana Num. 324, El Aguila Mexicana, Num. 324*, November 1828; Santa Anna's correspondence with Rincón, 20–21 November 1828, is reprinted in Bocanegra, *Memorias para la historia de México*, 1:478–84; also see Yáñez, *Santa Anna*, 109; González Pedrero, *País de un solo hombre*, 1:439.

9. Valadés, *México, Santa Anna y la guerra de Texas*, 87; Yáñez, *Santa Anna*, 108–9; Callcott, *Santa Anna*, 69; Muñoz, *Santa Anna*, 88–89; Jones, *Santa Anna*, 47–48.

10. AHSDN, Exp. XI/481.3/424: ff. 27–28, José María Calderón to Minister of War, Oaxaca, 2 December 1828; ff. 107–8, "Armisticio celebrado entre el Sr. General de Brigada Dn. José María Calderón y el de igual clase Dn. Antonio López de Santa Anna," Oaxaca, 11 December 1828; f. 117, copy of Agreement to end the hostilities in Oaxaca, Oaxaca, 14 December 1828. Arrom, "Popular Politics in Mexico City"; Fowler, *Tornel and Santa Anna*, 93–97; according to Valadés, Santa Anna found out about Zavala's victory in the capital from a letter his sister Francisca sent him from Puebla (Valadés, *México, Santa Anna y la guerra de Texas*, 88).

11. AHSDN, Exp. XI/481.3/424, ff. 121–22, Santa Anna to Vicente Guerrero, Sto Domingo de Oaxaca, 16 December 1828. For Santa Anna and Calderón's highly entertaining correspondence, see ff. 128–30, Calderón to Santa Anna, Santa Anna to Calderón, Calderón to Santa Anna, Oaxaca, 15 December 1828, and Santa Anna to Calderón, 16 December 1828.

12. AHSDN, Exp. XI/481.3/424: ff. 161–64, Calderón to Guadalupe Victoria, Oaxaca, 19 December 1828; f. 165, Santa Anna to Guerrero, Oaxaca, 20 December 1828; ff. 174–83, Santa Anna to Calderón, Calderón to Santa Anna, Santa Anna to the Governor of Oaxaca, Santa Anna to the Commisar General of Oaxaca, and Calderón to Santa Anna, Oaxaca, 21 December 1828; f. 173, Santa Anna to Minister of War, Oaxaca, 22 December 1828.

13. AHSDN, Exp. XI/481.3/424: f. 194, Santa Anna to Minister of War, Oaxaca, 25 December 1828; f. 196, Santa Anna to Colonel Mariano Rivera, Oaxaca, 25 December 1828; ff. 206–8, Santa Anna to Calderón, Calderón to Santa Anna, and copy of Peace Treaty signed by Calderón and Santa Anna, Oaxaca, 28 December 1828.

14. AHSDN, Exp. XI/481.3/531: ff. 11, 12, two letters by Santa Anna to Minister of War, Oaxaca, 3 January 1829; f. 24, Santa Anna to Minister of War, Oaxaca, 9 January 1829; Exp. XI/III/1-116 [1-15], vol. III, f. 552, Minister of Exchequer to Santa Anna, Mexico City, 29 August 1829. Regarding Santa Anna's banquet with Guerrero, Rivera Cambas claims the banquet took place in Tehuacán, and not Mexico City (Rivera Cambas, *Antonio López de Santa Anna*, 15). According to Cole, the banquet took place in Tepeaca

(Cole, "The Early Career," 287). Also see Valadés, *México, Santa Anna y la guerra de Texas,* 88–89; Yáñez, *Santa Anna,* 110; Callcott, *Santa Anna,* 70; Jones, *Santa Anna,* 48; Decree of 23 March 1829, AHAGEV, *Colección de decretos correspondientes al año de 1829* (Xalapa: Tipografía del gobierno del estado, 1903), 23–24 (all the decrees contained in this volume may also be found in Blázquez Domínguez and Corzo Ramírez [eds.], *Colección de Leyes y Decretos de Veracruz,* vol. 2); María Guadalupe Matilde Visenta Josefa Antonia López de Santa Anna, christened on 22 March 1829, Archivo Eclesiástico de la Parroquia del Sagrario de Xalapa, "Libro 32: Notaría Eclesiástica de la Parroquia del Sagrario de la Santa Iglesia Catedral, Bautizos 1826-1830, Xalapa," f. 104v. I thank David Carbajal López for checking this reference for me.

15. Quoted in Valadés, *México, Santa Anna y la guerra de Texas,* 88.

16. Decrees of 7 April 1829, AHAGEV, *Colección de decretos correspondientes al año de 1829,* 24–27.

17. Santa Anna's speech of 10 February 1829 is reprinted in Bocanegra, *Memorias para la historia de México,* 1:489–92.

18. Circular by Santa Anna, 11 April 1829, AHAGEV, *Colección de decretos correspondientes al año de 1829,* 29–32.

19. Decrees of 27 April and 28 October 1829, granting trade fair rights to Cosamaloapan and Tlacotalpan, respectively, AHAGEV, *Colección de decretos correspondientes al año de 1829,* 54–55, 88–90; Decrees of 22, 27, 29 April, 12 May, 30 June, and 31 October 1829, 34–40, 52–60 69–75, 109–35.

20. Sims, *The Expulsion of Mexico's Spaniards,* 115; Circulars of 29 April and 13 May 1829, AHAGEV, *Colección de decretos correspondientes al año de 1829,* 40–44, 63–69.

21. *Times,* 8 September 1829. I thank Michael Costeloe for kindly forwarding me this reference.

22. Rivera Cambas, *Antonio López de Santa Anna,* 24; Fowler, *Tornel and Santa Anna,* 97–100.

23. Rivera Cambas, *Antonio López de Santa Anna,* 16; *El Sol,* 17 July 1829; Bustamante quoted in Muñoz, *Santa Anna,* 94.

24. Frasquet, "Milicianos y soldados," 121; Callcott, *Santa Anna,* 72; Muñoz, *Santa Anna,* 93. Other "borrowed" boats were *Iris, Félix, Úrsula,* and *Concepción.*

25. Several accounts date Santa Anna's departure on 4 August. I have stated 9 August in line with Manuel María Escobar's memoirs of the campaign, reprinted as Escobar, "Campaña de Tampico," 56; also see Callcott, *Santa Anna,* 74; Jones, *Santa Anna,* 50; Cole, "The Early Career," 298–99; Sánchez Lamego, *La invasión española de 1829,* 107. For the action of 21 August, see AHSDN, Exp. XI/481.3/651.

26. Escobar, "Campaña de Tampico," 66–68.

27. Quoted in Méndez Reyes, *Eugenio de Aviraneta,* 88. According to Méndez Reyes, a study of all the existing correspondence points to the fact that it was Aviraneta and Barradas who were anxious to gain Santa Anna's support, and that Santa Anna had no interest in seeking an alliance with the invading army (Méndez Reyes, *Eugenio de Aviraneta,* 89). Also see Escobar, "Campaña de Tampico," 68.

28. Rivera Cambas, *Antonio López de Santa Anna*, 20–22; Callcott, *Santa Anna*, 74–75; Muñoz, *Santa Anna*, 96–101; Costeloe, *La primera república federal*, 225.

29. Mier y Terán is quoted in Muñoz, *Santa Anna*, 102; Santa Anna in Escobar, "Campaña de Tampico," 85–86.

30. Valadés, *México, Santa Anna y la guerra de Texas*, 92; Mier y Terán is quoted in Bustamante, *Memorias para la historia de la invasión española*, 11; Antonio López de Santa Anna, "Parte militar del general Antonio López de Santa Anna, fechado en el Cuartel General en Pueblo Viejo de Tampico, set. 11 de 1829," in *Noticia Extraordinaria* (Puebla), 23 September 1829; the treaty, "Artículos del convenio hecho en Pueblo Viejo de Tampico el 11 de septiembre entre los comisionados de las fuerzas españolas y mexicanas," is reprinted in full in Zavala, *Obras. El Historiador y el Representante Popular: Ensayo crítico*, 444–46.

31. Prieto, *Memorias de mis tiempos*, 19.

32. *Times*, 7 December 1829. I thank Michael Costeloe for kindly forwarding me this reference. Valadés claims Santa Anna arrived on the 25th (Valadés, *México, Santa Anna y la guerra de Texas*, 93).

33. For details of the numerous celebrations and festivities that were organized in Xalapa in October and November 1829, see Minutes of Town Council Meetings of 1, 21 October, 6, 20 November 1829, AHMX, "Libro de acuerdos del ilustre ayuntamiento constitucional de la villa de Jalapa, para el año del señor de 1829," vol. 40, ff. 57–69. Also see AHAGEV, *Colección de decretos correspondientes al año de 1829*, 85–86; Santa Anna, *Mi historia militar y política*, 14; Rivera Cambas, *Antonio López de Santa Anna*, 23–24; Muñoz, *Santa Anna*, 104–5; Jones, *Santa Anna*, 52; Díaz Díaz, *Caudillos y caciques*, 85–89. For two detailed studies of the nature and impact of the fiestas with which Santa Anna was celebrated, see Fowler, "Fiestas santanistas," and Zárate Toscano, "Héroes y fiestas en el México decimonónico: La insistencia de Santa Anna." Also see Fowler, "Antonio López de Santa Anna: 'El hombre visible por excelencia.'" See as well "Bando: El Prefecto del Distrito a sus habitants," signed by José Julián Gutiérrez, Xalapa, 10 September 1842, AHMX, "Libro de acuerdos del muy ilustre ayuntamiento de la ciudad de Jalapa, año de 1842," vol. 54, f. 557; AHAGEV, *Colección de decretos correspondientes al año de 1830* (Xalapa: Tipografía del Gobierno del Estado, 1904), 104–6. All the decrees contained in this volume may also be found in Blázquez Domínguez and Corzo Ramírez (eds.), *Colección de Leyes y Decretos de Veracruz*, vol. 2; Vázquez Mantecón, *La palabra del poder*, 21, 75; *El Sol*, 26 September and 1 October 1829.

34. González Pedrero, *País de un solo hombre*, 1:535; Fowler, *Tornel and Santa Anna*, 100–1, and "Antonio López de Santa Anna: 'El hombre visible por excelencia'"; Carlos Paris (1808–1860), *Acción militar en Pueblo Viejo, septiembre de 1829* (México City, 1835), cat. 71, Consejo Nacional de Cultura y Arte–Instituto Nacional de Antropología e Historia, Museo Nacional de Historia, Castillo de Chapultepec.

35. For a study that argues Guerrero was his own man, see Ávila, "La presidencia de Vicente Guerrero," in Fowler (ed.), *Presidentes mexicanos*, 1:59–85. According to José Antonio Aguilar Rivera, Guerrero's abuse of these emergency powers was such that Anas-

tasio Bustamante's government had to pass a law on 15 February 1831 that invalidated almost all of the laws Guerrero had passed, abusing the law of 25 August 1829, which granted him "facultades extraordinarias" (Aguilar Rivera, El manto liberal, 149–50).

36. Trueba, Santa Anna, 26; Bustamante and Santa Anna's manifesto of 31 October 1829 is reprinted in Zavala, Obras. El Historiador y el Representante Popular: Ensayo crítico, 599–600; Yáñez, Santa Anna, 118; Andrews, "The Political and Military Career of General Anastasio Bustamante," 128–34.

37. The 1829 Plan of Xalapa is reprinted in Bocanegra, Memorias para la historia de México, 2:55–56.

38. Santa Anna quoted in Yáñez, Santa Anna, 119. Also see Muñoz, Santa Anna, 109; AHSDN, Exp. XI/III/1-116 [1-15], vol. III, f. 555, Antonio Juille y Moreno to Santa Anna, Veracruz, 18 December 1829; and Santa Anna, Manifiesto y contramanifiesto del general de división Don Antonio López de Santa Anna (Mexico City: Imp. de Tomás Uribe y Alcalde, 1829) for his expressed commitment to defend Guerrero.

39. Fowler, Tornel and Santa Anna, 103; Callcott, Santa Anna, 84.

40. Tornel, Manifestación del C. José María Tornel, 41.

41. When Santa Anna donated Guadalupe a house worth 6,000 pesos house on the Calle del Vicario 692, in Veracruz, he did so to show her how much he loved her. See documents in Archivo General de Notarías del Estado de Veracruz, "Protocolo de instrumentos públicos que han de otorgarse en este oficio de Cárdena que es a cargo del escribano nacional don Eduardo Fernández de Castro en este presente año de 1841": Escritura de venta de casa, Veracruz, 26 June 1841, ff. 135–48; and "Donación graciosa," 7 July 1841, ff. 150–53.

42. This anomaly was eventually discovered in March 1831, and Rafael Mangino, then minister of finance, informed the minister of war, General José Antonio Facio, on 21 April, that as from 23 March Santa Anna would cease to get his pay. Mangino did wonder at this point whether Santa Anna should return the pay he had been awarded since January 1830. General Anastasio Bustamante, clearly fearful of provoking Santa Anna unnecessarily into coming out of his retreat, intervened personally in the matter. On 25 April 1831, Bustamante informed Mangino that Santa Anna should continue to receive his pay since he was still employed as general. He was not "inactive," he was simply "absent." See AHSDN, Exp. XI/III/1-116 [1-15], vol. III, ff. 587, 589, Mangino to Minister of War, Mexico City, 21 April 1831, and President [Bustamante] to Minister of Exchequer [Mangino], Mexico City, 25 April 1831.

43. Quoted in Callcott, Santa Anna, 87.

7. The Absentee President

1. See Potash, Mexican Government and Industrial Development in the Early Republic. Also see Tenenbaum, México en la éposa de los agiotistas, 57–62; Costeloe, La primera república federal, 304–5; Costeloe, Bonds and Bondholders, 27–32, 117; Andrews, "The Military and Political Career of General Anastasio Bustamante," 152–54.

2. Santa Anna to Gómez Pedraza, Orizaba, 9 August 1832, inserted in the *poblano* newspaper *Aurora de la libertad*, 24 November 1832; Santa Anna to Bustamante, Manga de Clavo, 15 February 1831, quoted in González Pedrero, *País de un solo hombre*, 2:193–94.

3. See Fowler, *Tornel and Santa Anna*, 117–18, 125.

4. According to Alfonso Trueba, Pedro Landero started the revolt to avoid being processed for embezzling 18,000 pesos that belonged to the Ninth Regiment (Trueba, *Santa Anna*, 28). See *Acta celebrada la noche de dos del corriente por los Sres. Gefes* [sic] *que componen la guarnición de esta plaza*. The Plan of Veracruz is reprinted in Bocanegra, *Memorias para la historia de México*, 2:265–68. Also see AHSDN, Exp. XI/481.3/775, ff. 17-18, *El Censor* (Veracruz), 8 January 1832, which contains the *Acta celebrada por la guarnición de Alvarado*, and ff. 78–81, copies of letters by Ciriaco Vázquez, 2 January 1832, and "Pronunciamiento de la guarnición de Veracruz," Veracruz, 2 January 1832. Quote is taken from Joseph Welsh to Richard Pakenham, Veracruz, 4 January 1832, PRO, FO 50/77, f. 18.

5. Quote from Welsh to Pakenham, Veracruz, 4 January 1832. Also see Fowler, "Joseph Welsh: A British Santanista."

6. Joseph Welsh to John Bidwell, Veracruz, 5 January 1832, PRO, FO 50/77, f. 15. This accusation, which became the main argument employed by the rebels to overthrow Bustamante's administration, was inaccurate. As several studies have shown, Bustamante's administration did not attempt to impose a centralist system. See Vázquez, "Iglesia, ejército y centralismo," 205–34; Fowler, *Mexico in the Age of Proposals*, 56–57; Andrews, "The Military and Political Career of General Anastasio Bustamante." However, Peter Guardino believes that "the regime was never able to leave behind the image it presented in early 1830 as it dissolved state governments and replaced them with its supporters": see Guardino, *Peasants, Politics, and the Formation of Mexico's National State*, 135. For the origins of the 1832 civil war, see Rodríguez O., "The Origins of the 1832 Rebellion," and Vázquez, "Los pronunciamientos de 1832," both in Rodríguez O. (ed.), *Patterns of Contention in Mexican History*.

7. AHSDN, XI/481.3/775: ff. 75–77, Santa Anna to Bustamante, Veracruz, 4 January 1832; ff. 145–46, Santa Anna to José María Calderón, Veracruz, 6 January 1832. AHSDN, XI/481.3/776: ff. 30–31, Santa Anna to Commander General of Guanajuato, Veracruz, 7 January 1832; f. 133, Santa Anna to Miguel Méndez [Commander of Garrison in Tuxpan], Veracruz, 10 January 1832; ff. 147–48, Santa Anna to Commander General of Michoacán [Antonio de Villaurrutia], Veracruz, 7 January 1832. AHSDN, XI/481.3/782, f. 15, Santa Anna to Francisco Palomino [Commander General of Tabasco], Veracruz, 7 January 1832. Santa Anna to Bustamante, Veracruz, 4 January 1832, BLAC, Mariano Riva Palacio Archive, 203; Santa Anna to Lucas Alamán, Veracruz, 1 January 1832, Centro de Estudios de Historia de México– Condumex, Archivo Lucas Alamán (Fondo CCLXXXVII), carpeta-expediente 11-933. I thank Eric Van Young for kindly forwarding me his annotated transcriptions of Santa Anna's correspondence with Lucas Alamán, held in the CEHM-Condumex, carpetas-expedientes: 10-854, 10-856, 11-885, 11-913, 11-920, 11-921, 11-924, 11-930, 11-933, 11-936, 20-1714; [Santa Anna], *El general de división Antonio López de Santa Anna a la guarnición de esta plaza y de Ulúa*.

8. See Fowler, *Tornel and Santa Anna*, 127–28, and *Mexico in the Age of Proposals*, 230–31, and "Valentín Gómez Farías," 47.

9. Samponaro, "La alianza de Santa Anna y los federalistas" 359.

10. Joseph Welsh to John Bidwell, Veracruz, 19 February 1832, PRO, FO 50/77, f. 61.

11. Jones, *Santa Anna*, 53; Callcott, *Santa Anna*, 89; Joseph Welsh to John Bidwell, Veracruz, 27 February 1832, PRO, FO 50/77, ff. 63–64; [Luz Romero], *Noticia estraordinaria sobre las operaciones del general Santa Anna contra el ejército ministerial*, held in "Criminal sobre la responsabilidad del impreso que dentro se expresa," AGN, galería 4, Ramo Civil, Legajo 130 3A (57 Num. 6), 1832.

12. Joseph Welsh to Richard Pakenham, Veracruz, 3 March 1832, PRO, FO 50/77, ff. 77–78.

13. AHSDN, Exp. XI/481.3/913, ff. 3, 8–18: Calderón to Minister of War, Tolome, 3, 5, 4, and 4 March 1832; and Exp. XI/481.3/783, f. 14, Calderón to Minister of War, Tolome, 6 March 1832.

14. AHSDN, Exp. XI/481.3/783, f. 75, Domingo Ramela to Calderón, Veracruz, 6 March 1832.

15. Joseph Welsh to John Bidwell, Veracruz, 18 March 1832, PRO, FO 50/77, ff. 74–75.

16. AHSDN, Exp. XI/481.3/783, ff. 83–85, *El Censor* (Veracruz), 5 March 1832, includes Antonio López de Santa Anna, "El general de división Antonio López de Santa Anna a las tropas de su mando," Veracruz, 4 March 1832.

17. AHSDN, Exp. XI/481.3/783, f. 78, Calderón, "Estado que manifiesta la fuerza y armas de que consta en la fecha," Tolome, 8 March 1832: 2 colonels; 3 lieutenant colonels; 7 first aides; 8 second aides; 3 surgeons; 39 captains; 46 lieutenants; 59 sublieutenants; 2 gunsmiths; 42 first sergeants; 86 second sergeants; 141 buglers and drummers; 0 musicians; 213 corporals; 1,656 soldiers; Valadés, *México, Santa Anna y la guerra de Texas*, 102. See also Callcott, *Santa Anna*, 91; Jones, *Santa Anna*, 54; Díaz Díaz, *Caudillos y caciques*, 117.

18. Sebastián Camacho to Anastasio Bustamante, Xalapa, 6 June 1832, inserted in *Registro Oficial del Gobierno de los Estados Unidos Mexicanos*, 20 June 1832. Much of the correspondence that was generated by the revolt, in June and July 1832, may be found in the *Registro Oficial del Gobierno de los Estados Unidos Mexicanos*, 20 June, 28 and 30 July 1832. I thank Cath Andrews for forwarding her transcriptions of these documents to me.

19. Santa Anna to José María Espinosa, 15 July 1832, AGN, Archivo de Guerra, vol. 484, "Causa de infidencia contra la Sra. Da. Francisca López de Santa Anna y socios," ff. 120–29.

20. Costeloe, *La primera república federal*, 336–38.

21. *El Sol*, 18 July 1832; Valadés, *México, Santa Anna y la guerra de Texas*, 104.

22. Letter inserted in *Aurora de la libertad*, 24 November 1832.

23. AHSDN, Exp. XI/481.3/821, f. 1, Santa Anna to Colonel José Antonio Barragán, cuartel general de Orizaba, 4 August 1832; Valadés, *México, Santa Anna y la guerra de Texas*, 104; AHSDN, Exp. XI/481.3/960, ff. 46–49, Facio to Minister of War, Hacienda de

San Juan, 1 October 1832; quote taken from Antonio López de Santa Anna, "Proclama," San Agustín del Palmar, 1 October 1832, inserted in the *poblano* newspaper *Aurora de la Libertad*, 11 October 1832.

24. AGN, Archivo de Guerra, vol. 484, Exp. s/n, 1832, Comandancia general de México [4747]: "Causa de infidencia contra la Sra. Doña Francisca López de Santa Anna y socios"; AHSDN, Exp. XI/481.3/861, ff. 2–3, Mariano Matamoros to Vice President Bustamante, Mexico City, 6 August 1832, and Declaration by Manuel Vázquez Aldama, Mexico City, 6 August 1832. For Francisca López de Santa Anna's arrest see Villavicencio y Varios Amigos de la Verdad, *Ya no muere fucilada*.

25. Callcott, *Santa Anna*, 93; Gómez Pedraza to Santa Anna, Bedford Springs, 28 September 1832, inserted in *Aurora de la Libertad*, 24 November 1832. Gómez Pedraza disembarked in Veracruz on 5 October (Muñoz, *Santa Anna*, 13).

26. Bocanegra, *Memorias para la historia de México*, 2:316–17; Jones, *Santa Anna*, 54; Valadés, *México, Santa Anna y la guerra de Texas*, 104–5.

27. Andrews, "The Political and Military Career of General Anastasio Bustamante," 196.

28. Richard Pakenham to Viscount Palmerston, Mexico City, 12 February 1833, PRO, FO 50/79, ff. 49–50; the Plan de Zavaleta is included in Bocanegra, *Memorias para la historia de México*, 2:366–69.

29. *El Fénix de la Libertad*, 15 January 1833; "Circular" by Santa Anna, Mexico City, 12 January 1833, included in *Aurora de la Libertad*, 19 January 1833.

30. Vázquez and Hernández Silva (eds.), *Diario histórico de México 1822–1848 de Carlos María de Bustamante*, CD-ROM 2, 23 March 1833.

31. Costeloe, *La primera república federal*, 365; Callcott, *Santa Anna*, 97–98; Jones, *Santa Anna*, 56.

32. Santa Anna to Gómez Farías, Manga de Clavo, 16 March 1833, BLAC, Valentín Gómez Farías Papers, no. 26.

33. *El Telégrafo*, 2 April 1833; Valadés, *México, Santa Anna y la guerra de Texas*, 108; Fowler, "Valentín Gómez Farías," 52–53; Vázquez, "La primera presidencia de Antonio López de Santa Anna," 89–112.

34. Callcott, *Santa Anna*, 98, 106; González Pedrero, *País de un solo hombre*, 2:334; Santa Anna to Gómez Farías, 16 February and 10 April 1833, BLAC, Valentín Gómez Farías Papers, nos. 20, 28; Pakenham to Palmerston, Mexico City, 11 November 1833, PRO, FO 50/80A, ff. 209–11.

35. Santa Anna to Gómez Farías, 13 April 1833, 4 January, and 12 March 1834, BLAC, Valentín Gómez Farías Papers, nos. 29, 231, 267.

36. Fowler, *Mexico in the Age of Proposals*, 244–45; quote taken from Pakenham to Palmerston, Mexico City, 29 June 1833, PRO, FO 50/79, ff. 264–65.

37. Costeloe, *La primera república federal*, 407.

38. Callcott, *Santa Anna*, 105; also see Cantrell, *Stephen F. Austin*, 274–75; and Gómez Farías to Francisco María Lombardo, Mexico City, 13 July 1834, printed in *El Telégrafo*, 6 August 1834. González Pedrero is persuaded that Santa Anna was responsible for the *Ley del Caso* (*País de un solo hombre*, 2:380–81).

39. Mora, *Obras sueltas*, 46–47.

40. Bocanegra, *Memorias para la historia de México*, 2:379, 383–385, 417–418, 421–422, 447.

41. Sordo Cedeño, *El congreso en la primera república centralista*, 25; Costeloe, *La primera república federal*, 383–85.

42. The Plan of Escalada is reprinted in Bocanegra, *Memorias para la historia de México*, 2:485–86; Santa Anna, *Manifestación del presidente a sus conciudadanos* ; Durán, *Carta y plan del señor general don Gabriel Durán*; Santa Anna, "El presidente de la república al ejército mexicano" (Mexico City: 1 June 1833), in *El Telégrafo*, 2 June 1833. This issue also contains copies of the following correspondence: Gabriel Durán to Santa Anna, Tlalpan, 1 June 1833; Santa Anna to Durán, Mexico City, 2 June 1833.

43. The Plan of Arista is reprinted in Bocanegra, *Memorias para la historia de México*, 2:486–91; Valadés, *México, Santa Anna y la guerra de Texas*, 110.

44. Santa Anna, *Mi historia militar y política*, 16; AHSDN, Exp. XI/481.3/968, f. 96, Santa Anna to Gómez Farías, Puebla, 13 June 1833. Santa Anna's account, albeit difficult to believe, is supported by the independent accounts of Juan Pablo Anaya (*La Antorcha*, 13 June 1833), and Gerónimo Cardona, "Relación de lo ocurrido al Escmo. Sr. Presidente de la República desde su salida de la ciudad federal, hasta su entrada en ésta, por el teniente coronel ciudadano Gerónimo" (held in Archivo Histórico del Instituto Nacional de Antropología e Historia, 3era serie, leg. 365, reg. 138, doc. 144 (Mexico, 1833).

45. Valentín Gómez Farías, "El vice-presidente de los Estados Unidos Mexicanos a sus compatriotas," (Mexico City, 7 June 1833), in *El Telégrafo*, 8 June 1833.

46. AHSDN, Exp. XI/481.3/968, ff. 97–98, Mariano Arista to Manuel Gómez Pedraza, Venta de Córdoba, 12 June 1833.

47. Pakenham to Palmerston, Mexico City, 11 June 1833, PRO, FO 50/79, ff. 241–46.

48. It was not just in the public documents, written for general consumption, that Santa Anna made his views on the matter known. He was equally categorical in condemning the revolt in private letters he addressed Arista. See *Cartas dirigidas al Exmo. Sr. General Presidente de la República D. Antonio López de Santa Anna por el general Mariano Arista y sus contestaciones*. Even the first half of Arista, *Reseña histórica de la revolución*, would appear to confirm the view that Santa Anna was not part of the conspiracy.

49. Santa Anna, *Manifiesto del Presidente de los Estados Unidos Mexicanos a sus Conciudadanos*.

50. *El Telégrafo*, 8 November 1833. According to González Pedrero there were four thousand men to begin with. Around two thousand died of cholera soon after they set off (*País de un solo hombre*, 2:383). Quote taken from Santa Anna, "El presidente de los Estados Unidos mexicanos al ejército de su mando" (Cuartel General en Querétaro, 10 August 1833), printed in *El Telégrafo*, 13 August 1833.

51. Santa Anna to Minister of War, Ciudad de Allende, 11 September 1833, printed together with his address "El general de división Antonio López de Santa Anna, presidente de los Estados Unidos Mexicanos, al ejército de su mando," in *El Telégrafo*, 14

September 1833; AHSDN, Exp. XI/481.3/1000, ff. 108–9, Santa Anna to Minister of War, Cuartel General en Valenciana, 6 October 1833. Also see El Telégrafo, 8 November 1833, for a more melodramatic account of the event.

52. AHSDN, Exp. XI/481.3/1000: f. 112, Santa Anna to Fernando Chico, Guanajuato, 5 October 1833; ff. 137–38, Santa Anna to Minister of War, Valenciana, 7 October 1832.

53. Martín Perfecto de Cos is often referred to as Santa Anna's brother-in-law. However, I have not found any evidence to support this claim. The only way Cos could have been Santa Anna's brother-in-law is if he married either his sister Guadalupe or his sister Mariana. Cos was not related to either of Santa Anna's wives and did not marry either of his other sisters, Francisca or Merced.

54. AHSDN, Exp. XI/481.3/1001, ff. 3–6, Santa Anna to José Joaquín de Herrera, Minister of War, Cuartel General de Mellado, 8 October 1833; quote taken from Santa Anna, "El presidente de los Estados Unidos Mexicanos, general en jefe del ejército federal, a los habitantes de Guanajuato," (Guanajuato, 10 October 1833), printed in El Telégrafo, 16 October 1833.

55. AHSDN, Exp. XI/III/1-116 [1-15], vol. III, f. 625, Julián Ferrera to Minister of War, Querétaro, 22 October 1833; Callcott, Santa Anna, 103; Valadés, México, Santa Anna y la guerra de Texas, 113; Santa Anna, Mi historia militar y política, 17; Fowler, Mexico in the Age of Proposals, 194–95.

56. For correspondence between Santa Anna and Bravo see El Fénix de la Libertad, 17 December 1833.

57. Mora, Obras sueltas, 153, 155; letters by Joaquín Huarriz, 30 January 1834, and Anonymous, 5 February 1834, warning Gómez Farías of Tornel's sedition and reactionary conspiracy, BLAC, Valentín Gómez Farías Papers, nos. 267, 271; Sordo Cedeño, El congreso en la primera república centralista, 50–54; Santa Anna to Gómez Farías, Manga de Clavo, 12 March 1834, BLAC, Valentín Gómez Farías Papers, no. 267; Callcott, Santa Anna, 109.

58. Mora, Obras sueltas, 3.

59. Santa Anna's Manifesto is quoted at length in González Pedrero, País de un solo hombre, 2:466, and see 468–71.

60. The Plan of Cuernavaca is reprinted in Bocanegra, Memorias para la historia de México, 2:573–74; also see Fowler, Tornel and Santa Anna, 136–42; Mora, Obras sueltas, 155.

61. Juan Álvarez to Tornel, Texas, 23 March 1834, included in Documentos relativos a la sublevación del general Don Juan Álvarez, 3; Bocanegra, Memorias para la historia de México, 2:547; Fowler, Military Political Identity and Reformism, 21–22; all plans are listed in Fowler, Mexico in the Age of Proposals, 281–82. Reynaldo Sordo Cedeño's research has shown, however, that resistance to the Plan of Cuernavaca was also fierce in a number of states (Sordo Cedeño, El congreso en la primera república centralista, 83–84).

62. Mora, Obras sueltas, 156; quote taken from Santa Anna, Mi historia militar y política, 17.

63. Quoted in Valadés, *México, Santa Anna y la guerra de Texas*, 116.

64. Valadés, *México, Santa Anna y la guerra de Texas*, 115–16.

65. Tenenbaum, *México en la época de los agiotistas*, 64.

66. Sordo Cedeño, *El congreso en la primera república centralista*, 61–106; Callcott, *Santa Anna*, 114.

8. The Warrior President

1. See Costeloe, *The Central Republic*, 46–65.

2. Quote taken from Sordo Cedeño, *El congreso en la primera república centralista*, 157; also see Callcott, *Santa Anna*, 115.

3. Manuel González Cosío and Marcos Esparza to Santa Anna, Zacatecas, 10 May 1835, inserted in *El Crepúsculo*, 16 May 1835.

4. All the details for Santa Anna's military operations in Zacatecas are taken from his dispatch of 24 May 1835 (Cuartel general de Zacatecas), "Detalle de la gloriosa acción del 11 de mayo de 1835 en Zacatecas, y documentos relativos," printed in *Diario del Gobierno*, 31 May 1835; also see Villa-Amor, *Biografía del General Santa-Anna*, 14; Pi-Suñer Llorens and Sánchez Andrés, *Una historia de encuentros y desencuentros*, 99; Amador, *Bosquejo histórico de Zacatecas*, 424–25; Callcott, *Santa Anna*, 115–16; Jones, *Santa Anna*, 62; González Pedrero, *País de un solo hombre*, 2:511.

5. AHSDN, Exp. XI/III/1-116 [1-15], vol. III, f. 661, Miguel Barragán to Tornel, Mexico City, 23 May 1835; Jones, *Santa Anna*, 62; Valadés, *México, Santa Anna y la guerra de Texas*, 120.

6. Bocanegra, *Memorias para la historia de México*, 2:613–14; the pronunciamiento of Orizaba is reprinted on 633.

7. Tornel, *Discurso pronunciado por el Exmo. Sr. general ministro de guerra y marina*, 6–8, 27; Costeloe, "Federalism to Centralism in Mexico," 184; Vázquez, "Los primeros tropiezos," 762.

8. Santa Anna, *Manifiesto que de sus operaciones en la campaña de Tejas*, reprinted in García (ed.), *Documentos inéditos*, 59:150.

9. Santa Anna, *Comunicación del Exmo. Sr. General Benemérito de la Patria*.

10. Cantrell, *Stephen F. Austin*, 6–7.

11. For the origins of the Texan revolution, see the work of Vito Alessio Robles, Julia Kathryn Garrett, William C. Binkley, Margaret Swett Henson, Alwyn Barr, Stephen L. Hardin, Paul D. Lack, Sam W. Haynes, Jaime E. Rodríguez O. and Kathryn Vincent, Gregg Cantrell, Andrés Reséndez, Josefina Zoraida Vázquez, and Richard Bruce Winders. Full details may be found in the bibliography.

12. See Mier y Terán, *Texas by Terán*, 29: "Its population [in 1828] consists of [deleted: "thirty"] 25 thousand savages, eight thousand North Americans with slaves, and four to five thousand Mexicans"; Tornel's quote taken from *Diario del Gobierno*, 3 November 1835; Santoni, *Mexicans at Arms*, 24–25; González Pedrero, *País de un solo hombre*, 2:519; Fowler, *Tornel and Santa Anna*, 101–2; Vázquez and Meyer, *México frente a Estados Unidos*, 42–43. Also see Vázquez, "The Colonization and Loss of Texas," 47–77.

13. Santa Anna, *Manifiesto que de sus operaciones en la campaña de Tejas*, 126; Santa Anna, *Mi historia militar y política*, 18.

14. Jones, *Santa Anna*, 64. Richard Pakenham confirmed this, noting that Santa Anna "rejected [the bribe] with the indignation which it deserved." See Pakenham to Palmerston, Mexico City, 15 December 1835, PRO, FO 50/93, ff. 282–87.

15. Quoted in Callcott, *Santa Anna*, 126. Richard Pakenham also noted Santa Anna's disposition to take on the United States in his correspondence. See Pakenham to Palmerston, Mexico City, 15 December 1835, PRO, FO 50/93, ff. 282–87.

16. Santa Anna, *Manifiesto que de sus operaciones en la campaña de Tejas*, 126.

17. AHSDN, Exp. 481.3/1102, f. 153, Santa Anna to Minister of War, San Luis Potosí, 10 December 1835; Filisola, *Memorias para la historia de la guerra de Tejas*, 2:321.

18. Callcott, *Santa Anna*, 122–23; Valadés, *México, Santa anna y la guerra de Texas*, 150–51; Fowler, "Valentín Gómez Farías," 44.

19. Santa Anna, *Manifiesto que de sus operaciones en la campaña de Tejas*, 127; Callcott, *Santa Anna*, 102, 128; Muñoz, *Santa Anna*, 125–26; González Pedrero, *País de un solo hombre*, 2:532–34; Jones, *Santa Anna*, 66; Trueba, *Santa Anna*, 38; Valadés, *México, Santa anna y la guerra de Texas*, 160–68; Vázquez, *Don Antonio López de Santa Anna*, 24.

20. AHSDN, Exp. XI/481.3/1897, ff. 1–2, Santa Anna to Minister of War, Béjar [San Antonio], 27 February 1836.

21. Santa Anna, *Manifiesto que de sus operaciones en la campaña de Tejas*, 128–29.

22. AHSDN, Exp. XI/481.3/1899, ff. 8–9, Santa Anna to Minister of War, José María Tornel, Béjar [San Antonio], 6 March 1836; Santa Anna, *Manifiesto que de sus operaciones en la campaña de Tejas*, 129; Callcott, *Santa Anna*, 130; Jones, *Santa Anna*, 66. Also see Costeloe, "The Mexican Press of 1836 and the Battle of the Alamo."

23. Villa-Amor, *Biografía del general Santa Anna*, 16.

24. Callcott, *Santa Anna*, 131–32. Valadés refused to believe this bogus wedding ever took place (*México, Santa Anna y la guerra de Texas*, 191).

25. Santa Anna, *Manifiesto que de sus operaciones en la campaña de Tejas*, 129–30.

26. Santa Anna, *Manifiesto que de sus operaciones en la campaña de Tejas*, 136; Valadés, *México, Santa Anna y la guerra de Texas*, 177–79.

27. Santa Anna, *Manifiesto que de sus operaciones en la campaña de Tejas*, 131; the "Tornel Decree" of 30 December 1835 is included as an appendix, 155–56; and see AHSDN, Exp. XI/III/1-116 [1-15], vol. III, ff. 718–19, Santa Anna to Urrea, Béjar, 24 March 1836.

28. AHSDN, Exp. XI/III/1-116 [1-15], Vol. III: ff. 697–99, Santa Anna to Minister of War, Manga de Clavo, 13 May 1837; ff. 713–16, José Urrea's declaration, Mexico City, 28 June 1837; ff. 776–79, Ignacio María de la Barrera's conclusions, Mexico City, 8 January 1838. For the Inquest on Goliad see Vol. III, ff. 695–723, and Vol. IV, ff. 751–779, "Sumaria instruida a solicitud del Exmo. Sr. General D. Antonio López de Santa Anna en depuración de los hechos ocurridos en la acción de guerra que dio el Exmo. Sr. General D. José Urrea, a los disidentes de Tejas, en el Llano del Perdido, el año próximo pasado." See also Valadés, *México, Santa Anna y la guerra de Texas*, 184.

29. AHSDN, Exp. XI/481.3/1146, ff. 5–26, Santa Anna to Minister of War, Manga de Clavo, 11 March 1837.

30. Santa Anna to Minister of War, Manga de Clavo, 11 March 1837; and Valadés, *México, Santa Anna y la guerra de Texas*, 197.

31. Santa Anna to Minister of War, Manga de Clavo, 11 March 1837.

32. According to Oakah Jones, Santa Anna's force numbered 1,150 and exceeded the strength of Houston's army by about three hundred men (*Santa Anna*, 68); Santa Anna to Minister of War, Manga de Clavo, 11 March 1837; Tornel y Mendívil, *Memoria del secretario de estado y del despacho de guerra y marina . . . 1835*, 6.

33. Santa Anna to Minister of War, Manga de Clavo, 11 March 1837.

34. Account written by Corporal Juan Reyes, quoted in González Pedrero, *País de un solo hombre*, 2:627; Santa Anna to Minister of War, Manga de Clavo, 11 March 1837.

35. Despite criticizing Fernández Castrillón for not remaining alert, Santa Anna praised him for the courage he displayed once the attack got under way. Fernández Castrillón died in battle, taking on the enemy with his sword.

36. Santa Anna to Minister of War, Manga de Clavo, 11 March 1837; for details of what Santa Anna was wearing, and an account of what happened to the diamond shirt stud, see Dittman, "Santa Anna's Battle of New Orleans."

37. Santa Anna, *Manifiesto que de sus operaciones en la campaña de Tejas*, 139–40; and Santa Anna to Minister of War, Manga de Clavo, 11 March 1837. He did not mention any encounter with the beautiful and captivating mulatta Emily West Morgan, the mythical "Yellow Rose of Texas," who according to Texan lore seduced Santa Anna near New Washington and cunningly led him into the trap of San Jacinto (González Pedrero, *País de un solo hombre*, 2:633–35).

38. Tornel, *Tejas y los Estados Unidos de América en sus relaciones con la república mexicana*, 1. For a discussion of Tornel's views on the United States see Fowler, *Tornel and Santa Anna*, 115–24, 158–63; Santa Anna, *Manifiesto que de sus operaciones en la campaña de Tejas*, 130.

39. González Pedrero, *País de un solo hombre*, 2:522–23; Valadés, *México, Santa Anna y la guerra de Texas*, 126–27, 154–55, 170, 176.

40. Dispatch included as an appendix in *Manifiesto que de sus operaciones en la campaña de Tejas*, 160; Santa Anna to Minister of War, Cuartel General de Béjar [San Antonio], 8 March 1836, included as appendix in *Manifiesto que de sus operaciones en la campaña de Tejas*, 179.

41. Trueba, *Santa Anna*, 46; Dunkerley, *Americana*, 481–547; Williamson quoted in Callcott, *Santa Anna*, 124 (my emphasis); Bustamante, *Continuación del Cuadro Histórico*, Vol. 8: *El gabinete mexicano*, 2:14.

42. Dittman, "Santa Anna's Battle of New Orleans," 189–90; James A. Sylvester, Open Letter, *Telegraph and Texas Register*, 2 August 1836. The accounts of the Texan eyewitnesses of Santa Anna's capture are remarkably contradictory. At one extreme we are shown a blubbering cowardly rascal desperate to take opium to cope with his ordeal, on the other a mighty warrior and a worthy adversary: the Napoleon of the West. Forbes is quoted in Jones, *Santa Anna*, 70.

43. AHSDN, Exp. XI/III/1-116 [1-15], vol. III: f. 637, José Urrea to Minister of War,

Matamoros, no date, 1836; f. 643, Mariano Garfias to Minister of War, Matamoros, 16 June 1836; Exp. XI/481.3/1146, ff. 5–26, Santa Anna to Minister of War, Manga de Clavo, 11 March 1837.

44. For the 14 May 1836 treaties, see El Paso Public Library, Rusk-Edwards Collection, Document no. 402 and/or AHSDN, Exp. XI/461.8/1146, ff. 47–53. They are also reprinted in García (ed.), *Documentos inéditos*, 59:190–95.

45. AHSDN, XI/481.3/1146, ff. 47–50, copy and translation of original draft of Treaty of Velasco, 14 May 1836. González Pedrero's recent biography of Santa Anna does not make clear that the appendix to chapter XX: "Artículos del convenio y pacto Solemne" (*País de un solo hombre*, 2:672–74) is *not* the signed public treaty of Velasco, but the original draft Santa Anna refused to sign, and which the other listed generals (Filisola, Urrea, Ramírez y Sesma, and Gaona) did not sign either; Santa Anna, *Manifiesto que de sus operaciones en la campaña de Tejas*, 145.

46. See AHSDN, XI/481.3/1146, ff. 41, 43: both letters are from Santa Anna to Filisola, San Jacinto, 22 April 1836.

47. Santa Anna, *Manifiesto que de sus operaciones en la campaña de Tejas*, 143–44.

48. Santa Anna, *Apelación al buen criterio de los nacionales y extranjeros*, 6.

49. AHSDN, XI/481.3/1146, f. 44, Filisola to Santa Anna, San Bernardo, 28 April 1836.

50. Fowler, *Tornel and Santa Anna*, 156; Sordo Cedeño, "El general Tornel y la guerra de Texas"; Santa Anna, *Manifiesto que de sus operaciones en la campaña de Tejas*, 125.

51. Ramón Martínez Caro was released on 13 September 1836 and stole Santa Anna's diamond shirt stud. He went on to publish a highly critical account of Santa Anna's behavior during and immediately after the campaign, "A True Account of the First Texas Campaign and the Events subsequent to the Battle of San Jacinto," in Castañeda (trans. and ed.), *The Mexican Side of the Texan Revolution*. Gabriel Núñez, also present at the time (Jones, *Santa Anna*, 70), was Santa Anna's brother-in-law, according to Dittman, "Santa Anna's Battle of New Orleans," 193.

52. Quoted in Valadés, *México, Santa Anna y la guerra de Texas*, 224 (and Jones, *Santa Anna*, 71).

53. This would be the very same Thomas J. Green who, several years later, would end up captive in Perote following his participation in the disastrous Mier expedition. See chapter 10.

54. AHSDN, Exp. XI/481.3/1146, f. 59, Santa Anna to President David Burnet, on board the *Invincible*, Port of Velasco, 1 June 1836; also see Haynes, *Soldiers of Misfortune*, 28–31; Callcott, *Santa Anna*, 144.

55. AHSDN, Exp. XI/481.3/1146, ff. 61–62, Santa Anna to President David Burnet, Velasco, 9 June 1836.

56. AHSDN, Exp. XI/481.3/1146, ff. 5–26, Santa Anna to Minister of War, Manga de Clavo, 11 March 1837; Jones, *Santa Anna*, 71–72; Santa Anna, *Manifiesto que de sus operaciones en la campaña de Tejas*, 146.

57. Santa Anna to Minister of War, Manga de Clavo, 11 March 1837; González Pedrero, *País de un solo hombre*, 2:661–68; Cantrell, *Stephen F. Austin*, 351–52.

58. AHSDN, Exp. XI/481.3/1146, ff. 63-65, Santa Anna to President Andrew Jackson, 4 July 1836; Santa Anna, *Manifiesto que de sus operaciones en la campaña de Tejas*, 147–49.

59. Andrew Jackson to Santa Anna, Hermitage, 4 September 1836, included as an appendix in *Manifiesto que de sus operaciones en la campaña de Tejas*, 203; Santa Anna to Minister of War, Manga de Clavo, 11 March 1837; Jones, *Santa Anna*, 73.

60. All quotes regarding Andrew Jackson's concern for Texas are taken from Remini, *Andrew Jackson*, 3:352–65. Also see Cole, *The Presidency of Andrew Jackson*, 130–36, and Bassett (ed.), *Correspondence of Andrew Jackson*, vol. 5.

61. Santa Anna to Minister of War, Manga de Clavo, 11 March 1837; Jones, *Santa Anna*, 73–74. Scott's biographer, Timothy D. Johnson, concurs with me that it is highly unlikely that they met; private communication (23 April 2004).

62. Remini, *Andrew Jackson*, 3:364; González Pedrero, *País de un solo hombre*, 2:725; Jones, *Santa Anna*, 74–75; Santa Anna, *Mi historia militar y política*, 20–21.

9. The Landowner President

1. AHSDN, Exp. XI/III/1-116 [1-15], vol. III, ff. 627–28, Antonio de Castro to Minister of War, Veracruz, 20 February 1837.

2. AHSDN, Exp. XI/III/1-116 [1-15], vol. III: f. 666, Order by Tornel, Mexico City, 11 January 1837; f. 667, Circular by Tornel, Mexico City, 23 February 1837. González Pedrero, *País de un solo hombre*, 2:727; Calderón de la Barca, *Life in Mexico*, 25. The quote refers to the reception she and her husband were given two years later. I am taking the liberty of using it here since there is every indication that Santa Anna's return in 1837 also took place before a large and curious crowd.

3. Santa Anna, *Mi historia militar y política*, 21–22.

4. AHSDN, Exp. XI/III/1-116 [1-15], vol. III, f. 678, J. M. Cervantes to Minister of War, Mexico City, 2 April 1837; for correspondence on Santa Anna's salary in the spring of 1837, see ff. 679–94. Santa Anna was eventually paid the salary of *general en cuartel*, as may be seen in f. 693, Santa Anna to Joaquín Lebrija, Manga de Clavo, 31 May 1837 .

5. Fowler, "Las propiedades veracruzanas de Santa Anna," 69.

6. Antonio López de Santa Anna, Dispatch, Veracruz, 27 November 1838, printed in *Diario del Gobierno*, 8 December 1838; AHSDN, Exp. XI/481.3/1287, ff. 22–23, Santa Anna to Manuel Rincón, Manga de Clavo, 22 November 1838; Jones, *Santa Anna*, 77.

7. Bustamante, *Continuación del Cuadro Histórico*, Vol. 8: *El gabinete mexicano*, 1:135.

8. Antonio López de Santa Anna, Dispatch, Veracruz, 5 December 1838, printed in *Diario del Gobierno*, 8 December 1838.

9. *Diario del Gobierno*, 8 December 1838.

10. Vázquez, *Don Antonio López de Santa Anna*, 25; Jones, *Santa Anna*, 78; *Diario del Gobierno*, 8 December 1838.

11. Díaz Díaz, *Caudillos y caciques*, 146.

12. *Diario del Gobierno*, 8 December 1838.

13. *Diario del Gobierno*, 8 December 1838.

14. *Diario del Gobierno*, 8 December 1838.

15. From what may be gathered from his "Hoja de servicios," he also had a finger amputated (see AHSDN, Exp. XI/III/1-116 [1-15], vol. I, ff. 17–19). However, since this is the only mention of an amputated finger, I am inclined to believe that this was not the case. Also see Jones, *Santa Anna*, 79.

16. AHSDN, Exp. XI/481.3/1287, ff. 1–2, Santa Anna to Minister of War, Los Pozitos, 13 December 1838.

17. Santa Anna, *Mi historia militar y política*, 24–25.

18. See AHSDN, Exp. XI/481.3/1287, ff. 44–46, Printed Decree "Sobre premios a la guarnición de Veracruz," Mexico City, 29 January 1839, and Exp. XI/III/1-116 [1-15] vol. IV, f. 782, Printed Decree of Supreme Conservative Power, Mexico City, 11 February 1839.

19. Runciman (ed.), *Weber: Selections in Translation*, 235–36.

20. AHSDN, Exp. XI/III/1-116 [1-15] vol. IV, f. 780, Printed Decree of Supreme Conservative Power, Mexico City, 23 January 1839. According to Andrews, surprising as it may seem, this decision was reached prompted by Anastasio Bustamante ("The Political and Military Career of General Anastasio Bustamante," 241). Also see Sordo Cedeño, *El congreso en la primera república centralista*, 311–12.

21. See Andrews, "The Political and Military Career of General Anastasio Bustamante," 201–76.

22. Callcott, *Santa Anna*, 161; Jones, *Santa Anna*, 79–80; Trueba, *Santa Anna*, 50; Rivera Cambas, *Antonio López de Santa Anna*, 46–48; Sordo Cedeño, *El congreso en la primera república centralista*, 316–28; Fowler, *Tornel and Santa Anna*, 171–73; Andrews, "The Political and Military Career of General Anastasio Bustamante," 245–47; Santa Anna quote is from *Diario del Gobierno*, 31 March 1839; ending quote is taken from Costeloe, *The Central Republic*, 154–55.

23. Tornel's ruthless side may be evidenced in his 1828 Ley de vagos y maleantes and his 1835 "Tornel Decree." See Fowler, *Tornel and Santa Anna*, 78–80, 119, 169, and Winders, *The United States, Mexico, and the Struggle for Texas*, 25. It is also captured in Manuel Payno's classic nineteenth-century novel *Los bandidos de Río Frío* (1891), in which one of the characters laments that crime has been on the increase since Tornel ceased to be at the head of the Federal District: "You only kill a viper if you stamp on its head, not on its tail, as the great Tornel would say" (213 in 1996 edition).

24. Dittman, "Santa Anna's Battle of New Orleans," 192–95; Callcott, *Santa Anna*, 162–63; Jones, *Santa Anna*, 80.

25. Bocanegra, *Memorias para la historia de México*, 2:792.

26. Fowler, "Las propiedades veracruzanas de Santa Anna," 68–76.

27. The figure for the value of cattle is noted in document listing his "Bienes raices" in 1844, held in Margarita O'Reilly Pavón's private collection. I thank her kindly for allowing me to see these documents.

28. For the detailed contracts Santa Anna drew up when renting parts of his haciendas see, as an example, the case of the Venta de Dos Ríos, in ANBUV, "Registro de instrumentos públicos: Año de 1842 [Xalapa]," Xalapa, 8 August 1842, ff. 300–2; 1845

Registro, 20 October 1845, ff. 533–35; 1847 Registro, 23 July 1847, ff. 166–69; 1848 Registro, 1 March 1848, ff. 46–48; 1849 Registro, 2 October 1849, ff. 362–64; 1853 Registro, 3 March 1853, ff. 92–95; 1854 Registro, 2 June 1854, ff. 270–72; 1856 Registro, 7 June 1856, ff. 194–96. Also see Fowler, "Las propiedades veracruzanas de Santa Anna," 76–85. For petition signed by the people of Turbaco on 10 February 1858, see Santa Anna, Mi historia militar y política, 56–58.

29. Archivo General de Notarías del Estado de Veracruz, "Protocolo de instrumentos públicos que han de otorgarse en este oficio de Cárdena que es a cargo del escribano nacional don Eduardo Fernández de Castro en este presente año de 1841": Escritura de venta de casa, Veracruz, 26 June 1841, ff. 135–48; and "Donación graciosa," 7 July 1841, ff. 150–53.

30. Francisca López de Santa Anna first married Lieutenant Colonel José Ventura García Figueroa, of the Fixed Regiment of Toluca. With him she had her first son, José Ventura Figueroa. Both her first husband and her first son died soon afterward, in a matter of two years, and Doña Francisca then married the Lic. José Agustín de Castro. Her second husband also died soon afterward, having fathered Francisco de Paula Castro. In later years, Francisca married Colonel Ricardo Dromundo, who walked out on her in 1837, having already made life very difficult for her in previous years, refusing to give her any money, and spending as much time as possible away from home. Dromundo was involved in the Texan campaign of 1836, and several sources point to the fact that he was horribly corrupt and abused his position, selling army rations to the troops for extortionate prices. I have put together this sequence of events using the following documents: "Bautismos," Exp. 42 640, 3 de octubre de 1791, and "Matrimonios," Exp. 42 664, 6 March 1808, both in Archivo Misceláneo General de la Catedral de Veracruz; ANBUV, "Registro de instrumentos de este oficio público de la villa de Xalapa para el año de 1820," Poder, 30 January 1820, ff. 23–26; Poder, 15 September 1820, ff. 177–78; Francisca López de Santa Anna to Town Hall of Xalapa, 8 August 1820, AHMX, "Libro de acuerdos y demás documentos del año 1820," vol. 29, ff: 246–47; AGN, Ramo Civil, Legajo 118 (59) 1837, "Francisca López de Santa Anna contra Mateo de la Tijera sobre pesos"; and Ramo Civil, Legajo 154 1B (3 num. 9) 1837, "Doña Francisca López de Santa Anna contra su esposo Sr. Coronel D. Ricardo Dromundo."

31. Santa Anna's 1874 will is reproduced in Potash, "Testamentos de Santa Anna," 435; also see Fowler, "Las propiedades veracruzanas de Santa Anna," 86–87; Arrendamiento, Xalapa, 20 October 1845, ANBUV, "Registro de instrumentos públicos: Año de 1845," ff. 533–35 (this is the earliest document I have found in which Francisco de Paula Castro features as the caudillo's legal representative. I have not found the document in which he awarded his son-in-law and nephew powers of attorney); and Giménez, Memorias, 398. Aurelia Castro López de Santa Anna married Emiliano Busto Antillón. They had four children: Adriana, Guadalupe, Aurelia, and Francisco. Adriana Busto Antillón y Castro López de Santa Anna married José Pavón Oviedo (son of the jurist José Ignacio Pavón). Don José and Doña Adriana had two children: José María Pavón, who married a Texan woman, Claudia Harvin, and Berta Pavón, who married

Francisco O'Reilly, descendant of an Irish family who moved to Mexico in the nineteenth century. Berta Pavón and Francisco O'Reilly had four children: Sergio, Adriana, Guadalupe, and Margarita. It is to Doña Margarita that I owe this genealogy. I thank her for forwarding it to me.

32. Santa Anna's 1874 Will, in Potash, "Testamentos de Santa Anna," 431, 435; Fowler, "Las propiedades veracruzanas de Santa Anna," 87. Carolina Maillard López de Santa Anna married Antonio Villalobos. They had only one son, Antonio Villalobos Maillard, who went on to serve as minister of labor under Lázaro Cárdenas (1934–40). His grandson, Hugo Villalobos Velasco, kindly forwarded these details to me.

33. Santa Anna's 1874 Will, in Potash, "Testamentos de Santa Anna," 431.

34. Santa Anna's 1874 Will, 438–39; and Fowler, "Las propiedades veracruzanas de Santa Anna," 78–79, 86–87; Giménez, Memorias, 347; Minutes of the Town Council Meeting of 11 December 1844, AHMX, "Libro de acuerdos del muy ilustre ayuntamiento de la ciudad de Jalapa" (1844), vol. 56, ff. 159–60.

35. AHSDN, Exp. XI/III/1-116 [1-15], vol. V, f. 1193, Santa Anna to President, Manga de Clavo, 30 December 1839; vol. IV, ff. 816–17, Santa Anna to Minister of War, Manga de Clavo, 27 January and 12 February 1840.

36. Jones, Santa Anna, 82–83; Costeloe, "A Pronunciamiento in Nineteenth Century Mexico."

37. Mora is quoted in Costeloe, The Central Republic, 170.

38. Gutiérrez Estrada, Carta dirigida al Exmo. Sr. Presidente de la República. Also see García Cantú (ed.), El pensamiento de la reacción mexicana, 1:209–17; Reyes Heroles, "Las ideas conservadoras en el siglo XIX"; and Palti (ed.), La política del disenso, 61–71. For a discussion of Gutiérrez Estrada's proposal see Fowler, Mexico in the Age of Proposals, 69–71.

39. Tornel, Discurso que pronunció el Escmo. Sr. General D. José María Tornel y Mendívil. For an analysis of Tornel's speech, see Fowler, Tornel and Santa Anna, 174–79.

40. See Costeloe, "The Triangular Revolt in Mexico," 338–43; Costeloe, The Central Republic, 159–72; Andrews, "The Political and Military Career of General Anastasio Bustamante," 258–69; Díaz Díaz, Caudillos y caciques, 156–57; Santa Anna, "Exposición dirigida al Escmo. Señor presidente de la república por el Escmo. Sr. D. Antonio López de Santa Anna," El Cosmopolita, 6 and 13 February 1841; José María Tornel, Manifestación presentada a la cámara de senadores por el general José María Tornel.

41. Jones, Santa Anna, 83.

42. Costeloe, "The Triangular Revolt in Mexico," 343–44.

43. Paredes y Arrillaga's Plan of 8 August 1841 is included in Bustamante, Continuación del Cuadro Histórico, Vol. 8: El gabinete mexicano, 133.

44. El Cosmopolita, 1 September 1841; Bustamante, Continuación del Cuadro Histórico, Vol. 8: El gabinete mexicano, 135–36; Costeloe, The Central Republic, 175.

45. Santa Anna to Minister of War, Perote, 2 September 1841, in Bustamante, Continuación del Cuadro Histórico, Vol. 8: El gabinete mexicano, 143–46.

46. El Cosmopolita, 4 September 1841, and Boletín Oficial, 6 September 1841; Costeloe, The Central Republic, 177.

47. Santa Anna, *Comunicación del Escmo. Sr. General Benemérito de la Patria*.

48. Costeloe, *The Central Republic*, 179–81.

49. Calderón de la Barca, *Life in Mexico*, 431; Vázquez and Hernández Silva (eds.), *Diario histórico de México 1822-1848 de Carlos María de Bustamante*, CD-ROM 2, 8 de octubre de 1841.

10. The Santanista Project

1. Pakenham to Palmerston, Mexico City, 9 October 1841, PRO, FO 50/147, ff. 97–107; see *Plan de Chilpancingo de los Bravos* and *El general en gefe del ejército del sur y departamento de México, a sus habitantes*; for a "Chronology of Major Revolts and Pronunciamientos, 1821–1853," see Fowler, *Mexico in the Age of Proposals*, 277–87.

2. Thompson, *Recollections of Mexico*, 66.

3. Costeloe, *The Central Republic*, 230–33.

4. Costeloe, "Generals versus Politicians: Santa Anna and the 1842 Congressional Elections in Mexico"; Noriega Elío, *El Constituyente de 1842*, 52–76.

5. Santa Anna, *Manifiesto del Exmo. Sr. Benemérito de la Patria y Presidente Constitucional de la República D. Antonio López de Santa Anna* (1844), 11.

6. Quoted in Bustamante, *Apuntes para la historia del gobierno del general don Antonio López de Santa Anna*, 2.

7. Tornel, *Memoria del secretario de estado y del despacho de guerra y marina . . . 1844*, 6. Also see Bocanegra, *Memorias para la historia de México*, 3:15, 17.

8. Tornel, *Memoria . . . 1844*, 8; Santa Anna, *Discurso pronunciado por el Exmo. Sr. Presidente Provisional, General Antonio López de Santa Anna, el 13 de junio de 1843*, is reprinted in Bocanegra, *Memorias para la historia de México*, 3:123–27. Also see Fowler, "El presidencialismo en México," in Fowler (ed.), *Presidentes mexicanos*, 1:16.

9. Santa Anna, *Manifiesto del Exmo. Sr. Benemérito de la Patria*, 9–10.

10. Warren, *Vagrants and Citizens*, 158–65. The 1843 Constitution is reprinted in Tena Ramírez, *Leyes fundamentales de México*, 403–36. For an analysis of the Bases Orgánicas, see Costeloe, *The Central Republic*, 226–27 and Arnold, *Política y justicia*, 125. Regarding the powers that the executive was awarded, the president could, without prior consultation, appoint and sack a whole range of government bureaucrats, impose fines, grant licenses and pensions, direct diplomatic negotiations, declare war, expel pernicious foreigners, etc. See articles 83–92.

11. Santa Anna to Juan Álvarez, Mexico City, 16 April 1842, quoted in Díaz Díaz, *Caudillos y caciques*, 166.

12. Costeloe, *The Central Republic*, 227; Olivera and Crété, *Life in Mexico under Santa Anna*, 219. See appendix to Tanck Estrada, *La educación ilustrada*, 259–60; Fowler, "The Compañía Lancasteriana," 94–104; and Staples, *Recuento de una batalla inconclusa*, 266–72.

13. Santa Anna, *Manifiesto del Exmo. Sr. Benemérito de la Patria*, 5–6; Staples (ed.), *Educar: Panacea del México Independiente*, 111. Staples's edited volume includes Manuel Baranda, *Memoria del secretario de estado y del despacho de justicia e instrucción pública a las cámaras del congreso nacional de la república mexicana, en enero de 1844*, 112–39; quote is taken from 139.

14. Arrom, *Containing the Poor*, 186–87.

15. ANBUV, "Registro de instrumentos públicos: Año de 1844 (Xalapa)," ff. 451–53: "Donación," Xalapa, 2 November 1844. The term *vara* (about one meter) was used for area as well as length.

16. Quote taken from Callcott, *Santa Anna*, 182; figures from Tornel, *Memoria . . . 1844*, 64.

17. Tornel, *Memoria . . . 1844*, 2; Fowler, *Military Political Identity*, 40–7; Loveman and Davies (eds.), *The Politics of Antipolitics*.

18. Vázquez Mantecón, *Santa Anna y la encrucijada del estado*, 25.

19. Callcott, *Santa Anna*, 192, 177.

20. Giménez, *Memorias*, 316; Costeloe, *The Central Republic*, 191; Bermúdez, "Meter orden e imponer impuestos," 205; Potash, *Mexican Government and Industrial Development in the Early Republic*, 135.

21. Dublán and Lozano, *Legislación mexicana*, 4:94–97, 134–44, 147–50; Costeloe, *The Central Republic*, 208–9, 223–25.

22. Tenenbaum, *México en la época de los agiotistas*, 85–86; Santa Anna, *Exposición que el Sr. D. Antonio López de Santa-Anna dirige desde la fortaleza de S. Carlos de Perote*, 6–7; quote taken from Costeloe, *The Central Republic*, 186.

23. *El Aguila Mexicana*, 25 January 1843; and *El Cosmopolita*, 31 May 1843. Also see Costeloe, *The Central Republic*, 216.

24. Callcott, *Santa Anna*, 186, 193.

25. Santa Anna, *Mi historia militar y política*, 25–26; Bustamante, *Apuntes*, 9.

26. Pakenham to Earl of Aberdeen, Mexico City, 29 August 1842, PRO FO 50/154, ff. 306–14.

27. Pakenham to Bocanegra, Mexico City, 6 September 1842, and Bocanegra to Pakenham, Mexico City, 23 September 1842, PRO, FO 50/155, ff. 50–56, 58.

28. Winders, *Crisis in the Southwest*, 51–63. Also see Haynes, *Soldiers of Misfortune*.

29. Quoted in Callcott, *Santa Anna*, 181; also see Winders, *Crisis in the Southwest*, 63; Pakenham to Earl of Aberdeen, Mexico City, 22 March 1843, PRO, FO 50/161, ff. 86–90.

30. Quoted in Callcott, *Santa Anna*, 179–80; also see 189–90.

31. Charles Bankhead to Earl of Aberdeen, Confidential, Mexico City, 29 November 1844, and copy of "Puntos sobre que puede convenir la República Mejicana a las indicaciones de S. M.Británica sobre el reconocimiento de Tejas en nación independiente," PRO, FO 50/177, ff. 76–82, 84–85.

32. Thompson, *Recollections of Mexico*, 53.

33. "Sobre fallecimiento y exequías de la E. S. Da. Inés García de Santa Anna, esposa del E. S. Presidente Constitucional," AGN, Justicia Archivo, vol. 139; see in particular Crescencio Rejón to Minister of Justice, Mexico City, 24 August 1844.

34. Sefchovich, *La suerte de la consorte*, 88–89.

35. ANBUV, "Registro de instrumentos públicos: Año de 1844 (Xalapa)," Poder, 28 September 1844, ff. 332–33.

36. Fowler, "Las propiedades veracruzanas de Santa Anna," 68–76; Jones, *Santa Anna*, 91.

37. Staples, "Las mujeres detrás de la silla presidencial mexicana," 1:164; Archivo General de Notarías de la Ciudad de México: Notario 169 Ramón de la Cueva, Poder General, 21 July 1844, and Notario 426 Francisco de Madariaga, Arras, 25 September 1846; Giménez, *Memorias*, 398–99; Sefchovich, *La suerte de la consorte*, 90, 92; Calderón de la Barca, *Life in Mexico*, 84–85; Fowler, "All the President's Women," 64–66. *Sévignés* are bow-and-drop ornaments and *parures* are pieces in matched sets.

38. Documents concerning the "Programa para el recibimiento de la Sra. Tosta de Santa Anna" and "Sobre el recibimiento de la Sra. Dolores Tosta de Santa Anna," AHMV, Caja 209, vol. 290, ff. 562, 564, show how Dolores accompanied Santa Anna on this occasion, providing a detailed account of the festivities that were organized in her honor on 9 August 1855. See also Santa Anna, *Mi historia militar y política*, 69–70; Sefchovich, *La suerte de la consorte*, 92; quote taken from Giménez, *Memorias*, 398.

39. Valadés, *Mexico, Santa Anna y la guerra de Texas*, 19–20; Galván Rivera, *Colección de las efemérides publicadas en el calendario del más antiguo Galván*, 27; and *Proceso del ex general Antonio López de Santa Anna, acusándole de infidencia de la patria*.

40. Giménez, *Memorias*, 398.

41. Bustamante, *Apuntes*, 250.

42. Vázquez Mantecón, *La palabra del poder*, 144.

43. Callcott, *Santa Anna*, 194.

44. Quoted in Callcott, *Santa Anna*, 194.

45. Fowler, *Tornel and Santa Anna*, 230–32; Bocanegra, *Memorias para la historia de México*, 3:209–10, 309–31.

46. AHSDN, Exp. XI/III/1-116 [1-15], vol. IV, ff. 909–10, Benito Quijano to Minister of War, Veracruz, 10 June 1844; Quijano, *El comandante general*.

47. Costeloe, *The Central Republic*, 237. Also see 238, 242–47.

48. Lynch, *Caudillos in Spanish America*, 344.

49. Callcott, *Santa Anna*, 202.

11. Our Man in Havana

1. Charles Bankhead to Earl of Aberdeen, Mexico City, 12 November 1844, PRO, FO 50/177, ff. 3–7.

2. Santa Anna, *Mi historia militar y política*, 26; also see Costeloe, "Los generales Santa Anna y Paredes y Arrillaga"; Vázquez, *Don Antonio López de Santa Anna*, 29.

3. AHSDN, Exp. XI/III/1-116 [1-15], vol. V, f. 1080, Santa Anna to Minister of War, Querétaro, 5 December 1844; Bankhead to Earl of Aberdeen, Mexico City, 31 December 1844, PRO, FO 50/177, ff. 147–58.

4. Costeloe, *The Central Republic*, 255–56.

5. Santa Anna, *Mi historia militar y política*, 27; Santa Anna to Herrera, Huehuetoca, 25 December 1844, in *Diario del Gobierno*, 13 January 1845.

6. Callcott, *Santa Anna*, 210–11; AHSDN, Exp. XI/481.3/2072, ff. 526–29, José J. Reyes, "Diario de las operaciones que se practicaron en el punto del convento de San Agustín desde el día primero del corriente enero, en que se avistaron las tropas sitiadoras," Puebla, 12 January 1845.

7. *Alcance al Diario del Gobierno Núm. 3.491* (Mexico City: Imp. del Águila, 1845).

8. Villa-Amor, *Biografía del general Santa Anna*, 21.

9. Callcott, *Santa Anna*, 212–14. Callcott was convinced the story was true. While in Xalapa in 1934, he claimed he "had the pleasure of hearing an Indian woman from Xico, herself entirely illiterate, relate the tale as told to her by her grandmother, who witnessed the episode." The local historian of Xico, Amado Manuel Izaguirre, while not denying that the episode occurred, offered me a slightly different interpretation of the event during a phone conversation in the autumn of 1999. According to Izaguirre, Santa Anna had had a particularly notorious affair with a woman from Xico, by the name of Gertrudis, who bore him two illegitimate children. As the caudillo had later abandoned her, it was Gertrudis's father and brothers who enjoyed pretending they were going to cook him, to avenge his cruel treatment of their relative. I was never able to verify Izaguirre's story.

10. AHSDN, Exp. XI/III/1-116 [1-15], vol. IV, ff. 941–46, 957–58, Santa Anna to Minister of War (Pedro García Conde), Xalapa, 16 January 1845; García Conde to Santa Anna, Mexico City, 20 January 1845; and Collection of pertinent documents put together by Ignacio de Mora y Villamil, Veracruz, 18 January 1845, which includes report by Amado Rodríguez, Xico, 15 January 1845.

11. Santa Anna, *Mi historia militar y política*, 27–28. In the same passage Santa Anna claimed that Rincón had served him on his hacienda. This is unlikely. The documents found in the ANBUV do not point to Rincón having been given any powers to administer El Encero during Santa Anna's absences. Such powers were awarded to his son-in-law Francisco de Paula Castro. It is to be presumed that Santa Anna was lying in the same way that he would lie about Benito Juárez having served him in Indian clothes in Oaxaca in 1828. He obviously got a kick out of showing some of his enemies as having been below him in social terms, whether serving him on his haciendas (Rincón) or waiting upon him while he had dinner (Juárez).

12. AHSDN, Exp. XI/III/1-116 [1-15], vol. IV, ff. 986–89, four letters by Santa Anna, Xalapa, 18 January 1845, addressed to Sres. Manning, Mackintosh y Compa., Dionisio J. de Velasco, Ramón Muñoz, and Manuel de Viya y Cosío; vol. V, ff. 1057–60, Santa Anna to Pedro García Conde, Perote, 1 March 1845. Also see *Diario del Gobierno*, 4 March 1845, and *Correspondencia entre el Supremo Gobierno y el general D. Antonio López de Santa Anna*. I thank Michael Costeloe for lending me a microfilm of the latter.

13. AHSDN, Exp. XI/III/1-116 [1-15], vol. IV, f. 967, Santa Anna to Minister of War, Perote, 22 January 1845; vol. V, ff. 1044–45, Santa Anna to Minister of War, Perote, 20 February 1845. According to another letter he addressed to the Minister of War, he had spent ninety thousand pesos on the army, all of which he claimed needed to be refunded by the government; see f. 1194, Santa Anna to Minister of War, Perote, 27 January 1845.

14. AHSDN, Exp. XI/III/1-116 [1-15], vol. V, f. 1024, Ignacio Inclán to Minister of War, Puebla, 23 January 1845; Bankhead to Earl of Aberdeen, Mexico City 29 January 1845, PRO, FO 50/184, ff. 1–7.

15. Bustamante, *Apuntes*, 435; Vázquez, "A manera de introducción," in Vázquez (ed.), *México al tiempo de su guerra*, 13.

16. Callcott, *Santa Anna*, 219; AHSDN, Exp. XI/III/1-116 [1-15], vol. V, ff. 1104–05, Pedro García Conde to Ignacio Inclán, "Muy reservado," Mexico City, 23 May 1845.

17. All the details of Santa Anna's departure may be found in AHSDN, Exp. XI/III/1-116 [1-15], vol. V, ff. 1153, 1160, 1162, 1168: Illegible to Minister of War, Veracruz, 31 May 1845; Santa Anna to Ignacio Inclán, La Banderilla, 29 May 1845; Illegible to Minister of War, Veracruz, 2 June 1845; Mariano Arista to Minister of War, Monterrey, 10 June 1845.

18. Santa Anna, *Mi historia militar y política*, 28; for Leopoldo O'Donnell's politics see, A. Martínez Gallego, *Conservar progresando*.

19. The quotes are from Callcott, *Santa Anna*, 231.

20. Manuel Crescencio Rejón to Gómez Farías, Havana, 13 February 1845, and Rejón to Gómez Farías, Havana, 7 July 1845, BLAC, Valentín Gómez Farías Papers, nos. 1069, 1225.

21. Santoni, *Mexicans at War*, 39–40.

22. Vázquez, "México y la guerra con Estados Unidos," in Vázquez (ed.), *México al tiempo de su guerra*, 33; also see Soto, *La conspiración monárquica en México*.

23. Santa Anna, *Antonio López de Santa Anna a sus conciudadanos*. The manifesto was signed in Havana, 20 May 1846.

24. AGN, galería 4, Ramo Civil (Legajos), Legajo 18 (2A 174) 1 (1846): "Sumaria contra Da. Francisca López de Santa Anna y sus criados Hilario Pérez y Juan López. Acusada la 1a. de haber mandado fijar en las esquinas papeles impresos contra el actual supremo gobierno; y los 2os. por haber fijado. 8 Junio–27 Julio 1846."

25. *La Reforma*, 21 March 1846, quoted in Santoni, *Mexicans at Arms*, 119–20.

26. Callcott, *Santa Anna*, 230.

27. Arrendamiento, Xalapa, 27 April 1844, ANBUV, "Registro de instrumentos públicos: Año de 1844 (Xalapa)," ff. 123–27; Polk, *Polk: The Diary of a President*, 50–53; Ward M. McAfee, "Alexander J. Atocha," in Frazier (ed.), *The United States and Mexico at War*, 32.

28. Accounts of the Mackenzie–Santa Anna interview may be found in Callcott, *Santa Anna*, 231–32, and Vázquez Mantecón, "Santa Anna y su guerra con los angloamericanos," 36–39.

29. Callcott, *Santa Anna*, 239; Bankhead to Earl of Aberdeen, Mexico City, 7 September 1846, and Bankhead to Palmerston, Mexico City, 29 September 1846, PRO, FO 50/199, ff. 31–35, 262–64.

30. *Manchester Guardian*, 16 September 1846.

31. Quoted in Callcott, *Santa Anna*, 236, and Jones, *Santa Anna*, 107, respectively.

32. Callcott, *Santa Anna*, 239; Santa Anna, *Apelación*, 16; quote taken from Santa

Anna to Minister of War, Puebla, 13 May 1847 (Scott's proclamation was published in Xalapa, on 11 May 1847), included in Smith (ed.), *Letters of General Antonio López de Santa Anna Relating to the War*, 426.

12. The Mexican-American War

1. AHSDN, Exp. XI/481.3/2181, f. 4, Santa Anna to General in Chief of the Republican Forces, responsible for the Executive Power, Veracruz, 16 August 1846; *Noticia Estraordinaria: ¡Viva la República Mexicana! ¡Viva el Héroe Inmortal de Tampico y Veracruz!*; AHSDN, Exp. XI/III/1-116 [1-15], vol. V, f. 1170, José María Ortiz Monasterio to Minister of War, Mexico City, 19 August 1846; Santa Anna, *Mi historia militar y política*, 28.

2. Villa-Amor, *Biografía del general Santa Anna*, 22; Santa Anna, *Exposición del general don Antonio López de Santa Anna*.

3. Bankhead to Earl of Aberdeen, Mexico City, 7 September 1846, PRO, FO 50/199, ff. 31–35; AHSDN, Exp. XI/481.3/2308, f. 26, Santa Anna to Minister of War, San Luis Potosí, 28 December 1846; quote taken from anonymous letter to Gómez Farías, 8 September 1846, BLAC, Valentín Gómez Farías Papers, no. 1741.

4. Bankhead to Earl of Aberdeen, Mexico City, 29 September 1846, PRO, FO 50/199, ff. 254–60; John Black to James Buchanan, Mexico City, 27 August 1846, quoted in Hutchinson, "Valentín Gómez Farías," 643.

5. Santa Anna, *Apelación*, 20; Santoni, *Mexicans at Arms*, 141–42.

6. Santoni, *Mexicans at Arms*, 143–46; Callcott, *Santa Anna*, 243; quote taken from Sordo Cedeño, "El congreso y la guerra con Estados Unidos de América," 52.

7. Santa Anna to Minister of War, Tacubaya, 25 September 1846, in Smith (ed.), *Letters of General Antonio López de Santa Anna*, 365.

8. See letters by Santa Anna to Minister of War, San Luis Potosí, 14 October, 16, 19 November, and 17 December 1846, in Smith (ed.), *Letters of General Antonio López de Santa Anna*, 372, 383–84, 385–86, 393–96; Santa Anna, *Apelación*, 22; Santa Anna to Congress, San Luis Potosí, 31 December 1846, AGN, Fondo de Guerra, 1846, sin sección, vol. 326, exp. 1.

9. Santa Anna to Rejón, San Luis Potosí, 2 January 1847, BLAC, Valentín Gómez Farías Papers, no. 2231.

10. AHSDN, Exp. XI/481.3/2308: f. 1, Santa Anna to Minister of War, San Luis Potosí, 13 January 1847; ff. 85, 86, two letters, Santa Anna to Minister of War, dated San Luis Potosí, 18 January 1847. Also Santa Anna to Gómez Farías, San Luis Potosí, 14 January 1847, BLAC, Valentín Gómez Farías Papers, no. 2337.

11. AHSDN, Exp. XI/481.3/2308, f. 37, Santa Anna to Minister of War, San Luis Potosí, 13 January 1847; Santa Anna, *Mi historia militar y política*, 29.

12. Santa Anna, *El general en gefe del ejército de operaciones del norte, a sus subordinados* (no place of publication or publisher). The document is dated San Luis Potosí, 27 January 1847. It can be found in AHSDN, Exp. XI/481.3/2363, f. 6; see also f. 70, Santa Anna to Minister of War, Matehuala, 7 February 1847; Santa Anna to Minister of War, San Luis

Potosí, 26 January 1847, in Smith (ed.), *Letters of General Antonio López de Santa Anna*, 410; Santa Anna, *Mi historia militar y política*, 29.

13. AHSDN, Exp. XI/III/1-116, vol. V, f. 1241, Unsigned and undated "Resumen de las fuerzas que se organizaron en San Luis Potosí, por el E. S. General Don Antonio López de Santa Anna para obrar contra el Ejército Americano mandado por el General Taylor." Also see Santa Anna to Minister of War, Matehuala, 11 February 1847, in Smith (ed.), *Letters of General Antonio López de Santa Anna*, 412.

14. AHSDN, Exp. XI/481.3/2363, ff. 4-5, Santa Anna to Minister of War, San Salvador, 17 February 1847. According to Zachary Taylor's dispatch, his army consisted of 334 officers and 4,425 men; Santa Anna's army rose to 20,000, (see *Parte circunstanciado del general Taylor, sobre la batalla de Buena-Vista o La Angostura*). Santa Anna's loyal aide Manuel María Giménez published this translation of Taylor's dispatch on 31 May 1847 to prove that the caudillo had shown great courage in the battle of Buena Vista–Angostura.

15. Roa Bárcena, *Recuerdos de la invasión norteamericana*, 1:144–93; DePalo, *The Mexican National Army*, 110–15; Alejandro García, *El comandante general del estado a los habitantes de él y tropas que lo guarnecen*, contains Santa Anna, "Parte de Santa Anna de la batalla de la Angostura de 23 de febrero de 1847," Campo de la Angostura sobre Buenavista, 23 February 1847; unsigned, undated "Resumen de las fuerzas" (see note 13); Jeffrey L. Patrick, "Battle of Buena Vista," in Frazier (ed.), *The United States and Mexico at War*, 58–61.

16. Santa Anna, "Parte de Santa Anna de la batalla de la Angostura de 23 de febrero de 1847," in García, *El comandante general del estado a los habitantes de él y tropas que lo guarnecen*.

17. AHSDN, Exp. XI/III/1-116 [1-15], vol. V, f. 1212, unsigned note, San Luis Potosí, 20 March 1847; DePalo, *The Mexican National Army*, 115; Santa Anna, *Mi historia militar y política*, 30–31; Santa Anna to Gómez Farías, Matehuala, 6 March 1847, BLAC, Valentín Gómez Farías Papers, no. 2707.

18. The Plan of 27 February 1847 is reprinted in Jiménez Codinach (ed.), *Planes de la nación mexicana*, 4:377–78; see also Costeloe, "The Mexican Church and the Rebellion of the Polkos."

19. Two letters by Santa Anna to Gómez Farías, San Luis Potosí, 9 March 1847, BLAC, Valentín Gómez Farías Papers, nos. 2717, 2722; Costeloe, "The Mexican Church and the Rebellion of the Polkos," 172.

20. *Los diputados que suscriben, a sus comitentes*.

21. Santa Anna, *Apelación*, 28.

22. Costeloe, "The Mexican Church and the Rebellion of the Polkos," 173.

23. Antonio López de Santa Anna, "A sus subordinados" (14 March 1847), in *El Zacatecano*, 1 April 1847, AHSDN, Exp. XI/481.3/2641, ff. 59–60; quote taken from Antonio López de Santa Anna, "Presidente interino de la república mexicana, a sus compatriotas" (31 March 1847), in *El soldado de la patria*, 7 April 1847, ff. 61–62.

24. Fowler, *Tornel and Santa Anna*, 244; Ramírez, *México durante su guerra con los Estados Unidos*, in García (ed.), *Documentos inéditos*, 59:534–35.

25. Callcott, *Santa Anna*, 257; AHSDN, Exp. XI/481.3/2466, f. 3, Antonio Gaona to Minister of War, Perote, 8 April 1847 (includes copy of Santa Anna to Minister of War, 7 April 1847); Santa Anna to Minister of War, El Encero, 6 April 1847, in Smith (ed.), *Letters of General Antonio López de Santa Anna*, 416.

26. Some historians, taking for granted Roswell S. Ripley's erred view that El Telégrafo and Cerro Gordo were two different hills, have since inspired a number of confusing accounts of the battle. See Roa Bárcena, *Recuerdos de la invasión norteamericana*, 2:39, note 1. Also see 65, and Santa Anna, *Apelación*, 37.

27. I thank Anne Staples, Renán Pérez, Juan Ortiz Escamilla, Juan Arturo Rivera, and Juanito Rivera Mandujano for taking the time to wander around Cerro Gordo with me on 15 September 2003, in an attempt to work out how and where the battle unfolded. See Timothy D. Johnson, *Winfield Scott*, 181.

28. Roa Bárcena, *Recuerdos de la invasión norteamericana*, 2:12; DePalo, *The Mexican National Army*, 121.

29. Roa Bárcena, *Recuerdos de la invasión norteamericana*, 2:15.

30. Santa Anna to Minister of War, Cerro Gordo, 17 April 1847, in Smith (ed.), *Letters of General Antonio López de Santa Anna*, 419; Santa Anna, *Apelación*, 38; Roa Bárcena, *Recuerdos de la invasión norteamericana*, 2:35.

31. DePalo, *The Mexican National Army*, 123–24; Ramírez, *México durante su guerra con los Estados Unidos*, 512.

32. Santa Anna, *Apelación*, 43–44; Santa Anna to Minister of War, Ayotla, 18 May 1847, inserted in *Diario del Gobierno*, 20 May 1847; Callcott, *Santa Anna*, 263.

33. Sordo Cedeño, "El congreso y la guerra con Estados Unidos de América," 84.

34. AHSDN, Exp. XI/III/1-116 [1-15], vol. V, ff. 1225–28, Minutes of a general meeting "en que se ventilase la importantísima cuestión de la guerra," Mexico City, 20 May 1847. The document is a copy of the original, transcribed by Manuel María de Sandoval, Mexico City, 30 March 1849. Present were Generals (*de División*) Nicolás Bravo, Antonio López de Santa Anna, Ignacio Mora, Manuel Rincón, Felipe Codallos, Gabriel Valencia, José María Tornel; Generals (*de Brigada*) Ignacio Inclán, Antonio Gaona, Lino J. Alcorta, Martín Carrera, Benito Quijano, Gregorio G. Palomino, Mariano Salas, Antonio Vireayno, Pedro Ampudia, Domingo Noriega, Julián Trueta, Manuel María Lombardini, and Casimiro Liceaga.

35. Minutes of general meeting, 20 May 1847.

36. Polk, *Polk: The Diary of a President*, 284–85; Callcott, *Santa Anna*, 262–63; Jones, *Santa Anna*, 114–15; Johnson, *Winfield Scott*, 195–96.

37. Santa Anna, *Apelación*, 45.

38. Antonio López de Santa Anna, "El presidente de la república, a los habitantes de la capital y al ejército que la defiende," in Ortiz de Zárate, ¡*Muy importante!*.

39. AHSDN, Exp. XI/481.3/2613, f. 10, "El presidente de la república mexicana a las tropas que vienen enganchadas en el ejército de los Estados Unidos de Norte América," Cuartel general del Peñón, 14 August 1847. Otero quoted and translated in Santoni, *Mexicans at Arms*, 232.

40. DePalo, *The Mexican National Army*, 127.

41. AHSDN, Exp. XI/481.3/2602, Santa Anna to Valencia, San Antonio, 19 August 1847; Santa Anna, *Mi historia militar y política*, 34; also see DePalo, *The Mexican National Army*, 129–31; Vázquez, *La intervención norteamericana 1846–1848*, 97–99.

42. DePalo, *The Mexican National Army*, 132; Adrian G. Trass, "Contreras and Churubusco," in Frazier (ed.), *The United States and Mexico at War*, 113; Johnson, *Winfield Scott*, 201; Santa Anna, *Mi historia militar y política*, 34.

43. Johnson, *Winfield Scott*, 201; DePalo, *The Mexican National Army*, 132 (quote).

44. Santa Anna, *Mi historia militar y política*, 35.

45. Santa Anna, *Mi historia militar y política*, 37.

46. Prieto, *Memorias de mis tiempos*, 270.

47. Santa Anna, *Mi historia militar y política*, 36. Also see Neal Mangum, "Battle of Molino del Rey," in Frazier (ed.), *The United States and Mexico at War*, 268.

48. Santa Anna, *Mi historia militar y política*, 36; DePalo, *The Mexican National Army*, 137–38.

49. Santa Anna, *Mi historia militar y política*, 38.

50. AHSDN, Exp. XI/481.3/2698, f. 12, unsigned "Circular," Guadalupe Hidalgo, 14 September 1847.

51. Roa Bárcena, *Recuerdos de la invasión norteamericana*, 3:140–45; Bustamante quoted in Vázquez, "México y la guerra con Estados Unidos," 17.

52. AHSDN, Exp. XI/III/1-116 [1-15], vol. IV: ff. 921–22, Santa Anna to Minister of War, Nopalucan, 4 October 1847; vol. VI: ff. 1258–68, Santa Anna to Minister of War, Puebla, 23 and 30 September 1847, and Santa Anna to Minister of War, Nopalucan, 5 October 1847.

53. AHSDN, Exp. XI/III/1-116 [1-15], vol. V, ff. 1220–22, Santa Anna to Minister of War, Huamantla, 13 October 1847; vol. VI, ff. 1266–67, Santa Anna to Minister of War, 5 October 1847.

54. Santa Anna, *Mi historia militar y política*, 40–43, 75; AHSDN, Exp. XI/III/1-116 [1-15], vol. IV, ff. 788–89, Santa Anna to Minister of War [?], undated, signature missing. Probably written in December 1847–January 1848. The U.S. troops set fire to part of Santa Anna's house in Manga de Clavo. In the fire, Santa Anna's personal archive burned to ashes. It goes without saying that we would know much more about the caudillo had all the correspondence and documents he kept there survived the Mexican-American War.

55. AHSDN, Exp. XI/III/1-116 [1-15], vol. VI, ff. 1292–93, Santa Anna to Minister of War, Coscatlán, 1 February 1848.

56. Santa Anna, *Mi historia militar y política*, 42–43.

57. Roa Bárcena, *Recuerdos de la invasión norteamericana*, 1:88, note 18; AGN, Archivo de guerra, vol. 954, "Correspondencia relativa a causa contra grales: Andrade y Jáuregui, por haber sido acusados de cobardía en el parte de Juan Álvarez sobre la batalla del Molino del Rey en 8 de septiembre de 1847," and "Documentos relativos a averiguación para establecer responsabilidad del gral. Nicolás Bravo y gral. Andrés Terrés que

pueda resultarles del parte del gral. Santa Anna sobre batalla de Chapultepec, el 13 de septiembre de 1847."

58. For a study that supports Gamboa's verdict see Jorge Veraza Urtuzuástegui's *Perfil del traidor.*

59. Gamboa, *Impugnación al informe del exmo. Sr. general D. Antonio López de Santa Anna,* included in García (ed.), *Documentos inéditos,* vol. 59, 213–76.

60. Bustamante, *El nuevo Bernal Díaz del Castillo o sea Historia de la Invasión de los angloamericanos en México,* 253; González Pedrero, *País de un solo hombre,* 2:346.

61. Vázquez Mantecón in her recent article on "Santa Anna y su guerra con los angloamericanos" surveys the historiographical discussion of Santa Anna's alleged betrayal and argues convincingly that he was not a traitor. Quote taken from Callcott, *Santa Anna,* 243.

62. See Vázquez (ed.), *México al tiempo de su guerra.* Also see Vázquez and Meyer, *México frente a Estados Unidos,* 63.

63. Quoted in Díaz Díaz, *Caudillos y caciques,* 204.

13. The Man Who Would Be King

1. Lecuna and Bierck (eds.), *Selected Writings of Bolívar,* 1:188, 189, 2:624, quotes taken from the following documents: Simón Bolívar, "Address delivered at the inauguration of the second national congress of Venezuela in Angostura," Angostura, 15 February 1819, and Bolívar to Francisco de Paula Santander, Magdalena, 8 July 1826. Longer quote taken from Bolívar to Juan José Flores, Barranquilla, 9 November 1830, in Pérez Vila (ed.), *Simón Bolívar, Doctrina del libertador,* 321–26.

2. See Mier y Terán, "Diary: Nacogdoches to Matamoros," in *Texas by Terán,* 103, 139; also Mora, *Obras sueltas,* 43.

3. *Undécimo calendario de Abraham López,* 23.

4. *El Universal,* 24 November 1848; Tornel, *Breve reseña histórica,* 135.

5. For regional indigenous and agrarian revolts and conflicts for this period, see González Navarro, *Raza y tierra;* Reina, *Las rebeliones campesinas;* Hu-Dehart, *Yaqui Resistance and Survival;* Lapointe, *Los mayas rebeldes de Yucatán;* Gou-Gilbert, *Una resistencia india;* Tutino, *From Insurrection to Revolution;* Katz (ed.), *Revuelta, rebelión y revolución;* Vázquez Mantecón, "Espacio social y crisis política,"; and Costeloe, "Mariano Arizcorreta and Peasant Unrest in the State of Mexico, 1849.". For the years 1848–53, see González Navarro, *Anatomía del poder en México.*

6. For a discussion of Alamán's proposals see Fowler, *Mexico in the Age of Proposals,* 75–84. Quote taken from Lucas Alamán to Santa Anna, 23 March 1853, in García Cantú (ed.), *El pensamiento político de la reacción mexicana,* 314.

7. *La Palanca,* 19 June 1849; Tornel, *Discurso . . . 1850,* 5; *La Palanca,* 3 May 1849.

8. *La Palanca,* 19 June, 5 June, 26 May, 10 May 1849.

9. The complete run of *La Palanca* (1 September 1848–16 November 1850) can be found in the British Library, Colindale [F. Misc. 181]. Also see Suárez y Navarro, *Historia*

de México y del General Antonio López de Santa Anna, 1821 a 1848, vol. 1, and Tornel, Breve reseña histórica.

10. Richard A. Johnson, *The Mexican Revolution of Ayutla*, 8–9; Vázquez Mantecón, *Santa Anna y la encrucijada del estado*, 28–29.

11. Vázquez Mantecón, *Santa Anna y la encrucijada del estado*, 30–31.

12. AHSDN, Exp. XI/III/1-116 [1-15], vol. VI, ff. 1440–47 contain Lombardini's dispositions concerning the conferral of the title of Captain General to Santa Anna, Mexico City, 11–12 April 1853; also see Johnson, *The Mexican Revolution of Ayutla*, 11; and Vázquez Mantecón, *Santa Anna y la encrucijada del estado*, 33.

13. For Santa Anna's stay in Colombia and the suggestion that he fathered several illegitimate children, see Velásquez Correa and Cuevas Fernández, "Antonio López de Santa Anna: Su vida en la Nueva Granada," (I thank David Carbajal López for forwarding me a copy of this article); also see Eduardo Posada, "El dictador Santa Anna en Colombia"; and Sebá Patrón, "Historia y leyenda de López de Santa Anna en Turbaco"; and Santa Anna, *Mi historia militar y política*, 43–44.

14. AHSDN, Exp. XI/III/1-116 [1-15], vol. VI, f. 1303, unsigned letter, Sección Central Mesa 2a., Mexico City, 15 May 1849; Fowler, "Las propiedades veracruzanas de Santa Anna," 80.

15. AHSDN, Exp. XI/III/1-116 [1-15], vol. VI, f. 1439, Manuel María de Sandoval to Director of Artillery, Mexico City, 1 April 1853; Fowler, *Tornel and Santa Anna*, 263; *Marcha patriótica dedicada al Exmo. Sr. Presidente de la República* (I thank Margarita O'Reilly Pavón for allowing me to see this document); Vázquez Mantecón, *Santa Anna y la encrucijada del estado*, 32–33, 39–41.

16. Santa Anna, *Mi historia militar y política*, 45; Percy Doyle to Lord Russell, Mexico City 2 April 1853, PRO, FO 50/259, ff. 149–55; *El Siglo XIX*, 21 April 1853; *Le Trait D'Union*, 23 April 1853.

17. Santa Anna, *Manifiesto del presidente de la república, a la nación* (1855), 6.

18. AGN, Archivo de Guerra, vol. 1280 (1853), "Correspondencia de la Comandancia Militar de México—Actas de adhesión a la determinación tomada por la guarnición de Guadalajara el 27 de noviembre, prorrogando la permanencia del gral. Santa Anna como presidente"; Portilla, *Historia de la revolución de México*, 168–71; Johnson, *The Mexican Revolution of Ayutla*, 63; Vázquez Mantecón, *Santa Anna y la encrucijada del estado*, 54, 56–57; Santa Anna, *Manifiesto del presidente*, 13.

19. Santa Anna, *Manifesto del presidente*, 10, 12; Decree of 1 February 1854, AGN, Archivo de Guerra, vol. 931; Dublán and Lozano (eds.), *Legislación mexicana*, 6:369–73, 39–V95, 400, 508–14, 594, 624–25, 662, 680–85,7:18–21, 47–48; Portilla, *Historia de la revolución*, 9, 88, 109, 143, 188; Johnson, *The Mexican Revolution of Ayutla*, 29–31; and Vázquez Mantecón, *Santa Anna y la encrucijada del estado*, 45, 94, 203, 218–33.

20. AGN, Gobernación, Legajo 116, Exp. 2, 22 April 1853; quote taken from Santa Anna, *Manifiesto del presidente*, 7–8; see also Dublán and Lozano (eds.), *Legislación mexicana*, 6:366–68, 395–99, 455, 525–26, 617–18, 680; Portilla, *Historia de la revolución*, 7–8; Johnson, *The Mexican Revolution of Ayutla*, 16, 18–19.

21. Santa Anna, *Manifiesto del presidente*, 7.

22. Numerous decrees were issued detailing the different uniforms the Mexican army was meant to wear. To note one example, see Decree of 13 January 1854, AGN, Archivo de Guerra, vol. 978, "Decretos de Santa Anna"; quote taken from Doyle to Clarendon, Mexico City, 3 July 1853, PRO, FO 50/260, ff. 51–56; Santa Anna, *Manifiesto del presidente*, 8; according to Johnson, the army reached the figure of 46,000 men (*The Mexican Revolution of Ayutla*, 22); also see Vázquez Mantecón, *Santa Anna y la encrucijada del estado*, 263; Santa Anna, Mi historia militar y política, 50.

23. Prieto, *Memorias de mis tiempos*, 318; Dublán and Lozano (eds.), *Legislación mexicana*, 6:403–5, 416, 427–30, 437, 440–62, 504–5, 524, 595–97, 627–28, 635, 646, 663, 701–7, 727, 734, 746, 798, 812–14,7:4–6, 39–40, 43, 54; also see Johnson, *The Mexican Revolution of Ayutla*, 23–24; and Vázquez Mantecón, *Santa Anna y la encrucijada del estado*, 138–46.

24. Santa Anna, *Manifiesto del presidente*, 14; Johnson, *The Mexican Revolution of Ayutla*, 27; Dublán and Lozano (eds.), *Legislación mexicana*, 6:671–72; Callcott, *Santa Anna*, 284.

25. *El Siglo XIX*, 17 December 1853; Dublán and Lozano (eds.), *Legislación mexicana*, 6:752–60; AGN, Relaciones Exteriores, Bonilla. Indiferente. Leg. 247, Exp. 3, 17 June and 1 July 1853. Also see Decree of 4 January 1854, AGN, Archivo de Guerra, vol. 978, "Decretos de Santa Anna."

26. Fowler, "Fiestas santanistas," 434; Fernández Ledesma, "Santa Anna and the Order of Guadalupe". The current Mexican national anthem is the very same one that was written and composed by Francisco González Bocanegra and Jaime Nunó, originally published in the *Diario Oficial*, on 5 February 1854, and first sung on 15 September 1854.

27. Santa Anna, *Manifiesto del presidente*, 6–7.

28. Santa Anna, *Manifiesto del presidente*, 4–5.

29. See Vázquez Mantecón, *Santa Anna y la encrucijada del estado*, 18, 70–78, 155–57; AGN, Archivo de Guerra, vol. 978, contains numerous Decrees by Santa Anna. Also see vol. 931 and AGN, Justicia Archivo, vol. 165, "Leyes y decretos y órdenes expedidas por la administración dictatorial de Santa Anna."

30. Vázquez Mantecón, *Santa Anna y la encrucijada del estado*, 154, 158–59, 264–65; Decrees of 23 February 1855 and 12 April 1855, AGN, Archivo de Guerra, vol. 978, "Decretos de Santa Anna."

31. Santa Anna, *Manifiesto del presidente*, 11. He offered an even longer list of his achievements in his *Mi historia militar y política*, 47–48; also see Johnson, *The Mexican Revolution of Ayutla*, 25; Dublán and Lozano (eds.), *Legislación mexicana*, 6:393–94, 425–26, 431–34, 438–53, 608–9, 612-615, 621–24, 629, 642–46, 648, 669–70, 707–9, 713–14, 722–24, 726, 811, 817–61; 7:4–5, 17–21, 51–53; *El Siglo XIX*, 23 June 1853; Vázquez Mantecón, *Santa Anna y la encrucijada del estado*, 48, 80.

32. See Johnson, *The Mexican Revolution of Ayutla*, 31–35; Doyle to Earl of Clarendon, Mexico City, 3 May 1853, PRO, FO 50/259, ff. 229–35.

33. Johnson, *The Mexican Revolution of Ayutla*, 32; Vázquez Mantecón, *Santa Anna y la*

encrucijada del estado, 119; Pi-Suñer Llorens and Sánchez Andrés, *Una historia de encuentros y desencuentros,* 108.

34. Percy Doyle to Earl of Clarendon, "Secret," Mexico City, 3 December 1853, PRO, FO50/261, ff. 267–86 (my emphasis).

35. Doyle to Clarendon, Mexico City, 3 July 1853, PRO, FO 50/260, ff. 34–45.

36. Johnson, *The Mexican Revolution of Ayutla,* 33–35; Vázquez Mantecón, *Santa Anna y la encrucijada del estado,* 184–86.

37. Vázquez Mantecón, *Santa Anna y la encrucijada del estado,* 186–87; and Santa Anna to Corona, Mexico City, 2 January 1854, quoted in Johnson, *The Mexican Revolution of Ayutla,* 37.

38. Quotes taken from Santa Anna, *Manifiesto del presidente,* 8–9; also see Santa Anna, *Mi historia militar y política,* 49.

39. Valadés, *México, Santa Anna y la guerra de Texas,* 122.

40. Johnson, *The Mexican Revolution of Ayutla,* 95; Vázquez Mantecón, *Santa Anna y la encrucijada del estado,* 189–96.

41. Marx to Engels, London, 2 December 1854, quoted in Dunkerley, *Americana,* 127.

42. See Bazant, *Antonio Haro y Tamariz,* for an excellent biography of Santa Anna's 1853 minister of finance. Also see Doyle to Clarendon, Mexico City, 3 July 1853, PRO, FO 50/260, ff. 51–56.

43. Vázquez Mantecón, *Santa Anna y la encrucijada del estado,* 25–26.

44. Bazant, *Antonio Haro y Tamariz,* 72.

45. The first Mexican production of Zorrilla's *Don Juan Tenorio* took place in the Teatro de Santa Anna in December 1844. Juan de Mata, Antonio Castro, and María Cañete played the leading roles of Don Juan, Don Luis Mejía, and Doña Inés, respectively. See Reyes de la Maza, *El teatro en México,* 47. For a study of Zorrilla's Mexican stay, see Cardwell, "José Zorrilla y la visión especular de México.".

46. Zorrilla, *Recuerdos del tiempo viejo,* 2:143, 149, 152, 154, 158–59. I thank María Asunción Pérez, at the Casa Museo Zorrilla in Valladolid (Spain), for assisting me during the two days I worked in Zorrilla's library in 1999. Also see Portilla, *Historia de la revolución,* 34–35.

47. Portilla, *Historia de la revolución,* 6, 58.

48. The *Plan de Ayutla* (1 March 1854) and the *Plan de Ayutla, reformado en Acapulco* (11 March 1854) are both reprinted as appendices in Portilla, *Historia de la revolución,* xv–xix, xix–xxvii, respectively; also see Johnson, *The Mexican Revolution of Ayutla,* 43. Final quote taken from Guardino, *Peasants, Politics, and the Formation of Mexico's National State,* 188.

49. Portilla, *Historia de la revolución,* 65–74.

50. Portilla, *Historia de la revolución,* 74–85.

51. Portilla, *Historia de la revolución,* 85–93; Johnson, *The Mexican Revolution of Ayutla,* 47–50.

52. Portilla, *Historia de la revolución,* 187–200.

53. Quote taken from Johnson, *The Mexican Revolution of Ayutla,* 58–59; also see Portilla, *Historia de la revolución,* 215–19.

54. Portilla, *Historia de la revolución*, 220–24, 229–31; Vázquez Mantecón, *Santa Anna y la encrucijada del estado*, 60–61; Johnson, *The Mexican Revolution of Ayutla*, 100; Galván Rivera, *Colección de efemerides publicadas en el calendario del más antiguo Galván*, 27.

55. Minutes of Town Council Meetings of 10 August and 18 September 1855, AHMX, "Libro de acuerdos del ilustre ayuntamiento de la ciudad de Jalapa año de 1855," vol. 67, ff. 110–11, 128–30; "Programa para el recibimiento de la Sra. Tosta de Santa Anna," and "Sobre el recibimiento de la Sra. Dolores Tosta de Santa Anna," Veracruz, August 1855, AHMV, Caja 209, vol. 290, ff. 562, 564; Jones, *Santa Anna*, 131; for the correspondence of the rebels of Ayutla, see García (ed.), *Documentos inéditos*, Vol. 26: *La revolución de Ayutla según el archivo del general Doblado*; *El Siglo XIX*, 17 September 1855.

56. Agustín de Iturbide (1783–1824), Vicente Guerrero (1783–1831), Manuel de Mier y Terán (1789–1832), José María Calderón (1780–1834), Miguel Barragán (1789–1836), Lorenzo de Zavala (1788–1836), José Antonio Mejía (1790–1839), Guadalupe Victoria (1786–1843), José Antonio Rincón (1781–1846), Francisco Sánchez de Tagle (1782–1847), Ciriaco Vázquez (1794–1847), Gabriel Valencia (1799–1848), Carlos María de Bustamante (1774–1848), Mariano Paredes y Arrillaga (1797–1849), José Urrea (1797–1849), Manuel Rincón (1784–1849), Mariano Otero (1817–50), José María Luis Mora (1794–1850), Vicente Filisola (1785–1850), and Manuel Gómez Pedraza (1789–1851).

57. Fowler, "Valentín Gómez Farías," 50; *El Siglo XIX*, 5 and 8 July 1858.

58. See Sierra, *Obras completas XII*, 269–70.

14. The General in His Labyrinth

1. For Juárez, see Hamnett, *Juárez*; for Lerdo, see Pi-Suñer Llorens, *Sebastián Lerdo de Tejada: Canciller-estadista*, and "Sebastián Lerdo de Tejada.".

2. John Forsyth to Lewis Cass, Mexico City, 18 March 1858, quoted in Jones, *Santa Anna*, 134.

3. See Santa Anna, *Mi historia militar y política*, 55–58; and Velásquez Correa and Cuevas Fernández, "Antonio López de Santa Anna," 27.

4. According to Jones, "El Encero passed on to an agricultural society, and Manga de Clavo was purchased by private individuals" (*Santa Anna*, 134). See also Santa Anna to Gutiérrez Estrada, St. Thomas, 15 October 1861, in *Proceso del ex general Antonio López de Santa Anna, acusándole de infidencia a la patria*, with introduction by Ciro B. Ceballos,14. This letter was reproduced in *El Diario del Imperio*, 22 January 1866. The original documents compiled in *Proceso del ex general* (hereafter cited simply as *Proceso*) may be found in AHSDN, Exp. XI/III/1-116 [1-15], vol. VII, ff. 1517–1750.

5. *Manifiesto: Antonio López de Santa Anna, Benemérito de la Patria y general de división de los ejércitos nacionales, a sus compatriotas*, in *Proceso*, 221, 223–24.

6. *Proceso*, 225–27.

7. Santa Anna to Gutiérrez de Estrada, St Thomas, 30 November 1861, in *Proceso*, 9. Also in *El Diario del Imperio*, 20 January 1866.

8. Santa Anna to Maximilian, St Thomas, 22 December 1861, in *Proceso*, 12–13. Also in *El Diario del Imperio*, 22 January 1866.

9. Santa Anna to Gutiérrez de Estrada, St. Thomas, 25 March 1863, in *Proceso*, 17–18. Also in *El Diario del Imperio*, 23 February 1866; Jones, *Santa Anna*, 136.

10. Santa Anna, *Manifiesto: Antonio López de Santa Anna, Benemérito de la Patria y general de división de los ejércitos nacionales, a sus compatriotas* (1864), in *Proceso*, 225.

11. Jones, *Santa Anna*, 136. Also see Corti, *Maximilian and Charlotte of Mexico*, 1, 141. Quote taken from Giménez, *Memorias*, 345.

12. AHSDN, Exp. XI/III/1-116 [1-15], vol. VI, ff. 1497–98, Santa Anna to Minister of War, Veracruz, 27 February 1864; Giménez, *Memorias*, 342; French declaration translated into English and quoted in Jones, *Santa Anna*, 137.

13. General Bazaine to Santa Anna, Mexico City, 7 March 1864, in *Proceso*, 218; Santa Anna to Bazaine, Veracruz, 12 March 1864, in *Proceso*, 218–20.

14. Santa Anna, *Mi historia militar y política*, 59.

15. Santa Anna to Francisco de Mora, St. Thomas, 15 January 1866, BLAC, G-518; Jones, *Santa Anna*, 139–45.

16. *El Diario del Imperio*, 9 June 1866, in *Proceso*, 19–23 (my emphasis). A year before the trial even took place, the *juaristas* were committed to punishing Santa Anna for high treason.

17. Matías Romero to Santa Anna, Washington, 25 May 1866, in *Proceso*, 44–46 (my emphasis).

18. Santa Anna to Matías Romero, Elizabethport, 21 May 1866, in *Proceso*, 40–43; *Manifiesto del general Antonio López de Santa Anna*, Elizabethport, 5 June 1866, reprinted in *El Diario del Imperio*, 10 July 1866, and in *Proceso*, 24–39. Last quote taken from 38.

19. Santa Anna to Matías Romero, Elizabethport, 21 May 1866, in *Proceso*, 43; Santa Anna to Matías Romero, Calle 28 al Oeste, New York, 5 September 1866, in *Proceso*, 51–57; *Manifiesto del general Antonio López de Santa Anna*, Elizabethport, 5 June 1866, in *Proceso*, 26, 27, 29–37.

20. *Manifiesto del general Antonio López de Santa Anna*, Elizabethport, 5 June 1866, in *Proceso*, 29–36.

21. *Manifiesto*, 5 June 1866.

22. Jones, *Santa Anna*, 144.

23. This document was reprinted and translated into Spanish in Rea (ed.), *Antonio López de Santa Ana*. Santa Anna went on to suffer the consequences of Naphegyi's abuse of the powers the general awarded him. The "Post Scriptum" he added at the end of his *Mi historia militar y política*, 80–82, on 12 March 1874, is almost entirely dedicated to the Hungarian's misdeeds.

24. See Dublano and Lozano (eds.), *Legislación mexicana*, 9:367–71. See also Hamnett, "La ejecución del emperador Maximiliano de Habsburgo."

25. Just before Santa Anna left the United States, his local secretary John Adams, who had noticed and questioned his employer about the tropical vegetable he chewed regularly (chicle), persuaded Santa Anna to "leave his supply of chicle behind. The young, enterprising secretary then added sweetening elements to it and began to market the new product, later founding the Adams Chewing Gum Company" (Jones, *Santa Anna*,

145). See also "Declaración de don Antonio López de Santa Anna, 14 September 1867, in *Proceso*, 119–20; General Francisco Zérega to General Ignacio Alatorre, Veracruz, 30 July 1867, in *Proceso*, 74; "Declaración de don Luis G. de Vidal y Rivas" (14 September 1867), and the transcript of the interrogrations of Manuel Sánchez, Ángel Arzamendi, Vicente Sánchez, and Jorge Murcía (15 September 1867), in *Proceso*, 124–28, 131–35.

26. See "Declaración jurada del capitán del vapor "Virginia," de los Estados Unidos del Norte, y de los individuos presentes" (23 August 1867), in *Proceso*, 95–99; "Díalogo entre el comandante F. A. Roe, del vapor de guerra "Tacony," y el general Santa Anna," testified by the interpreter Eduardo Gottliet (23 August 1867), in *Proceso*, 99–102; Jones, *Santa Anna*, 146; Agustín O'Horán's declaration (23 August 1867), in *Proceso*, 89–93.

27. "Antonio López de Santa Anna, general de división de los ejércitos nacionales, benemérito de la patria, a sus conciudadanos" (Aboard the *Virginia* off the shore of Sisal, 30 June 1867), in *Proceso*, 94.

28. General I. R. Alatorre's transcription of Juárez's orders, in *Proceso*, 84.

29. Order of 31 July 1867, and Manuel Santibáñez to Minister of War, Ulúa, 4 and 8 August 1867, in *Proceso*, 76, 80–81; "Diligencia del estado de salud del preso," in *Proceso*, 114–15; Santibáñez to Minister of War, Ulúa, 4 August 1867, in *Proceso*, 80; and Santa Anna to Francisco de Paula Castro, Veracruz, 30 July 1867, letter held in Margarita O'Reilly Pavón's private collection. I thank Doña Margarita for allowing me to have access to this document.

30. "Oficio No. 316," 2 September 1867, in *Proceso*, 86; Vázquez Mantecón, *Santa Anna y la encrucijada del estado*, 297; "Parecer fiscal," in *Proceso*, 163–64

31. "Confesión con cargos del acusado" and "Protesta de Antonio López de Santa Anna," in *Proceso*, 140–46, 150.

32. For jury deliberations, verdict, and assessor's comments, see *Proceso*, 168–80; Juárez's communiqué, sent to Assessor and the Jury, and dated in Mexico City, 24 October 1867, is on 181–82.

33. Santa Anna, *Mi historia militar y política*, 43; Vázquez, "Benito Juárez y la consolidación del estado mexicano," 75; Hamnett, "Benito Juárez," 11; Zayas Enríquez, *Benito Juárez*, 67–68; Tamayo, *Epistolario de Benito Juárez*, 634, 33, 55; Hamnett, *Juárez*, 39, 44; Díaz Díaz, *Caudillos y caciques*, 246; *El Siglo XIX*, 17 September 1855.

34. "Apuntes para mis hijos," in Tamayo, *Epistolario de Benito Juárez*, 31, 35, 41.

35. Juárez to Pedro Santacilia, Chihuahua, 22 June 1866, in Tamayo, *Epistolario de Benito Juárez*, 616.

36. Hamnett, *Juárez*, 191, 195; Hamnett, "La ejecución del emperador Maximiliano de Habsburgo," 227–44; Hamnett, "Mexican Conservatives, Clericals, and Soldiers," 205; Santa Anna, *Mi historia militar y política*, 70.

37. According to Jones, on this occasion (June 1867) Santa Anna "seems to have desired at this time to promote a revolt against Juárez, to establish a conservative republic in Mexico and to replace Juárez with Porfirio Díaz" (Jones, *Santa Anna*, 146). Juárez took for granted that Santa Anna and González Ortega were plotting together to have him replaced as leader of the republican movement. See Juárez to Santaclia, Chihuahua, 24 July 1866, in Tamayo, *Epistolario de Benito Juárez*, 625.

38. Santa Anna, *Mi historia militar y política*, 37.

39. Jones, *Santa Anna*, 147–48; AHSDN, Exp. XI/III/1-116 [1-15], vol. VIII, f. 1796, Matías Romero to Minister of War, Mexico City, 2 October 1869.

40. Potash, "Testamentos de Santa Anna," 435; Jones, *Santa Anna*, 95. Among the documents in Margarita O'Reilly Pavón's private collection are an inventory of Santa Anna's estate following Doña Inés's death in 1844, several "Lista[s] de alhajas" of Santa Anna's, and a later inventory that dates from 22 July 1862.

41. Potash, "Testamentos de Santa Anna," 429.

42. Santa Anna, *Mi historia militar y política*, 75.

43. Santa Anna, *Mi historia militar y política*, 78–80.

44. Jones, *Santa Anna*, 148; AHSDN, Exp. XI/III/1-116 [1-15], vol. VIII, ff. 1804–5: Ramses J. Álvarez to Minister of War, Mexico City, 19 October 1871, and [?] Mejía to [?], Mexico City, 24 October 1871.

45. Antonio López de Santa Anna "Protesta," Nassau, 23 November 1870, included *Mi historia militar y política*, 75–78.

46. Giménez, *Memorias*, 397; Jones, *Santa Anna*, 148–49.

47. AHSDN, Exp. XI/III/1-116 [1-15], vol. VIII, f. 1806, Santa Anna to the President of the Republic, Mexico City, 24 June 1874; ff. 1808–9, J. J. Álvarez to Minister [of War?], 1 July 1874; vol. VI, f. 1428, Illegible to Minister of War, Mexico City, 13 May 1859; and see Jones, *Santa Anna*, 149.

48. Obituary quoted and translated in Jones, *Santa Anna*, 151, and see 149–51, and Giménez, *Memorias*, 381–86.

15. Conclusion

1. Giménez, *Memorias*, 398; *Diccionario Porrúa*, 268; Jones, *Santa Anna*, 150.

2. It is worth noting that there were no caudillos as such either in Cuba or Puerto Rico, since the elite in both of these islands chose to remain affiliated to Spain at the time, fearful of unleashing a slave revolt like the Haitian Revolution of 1791. Without the rupture and turmoil of revolution and independence, the need for caudillos was postponed. In the case of Brazil, *caudillismo* surfaced following the demise of Dom Pedro II's rule toward the end of the nineteenth century, with the emergence of the *coroneis*.

3. Fowler, *Mexico in the Age of Proposals*, and *Latin America 1800–2000*, 33–40.

4. Lynch, *Caudillos in Spanish America*; Guerra, *Modernidad e independencias*, 150–62. For caudillos also see Hamill (ed.), *Caudillos: Dictators in Spanish America*; Cunninghame Graham, *José Antonio Páez*; Bushnell, *The Santander Regime in Gran Colombia*; Chaves, *El supremo dictador*; Lynch, *Argentine Dictator: Juan Manuel de Rosas*; Woodward, *Rafael Carrera*.

5. Santa Anna, *Manifiesto del General de Division don Antonio López de Santa Anna* (1858), quoted in Jones, *Santa Anna*, 134.

6. Holmes, *Wellington: The Iron Duke*, 144, 257, 272.

7. Ellis, *Napoleon*, 54.

8. See Veraza Urtuzuástegui, *Perfil del traidor*, 16, where he compares Santa Anna to Carlos Salinas de Gortari and Ernesto Zedillo.

Bibliography

Libraries, Archives, and Collections
Britain

British Library, London
Public Record Office, Foreign Office Papers, London

Mexico

Archivo Eclesiástico de la Parroquia del Sagrario, Iglesia del Sagrado Corazón, Xalapa, Veracruz (ANBUV)
Archivo General de la Nación, Mexico City
Archivo General de Notarías de la Ciudad de México, Mexico City
Archivo General de Notarías del Estado de Veracruz, Xalapa, Veracruz
Archivo Histórico del Archivo General del Estado de Veracruz, Xalapa, Veracruz (AHA-GEV)
Archivo Histórico del Estado de San Luis Potosí, San Luis Potosí
Archivo Histórico del Ex. Ayuntamiento de México, Mexico City
Archivo Histórico del Instituto Nacional de Antropología e Historia, Mexico City
Archivo Histórico Municipal de Veracruz, Veracruz
Archivo Histórico Municipal de Xalapa, Xalapa, Veracruz (AHMX)
Archivo Histórico de la Secretaría de la Defensa de la Nación, Mexico City (AHSDN)
Archivo Misceláneo General de la Catedral de Veracruz, Veracruz
Archivo de Notarías de la Biblioteca de la Universidad Veracruzana, Xalapa, Veracruz
Biblioteca Nacional, Colección Lafragua, Mexico City
Biblioteca Nacional, Hemeroteca, Mexico City
Centro de Estudios de Historia de México Condumex, Mexico City

Spain

Casa Museo Zorrilla, Valladolid

United States

El Paso Public Library, Rusk-Edwards Collection, El Paso
Nettie Lee Benson Latin American Collection (BLAC), University of Texas at Austin, Austin
Antonio López de Santa Anna Collection (BLAC)
Hernández y Dávalos Papers (BLAC)
Latin American Manuscripts (BLAC)
Mariano Riva Palacio Archive (BLAC)
Valentín Gómez Farías Papers (BLAC)
W. B. Stephens Collection (BLAC)

Books, Pamphlets, and Articles

Acta celebrada la noche de dos del corriente por los Sres. Gefes [sic] que componen la guarnición de esta plaza. Veracruz: Imp. de Antonio María Valdés, 1832.

Aguilar Rivera, José Antonio. El manto liberal: Los poderes de emergencia en México 1821–1876. Mexico City: UNAM, 2001.

Aguirre Beltrán, Gonzalo. La población negra de México. Vol. I: (1519–1810). Mexico City: Editorial Fuente Cultural, 1946.

Alamán, Lucas, Historia de Méjico. Vol. 5. Mexico City: Libros del Bachiller Sansón Carrasco, 1986.

———. Historia de México, 4 vols. Mexico City: Fondo de Cultura Económica, 1985.

Alatriste de la Fuente, Miguel. Un liberal de la Reforma: Ensayo biográfico del General Miguel C. de Alatriste, 1820–1862. Mexico City: Secretaría del Patrimonio Nacional, 1962.

Alberdi, Juan Bautista. Bases y puntos de partida para la organización política de la República Argentina. Buenos Aires: Imp. Argentina, 1852.

Alberro, Solange, Alicia Hernández Chávez, and Elías Trabulse (eds.). La revolución francesa en México. Mexico City: El Colegio de México, 1992.

Alessio Robles, Vito. Coahuila y Texas en la época colonial. Mexico City: Editorial Cultura, 1938.

Alessio Robles, Vito (ed.). Archivo Histórico Militar Mexicano: La correspondencia de Agustín de Iturbide después de la proclamación del Plan de Iguala. 2 vols. Mexico City: Taller Autográfico, 1945.

Altamirano, Ignacio M. Historia y política de México (1821–1882). Mexico City: Empresas Editoriales, 1947.

Amador, Elías. Bosquejo histórico de Zacatecas. Zacatecas: PRI–Comité Directivo, 1982.

Amaya, Juan Gualberto. Santa Anna no fue un traidor: "Federalismo" y "Centralismo," depuraciones y refutaciones históricas, 1831 a 1855. Mexico City: Editora Impresora Cicerón, 1952.

Ancona, Eligio. Historia de Yucatán: Desde la época más remota hasta nuestros días. Vol. 3. Mérida: Club del Libro, 1951.

Andrews, Catherine. "Indecisión y pragmatismo en la presidencia de Anastasio Bustamante (1837–1841): El ministerio de tres días, diciembre de 1838." In Will Fowler (ed.), *Presidentes mexicanos*, vol. 1. Mexico City: INEHRM, 2004. 115–35.

———. "The Political and Military Career of General Anastasio Bustamante (1780–1853)." Ph.D. diss., University of St. Andrews, 2001.

Anna, Timothy E. "Demystifying Early Nineteenth-Century Mexico." *Mexican Studies/Estudios Mexicanos* 9, no. 1 (Winter 1993): 119–37.

———. *El imperio de Iturbide*. Mexico City: Alianza Editorial, 1991.

———. *Forging Mexico 1821–1835*. Lincoln: University of Nebraska Press, 1998.

———. "Guadalupe Victoria." In Will Fowler (ed.), *Presidentes mexicanos*, vol. 1. Mexico City: INEHRM, 2004. 27–55.

———. *The Mexican Empire of Iturbide*. Lincoln: University of Nebraska Press, 1990.

Annino, Antonio (ed.). *Historia de las elecciones en Iberoamérica, siglo XIX*. Mexico City: Fondo de Cultura Económica, 1995.

Aquino Sánchez, Faustino A. *Intervención francesa 1838–1839: La diplomacia mexicana y el imperialismo del libre comercio*. Mexico City: INAH, 1997.

Archer, Christon I. (ed.). *The Army in Bourbon Mexico, 1760–1810*. Albuquerque: University of New Mexico Press, 1977.

———. "Discord, Disjunction, and Reveries of Past and Future Glories: Mexico's First Decades of Independence, 1810–1853." *Mexican Studies/Estudios Mexicanos* 16, no. 1 (Winter 2000): 189–210.

———. "Politicization of the Army of New Spain during the War of Independence, 1810–1821." In Jaime E. Rodríguez O. (ed.), *The Origins of Mexican National Politics, 1808–1847*. Wilmington DE: Scholarly Resources, 1997. 11–38.

———. (ed.). *The Wars of Independence in Spanish America*. Wilmington DE: Scholarly Resources, 2000.

———. "The Young Antonio López de Santa Anna: Veracruz Counterinsurgent and Incipient Caudillo." In Judith Ewell and William H. Beezley (eds.), *The Human Tradition in Latin America: The Nineteenth Century*. Wilmington DE: Scholarly Resources, 1992. 3–16.

Arista, Mariano. *Reseña histórica de la revolución que desde 6 de junio hasta 8 de octubre tuvo lugar en la República a favor del sistema central*. Mexico City: Imp. de Mariano Arévalo, 1837.

Arnold, Linda. *Bureaucracy and Bureaucrats in Mexico City, 1742–1835*. Arizona: University of Arizona Press, 1988.

———. *Burocracia y burócratas en México, 1742–1835*. Mexico City: Grijalbo, 1991.

———. *Política y justicia: La suprema corte mexicana (1824–1855)*. Mexico City: UNAM, 1996.

Arrom, Silvia Marina. *Containing the Poor: The Mexico City Poor House 1774–1871*. Durham NC: Duke University Press, 2000.

———. *Las mujeres de la ciudad de México 1790–1857*. Mexico City: Siglo XXI Editores, 1988.

———. "Popular Politics in Mexico City: The Parián Riot, 1828," *Hispanic American Historical Review* 68, no. 2 (1988): 245–68.

Arroyo Cabrera, Miguel. "¿Don Antonio López de Santa Anna, nació en Veracruz?," *El Universal*, 3 January 1933.

Ávila, Alfredo. *En nombre de la nación: La formación del gobierno representativo en México (1808–1824)*. Mexico City: Taurus, 2002.

———. "La presidencia de Vicente Guerrero." In Will Fowler (ed.), *Presidentes mexicanos*, vol. 1. Mexico City: INEHRM, 2004. 59–85.

———. *Para la libertad: Los republicanos en tiempos del imperio 1821–1823*. Mexico City: UNAM, 2004.

Aviraneta e Ibargoyen, Eugenio de. *Mis memorias íntimas o apuntes para la Historia de los últimos sucesos ocurridos en la emancipación de la Nueva España, 1825–1829*. Mexico City: Moderna Librería Religiosa de José L. Vallejo, 1906.

Barr, Alwyn. *Texans in Revolt: The Battle for San Antonio, 1835*. Austin: University of Texas Press, 1990.

Bassett, John Spencer (ed.). *Correspondence of Andrew Jackson*, vol. 5 (1833–1838). Washington DC: Carnegie Institution of Washington, 1931.

Bazant, Jan. *Alienation of Church Wealth in Mexico: Social and Economic Aspects of the Liberal Revolution 1856–1875*. Ed. and trans. Michael P. Costeloe. Cambridge: Cambridge University Press, 1971.

———. *Antonio Haro y Tamariz y sus aventuras políticas 1811–1869*. Mexico City: El Colegio de México, 1985.

———. *Cinco haciendas mexicanas: Tres siglos de vida rural en San Luis Potosí (1600–1910)*. Mexico City: El Colegio de México, 1980.

———. "From Independence to the Liberal Republic, 1821–1867." In Leslie Bethell (ed.), *Mexico Since Independence*. Cambridge: Cambridge University Press, 1992. 1–48.

Benson, Nettie Lee. *La diputación provincial y el federalismo mexicano*. Mexico City: El Colegio de México, 1994.

Bermúdez, María Teresa. "Meter orden e imponer impuestos, la política de Ignacio Trigueros Olea." In Leonor Ludlow (ed.), *Los secretarios de hacienda y sus proyectos (1821–1933)*. Tomo 1. Mexico City: UNAM, 2002. 197–228.

Binkley, William C. *The Texas Revolution*. Baton Rouge: Louisiana State University Press, 1952.

Blanco Moheno, Roberto, *Iturbide y Santa Anna: Los años terribles de la infancia nacional*. Mexico City: Editorial Diana, 1991.

Blázquez Domínguez, Carmen (ed.). *Veracruz: Textos de su historia*. 2 vols. Mexico City: Instituto Mora, 1988.

———. *Políticos y comerciantes en Veracruz y Xalapa 1827–1829*. Xalapa: Gobierno del Estado de Veracruz, 1992.

———. *Veracruz: Una historia compartida*. Mexico City: Instituto Mora, 1988.

Blázquez Domínguez, Carmen, and Ricardo Corzo Ramírez (eds.). *Colección de Leyes y Decretos de Veracruz, 1824–1919*. 10 vols. Xalapa: Universidad Veracruzana, 1997.

Bocanegra, José María. *Memorias para la historia de México independiente, 1822–1846*. 3 vols. Mexico City: Fondo de Cultura Económica, 1987.

Booker, Jackie R. *Veracruz Merchants, 1770–1829: A Mercantile Elite in Late Bourbon and Early Independent Mexico*. Boulder, CO: Westview Press, 1993.

Brading, David. A. *Church and State in Bourbon Mexico: The Diocese of Michoacán 1749–1810*. Cambridge: Cambridge University Press, 1994.

———. *The First America: The Spanish Monarchy, Creole Patriots, and the Liberal State 1492–1867*. Cambridge: Cambridge University Press, 1991.

———. "Mexican Intellectuals and Political Legitimacy." In Roderic A. Camp, Charles A. Hale, and Josefina Zoraida Vázquez (eds.), *Los intelectuales y el poder en México*. Mexico City: El Colegio de México–UCLA Latin American Center Publications, 1991. 833–41.

———. *Mexican Phoenix, Our Lady of Guadalupe: Image and Tradition across Five Centuries*. Cambridge: Cambridge University Press, 2001.

———. *Miners and Merchants in Bourbon Mexico 1763–1810*. Cambridge: Cambridge University Press, 1971.

———. *The Origins of Mexican Nationalism*. Cambridge: Centre of Latin American Studies, 1985.

———. *Prophecy and Myth in Mexican History*. Cambridge: CLAS, 1984.

Briseño Senosiain, Lillian, Laura Solares Robles, and Laura Suárez de la Torre. *Guadalupe Victoria Primer presidente de México*. Mexico City: Instituto Mora/SEP, 1986.

———. *Valentín Gómez Farías y su lucha por el federalismo 1822–1858*. Mexico City: Instituto Mora, 1991.

Bulnes, Francisco. *Las grandes mentiras de nuestra historia*. Mexico City: Editorial Nacional, 1951.

Burkholder, Mark A., and D. S. Chandler. *From Impotence to Authority: The Spanish Crown and the American Audiencias, 1687–1808*. Columbia: University of Missouri Press, 1977.

Bushnell, David. *The Santander Regime in Gran Colombia*. Westport CT: Greenwood Press, 1970.

Bustamante, Carlos María de. *Apuntes para la historia del gobierno del general don Antonio López de Santa Anna*. Mexico City: Fondo de Cultura Económica, 1986.

———. *Continuación del Cuadro Histórico*. Vol. 8: El Gabinete Mexicano durante el segundo periodo de la administración del Exmo. Sr. Presidente D. Anastasio Bustamante hasta la entrega de mando al Exmo. Señor Presidente interino D. Antonio López de Santa Anna. 2 vols. Mexico City: Fondo de Cultura Económica, 1985.

———. *Cuadro histórico de la revolución mexicana*. 8 vols. Mexico City: Fondo de Cultura Económica, 1985.

——. *Diario histórico de México.* 3 vols. Mexico City: SEP/INAH, 1980.

——. *El nuevo Bernal Díaz del Castillo o sea Historia de la Invasión de los anglo-americanos en México.* Mexico City: SEP, 1949.

——. *Memorias para la historia de la invasión española.* Mexico City: Imp. de Alejandro Valdés, 1831.

Calderón de la Barca, Madame. *Life in Mexico.* London: Century, 1987.

Calderón, Fernando I. *Tres campañas nacionales y una crítica falaz.* Vol. 1. Mexico City: Tipográfica Económica, 1906.

Callcott, Wilfrid Hardy. *Santa Anna: The Story of an Enigma Who Once Was Mexico.* Hamden CT: Archon Books, 1964.

Cantrell, Gregg. *Stephen F. Austin: Empresario of Texas.* New Haven: Yale University Press, 1999.

Cardwell, Richard A. "José Zorrilla y la visión especular de México: Recuperación del tiempo primero." *Explicación de textos literarios* 22, no. 2 (1993–94): 29–42.

Carlyle, Thomas. *Heroes, Hero-Worship and the Heroic in History.* London: Chapman and Hall, 1897.

Carmagnani, Marcello. *Estado y mercado: La economía pública del liberalismo mexicano, 1850–1911.* Mexico City: El Colegio de México, 1994.

Carrera Stampa, Manuel. "Las ferias novohispanas." *Historia Mexicana* 2, no. 3 (1953): 319–42.

Cartas de los señores generales D. Agustín de Iturbide y D. Vicente Guerrero. Mexico City: Imp. Imperial, 1821.

Cartas dirigidas al Exmo. Sr. General Presidente de la República D. Antonio López de Santa Anna por el general Mariano Arista y sus contestaciones. Mexico City: Imp. del Águila, 1833.

Castañeda, Carlos E. (trans. and ed.). *The Mexican Side of the Texan Revolution (1836), by the Chief Mexican Participants.* Dallas: P. L. Turner Company, 1928.

Castañeda, Jorge. *Compañero: The Life and Death of Che Guevara.* London: Bloomsbury, 1997.

Chartrand, René, and Bill Younghusband. *Santa Anna's Mexican Army 1821–48.* Oxford: Osprey Publishing, 2004.

Chaves, Julio César. *El supremo dictador.* Madrid: Atlas, 1964.

Chávez Orozco, Luis, and Enrique Florescano. *Agricultura e industria textil de Veracruz: Siglo XIX.* Xalapa: Universidad Veracruzana, 1965.

——. "La herencia colonial." In Carmen Blázquez Domínguez (ed.), *Veracruz: Textos de su historia.* Mexico City: Instituto Mora, 1988. 48–50.

——. *Un esfuerzo de México por la independencia de Cuba.* Mexico City: Secretaría de Relaciones Exteriores, 1930.

Chowning, Margaret. "Elite Families and Popular Politics in Early Nineteenth-Century Michoacán: The Strange Case of Juan José Codallos and the Censored Genealogy." *Americas* 55, no. 1 (1998): 35–61.

——. *Wealth and Power in Provincial Mexico: Michoacán from the Late Colony to the Revolution.* Stanford: Stanford University Press, 1999.

Churchill, Winston S. *My Early Life, 1874–1908*. Glasgow: Fontana, 1985.

Chust, Manuel (ed.). *Revoluciones y revolucionarios en el mundo hispano*. Castellón: Universitat Jaume I, 2000.

———. *La cuestión nacional americana en las Cortes de Cádiz*. Alzira (Valencia) and Mexico City: UNED-IIH/UNAM, 1995.

Cogner, John Janeway, and Anne C. Petersen. *Adolescence and Youth: Psychological Development in a Changing World*. 3rd ed. New York: Harper & Row, 1984.

Cole, David A. "The Early Career of Antonio López de Santa Anna." Ph.D. diss., Christ Church, University of Oxford, 1977.

Cole, David B. *The Presidency of Andrew Jackson*. Kansas: University Press of Kansas, 1993.

Connaughton, Brian F., and Andrés Lira González (eds.). *Las fuentes eclesiásticas para la historia social de México*. Mexico City: UAM–Instituto Mora, 1996.

———. *Ideología y sociedad en Guadalajara (1788–1853)*. Mexico City: Conacyt, 1992.

Correspondencia entre el Supremo Gobierno y el general D. Antonio López de Santa Anna. Mexico City: Imp. de Vicente García Torres, 1845.

Corro, José Justo. *El presidente interino de la república mexicana: A sus conciudadanos*. Puebla: Imp. Del Gobierno, 19 May 1836.

Corti, Count Egon Caesar. *Maximilian and Charlotte of Mexico*. Trans. Catherine A. Phillips. New Cork: Alfred A. Knopf, 1928.

Costeloe, Michael P. *Bonds and Bondholders: British Investors and Mexico's Foreign Debt, 1824–1888*. Westport CT: Praeger Publishers, 2003.

———. *The Central Republic, 1835–1846: Hombres de Bien in the Age of Santa Anna*. Cambridge: Cambridge University Press, 1993.

———. *Church and State in Independent Mexico: A Study of the Patronage Debate 1821–1857*. London: Royal Historical Society, 1978.

———. *Church Wealth in Mexico: A study of the "Juzgado de Capellanías" in the Archbishopric of Mexico 1800–1856*. Cambridge: Cambridge University Press, 1967.

———. "Federalism to Centralism in Mexico: The Conservative Case for Change, 1834–1835." *Americas* 45 (1988): 173–85.

———. "Generals versus Politicians: Santa Anna and the 1842 Congressional Elections in Mexico." *Bulletin of Latin American Research* 8, no .2 (1989): 257–74.

———. *La primera república federal de México (1824–1835): Un estudio de los partidos políticos en el México independiente*. Mexico City: Fondo de Cultura Económica, 1975.

———. "Los generales Santa Anna y Paredes y Arrillaga en México, 1841–1843: Rivales por el poder o una copa más." *Historia Mexicana* 39, no. 2 (1989): 417–40.

———. "Mariano Arista y la élite de la ciudad de México, 1851–1852." In Will Fowler and Humberto Morales Moreno (eds.), *El conservadurismo mexicano en el siglo XIX (1810–1910)*. Puebla: BUAP–University of St. Andrews, 1999. 187–212.

———. "Mariano Arizcorreta and Peasant Unrest in the State of Mexico, 1849." *Bulletin of Latin American Research* 15, no. 1 (1996): 63–79.

———. "The Mexican Church and the Rebellion of the Polkos." *Hispanic American Historical Review* 46, no. 2 (1966): 170–78.

―――. "The Mexican Press of 1836 and the Battle of the Alamo." *Southern Historical Quarterly* 61 (1988): 533–43.

―――. "A Pronunciamiento in Nineteenth Century Mexico: '15 de julio de 1840.'" *Mexican Studies/Estudios Mexicanos* 4, no. 2 (1988): 245–64.

―――. "The Triangular Revolt in Mexico and the Fall of Anastasio Bustamante, August–October, 1841." *Journal of Latin American Studies* 20 (1988): 337–60.

Cotner, Thomas Ewing. *The Military and Political Career of José Joaquín de Herrera, 1792–1854.* Austin: University of Texas Press, 1949.

Cunninghame Graham, R. B. *José Antonio Páez.* London: Heinemann, 1929.

Dawson, G. *Soldier Heroes: British Adventure, Empire and the Imagining of Masculinities.* London: Routledge, 1994.

Delgado, Ana Laura (ed.). *Cien viajeros en Veracruz: Crónicas y relatos. Vol. 4. 1831–1832.* Veracruz: Gobierno del Estado de Veracruz, 1992.

DePalo, William A., Jr. *The Mexican National Army, 1822–1852.* College Station: Texas A&M University Press, 1997.

Di Tella, Torcuato S. *National Popular Politics in Early Independent Mexico, 1820–1847.* Albuquerque: University of New Mexico Press, 1996.

Díaz Díaz, Fernando. *Caudillos y caciques: Antonio López de Santa Anna y Juan Álvarez.* Mexico City: El Colegio de México, 1972.

Diccionario Porrúa: Historia, biografía y geografía de México. 2 vols. 3rd ed. Mexico City: Porrúa, 1970.

Dittman, Ralph E. "Santa Anna's Battle of New Orleans." *Louisiana History* 25 (1984): 189–97.

Documentos relativos a la sublevación del general Don Juan Álvarez en el Sur del Estado de México y a los últimos sucesos del Estado de Zacatecas. Mexico City: Imp. de Ignacio Cumplido, 1835.

Dublán, Manuel, and José M. Lozano. *Legislación mexicana o colección completa de las disposiciones legislativas expedidas desde la independencia de la república.* Vols. 4–9. Mexico City: Imp. del Comercio, 1877–1902.

Ducey, Michael T. "From Village Riot to Rural Rebellion: Social Protest in the Huasteca, Mexico, 1760–1870." Ph.D. diss., University of Chicago, 1992.

―――. "La causa justa: Los defensores del dominio español en el norte de Veracruz, 1810–1821." In Will Fowler and Humberto Morales Moreno (eds.), *El conservadurismo mexicano en el siglo XIX (1810–1910).* Puebla: BUAP–University of St Andrews, 1999. 37–57.

―――. "Village, Nation and Constitution: Insurgent Politics in Papantla, Veracruz, 1810–1821," *Hispanic American Historical Review* 79. No. 3 (1999): 1–31.

Duncan, Robert. "Political Legitimation and Maximilian's Second Empire in Mexico, 1864–1867." *Mexican Studies/Estudios Mexicanos* 12, no. 2 (Winter, 1996): 27–66.

Dunkerley, James. *Americana: The Americas in the World, around 1850.* London: Verso, 2000.

Durán, Gabriel. *Carta y plan del señor general don Gabriel Durán*. Mexico City: Imp. de Tomás Uribe y Alcalde, 1833.

Earle, Rebecca. "'A Grave for Europeans'? Disease, Death, and the Spanish-American Revolutions." *War in History* 3 (1996): 371–83.

El general en gefe del ejército del sur y departamento de México, a sus habitantes. Chilpancingo: n.p., 23 October 1841.

Ellis, Geoffrey. *Napoleon*. London: Longman, 1997.

Escobar Ohmstede, Antonio. *Ciento cincuenta años de historia de la Huasteca*. Mexico City: Consejo Nacional para la Cultura y las Artes–Gob. Del Estado de Veracruz, 1998.

———. *Indio, nación y comunidad en el México del siglo XIX*. Mexico City: CIESAS-CEMCA, 1993.

Escobar, Manuel María. "Campaña de Tampico de Tamaulipas, año de 1829." *Historia Mexicana* 9 no. 1 (1959): 44–96.

Esteva, José Ignacio, *Exposición de las ocurrencias que motivaron la salida de Veracruz del Ciudadano José Ignacio Esteva*. Puebla: Imp. del Gobierno, 1827.

———. *José Ignacio Esteva, Secretario del Despacho de Hacienda, y encargado en comisión del gobierno del distrito federal*. Mexico City: Imp. del Águila, September 1828.

Ewell, Judith, and William H. Beezley (eds.). *The Human Tradition in Latin America: The Nineteenth Century*. Wilmington DE: Scholarly Resources, 1992.

Fernández Ledesma, Enrique. "Santa Anna and the Order of Guadalupe." *Mexican Art and Life* 6 (April 1939).

Ferrer Muñoz, Manuel. *La formación de un Estado nacional en México: El Imperio y la República federal, 1821–1835*. Mexico City: UNAM, 1995.

Filisola, Vicente. *Memorias para la historia de la guerra de Tejas*. 2 vols. Mexico City: Tipografía de Rafael Rafael, 1849.

Fisher, John. *Commercial Relations between Spain and Spanish America in the Era of Free Trade, 1778–1796*. Liverpool: Institute of Latin American Studies, 1985.

Flaccus, Elmer William. "Guadalupe Victoria, Mexican Revolutionary Patriot and First President, 1786–1843." Ph.D. diss., University of Texas, Austin, 1951.

Flores Mena, Carmen. *El general don Antonio López de Santa Anna (1810–1833)*. Mexico City: UNAM, 1950.

Florescano, Enrique, *Precios del maíz y crisis agrícolas en México, 1708–1810*. Mexico City: El Colegio de México, 1969.

Fowler, Will. "All the President's Women: The Wives of General Antonio López de Santa Anna in 19th Century Mexico." *Feminist Review* 79 (2005): 52–68.

———. "Antonio López de Santa Anna: 'El hombre visible por excelencia' (México, 1821–1855)." In Manuel Chust and Víctor Mínguez (eds.), *La construcción del héroe en España y México (1789–1847)*. Valencia: Universitat de Valencia, 2003. 357–80.

———. "Carlos María Bustamante: Un tradicionalista liberal." In Will Fowler and Humberto Morales Moreno (eds.), *El conservadurismo mexicano en el siglo XIX (1810–1910)*. Puebla: BUAP, 1999. 59–85.

———. "Civil Conflict in Independent Mexico, 1821–57: An Overview." In Rebecca Earle (ed.), *Rumours of Wars: Civil Conflict in Nineteenth-Century Latin America.* London: ILAS, 2000. 49–86.

———. "The Compañía Lancasteriana and the Élite in Independent Mexico, 1822–1845," *Tesserae, Journal of Iberian and Latin-American Studies* 2, no. 1 (Summer 1996): 81–110.

———. "Dreams of Stability: Mexican Political Thought during the 'Forgotten Years.' An Analysis of the Beliefs of the Creole Intelligentsia (1821–1853)." *Bulletin of Latin American Research* 14, no. 3 (September 1995): 287–312.

———. "El pensamiento político de los moderados, 1838–1850: el proyecto de Mariano Otero." In Brian Connaughton, Carlos Illades, and Sonia Pérez Toledo (eds.), *Construcción de la legitimidad política en México.* Mexico City: El Colegio de Michoacán–UAM–UNAM–El Colegio de México, 1999. 275–300.

———. "El pensamiento político de los santanistas, 1821–1855." In Luis Jáuregui and José Antonio Serrano Ortega (eds.), *Historia y nación*, vol. 2: *Política y diplomacia en el siglo XIX mexicano.* Mexico City: El Colegio de México, 1998. 183–226.

———. "Fiestas santanistas: La celebración de Santa Anna en la villa de Xalapa, 1821–1855." *Historia Mexicana* 52, no. 2 (Octubre–Diciembre 2002): 391–447.

———. "Introducción: El presidencialismo en México." In Will Fowler (ed.), *Presidentes mexicanos*, vol. 1. Mexico City: INEHRM, 2004. 11–24.

———. "Joseph Welsh: A British Santanista (Mexico, 1832)." *Journal of Latin American Studies* 36, no. 1 (February 2004): 29–56.

———. "Las propiedades veracruzanas de Santa Anna." *Memorias de la Academia Mexicana de la Historia* 43 (2000): 63–92.

———. *Latin America 1800–2000.* London: Arnold, 2002.

———. *The Mexican Press and the Collapse of Representative Government during the Presidential Elections of 1828.* Liverpool: ILAS Research Paper 21, 1996.

———. *Mexico in the Age of Proposals, 1821–1853.* Westport CT: Greenwood Press, 1998.

———. *Military Political Identity and Reformism in Independent Mexico: An Analysis of the Memorias de Guerra (1821–1855).* London: ILAS, 1996.

———. "The Repeated Rise of General Antonio López de Santa Anna in the So-Called Age of Chaos (Mexico, 1821–55)." In Will Fowler (ed.), *Authoritarianism in Latin America since Independence* (Westport CT: Greenwood Press, 1996). 1–30.

———. *Tornel and Santa Anna, the Writer and the Caudillo (Mexico 1795–1853).* Westport CT: Greenwood Press, 2000.

———. "Valentín Gómez Farías: Perceptions of Radicalism in Independent Mexico, 1821–1847." *Bulletin of Latin American Research* 15, no. 1 (January 1996): 39–62.

Fowler, Will, and Juan Ortiz Escamilla. "La revuelta del 2 de diciembre de 1822: Una perspectiva regional." *Historias* 47 (2000): 19–37.

Fowler, Will, and Humberto Morales Moreno (eds.). *El conservadurismo mexicano en el siglo XIX (1810–1910).* Puebla: BUAP, 1999.

Fowler, Will, and Peter Lambert (eds.). *Political Violence and the Construction of National Identity in Latin America.* New York: Palgrave Macmillan, 2006.

Frasquet, Ivana. "Milicianos y soldados: La problemática social mexicana en la invasión de 1829." In Salvador Broseta, Carmen Corona, Manuel Chust, et al. (eds.), *Las ciudades y la guerra, 1750–1898* (Castelló: Universitat Jaume I, 2002). 115–32.

Frazier, Donald S. (ed.). *The United States and Mexico at War: Nineteenth-Century Expansionism and Conflict.* New York: Simon & Schuster Macmillan, 1998.

Fuentes Mares, José. *Santa Anna: Aurora y ocaso de un comediante.* Mexico City: Jus, 1956.

Fuentes, Carlos, *The Death of Artemio Cruz.* London: Panther, 1969.

Galindo y Galindo, Miguel. *La gran década nacional o relación histórica de la Guerra de Reforma, intervención extranjera y gobierno del archiduque Maximiliano, 1857–1867.* 3 vols. Mexico City: Fondo de Cultura Económica, 1987.

Galván Rivera, Mariano. *Colección de las efemérides publicadas en el calendario del más antiguo Galván: Desde su fundación hasta el 30 de junio de 1950. Primera parte.* Mexico City: Antigua Librería Murguía, 1950.

Gamboa, Ramón. *Impugnación al informe del exmo. Sr. general D. Antonio López de Santa Anna y constancias en que se apoyan las ampliaciones de la acusación del Sr. diputado D. Ramón Gamboa.* Mexico City: Imp. de Vicente García Torres, 1849.

García, Alejandro. *El comandante general del estado a los habitantes de él y tropas que lo guarnecen.* San Juan Bautista: Imp. de José María Abalos, 1847.

García, Genaro (ed.). *Documentos inéditos o muy raros para la historia de México.* Vol. 59: *Antonio López de Santa Anna.* Mexico City: Porrúa, 1991.

———. *Documentos inéditos o muy raros para la historia de México.* Vol. 26: *La revolución de Ayutla según el archivo del general Doblado.* Mexico City: Librería de la Vda. De Ch. Bouret, 1909.

García Cantú, Gastón (ed.). *El pensamiento de la reacción mexicana: Historia documental.* Vol. 1. Mexico City: UNAM, 1994.

García Márquez, Gabriel. *One Hundred Years of Solitude.* London: Picador, 1978.

García Morales, Soledad. *Hacendados y capitales: Análisis de propietarios de la región de Coatepec, Veracruz. 1790–1810.* Xalapa: Universidad Veracruzana, 1994.

Garner, Paul. *Porfirio Díaz.* London: Pearson Education, 2001.

Garrett, Julia Kathryn. *Green Flag over Texas: A Story of the Last Years of Spain in Texas.* Austin: Jenkins Publishing Company, c. 1939.

Giménez, Manuel María. *Memorias del coronel Manuel María Giménez (1798–1878).* In Genaro García (ed.), *Documentos inéditos o muy raros para la historia de México,* Vol. 59: *Antonio López de Santa Anna.* Mexico City: Porrúa, 1991. 277–408.

Gonzalbo Aizpuru, Pilar, and Véronica Zárate Toscano (eds.). *Gozos y sufrimientos en la historia de México.* Mexico City: El Colegio de México, 2007.

González Navarro, Moisés. *Anatomía del poder en México (1848–1853).* Mexico City: El Colegio de México, 1977.

———. *Raza y tierra: La guerra de casta y el henequén.* Mexico City: El Colegio de México, 1970.

González Pedrero, Enrique. *País de un solo hombre: El México de Santa Anna*. Vol. 1: *La ronda de los contrarios*. Mexico City: Fondo de Cultura Económica, 1993.

————. *País de un solo hombre: El México de Santa Anna*. Vol. 2: *La sociedad del fuego cruzado 1829–1836*. Mexico City: Fondo de Cultura Económica, 2003.

Gou-Gilbert, Cecile. *Una resistencia india: Los yaquis*. Mexico City: INI–Centro de Estudios Mexicanos y Centroamericanos, 1985.

Green, Stanley C. *The Mexican Republic: The First Decade, 1823–1832*. Pittsburgh: Pittsburgh University Press, 1987.

Gregory, Desmond. *Brute New World: The Rediscovery of Latin America in the Early Nineteenth Century*. London: British Academic Press, 1992.

Groneman, Bill. *Battlefields of Texas*. Plano TX: Republic of Texas Press, 1998.

Guardino, Peter F. *Peasants, Politics, and the Formation of Mexico's National State: Guerrero, 1800–1857*. Stanford: Stanford University Press, 1996.

————. *The Time of Liberty: Popular Political Culture in Oaxaca, 1750–1850*. Durham NC: Duke University Press, 2005.

Guedea, Virginia. "El golpe de estado de 1808." *Universidad de México* 48 (1991): 21–24.

————. *En busca de un gobierno alterno: Los Guadalupes de México*. Mexico City: UNAM, 1992.

————. *La insurgencia en el Departamento del Norte: Los llanos de Apan y la sierra de Puebla 1810–1816*. Mexico City: UNAM–Instituto Mora, 1996.

Guedea, Virginia (ed.). *La revolución de independencia*. Mexico City: El Colegio de México, 1995.

Güemez Pineda, Arturo. *Liberalismo en tierras del caminante: Yucatán 1812–1840*. Zamora: El Colegio de Michoacán, 1994.

Guerra, François-Xavier. *Modernidad e independencias: Ensayos sobre las revoluciones hispánicas*. Mexico City: Fondo de Cultura Económica, 1993.

Gutiérrez Casillas, José. *Papeles de Agustín de Iturbide*. Mexico City: Editorial Tradición, 1997.

Gutiérrez Estrada, José María. *Carta dirigida al Exmo. Sr. Presidente de la República, sobre la necesidad de buscar en una convención el posible remedio de los males que aquejan a la República y opiniones del autor acerca del mismo asunto*. Mexico City: Imp. de Ignacio Cumplido, 1840.

Hale, Charles A. *El liberalismo mexicano en la época de Mora 1821–1853*. Mexico City: Siglo XXI Editores, 1972.

Hamill, Hugh M. (ed.). *Caudillos: Dictators in Spanish America*. Norman: University of Oklahoma Press, 1992.

Hamnett, Brian R. "Benito Juárez, Early Liberalism, and the Regional Politics of Oaxaca, 1828–1853." *Bulletin of Latin American Research* 10, no. 1 (1991): 1–21.

————. *A Concise History of Mexico*. Cambridge: Cambridge University Press, 1999.

————. *Juárez*. London: Longman, 1994.

————. "La ejecución del emperador Maximiliano de Habsburgo y el republicanismo mexicano." In Luis Jáuregui and José Antonio Serrano Ortega (eds.), *Historia y Nación*, vol. 2: *Política y diplomacia en el siglo XIX mexicano*. Mexico City: El Colegio de México, 1998. 227–44.

———. "Mexican Conservatives, Clericals, and Soldiers: The 'Traitor' Tomás Mejía through Reform and Empire, 1855–1867." *Bulletin of Latin American Research* 20, no. 2 (April 2001): 187–209.

———. "Partidos políticos mexicanos e intervención militar, 1823–1855." In Antonio Annino et al. (eds.), *America Latina dallo stato coloniale allo stato nazione*. Vol. 2. Milan: Franco Angeli, 1987. 573–91.

———. *Politics and Trade in Southern Mexico 1750–1821*. Cambridge: Cambridge University Press, 1971.

———. *Raíces de la insurgencia en México: Historia regional 1750–1824*. Mexico City: Fondo de Cultura Económica, 1990.

Hancock, Walter Edgar. "The Career of General Antonio López de Santa Anna." Ph.D. diss., University of Texas, Austin, 1930.

Hanighen, Frank C. *Santa Anna: The Napoleon of the West*. New York: Coward-McCann, 1934.

Hardin, Stephen L. *Texian Iliad: A Military History of the Texas Revolution 1835–1836*. Austin: University of Texas Press, 1994.

Haynes, Sam W. *Soldiers of Misfortune: The Somervell and Mier Expeditions*. Austin: University of Texas Press, 1990.

Henson, Margaret Swett. *Juan Davis Bradburn: A Reappraisal of the Mexican Commander at Anahuac*. College Station: Texas A&M University Press, 1982.

———. *Lorenzo de Zavala: The Pragmatic Idealist*. Fort Worth: Texas Christian University Press, 1996.

Holmes, Richard. *Wellington: The Iron Duke*. London: HarperCollins, 2003.

Hu-Dehart, Evelyn. *Yaqui Resistance and Survival: The Struggle for Land and Autonomy, 1821–1910*. Madison: University of Wisconsin Press, 1984.

Humboldt, Alexandre. *Essai politique sur le Royaume de la Nouvelle-Espagne*. 2 vols. Paris: Imp. de J. H. Stone, 1811.

Hutchinson, Cecil Alan. "Valentín Gómez Farías: A Biographical Study." Ph.D. diss., University of Texas, Austin, 1948.

Jiménez Codinach, Guadalupe (ed.). *Planes en la Nación Mexicana*. 4 vols. Mexico City: Senado de la República–El Colegio de México, 1987.

Johnson, John J. *The Military and Society in Latin America*. Stanford: Stanford University Press, 1964.

Johnson, Richard A. *The Mexican Revolution of Ayutla, 1854–1855: An Analysis of the Evolution and Destruction of Santa Anna's Last Dictatorship*. Westport CT: Greenwood Press, 1974.

Johnson, Timothy D. *Winfield Scott: The Quest for Military Glory*. Kansas: University Press of Kansas, 1998.

Jones, Oakah L., Jr. *Santa Anna*. New York: Twayne Publishers, 1968.

Karsten, Peter. *Patriot-Heroes in England and America: Political Symbolism and Changing Values over Three Centuries*. Madison: University of Wisconsin Press, 1978.

Katz, Friedrich. *The Life and Times of Pancho Villa*. Stanford: Stanford University Press, 1998.

Katz, Friedrich (ed.). *Revuelta, rebelión y revolución: La lucha rural en México del siglo xvi al siglo xx*. 2 vols. Mexico City: Era, 1990.

———. *Riot, Rebellion and Revolt: Rural Social Conflict in Mexico*. Princeton: Princeton University Press, 1988.

Kipling, Rudyard. *Wee Willie Winkie*. London: Macmillan, 1982.

Knight, Alan. *Mexico: The Colonial Era*. Cambridge: Cambridge University Press, 2002.

Krauze, Enrique. *Siglo de caudillos*. Barcelona: Tusquets Editores, 1994.

La Excelentísima Señora Doña Inés García de Santa Anna, digna esposa del Supremo Magistrado de la Nación, vino buscando la salud, y la Puebla que habría querido inspirarle vida, llena de sentimiento vio su muerte el día 23 de agosto de 1844: Llora su familia una virtuosa y tierna madre: Llórala Veracruz su patria y la llora también la sociedad Mexicana. Puebla: Imp. de Rivera, 1844.

Lack, Paul D. *The Texas Revolutionary Experience: A Political and Social History, 1835–1836*. College Station: Texas A&M University Press, 1992.

Landavazo, Marco Antonio. *La máscara de Fernando VII: Discurso e imaginario monárquicos en una época de crisis, Nueva España, 1808–1822*. Mexico City: El Colegio de México, 2001.

Lapointe, Marie. *Los mayas rebeldes de Yucatán*. Mexico City: El Colegio de Michoacán, 1983.

Latrobe, Charles Joseph, *The Rambler in Mexico: 1834*. London: Seeley and Burnside, 1836.

Lecaillon, Jean-François. *Napoléon III et le Mexique: Les illusions d'un grand dessein*. Paris: Éditions L'Harmattan, 1994.

Lecuna, Vicente, and Harold A. Bierck, Jr. (eds.). *Selected Writings of Bolívar*. 2 vols. New York: Colonial Press, 1951.

León Fuentes, Nelly Josefa. "Los antagonismos empresariales de Xalapa en el siglo XIX." In *Anuario IX Instituto de Investicaciones Histórico-Sociales Universidad Veracruzana*. Xalapa: Universidad Veracruzana, 1994. 79–97.

Lerdo de Tejada, Miguel. *Apuntes históricos de la heróica ciudad de Veracruz*. 2nd ed. 2 vols. Mexico City: SEP, 1940.

Lira, Andrés (ed.). *Lucas Alamán*. Mexico City: Cal y Arena, 1997.

Liss, Peggy K. *Atlantic Empires: The Network of Trade and Revolution, 1713–1826*. Baltimore: John Hopkins University Press, 1983.

Los diputados que suscriben, a sus comitentes. Mexico City: Imp. de Santiago Pérez, 1847.

Loveman, Brian, and Thomas Davies (eds.). *The Politics of Antipolitics: The Military in Latin America*. Lincoln: University of Nebraska Press, 1978.

Luz Romero, José de la. *Noticia estraordinaria sobre las operaciones del general Santa Anna contra el ejército ministerial*. Mexico City: Imp. Libre, 1832.

Lynch, John. *Argentine Dictator: Juan Manuel de Rosas 1829–1852*. Oxford: Clarendon, 1981.

————. *Caudillos in Spanish America 1800–1850*. Oxford: Clarendon Press, 1992.

————. *The Spanish American Revolutions 1808–1826*. London: Weidenfeld and Nicolson, 1973.

Manzur Ocaña, Justo. *Don José Joaquín de Herrera, héroe de Córdoba*. Mexico City: Federación Editorial Mexicana, 1984.

Marcha patriótica dedicada al Exmo. Sr. Presidente de la República Mexicana, General de División y Benemérito de la Patria, Don Antonio López de Santa Anna. Guadalajara: Tipografía de Brambila, 1853.

Martínez Gallego, Francisco A. *Conservar progresando: La Unión Liberal (1856–1868)*. Valencia: Centro Francisco Tomás y Valiente UNED Alzira-Valencia, 2001.

Mateos, Juan Antonio. *Historia parlamentaria de los congresos mexicanos*. Vol. 2, tomos 1–2. Mexico City: Porrúa, 1997.

Matute, Álvaro, Evelia Trejo, and Brian Connaughton (eds.). *Estado, iglesia y sociedad en México: Siglo XIX*. Mexico City: UNAM-Porrúa, 1995.

McAlister, Lyle N. *The "Fuero Militar" in New Spain, 1764–1800*. Gainesville: University of Florida Press, 1957.

————. "The Reorganization of the Army of New Spain, 1763–1766." *Hispanic American Historical Review* 33, no. 1 (1953): 1–32.

Medina Peña, Luis. *Invención del sistema político mexicano: Forma de gobierno y gobernabilidad en México en el siglo XIX*. Mexico City: Fondo de Cultura Económica, 2004.

Méndez Reyes, Salvador. *Eugenio de Aviraneta y México*. Mexico City: UNAM, 1992.

Menéndez, Carlos R. *La huella del general don Antonio López de Santa Anna en Yucatán*. Mérida: Compañía Tipográfica Yucateca, n.d.

Mier y Terán, Manuel de. *Texas by Terán: The Diary kept by General Manuel de Mier y Terán on His 1828 Inspection of Texas*. Ed. Jack Jackson, trans. John Wheat. Austin: University of Texas Press, 2000.

Moctezuma, Esteban. *El general ciudadano Esteban Moctezuma, a sus compatriotas*. Tampico de Tamaulipas: n.p., 16 March 1832.

Molina Solís, Juan Francisco. *Historia de Yucatán desde la Independencia hasta la época actual*. Vol. 1. Mérida: Yucateca Editorial, 1921.

Mora, José María Luis. *Obras sueltas de José María Luis Mora, ciudadano mexicano*. Mexico City: Porrúa, 1963.

Muñoz, Rafael F. *Santa Anna: El dictador resplandeciente*. Mexico City: Fondo de Cultura Económica, 1983.

Muro, Manuel. *Historia de San Luis Potosí*. 2 vols. Mexico City: Sociedad Potosina de Estudios Históricos, 1973.

Noriega Elío, Cecilia. *El Constituyente de 1842*. Mexico City: UNAM, 1986.

Noriega, Alfonso. *El pensamiento conservador y el conservadurismo mexicano*. 2 vols. Mexico City: UNAM, 1993.

Noticia Estraordinaria: ¡Viva la República Mexicana! ¡Viva el Héroe Inmortal de Tampico y Veracruz! Mexico City: Imp. de M. Barte, 1846.

O'Gorman, Edmundo. *México: El trauma de su historia*. Mexico City: UNAM, 1977.

Ocampo, Javier. *Las ideas de un día: El pueblo mexicano ante la consumación de su independencia.* Mexico City: El Colegio de México, 1969.

Olivera, Ruth R., and Liliane Crété. *Life in Mexico under Santa Anna, 1822–1855.* Norman: University of Oklahoma Press, 1991.

Ortiz de Zárate, Francisco. *¡Muy importante! Francisco Ortiz de Zárate, general de brigada graduado y vice-gobernador en ejercicio del supremo poder ejecutivo del estado, a los habitantes del mismo.* Oaxaca: Imp. de Ignacio Rincón, 1847.

Ortiz Escamilla, Juan. "El federalismo veracruzano, 1820–1826." In Josefina Zoraida Vázquez (ed.), *El establecimiento del federalismo en México (1821–1827).* Mexico City: El Colegio de México, 2003. 505–32.

———. *Guerra y gobierno: Los pueblos y la independencia de México.* Sevilla: Colección Nueva América, 1997.

———. "La élites novohispanas ante la guerra civil de 1810." *Historia Mexicana* 46, no. 2 (1996): 325–57.

Palti, Elías José (ed.). *La política del disenso: La "polémica en torno del monarquismo" (México, 1848–1850) . . . y las aporías del liberalismo.* Mexico City: Fondo de Cultura Económica, 1998.

Pani, Erika. *Para mexicanizar el Segundo Imperio: El imaginario político de los imperialistas.* Mexico City: El Colegio de México–Instituto Mora, 2001.

Pantoja Morán, David. *El Supremo Poder Conservador: El diseño institucional en las primeras constituciones mexicanas.* Mexico City: El Colegio de México–El Colegio de Michoacán, 2005.

Payno, Manuel. *Los bandidos de Río Frío.* Mexico City: Porrúa, 1996.

Parte circunstanciado del general Taylor, sobre la batalla de Buena-Vista o La Angostura. Mexico City: Imp. de la Calle de Chiquis, Núm. 6, 1847.

Pasquel, Leonardo. *Antonio López de Santa Anna.* Mexico City: Instituto de Mexicología, 1990.

Pérez Herrero, Pedro (ed.). *Región e historia en México (1700–1850): Métodos de análisis regional.* Mexico City: Instituto Mora, 1997.

Pérez Vila, Manuel (ed.). *Simón Bolívar, doctrina del libertador.* Los Ruices, Colombia: Biblioteca Ayacucho, 1976.

Pietschmann, Horst. *Las reformas borbónicas y el sistema de intendentes en Nueva España.* Mexico City: Fondo de Cultura Económica, 1996.

Pi-Suñer Llorens, Antonia. "Sebastián Lerdo de Tejada." In Will Fowler (ed.), *Presidentes mexicanos,* vol. 1. Mexico City: INEHRM, 2004. 217–45.

———. *Sebastián Lerdo de Tejada: Canciller-estadista.* Mexico City: SRE, 1989.

Pi-Suñer Llorens, Antonia, and Agustín Sánchez Andrés. *Una historia de encuentros y desencuentros: México y España en el siglo XIX.* Mexico City: Secretaría de Relaciones Exteriores, 2001.

Pitner, Ernst. *Maximilian's Lieutenant: A Personal History of the Mexican Campaign, 1864–7.* Trans. and ed. Gordon Etherington-Smith. London: I. B. Tauris and Company, 1993.

Plan de Chilpancingo de los Bravos. No location: Imp. de M. Cordero, 22 October 1841.

Poinsett, Joel Roberts. *Notes on Mexico, made in the autumn of 1822: Accompanied by an historical sketch of the revolution and translations of official reports on the present state of the country.* London: Shackell and Arrowsmith, 1825.

Polk, James K. *Polk: The Diary of a President 1845–1849, Covering the Mexican War, the Acquisition of Oregon, and the Conquest of California and the Southwest.* Ed. Allan Nevins. London: Longmans, Green and Company, 1952.

Portilla, Anselmo de la. *Historia de la revolución de México contra la dictadura del General Santa Anna 1853–1855.* Prólogo de Andrés Henestrosa. Mexico City: Fondo de Cultura Económica, 1993.

Posada, Eduardo. "El dictador Santa Anna en Colombia." *Boletín Historial* 54 (September 1929): 136–40.

Potash, Robert A. *Mexican Government and Industrial Development in the Early Republic: The Banco de Avío.* Amherst: University of Massachusetts Press, 1983.

———. "Testamentos de Santa Anna." *Historia Mexicana* 13, no. 3 (1964): 428–40.

Prieto, Guillermo. *Memorias de mis tiempos.* Mexico City: Porrúa, 1996.

Proceso del ex general Antonio López de Santa Anna, acusándole de infidencia a la patria. Veracruz: Imprenta de David, 1867; reprinted by Secretaría de Guerra y Marina, Mexico City: Talleres Gráficos de la Nación, 1926.

Prucha, Francis Paul. *The Great Father: The United States Government and the American Indians.* Lincoln: University of Nebraska Press, 1984.

Quijano, Benito. *El comandante general del departamento, a las tropas de su mando ¡Soldados!.* Veracruz: n.p., 13 June 1844.

Quinlan, David M. "Issues and Factions in the Constituent Congress, 1823–1824." In Jaime E. Rodríguez O. (ed.), *Mexico in the Age of Democratic Revolutions, 1750–1850* Boulder CO: Lynne Rienner Publishers, 1994. 177–207.

Ramírcz, José Fernando. *México durante su guerra con los Estados Unidos.* In Genaro García (ed.), *Documentos inéditos o muy raros para la historia de México,* Vol. 59: *Antonio López de Santa Anna.* Mexico City: Porrúa, 1991. 409–548.

Ramos, Luis (ed.). *Del Archivo Secreto Vaticano: La Iglesia y el Estado Mexicano en el Siglo XIX.* Mexico City: UNAM–SRE, 1997.

Rea, Vargas (ed.). *Antonio López de Santa Ana: Importante documento para juzgar si traicionó a México.* Mexico City: Biblioteca Aportación Histórica, 1947.

Real Díaz, José Joaquín. *Las ferias de Jalapa.* Sevilla: Publicaciones de la Escuela de Estudios Hispanoamericanos de Sevilla, 1959.

Reed, Nelson. *La guerra de castas de Yucatán.* Mexico City: Biblioteca Era, 1987.

Reina, Leticia. *Las rebeliones campesinas en México, 1819–1906.* Mexico City: Siglo XXI, 1980.

Remini, Robert V. *Andrew Jackson and the Course of American Democracy, 1833–1845.* Vol. 3. New York: Harper & Row, 1984.

Reséndez, Andrés. *Changing National Identities at the Frontier: Texas and New Mexico, 1800–1850.* Cambridge: Cambridge University Press, 2005.

Reséndez, Andrés (ed.). *A Texas Patriot on Trial in Mexico: José Antonio Navarro and the Texan Santa Fe Expedition.* Library of Texas Series. Dallas: Southern Methodist University Press, 2005.

Reyes de la Maza, Luis. *El teatro en México en la época de Santa Anna (1840–1850).* Tomo 1. Mexico City: UNAM, 1972.

Reyes Heroles, Jesús. "Las ideas conservadoras en el siglo XIX." In Ernesto de la Torre Villar (ed.), *Lecturas históricas mexicanas,* vol. 5. Mexico City: UNAM, 1994. 404–18.

Rincón, José [Antonio]. *Conducta que adopta la mayoría de la guarnición de esta plaza, para sostener los altos poderes de la Federación, contrariando la que se ha acreditado por los unidos para un trastorno político en este estado que destruyera nuestras actuales instituciones.* Veracruz: Imp. de Papaloapan, 31 July 1827.

Rivera Cambas, Manuel. *Antonio López de Santa Anna.* Mexico City: Editorial Citlaltépetl, 1958.

———. *Historia antigua y moderna de Jalapa y de las revoluciones del Estado de Veracruz.* 2 vols. Mexico City: Editorial Citlaltépetl, 1959.

Roa Bárcena, José María. *Recuerdos de la invasión norteamericana (1846–1848).* 3 vols. Edición y prólogo de Antonio Castro Leal. Mexico City: Porrúa, 1947.

Rochfort, Desmond. *The Murals of Diego Rivera.* London: Journeyman Press, 1987.

Rodríguez O., Jaime E. "The Constitution of 1824 and the Formation of the Mexican State." In Jaime E. Rogríguez O. (ed.), *The Evolution of the Mexican Political System.* Wilmington DE: Scholarly Resources, 1993. 71–90.

———. *El nacimiento de Hispanoamérica: Vicente Rocafuerte y el hispanoamericanismo, 1808–1832.* Mexico City: Fondo de Cultura Económica, 1980.

———. *The Independence of Mexico and the Creation of the New Nation.* Berkeley: University of California Press, 1989.

———. *The Independence of Spanish America.* Cambridge: Cambridge University Press, 1998.

———. "Intellectuals and the Mexican Constitution of 1824." In Roderic A. Camp, Charles A. Hale, and Josefina Zoraida Vázquez (eds.). *Los intelectuales y el poder en México.* Mexico City: El Colegio de México–UCLA Latin American Center Publications, 1991. 63–74.

———. "The Origins of the 1832 Rebellion." In Jaime E. Rodríguez O. (ed.), *Patterns of Contention in Mexican History.* Wilmington DE: Scholarly Resources, 1992. 145–162.

Rodríguez O., Jaime E. (ed.). *Mexico in the Age of Democratic Revolutions, 1750–1850.* Boulder CO: Lynne Rienner Publishers, 1994.

———. *The Origins of Mexican National Politics, 1808–1847.* Wilmington DE: Scholarly Resources, 1997.

Rodríguez O., Jaime E., and Kathryn Vincent (eds.). *Myths, Misdeeds and Misunderstandings: The Roots of Conflict in U.S.-Mexican Relations.* Wilmington DE: Scholarly Resources, 1997.

Runciman, W. G. (ed.). *Weber: Selections in Translation* Cambridge: Cambridge University Press, 1978.

Salinas Sandoval, Ma. Del Carmen. *Política y sociedad en los municipios del Estado de México (1825–1880)*. Toluca: El Colegio Mexiquense, 1996.

Samponaro, Frank N. "La alianza de Santa Anna y los federalistas 1832–1834. Su formación y desintegración." *Historia Mexicana* 30, no. 3 (1981): 358–90.

Sánchez Lamego, Miguel A. *La invasión española de 1829*. Mexico City: Editorial Jus, 1971.

Santa Anna, Antonio López de. *Antonio López de Santa Anna a sus conciudadanos*. Puebla: Imp. Liberal, 1846.

———. *Apelación al buen criterio de los nacionales y extranjeros: Informe que el Exmo. Sr. General de División, Benemérito de la Patria, Antonio López de Santa Anna dió por acuerdo de la Sección del Gran Jurado, sobre las acusaciones presentadas por el Sr. diputado don Ramón Gamboa*. Mexico City: Imp. de Ignacio Cumplido, 1849.

———. *Comunicación del Escmo. Sr. General Benemérito de la Patria, D. Antonio López de Santa Anna, en que desconoce al poder dictatorial que se ha abrogado el Escmo. Sr. General D. Anastasio Bustamante*. Mexico City: Imp. de Luis Heredia, 1841.

———. *El Comandante General del Estado Libre de Yucatán a sus habitantes*. Campeche: n.p., 29 May 1824.

———. *El general de división Antonio López de Santa Anna a la guarnición de esta plaza y de Ulúa*. Veracruz: Imp. Liberal de Antonio María Valdés, 1832.

———. *Exposición del general don Antonio López de Santa Anna a sus compatriotas con motivo del programa proclamado para la verdadera regeneración de la República*. Mexico City: Imp. de la Sociedad Literaria, 1846.

———. "Exposición dirigida al Escmo. Señor presidente de la república por el Escmo. Sr. D. Antonio López de Santa Anna." *El Cosmopolita*, 6 and 13 February 1841.

———. *Exposición que el Sr. D. Antonio López de Santa-Anna dirige desde la fortaleza de S. Carlos de Perote a los exmos. Señores secretarios de la cámara de diputados para que se sirvan dar cuenta en la sesión del gran jurado señalada para el día 24 de febrero del corriente año*. Mexico City: Imp. Calle de la Palma, Núm. 4, 1845.

———. *Manifestación del presidente a sus conciudadanos*. Puebla: Imp. del Supremo Gobierno del Estado de Puebla, 1833.

———. *Manifiesto: Antonio López de Santa Anna, Benemérito de la Patria y general de división de los ejércitos nacionales, a sus compatriotas*. Veracruz: n.p., 28 February 1864.

———. *Manifiesto de Antonio López de Santa Anna a sus conciudadanos*. Mexico City: Imp. de Martín Rivera, 10 August 1823.

———. *Manifiesto del Exmo. Sr. Benemérito de la Patria y Presidente Constitucional de la República D. Antonio López de Santa Anna*. Mexico City: Imp. de Vicente García Torres, 1844.

———. *Manifiesto del general de división, benemérito de la patria, Antonio López de Santa Anna, a sus conciudadanos, 24 de marzo de 1848*. Mexico City: Imp. de Navarro, 1848; reprinted in Genaro García (ed.), *Documentos inéditos o muy raros para la historia de México*, Vol. 59: *Antonio López de Santa Anna*. Mexico City: Porrúa, 1991. 207–12.

———. *Manifiesto del presidente de la república, a la nación.* Mexico City: Imp. de Antogenes Castillero, 1855.

———. *Manifiesto del Presidente de los Estados Unidos Mexicanos a sus Conciudadanos.* Mexico City: Imp. del Águila, 18 June 1833.

———. *Manifiesto que de sus operaciones en la campaña de Tejas y en su cautiverio dirige a sus conciudadanos el general Antonio López de Santa Anna, 10 de mayo de 1837.* Veracruz: Imp. Liberal, 1837; reprinted in Genaro García (ed.), *Documentos inéditos o muy raros para la historia de México,* Vol. 59: *Antonio López de Santa Anna.* Mexico City: Porrúa, 1991. 123–206.

———. *Manifiesto que hace a la Nación Americana el Teniente Coronel D. Antonio López de Santa Anna, de la conducta política y militar que á observado en el sitio y asalto que dió a la plaza de Veracruz la mañana de 7 de julio de 1821; satisfaciendo a las imputaciones con que ha osado tiznar su reputación cierto papel impreso publicado en aquella ciudad.* Puebla: Oficina del Gobierno Imperial, 1821.

———. *Manifiesto que hace público el teniente coronel D. A. López de Santa Anna, comandante general de la provincia de Veracruz, sobre lo ocurrido con la persona del coronel D. Manuel de la Concha, asesinado al amanecer del día 5 del corriente en los estramuros de la villa de Jalapa, camino de Veracruz.* Puebla: Imp. de Pedro de la Rosa, 1821.

———. *Manifiesto y contramanifiesto del general de división Don Antonio López de Santa Anna.* Mexico City: Imp. de Tomás Uribe y Alcalde, 1829.

———. *Mi historia militar y política 1810–1874: Memorias inéditas.* In Genaro García (ed.), *Documentos inéditos o muy raros para la historia de México,* Vol. 59: *Antonio López de Santa Anna.* Mexico City: Porrúa, 1991. 1–118.

———. *Oficios dirigidos al Soberano Congreso y Supremo Poder Ejecutivo de la Nación, por el Ciudadano General Santana; que se imprime para que se imponga el Público de las sanas intenciones de este jefe, y acontecimientos que le mueven a suspender sus operaciones militares.* San Luis Potosí: Imp. del Ciudadano Estrada, 1823.

———. *Plan de San Luis Potosí.* San Luis Potosí: Imp. de Estrada, 5 de junio de 1823.

———. *Proclama del impávido teniente coronel D. Antonio López de Santana, avisando a los habitantes del pueblo de Perote la toma de aquel fuerte.* Puebla: Imp. Americana de D. José María Betancourt, 1821.

———. *Proclama del sr. coronel D. Antonio López de Santa-Ana á los habitantes de Veracruz en la ocupación de aquella plaza.* Mexico City: Imp. de Mariano Ontíveros, 1821.

Santoni, Pedro. *Mexicans at Arms: Puro Federalists and the Politics of War, 1845–1848.* Fort Worth: Texas Christian University Press, 1996.

Santos, Richard G. *Santa Anna's Campaign against Texas 1835–1836.* Waco: Texian Press, 1968.

Sarmiento, Domingo F. *Facundo: Civilización y barbarie.* Madrid: Editora Nacional, 1975.

Scheina, Robert L. *Santa Anna: A Curse upon Mexico.* Washington DC: Brassey's, 2002.

Sebá Patrón, Francisco. "Historia y leyenda de López de Santa Anna en Turbaco." *Boletín Historial* 146 (June 1969): 11–25.

Sefchovich, Sara. *La suerte de la consorte.* Mexico City: Océano, 2002.

Selby, John. *The Eagle and the Serpent: The Spanish and American Invasions of Mexico, 1519 and 1846*. London: Hamish Hamilton, 1978.

Sentimientos y heroismo del general de la provincia de Veracruz. Puebla: Imp. de Pedro de la Rosa, 1821.

Serna, Enrique. *El seductor de la patria*. Mexico City: Editorial Joaquín Mortiz, 1999.

Shakespeare, William. *Macbeth*. Ed. Kenneth Muir. London: Methuen, 1982.

Siemens, Alfred H. *Between the Summit and the Sea: Central Veracruz in the Nineteenth Century*. Vancouver: University of British Columbia Press, 1990.

Sierra, Justo. *Historia patria*. Mexico City: Departamento Editorial de la Secretaría de Educación Pública, 1922.

———. *Obras completas XII: Evolución política del pueblo mexicano*. Mexico City: UNAM, 1991.

Sims, Harold Dana. *The Expulsion of Mexico's Spaniards 1821–1836*. Pittsburgh: University of Pittsburgh Press, 1990.

Smith, Justin H. (ed.). *Letters of General Antonio López de Santa Anna Relating to the War between the United States and Mexico, 1846–1848*. In *Annual Report of the American Historical Association for the Year 1917*. Washington DC, 1920.

Solares Robles, Laura. *Una revolución pacífica: Biografía política de Manuel Gómez Pedraza, 1789–1851*. Mexico City: Instituto Mora, 1996.

Solís Vicarte, Ruth. *Las sociedades secretas en el primer gobierno republicano (1824–1828)*. Mexico City: Editorial ASBE, 1997.

Sordo Cedeño, Reynaldo. "Benito Juárez y el soberano congreso constituyente, 1846–1847." In Luis Jáuregui and José Antonio Serrano Ortega (eds.), *Historia y nación*, vol. 2: *Política y diplomacia en el siglo XIX mexicano*. Mexico City: El Colegio de México, 1998. 355–78.

———. "El congreso y la guerra con Estados Unidos de América, 1846–1848." In Vázquez (ed.), *México al tiempo de su guerra con Estados Unidos (1846–1848)*. Mexico City: El Colegio de México/FCE, 1997. 47–103.

———. *El congreso en la primera república centralista*. Mexico City: El Colegio de México/ITAM, 1993.

———. "El general Tornel y la guerra de Texas." *Historia Mexicana* 42, no. 4 (1993): 919–53.

Sosa Rodríguez, Enrique. *Proyectos de invasión a Yucatán desde Cuba 1828–1829*. Mérida: Universidad Autónoma de Yucatán–Universidad de la Habana, 1996.

Soto, Miguel. *La conspiración monárquista en México, 1845–1846*. Mexico City: EOSA, 1988.

Staples, Anne. *Bonanzas y borrascas mineras: El Estado de México, 1821–1876*. Mexico City: El Colegio de México, 1994.

———. "Clerics as Politicians: Church, State and Political Power in Independent Mexico." In Jaime E. Rodríguez O. (ed.), *Mexico in the Age of Democratic Revolutions*. Boulder CO: Lynne Rienner Publishers, 1994. 223–41.

———. *La iglesia en la primera república federal mexicana (1824–1835)*. Mexico City: SepSetentas, 1976.

———. "Las mujeres detrás de la silla presidencial mexicana en el siglo XIX." In Will Fowler (ed.), *Presidentes mexicanos*, vol. 1. Mexico City: INEHRM, 2004. 139–69.

———. *Recuento de una batalla inconclusa: La educación mexicana de Iturbide a Juárez*. Mexico City: El Colegio de México, 2005.

Staples, Anne (ed.). *Educar: Panacea del México Independiente*. Mexico City: SEP, 1985.

Stevens, Donald Fithian. "Autonomists, Nativists, Republicans, and Monarchists: Conspiracy and Political History in Nineteenth-Century Mexico." *Mexican Studies/ Estudios Mexicanos* 10, no. 1 (Winter 1994): 247–66.

———. *Origins of Instability in Early Republican Mexico*. Durham NC: Duke University Press, 1991.

———. "Temerse la ira del cielo: Los conservadores y la religiosidad popular en los tiempos del cólera." In Will Fowler and Humberto Morales Moreno (eds.), *El conservadurismo mexicano en el siglo XIX (1810–1910)*. Puebla: BUAP University of St Andrews, 1999. 87–101.

Strode, George K. (ed.). *Yellow Fever*. New York: McGraw-Hill, 1951.

Suárez Argüello, Ana Rosa, and Marcela Terrazas Basante (eds.). *Política y negocios: Ensayos sobre la relación entre México y los Estados Unidos en el Siglo XIX*. Mexico City: UNAM–Instituto Mora, 1997.

Suárez y Navarro, Juan. *Historia de México y el general Antonio López de Santa Anna: Comprende los acontecimientos políticos que han tenido lugar en la nación, desde el año de 1821 hasta 1848*. 2 vols. Mexico City: Imp. de Ignacio Cumplido, 1850.

Suárez, Federico. *Las Cortes de Cádiz*. Madrid: Rialp, 1982.

Tamayo, Jorge L. *Epistolario de Benito Juárez*. Mexico City: Fondo de Cultura Económica, 1972.

Tanck Estrada, Dorothy. *La educación ilustrada 1786–1836*. Mexico City: El Colegio de México, 1977.

Taylor, William B. *Magistrates of the Sacred: Priests and Parishioners in Eighteenth-Century Mexico*. Stanford: Stanford University Press, 1996.

Tena Ramírez, Felipe. *Leyes fundamentales de México 1808–2002*. Mexico City: Porrúa, 2002.

Tenenbaum, Barbara A. "Development and Sovereignty: Intellectuals and the Second Empire." In Roderic A. Camp, Charles A. Hale, and Josefina Zoraida Vázquez (eds.), *Los intelectuales y el poder en México*. Mexico City: El Colegio de México/ UCLA Latin American Center Publications, 1991. 77–88.

———. *México en la época de los agiotistas, 1821–1857*. Mexico City: El Colegio de México, 1985.

Thomas, Hugh. *The Conquest of Mexico*. London: Hutchinson, 1993.

Thompson, Waddy. *Recollections of Mexico*. New York: Wiley and Putnam, 1847.

Thomson, Guy P. C. "Popular Aspects of Liberalism in Mexico, 1848–1888," *Bulletin of Latin American Research* 10, no. 3 (1991): 265–92.

Thomson, Guy P. C., with David G. LaFrance. *Patriotism, Politics, and Popular Liberalism in*

Nineteenth-Century Mexico: Juan Francisco Lucas and the Puebla Sierra. Wilmington DE: Scholarly Resources, 1999.

Tornel y Mendívil, José María. "A D. José María Gutiérrez Estrada, o sean, Algunas observaciones al folleto en que ha procurado la destrucción de la república, y el llamamiento al trono mexicano de un príncipe extranjero." El Cosmopolita, 31 October 1840.

———. Breve reseña histórica de los acontecimientos más notables de la nación mexicana. Mexico: INEHRM, 1985.

———. Discurso pronunciado en la alameda de la ciudad de México en el día 27 de septiembre de 1850. Mexico City: Imp. de Ignacio Cumplido, 1850.

———. Discurso pronunciado por el Exmo. Sr. general ministro de guerra y marina, don José María Tornel, en la sesión del 12 de octubre de 1842 del congreso constituyente, en apoyo del dictamen de la mayoría de la comisión de constitución del mismo. Mexico City: Imp. de Ignacio Cumplido, 1842.

———. Discurso que pronunció el Escmo. Sr. General D. José María Tornel y Mendívil, individuo del Supremo Poder Conservador, en la alameda de la ciudad de México, en el día del solemne aniversario de la independencia. Mexico City: Imp. de Ignacio Cumplido, 1840.

———. El grito de la patria. Puebla: Imp. de Pedro de la Rosa, 1821.

———. Fastos militares de iniquidad, barbarie y despotismo del gobierno español, ejecutados en las villas de Orizaba y Córdoba en la guerra de once años. Mexico City: Imp. de Ignacio Cumplido, 1843.

———. La aurora de México. Mexico City: Imp. de Celestino de la Torre, 1821.

———. Manifestación del C. José María Tornel. Mexico City: n.p., 1833.

———. Manifestación presentada a la cámara de senadores por el general José María Tornel, apoderado de las diputaciones de cosecheros de tabaco de las ciudades de Jalapa y Orizaba, pidiendo la reprobación del acuerdo sobre amortización de la moneda de cobre, por medio del estanco de aquel ramo. Mexico City: Imp. de Ignacio Cumplido, 1841.

———. Manifiesto del origen, causas, progresos y estado de la revolución del imperio mexicano con relación a la antigua España. Puebla and Mexico City: Imp. de Ontíveros, 1821.

———. Memoria de la secretaría de estado y del despacho de guerra y marina, leída por el Exmo. Sr. General José María Tornel, en la cámara de diputados el día 7 de enero de 1839, y en la de senadores el 8 del mismo. Mexico City: Imp. de Ignacio Cumplido, 1839.

———. Memoria del secretario de estado y del despacho de guerra y marina, leída a las cámaras del congreso nacional de la república mexicana, en enero de 1844. Mexico City: Imp. de Ignacio Cumplido, 1844.

———. Memoria del secretario de estado y del despacho de guerra y marina, leída en la cámara de representates en la sesión del día veinte y tres de marzo, y en la de senadores en la del veinte y cuatro del mismo mes y año de 1835. Mexico City: Imp. de Ignacio Cumplido, 1835.

———. Respuesta del general José María Tornel y Mendívil al escrito que formó el Escmo. Sr. Lic. D. Manuel de la Peña y Peña, que acogió el Supremo Poder Conservador, e imprimió y circuló el gobierno como suplemento de su diario, contra la protesta que el espresado publicó en 30 de noviembre del año anterior, sobre el decreto espedido en 9 del mismo mes, acerca de las reformas de la constitución. Mexico City: Imp. de Ignacio Cumplido, 1840.

———. Tejas y los Estados Unidos de América en sus relaciones con la república mexicana. Mexico City: Imp. de Ignacio Cumplido, 1837.

———. Valor y constancia es nuestra divisa. Puebla: Imp. de Pedro de la Rosa, 1821.

Torre, Ernesto de la. La independencia de México. Madrid: Editorial Mapfre, 1992.

Trens, Manuel B. "Santa Anna, realista." Boletín del Archivo General de la Nación 28, no. 1 (1957): 1–31.

Trueba, Alfonso. Santa Anna. Mexico City: Jus, 1958.

Tutino, John. From Insurrection to Revolution in Mexico: Social Bases of Agrarian Violence, 1750– 1940. Princeton: Princeton University Press, 1986.

Un ciudadano que no tomó la más mínima parte en aquellos acontecimientos, Pronunciamiento de Perote por el general Antonio López de Santa Anna y sucesos de campaña hasta la derogación de la Ley que los proscribió. Mexico City: Imp. del Águila, 1829.

Undécimo calendario de Abraham López; arreglado al meridiano de México y antes publicado en Toluca para el año de 1849. Mexico City: Imp. de A. López, 1849.

Vagts, Alfred. A History of Militarism: Civilian and Military. London: Blackwell, 1959.

Valadés, José C. Alamán: Estadista e historiador. Mexico City: UNAM, 1977.

———. México, Santa Anna y la guerra de Texas. Mexico City: Editorial Diana, 1979.

———. Santa Anna y la guerra de Texas. Mexico City: Porrúa, 1951.

Van Young, Eric. The Other Rebellion: Popular Violence, Ideology, and the Mexican Struggle for Independence, 1810–1821. Stanford: Stanford University Press, 2001.

———. "Recent Anglophone Scholarship on Mexico and Central America in the Age of Revolution (1750–1850)." Hispanic American Historical Review 65 (1985): 725–43.

Vázquez Mantecón, Maria del Carmen. "Espacio social y crisis política: La Sierra Gorda 1850–1855." Mexican Studies/Estudios Mexicanos 9, no. 1 (1993): 47–70.

———. "La Jura de Obediencia al Emperador o el fin de la fiesta iturbidista: Sus episodios en la Ciudad de México, en enero de 1823." Trace 39 (June 2001): 21–29.

———. La palabra del poder: Vida pública de José María Tornel 1795–1853. Mexico City: UNAM, 1997.

———. "La prostitución de la sexualidad durante el siglo XIX mexicano." Históricas 61 (2001): 36–62.

———. Santa Anna y la encrucijada del estado: La dictadura (1853–1855). Mexico City: Fondo de Cultura Económica, 1986.

———. "Santa Anna y su Guerra con los angloamericanos: Las versiones de una polémica." Estudios de Historia Moderna y Contemporánea de México 22 (julio-diciembre 2001): 23–52.

Vázquez, Josefina Z. "Benito Juárez y la consolidación del estado mexicano." In Juana Inés Abreu (ed.), Juárez: Memoria e imagen. Mexico City: Secretaría de Hacienda y Crédito Público, 1998. 35–III.

———. "Centralistas, conservadores y monarquistas 1830–1853." In Will Fowler and Humberto Morales Moreno (eds.), *El conservadurismo mexicano en el siglo XIX (1810–1910)*. Puebla: BUAP–University of St Andrews, 1999. 115–33.

———. "The Colonization and Loss of Texas: A Mexican Perspective." In Jaime E. Rodríguez O. and Kathryn Vincent (eds.), *Myths, Misdeeds and Misunderstandings: The Roots of Conflict in U.S.-Mexican Relations*. Wilmington DE: Scholarly Resources, 1997. 47–77.

———. *Don Antonio López de Santa Anna: Mito y enigma*. Mexico City: Condumex, 1987.

———. "De la difícil constitución de un estado: México, 1821–1854." In Josefina Zoraida Vázquez (ed.), *La fundación del estado mexicano*. Mexico City: Nueva Imagen, 1994. 9–37.

———. "Iglesia, ejército y centralismo." *Historia Mexicana* 39, no. 1 (1989): 205–34.

———. *La intervención norteamericana 1846–1848*. Mexico City: SRE, 1997.

———. "La primera presidencia de Antonio López de Santa Anna." In Will Fowler (ed.), *Presidentes mexicanos*, vol. 1. Mexico City: INEHRM, 2004. 89–112.

———. "Los años olvidados." *Mexican Studies/Estudios Mexicanos* 5, no. 2 (Summer 1989): 313–26.

———. "Los primeros tropiezos." In Daniel Cosío Villegas (ed.), *Historia general de México*, vol. 2. Mexico City: El Colegio de México, 1988. 735–818.

———. "Los pronunciamientos de 1832: Aspirantismo político e ideología." In Jaime E. Rodríguez O. (ed.), *Patterns of Contention in Mexican History*. Wilmington DE: Scholarly Resources, 1992. 163–86.

———. *Nacionalismo y educación en México*. Mexico City: El Colegio de México, 1975.

———. "Political Plans and Collaboration between Civilians and the Military, 1821–1846," *Bulletin of Latin American Research* 15, no. 1 (January 1996): 19–38.

———. "Soldados alemanes en las huestes santanistas." *Jahrbuch für geschichte von staat, wirtschaft und gesellschaft Lateinamerikas* 25 (1988): 415–36.

———. "Un viejo tema: El federalismo y el centralismo." *Historia Mexicana* 42, no. 3 (Enero–Marzo 1993): 622–31.

Vázquez, Josefina Z. (ed.). *El establecimiento del federalismo en México (1821–1827)*. Mexico City: El Colegio de México, 2003.

———. *México al tiempo de su guerra con Estados Unidos (1846–1848)*. Mexico City: Fondo de Cultura Económica, 1997.

Vázquez, Josefina Z., and Héctor Cuauhtémoc Hernández Silva (eds.). *Diario histórico de México 1822–1848 de Carlos María de Bustamante*, 2 CD-ROMS (1822–1848). Mexico City: CIESAS/El Colegio de México, 2001, 2004.

Vázquez, Josefina Z., and Lorenzo Meyer. *México frente a Estados Unidos: Un ensayo histórico 1776–1988*. Mexico City: Fondo de Cultura Económica, 1989.

Velázquez Correa, Ma. Cristina, and Héctor Cuevas Fernández. "Antonio López de Santa Anna: Su vida en la Nueva Granada." *Boletín del Consejo de la Crónica de la Ciudad de Xalapa-Enríquez* 1 (July 2001): 25–28.

Velázquez, María del Carmen. *El Estado de Guerra en Nueva España, 1760–1808*. Mexico City: El Colegio de México, 1950.

Veraza Urtuzuástegui, Jorge, *Perfil del traidor: Santa Anna en la historiografía y en el sentido común*. Mexico City: Itaca, 2000.

Victoria, Guadalupe. *El Presidente de los Estados Unidos Mejicanos a sus Conciudadanos*. Mexico City: Imp. del Águila, 17 September 1828.

Villa-Amor, Manuel. *Biografía del general Santa Anna, aumentada con la segunda parte*. Mexico City: Imp. de Vicente G. Torres, 1857.

Villavicencio, Pablo y Varios Amigos de la Verdad. *Ya no muere fucilada, Doña Francisca Santa Anna*. Mexico City: Imprenta Liberal, 1832.

Villegas Revueltas, Silvestre. *Deuda y diplomacia: La relación México–Gran Bretaña 1824–1884*. Mexico City: UNAM, 2005.

———. *El liberalismo moderado en México, 1852–1864*. Mexico City: UNAM, 1997.

Villoro, Luis. *El proceso ideológico de la revolución de independencia*. Mexico City: UNAM, 1967.

Vincent, Theodore G. *The Legacy of Vicente Guerrero, Mexico's First Black Indian President*. Gainesville: University Press of Florida, 2001.

Ward, Henry George. *México en 1827*. Mexico City: Fondo de Cultura Económica, 1995.

Warren, Harris Gaylord. *The Sword Was Their Passport: A History of American Filibustering in the Mexican Revolution*. Port Washington NY: Kennikat Press, 1972.

Warren, Richard A. *Vagrants and Citizens: Politics and the Masses in Mexico City from Colony to Republic*. Wilmington DE: Scholarly Resources, 2001.

Wasserman, Mark. *Everyday Life and Politics in Nineteenth-Century Mexico: Men, Women, and War*. Albuquerque: University of New Mexico Press, 2000.

Whitaker, A. P. (ed.). *Latin America and the Enlightenment*. Ithaca: Cornell University Press, 1961.

Winders, Richard Bruce. *Crisis in the Southwest: The United States, Mexico, and the Struggle over Texas*. Wilmington DE: SR Books, 2002.

———. *Sacrificed at the Alamo: Tragedy and Triumph in the Texas Revolution*. Abilene: State House Press, 2004.

Woodward, Ralph Lee, Jr. *Rafael Carrera and the Emergence of the Republic of Guatemala, 1821–1871*. Athens: University of Georgia Press, 1993.

Yáñez, Agustín. *Santa Anna: Espectro de una sociedad*. Mexico City: Fondo de Cultura Económica, 1993.

Zamora Plowes, Leopoldo. *Quince uñas y Casanova aventureros*. 2 vols. Mexico City: Patria, 1984.

Zárate Toscano, Verónica. "Héroes y fiestas en el México decimonónico: La insistencia de Santa Anna." In Manuel Chust and Víctor Mínguez (eds.), *La construcción del héroe en España y México, 1789–1847*. Castellón: Universitat Jaume I, 2003. 133–53.

———. *Los nobles ante la muerte en México: Actitudes, ceremonias y memoria (1750–1850)*. Mexico City: El Colegio de México–Instituto Mora, 2000.

————. "Los testamentos de los presidentes del siglo XIX." In Luis Jáuregui and José Antonio Serrano Ortega (eds.), *Historia y nación*, vol. 2: *Política y diplomacia en el siglo XIX mexicano*. Mexico City: El Colegio de México, 1988. 245–62.

Zavala, Lorenzo de. *Obras. Viaje a los Estados Unidos del Norte de América*. Mexico City: Porrúa, 1976.

————. *Obras. El historiador y el representante popular: Ensayo crítico de las revoluciones de México desde 1808 hasta 1830*. Mexico City: Porrúa, 1969.

Zayas Enríquez, Rafael de. *Benito Juárez: Su vida y su obra*. Mexico City: Sepsetentas, 1979.

Zorrilla, José. *Recuerdos del tiempo viejo*. Vol. 2. Madrid: Tipografía Gutenberg, 1882.

Index